THE ABOLITION OF FEUDALISM

John Markoff

The Abolition of Feudalism

Peasants, Lords, and Legislators in the French Revolution

The Pennsylvania State University Press
University Park, Pennsylvania

This publication has been supported by the National Endowment for the Humanities, a federal agency which supports the study of such fields as history, philosophy, literature, and languages.

Library of Congress Cataloging-in-Publication Data

Markoff, John, 1942–
The abolition of feudalism : peasants, lords, and legislators in the French Revolution / John Markoff.

p. cm.
Includes bibliographical references and index.
ISBN 0-271-01538-1 (cloth : alk. paper)
ISBN 0-271-01539-X (pbk. : alk. paper)
1. Land tenure—France—History. 2. Peasantry—France—History. 3. Feudalism—France. 4. France—History—Revolution, 1789–1799–Causes. I. Title.
HD644.M37 1996
333.3′22′0994—dc20 95-50657
CIP

Printed in the United States of America
Published by The Pennsylvania State University Press,
University Park, PA 16802-1003

It is the policy of The Pennsylvania State University Press to use acid-free paper for the first printing of all clothbound books. Publications on uncoated stock satisfy the minimum requirements of American National Standard for Information Sciences—Permanence of Paper for Printed Library Materials, ANSI Z39.48-1992.

For my parents,
Maxine and Sol Markoff

Contents

List of Figures and Maps

List of Tables

Acknowledgments

On the cover a solitary name stakes a claim that this book has a single author; but the references at the bottoms of the pages within show something of the community without which this book couldn't exist. The footnotes indicate only some of what is owed to others. Gilbert Shapiro thought up the systematic study of the *cahiers de doléances* and, together with Sasha Weitman, had carried out much preliminary work toward the coding of these documents when I joined them. It's easy enough to thank them for the creation of an essential data set; I cannot begin, however, to thank them for all I've learned from them. It's been a long time since I attended Robert Forster's graduate seminar on the French Revolution, the first course in history in which I'd ever formally enrolled, but it remains with me as a model of how to work with students. Like others who were graduate students in the same time and place, I found the sociology department created by James Coleman and Arthur Stinchcombe a garden that in exile, I'd hope to re-create.

Some of the analyses and arguments in this book and some of its words had earlier versions as articles or talks and I found many people willing to read these early drafts of chapters. I'm grateful to all those who generously gave me comments on these versions: Silvio Baretta, Seymour Drescher, Jack Goldstone, Peter Jones, D. Carroll Joynes, John Marx, Peter McPhee, James Riley, Eugen Weber, Arthur Stinchcombe, Rainer Baum, William Brustein, Lynn Hunt, Daniel Regan, Charles Tilly, Donald Sutherland, Jeremy Popkin, Isser Woloch, Colin Lucas, Lloyd Moote, Sidney Tarrow, George Taylor, Sasha Weitman, Susan Olzak, Gilbert Shapiro, Norman Ravitch, François Furet, and Harvey Graff. Later, others commented, sometimes in extraordinarily generous detail, on complete or nearly complete drafts of the book: Arthur Stinchcombe, Peter Jones, Cynthia Bouton, Carmenza Gallo, John Marx, Timothy Tackett, Peter McPhee, Anatoly Ado, Ludmila Pimenova, Robert Forster, William Doyle, and Mounira Charrad.

Other scholars managed to find the time to answer queries about their own work or let me make use of their unpublished or even unfinished research. For these and other sorts of help I thank Timothy Tackett, Melvin Edelstein, Anthony Crubaugh, Nancy Fitch, Cynthia Bouton, Jean Nicolas,

André Fel, Bernard Sinsheimer, Donald Sutherland, Bryant Ragan, Steven Reinhardt, Thomas Fox, Jeffrey Merrick, Hilton Root, Lionel Rothkrug, Lloyd Moote, and Sarah Maza. (The particular generosity in sharing unfinished work is obscured in my references by how much of that work got into print long before this book finally did.) Many, many others I can only thank collectively—my students, colleagues, friends—for putting up with my obsessions. Beyond the gift of time taken away from their own projects for which I thank all, I found the particular helpfulness of scholars with whose own work I quarrel in these pages to be a model of generosity. Where I have not taken an excellent scholar's advice, let it be called obstinacy, but not ingratitude.

The University of Pittsburgh's Center for International Studies provided essential financial support on a number of occasions: I'm deeply grateful to its director and associate director, Burkart Holzner and Thomas McKechnie. The endless revisions seductively invited by word-processing technology were actually carried out by Josephine Caiazzo. Without her work, I'm not sure that this book would ever have been completed.

CHAPTER

1

INTRODUCTION: GRIEVANCES, INSURRECTIONS, LEGISLATION

In the 1780s young men seeking employment under Alpine lords used to place notices in the ad columns of the *Dauphiné Announcements* vaunting their fine handwriting, their skill in mathematics, their moral character, their knowledge of Latin, their respectable families and, of course, their grasp of the intricacies of land surveys, the law of fiefs, and seigneurial rights.[1] In 1967, a villager in Upper Provence, whose family had lived there a long time, was heard to tell of the day in December 1789—the story was nowhere written down in any detail—when a boisterous group of villagers marched to the local *château,* dug a hole in the courtyard, and informed the lord that his continuing refusal to make a written renunciation of his rights would straightway lead to throwing him in. (Monsieur de Robert complied.)[2]

1. Jean Nicolas, "Le paysan et son seigneur en Dauphiné à la veille de la Révolution," in *La France d'ancien régime: Etudes réunies en l'honneur de Pierre Goubert* (Toulouse: Privat, 1984), 2:497.

2. Daniel Solakian, "Mouvements contestataires de communautés agro-pastorales de Haute-

In the 1780s a French lord could collect a variety of monetary and material payments from his peasants; could insist that nearby villagers grind their grain in the seigneurial mill, bake their bread in the seigneurial oven, press their grapes in the seigneurial winepress; could set the date of the grape harvest; could have local cases tried in his own court; could claim particularly favored benches in church for his family and proudly point to the family tombs below the church floor; could take pleasures forbidden the peasants—hunting, raising rabbits, or pigeons—in the pursuit of which pleasures the peasants' fields were sometimes devastated. It was a world that could sustain the careers of young men who would bring their knowledge of agricultural practice, of law, and of household finances to keeping the lord's affairs in order.

Between 1789 and 1793, the people of the French countryside mounted attacks on their enemies; a very significant part of these thousands of incidents were attacks on the claims of the lords. At the same time, the articulate, educated, and energetic members of the revolutionary legislatures in Versailles and Paris produced a stream of words laying out their blueprint for the new rural order. For those who lived through this time, it was not just a diminution in the power of a social group, but the collapse of a world. Those who had lived in this world suddenly had new choices to make and made them differently. One highly successful lawyer sometimes in seigneurial employ, Philippe-Antoine Merlin, well known as collaborator on one of the last major legal treatises of the Old Regime, found a new use for his skills in serving as secretary of the National Assembly's Committee on Feudal Rights where he was chief architect of the detailed legislation on the seigneurial rights. Meanwhile in Picardy, François-Noël Babeuf, traveling quite a different road, abandoned the lords whom he had advised, and found a new (and brief) life in championing the peasant cause as he understood it, through proposals intolerable to any of the governments of the decade of revolution.

The sense of a dramatic break was such a deep experience that one historian of rural France could recall that when he was growing up in rural Brittany in the 1920s the country people spoke of the distant past as "the time of the lords."[3] In how many villages was that experience recounted to the young over generations—and, when recounted, with what alterations as the events receded in time? We do not usually have easy access to the ways in which the great upheaval was experienced in France's forty thousand rural communities but we do at least know a great deal about what many of those villages were demanding at one early moment when they set down

Provence au XVIIIe siècle dans le témoignage écrit et la mémoire collective," in Jean Nicolas, ed., *Mouvements populaires et conscience sociale, XVIIe–XIXe siècles* (Paris: Maloine, 1985), 249.

3. Pierre Goubert, *L'Ancien Régime,* vol. 1, *La société* (Paris: Armand Colin, 1969), 17.

their grievances. The legislators of the National Assembly (1789–91), the Legislative Assembly (1791–92) and the Convention (1792–95), on the contrary, have left us an elaborate written account of their revolution, in the form of the written record of the legislature as a collectivity—their laws and the surrounding debates and reports by relevant committees—as well as such personal documents as letters, journals, memoirs, and position-taking brochures. This ocean of words contains a great deal on the legislators' views on rural revolt and on the rights of the lords.

The seigneurial rights were a central focus of attention in the years of revolution. They were a principal target of rural insurrection; they were on center stage in the National Assembly's dramatic renunciation of privilege on August 4, 1789; they were a continual bone of contention between rural communities who found the early enactments of the legislators to be thoroughly inadequate and legislators faced with continuing rural turbulence; they were an essential element in the revolutionaries' notions of the "feudal regime" being dismantled; they were the concrete subject matter addressed in the first legislation that tested the tensions inherent in the thorny constitutional issue of a royal veto (and they thereby contributed to the difficulty of embodying the Revolution in some monarchical form); they were invoked in the rhetoric with which those in high places addressed the growing international tension surrounding the revolutionary state, a rhetoric which imbued the revolutionaries with a self-righteous sense of a national mission to liberate the victims of feudalism outside of France, altering the character of European warfare.

The assault upon the lords' rights has been variously interpreted in the historical literature but it is widely seen as a central element in the entire upheaval. For Marcel Reinhard, the struggle against seigneurial rights was what gave the multifarious Revolution its unity.[4] Albert Soboul, who views the seigneurial institutions within the Marxist conception of the transition from feudalism to capitalism, finds the attack on those rights to be a large part of what made the French Revolution "truly revolutionary."[5] Pierre Goubert argues that the seigneurial regime was a constitutive element in the revolutionary actors' own conception of the Old Regime. The National Assembly was clearly of the view, he writes, that what they called the feudal regime "was one of the foundations of the Old Regime."[6] For Jerome Blum, the struggle against these rights was the French contribution to "the end of the old order in rural Europe."[7] Emmanuel Le Roy Ladurie has

4. Marcel Reinhard, "Sur l'histoire de la Révolution française," *Annales: Economies, Sociétés, Civilisations* 14 (1959): 555–58.

5. Albert Soboul, *The French Revolution, 1787–1799: From the Storming of the Bastille to Napoleon* (New York: Vintage Books, 1975), 7–8.

6. Goubert, *L'Ancien Régime,* 12.

7. Jerome Blum, *The End of the Old Order in Rural Europe* (Princeton: Princeton University Press, 1978).

proposed that what most sharply distinguished the rural risings of 1789 from the great peasant upheavals of the seventeenth century was precisely their focus on seigneurial rights rather than the fiscal exactions of the state.[8] In Tocqueville's search for the central issues posed by the Revolution, the attempt to understand "why feudalism had come to be more detested in France than in any other country," as one of his chapter titles has it, occupies a strategic place.[9] It was not, Tocqueville contends, that what he calls the yoke of medieval institutions was still strong. Rather, the centuries-long growth of the central state bureaucracy had to such an extent eroded the public powers and responsibilities of the lords, that their prerogatives were now so many unjustifiable privileges, and therefore vulnerable.[10]

In this book, I shall address the ways in which insurrectionary peasants and revolutionary legislators joined in bringing the time of the lords to an end and how, in that ending, the seigneurial rights came to be so central to the very sense of revolution as a sudden and radical break. I shall examine French views of seigneurial rights toward the onset of revolution and shall then trace the subsequent actions of peasants and legislators. How did France's peasants view their obligations to their lords? In what ways were these particular burdens felt to be like the other obligations that weighed upon them, especially state taxation and ecclesiastical exactions—and how were they felt to be different? How did the nobility see these rights? Did they defend their existence and, to the extent they did so, in what ways? And the urban notables who came to national power in the revolutionary decade—how did their views resemble those of peasants (or of nobles) and in what ways were they distinctive? And what made the seigneurial rights occupy such an important place in how they came to characterize France's past?

Peasant insurrection was a significant element of the collapse of the Old Regime. The French countryside teemed with groups who challenged the existing order and whose continued turbulence for the next several years posed difficult problems for those who sought, in Paris, to assert their claims to be at the head of the new revolutionary order. The forms assured in the mobilization of the countryside were many. Small-town marketplaces were occupied by country people demanding grain at prices they could afford; lords were dragged out of their residences and compelled to issue public renunciations of their seigneurial rights; monasteries were broken into; administrative offices of tax agencies were burned; arms were sought as villages mobilized for self-defense against what were believed to be

8. Emmanuel Le Roy Ladurie, "Révoltes et contestations rurales en France de 1675 à 1788," *Annales: Economies, Sociétés, Civilisations* 29 (1974): 6–22.

9. Alexis de Tocqueville, *The Old Regime and the French Revolution* (Garden City, N.Y.: Doubleday, 1955), 22.

10. Ibid., 22–32.

imminent invasions by criminals or foreign armies or aristocrats' lackeys. Later on there was bitter and violent engagement on one side or or the other of the church that divided in its allegiances; there were risings over conscription and other claims of the new central authorities; there were battles for access to land in which fences were knocked down, forests invaded, and commons divided; less commonly, there were struggles in which rural wage laborers sought better earnings. What role did the seigneurial rights play among all the diverse forms of peasant insurrection?

The Revolution was not just popular ferment, however. It was also the attempt at reconstructing central authority upon new institutional foundations. How did the legislators envisage the new order in the countryside? How did they cope, not only with their own sense of what was desirable, but with the waves of rural turbulence? In light of the variety of peasant targets, how did the seigneurial rights come to assume such a central role in the legislators' conception of a break with the past? From the beginning of their debates, these rights were placed within a discussion of "the feudal regime," to be done away with. But what was this "feudal" regime and why was it central to their vision of France's past and future?

I shall show in this book how revolutionary legislators and revolutionary peasants confronted one another, posed problems for one another, and implicitly negotiated with one another. To explore the desires of both peasants and elites toward the beginning of the crisis as well as the ensuing interplay of rural insurrection and legislative actions, I explore several sorts of evidence. First of all, the expression of the views of rural communities, nobles, and urban notables as the Old Regime broke down: here I draw upon a series of studies of the grievance lists of 1789 that I have been engaged in with Gilbert Shapiro.[11] As the Old Regime disintegrated about them that

11. Gilbert Shapiro and John Markoff, *Revolutionary Demands: A Content Analysis of the Cahiers de Doléances of 1789* (Stanford: Stanford University Press, 1997); John Markoff, "Governmental Bureaucratization: General Processes and an Anomalous Case," *Comparative Studies in Society and History* 17 (1975): 479–503; "Some Effects of Literacy in Eighteenth-Century France," *Journal of Interdisciplinary History* 17 (1986): 311–33; "Allies and Opponents: Nobility and Third Estate in the Spring of 1789," *American Sociological Review* 53 (1988): 477–96; "Images du roi au début de la Révolution," in Michel Vovelle, ed., *L'image de la Révolution française: Communications présenteés lors du Congrès Mondial pour le Bicentenaire de la Révolution* (Paris: Pergamon, 1989), 1:237–45; "Peasants Protest: The Claims of Lord, Church and State in the *Cahiers de Doléances* of 1789," *Comparative Studies in Society and History* 32 (1990): 413–54; "Peasant Grievances and Peasant Insurrection: France in 1789," *Journal of Modern History* 62 (1990): 445–76; "Prélèvements seigneuriaux et prélèvements fiscaux: Sur l'utilisation des cahiers de doléances," in *Mélanges de l'Ecole Française de Rome* 103 (1991): 47–68; Gilbert Shapiro and Phillip Dawson, "Social Mobility and Political Radicalism: The Case of the French Revolution of 1789," in William O. Aydelotte, Alan G. Bogue, and Robert Fogel, eds., *The Dimensions of Quantitative Research in History* (Princeton: Princeton University Press, 1972), 159–92; Gilbert Shapiro, John Markoff, and Sasha R. Weitman, "Quantitative Studies of the French Revolution," *History and Theory: Studies in the Philosophy of History* 12 (1973): 163–91; John Markoff, Gilbert Shapiro, and Sasha R. Weitman, "Toward the

spring, Frenchmen met in tens of thousands of assemblies to draw up *cahiers de doléances,* lists of grievances that were intended to instruct and often to control the deputies chosen in the complex multistage elections for the Estates-General. These documents offer precious glimpses into the thinking of many groups, and offer a virtually unique perspective on the aspirations of civil society at the onset of a revolutionary upheaval. The *cahiers* are unmatched in their capacity to give us the range of views expressed by social groups around the country: they are not only invaluable as a source for the positions being staked out in France's forty thousand rural communities; they are an utterly unparalleled source for the study of peasants in revolution. There is simply no similar body of evidence bequeathed to us by any other revolutionary upheaval. The structure of the convocation process, moreover, permits comparisons among the positions being staked out by the country people, the non-noble urban elites and the nobility in a way that no other source allows.

It is usually only elites of one sort or another whose positions on public issues may be assessed in anything resembling a systematic fashion at the time of crisis. The thinking of intellectuals, officials, upper economic groups, or revolutionary leaders is often known to us through decrees, public debates, manifestos, memoirs, letters. Even then, there are often serious issues: depending on our source we might be concerned about representativeness, concealment, or failures of memory. When we deal with "the people" however, our problems of assessing outlooks in times of crisis are vastly multiplied, for they generally control few newspapers, publish few memoirs, and are not among the public representatives who articulate the positions of political parties (even those parties that claim to speak on their behalf). Those who study crises must often exercise considerable ingenuity to attempt to gauge crucial attitudes from recalcitrant sources. Consider two impressive instances of this sort. Richard Merritt explored a developing American identity over the four decades that preceded the Declaration of Independence by systematically exploring the terms used in several colonial newspapers to denote the inhabitants of the thirteen colonies ("His Majesty's subjects" versus "Americans," for example) or the land they dwelt in

Integration of Content Analysis and General Methodology," 1–58, in David Heise, ed., *Sociological Methodology, 1975* (San Francisco: Jossey-Bass, 1974); John Markoff and Gilbert Shapiro, "Consensus and Conflict at the Onset of Revolution: A Quantitative Study of France in 1789," *American Journal of Sociology* 91 (1985): 28–53; Gilbert Shapiro, John Markoff, and Silvio R. Duncan Baretta, "The Selective Transmission of Historical Documents: The Case of the Parish *Cahiers* of 1789," *Histoire et Measure* 2 (1987): 115–72; Gilbert Shapiro and John Markoff, "L'authenticité des cahiers," in *Bulletin d'Histoire de la Révolution Française* (1990–91): 17–70; Gilbert Shapiro, "Les demandes les plus répandues dans les cahiers de doléances," in Vovelle, ed., *L'image de la Révolution française,* 1:7–14.

("British North America" versus "the colonies in America," say).[12] Marc Ferro explored the common threads as well as the divergences of Russian workers, peasants, and soldiers in the crisis of 1917 through letters and resolutions sent to party newspapers and various claimants to governmental authority.[13] Rather more commonly, scholars hoping for a glimpse of plebeian rebels scour the archives of the police and the magistrates for reports, depositions, and trial records. Serious difficulties with such sources[14] hardly interferes with our sense of how precious they are for their vital, if imperfect, glimpse of the thinking of people who are largely inaccessible to us but whose outlook is fundamental to an understanding of the societal crisis in which they were enmeshed.

Scholars of the French Revolution are in the exceptionally fortunate position of having in their possession the *cahiers* of the spring of 1789, which provide a magnificent and unrivaled snapshot of the complaints and aspirations of those below as well as above at the beginning of the great revolution. To track the course of revolutionary conflict, however, even a marvelous snapshot is inadequate: I wanted a movie. I wanted to see what sorts of actions were engendered in regions of France with particular constellations of grievances, so I initially set about constructing a little data file of what I took to be the major kinds of insurrectionary events in the countryside in the spring and summer of 1789. It was now possible to search for the roots of distinctive forms of rural upheaval over space.[15] But although it was now beginning to be possible to study the relationship of demanding and of acting, I still did not have my movie. I had two snapshots

12. Richard L. Merritt, *Symbols of American Community, 1735–1775* (New Haven: Yale University Press, 1966).

13. Marc Ferro, "The Russian Soldier in 1917: Undisciplined, Patriotic and Revolutionary," *Slavic Review* 30 (1971): 483–512; "The Aspirations of Russian Society," in Richard Pipes, ed., *Revolutionary Russia* (Cambridge: Harvard University Press, 1968), 143–57.

14. To what degree does newspaper content, sometimes written in England, enlighten us on colonial *readers'* views—and just who read these periodicals? How representative are the *particular* periodicals chosen by Merritt? What sort of sample of workers, soldiers, and peasants wrote letters to *Isvestiia* or to the Soviet—and how did editors decide which letters to publish (and with what alterations)? Of the many letters deposited in archives or published in newspapers (itself an apparently haphazard sample of a much larger number actually written), how representative are the much smaller number actually analyzed by Ferro? To what degree do the concerns of the powerful whose records we plow through distort our picture of the powerless we hope to encounter? To what degree, for example, do administrative records overrepresent popular turbulence in and around major administrative centers?

15. John Markoff, "The Social Geography of Rural Revolt at the Beginning of the French Revolution," *American Sociological Review* 50 (1985): 761–81; "Contexts and Forms of Rural Revolt: France in 1789," *Journal of Conflict Resolution* 30 (1986): 253–89; "Literacy and Revolt: Some Empirical Notes on 1789 in France," *American Journal of Sociology* 92 (1986): 323–49; "Peasant Grievances and Peasant Insurrection."

(and of different objects at that). The concept of process, so central to understanding both the peasant movement(s) and the legislative actions, was still not mirrored in my data. The rural upheavals had, no doubt, some relation to environing social, economic, and political structures and, no doubt as well, some relation with grievances; and these matters could be explored with the two snapshots. But the insurrections had not only causes, but also consequences. And one important consequence of insurrection was the impact on future insurrections: by demonstrating the effectiveness of certain tactics and the folly of others, by inspiring countermobilization of those fearful of the intentions and capacities of the earlier rebels, by leading the authorities to take action, whether by way of repression or reform. And these consequences, in turn, became part of the context within which, a week or a month or a year hence, the same and different rural communities rose again (or failed to do so). What was really needed, I reasoned, was the capacity to see the insurrections unfold over time as well as space in a dialogue with each other as well as with the powerful of the new revolutionary regime.

The second major task of this book, then, is tracking rural insurrection through time and space. When does the rural upheaval take on a markedly antiseigneurial character, and where? How are antiseigneurial events related to the multifarious forms of peasant revolt more generally? What are the specific forms and targets of actions against the rights of the lords? To this end I explore a second data set, a body of information on some 4,700 incidents of rural disruption that took place between the summer of 1788 and the summer of 1793, covering roughly the period from the political crisis that produced the decision to convoke an Estates-General up to the Convention's passage of major pieces of legislation on rural issues, among them the termination of seigneurial rights.

As for the legislative side of the peasant-legislator dialogue that began in the summer of 1789, the task is easier; this particular field happily has been carefully tilled by many very able scholars. Although that legislative history is broadly familiar,[16] to examine it anew with an eye on the waves of peasant insurrection, on the shifts of timing, targets, and tactics of rebellious country people, suggests new insights into the legislative half of that dialogue.

The focus on the national pattern of rural insurrection as one side of a dialogue—itself set against a background of a national survey of positions—inevitably commits one to statistical argument. It will be important to ask

16. Henri Doniol, *La Révolution française et la féodalité* (Paris: Guillaumin, 1876); Emile Chénon, *Les démembrements de la propriété foncière en France avant et après la Révolution* (Paris: Recueil Sirey, 1923); Philippe Sagnac, *La législation civile de la Révolution française* ((Paris: Hachette, 1898); Alphonse Aulard, *La Révolution française et le régime féodal* (Paris: Alcan, 1919); Marcel Garaud, *La Révolution et la propriété foncière* (Paris: Recueil Sirey, 1958); Peter M. Jones, *The Peasantry in the French Revolution* (Cambridge: Cambridge University Press, 1988).

which aspects of the seigneurial regime are more important to the peasants and which to the urban notables; to ask at which times and at which places was the seigneurial regime a significant target of peasant action; to ask whether the pattern of grievances expressed in the spring of 1789 by rural communities, urban notables, and nobles helps us understand actions subsequently undertaken in the countryside and legislature; and to ask what impact, if any, the nature and timing of those actions taken by peasants or legislators had on the actions of the other. In such matters I favor actual counts of various events, whether the expression of particular sorts of grievances or the carrying out of particular forms of collective action, rather than the exclusive reliance on quasi-quantitative statistical claims conveyed primarily by terms like "few" or "many" and the like: hence the large number of tables, graphs, and maps. This has the consequence that a reader's own sense of what "few," "many," "large," or "small" might mean in a particular context can readily be checked against the evidence.

A narrative whose actors are usually collectivities—rural gatherings, for example, or legislative committees—and whose actions are largely presented as counts of one sort or another has an impersonal quality. Is this a distortion of the participants' experience? There was an impersonal aspect to the interchanges of villages and lawgivers. To a large extent those in the revolutionary assemblies experienced an abstract world of "sedition" and "insurrection" populated by sketchily and abstractly conceived "brigands" or "the people." And for sharecroppers in Périgord, rural weavers in Normandy, smallholders in Maine, serfs around Amont, wage laborers in Flanders, the lawgivers were equally remote. But there is a less impersonal set of encounters as well and precious are the documents that reveal them, usually in flashes: the noble deputy Ferrières' letters home to his wife, full of anxious advice on how to avoid an attack on their home (and what to do, should that happen) or the country priest's Barbotin's sudden and permanent shift toward the political right, in his letters to a clerical colleague, on discovering the tenacity of peasant hostility to the tithe. (From this point of view, the report of two agents of the National Assembly on their travels in an insurgent zone stands alone.)

An appraisal of the seigneurial regime as a subject of complaint as the Old Regime fell apart and as a target of insurrection and object of legislation into the 1790s bears on many important assessments and debates about the nature of the French Revolution. Georges Lefebvre[17] saw the peasant revolt as a defensive reaction of peasant communities confronted by increasingly

17. Georges Lefebvre, "La Révolution française et les paysans," in his *Etudes sur la Révolution française* (Paris: Presses Universitaires de France, 1963), 343, 350–53; and *Les Paysans du Nord pendant la Révolution française* (Paris: Armand Colin, 1972), 148. The theme of the lords' tightening the screws is also stressed in "La Révolution française dans l'histoire du monde" in *Etudes sur la Révolution française,* 438.

demanding lords who were themselves increasingly inclined to participate in a developing rural capitalism. Alexis de Tocqueville,[18] in contrast, directed us away from the level of burden as such to the increasing sense of that burden as unjust, as the genuine services once provided by the lord atrophied. Rather than seeing the marketplace as the external context that encroached on local social relations, Tocqueville maintained it was the increasingly demanding central state that eroded the once genuine social functions of the lords. George Taylor[19] supported neither view: he urged us to see agrarian radicalism as minimal; he denied, in consequence, that the countryside made much of a contribution to the radicalism of the Revolution. For Taylor, to the extent that any group can be said to be the bearer of a radical message, it was the urban elites—even when the matter at hand was a rural issue. Taylor's thesis is a major challenge to the view urged by Albert Soboul[20] who, incarnating the Marxism that non-Marxists most love to attack, insisted that one see a bourgeois-peasant alliance against the bulwarks of feudalism. For Soboul it was the joint peasant and bourgeois action that gave the French Revolution its unique character. Alfred Cobban challenged this portrait with a denial of any bourgeois radicalism at all, at least insofar as the seigneurial regime was concerned, thereby undermining the notion of a bourgeois-peasant alliance against feudalism.[21] This was almost the inverse of George Taylor's critique which saw little but bourgeois radicalism in the Revolution's moves against the lords; Taylor's peasants have nothing in the way of revolutionary consciousness at all. More recently, Hilton Root[22] has argued that peasant insurrections against the lords have been much exaggerated by all concerned and that, moreover, such insurrectionary activity as did take place was of little concern to revolutionary governments.

In a very different vein, we have all the many issues that have swirled around the notion of "feudalism." During the Revolution, the seigneurial rights were invariably discussed in the context of "the feudal regime" and questions of what, if anything, that phrase meant and what relationship, if any, the Revolution had to that feudal regime have been among the central big questions, at least until the very recent shift by historians away from

18. Tocqueville, *Old Regime and Revolution.*

19. George V. Taylor, "Revolutionary and Nonrevolutionary Content in the Cahiers de Doléances of 1789: An Interim Report," *French Historical Studies* 7 (1972): 479–502.

20. Soboul, *The French Revolution.*

21. Alfred Cobban, *The Social Interpretation of the French Revolution* (Cambridge: Cambridge University Press, 1965).

22. Hilton Root, "The Case Against George Lefebvre's Peasant Revolution," *History Workshop* 28 (1989): 88–102; see also Peter M. Jones, "A Reply to Hilton Root," *History Workshop* 28 (1989): 103–6 and "Root's Response to Jones," *History Workshop* 28 (1989): 103–10.

economic relationships and toward placing revolutionary discourse at the center of things.[23]

Thus, peasant risings against their lords have been held to be one of the engines of the entire revolutionary upheaval and trivial to the point of nonexistence. Peasants are held to have been the allies of a revolutionary elite, to have pushed that elite where it did not want to go and to have been an apathetic and conservative force only galvanized by that elite. Peasant risings have been explained by the development of the market, the growth of the state, the harvest disasters of the late 1780s, the sudden jump in consciousness and opportunity produced by the convocation of the Estates-General and the long-term impact of literacy. And very different notions of the microstructures of motivation are deployed to connect one or more of these surrounding circumstances to disruptive rural politics: peasant violence is seen as a strategy adopted in a struggle over material resources, as an expression of the angry resentment associated with a sense of injustice, or as a sign of continued participation in a traditional culture as yet unconquered by the civilizing process described by Norbert Elias.

I shall show that both peasants and legislators undertook major initiatives but that the central impetus for rural social transformation came from how each reacted to the other; that their common movement against the seigneurial regime was not present at the onset of the Revolution in more than embryonic form; that the antiseigneurial forces of rural mobilization developed in the course of the Revolution as legislative action presented opportunities to the countryside; and—a more widely appreciated matter—that the legislative dismantling of seigneurialism is, in substantial part, an adaptation to peasant insurrection. As for the new and still current scholarly stress on discourse, the conception of the feudal regime was an important building-block of that discourse, but rather than examine an intellectual construction in splendid isolation, we need to reinsert it into the turbulent, confusing, and conflicting demands that revolutionary legislators confronted every day, even as, in explaining and defending their actions, they elaborated upon their notions of the feudal.

The tactic of investigation throughout will be systematically comparative. In exploring the theme of seigneurial rights in the *cahiers,* we shall compare the *cahiers* of peasants, elite town-dwellers, and nobles. We shall search among the seigneurial rights for the ways these groups distinguish one seigneurial right from another; to check our understandings we shall then

23. On recent trends in revolutionary historiography, see Jack Censer, "The French Revolution After Two Hundred Years," in Joseph Klaits and Michael Haltzel, eds., *The Global Ramifications of the French Revolution* (Washington, D.C.: Woodrow Wilson Center Press, 1994), 7–25; and Sara Maza, "Politics, Culture and the Origins of the French Revolution," *Journal of Modern History* 61 (1989): 704–23.

explore the comparison of grievances about one tax with another. We shall also try to understand what is special about seigneurial rights by seeing how, in the aggregate, grievances about seigneurial rights differ from grievances about other matters. We hope to arrive at a sense not merely of the distinctive characteristics of antiseigneurial grievances but how they fitted with other grievances into an overarching whole. We shall pursue the same strategy of systematic comparison when we turn to insurrection: not just where and when did insurrection occur, but how (and with luck, why) did the spatial and temporal patterns of antiseigneurial events differ from those of other forms of rural insurrection? Among antiseigneurial actions, where and when were the lord's documents seized, his fences torn down, or his *château* invaded? And how did seigneurial rights fit into a larger, overarching whole; namely, the ebb and flow of rural rebellion? When, finally, we turn to legislation, we shall ask how the trajectory of legislation on seigneurial rights resembles—and yet is distinct from—legislation on other concerns of insurrectionary peasants; and we shall also ask how the legislative program on seigneurial rights took its place alongside other arenas of legislation to form yet another overarching whole. In all areas we search for points of distinction but also for encompassing larger patterns.

We shall see in the earlier chapters of this book that the grievances of France's villagers were very much focused on their burdens. The claims upon them of lord, church, and state, however, were experienced quite differently. Although nothing else in French life occasioned so many complaints in the countryside as did taxation, there was a very strong propensity to demand an improved tax system. Demands about the seigneurial regime, in contrast, were in large part demands that the lord's claims be done away with. But even the seigneurial rights were not seen simply as an undifferentiated and hated ensemble; France's country people distinguished one right from another, and significant minorities held some aspects of the seigneurial regime worthy of reform; in particular, those attached to services valued in the rural community.

When, in the book's middle chapters, we look at the pattern of peasant insurrection, we clearly see that this collection of grievances was not instantly translated into antiseigneurial action. The major target of peasant revolt in the major risings of the seventeenth century had been royal taxation. Antitax actions continued to be a significant part of the rural protest repertoire in the more generally peaceful eighteenth century but were now joined by major waves of actions over questions of food supply. Toward the end of the Old Regime, there appears to have been an increasing tendency to go after seigneurial targets, but conflict over food or taxes continued to be far more common down to the eve of the Revolution.

The evidence that we shall examine will show that, initially, subsistence questions are what occasioned collective action as the Old Regime began to break down. Between the summer of 1788 and the spring of 1789, however, antiseigneurial actions were on the rise and grew still stronger in the dramatic summer. By the fall of 1789, the seigneurial regime had become the target of choice of insurrectionary peasants, and remained so for the next three years, although at some moments and in some places other targets were attractive as well. So what needs to be explained is not just how the structures of French society formed an antiseigneurial peasantry, but how peasants with a variety of grievances came to turn to antiseigneurial struggle in the course of revolution and to make antiseigneurial actions the dominant as well as most distinctive form of insurrection of the entire period 1788–93.

Let me stress that they *turned to* antiseigneurial actions. Claims that antiseigneurialism was a response to the enduring structures of French history will be hard put to explain a *process* occurring over a period of months. We need to look for a revolutionary process, not a revolutionary reflex. When we examine the geography of revolt, we shall see that we need to take both space and time into account. At one or another moment, different regions were at the cutting edge of antiseigneurial challenge. Provence was in the forefront at an early moment; the summer of 1789 saw the northern countryside on center stage; beyond that summer the battle against the lords was carried forward, at different moments, in eastern Brittany, in the Southeast, and in the Southwest (while various northern zones focused on subsistence, on conflicts over land, more rarely on wages, and at times fell silent). We shall see that explanations in terms of the impact of the market and the state make sense of our data, to some extent, but do not get to the heart of the Revolution as process.

In the later chapters, we look at the Revolution and the role of the countryside within it from the vantage point of the legislators. In staking out positions in the spring of 1789, the assemblies around the country that elected Third Estate deputies to the Estates-General gave their deputies documents whose position on the seigneurial regime tended to be distinctive in a number of ways, including the strength of their support for indemnifying the lords whose seigneurial rights were to be ended. The nobles' deputies brought documents that did not go that far; indeed they often avoided taking up the seigneurial rights at all or, sometimes, in taking them up, opted to maintain them. Yet it was the delegates of these assemblies that in August 1789 proclaimed the abolition of "the feudal regime in its entirety." In practice, subsequent legislation made clear that "abolition" was often to involve indemnification. Peasant insurrection resumed and the National Assembly and its successors continued to grope for a formula to pacify the countryside, ultimately finding it in abandoning the initial plan.

So peasants came to focus on seigneurial rights as their major target and legislators came to move to a far more radical notion of what to do about the seigneurial regime than is evident in the *cahiers* of the spring of 1789, in the early rural insurrections and in the initial legislation. There was, I shall argue, a dialogic process that led, not to a compromise, but to a mutual radicalization. The form "abolition" was to take was altered by revolutionary peasants and revolutionary legislators in their angry, violent, frustrating, antagonistic (but sometimes cooperative) dialogue. But what was "feudalism"? This master concept itself was being imbued with new significance. But the discourse of feudalism did not evolve in a world made up of nothing but words. The legislators deployed it as they grappled, at various times and in various ways, with sharecroppers, smallholders, forest workers, weavers, renters, and serfs willing to challenge the lords' claims upon them openly, collectively, and aggressively. The legislators groped for a narrow definition that would square with the claim that they had already abolished feudalism (and need do no more in the future). But they also claimed that abolition to be so profound as to explain the fearful enmity of other European states; and they threatened those states with a similar overthrow of their own feudal regimes in the event of war. Some in the legislature thought that the definition and deployment of words could control the flow of events; but they uttered those words in response to the thousands of rural mobilizations whose ebb and flow we shall explore.

Lynn Hunt[24] has suggested that much writing on the Revolution is focused on causes and consequences in a way that leaves the revolutionary events themselves as a blank. The development of national and international markets, we are sometimes told, created an energetic and prosperous class looking to further opportunities for economic change; a peasantry in part buying into the new possibilities of prosperity and in part resentful of the new possibilities of impoverishment; and a nobility in part won over to and eagerly participating in the new order and in part attempting to halt the march of change. This is social dynamite; and when the dust of the social explosion cleared, we have the bourgeois France of the nineteenth century. A rather different story focuses on the state, rather than the market. The rationalizing propensities of a growing state undermines the pretensions of local institutions to wield authority, of the traditionally privileged to have their advantages tolerated and of the very claims of hallowed tradition as a justification of social arrangements. Peasants come to experience their lords as thieves rather than honored patrons; educated and well-off commoners see legally defined hierarchy as an unjust refuge for incompetence and a barrier to progress; and even some among the privileged themselves no longer believe their own privilege is justified and hope to find a renewed sense of their own worth in joining in the struggle for an enlightened future.

24. Lynn A. Hunt, *Politics, Culture and Class in the French Revolution* (Berkeley and Los Angeles: University of California Press, 1984), 1–16.

This, too, is social dynamite, and when the dust clears, we have the modern French state presiding over a society of individuals, the old corporate and hierarchical structures consigned to history's dustbin.

In either of these stories, Lynn Hunt suggests, we are led away from what happens in the Revolution itself: we move from the seeds of the new order germinating in the Old Regime to its bearing fruit in the modern world. Causes lie in the decades or even centuries that precede and consequences in the two centuries that follow. The point of her comment is to try to get us to look anew at the possibility that something was created in the Revolution itself. I shall be arguing here that accounts of long-term structures do help us understand patterns of grievance-making, patterns of rural insurrection and revolutionary legislation. Both accounts of how interests were shaped by economic changes (which I shall call, approximately, Marxian) and of cultural changes that accompanied the growth of a rationalizing state (which I shall call, approximately, Tocquevillean) help make sense of a good deal of the data I shall present. But what they do not explain is critical: they do not explain the shift in peasant targets and the radicalization of legislation. Something happened in the Revolution (Lynn Hunt's point). What happened, or so I shall argue, is that villagers and legislators dealt with each other and altered their actions; the convergence of their actions was what ended the seigneurial regime.

Whatever contribution this book makes to understanding one revolution, it is not primarily in any novelty of facts wrested from archival documents. But counting grievances or insurrections of one sort or another does reveal unseen patterns and confirms some familiar claims (but refutes others). This book proposes to sift through the spatial and temporal patterns of grievance and of insurrection, in order to assay established theories and try to develop new ones. It aims to break new ground by charting the relationship of grievance and revolt. Most fundamentally, in exploring the dialogue of insurrectionary peasants and revolutionary legislators, it sheds, I believe, a revealing light on both.

CHAPTER

2

SEIGNEURIAL RIGHTS ON THE REVOLUTIONARY AGENDA

For all the attention the rural insurrections of 1789 have received, there is still a great deal to learn. Emmanuel Le Roy Ladurie has suggested that the revolts provide us with a window into a great transformation of the French countryside. He is struck by the contrast with the great seventeenth-century movements of violent resistance to the fiscal pressures of the growing state. After a long interval in which the defeated peasantry raised no major challenge, the distinctive target of the rural upheavals of the early Revolution had switched from the claims of the state to those of the lord. Understanding this shift, Le Roy Ladurie contends, should illuminate the rural history of France in modern times. Behind the change in peasant actions must lie major changes in French institutions.[1]

We can try to understand what had made the demands of their lords so central a focus of the revolutionary mobilization of the French countryside

1. Emmanuel Le Roy Ladurie, "Révoltes et contestations rurales en France de 1675 à 1788," *Annales: Economies, Sociétés, Civilisations* 29 (1974): 6–22.

through an exploration of the rural grievances expressed at the Revolution's onset. Those grievances reveal a great deal and through those grievances we will be able to see something of the larger social contexts that the people of the countryside were addressing. But we shall also see that the role played by the seigneurial rights is more than the inexorable working-out of forces clearly in play at the beginning of the great upheaval. The long-term processes that Le Roy Ladurie asks us to study are essential to understanding the attack on the rights of the lords; but we shall see that we need as well to consider the Revolution itself as a process in which the countryside and the legislature confronted one another and in this confrontation nurtured the insurrections and the legislation that brought the time of the lords to an end.

Why do peasants rise against one target rather than another? To date there is little scholarly consensus on the causes and significance of the rural insurrection. In one view there is a direct connection between the burden of claims on peasant resources and the vehemence of defensive peasant action. Georges Lefebvre[2] stresses the weight of taxes, tithes, and seigneurial rights. In accounting for the revolt, he asserts that seigneurial rights were increasingly heavy and that taxes probably were. The burning of the *châteaux* is central to his summary account of the risings, while tax disturbances are clearly secondary. The implicit yet clear explanation rests on his reading of the *cahiers:* "The petitions call attention to the crushing weight of all these dues taken together, finding it heavier than the parallel burden of the royal taxes."[3] The rural movement was a significant pressure on revolutionary legislators: without it, it is unlikely that the new regime would have so profoundly attacked the seigneurial rights.[4] Lefebvre's more microscopic treatments also stress the weight of exactions. At one point in his minute account of the claims upon the peasants of the Nord, for example, he writes: "The feudal rights made up a heavy weight, often irritating but above all customary. If they so strongly excited the animosity of the peasants at the end of the Old Regime, wasn't this because the lords insisted upon them with more exactitude and rigor or were even increasing them?"[5]

He briefly considers the possibility of a change in peasant attitudes as an autonomous element: "It may be that they judged intolerable what their

2. Georges Lefebvre, *The Coming of the French Revolution* (Princeton: Princeton University Press, 1947), 131–51.

3. Ibid., 141.

4. Georges Lefebvre, "La Révolution française et les paysans," in his *Etudes sur la Révolution française* (Paris: Presses Universitaires de France, 1963), 343.

5. Lefebvre, *Les paysans du Nord pendant la Révolution française* (Paris: Presses Universitaires de France, 1972), 148. The theme of the lords tightening the screws is also stressed in "La Révolution française et les paysans," 350–53.

fathers had supported."[6] But he returns quickly to the theme of a seigneurial crackdown. Explaining regional variations in the pattern of revolt, he points to differences in the weight of the seigneurial rights: One zone has fewer lords and many possible rights were nonexistent; a second has a full panoply of rights rigorously enforced. The former zone is relatively prosperous; the latter, poorer, finds the greater weight all the harder to support. Hence it is in the latter, where rights were heavier and peasant resources lighter, that one finds the risings of the summer of 1789.[7]

Elements of this picture are shared by many. The much-debated notion of a "feudal reaction" according to which the lords were pushing to extract more toward the end, would, if accepted, constitute strong evidence that an increase in the burden was central to the rising.[8] A less common tactic, but also concordant with Lefebvre's account, has been the attempt to show that, increasing or not, the level of seigneurial exactions was frequently high.[9]

By contrast, Tocqueville urges us to look not to the sheer level of burden, but to the collapse of services provided by the lords, services that constituted justifications for payments.[10] To the extent that local lords protected the community, repaired and policed the roads, resolved communal disputes, supported the true Church, inspected weights and measures, and provided grain in hard times the payments to the lords supported vital services. As these functions were seized by the developing state, however, the lord's powers and prerogatives, though in some ways diminished, were experienced as unjust and detested. It was not the weight of the seigneurial system that led peasants to rise in anger, but its loss of utility. For Tocqueville the issue is not burden as such at all, but justice. A heavy burden that purchases a genuine service, a lord whose revenues are compensations for his filling a communal need are tolerated, but even a lightened burden that purchases nothing is not to be borne. In comparative

6. Lefebvre, *Paysans du Nord,* 149.

7. Ibid., 162–63.

8. Various views within an enormous literature may be sampled in William Doyle, "Was There an Aristocratic Reaction in Pre-Revolutionary France?" in Douglas Johnson, ed., *French Society and Revolution* (Cambridge: Cambridge University Press, 1976), 3–28; Guy Lemarchand, "La féodalité et la Révolution française: Seigneurie et communauté paysanne (1780–1799)," *Annales historiques de la Révolution française* 242 (1980): 536–58; Jonathan Dewald, *Pont-St.-Pierre, 1398–1789: Lordship, Community and Capitalism* (Berkeley and Los Angeles: University of California Press, 1987), 232.

9. For example, Guy Lemarchand, "Le féodalisme dans la France rurale des temps modernes: essai de caractérisation," *Annales historiques de la Révolution française* 41 (1969): 77–108. Henri Sée regards it as reasonable supposition that where complaints about taxes outran complaints about seigneurial rights, the tax burden was probably heavier than the seigneurial. See Henri Sée, "La rédaction et la valeur historique des cahiers de paroisses pour les états-généraux de 1789," *Revue Historique,* no. 103 (1910): 305–6.

10. Alexis de Tocqueville, *The Old Regime and the French Revolution* (Garden City, N.Y.: Doubleday, 1955).

perspective Tocqueville suggests we note how, heavy as the demands of lord and church might be, they were less heavy than elsewhere in Europe. The relative lightness is a sign of decay, and it is the decay of a genuine public role for the lord that made his decreased exactions into intolerable theft.[11] This position, too, has its recent adherents. William Brustein and Hudson Meadwell have recently tried to marshal evidence to demonstrate that where the lord's authority was coupled with the control of resources adequate for the performance of a genuine public role, the lords were not a principal target of peasant action.[12]

Where Lefebvre tends to explain peasant risings by a heavy and rising burden, then, Tocqueville points to the decline of services. Both, however, converge on what is to be explained; namely, an intense rural hostility to the seigneurial regime that made the peasantry a formidable force whose pressures on the new revolutionary government significantly contributed to an overall radicalization. More recently, a third judgment on the peasants' revolution has emerged. In an influential article on the grievance lists of 1789—the *cahiers de doléances*[13]—George Taylor contended that those documents show a France far less ready for social revolution than a reader of Tocqueville would expect. The parish *cahiers* in particular show a narrowness of vision and a lack of concern with national political questions. Even on the issue of seigneurial rights, it was upper urban groups who were the carriers of radicalism. On his reading of the evidence, Taylor is quite skeptical of claims that the peasants radicalized the revolution; he specifically dismisses Alfred Cobban's attempt to show that it was the militant countryside and not a rather conservative group of revolutionary legislators that drove the revolution forward.[14]

What no party to this debate has done is to examine peasant attitudes toward their various burdens in detail, right by right and tax by tax. Such a procedure, of course, sheds no light on the objective level of burdens borne

11. Ibid., 22–31.

12. William Brustein, "Regional Social Orders in France and the French Revolution," *Comparative Social Research* 9 (1986): 145–61; Hudson Meadwell, "Exchange Relations Between Lords and Peasants," *Archives Européenes de Sociologie* 28 (1987): 3–49. A more or less Tocquevillean perspective on lord-peasant relations is now common in comparative studies of rural insurrection. James Scott and Samuel Popkin, who disagree on much, are in accord that rebellious peasant action is oriented not to what dominant strata take from them, but to the balance of what is taken and what is given. See James C. Scott, *The Moral Economy of the Peasant: Rebellion and Subsistence in Southeast Asia* (New Haven: Yale University Press, 1976) and Samuel Popkin, *The Rational Peasant* (Berkeley and Los Angeles: University of California Press, 1979).

13. George V. Taylor, "Revolutionary and Nonrevolutionary Content in the Cahiers de Doléances of 1789: An Interim Report," *French Historical Studies* 7 (1972): 479–502.

14. The Cobban position disputed by Taylor was itself developed as part of a critique of Marxist claims of bourgeois antipathy to the lords. See Alfred Cobban, *The Social Interpretation of the French Revolution* (Cambridge: Cambridge University Press, 1965).

(let alone services received). It does, however, permit us to examine almost microscopically how the people of the countryside conceived of what was demanded of them and of those who demanded it. I shall show in this chapter and Chapter 3 that French villagers engaged in a multifaceted evaluation of their burdens, making at times rather fine judgments about the tolerable and the intolerable. Their burdens were central to their wishes, as Lefebvre indicates, but their evaluation of these burdens raised issues of utility and fairness in ways broadly consonant with Tocqueville's picture. In considering the payments to the lord, the church, or the state, the French countryside was animated by considerations of services received, of equity, and even of something verging on a sense of potential citizenship not often ascribed to village France. I shall reaffirm Taylor's view that the broad political issues found in the *cahiers* of higher-status groups preoccupy the peasants very little, but I shall also show the peasants to be animated by their own broad concerns and to be, in some regards, more radical than those elites.

The parish *cahiers* show that France's villages were settings for considerable thought about the French institutions that impinged upon them, more thought than is always recognized. Abel Poitrineau writes of the peasants of Auvergne whose poverty and illiteracy "make them unused to and perhaps incapable of linking their spontaneous protest to a coherent body of general ideas on social or political organization."[15] And William Doyle explains the failure of their *cahiers* to condemn "feudalism as a whole": "Such an idea was beyond the intellectual grasp of illiterate or semi-literate peasants."[16] I believe, on the contrary, the evidence does show the capacity of the peasants to distinguish one seigneurial right from another, one tax from another, one church exaction from another demonstrates a considerable intellectual grasp of their world.[17]

The Cahiers de Doléances

We shall explore the discussions of seigneurial rights in the *cahiers de doléances,* the remarkable collection of political documents produced in the course of the convocation of the Estates-General of 1789. Financial crisis forced the government to convene this body, by means of which His

15. Abel Pointrineau, "Le détonateur économico-fiscal des rancoeurs catégorielles profondes, lors des explosions de la colère populaire en Auvergne, au XVIIIe siècle," in Jean Nicholas, ed., *Mouvements populaires et conscience sociale, XVIe–XIXe siècles,* (Paris: Maloine, 1985), 361.

16. William Doyle, *Origins of the French Revolution* (Oxford: Oxford University Press, 1980), 198.

17. We shall examine in Chapter 9 the intellectual constructions of those who did speak of the feudal regime as a whole.

Majesty's subjects, through their representatives, conveyed their views to the throne. No such body had met since 1614, as kings sought to assert their independence of all merely human institutions. When the monarchy acceded to the resuscitation of the Estates-General it sought to enhance its legitimacy while denying obstreperous elite forces a platform to pursue their program of restricting royal authority. Although the tradition of separate elections of delegates from the three estates of the realm—the clergy, nobility, and Third Estate—was maintained, the electoral process allowed a wide suffrage and saw the representation, to one degree or another, of virtually the entire kingdom and most of the significant social groupings of the Old Regime.[18] The mix of traditionally hierarchical and corporate conceptions and more individualistic and egalitarian ones that is visible in fusing a wide suffrage with three distinct orders permeated the entire electoral process.[19]

The electoral district used for the previous Estates-General, in 1614, had been the *bailliage,* a judicial unit defining the territorial jurisdiction of a lower-level royal court. It was adopted, with modifications here and there, as the basis of the elections of 1789. The Estates-General was a gathering of delegates from the three estates of the realm. As had been done in the past, each estate—clergy, nobility, and Third Estate (a residual category that included most of the population)—followed its own electoral procedure. The rules defining eligibility were different for each estate, but gave most adult men an opportunity to attend an assembly.[20] While the convocation varied a great deal from region to region, there was a basic regulation and a modal procedure. Although the clergy's elections acknowledged ecclesiastical hierarchy in the selection of the chair of the *bailliage* meeting, the parish clergy were numerically dominant. As for the Second Estate, fief-holding nobles were honored by a personal letter of convocation (while other nobles were invited only by a collective notice), but virtually all noblemen could show up and vote. In the case of the numerous Third Estate, a similarly broad suffrage obviously required a sequence of indirect elections. Each *bailliage* contained towns and rural parishes. Within each of the rural parishes a meeting of all the eligible members of the Third Estate was held, to elect delegates to a *bailliage* assembly. Decisions were made by public

18. Standard sources on the convocation are Armand Brette, *Receuil de documents relatifs à la convocation des états généraux de 1789* (Paris: Imprimerie Nationale, 1894–1915) and Beatrice Fry Hyslop, *A Guide to the General Cahiers of 1789, with the Texts of Unedited Cahiers* (New York: Octagon, 1968).

19. For a detailed analysis of the convocation rules, see Gilbert Shapiro and John Markoff, *Revolutionary Demands: A Content Analysis of the Cahiers de Doléances of 1789* (Stanford: Stanford University Press, 1997), chap. 7.

20. The formal rules excluded most women and some poor men but even those women who were eligible tended to stay away, and something similar may be said of the poor in many places.

voice vote. In the towns there was a similar meeting of each guild or corporation, as well as a meeting of those not organized into corporate bodies. These meetings elected deputies to a town meeting, which in turn elected representatives to the *bailliage* assembly, where they met with the rural delegates. Sometimes this *bailliage* assembly elected delegates to the Estates-General at Versailles. In other cases there might be still another step in which delegates from several *bailliages* met together to choose representatives. Every one of these assemblies—parish, guild, town, *bailliage,* or group of several *bailliages*—was a deliberative as well as an electoral body. That is, it not only picked representatives, but also drew up a *cahier de doléances,* a record of grievances, suggestions, complaints, and proposals. The assemblies of the nobles and the clergy also drafted *cahiers* as well as elected deputies.

What is remarkable about the *cahiers,* and gives them their special interest to students of social change, is that the French Revolution is the only major revolution at the beginning of which so much of the nation gathered in public assemblies and recorded its grievances, aspirations, and demands for change. Since little would appear as patently significant in the study of a revolution as the range, intensity, and distribution of grievances among groups in the population, the *cahiers de doléances* are absolutely unique in importance as a documentary source.

More than 40,000 corporate and territorial entities (craft guilds, parishes, towns, *bailliages,* and so forth) drew up these documents. The *cahiers* were to serve as mandates for the delegates elected for the national convocation of the Estates-General in the spring of 1789. As open-ended lists of grievances and proposals for reform, the *cahiers* are extraordinarily varied in length, tone, range of subjects covered, mode of exposition, and opinions. A content analysis of these documents provides the statistical database on which this study will draw.[21]

Of the many types of documents produced we have coded three collections.

1. The general *cahiers* that assemblies of the nobility endorsed (166 documents).
2. The general *cahiers* that assemblies of the Third Estate endorsed (198 documents).[22] For convenience, we shall refer to these as the "Third Estate *cahiers.*"
3. A national sample of the *cahiers* of rural parishes (748 documents).

21. The development of this database was carried out together with Gilbert Shapiro. For a general discussion of this research program, see Gilbert Shapiro, John Markoff, and Sasha R. Weitman, "Quantitative Studies of the French Revolution," *History and Theory* 12 (1973): 163–91, and Shapiro and Markoff, *Revolutionary Demands*.

22. A "general" *cahier* is one drawn up at the last stage of the convocation; that is, one that was carried to the meetings of the Estates-General in Versailles rather than any higher level intermediary

Coding the Cahiers

To appreciate the analyses that follow, the coding of the *cahiers* must be briefly described.[23] In the construction of our code for the *cahiers,* our objective was to translate every grievance in the documents into a language that is convenient for computer analysis, particularly since it has only one way to express a particular demand. We attempted to capture as much of the concrete meaning (as distinguished from the analytical significance) of the text in its coded representation. The code for a given demand includes, first of all, a designation of the *subject* of the grievance (ordinarily an institutional or problem area) and, second, a code for the *action* that is demanded in the document.[24] The code guide has a very large number of institutional and action codes intended to capture all grievances that appear in the *cahiers* with any significant frequency.

The action codes are relatively simple. The action may be quite precise, such as "reestablish," or it may be extremely vauge: for example, "do something about" some subject. Other codes represent such simple and commonly demanded actions as "abolish" or "maintain" something or other, "equalize," "simplify," or "standardize."

The code for the subject of the grievance, its institutional or problem area, is somewhat more complex: it is organized as a four-level hierarchy. The first level of the hierarchy represents major institutional categories of eighteenth-century France:

0 Miscellaneous[25]
1 General
C Constitution
E Economy
G Government

assembly. I phrase this description in a rather clumsy way since there were *joint cahiers* endorsed by more than one estate, and we included them in the group of documents coded so long as the relevant estate endorsed the grievances.

23. For a fuller treatment of the coding methods and their rationale, see John Markoff, Gilbert Shapiro, and Sasha R. Weitman, "Toward the Integration of Content Analysis and General Methodology," in David Heise, ed., *Sociological Methodology 1975* (San Francisco: Jossey-Bass, 1974), 1–58, as well as Shapiro and Markoff, *Revolutionary Demands.*

24. We also provide the coder the option of expressing qualifications and detailed notes clarifying coding decisions, in the form of a Conventional and a Free Remarks field. For example, the coder might indicate that the text is more specific than the code by writing SPEC in the conventional field and the details in the Free Remarks field.

25. In any position of the hierarchy, or in the action field, a "0" or miscellaneous code refers to a grievance that does not fit *any* of the categories provided: in the present instance, the first hierarchical level, it would mean a grievance neither constitutional nor economic nor governmental, nor referring to the judiciary, religion, or stratification. A "1" is very different: it refers to a *general* grievance, which falls under most or all of the categories provided.

J Judiciary
R Religion
S Stratification System

We shall illustrate the hierarchical principle by showing those sections of the code that are required to encode the demand that the *gabelle* (the salt tax) be standardized; that is, that it be subject to the same rate and administrative rules throughout the country. The full code would read: G TA IN GA ST (i.e., Government, Taxation, Indirect Taxes, Gabelle, Standardize). To begin with, the Level 1 category, "Government," is broken down into the following Level 2 codes:

G 0 Government—Miscellaneous
G 1 Government—General
G AA Administrative Agencies
G FI Government—Finances
G KI The King
G MI Military
G RL Regional and Local Government
G TA Government—Taxation

"Taxation" is divided into Level 3 categories as follows:

G TA 0 Government—Taxation—Miscellaneous
G TA 1 Government—Taxation—General
G TA AD Tax Advantages
G TA DA Direct Tax Agencies
G TA DI Existing Direct Taxes
G TA IA Indirect Tax Agencies
G TA IN Existing Indirect Taxes
G TA NT New Taxes
G TA TA Tax Administration

Finally, G TA IN, "Indirect Taxes," is divided into the following relatively concrete Level 4 coding categories representing particular taxes:

G TA IN 0 Existing Indirect Taxes—Miscellaneous
G TA IN 1 Existing Indirect Taxes—General
G TA IN AI Aides
G TA IN CD Centième Denier
G TA IN CU Cuir
G TA IN DC Droits de Contrôle
G TA IN DD Droits Domaniaux

G TA IN DF	Droits sur la Fabrication
G TA IN DJ	Droits Joints aux Aides
G TA IN ES	Droits D'Entrée et de Sortie
G TA IN FE	Fer
G TA IN GA	Gabelle
G TA IN HU	Huiles
G TA IN IN	Insinuation
G TA IN OC	Octrois des Villes
G TA IN OF	Centième Denier des Offices

As we shall see, the main advantage of this kind of hierarchical organization is that it facilitates analysis at multiple levels. We can study, in other words, the frequencies (and the consensus) of various groups not only on the *gabelle* but also on the more general categories of *indirect taxes* or of *taxes in general* or even of demands relative to *government,* taxes, of course included. An assessment of this study depends not only on the quality of the discussion of evidence but also on the quality of the evidence itself. I shall introduce two questions here: (1), the adequacy of the *cahiers* as a source for the views of the French people, and (2), the adequacy of our sample of the *cahiers.* Each of these questions requires a rather lengthy response and is in fact dealt with fully in a book with Gilbert Shapiro, *Revolutionary Demands.* I shall limit myself here to the briefest of assertions.[26]

First of all, the *cahiers* need to be critically evaluated as sources of information on political grievances. Many historians have criticized them for a wide variety of alleged shortcomings as public opinion data. For example, certain individuals are supposed to have been too influential at the assemblies (the presiding officers, for example), and others (like the duke of Orléans) deliberately circulated "model *cahiers*" that were sometimes closely imitated by some of the actual *cahiers.* In addition there are serious questions regarding the extent of participation in the parish electoral process.[27] Moreover, it has often been argued, the collective nature of the assemblies makes it difficult to know just whose opinions are expressed in these documents. Much of this criticism is misplaced.[28]

26. There is also a third significant question, namely, the adequacy of our coding. This is discussed in *Revolutionary Demands* and I will not repeat that discussion here.

27. A few high points from an enormous literature: Marc Bouloiseau, "Elections de 1789 et communautés rurales en Haute-Normandie," *Annales Historiques de la Révolution Française* 28 (1956): 29–47; Melvin Edelstein, "Vers une 'sociologie electorale' de la Révolution française: La participation des citadins et campagnards (1789–1793)," *Revue d'Histoire Moderne et Contemporaine* 22 (1975): 508–29; Ran Halévi, "La Monarchie et les élections: position des problèmes," in Keith Michael Baker, ed., *The French Revolution and the Creation of a Modern Political Culture,* vol. 1, *The Political Culture of the Old Regime* (Oxford: Pergamon Press, 1987), 387–402.

28. Let us consider, for example, the charge that the *cahiers* reveal little about the views of assemblies that drafted them because they contain material copied from other *cahiers* or from

We need to see the assemblies that adopted the *cahiers* as engaged in a political action. There are judgments being made of what is possible to obtain and other judgments of what it is impolitic to mention. There are decisions by some in the assemblies not to object to certain grievances whose inclusion is proposed by others—so long, that is, as the proposers will not object to one's own pet projects. There are also, no doubt, topics best avoided because they are hopelessly divisive. The *cahiers,* in short, constitute a form of strategic speech. If noble assemblies say little on many seigneurial rights, we suspect (and shall argue below) that it is not because they had no wishes, as individuals, but because they frequently disagreed among themselves and also because it was an area some wished out of public debate. The demands expressed in *cahiers* are those that groups constituted in specific ways could manage to agree upon at a specific moment and with a complex audience in mind: at an assembly one had not only to come to terms with the other nobles, urban notables, or villagers with whom one was trying to agree on a text, but one had to also bear in mind the ultimately public nature of the act, the Estates-General ahead, and one's sense—possibly shared with one's fellows at the assembly, possibly not—of what it was shrewd and what it was prudent to demand.

A *cahier,* then, is a marvelous snapshot of the staking-out of positions, but it is only a snapshot. A year down the line, in changing circumstances, the same assemblies might well have seen things differently. A year down the line, those who had been constituted as electoral assemblies might constitute themselves differently. By March 1792 or March 1793 a portion of the villagers may have found a basis for acting on their own whether as consumers of grain, earners of wages, or payers of rent; the urban notables who joined in passing a text would very likely have divided into various politicized factions (and some would have dropped out of politics); some nobles would now be in exile and others would have learned to keep quiet. The *cahiers* are not a window through which we see some presocial "attitudes"; they show us speech-in-context.

In a meditative essay on the dialogue of domination and subordination,

---

propaganda designed specifically to influence them. But a comparison of the bona fide *cahiers* with such electoral campaign materials reveals that choice was exercised in selecting among available models; that frequently only a few articles were copied; that models were rarely if ever copied in toto; that even when totally copied, new demands were usually added. (See, for example, the revealing analysis by Paul Bois, *Cahiers de doléances du tiers état de la sénéchaussée de Château-du-Loir pour les Etats généraux de 1789* [Gap: Imprimerie Louis-Jean, 1960], chap. 4.) In short, everything suggests deliberate selection. And why not select a more articulate, expressive, and forceful statement of one's own genuinely held demands? Numerous other charges and objections have been raised against the *cahiers,* discussion of which will be found in Gilbert Shapiro and John Markoff, "L'authenticité des cahiers," *Bulletin d'Histoire de la Révolution Française* (1990–91): 17–70, and *Revolutionary Demands.*

James Scott[29] urges us to accept "the public transcript," the statements that the top dogs and bottom dogs make to each other, as having only the most uncertain relationship to the several "hidden transcripts," what the dominators or the underclass say among themselves. The *cahiers* are doubly public: first, they are negotiated in a public forum among villagers, nobles or elite urbanites; second, they are addressed to a much wider audience. We might sometimes imagine several possible models of private transcripts that are consistent with the public one, but direct glimpses of anything but another public one, adopted to other circumstances, are rare.[30] When we shift away from grievances toward insurrections and legislation in Chapter 5, we are seeing other public acts, too. When peasants tell a pair of visiting investigators what a maypole means (see p. 604) we may wonder, even if the investigators do not, whether they have been told what the villagers say among themselves.

Consider the three sorts of documents we shall be exploring here. Who speaks in them? As a rough approximation: In the *cahiers* of the parishes we hear the peasants of rural France, even though such outsiders as local priests, urban lawyers, and seigneurial judges may have aided or hindered in their drafting. No doubt, it was the more affluent members of the rural community whose voices weighed most heavily. In the *cahiers* the deputies of the Third Estate carried to Versailles, we probably hear the positions of the non-noble portion of the upper reaches of urban France. By way of simplification, but not, we contend, oversimplification, we may speak of those represented in these texts as the ***urban notables;*** notables who have an eye on the upheavals around them and who are certainly responsive to some degree to the rural grievances carried by the delegates from the parishes. In light of the role played by these "general" *cahiers* of the Third Estate in our subsequent discussion, it is important to forestall some terminological confusion. Although "Third Estate" had the very broad meaning of the overwhelming majority of the French people, those neither clergy nor noble, in the context of the *cahiers* we shall sometimes refer much more narrowly to the well-to-do higher reaches of non-noble France: the legal, medical, scientific professionals; the writers, merchants, and financiers; the substantial landholders and those vying as the common phrase had it, "to live nobly"; in a word, the "notables." It was these notables who dominated the drafting of those *cahiers*. Particularly when comparing various *cahiers* with one another, by "Third Estate" we shall often mean, not the entire range of non-noble France, but this non-noble

29. James C. Scott, *Domination and the Arts of Resistance: Hidden Transcripts* (New Haven: Yale University Press, 1990).

30. And, arguably, nonexistent. Even one's memories of one's dreams may be tailored to an imagined audience.

elite. As for the nobility, this first genuinely democratic election among the privileged produced a number of surprises, and we would judge these documents broadly representative of France's Second Estate and not just the greatest and the most powerful. But we must remember that these are all public statements: they are what villagers, urban elites, and nobles thought shrewd or prudent to say to each other, and to other significant actors as well, such as the clergy (whose own *cahiers* are not represented here), or the king and his agents and supporters. These are, to be sure, very important assertions—fundamental, in fact.[31]

Which documents should we include in our sample? A large number of *cahiers* representing many groups was produced, and the statistical analysis of all of them is altogether impossible.[32] Some sort of sample is necesary. We decided to code the extant general *cahiers* of the Third Estate and nobility and a sample of the *cahiers* of the parishes. We feel that this choice of document type gives a good coverage of the diversity of political leanings, at the cost, to be sure, of omitting the enormously significant clergy. The samples of the noble and Third Estate *cahiers* are not particularly problematic but our coding of fewer than 2% of the parish *cahiers* requires more comment. We believe we have good reason to regard this as a rather representative national sample.

A rather detailed exploration that compared the *bailliages* from which the parish *cahiers* were sampled to France as a whole revealed that our sample is a bit too urban.[33] Our parishes, in other words, tend to be more likely to have a large town nearby than would a fully representative sample. Other elements that go along with a large town are also overrepresented—most important, insurrection.[34] The parishes whose *cahiers* we examine were,

31. For further discussion of some of these issues, see Shapiro and Markoff, "L'authenticité des cahiers."

32. Opinions differ widely as to the total number of *cahiers* produced. Edmé Champion suggests that there were more than fifty thousand. Beatrice Hyslop, a more recent authority, guesses "more than twenty-five thousand." Albert Soboul offers sixty thousand. The estimate of the total number of *cahiers* actually written is an extremely hazardous task. In the first place, there were roughly forty thousand rural communes; but in some instances the "parish" in the convocation sense encompassed a number of such districts. The number of preliminary *cahiers* of the clergy, while conceivably enormous, is totally unknown, for these documents have rarely been studied, reprinted, or even catalogued. The number of *cahiers* written by urban corporate groups is also rather obscure, because unlike the rural parishes, urban groups often failed to exercise their option of writing down their grievances; we cannot therefore assume that the number of assemblies entitled to draft *cahiers* is a good approximation of the number who did so. (Edmé Champion, *La France d'après les cahiers de 1789* (Paris: A. Colin, 1897), 21; Hyslop, *Guide,* ix–x; Soboul, *Precis d'Histoire de la Révolution Française* (Paris: Editions Sociales, 1962), 103–4.

33. For a much more detailed account, see Gilbert Shapiro, John Markoff, and Silvio R. Duncan Baretta, "The Selective Transmission of Historical Documents: The Case of the Parish Cahiers of 1789," *Histoire et Mesure* 2 (1987): 115–72.

34. For the relationship of towns and rural insurrection, see Chapter 7, as well as John Markoff,

therefore, somewhat more likely than a perfectly randomly chosen group would be to have had insurrectionary events nearby in 1789. But these effects are small and almost anything else we could measure is unrelated to inclusion in our sample.

The Rural World of Burdens

Table 2.1 displays the fifty most widely discussed institutions of eighteenth-century France.[35] For each group of *cahiers,* the subjects are arranged in the order of frequency of discussion, with those most discussed listed first. For example, "taxation in general" is discussed in more *cahiers* of the parishes and of the Third Estate than any other subject; for the nobility, however, pride of place goes to "regular meetings of the Estates-General." Those entries linked by brackets are tied in frequency.[36]

A look at the three groups of *cahiers* brings out the special character of each group's grievances. Despite some common concerns, there are clear differences in priorities. The nobility are particularly likely to address the organization and authority of the coming Estates-General. Not only is the issue of regular meetings (as opposed to infrequent convocation at the whim of the monarch) their most widely discussed subject, but there are also a large number of other demands concerning either the procedures ("vote by order")[37] or the authority ("veto on taxation," "ministerial responsibility") of that body. The nobility, moreover, are unusually keen to treat civil liberties: notice the presence on this list of such subjects as censorship, personal liberties, *lettres de cachet* (arbitrary authorizations of imprisonment), and secrecy of the mails. The common thread that links these subjects is no doubt a concern with arbitrary central authority, also shown in discussions of a written constitution or of the royal authority to transfer cases from one court to another. It seems likely that the weight of noble concern for "laws," as well as the codification of law into criminal and civil codes is also part and

"The Social Geography of Rural Revolt at the Beginning of the French Revolution," *American Sociological Review* 50 (1985): 761–81, and "Contexts and Forms of Rural Revolt: France in 1789," *Journal of Conflict Resolution* 30 (1986): 253–89.

35. In the terminology developed earlier, we are exploring our Level 4 categories.

36. Several subjects shared last place for the nobility, which forced a relaxation of the restriction to fifty subjects. This restriction to the top fifty is, to be sure, quite arbitrary, but it is adequate for illuminating the gulf that separated the great rural majority from the elites. For another analysis of the most widespread demands, see Shapiro and Markoff, *Revolutionary Demands,* chap. 14.

37. A major debate raged over whether the deputies at the Estates-General were to vote individually ("by head") or "by order," with each of the three orders having one vote, the latter procedure widely viewed as a brake on reforms that might threaten the privileged.

Table 2.1. Subjects Most Widely Discussed in *Cahiers*, Ranked by Frequency of Discussion

Rank[a]	Parishes	Third Estate	Nobility
1	Taxation in general	Taxation in general	Regular meetings of Estates-General
2	Salt tax *(gabelle)*	Provincial Estates	Taxation in general
3	Tax on alcoholic beverages *(aides)*	Regular meetings of Estates-General	Veto on taxation for Estates-General
4	Salt monopoly	Vote by head at Estates-General	Provincial Estates
5	Tax on legal acts *(droit de contrôle)*	Veto on taxation for Estates-General	Censorship
6	Compulsory labor service on roads *(corvée royale)*	Customs duties *(traites)*	Personal liberties
7	Provincial Estates	Tax on legal acts *(droit de contrôle)*	Allocation of taxes
8	Principal direct tax *(taille)*	Censorship	Government pensions
9	Praise of Louis XVI	Government pensions	Authorizations to arrest *(lettres de cachet)*
10	Tax advantages of clergy	Career opportunities in military	Customs duties *(traites)*
11	Tax advantages of nobility	Tax on commoner acquisition of noble land *(franc-fief)*	Collection of taxes
12	Court officers who supervised auctions *(priseurs)*	Authorizations to arrest *(lettres de cachet)*	Private property
13	Customs duties *(traites)*	Allocation of taxes	Vote by order in Estates-General
14	Lord's right to raise pigeons	Weights and measures	Royal domain
15	Legal procedures	Personal liberties	Royal removal of cases to higher court *(évocation)*
16	Regional and local roads	Court officers who supervised auctions *(priseurs)*	Tax on legal acts *(droit de contrôle)*

17	Veto on taxation for Estates-General	Noble right to trial in high court *(committimus)*	Salt tax *(gabelle)*
18	Single tax *(impôt unique)*	Seigneurial tolls	Ministerial responsibility to Estates-General
19	Regular meetings of Estates-General	Salt tax *(gabelle)*	Government debt
20	Miscellaneous local subjects	The courts	Praise of Louis XVI
21	Allocation of taxes	Ministerial responsibility to Estates-General	Financial accountability of government
22	*Corvée* modified as money tax	Praise of Louis XVI	Right to be tried locally
23	Militia	Tax collection	Constitution
24	Head tax *(capitation)*	Compulsory labor services for lord	Means to repay government debt
25	Seigneurial courts in general	Royal domain	Nobility
26	Tithe in general	Officers of local government	Laws in general
27	Seigneurial regime in general	Lord's right to hunt	Veto on government borrowing for Estates-General
28	The courts in general	Royal removal of cases to high court *(évocation)*	Criminal code
29	Lord's right to hunt	Veto on government borrowing for Estates-General	Tax advantages of nobility
30	Government monopoly and tax on tobacco	Irregular payments to clergy *(casuels)*	Government loans
31	Territorial tax *(impôt territorial)*	Lord's monopolies in general	Publicity and consolidation of government debt
32	Tax administration, miscellaneous	Doubling of the Third Estate	Ennoblement through achievement
33	Tax on commoner acquisition of noble land *(franc-fief)*	Means to repay government debt	Government finances
34	Lord's monopoly on milling	Legal procedures	Registering decrees with courts

Table 2.1 *(Continued)*

35	Tax advantages in general	Tax on alcoholic beverages *(aides)*	Ennoblement through office-holding
36	Twentieth tax *(vingtièmes)*	Private property	Military organization, miscellaneous
37	Effectiveness or efficiency of courts	Militia	Vote by head at Estates-General
38	The poor	Tax administration, miscellaneous	Expenses of government agencies
39	Weights and measures	Lord's right to raise pigeons	The courts
40	Vote by head in Estates-General	Miscellaneous indirect taxes	Secrecy of the mails
41	Draft by lot for militia	Tax on legal acts transferring property *(centième denier)*	Provincial Estates, miscellaneous
42	Fees for legal professions	Criminal penalties	Civil code
43	Direct tax agencies	Exceptional courts	General
44	Irregular payments to clergy *(casuels)*	Monastic institutions	Emergency sessions for Estates-General
45	A periodic cash payment to lord *(cens et rentes)*	Financial accountability of government	Government deficit
46	Major roads	Taxes on manufacture	Legislative veto for Estates-General
47	Taxation, miscellaneous	Beggars	Exceptional courts
48	Taxes on manufacture	Provincial Estates, miscellaneous	Estates-General in general
49	Tithe use for maintenance of church	Salary of parish priest *(portion congrue)*	Powers and functions of Estates-General, miscellaneous
50	Dues on property transfers to lord *(lods et ventes)*	Seigneurial regime in general	Government ministers
			Tax on alcoholic beverages *(aides)*
			New taxes in general

[a]Brackets indicate tied ranks.

parcel of this aristocratic sensitivity to *l'arbitraire.*[38] In this concern with the arbitrary prerogatives of central authority, we may discern the deep aristocratic roots of the liberal assault on the Old Regime, as argued, for example, by Denis Richet.[39]

If the greater stress on civil liberties by the nobility compared to the Third Estate surprises, we need only recall whose local, traditional, or group "liberties" were continually nibbled away by the expanding authority of the monarchical state. The nascent bureaucratic structures of this state evinced tendencies to standardization and uniformity that threatened to iron out the quirky distinctions that made one region and one social group unlike another. The noble-dominated high courts—the *parlements*—had for some time been at the forefront of open and explicit confrontation with royal authority and were thus especially sensitive to high-handed arbitrary tactics used against them that denied their liberty to protest, jailed or exiled them without much by way of legal procedures, and the like. It is plausible that what began as a reactive defense of their liberties (in the plural) had become, by 1789, a championing of liberty.

The classic statement of the great historic significance of the struggles of the monarchical state to penetrate, control, and rationalize the kingdom is Tocqueville's.[40] For Tocqueville the nobility are significant not merely as the purveyors of a liberal critique of the state's capricious power but also as the target of attacks on their own position: The slow strangulation of their independent action by the growing state removed from them the functions that alone permitted others—whether well-off, educated, elite commoners or impoverished, perhaps semiliterate peasants—to tolerate their status. As we glance at their positions in their own *cahiers* we shall certainly see (in this and the next chapter) such a hostility to privilege on the part of elite commoners and peasants; and we shall have an opportunity to explore later on whether the regional pattern of antiseigneurial rural revolt is consistent

38. The range of liberal sentiment in the noble *cahiers* has been copiously documented in two fine studies: Guy Chaussinand-Nogaret, *La noblesse au XVIIIe siècle: De la féodalité aux lumières* (Paris: Hachette, 1976), 181–226; and Sasha R. Weitman, "Bureaucracy, Democracy and the French Revolution" (Ph.D. diss., Washington University, 1968). By contrast Ludmila Pimenova stressed the extent of noble conservatism. See her *Dvorianstvo nakanune velikoi frantsuzskoi revoliutsii* (Moscow: Izdatel'stvo Universiteta, 1986), summarized in "La Noblesse à la veille de la Révolution" in *La Grande Révolution française* (Moscow: Editions "Naouka," 1989), 37–64, and "Das sozialpolitische Programm des Adels am Vorabend der Französischen Revolution," *Jahrbuch für Geschichte* 39 (1989): 179–201.

39. For Richet the "bourgeois" contribution to the Enlightenment is a relatively late graft on an already well developed tree. Denis Richet, "Autor des origines idéologiques lointaines de la Révolution française: élites et despotisme," *Annales: Economies, Sociétés, Civilisations* 9 (1969): 1–23; *La France moderne: L'esprit des institutions* (Paris: Flammarion, 1973).

40. Alexis de Tocqueville, *The Old Regime and the French Revolution.*

wtih the Tocquevillean expectation that it would be particularly common where the hand of the state was particularly heavy (see Chapter 7).

If noble concern for political liberties is striking, the salience of "private property" may strike some as little short of astonishing. If it may be paradoxical, in terms used by some Marxists, to note a relatively greater concern with "bourgeois liberties" among the nobility than the Third Estate, it is downright startling that "private property," that watchword of the bourgeois order, is the nobles' 12th most common subject and only 36th for the Third. Tocqueville and Denis Richet helped us with the first paradox, but what of the second? One bridge may be suggested by those noble *cahiers* that couple liberty and property, perhaps invoking natural law.[41] The nobility often appeal to "property" when defending themselves against state taxation[42] as well as threats to seigneurial rights.[43] Property is often held to be "inviolable and sacred."[44] The nobles of Belley go so far as to assert that the only purpose of society is the protection "of the property and persons of each individual by the strength of all" (*AP* 2:480). This linkage of property and liberty in a context of wariness about state taxation in particular and state authority in general—indeed the subordination of state purposes to the defense of property—shows the deep penetration of a Lockean rhetoric into the French nobility.[45]

We shall see below that when the nobility defend seigneurial rights in their *cahiers,*[46] it is often done by invoking the sacred character of property.

41. For example, the *cahier* of the nobility of Angers; see Jérôme Mavidal and E. Laurent, eds., *Archives parlementaires de 1787 à 1860,* 1st ser. (Paris: Librairie Administrative de Paul Dupont, 1862–), 2:32. This work will be abbreviated *AP* throughout.

42. For example, the joint *cahier* of the nobility and clergy of Lixheim, *AP* 5:714.

43. For example, in the course of the failed efforts of the three orders at a consensual document in Bourg-en-Bresse, the Third Estate proposal of restoring the tithe to its intended function was opposed by the nobility as an infringement of property rights. While they did not specify whose property rights, the clergy's response probably illuminates a discussion that did not enter the document: the clergy supported the Third's proposal, but specified that it was the "infeudated tithe," the tithe that had passed from clerics into the hands of lay lords, that was to be addressed. See *AP* 2:458.

44. For example, *AP* 2:281.

45. John Locke, *Of Civil Government, Two Treatises* (London: J. M. Dent, 1924), 180: "The great and chief end, therefore, of men uniting into commonwealths, and putting themselves under government, is the preservation of their property." The specific phrase "inviolable and sacred" had cropped up among champions of property rights in and out of France for some decades, as in the physiocrat Lemercier in 1770 or Adam Smith in 1776. See Adam Smith, *An Inquiry into the Nature and Causes of the Wealth of Nations* (London: Everyman's Library, 1910), 110; Steven L. Kaplan, *La Bagarre: Galiani's "Lost" Parody* (The Hague: Martinus Nijhoff, 1979), 39. (For other examples from physiocratic writing see Weulersse, *Le mouvement physiocratique en France (de 1756 à 1770)* [Paris: Félix Alcan, 1910], 1:4–5.)

46. See Chapter 3. Later, when anyone defended the continued collection of seigneurial dues on the floor of the National Assembly, it was almost exclusively in terms of property rights. See Chapter 9.

Is this noble stress on property—and not an immutable and perhaps divinely sanctioned social order—a powerful symptom of some Tocquevillean process of cultural adaptation to the antihierarchical leveling of the state? Or might it be better described as the cultural aspect of an increasing centrality of the market, a process that Marxists might speak of as an embourgeoisement of the nobility? And what sort—or sorts—of property do they have in mind? We shall return to these questions below.

The nobility are also distinctive for the salience of their concern with government expenditures. Their *cahiers* are the most likely to take up government borrowing and indebtedness, the means of repayment (including the royal domain, whose possible sale was widely bruited about as a partial solution to government debt), the expenses of the government (including the pensions by which obligations to the loyal and fears of the dangerous were met), accountability for government expenditures, as well as the issue of a veto for the Estates-General in taxation matters. Not that these issues are nonexistent for the others, but they occupy relatively greater salience for the nobility, as demonstrated by their ranking on Table 2.1. The link with other distinctive noble concerns is not hard to find: the growth of central state authority and the consequent loss of their proud autonomy is of a piece with the growth of uncontrolled state expenditures and the mounting shortages of revenues. The state debt is at the same time a consequence of state expansion and a likely cause of further expansion as the state grapples for new powers to fill its empty coffers even as it further encroaches on any independent forces in civil society.[47] And last but assuredly not least, government debt was among the strongest motives that energized a series of ministerial attempts to weaken the claims of fiscal privilege.[48]

For its part, the Third Estate is noteworthy for its emphases on privilege and on barriers to the development of the market. In the general area of privilege, note the relatively widespread concern with whether the Estates-General is to maintain the traditional distinctions among the orders under which the clergy, nobility, and Third Estate each get one vote collectively or whether each deputy has an individually counted vote. Note, too, the

47. Consider our entire corpus of 26,230 grievances of the nobles and 46,376 grievances of the Third Estate. Of these a rather higher proportion of noble demands concern the very broad area of "government" (38% vs. 32%). Among grievances that deal with "government," we find that "government finances" are more salient for the nobility (21% vs. 14%).

48. One might find in the joint stress on liberties and finances support for (and greater specification of) James Riley's proposal that the central liberties under debate from the 1760s on were precisely concerned with "the despotism of the tax collector." Our data suggest the conjunction of liberty and finance to be particularly characteristic of the nobility. See James C. Riley, *The Seven Years War and the Old Regime in France: The Economic and Financial Toll* (Princeton: Princeton University Press, 1986), 218.

concerns over blocked careers in the military, the heavy tax on sales of noble land to commoners (*franc-fief*) and the privileged access of nobles to higher courts in first instance (*committimus*). By way of contrast to this last item, the nobles, not overconcerned with issues of privilege, are very concerned with royal authority over court procedure and tend to discuss royal prerogatives to shift cases from one court to another—or even to an administrative authority. The premier problem in the judicial system for the Third is a noble privilege; for the nobility, it is an instance of the heavy hand of royal interference.

As for hindrances to the market, note that among those taxes or seigneurial rights of greatest concern among the urban notables, one finds precisely those that most interfere with the free movement of commodities, the sale of land, or the price of labor. Thus, they are especially prone to take up customs duties, the tax on noble land sales mentioned above, the lord's right to collect tolls, seigneurial claims on compulsory peasant labor in field or *château*, or the whole range of seigneurial monopolies. The notables' concern with the weights and measures whose great and mysterious variety was a considerable nuisance to long-distance commerce is also a clear instance of such a concern, especially when taken in conjunction with seigneurial and royal tolls. What could more vividly summon up an image of human folly creating obstacles to social wealth than the multiple inspections and associated losses of time and money occasioned by searches, unloadings, arguing, tolls, taxes, consultation of rate-schedules, bribes, breakage, and spoilage at the vast number of collection points at which goods might be assessed at different rates and in different units of measurement?

As different as nobility and Third Estate are from one another, however, the greater contrast, by far, is between the nobility and Third Estate on the one hand, and the parishes on the other. The people of the French countryside voice the concerns of the elites in very limited measure. The rural people appear minimally interested in political structures; somewhat in economic development, in government finances only insofar as taxation is concerned, and in tax privilege (but not other forms of privilege); and not at all in civil liberties.[49] But what is impressive is the frequency with which they take up the material exactions with which they are burdened. Like the Third Estate, their single most common subject is taxation in general, but unlike the Third Estate—for whom matters concerning the Estates-General or regional self-government in the form of Provincial Estates are almost as significant—these rather general complaints are followed by grievances about specific taxes. At the head of the list, the salt tax, which was assessed at rates that varied considerably with region but that were often quite high,

49. While censorship, for example, is among the top ten topics for nobility and Third Estate, it is relegated to the 233d position by the parishes.

was made more burdensome still in those parts of the kingdom in which a minimum salt purchase was mandated.[50] Close behind the salt tax is a complex group of taxes, known as the *aides,* which were levied principally though not exclusively on alcoholic beverages. These in turn are followed by the *droit de contrôle,* an omnipresent tax on the registration of legal transactions. Our data indicate that the significance of this tax as a focus of resentment in the French countryside is not adequately reflected in most of the historical literature in which this levy is overshadowed by others like the *taille,* which are actually rather less widely made the subjects of grievances.[51]

Looking further down the list one may observe many other taxation concerns. There is the royal *corvée,* the compulsory labor services on the royal roads, transmuted in a recent reform into a money tax; there is the *taille,* the main direct tax of the Old Regime, in principle assessed with an eye on landed wealth, but hopelessly riddled with regional variations and so saddled with privileged exemptions that it was a mark of low status to pay it. There are various taxes that initially were intended to be more uniform in their assessment (*capitation, vingtième*). There are proposals for tax reform (*impôt unique, impôt territorial*), discussions of tax privileges, discussions of agencies of tax collection.[52]

This rural concern for taxes is simply unmatched by the elites. Of the ten subjects most widely discussed in the parish *cahiers,* eight concern taxes, in contrast with four each for the Third Estate and the nobility. The most frequent peasant demand that bears on the Estates-General is symptomatic. While various matters concerning the anticipated gathering of that body are toward the very top of the lists for the Third Estate and nobility, the Estates-General is only mentioned in 17th place by the parishes—and the

50. To these demands might be added those many rural grievances concerning the government's salt monopoly, for which we have created a distinct category but which is part and parcel of the institutional context of the *gabelle.*

51. The valuable essay by François Hincker, for example, virtually ignores the *droit de contrôle* and related taxes. See François Hincker, *Les français devant l'impôt sous l'ancien regime* (Paris: Flammarion, 1971). I defer reflecting on the significance of the frequency of grievances about this particular tax until Chapter 3, p. 107.

52. On taxation, see Marcel Marion, *Les impôts directs sous l'ancien régime principalement au XVIIIe siècle* (Geneva: Slatkine-Megariotis Reprints, 1974) as well as *Histoire financière de la France depuis 1715* (Paris: Rousseau, 1914), vol. 1; Gabriel Ardant, *Théorie sociologique de l'impôt* (Paris: Service d'Edition et de Vente des Publications de l'Education Nationale, 1965); J. F. Bosher, *French Finances, 1770–1795. From Business to Bureaucracy* (Cambridge: Cambridge University Press, 1970); George T. Matthews, *The Royal General Farms in Eighteenth-Century France* (New York: Columbia University Press, 1958) as well as a great deal of material on tax reform debates in the various works of Georges Weulersse on the physiocratic movement: *Mouvement physiocratique; La physiocratie sous les ministères de Turgot de Nicker (1774–1781)* (Paris: Presses Universitaires de France, 1950); *La physiocratie à l'aube de la Révolution (1781–1792)* (Paris: Editions de l'Ecole des Hautes Etudes en Sciences Sociales, 1985).

specific subject is a proposed veto on taxation. The intensely debated issue of the voting rules for the Estates-General (vote by head vs. vote by order), one of the questions that most deeply divided the Third Estate from the nobility, only figures in 40th place as a rural concern. The even more divisive subject[53] of opportunities to achieve high office is not represented among the peasant top fifty at all.

The claims of the state, weighty as they are, hardly exhaust the rural sense of burden, for the claims of church and lord must be considered as well. Two rather different forms of ecclesiastical exaction are treated with some frequency. The tithe, a compulsory payment of a portion of the crop, was subject to wide variation in the rate at which it was assessed and the crops on which it was to be levied. While it was in principle justified as support of the pastoral activities of the parish priest, it often went in practice to a tithe-holder who was expected to provide for the priest and the upkeep of the church building. The *casuels* were irregular payments rendered upon the performance of special functions, for example, a marriage ceremony.[54] Notice that only the *casuels* are among the Third Estate's top fifty and both tithe and *casuels* are omitted by the nobles.

If clerical exactions came in two main kinds, the lord's claims came in many. Among the most common objects of complaint we find a number of seigneurial recreational privileges. The lord's pigeons and the lord's hunts were sometimes experienced as airborne and groundbased assaults on peasant crops, as John Q. C. Mackrell puts it.[55] The seigneurial court, as the institutional mechanism by which the lord could compel payments, has often been seen as critical to the entire system of seigneurial rights (although recently there has been some challenge to this view).[56] The monopoly on milling was one of several seigneurial monopolies. The miller was charged quite a high fee for his protected monopoly and he passed it on to his customers. Mutation fees (*lods et ventes*) were assessed (at a generally high rate) when land changed hands. *Cens et rentes,* finally, was a periodic cash payment often composed, as its compound name suggests, as an amalgam of a variety of payments that might individually bear a very wide range of designations. These seigneurial subjects are far less salient for the urban notables and the nobles: the *cahiers* of the Third Estate include only four

53. For one attempt at measuring the extent of the differences between the Third Estate and nobles over various issues, see Shapiro and Markoff, *Revolutionary Demands,* chap. 15.

54. Timothy Tackett, *Priest and Parish in Eighteenth-Century France. A Social and Political Study of the Curés in the Diocese of Dauphiné, 1750–1791* (Princeton: Princeton University Press, 1977), 130–31.

55. John Q. C. Mackrell, *The Attack on "Feudalism" in Eighteenth-Century France* (London: Routledge and Kegan Paul, 1973), 4–5.

56. Lefebvre, *Paysans du Nord,* 117–18, 124–25; Olwen H. Hufton, "Le paysan et la loi en France au XVIIIe siècle," *Annales: Economies, Sociétés, Civilisations* 38 (1983): 679–701.

seigneurial subjects among their most widely discussed issues; for the nobles the count is a very eloquent zero.

The world of the country people is a world of burdens. We have concentrated on taxes, seigneurial claims, clerical payments; yet when we examine the other topics in Table 2.1, we find that what is left over still includes various claims on resources in the parish *cahiers* to a greater extent than in the other two collections of documents. The militia, a low-status conscripted adjunct to the army whose members were virtually all peasants, ranks 23d among peasant grievances (and the draft by lot specifically ranks 41st); for the urban notables the former category is 37th and for the nobility not among the first fifty at all; the specific subject of the draft is not among the most widespread concerns of the elites. Serving for years as a "soldier dishonored by his situation"[57] (or the difficult efforts to evade such service) surely added to the rural sense of burden.[58]

The differences among the three groups are often revealing when they confront the same institutional sphere. On military matters, the nobility, for whom a martial image was often an important component of a public identity,[59] have a substantial number of grievances on such varied subjects that they constitute a large but quite "miscellaneous" category. The Third Estate's primary concern is with a military career in which any aspiration to high rank was essentially blocked. But the rural communities are interested neither in the details of military affairs nor in career problems. The militia ("also a tax" as the village of Beaulieu-en-Argonne observes)[60] and the associated draft are the salient military issues for them.

To examine a very different institutional arena, all three collections of documents evince a concern for legal procedures and the judicial apparatus. While the arbitrary powers embodied in the *lettres de cachet* head such concerns for nobility and Third Estate (and more so for the former than the latter), such issues are not the principal concerns of the rural communities.

57. *Cahier* of the parish of Hiis, *bailliage* of Bigorre (Gaston Balencie, ed., *Cahiers de doléances de la sénéchausée de Bigorre pour les états généraux de 1789* [Tarbes: Imprimerie Lesbordes, 1925], 297).

58. On rural evasion and resistance to conscription, see André Corvisier, *L'armée française de la fin du XVIIe siècle au ministère de Choiseul. Le soldat* (Paris: Presses Universitaires de France, 1964), 1:222–31.

59. Consider the frequency with which the French nobility chose military officers to represent them at the Estates-General. See David Bien, "La réaction aristocratique avant 1789: L'exemple de l'armée," *Annales: Economies, Sociétés, Civilisations* 29 (1974): 23–48, 505–34; Edna Hindie Lemay, "Les révélations d'un dictionnaire: du nouveau sur la composition de l'Assemblée Nationale Constituante (1789–1791)," *Annales Historiques de la Révolution Française,* no. 284 (1991): 175; Timothy Tackett, *Becoming a Revolutionary: The Deputies of the French National Assembly and the Emergence of a Revolutionary Culture (1789–1790)* (Princeton: Princeton University Press, 1996).

60. Gustave Laurent, ed., *Cahiers de doléances pour les états généraux de 1789,* vol. 1, *Bailliage de Châlons-sur-Marne* (Epernay: Imprimerie Henri Villers, 1960), 71.

Pride of place, for them, goes to the seizures of property and subsequent court-ordered auctions that made life miserable for the indebted and indigent. While the urban notables evince a similar, if not quite so pressing, concern along these latter lines, it is only in the countryside that one finds the fees for the services of legal professionals to be much of an issue. While in 42d place in the villages, legal fees are only tied for 125th place among Third Estate demands. Certainly the urban attorneys who played a central role in the assemblies of the Third Estate were unlikely to complain bitterly, as did a village in Lorraine, of the financial ruin wreaked by "Jews, guards, and lawyers."[61]

In village France, the significant institutions are burdens. I would judge thirty-eight of the fifty most widely discussed institutions to fall under that rubric.[62] This may be contrasted with twenty-two for the Third Estate, at most ten for the nobility.[63] A different computation permits us to see even more vividly the significance of the extraction of resources from the peasantry, whether in cash, kind, or labor. Table 2.2 treats the demands in the *cahiers* as an aggregate. By thus examining the entire body of grievances, we see that grievances concerning material exactions acount for more than two peasant grievances in five, a considerably higher proportion than is the case for the higher-status groups. At least as striking from this perspective is the observation that for all the real difference between the Third Estate and the nobility in the salience of such issues, that difference is dwarfed by the abyss that separates either from the countryside.[64]

Regardless of the weight of specific exactions, Lefebvre's focus on peasant burdens is thus true to their own expressed concerns. The present analysis also confirms Taylor's case that the specific constitutional issues that agitated the revolutionary leadership are virtually absent from the parish assemblies. Equally worthy of attention is the relative weight of different sorts of burden. In the countryside taxation is the focus of considerably more discussion than seigneurial rights. Indeed there are

61. P. Lesprand and L. Bour, eds., *Cahiers de doléances des prévôtés bailliagères de Sarrebourg et Phalsbourg et du bailliage de Lixheim pour les états généraux de 1789* (Metz: Imprimerie Paul Even, 1938), 248.

62. I considered a subject to be an instance of a burden if it dealt with claims by state, church, or lord but not if the central focus is on the use or management of resources once exacted. I did not consider the subject of roads, for example, as a burden—even though they were constructed by exaction of labor and money. (But one wonders whether the great salience of roads in the parish *cahiers* might not be due to the coerced rural labor that built and maintained them.) Others might, therefore, differ slightly on how many of these topics they would call burdens.

63. The ambiguity of the nobility resides in the tie for last place, which includes taxes and other grievances.

64. If we considered other appropriations of resources (legal fees, for example, or militia service) these figures would not only be a bit higher, but the difference between village France and the elites would be also somewhat greater.

Table 2.2. Grievances Concerning Burdens (%)

Type of Burden	Parishes	Third Estate	Nobility
Taxation	32%	16%	15%
Clerical tithe and *casuels*	4	2	1
Seigneurial regime	10	7	3
Total burdens	46	24	19
(*N*)	(27,742)	(46,376)	(26,230)

parish *cahiers* that do not even mention the seigneurial regime at all. Table 2.3 shows a number of other things as well. Although a smaller proportion of Third Estate grievances treat it, almost all Third Estate *cahiers* have at least some discussion.[65] By comparison, the fact that more than one-fifth of noble *cahiers* pay no attention whatsoever is quite striking. The noble *cahiers* are far longer than those of the parishes, yet they typically contain no more discussion of seigneurial institutions. In short, the nobility tend to be silent on the seigneurial system, a critical point to which we shall return. But a significant minority of parishes are also silent.

At the onset of revolution, then, the seigneurial rights were simply not the predominant rural concern, if the *cahiers* are any guide. It would be hard to predict, from the sheer foci of attention of their *cahiers,* the antiseigneurial character coming to be taken by the growing rural insurrection (see Chapter

Table 2.3. Grievances on Seigneurial Regime (%)

Attention to Seigneurial Regime	Parishes	Third Estate	Nobility
Documents that have at least one grievance treating any aspect of seigneurial regime	77% (*N* = 748)	98% (*N* = 198)	79% (*N* = 166)
Mean number of grievances on seigneurial regime in document (Base: all documents)	4.4	16.9	4.4
Mean number of grievances on seigneurial regime among documents mentioning seigneurial regime at least once	5.7	17.4	5.5
Mean number of all grievances in document (Base: all documents)	40	234	158

65. We see an important element of claims that the Third Estate is more radical than the parishes. The considerably greater length of the general *cahiers* of the Third means that they will tend to have more grievances about anything even if those matters are relatively less weighty. The sheer number of demands implies nothing about which aspects of the seigneurial regime are discussed let alone what is said about those aspects.

6, p. 281). And as we shall see in Chapter 6, in the early stages of breakdown of the old order, and certainly through March 1789 when most parish documents were written, they were not the dominant target of collective action in the countryside either. We need to rethink the question posed by Le Roy Ladurie, of identifying the structural changes that led the Old Regime to go down under the blows of an antiseigneurial countryside that had moved away from the anti-taxation focus of the great movements of the seventeenth century. As late as that first spring of revolution the parish grievances were far more focused on taxation. Indeed, as we shall see below, throughout the eighteenth century taxation was more often a target of insurrection than seigneurial rights (see p. 16; Chapter 5, p. 264).

We will need, then, to consider why the revolutionary countryside *came* to take an overwhelmingly antiseigneurial course. The *cahiers* may yet tell us something of why that antiseigneurial turn came about, rather than the more traditional anti-taxation thrust whose continuation into the great revolution might well have been anticipated on the basis of the overall quantity of demands.[66] If the claims of the distant and abstract state occupied more rural attention, we shall see (in Chapter 3) that at the beginning of the Revolution the claims of the lord and church were seen as having a different and fundamentally less tolerable character.

Faces of the Seigneurial Regime

Which particular seigneurial rights mattered most to peasants, to nobles, and to urban elites? First of all we shall group the discussions of the seigneurial regime under a number of broad rubrics. Table 2.4 shows the percentage of documents that have at least one grievance concerning any of nineteen broad aspects of the seigneurial regime, among all documents that discuss the lord's rights at all. We see, for example, that among those parish documents that discuss the seigneurial regime the seigneurial courts are discussed in 29%. Table 2.4, then, indicates how widespread concern with that category was.

Peasants: Still More Burdens

The three groups of documents not only differ from one another in their attention to seigneurial rights, but they also differ in which kinds of rights they would place on the public agenda. We are struck first of all by the vast

66. Looking ahead to Chapter 6 we will see that attacks on the seigneurial regime had risen from very small numbers to 28% of all rural revolts by March 1789 (and would be climbing much higher). See Table 6.3.

Table 2.4. Documents that Discuss Particular Aspects of Seigneurial Regime (%)

Aspect of Seigneurial Regime	Parishes	Third Estate	Nobility
Seigneurial courts	29%	65%	32%
Seigneurial regime in general	24	47	26
Seigneurial monopolies	38	79	15
Symbolic deference	11	30	48
Labor services	18	57	10
Periodic dues (in cash or kind)	50	65	15
Dues on property transfers	24	44	8
Formal acts of recognition of seigneurial rights	2	15	8
Recreational privileges	42	71	24
Seigneurial agents	5	25	8
Serfdom	9	28	8
Seigneurial tolls	13	61	30
Rights over fairs and markets	3	24	6
Protection rights	0	17	2
Requisition rights	1	0	0
Seigneurial aspects of land tenure	13	37	26
Seigneurial aspects of communal rights	11	18	2
Tax advantages of seigneurs	2	3	1
Other[a]	19	51	20
(*N*)[b]	(564)	(193)	(131)

Note: Totals sum to over 100% since documents may have more than one grievance concerning seigneurial regime.
[a]Combines: (1) Miscellaneous seigneurial rights which have no more specific code; (2) seigneurial aspects of any institution not indicated here; (3) incomplete seigneurial codes.
[b]Only includes documents that discuss the seigneurial regime.

gulf that separates the peasants from their noble lords. For the peasants, the most widely discussed aspects of the regime are the periodic dues. These payments were quite varied in character. The *cens* was an annual cash payment whose value had generally been eroded with several centuries of inflation, but whose payment was taken to signify recognition of the entire body of rights due the lord. In the legal language of the day, payment of the *cens* constituted acknowledgment of the lord's "direct," which is to say the body of seigneurial rights.[67] Eighteenth-century jurists distinguished two

67. Robert Pothier, *Traité des fiefs, avec un titre sur le cens* (Orléans: Montaut, 1776) 2:373–75; Joseph Renauldon, *Dictionnaire des fiefs et des droits seigneuriaux utiles et honorifiques* (Paris:

clusters of property rights: *domaine direct* and *domaine utile. Domaine utile* consisted of the rights to exploit, rent, sell, and bequeath land, although these rights might be subject to various restrictions as a consequence of *la directe.* Thus *domaine utile* resembles what we mean today by ownership; and in the eighteenth century the person who held land as *domaine utile* was far more likely to be called the *propriétaire* than the holder of *la directe.*[68]

The *domaine direct* consisted of rights owed a seigneur by those whose land was regarded as being held from that seigneur. A modern property owner's rights are limited by the claims of the state to taxation, to eminent domain, to the enactment of criminal statutes, and to the regulation of inheritance, sale, and gift. Before the Revolution, the rights of *domaine utile* were similarly hemmed in by the claims of the lord as well as those of the state. In theory there was a relation of personal dependence of the proprietor on the lord; and, again in theory, some expression of this personal dependence—an act of "fealty and hommage" (*foi et hommage*) for noble land, the payment of the *cens* for common land—was required for *la directe* to be recognized.[69]

The web of property relationships, then, was conceived as intertwined with a web of personal relations among unequals. A whole language of inequality flourished in which persons, land, and even the dependency relationshps among unequals were distinguished by their honorable or vile qualities. "Noble" land might be held from a *suzerain* as a *fief* by a *vassal,* a set of relationships of men and land acknowledged by fealty and homage; a less honorable set of terms was used when "common" land was held as a *censive* by a lord's *censitaire,* a set of relationships acknowledged by a cash payment (the *cens*). For some, such distinctions remained fundamental. Pothier, for example, devoted the very first page of his *Treatise on Fiefs* to their exposition.[70] Yet their force was eroding. One symptom of the declining power of this conceptual scheme to grip the imagination in the eighteenth century was the failure to maintain the full panoply of status distinctions: "vassal" was widely used now in place of "censitaire" for the peasant with obligations to a lord; the adjectival form of fief ("feudal") was now often used to cover a much wider range of seigneurial relationships. (In Chapter

Delalain, 1788), 1:175; Marcel Garaud, *Histoire générale du droit privé français,* vol. 2, *La Révolution et la propriété foncière* (Paris: Recueil Sirey, 1958), 29–35.

68. See, for example, Renauldon's entries on *seigneur direct* and *seigneur utile* (*Dictionnaire des fiefs,* 2:394–95).

69. The land over which the seigneur himself exercised *domaine utile* was the *domaine proche* which he might exploit by hiring laborers, leasing to sharecroppers or farming it out to someone. Some of these concessions of the lord's *domaine proche* tended to become permanent tenures which were difficult to distinguish from the *mouvances,* the land over which the lord exercised *la directe* and someone else (the *vassal* or the *censitaire*) exercised *domaine utile.*

70. Pothier, *Traité des fiefs,* 1:1.

4 we shall try to understand the conceptual scheme of those who wrote the *cahiers.*)

The *champart*[71] only rarely carried the symbolic weight of the *cens,* but since it was assessed in kind as a portion of the crop, its value did not deteriorate with inflation. Its precise value varied as widely as the names under which it was known, but it could be very burdensome indeed, especially when considered in conjunction with the similarly assessed church tithe.[72] Also rather common were a variety of other cash payments known as *rentes seigneuriales* or *rentes foncières,* sometimes lumped together with the *cens* as *cens et rentes.*[73] Whether or not such *rentes* were regarded, like the *cens,* as recognizing the lord or as merely a transfer of money with no implicit acknowledgment of the domination of one person over another was one of those matters over which jurists demonstrated their intellectual powers and everyone else their bafflement. (The legal reasoning about such things differed in the parts of France under what was called "customary law" from those under "written law.") Whatever these variously denominated annual payments evoked in the conceptual universe of the legal theorists, the parish *cahiers* show that they plainly evoked a response among the country people. We see that half of those parish *cahiers* that discuss the seigneurial regime take up these periodic dues, in contrast to a mere one noble *cahier* in seven. And let us not forget we are speaking here only of those noble *cahiers* that take up the seigneurial regime at all.

The lord's recreational privileges were also weighty for the peasants; indeed, they are the second most widely discussed group of rights.[74] The lord's monopoly on hunting was a double deprivation.[75] Not only was the

71. Renauldon, *Dictionnaire des fiefs,* 1:95; see also the discussion in Garaud, *Révolution et propriété foncière,* 35–38.

72. The *champart* was sometimes known as the "seigneurial tithe." Some Burgundian villagers called it "the devil's tithe" (Pierre de Saint Jacob, *Les paysans de la Bourgogne du Nord au dernier siècle de l'Ancien Régime* [Paris: Société Les Belles Lettres, 1960], 120). Garaud, (*Révolution et propriété foncière,* 37) suggests it could run as high as 20% of the crop. If the *cens,* somewhat unusually, was assessed in kind it could rival the *champart* in its weight. See Jacques Peret, *Seigneurs et seigneurie en Gâtine poitevine: La duché de la Meilleraye, XVIIe–XVIIIe siècles* (Poitiers: Société des Antiquaires de l'Ouest, 1976), 97–98.

73. Garaud, *Révolution et propriété foncière,* 38. The adjectival distinction (*seigneurial* vs. *foncier*) often, but not always, corresponded to the distinction between a recognition of lordship and a "simple"—to use the terminology of the day—payment.

74. If one considers the proportion of grievances of a particular kind, rather than the number of documents with at least one such grievance as the measure of peasant concern, one would actually note that among those parish grievances that consider the seigneurial regime, rather more concern the recreational privileges than the periodic dues (19% vs. 17%).

75. On the long identification of hunting as part of the distinctive lifestyle of a warrior class at leisure, with the consequent unending struggle to preserve that monopoly against both needy peasants and status-envious bourgeois, see the essays in André Chastel, ed., *Le Château, la chasse et la forêt* (Bordeaux: Editions Sud-Ouest, 1990).

rural underclass deprived of an occasional source of protein but they were not free to guard their crops from animal incursions—or human incursions, for that matter. Apart from the damages of thieves—and hungry people passing through were always feared—abusive lords, hunting, might trample fields.[76] The lord's hunting rights might, in turn, be limited by the king's own game preserves on which the lords dared not infringe, but such a limit hardly helped the country people. To make matters worse, under the "right of warren" (*droit de garenne*), it might be the lord himself who was raising the intruding rabbits. Under the similar "right of dovecote" (*droit de colombier*), the lord was permitted to raise pigeons whose depredations could hardly be prevented by scarecrows. Rights to hunt or raise animals were sometimes surrounded, in principle, by customary restrictions that, if enforced, would significantly limit damage to peasant property.[77] Hunting might be prohibited while grain was ripening, for example, and warren and dovecote construction might be regulated. But such limits were not universal nor, even where they were on the books, were they universally enforced. If the lord's right to fish, like the right to hunt, was sometimes limited by royal prerogatives (in this case the king's claims on navigable rivers), the peasants were similarly barred in principle from a source of food. Sometimes, the lord had the additional right to construct a fishpond, which might well damage the peasants' land. This entire bundle of recreational rights, we see, was far more widely a subject of peasant concern than of the nobility.

Peasant *cahiers* were also two and one-half times more likely to take up seigneurial monopolies than were the *cahiers* of the nobility. These monopolies most commonly included the requirement that grain be ground at the lord's mill (*banalité du moulin*), that the lord's oven be used for baking (*banalité du four*), or that the lord's winepress be used (*banalité du pressoir*). The lord might have the right to fix a date prior to which wine could not be sold (*banvin*), grapes picked (*ban de vendange*), crops harvested (*ban de moisson*), or mowing carried out (*ban de fauchaison*). By jumping the gun, so to speak, the lord for a few decisive days could have a local monopoly on marketing. Examining other classes of grievances that constituted burdens borne by the peasants reveals the same pattern: the parish *cahiers* are twice as likely as the noble documents to discuss compulsory labor services on the lord's lands and three times as likely to take up any of the variety of payments due the lord when property changed hands. In short, the demands most characteristic of the peasant *cahiers* deal with the material costs

76. A collateral right might be joined to the lords' monopolies on hunting and weapons, a monopoly on hunting dogs. On occasion, lords chasing game across peasant plots would kill the dogs they came across, thereby eliminating any nearby rivals to their own canine servitors (and depriving the nearby peasants of a valuable guard, herder and, perhaps, companion). See Renauldon, *Dictionnaire des fiefs,* 1:205–6; Garaud, *Révolution et propriété foncière,* 93.

77. See Renauldon, *Dictionnaire des fiefs,* 1:223–26, 513–17.

imposed on them by seigneurial privilege; these areas are far less frequently taken up by the nobility.

Nobility: Honor

What does the nobility want on the public agenda? If half the parish *cahiers* that take up the seigneurial regime regard periodic dues as worth discussing, we also find that half the noble *cahiers* take up claims to symbolic deference. These are rights that permit some distinguishing behavior or dress for the seigneur[78] that is denied to others. This would include the right to bear arms,[79] which constituted for the nobility an outward reminder of their place in that substratum of Indo-European social mythology that saw the world divided into those who prayed, those who fought, and those who worked.[80]

Symbolic deference patterns included other "honorific rights" that could not be sold, rented, exchanged, or given to someone else, for example, rights to precedence in public processions or in seating arrangements at Sunday church services. The latter was the most noticeable portion of an entire lord-church nexus.[81] The lord's ancestors might be buried below the church; his marriage, procreation, death especially marked; his place particularly notable in the endless ceremonial observances of the liturgical year. In a few places, he might have a traditional claim on naming the priest.[82] Noble lords also had something more than a house: the *château* might be decorated with a family coat-of-arms, a weathervane—was this a claim to rights over air to match those over land and water?[83]—and architectural themes of a distinctly military cast. A lord with rights of high justice could have a gallows.

This category of symbolization, the category of most pertinence to the

78. We include here several rights that some eighteenth-century jurists held to be privileges of the noble rather than of the seigneur. The distinction is not always clear, nor do we have a sense that it was always clearly recognized by those who wrote the *cahiers* (on which more below).

79. The history of the interdiction on weapons is little researched. The essay of Christian Desplat stands out: "Le Peuple en armes dans les Pyrénées occidentales françaises à l'époque moderne," in Jean Nicolas, ed., *Mouvements populaires et conscience sociale, XVI–XIXe siècles* (Paris: Maloine, 1985), 217–27.

80. Georges Duby, *The Three Orders: Feudal Society Imagined* (Chicago: University of Chicago Press, 1980).

81. The variety of ways the lord might be linked through the church to the sacred can be seen by leafing through Renauldon's manual. Renauldon, indeed, informs us that "honorific rights" has as its core meaning precisely the halo of religious ceremonial surrounding the lord (*Dictionnaire des fiefs*, 1:346).

82. For some Alsatian examples, see Erich Pelzer, "Nobles, paysans et la fin de la féodalité en Alsace," in *La Révolution française et le monde rural* (Paris: Editions du Comité des Travaux Historiques et Scientifiques, 1989), 50–51.

83. The lord claimed rights that no peasant had over denizens of earth, water, and air in the hunting rights and the rights to rabbits, fish, and pigeons.

nobility, is of relatively little concern to the peasantry. While 48% of all the nobles' grievances concerning the seigneurial regime fall in this group, making it the most numerous of the 19 categories in Table 2.4, for the peasants a scant 11% of all grievances are on such subjects and it is their 12th most widely grieved about class of demands. It is moreover, the *only* class of seigneurial subjects taken up by a higher proportion of noble documents than by those of the Third Estate. In an era of royal armies and royal courts, lords had not raised feudal levies nor tried capital offenses for a long time. Turrets and gallows alike were no longer material implements of seigneurial power; yet they were so plainly meaningful to the nobility that one balks at describing them as mere decoration. To look ahead to Chapter 8 (see p. 463), the pain expressed by noble deputies on the suppression of such symbolizations, rivals any other single expression of dismay at the course of the Revolution.)

Such dramatic markers of status might have other meanings as well. Consider the barring of most Frenchmen from the display of arms. An enforced monopoly of arms promoted a disarmed rural underclass, a matter of royal concern since the great peasant risings of the seventeenth century.[84] Despite the prohibition and searches, a taste for firearms had insinuated itself into masculine popular culture, as Roger Dupuy observes, a taste that revealed itself in shooting competitions at village fairs or firing of muskets at weddings.[85] Nonetheless, the ostentious bearing of arms was not very salient to the peasantry, as indicated by the relatively low interest of the peasants in this issue. But a disarmed peasantry could not defend their crops against wild animals, let alone the lord's rabbits. If we glance ahead at Table 2.5, we see that in the parishes, it was far more important to have hunting rights discussed than the right to bear arms: The peasants wanted to kill crop-menacing birds and animals and they wanted a little more meat; they had no great interest in showing off their weapons. For the nobles, on the contrary, it is the status marker that is more commonly on the agenda. Hunting mattered a good deal to the peasants, but the right to walk around with a sword did not. Or, more precisely, the peasantry were concerned with food and with crops, but not with the honor involved in the right to bear arms, if conceived of separately from the burden of the recreational privileges. For the nobility, the priority of concerns was reversed.

84. The high rate of military desertion assured the continual availability of arms, even though confiscation was one of the major tasks of France's militarized national police, the *maréchausée*. The need of the cultivators to protect their crops, of the impoverished for meat, of minor officials for protection against a potentially dangerous populace, of bourgeois for self-respect in emulation of the nobility, combined to make the intermittent disarmament campaigns a continual focus of contestation and rebellion. See Iain A. Cameron, *Crime and Repression in the Auvergne and the Guyenne, 1720–1790* (Cambridge: Cambridge University Press, 1981), 79–88, 224–26.

85. See Roger Dupuy, *La Garde Nationale et les débuts de la Révolution en Ille-et-Vilaine (1789–mai 1793)* (Rennes: Université de Haute-Bretagne, 1972), 28.

One sort of status marker the nobles did not address, however, was ritualized humiliation. To the limited extent that the nobles could be said to have been keen to discuss anything connected with the seigneurial regime, it was their claims to a positive public display of their superiority. Occasionally, lords held the right to a negative display: to compel a humiliating act. The Third Estate of Lannion speaks of "practices degrading to humanity," including the lord's right to compel singing in public or jumping in the water on which they comment: "no lord can oppose the abolition of such rights unless he finds honor in humiliating his fellows" (*AP* 4:76). Discussions of such humiliating practices, including the right to get villagers to chase frogs away or the lord's right to put his foot in his peasants' marriage bed ("frogging" and "thighing"),[86] are rare for the parishes and the Third Estate; they are nonexistent on the part of the nobility. To be sure, the mere denial to some of what is granted to others may be experienced as humiliating, regardless of the particular acts that are permitted/forbidden. Not far from the assembly of Lannion, whose sense of humiliation we just examined, the assembly of the Third Estate of Auray demands the suppression of "useless" and "ridiculous" rights that are leftovers of "centuries of fury and blindness" in which "the hard and ambitious man made himself vile while degrading his fellows." They are not speaking of "frogging" or "thighing," but of the rights to raise rabbits and hunt (*AP* 6:115). If, for some in the Third Estate, not being allowed to do what was allowed another, was a humiliation, the other side of that particular coin was that for some noble assemblies, an expansive sense of honor included virtually the entire seigneurial regime, including some very lucrative rights (see Chapter 3, p. 80).

Those who dealt with the seigneurs in the Old Regime understood the intensity of concern for the forms and formalities of public recognition. The lawyer Renauldon used the introduction to a manual of seigneurial rights to boast of the particular distinction of his book in the area of symbolic prerogatives. A predecessor in the writing of such manuals, he informs his prospective readers, correctly noted that the honorific rights were those most jealously guarded by the seigneurs. The earlier manual, however, managed to omit many, a fault Renauldon promises to remedy.[87] But even Renauldon is cursory on rights whose sole purpose is humiliation.[88]

86. Garaud, *Révolution et propriété foncière,* 102–9.

87. Renauldon, *Dictionnaire des fiefs,* 1:iii. Note that this eighteenth-century equivalent of today's book-jacket puffery is addressed to the seigneurs themselves, a part of the work's intended audience. (The title page describes the book as a "most useful and suitable work for all *seigneurs,* judges, and lawyers.")

88. Out of alphabetical sequence, as if it is an afterthought, there is a brief discussion of "rights that are abusive, ridiculous, and contrary to good morals" (Renauldon, *Dictionnaire des fiefs,* 1:357–58). It is interesting that a manual for lords and their advisers had such a category at all. Is this an attempt to disown some claims to save the rest in the threatening climate of 1788, when this dictionary appeared? If so, this may be a forerunner of the renunciations of August 4, 1789.

We see here a system that at the top is thought of in largely but hardly exclusively symbolic terms, but at the bottom seems rather exclusively a system of material exactions. Or, more precisely, the nobles' public transcript stresses the symbols by which their distinctiveness is to be recognized. Theirs is a discourse of honor.

Third Estate: Freedom of the Market

If the seigneurial regime's burdens are the peasant's concerns and its honorific distinctions a uniquely striking part of the nobility's, what is most distinctive to the Third Estate is different yet again. Returning to Table 2.4, we see first of all a consequence of the vastly larger number of demands a typical Third Estate text has than either of the other two groups.[89] Seventeen of the nineteen categories of grievance are most widely discussed in the Third Estate *cahiers*.

We note that those burdens that the peasants treated far more frequently than the nobility are even more widely discussed by the Third Estate: seigneurial monopolies, compulsory labor services, periodic dues, dues on property transfers, and recreational privileges. When we examined the most common grievances earlier, we saw that the Third Estate was especially concerned with restrictions on the market (see p. 35). That conclusion is reaffirmed by Table 2.4. Seigneurial monopolies, taken up by four Third Estate *cahiers* in five, are taken up less than half so widely in the parish documents; the same holds for the labor services. Although a higher proportion of the *cahiers* of all three groups deal with periodic dues than with dues on property transfers, the latter occurs in almost twice as many Third Estate *cahiers* than parish documents, as contrasted with far less of a difference in the former. (Property transfer dues inhibited free commerce in land.) In short, of those categories particularly characteristic of the peasantry, Third Estate concern leans toward those aspects of the seigneurial regime that have particularly dampening effect on trade.

The seigneurial *corvées,* the compulsory labor services, were no doubt far less onerous in the eighteenth century than in past centuries, having been partially supplanted by the king's increasing capacity to extract such services, most importantly for work on the royal roads. But the lord's claim to unpaid labor in his fields, perhaps including the peasant's draft animals, and occasionally including claims to artisanal services or even labor on his *château,* were still quite widespread and felt to be onerous enough.[90]

89. The median number of demands (seigneurial and otherwise) in Third Estate *cahiers* is 203; in noble *cahiers,* 141; and in parish *cahiers,* 33 (for means see Table 2.3).

90. Garaud, *Révolution et propriété foncière,* 51–56. The *corvées* were also sometimes important enough for the lords to use their judicial resources to insist on their collection, at least in the region around St. Jean d'Angély studied by Anthony Crubaugh in research not yet published.

The seigneurial monopolies, of course, radically curtailed competition for the provision of essential services.[91] By charging the miller, say, a high fee for the exclusive right to do the local milling and then compelling the nearby peasants, backed by the weight of French law, to use the miller's services, the costs of agricultural production were kept high. The milling monopoly, indeed, not only prevented millers and peasants from associating freely, but it prevented the construction of new mills that might compete with the lord's. In this sense the miller may be said to have paid the lord at a high rate in return for security.[92]

Examining other classes of grievance that are not major peasant concerns but that the Third Estate focuses on, we see a rather similar pattern. Seigneurial tolls were an often lucrative source of seigneurial revenue that had been opposed on and off over the centuries by the central government. If the short-term interests of the royal fisc favored the maintenance of at least the royal tolls—the king, after all, was the first seigneur of the land—since Colbert in the seventeenth century the campaign for abolition had been particularly lively.[93] The struggle for national integration and economic development had made the eradication of internal barriers to commerce a central mercantilist concern, one point on which the newer doctrines of their intellectual enemies, the physiocrats, were in agreement.[94] The tolls are not notable among parish grievances, while they are a relatively common subject for the nobility. But they are treated in twice as many *cahiers* of the Third Estate. On the general theme, we note that the subject of rights over fairs and markets[95] is not a common one. But Table 2.4 shows that concern over such rights was far more widespread among the Third Estate than among the nobility and rather unusual among the peasantry.

Serfdom, as it still existed in a few regions in the eighteenth century,[96] was largely reduced to *mainmorte,* whereby a serf could bequeath his land

91. Here is the Third Estate of Alençon: "Let all monopoly rights—on mills, ovens, winepresses and others—be irrevocably abolished as contrary to natural liberty. In consequence, the commerce in flour shall be made free throughout the realm, free of all dues and extricated from all impediments" (*AP* 1:718.)

92. The revolutionary end of the *banalités* brought to a close the lord's capacity to squeeze the miller, yet we find the millers of Hainaut in 1790 protesting the new legislation: in the new legal environment many new mills were rapidly constructed (Lefebvre, *Paysans du Nord,* 377).

93. J. F. Bosher, *The Single Duty Project: A Study of the Movement for a French Customs Union in the Eighteenth Century* (London: Athlone, 1964).

94. Eli F. Heckscher, *Mercantilism* (New York: Macmillan, 1955), 1:78–109; Weulersse, *Mouvement physiocratique,* 1:510–14.

95. Seigneurs sometimes had the exclusive right to institute and administer fairs or markets in their localities or to collect a variety of fees there.

96. Marcel Garaud, *Histoire générale du droit privé français,* vol. 1, *La Révolution et l'égalité civile* (Paris: Recueil Sirey, 1953), 15–34; Charles-Louis Chassin, *L'Eglise et les derniers serfs* (Paris: Dentu, 1880).

only to a child living at home, in the absence of whom the land reverted to the seigneur. This necessarily implied that the peasant *mainmortable* could not sell the land and therefore could leave the community only by sacrificing his birthright. This institution was a clear barrier to free mobility of labor and free commerce in land. Although fairly uncommon outside of Franche-Comté and Burgundy, serfdom was dramatically quite striking: what other aspect of the seigneurial regime was more reminiscent of the medieval past?[97] Yet it did not inspire much comment among the nobles or peasants of most *bailliages;* only the Third Estate shows much interest.

Second only to monopolies in how widespread was Third Estate concern, the recreational privileges had at least an element of hindrance of enterprise. The ban on hunting reduced the capacity of peasants to provide themselves with protein. The whole array of rights barred large proprietors without the particular privilege needed from raising their own pigeons, say, perhaps in an effort to develop a luxury market.

If the peasants seem almost exclusively concerned with their burdens, and the nobility are quite distinctively interested in their claims to prestige (although hardly to the exclusion of other concerns), the Third Estate's focus on market barriers is less clear-cut. Almost half their documents take up the seigneurial regime as a whole;[98] almost two-thirds take up the seigneurial courts, both of which plainly have to do with much besides barriers to enterprise. Indeed the very diversity of Third Estate concerns is reflected in the large size of the "other" category. Half of the Third Estate documents have at least one demand that fits none of our seigneurial categories, as contrasted with one-fifth of the other documents.

We may complete our survey of Table 2.4 by briefly examining the less common subjects of grievance. "Seigneurial aspects of land tenure" refers to rather abstractly conceived issues of rights framed in the archaic and arcane legal categories of the Old Regime. Distinctions between *fiefs* and *censives,* the status of *alleux* (allodial land or freeholds) and the complexities of *emphytéose* seem not to have been terribly common, and far less common for the peasants than anyone else.[99] Uncommon as they were, such matters

97. The Third Estate of Poitiers: "If, for many centuries, France languished in ignorance, anarchy and confusion, those were the centuries of the feudal regime, when the seigneurs, enjoying their usurped authority, crushed goods and persons alike under an equal servitude. The odious time of personal servitude has at last disappeared; or, if in some parts of the realm, the right of *mainmorte* still exercises its empire, this right . . . can not fail to disappear soon in its turn" (AP 5:412).

98. Grievances that address the seigneurial rights as a collectivity rather than restrict themselves to particular rights are coded by us under the heading of "Seigneurial Regime in General." If a *cahier* contains such grievances and *also* contains demands about particular rights, both are coded.

99. Looking ahead, one notes that the parish *cahiers* were showing very little interest in just those sorts of distinctions that would be so important in revolutionary legislation (see Chapters 8 and 9).

were for the nobility more commonly discussed than many other things. There is even less interest in the various institutions that to the legal-minded signified a vassal's acknowledgment of his lord or in the lord's occasional attempted exercise of his prerogative to seize temporarily the land of one who withheld such acknowledgment.[100] For the peasants these practices appear utterly insignificant.

Let us consider now the seigneurial aspects of "communal rights." Rural communities' claims of collective rights of various kinds had largely defeated the sporadic attempts of the central authorities to promote what Marc Bloch referred to as agrarian individualism.[101] These rights included obligatory fallow land; bans on close-cutting agricultural tools; claims to access of communal animals to postharvest stubble, to fallow, to communally owned land; and various rights to forest products. These rights were articulated with the rights of the lord and were sometimes the occasion of competing claims on woods, pastures, harvests. While raised as an issue by only one parish *cahier* in ten and in rather more Third Estate documents, we see, in contrast, that the nobles avoided this area almost completely (or were they merely indifferent?).

The various legal specialists, rent-collectors, and stewards who served the seigneurs and mediated the lord-peasant relationship, seem to have held little interest for either nobles or peasants, for all their significance in the operation of the system.[102] The role of the *feudistes,* authorities on seigneurial law who advised the lords on maximizing their exactions from the peasantry, has been the subject of much comment in the historical literature;[103] the mini-technocrats of estate management have been much less discussed.[104] But it may be a bit surprising to see that in 1789 only

100. The rights I have in mind here include *foi et hommage, aveu et dénombrement, commise,* and *saisie,* on all of which see Garaud, *Révolution et propriété foncière,* 17–29. On land other than fiefs, recognition of the seigneur's claims was taken to go with payment of *cens, champart,* or *rente seigneuriale,* which we have examined under the category of "periodic payments."

101. Marc Bloch, "La Lutte pour l'individualisme agraire dans la France du XVIIIe siècle," *Annales d'Histoire Economique et Sociale* 2 (1930): 329–83; 511–84.

102. The other aspects of the seigneurial regime that the tables show to have been of little weight in 1789 were the "protection rights," a variety of now unusual dues paid in the Middle Ages in return for the lord's military protection *(taille seigneuriale, cens en commande, le guet et la garde)* and various equally archaic claims of the lord to being lodged or fed *(gîte, prise).*

103. See, for example, Saint Jacob, *Paysans de la Bourgogne du Nord,* 432–34; Jean Bastier, *La féodalité au siècle des lumières dans la région de Toulouse (1730–1790)* (Paris: Bibliothèque Nationale, 1975), 64–71.

104. Robert Forster, "Seigneurs and Their Agents," in Ernst Hinrichs, Eberhard Schmitt, and Rudolf F. Vierhaus, eds., *Vom Ancien Régime zur Französischen Revolution: Forschungen und Perspektiven* (Göttingen: Vandenhoeck & Ruprecht, 1978), 169–87; "The 'World' Between Seigneur and Peasant," in Ronald C. Rosbottom, ed., *Studies in Eighteenth-Century Culture* (Madison: University of Wisconsin Press, 1976), 5:401–21.

the *cahiers* of the Third Estate seem to have paid any of these figures much attention.[105]

These agents have often been seen as deeply implicated in a rationalization of the seigneurie that destroyed whatever responsible paternalism may have at some point existed and stepped up the exactions on the peasantry as well. Saint Jacob sees the renters of seigneurial rights, the *fermiers,* as well on their way to becoming the real bosses of the estates in northern Burgundy.[106] Pierre Goubert, in the course of an astute commentary on the unresolved question of whether there was a radical increase in the lords' efforts to collect dues as the Old Regime approached its end, suggests that whatever reality there may have been to this phenomenon, a dramatic systematization of estate management in the eighteenth century was central.[107] Robert Forster finds, in the papers of the seigneurial agents, evidence of a world coming apart, evidence of a seigneur whose distance from the peasants is more than spatial and whose local agents take without giving.[108] In this light Alfred Cobban's claim that the *cahiers* are full of complaints about the "excesses of seigneurial agents"[109] is unsurprising. What is a bit startling is that, as far as the peasants are concerned, Cobban is mistaken: the peasants have little to say.[110] That the nobility also seem oblivious is only less startling in light of their capacity to avoid discussing many other facets of the seigneurial regime.

Seigneurial Rights in the Cahiers: Peasant Burdens, Third Estate Market Freedom, Noble Silence and Honor

We have explored in some detail the differences among our three groups of documents in stressing specific aspects of the seigneurial regime. Let us

105. It is conceivable that some of the grievances directed against the lord's agents merely name that agent as a renter of land *(fermier),* particularly in northern France where such renters often also functioned as estate-managers. To the extent that the agent is named by villagers in this fashion, the counts presented here would be undercounts. (I owe this observation to Cynthia Bouton.) The presence of such agents at parish assemblies might have deterred otherwise open criticism on occasion, but peasants who were often undeterred from criticizing seigneurial justice by the presiding seigneurial judge prescribed in the royal regulations, would hardly have been intimidated into nearly total silence by accountants and rent-collectors.

106. Saint Jacob, *Paysans de la Bourgogne du Nord,* 428–32.

107. Pierre Goubert, "Sociétés rurales françaises du XVIIIe siècle: Vingt paysanneries contrastées. Quelques problèmes," in his *Clio parmi les hommes: Recueuil d'articles* (Paris: Mouton, 1976), 70.

108. Forster, "The 'World' Between Seigneur and Peasant," 418.

109. Cobban, *Social Interpretation,* 48. On Cobban's misreadings of the *cahiers,* see Chapter 10.

110. On the significance of peasant lack of concern with the lord's agents, see Chapter 5.

now, more briefly, approach the same comparisons in another way, by comparing the relative frequencies with which each group takes up particular seigneurial rights, the same sort of data that was used in Table 2.1, but now exclusively focusing on the seigneurial regime. Going through all our code categories, let us select the dozen most commonly discussed seigneurial matters for each of the three groups. Table 2.5 lists them in their order of salience to the parishes. For each right we indicate its rank among all subjects including those that are not aspects of the seigneurial regime. The seigneurial institution most widely discussed by the parishes, for example, is the lord's right to raise pigeons; this right is 39th among all subjects complained about by the Third Estate.

Table 2.5. Frequencies[a] with Which Documents Treat Often-Discussed Seigneurial Subjects

Subject	Parishes	Third Estate	Nobility
Right to raise pigeons (*droit de colombier*)	14*	39*	399*
Seigneurial courts in general	25*	52*	174*
Seigneurial regime in general	27*	48.5*	125.5*
Right to hunt (*droit de chasse*)	29*	27*	174*
Use of seigneur's mill is compulsory (*banalité du moulin*)	34*	87.5*	689
A periodic cash payment (*cens et rentes*)	45*	264.5	836.5
Dues on property transfers (*lods et ventes*)	50*	175	582.5
Compulsory labor services (*corvées*)	51*	24*	380.5*
Seigneurial monopolies in general (*banalités*)	52*	31*	338.5*
Periodic dues in general	55*	329	633.5
Periodic dues in kind (*champart*)	58*	120.5*	470
Seigneurial tolls	78*	17.5*	98.5*
Miscellaneous aspects of seigneurial courts	88	140*	303.5*
Miscellaneous aspects of seigneurial regime	105	70.5*	260.5*
Right to bear arms	131	233.5	148.5*
Use of seigneur's oven for baking is compulsory (*banalité du four*)	156	167.5*	753
Honorific rights	511	713.5	246.5*
Symbolic deference patterns in general	548.5	652.5	174*
Median rank of 12 most widely grieved-about seigneurial topics	47.5	50.25	210

[a]Values other than integers indicate tied ranks. For example, grievances concerning "seigneurial tolls" occur in the same number of Third Estate *cahiers* as grievances concerning the noble right to trial in a high court (see Table 2.1), which is not a seigneurial right. Among subjects treated in Third Estate *cahiers*, these two subjects are tied as the seventeenth and eighteenth most common; hence a rank for "seigneurial tolls" of 17.5.

*Indicates that a subject is among the dozen most frequently treated in the *cahiers* of the parishes, Third Estate, or nobility.

The relative silence of the nobility on the seigneurial regime stands out once again. Most of the rights itemized in Table 2.5 are far less salient for the nobles than the others. There is only one aspect of the seigneurial regime among the nobles' hundred most widely discussed subjects. This may be contrasted with 13 for the parishes and 9 for the Third Estate. The peasants may have widely protested pigeon-raising; the nobility finds 398 subjects more worthy of attention. The median rank among the dozen seigneurial institutions most commonly discussed by the nobility is an unimpressive 210. The nobles appear far away from the concerns of the peasants or the urban notables.

Table 2.5 not only reinforces the picture of a nobility keeping its own counsel, but also demonstrates that when the nobility does discuss the seigneurial regime, its agenda is distinctive. Consider again the right to bear arms and the intimately associated right to hunt, clearly distinguished in this table. The complex of a hunting-arms monopoly has a material component in the form of crop damage and loss of meat, a symbolic-identity component as the maintenance of an especially powerful status marker and a political component as a guarantor of the military superiority of the powerful. That the peasants are far more prone to single out the hunting aspect, rather than the arms aspect, for discussion argues that it is their economic situation that is their paramount concern. For the nobility, the discrepancy between the two rankings is far less, with the right to bear arms enjoying pride of place. This suggests the degree to which these institutions were seen by the nobles through the prism of their concerns for public tokens of respect. And it also permits one to wonder about the degree to which the language of honor functions as a form of publicly expressible speech that conceals other concerns. It is possible that the nobles had political worries as well as threatened pride in mind: By March 1789 perhaps some of the nobles could see in the storm around them those greater storms yet to come and looked to reaffirm a disarmed countryside. As for the Third Estate, the discrepancy in ranking is of the same sort as for the rural parishes, although far more extreme. But one could not conclude that the symbolic issues, for the urban notables, pale in significance before the economic ones. For a large number of rural people hunting could spell the difference between a measure of security in poverty and utter destitution.[111] But for how many of the upper Third Estate was hunting significant for adding a bit of meat to one's table and for how many was the issue the enjoyment of the lord's forbidden pleasures? (Perhaps an upper-village stratum might have had a similar viewpoint.)

111. On the makeshift economy by which large numbers of people managed to keep themselves barely above total ruin, see Olwen H. Hufton, *The Poor of Eighteenth-Century France: 1750–1789* (Oxford: Clarendon Press, 1974).

When we turn to the financial burdens of the seigneurial regime, so important to the peasantry, the gap between the French nobility and the people of the French countryside appears even greater. The compulsory use of the lord's mill, the various annual payments (*cens et rentes, champart*), the very high mutation fee exacted when property changed hands (*lods et ventes*), the various monopolies considered as a group, the ensemble of periodic dues—all figure importantly in the parish *cahiers,* though astonishingly little is said of them by the nobles.

There are, indeed, only two categories in this table that are actually more salient for the nobility for either of the other two groups: "honorific rights" and "symbolic deference patterns in general."[112] The peasants as well as the urban notables have about as little time to pay attention to the appropriateness of particular forms of dress on ceremonial occasions, the occupancy of particular pews in church, the proper sequence of march in parades or the formulas with which people greeted one another as the nobles had to consider the financial burdens on rural France; but these are the most discussion-worthy matters to the system's chief beneficiaries.

If the peasants are not quite so indifferent to these public emblems of differential honor as is the Third Estate (and we may group the right to bear arms here as well) they hardly loom as major peasant concerns. This may surprise some. There is well-attested evidence of peasant attack, in the risings of 1789 and beyond (see Chapter 5, p. 223), on the symbolic trappings of the seigneurial regime. Weathervanes were destroyed, gallows and pillories burned, the lords' church benches ripped out, coats-of-arms smashed, and rural France inaugurated and sustained its own countersymbolism of liberty in the erections of maypoles in front of the *châteaux.*[113] In this discrepancy between the reticence of the *cahiers* and the vigorous actions soon to follow, we catch another glimpse of a theme we shall be pursuing further. The peasant *cahiers* are not the frozen embodiment of eighteenth-century opinion on seigneurial rights; they are an expression of the positions held at a particular moment in the eighteenth century. These positions evolved along with the Revolution they helped inaugurate, evolved rapidly, in fact. The indifference to the symbolic dimension of the seigneurial

112. Just as "seigneurial rights in general" refers to grievances that focus on seigneurial rights as a collectivity, "symbolic deference patterns in general" includes demands addressed to a range of such signs of deference conceived of as a group. Similarly, "seigneurial monopolies in general" will refer to attacks on (or defenses of) *banalités* as a group; etc. To reiterate, the very same *cahiers* that speak of a class of seigneurial institutions may also speak of particular instances. If so, both the general and the particular grievances are coded and counted.

113. For some examples, see Sydney Herbert, *The Fall of Feudalism in France* (New York: Barnes and Noble, 1921), 124–27, 161–62, 165–71; Mona Ozouf, *La Fête révolutionnaire, 1789–1799* (Paris: Gallimard, 1976), 281–316; Alphonse Aulard, *La Révolution française et le régime féodal* (Paris: Félix Alcan, 1919), 129, 142, 167–68.

regime that we have seen, for example, is mirrored in a rather low level of attacks on coats-of-arms, weathervanes, or turrets early in the Revolution. The choice of such symbolic targets, however, rose by the summer and fall of 1789 and was quite substantial by the winter rising of 1789–90 (see Chapter 8, p. 499).

As for the Third Estate, we may note the subjects more salient to them than to the others: the right to hunt, the compulsory labor services, the seigneurial monopolies in general and the seigneurial tolls.[114] Apart from the right to hunt, these are clearly interferences with the operation of the market. The right to hunt probably taps into the particular Third Estate concern with privilege. Why ought landholding commoners not be able to hunt, whether they are lords or not? Just such resentment may have fueled a growing propensity for the lords' zealous defense of their hunting monopolies to set them at odds not just with plebeian poachers but with status-conscious bourgeois landowners out to demonstrate that they liked a good hunt as much as the style-setting aristocrats.[115]

We began this chapter by trying to identify the distinctive traits of each group's agenda by considering grievances on all subjects. We found distinctive emphases: burdens, the market and privilege, state expansion, and personal liberties. When we look at the more specific agendas for the seigneurial regime, the more general parish and Third Estate patterns hold up within the more specific seigneurial arena as well. For the nobles what was striking when we examined their agenda as a whole was a general avoidance of seigneurial matters altogether; when we look at those seigneurial matters that are discussed we found that those matters that touch on their honor were the ones more likely to be brought forward. The picture we have been assembling has largely (although not exclusively) been drawn from the study of the more common items on the various agendas. Might it be the case that these patterns only obtain for the most widely discussed seigneurial matters? To answer this question, we examined the relative salience, for the three groups, of a much larger range of seigneurial subjects. The results are summarized in Table 2.6.[116]

The dominant pattern here is quite plain: half of the aspects of the seigneurial regime our code distinguishes are discussed most widely, compared to other institutions, in the parish *cahiers* and least in the *cahiers* of the nobility. This is what one might well expect on the basis of the foregoing

114. "Miscellaneous aspects of the seigneurial regime" also belongs on this list. We see here again the greater range of Third Estate concerns, great enough to strain at the limits of our coding.

115. Anne-Marie Cocula-Vaillières, "La contestation des privilèges seigneuriaux dans le fonds des Eaux et Forêts. L'exemple acquitain dans la seconde moitié du XVIIIe siècle," in Jean Nicolas, ed., *Mouvements populaires et conscience sociale, XVI–XIXe siècles* (Paris: Maloine, 1985), 214.

116. We omitted subjects that were not treated in at least 5% of the documents of at least one group to avoid extremely rare institutions on which our frequencies would be highly unstable.

Table 2.6. Relative Frequencies with Which Seigneurial Subjects Are Treated by Parishes, Third Estate, and Nobility

Relative Frequency[a]	Number of Seigneurial Subjects ($N = 47$)
P > T > N	27
P = T > N	1
T > P > N	10
P > N > T	5
T > N > P	1
N > P > T	2
N > T > P	1

Note: Seigneurial subjects in this analysis were those in which at least one class of documents (P, T, N) had at least one grievance on the subject in at least 5% of its *cahiers*.

[a]For each subject, the rank of that subject is examined for the parishes, Third Estate, and nobility; the parishes, Third Estate, and nobility in turn are ordered according to which has the highest, lowest, and intermediate ranking for that subject. For example, consider the *droit de colombier,* the right to raise pigeons. For the parishes this ranks 14 in terms of the number of *cahiers* treating it, for the Third Estate 39 and for the nobility 399. This subject then is one of the 27 assigned to the modal pattern, P > T > N.

discussion. Clearly, however, there are seigneurial institutions that are exceptions to the rule of great parish interest, little noble interest, and intermediary levels for the Third Estate. Taking the modal pattern as the standard, it may be of interest to examine two sorts of deviations: (1) those institutions for which the nobility is not the least interested of the three and (2) those for which the Third Estate is more concerned than the parishes.

The first group, those that receive atypically large noble attention, are enumerated in Table 2.7. With the exception of the last item, the *rentes foncières,* these are all matters whose symbolic significance is far clearer than their material import. In addition to the arenas of symbolic deference already discussed, our broader survey now turns up a variety of aspects of fief-holding that in the eighteenth century contributed far more to the lords' mystique than to their pocketbooks, now that vassals no longer owed military service to their suzerains. The very notion of a fief attracted little attention in the *cahiers.* By the late eighteenth century, fiefs without obligations were not always easy to distinguish from freeholds and fiefs carrying obligations in cash or kind were not always easy to distinguish from *censives,* a point acknowledged at the very beginning of Hervé's seven-volume *Theory of Feudal Matters,* one of the last treatises on feudal law to appear before the Revolution.[117]

117. François Hervé, *Théorie des matières féodales et censuelles* (Paris: Knapen, 1785–88), 1:1 et seq.

Table 2.7. Seigneurial Subjects of Relatively Greater Salience to the Nobility than to the Parishes, Third Estate, or Both

I. Nobles more concerned than both parishes and Third Estate
- Symbolic deference patterns in general
- Honorific rights
- Fealty and homage (*foi et hommage*) (vassal's acknowledgment of receipt of a fief and of his responsibilities to his lord)

II. Nobles more concerned than Third Estate
- Right to bear arms
- Avowal and enumeration (*aveu et dénombrement*) (a detailed description of the fief a new vassal owed to his seigneur)
- Allodial land (*alleux:* land subject to no seigneur)
- Seigneur's domain (*domaine proche*) (the portion of a *seigneurie* directly controlled by the lord)
- Fiefs

III. Nobles more concerned than parishes
- *Rentes foncières*

Although it had become essentially hereditary, the relation of vassal and suzerain was regarded as the result of a contract freely entered. The "fealty and homage" that acknowledged that relationship was a very uncommon subject of discussion, and like other symbolic trappings of the seigneurial regime, was a largely noble concern. Nobody besides the nobles seemed to care at all about the streamlined eighteenth-century version of the once powerful drama in which the lord held the hands of the vassal kneeling before him and kissed him on the mouth.[118] After fealty and homage there followed "avowal and enumeration" (*aveu et dénombrement*), a detailed declaration of the resources of the fief into whose possession one had entered. As for the other terms in Table 2.7, a freehold *alleu* was a landholding that had no seigneur of any kind, while by *rentes foncières* we refer to regular payments devoid of seigneurial implications.

I have already commented on the limited interest the *cahiers* express in fiefs, freeholds, avowal and enumeration and discussions of the land over which the lords had "useful" rights (the *domaine proche*). Next to no interest is expressed by the Third Estate, although the parishes pay some attention. As for *rentes foncières,* the peasants take no note and the nobility not much more. A small but notable number of Third Estate assemblies have something to say on the subject of regular payments to the lord that do not acknowledge the corpus of seigneurial rights.[119] In the general lack of

118. Marc Bloch, *Feudal Society* (Chicago: University of Chicago Press, 1964), 145–46.

119. Discussions of *rentes foncières* as an aspect of the seigneurial regime are found in 0% of parish *cahiers,* 2% of noble *cahiers,* and 14% of Third Estate *cahiers.*

interest in what some would have held to be feudal claims in a strict sense, we see here a small forerunner of the thinking of the National Assembly. We shall see others.

That the nobility are a little more likely to bring aspects of the feudal hierarchy into the public limelight should not obscure, however, the more essential fact that raising such matters is rather rare even for them. While many of those assemblies who chose speech rather than silence on the subject of seigneurialism are apt to stress status distinctions, few noble assemblies care to go near those status markers that differentiate one lord from the next. The noble concern with maintaining a status boundary between themselves and commoners cannot be equated with anything that even begins to resemble a nostalgia for a fully elaborated hierarchical image of society, where noble vassals owed allegiance to noble suzerains.

One might be tempted to argue that this lack of support for an internal hierarchy within the nobility is the result of the particular way of constituting the assemblies that adopted noble *cahiers*. The convocation rules enabled lesser nobles, poorer nobles, and nobles without fiefs to participate[120]—although not going quite so far as to embrace those among the ennobled whose newly granted status was not transmissible to heirs. The assemblies were not restricted to the great lords who generally spoke for their order and who could be outvoted by their usually more obscure fellows. If the rules produced this effect, however, is this not a sign that those lesser nobles had bought into the vision of an internally undifferentiated brotherhood of warriors' descendants put forward by Count Henri de Boulainvillers[121] rather than the minutely graded structure of hierarchical nuance associated with the high Princes of the Blood?[122] If the Third Estate's voice on feudal hierarchy was nearly still, the nobility did not offer much more than a whisper; was that a lack of interest—or was it paralysis in assemblies

120. This was a subject of the most bitter intra-noble controversy in Provence. See Jean Egret, "La prérévolution en Provence," *Annales historiques de la Révolution française* (1954): 97–126; Jules Viguier, *La convocation des états généraux en Provence* (Paris: Lenoir, 1896); Monique Cubells, *Les horizons de la liberté: Naissance de la Révolution en Provence (1787–1789)* (Aix: Edisud, 1987).

121. François Furet and Mona Ozouf speak of Boulainvilliers reinstalling "equality inside inequality" ("Deux légitimations historiques de la société française au XVIIIe siècle: Mably et Boulainvilliers," *Annales: Economies, Sociétés, Civilisations* 34 [1979]: 444). On the eve of revolution antihierarchical conceptions were emerging even among social forces most devoted to hierarchy. Although the fief-holding nobility of Provence continued to insist on excluding non-fief-holders from provincial bodies representing the nobility, and were to attempt to have them excluded from the noble elections to the Estates-General, they decided, in 1787, on something resembling equality among themselves: in public ceremonials they would march in order of age, rather than in order of the dignity of their fiefs. (Even this "little revolution" as Monique Cubells calls it, drew some protests from the most conservative.) See Cubells, *Horizons de la liberté*, 11.

122. Franklin L. Ford, *Robe and Sword: The Regrouping of the French Aristocracy after Louis XIV* (New York: Harper and Row, 1965), 173–87.

containing both the great and the lowly? Regardless, it is clear that the nobles are very far from an organic conservatism.[123]

Now consider *rentes foncières,* the last item in Table 2.7, and the only category more salient to the nobility than to the parishes but not the Third Estate. The term was used to indicate regular payments to the lord that were "simple" payments, that unlike the *cens* were not used to acknowledge the fact of lordship. The term then has nothing to do with the status markers that the lords are more prone to discuss than the Third Estate; and it is used in establishing the sorts of fine distinction in which the people of the countryside have little interest. Indeed, as we shall repeatedly see, peasants would have the greatest interest in ignoring such distinctions when they reacted to the new revolutionary legislation that was soon to come. The legislators would attempt to distinguish some seigneurial rights, to be simply abolished as mere relics of a feudal past, from seigneurial rights that retained some legitimacy (see Chapters 8 and 9). While the *cahiers* of nobles and Third Estate show little interest in the particular distinction embodied in the notion of nonseigneurial *rentes foncières,* the peasants show none. The exceptional character of the last item in Table 2.7, then, is not so much that the nobles are unusually concerned as that the peasants are unusually unconcerned. Does this mean that the peasants are insensitive to fine distinctions of any kind? We shall consider their own distinctions in Chapter 3.

The subjects distinctively salient to the Third Estate are presented in Table 2.8. Reinforcing the picture painted above, we see that six of the eleven categories constitute constraints on the market: monopolies, dues on fairs and markets, compulsory labor services, mutation fees, rights to first wine sales, and tolls. But the *cens,* the obligation of "watch and ward" (*le guet et la garde*), hunting rights, and the *rentes foncières* do not have this character. The picture here is less clear-cut than was that of the nobility. The stress on market hindrances in the *cahiers* of the urban notables, while marked, does not exclude other concerns, among them the strong focus on privilege that may underlie the special attention to hunting. Indeed, it may

123. Consider the alienation of the royal domain, one of the issues most widely voiced by the nobility as part of its particular stress on state finances. While a handful of noble assemblies asserted the traditional inalienability of crown holdings—an element of an integralist vision of an immutable social order—the great majority were eager to do anything with royal land that would speed the flow of resources to the treasury, including the traditionally forbidden sale of this land. Nobles were in the forefront, then, both of sacralizing "property" in defense against state claims and excluding royal lands from this defense (thereby sharpening the demarcation of the public and the private). The major point here, to which we will refer repeatedly, is that the nobles, when they defended seigneurial rights at all, did so with modern notions of property and not older notions of hierarchy. The secondary point is that what was covered by the sacred aura of "property" was quite flexible; and if nobles could be flexible in deploying this powerful word in their *cahiers,* revolutionary legislators, we shall see, could be similarly flexible soon afterward.

be the theme of privilege that distinguishes the other rights most salient to the Third Estate. The *cens* was not just any monetary payment, but acknowledged a dependency on the lord; *rentes foncières* were quite the opposite, and, therefore, tend to be mentioned in the *cahiers* precisely when what was at issue was what makes a lord more than another proprietor. As for "watch and ward," even in its attenuated form as a cash payment, wasn't this a reminder that a *château* was more than just a large house?

To the extent that peasants, urban notables, and nobles attended to the seigneurial regime in March and April 1789 they differed in the foci of their expressed concerns. France's rural majority saw a cluster of claims upon their often precarious resources while the nobles were particularly likely to stress public displays of deference. And the Third Estate, among its many concerns, stands out for its attention to market barriers.

The Third Estate is at least as striking for the range and variety of its concerns as it is for precisely what those concerns were. For if the rural *cahiers* are relatively more preoccupied with the seigneurial exactions, the lengthy and complex documents of the urban notables have a lengthier and more complex agenda. Rural France, we shall see in Chapter 3, expresses the stronger urge to abolish seigneurial institutions; but it is the urban commoners who have the most to say and say it with the greatest complexity.

As for the nobles, their silent reserve is no less dramatic than the subjects they address. And when they speak, as we shall see in Chapter 3, a significant group of "maintainers" vies with their "abolitionists." They are divided with an intensity that has no parallel among the unprivileged. There is a magnificent study of another revolutionary upheaval that is very suggestive here. Oliver Radkey has exhaustively explored the question of

Table 2.8. Seigneurial Subjects of Relatively Greater Salience to the Third Estate than to the Peasantry

- Miscellaneous seigneurial rights
- Seigneurial monopolies, in general
- *Le guet et la garde* (in former times, service of watching over the *château;* now commuted into a money fee)
- Right to collect dues at fairs or markets; includes exclusive right to establish a market
- Compulsory labor services
- *Cens*
- *Rentes foncières*
- Mutation fees on property transfer, in general
- Hunting rights
- Right to forbid peasants to sell wine before seigneur does (*banvin*)
- Seigneurial tolls

how the Socialist Revolutionary party, overwhelmingly the largest party following the abdication of the czar, managed to fritter away its apparently commanding lead. A minute examination of its internal debates, meetings, writings, and public positions shows it frequently unable to arrive at anything resembling a consensus. In many party congresses and assemblies in 1917, on many critical issues, its internal vote was deeply split; moreover, a large number of party delegates abstained. Abstention was so characteristic of the ill-fated SRs that it was often the position (nonposition?) of a plurality of voting members. The SRs were a great party of abstainers, Radkey concludes, a fatal weakness in the climate of intensive and extensive mobilization of a multiplicity of groups passionately struggling for their shifting interests and their evolving beliefs.[124] The nobles in the spring of 1789 were hardly a party, and they had already lost the leadership of the movement to regenerate France, but on a central pillar of the Old Regime, more bitterly attacked than most, they were certainly abstainers.

124. Oliver Radkey, *The Agrarian Foes of Bolshevism: Promise and Defeat of the Russian Socialist Revolutionaries, February to October, 1917* (New York: Columbia University Press, 1958).

CHAPTER

3

THREE REVOLUTIONARY PROGRAMS

Openness to Change

In the last chapter, we considered the distinct agendas of parishes, Third Estate, and nobility. In this chapter, we turn to what we may call their programs. We shall explore what they want to do about seigneurial rights. In terms of our coding of grievances (see Chapter 2, pp. 23–25), we are shifting from a focus on the subjects of grievances to their actions. As in Chapter 2, we may sharpen our analysis of rural grievances over seigneurial rights through comparison with demands about other obligations of the peasantry, namely, state taxation and ecclesiastical exactions. We shall do this in three specific ways. First, we may deepen our search for what is distinctive about seigneurial rights through establishing contrasts with other burdens. Second, we may test (and refine) our hypotheses about the ways in which villagers distinguish one seigneurial right from another by seeing if they distinguish one tax from one another (or one ecclesiastical claim from another) along the same lines. And, third, we may see grievances about the seigneurial regime as part of a larger whole, as one portion of a mosaic of grievances.

To compare our three groups is to look for significant variations on the theme of change. How open to change were France's villagers, elite urbanites, and nobles? Tocqueville argued that the repercussions of centuries of monarchical centralization had so greatly strained social relations that virtually all were eager for radical measures. Their dealings with the standardization imposed by the growing state had imbued France's elite, noble and commoner alike, with an openness toward change, a commitment to rationality and a disparagement of social arrangements bequeathed by the past. In a classical summary of his analysis of the *cahiers* of the nobility, Tocqueville wrote: "Like all other Frenchmen, they regard France as a trial field—a sort of political model farm—in which everything should be tried, everything turned upside down, except the little spot in which their particular privileges grow. To their honor, it may even be said that they did not wholly spare that spot. In a word, it is seen from these *cahiers* that the only thing the nobles lacked to effect the Revolution was the rank of commoners."[1]

Were the nobles almost as open to change as the Third Estate? Tables 3.1 and 3.2 show some of the broad orientations of the French with regard to the claims of lord, church, and state as well as their grievances on other subjects.[2] I have classified the demands under a few broad rubrics. We see that noble assemblies only rarely called for the integral maintenance of French institutions. It is true that with such large numbers of grievances the 2% of noble demands that were dead set against change on matters other than the three burdens is reliably greater than the Third Estate's 1%. But this marginally greater noble conservatism hardly invalidates the essentially Tocquevillean picture, particularly when one notes how much stronger is the degree to which both groups favored abolition over conservation. Apart from seigneurial rights, even the nobles were more likely to propose abolition than preservation. One might wish to dispute Tocqueville's picture in a relative sense, however, for the propensity to abolish is far greater still in the general *cahiers* of the Third Estate and still more so out in the countryside. (Table 3.3 emphasizes this.) That the nobles may have been significantly open to change and thereby helped bring on the collapse, does not mean that they were so eager for change as potential non-noble elite rivals (a point Tocqueville does not give its due weight) let alone their rural dependents (a matter not on Tocqueville's mind at all). More striking

1. Alexis de Tocqueville, *The Old Regime and the French Revolution* (Garden City, N.Y.: Doubleday, 1955), 272.

2. Tables 3.1 and 3.2 are fundamental to this chapter and shall be referred to at many points in the discussion.

is the extent of genuine noble conservatism on that "little spot," as Tocqueville so disarmingly puts it, of their own concerns. Noble enthusiasm for defending the seigneurial rights outruns any propensity to abolish them. Alongside the substantial noble avoidance of discussing the seigneurial rights at all that we saw in Chapter 2, we now must place the conservatism of a portion of those nobles who are not silent, a conservatism all the more striking since even the nobles are pushing, like the others, for change in most arenas, even if perhaps not so radically. But should we be willing to minimize, along with Tocqueville, the arenas of noble intransigence? The "little spot" includes, along with seigneurial rights, issues of privileged access to high posts and the voting rules to be followed in the Estates-General.[3] Are the nobles overwhelmingly and fundamentally liberal or are they—or rather a portion of them—intransigent when it really counts?

Ways of Changing and Ways of Keeping

George Taylor raised the issue of the revolutionary consciousness of the French at the onset of the Revolution and, drawing on his study of the *cahiers,* urged us to see little such consciousness anywhere and virtually none as far as the parishes are concerned.[4] But we have just seen that all groups share an openness to change, although to different degrees and with different manifestations. Proposals that institutions be maintained without substantial alteration are generally quite rare; they only characterize the nobility on seigneurial rights.[5] This is rather closer to Tocqueville's view than it is to Taylor's.[6]

My analysis departs from Taylor's in another particular: the radicalism of the countryside. In noting how little advanced Enlightenment ideas were

3. John Markoff and Gilbert Shapiro, "Consensus and Conflict at the Onset of Revolution: A Quantitative Study of France in 1789," *American Journal of Sociology* 91 (1985): 44–47.

4. George V. Taylor, "Revolutionary and Nonrevolutionary Content in the *Cahiers* of 1789: An Interim Report," *French Historical Studies* 7 (1972): 479–502.

5. *Cahiers* that call for reform but also insist that an institution be maintained are also only characteristic of the nobility on seigneurial rights.

6. This is the first of several points where my sifting of evidence diverges in important ways from George Taylor's. One reason is the difference in coding: Taylor does not distinguish the *agenda* from the *program;* that is, he does not separately code the subject under discussion as well as the action demanded. He therefore cannot count demands to abolish something independently of that something. I do not dispute Taylor's contention that few *cahiers* at all (and fewer parish *cahiers* in particular) closely approximate the programs of the revolutionary assemblies, but their support for change of some sort (as assessed by examining the actions demanded) is very substantial; although I find with Taylor that individual seigneurial rights are discussed in fewer parish *cahiers* than general *cahiers* of the Third Estate, I also find that those parishes that do discuss a particular right tend to be more radical, a significant element that Taylor's method does not detect.

Table 3.1. Demands Concerning Burdens (%)

Actions Demanded	Parishes			Third Estate			Nobility		
	Taxation	Ecclesiastical Payments	Seigneurial Rights	Taxation	Ecclesiastical Payments	Seigneurial Rights	Taxation	Ecclesiastical Payments	Seigneurial Rights
Abolish without compensation	24%	42%	36%	25%	54%	27%	16%	41%	10%
Indemnify	0	1	9	1	3	17	0	3	15
Maintain substantially unaltered	1	0	1	0	0	1	1	2	13
Maintain with reforms	0	0	0	1	1	1	2	1	8
Reform	42	23	15	39	22	16	42	18	17
Replace	4	0	2	6	2	1	7	3	1
Unfavorable	14	15	16	5	2	5	6	5	3
Favorable	1	0	0	0	0	0	2	0	1
"Do Something"	0	0	0	1	1	2	1	2	2
Local demand	9	19	15	5	2	4	2	0	2
Provincial demand	1	1	0	5	5	5	7	2	5
(*N*)	(6,032)	(357)	(2,174)	(4,795)	(394)	(2,817)	(2,409)	(103)	(583)

Table 3.2. Demands Concerning Institutions Other than Taxation, Ecclesiastical Payments, and Seigneurial Rights (%)

Action Demanded	Parishes	Third Estate	Nobility
Abolish without compensation	12%	10%	8%
Indemnify	1	1	1
Maintain substantially unaltered	1	1	2
Maintain with reforms	1	1	2
Reform	24	24	22
Replace	1	1	1
Unfavorable	11	3	4
Favorable	2	1	2
"Do Something"	1	1	2
Local demand	9	5	2
Provincial demand	2	5	5
(*N*)	(19,874)	(38,691)	(23,262)

Table 3.3. Ratio of Propensity to Demand "Abolish" to Propensity to Demand "Maintain"

Subject of Grievances	Parishes	Third Estate	Nobility
Seigneurial grievances	37.8	14.7	0.6
Other grievances	11.9	6.7	2.7

evident in rural demands and how little the parish *cahiers* addressed the great questions that the National Assembly was to take up, Taylor urged us to see the peasantry as far less of a force for change than has sometimes been held.[7] If we accept that one element of the idea of "radicalism" is captured by the ratio of "abolish" to "maintain," we see in Table 3.3 that by this measure the parishes are the most radical and the nobles least. The specific targets of the most extreme peasant demands also distinguish their *cahiers*. While all three groups are more prone to abolish burdens than other institutions (with the usual and significant exception of the nobility on seigneurial rights), the peasants are even more unyielding on the seigneurial rights than the urban notables.[8]

7. Alfred Cobban's view of the peasants as markedly more radical on the seigneurial regime than the triumphant urban groups that they had to push beyond foot dragging is specifically repudiated by Taylor. See Cobban, *The Social Interpretation of the French Revolution* (Cambridge: Cambridge University Press, 1965), 53; Taylor, "Revolutionary and Non-revolutionary Content in the *Cahiers*," 495–96.

8. Note by way of contrast that the parishes are marginally less radical than the Third Estate on taxation and markedly less radical on ecclesiastical exactions.

Peasant hostility to the seigneurial regime is simply greater than the elites', as is their hostility to institutions other than burdens. If one asks how completely the peasants anticipate the National Assembly in its work of reconstruction as well as destruction, there is little in the present analysis that departs from George Taylor's conclusions about the countryside. (The parishes also make fewer demands and tend not to discuss the same institutions as each other.)[9] But if one asks how hostile was village France to those Old Regime institutions they chose to discuss in their own texts, one forms quite a different picture. The reconstruction of a new France may not have been their work, but their *cahiers* are more enthusiastic than the elites' about the destruction of the old; among the old institutions they are particularly hostile to their burdens; and among their burdens, the seigneurial regime.

We can more fully appreciate the more extreme demands for abolition or maintenance by taking a look at rather more complex actions. The proposal that someone may be dispossessed of a right in return for financial compensation (which we call "indemnify" here) is for all groups less common than "abolish," but it is an action that hardly occurs in the *cahiers* at all except in the context of seigneurial institutions. If there is anything that most clearly distinguishes grievances about the seigneurial regime from other grievances, it is the frequency of the call for this action. And if there is anything that most clearly distinguishes the positions of the people of the countryside from the Third Estate elite it is this same issue. It is not often applied to ecclesiastical payments (and hardly at all by the rural communities) and is almost totally irrelevant in the area of taxation or in institutional areas other than burdens. Indemnification is most marked as a predilection of the Third Estate, whose *cahiers* urge this particular compromise on seigneurial rights almost twice as frequently as do the documents of the countryside (I shall discuss indemnification in greater detail shortly. See p. 88.)

Another intermediary position between uncompensated abolition and integral maintenance is "reform." Proposals to improve the way in which an institution functions include demands to eliminate its abuses (as opposed to eliminating the institution itself); to abolish an aspect of an institution while leaving the basic structure in place; to improve, modify, or reorganize an activity or practice; to standardize, simplify, make predictable, clarify, or otherwise circumscribe it within definite rules; to redistribute its burdens according to some principle of equity (by decreasing costs or by equalizing costs or by making costs proportional to the ability to pay); to place an institution under the control of some superior authority or to remove it from

9. The mean number of demands is 40 for parishes, 234 for the Third Estate, and 158 for the nobility. See Table 2.3 and Markoff and Shapiro, "Consensus and Conflict," 39.

such control; to combine it with (or separate it from) another institution or to change administrative boundaries; to increase its speed or responsiveness; to change the modalities of a burden (for example, commuting a payment in labor or kind into a cash payment). Such proposals are strikingly less likely to be evoked by the seigneurial rights than other institutions.

A third intermediary position is that an institution be *replaced* by another. Such demands for replacement are consistently less frequent for seigneurial institutions than for taxation and, apart from the parishes, less frequent than for ecclesiastical exactions. Demands for replacement or reform are both acknowledgments of a certain vitality by the dissatisfied. An institution may be held to serve a purpose but to be operating inadequately or in a way that, adequate or not, carries associated and unnecessary costs. Wisdom suggests improving the institution rather than destroying it; or, if destroyed, creating a substitute. Alternatively, an institution may be held to be without value or its purpose may be rejected, yet a sense of political realism suggests that abolition is beyond attainment. Amelioration then becomes the best one may hope for. Those who wish a seigneurial institution eliminated, on the other hand, see no harmful void that needs to be filled. As for the satisfied, they may say nothing if complacent or embarrassed; they may call for preservation if threatened; or they may propose a compromise amelioration under challenge. Such a reform acknowledges the value to them of an institution hard to defend in its present form.

The Third Estate and parishes are markedly less likely to propose reform for a seigneurial institution than they are for ecclesiastical exactions or for institutions other than burdens; and a great deal less likely than for taxes (with these differences all tending to be smaller for the nobility). Compared to other institutions the seigneurial regime is neither seen as reformable nor worth replacing. Its enemies want it gone and its smaller number of vocal friends want it as it was. It had a life of sorts but it could not stimulate visions of vital change. By way of striking contrast, taxation is not merely seen as more reformable than seigneurial rights, it is far more prone to attract reform demands than most institutions (compare Tables 3.1 and 3.2).

In sum the seigneurial regime is the occasion of more extreme proposals than many other facets of the Old Regime. But it also is the occasion of an almost unique moderate demand for indemnification. It is an occasion as well for the nobility to keep their thoughts to themselves—but when those thoughts are expressed they show a profoundly divided nobility, in which the conservative thrust has an edge. The noble conservative thrust, indeed, is more pronounced than for most other institutions; nonetheless, a significant number of noble documents propose abolition while reform is as much a part of their agenda as anyone else's. The seigneurial regime is also the occasion for the peasantry to show themselves more inclined to abolition pure and simple than are the urban notables, among whom there is significant support for financial compensation.[10]

To Abolish or to Maintain

Peasant and Third Estate Radicalism

If seigneurial rights stand apart from other burdens—and, indeed, from other grievances generally—by the extent of rural radicalism as well as by the extent of both noble silence and noble conservatism, a closer scrutiny should prove enlightening. While peasant attitudes toward the seigneurial regime have been the subject of considerable scrutiny and even more *obiter dicta,* what is needed is a more minute analysis. The same is true with regard to other peasant burdens. Some have seen peasant proposals to reform parts of the seigneurial regime, rather than condemnation of it as a totality, as signs of an intellectual incapacity to grasp a social whole or a powerful conservatism impermeable to Enlightenment ideas (as have, for example, William Doyle or George Taylor; see Chapter 2, p. 19). In contrast, I shall argue here that French villagers show a thoughtful and nuanced capacity to differentiate among their burdens and that they had their own sort of radicalism. To see this, we need to go beyond the seigneurial regime as a whole and consider its distinct components.

Table 3.4 presents the proportion of parish and Third Estate *cahiers* that demand that a particular seigneurial right[11] be maintained essentially without change or that it be abolished outright. We are concerned, for the moment, only with the drastic step of abolition without providing financial compensation for the lord. We will turn to that other very important option shortly. Similarly, by "maintain" we have in mind only proposals to retain an institution essentially as is; proposals for institutional reform will also be taken up below.

Among the urban notables as among peasants and rural artisans, there is

10. A more complex statistical analysis of these matters is possible. Stanley Lieberson developed a measure of agreement that may be extended to analyze consensus (or its absence) in the sort of data we have here. This analysis reveals the degree to which the nobles had less consensus on the seigneurial regime than on most other facets of French society, as well as the degree to which the seigneurial regime stands out as one of the arenas in which the Third Estate and nobility most strongly differ. See John Markoff, "Suggestions for the Measurement of Consensus," *American Sociological Review* 47 (1982): 290–98; Markoff and Shapiro, "Consensus and Conflict."

11. This table includes all seigneurial rights discussed by at least 20 *cahiers* of the parishes or 20 of the Third Estate. Omitted from this analysis are aspects of the seigneurial system that are not seigneurial claims to money, goods, services, or honor (e.g., "allodial land" or "seigneurial legal specialists").

virtually no support for retaining any aspect of the seigneurial regime in its current form. The closest to being an acceptable institution to the Third Estate is the financially trivial but symbolically enormous money rent, the *cens,* whose maintenance is advocated by a scant 7% of those *cahiers* that treat it. The lord's possession of an exclusive right to bear arms is acceptable as it stands to 5% of the peasant assemblies. Of the 25 rights in this table, 21 are unacceptable in their present form to every rural assembly in our sample, 15 to all those of the Third Estate. Demands for outright abolition of seigneurial rights, without compensation, occur in a majority of the parish *cahiers* in regard to 14 types of rights; the corresponding figure for the Third Estate is eight. The parishes and Third Estate tend to be relatively tough on the same institutions as each other,[12] but the parishes tend to be more extreme on more categories: for 18 seigneurial rights, the parishes are more likely to insist on abolition. The most striking evidence of both the existence and limitations of peasant radicalism, however, is the significant minority that wants to abolish the seigneurial regime as a whole. It is actually a larger minority than is found among the *cahiers* of the Third Estate.

Of the various material burdens, both the parishes and the Third Estate are far more prone to insist on the abolition of the various seigneurial monopolies, the dues on fairs and markets, the compulsory labor services, the seigneurial tolls, or the property transfer dues than they are with regard to periodic dues. None of the half-dozen forms of regular payments is nearly so likely to have its outright abolition demanded as almost any of the specific rights in the other broad categories listed above. Indeed, apart from the right to bear arms and "seigneurial courts, miscellaneous," the regular payments in cash or kind actually seem the least loathed feature of the seigneurial regime in the villages as well as the towns. It is easy enough to suggest that the petty amount of the *cens*[13] accounts for the low proportion of demands to abolish. The *champart* was a far heavier burden, which may account for the considerably greater tendency shown by the peasants to demand its suppression; nevertheless assemblies that demand abolition of *champart* are far less numerous than those who make radical proposals about most seigneurial rights other than regular dues. Why aren't the dues treated so harshly as the lords' other claims? We shall return to this question after considering the other distinctions Table 3.4 displays.

The various recreational privileges were not treated with anything resembling uniformity. While nearly four parish *cahiers* in five (of those discussing the subject) favored abolishing the right to raise rabbits, a relatively low two

12. The correlation of the proportion of documents calling for abolition in the two groups is .75 (computed for the 27 subjects discussed in at least ten *cahiers*).

13. The *cens* was often not worth the trouble of collecting. See Marcel Garaud, *Histoire générale du droit privé français,* vol. 1, *La Révolution et l'égalité civile* (Paris: Recueil Sirey, 1953), 167.

Table 3.4. Parish and Third Estate Documents Demanding that Seigneurial Rights Be Abolished (Without Compensation) or Maintained (%)

Right[a]	Parishes Abolish	Parishes Maintain	Parishes (*N*)	Third Estate Abolish	Third Estate Maintain	Third Estate (*N*)
Periodic dues						
Cens	3%	0%	(17)	4%	7%	(28)
Champart	21	0	(92)	13	2	(61)
Cens et rentes	24	0	(86)	0	3	(37)
Periodic dues in general	15	1	(86)	7	0	(30)
Miscellaneous periodic dues	10	0	(38)	23	0	(22)
Seigneurial monopolies						
Monopoly on ovens	66	0	(39)	56	2	(50)
Monopoly on milling	79	0	(128)	44	0	(70)
Monopoly on wine press	72	0	(37)	59	0	(44)
Monopolies in general	66	0	(90)	40	0	(103)
Assessments on economic activity						
Seigneurial tolls	60	0	(61)	53	0	(117)
Dues on fairs and markets	51	0	(17)	36	0	(45)
Property transfer rights						
Dues on property transfers (*lods et ventes*)	49	0	(60)	37	0	(49)
Retrait	75	0	(36)	44	4	(48)
Justice						
Seigneurial courts in general	53	0	(104)	53	3	(90)
Seigneurial courts, miscellaneous	21	3	(41)	23	2	(56)
Recreational privileges						
Hunting rights	39	2	(97)	14	2	(107)
Right to raise pigeons	57	0	(152)	38	0	(96)
Right to raise rabbits	79	0	(35)	51	0	(39)
Fishing rights	45	0	(17)	21	0	(24)
Symbolic deference						
Right to bear arms	12	5	(27)	24	0	(41)
Serfdom						
Mainmorte	55	0	(9)	56	0	(36)
Serfdom in general	64	0	(18)	69	0	(26)
Other						
Compulsory labor services	66	0	(102)	51	0	(109)
Miscellaneous right	51	0	(54)	44	3	(79)
Regime in general	29	0	(112)	18	2	(91)

[a]Rights discussed in at least 20 parish or 20 Third Estate *cahiers* (and in at least 5 of each).

Note to Tables 3.4 and 3.5: Since our action code "Abolish" includes proposals to eliminate an institution with or without compensation, and since, moreover, a document calling for the abolition of, say, seigneurial tolls in one article might, in another article, discuss the subject of indemnitites, we only counted an instance of "abolish" if a *cahier* does not also demand indemnification. There are several possible ways in which demands to abolish coexist with demands to indemnify and we adopted the following rules:

- If "abolish without compensation" was presented as the preferred option, with indemnification merely an acceptable second best, we count this as a demand for abolition without compensation only.

Table 3.5. Noble Documents Demanding that Seigneurial Rights Be Abolished (Without Compensation) or Maintained (%)

Right[a]	Abolish	Maintain	*(N)*
Periodic dues			
Cens	14%	14%	(7)%
Champart	0	22	(9)
Periodic dues in general	0	0	(5)
Seigneurial monopolies			
Monopolies in general	7	20	(15)
Assessments on economic activity			
Seigneurial tolls	26	3	(39)
Dues on fairs and markets	33	0	(6)
Property transfer rights			
Dues on property transfers (*lods et ventes*)	0	17	(6)
Justice			
Seigneurial courts in general	7	41	(27)
Seigneurial courts, miscellaneous	12	18	(17)
Recreational privileges			
Hunting rights	4	26	(27)
Right to raise pigeons	0	8	(12)
Symbolic deference patterns			
Right to bear arms	3	17	(30)
Honorific rights	0	43	(21)
Fealty and homage (*foi et hommage*)	11	0	(9)
Avowal and enumeration (*aveu et dénombrement*)	0	0	(9)
Symbolic deference patterns in general	0	67	(27)
Serfdom			
Mainmorte	40	0	(5)
Serfdom in general	71	0	(7)
Other			
Compulsory labor services	15	8	(13)
Miscellaneous right	20	15	(20)
Regime in general	3	26	(34)

[a]Institutions discussed in at least 5 Noble *cahiers.*

- If, on the other hand, the two options are posed as equally desirable alternatives we count *both* demands on the grounds that the *cahier* evinces half-hearted support for both positions. (While this situation was most difficult to classify, it is also so rare as not to be of any statistical consequence.)
- If, on yet a third hand, there is no statement in the text clarifying the relationship of the two demands, we treat this as only a demand for indemnification.
- For a miscellaneous category, for example, "miscellaneous periodic dues," we examine the Free Remarks that our coders are permitted to write to see if "abolish" and "indemnify" refer to the same or different institutions. If different, we have two (or more) distinct demands; if identical, we apply one of the other decision rules.
- If a seigneurial right is to be abolished under some circumstances but indemnified under others, we regard this as a demand for indemnification. We treat this as a complex demand spelling out the modalities of indemnification. (Such demands typically ask that there be indemnification if there is a title deed, but not otherwise; or insist on abolition of the king's seigneurial rights, but indemnification for others.)

in five wanted an end to exclusive hunting rights and a mere 14% of the Third Estate favored such a move. What is the basis for the sharp distinction drawn among these similar rights? For now, we merely pose the question.

Unlike the periodic dues, serfdom was clearly loathed by those who addressed it, and along with seigneurial tolls, it invited the most consistently radical position of the Third Estate. Serfdom had been the subject of much discussion during the eighteenth century and provided the subject for some of Voltaire's most successful polemics. Serfdom was also the target of one of the Old Regime's few reforms of seigneurial rights. In 1779, perhaps following the lead of the neighboring duchy of Savoy,[14] Louis XVI ended serfdom on royal lands. (Although the royal edict called on other lords to do the same,[15] few did so, and these few often seem to have obtained compensation from the serfs in cash or land in return for emancipation.)[16] In light of this campaign it is not surprising that the *cahiers* of the Third Estate are so bitterly hostile to "a crime against humanity,"[17] a hostility matched by those peasant documents that address the issue. But what is perhaps more remarkable is the level of peasant indifference. Mackrell sees serfdom as a picturesque literary issue with which intellectuals amused themselves rather than as a central concern of a burdened peasantry.[18] The evidence seems broadly consistent with Mackrell's suggestion. Parish *cahiers* that take up serfdom are as antagonistic as those of the Third Estate, but to return for a moment to Table 2.4, very few rural documents have any discussion at all.[19] Why was the French peasantry so often silent on an institution that, when discussed, was clearly hated? Was it not they, after all, who were serfdom's victims?

Perhaps we may attribute the lack of widespread peasant hatred for a rural institution so repeatedly described as morally loathsome by the urban notables to a peasant inability to forge a national agenda. Serfdom, after all, was highly localized by the late eighteenth century in Franche-Comté and Burgundy. Conceivably, the peasants of those provinces were the only ones

14. Max Bruchet, *L'Abolition des droits seigneuriaux en Savoie (1761–1793)* (Annecy: Hérisson Frères, 1908).

15. Garaud, *Révolution et égalité civile,* 26–29; Jean Millot, *Le régime féodal en Franche-Comté au XVIIIe siècle* (Besançon: Imprimerie Millot Frères, 1937), 127–82; Jacques Necker, *Oeuvres complètes* (Paris: Treuttel and Würtz, 1820), 3:488–96.

16. Alphonse Aulard, *La Révolution française et le régime féodal* (Paris: Librairie Félix Alcan, 1919), 36.

17. Third Estate of Clermont-en-Beauvaisis, *AP* 2:755. Necker's recommendation to the king speaks of *mainmorte* as "a form of servitude contrary to humanity" (Necker, *Oeuvres,* 3:488).

18. On the polemic against serfdom see John Q. C. Mackrell, *The Attack on "Feudalism" in Eighteenth-Century France* (London: Routledge and Kegan Paul, 1973), 104–32.

19. Chassin attempted to collect grievances about serfdom in the *cahiers,* and, strikingly, found most of his material in the general *cahiers* of the Third Estate (Charles-Louis Chassin, *L'église et les derniers serfs* [Paris: Dentu, 1880], 155–91).

with much awareness.[20] Perhaps, however, we may see something else as well. Might eighteenth-century peasants have seen some benefits to which serfdom's critics were indifferent? Paternalistic apologists for serfdom, after all, insisted on its protection of the serfs.[21] Protection from what? Protection against loss of land under seigneurial pressures. Seigneurial institutions were often used to force out marginal peasant proprietors, to seize land through *retrait,* or to lay claim to pasture or forest. Lords might let arrears accumulate on periodic dues for years, then demand that peasants pay up, and accept a land-for-debt swap; under *retrait,* a lord had the optional right to substitute himself for the purchaser of peasant land; and lords might hold or fabricate a claim on a portion of common land. Many seigneurial rights could thus be put at the service of landholders oriented to a growing agricultural market, to such an extent that some historians have wondered whether peasant contestation might not be better described as a losing, rear-guard struggle against a growing capitalism than a vanguard battle against a dying feudalism in conjunction with the victorious bourgeoisie.[22] In such a context, did not the "archaic" *mainmorte* actually preserve peasant smallholdings at the same time as limiting their rights? Certainly this was the judgment of Pierre de Saint Jacob in his unsurpassed study of the seigneurial regime in a region where serfdom was far from dead. "*Mainmorte,*" he wrote, "was in fact a protection."[23] Analyzing the varying success of efforts at estate enlargement through dispossession of small peasant proprietors, he concludes that "the regions of *mainmorte* were alone in exhibiting an extreme stability of peasant property" (462).

This paternalistic defense of serfdom was scorned by no less a critic than Voltaire. The lords, Voltaire writes, may well contend that liberty will be "pernicious to those held to the soil." These lords are forgetting the great social transformation that accompanies liberty, namely, industry and prosperity.[24] But the sage of Ferney forgets something himself: the proletarianization that accompanies industry and prosperity. We do not necessarily

20. The peasants of the *bailliage* of Baume, for example, overwhelmingly condemned *mainmorte.* See Maurice Gresset, *Gens de justice à Besançon de la conquête par Louis XIV à la Révolution française (1674–1789)* (Paris: Bibliothèque Nationale, 1978), 2:730.

21. For example, the Academy of Besançon in 1778 awarded a prize to an essay by a member of the serf-holding abbey of Luxeuil that argued that many peasants actually preferred the economic security of serfdom to the freedom to become destitute (Aulard, *Révolution française et régime féodal,* 31–33).

22. Georges Lefebvre introduced the idea of an anticapitalist aspect to peasant action in 1789 and beyond. See Georges Lefebvre, "La Révolution française et les paysans," in *Etudes sur la Révolution française* (Paris: Presses Universitaires de France, 1963), 343.

23. Pierre de Saint Jacob, *Les paysans de la Bourgogne du Nord au dernier siècle de l'Ancien Régime* (Paris: Société Les Belles Lettres, 1960), 48.

24. Voltaire, "Coutume de Franche-Comté, sur l'esclavage imposé à des citoyens par une vieille coutume," *Oeuvres complètes* (Paris: Garnier Frères, 1879), 28:378.

need to see in the failure of the parish *cahiers* to write so frequently of serfdom with envenomed passion as do the urban notables, a sign of the intellectual backwardness of village France, nor of widespread ignorance or indifference to an abuse confined to a few provinces. On the contrary, abstaining on serfdom may be a sign of peasant intellectual independence from those who claimed to know their interests, but whose own interests were far from identical with theirs. Indeed, let us look ahead to the revolutionary legislation. The initial form assumed by the abolition of serfdom a year after the *cahiers* were written, in fact, left the newly emancipated serfs heavily burdened by their lords' claims (see Chapter 8, p. 461). The Third Estate's disgust with the humiliation of servile status may not have been the main issue for those held to be humiliated.

The indifference of the countryside to what the upper reaches of the Third Estate took to be the degraded serf status appears part of a broader syndrome. The peasants were particularly hostile to rights where the material exaction was severe and far less hostile where the symbolization of status was central (see Chapter 2, p. 42). There was a lack of peasant interest in abolishing the financially insignificant *cens* as there was in the monopoly on bearing arms. The *cens* had an important symbolic value, however, as a mark of the seigneur's "direct" rights generally.[25] This seems not to have impressed the peasants, but when fused with other, higher payments as *cens et rentes,* a markedly higher proportion opted for abolition. (The Third Estate, with no proposals to abolish *cens et rentes,* had other ideas concerning periodic payments as we shall see, p. 124 et seq.)

Similarly, the right to bear arms is not a target for abolition pure and simple for the peasants, while the right to hunt is.[26] In this regard the peasants are quite consistent: they separate symbolization of hierarchy from material burdens and complain more bitterly about the latter. Few parish *cahiers* concern themselves with such honorific rights as the claim on the best seat in church or the most visible place in a procession and none of those few demands abolition. Nor do they take up symbolic deference patterns in general: we find not a single parish *cahier* in our sample to have demanded their abolition, while a handful actually insist on their retention.

25. Pothier, for example, speaks of the *cens* as a "recognition of lordship" (Robert Pothier, *Traité des fiefs, avec un titre sur le cens* [Orléans: Montaut, 1776], 2:378). Note the common lawyer's formula: "Cens portant tous droits censaux et seigneuriaux" (Saint Jacob, *Paysans de la Bourgogne du Nord,* 66).

26. Not that a sensitivity to the symbolism of honor is totally absent. At the head of the bitter denunciation of hunting rights composed by the parish of Marly-la-ville (*bailliage* of Paris-hors-les-murs), stands a condemnation of its characteristics as a status marker: "How great is the attachment for an amusement which is only keenly felt because it is licit for some but illicit for others; for an amusement which often raises the unreasoning beast above the fortune, the freedom and the life of man, who God has given to the animal for master" (*AP* 4:678).

On the other hand, privileges maintaining the most visible status distinctions could be bitterly opposed by the peasants, if they were experienced as severe financial burdens. The most detested seigneurial claim of all in terms of the proportion of rural documents insisting on abolition is the monopoly on milling. Pierre de Saint Jacob argues that the monopoly on milling both existed more widely in the eighteenth century than the other forms of monopoly and that, when present, it was harder to evade.[27] Perhaps this explains why it stands out among the monopolies treated in the rural *cahiers* for the frequency and the bitterness of the discussions. The monopoly on ovens for baking bread, by way of contrast, was continually threatened by small, privately held ovens.[28] In the Toulouse region some lords were abandoning this right and those who clung to it had to struggle ceaselessly to enforce it.[29]

Noble Conservatism

Table 3.5 presents the data on "abolish" and "maintain" for the nobility[30] and the contrast with Table 3.4 could not be more striking. For most categories, unsilent noble assemblies have a substantial tendency to insist on maintaining the institution as is; for most categories shown on both Tables 3.4 and 3.5, the nobles correspondingly have a markedly lower propensity than the Third Estate, let alone the parishes, to propose abolition. Note especially the differences with regard to the seigneurial regime in general: the nobility's propensity to preserve it matches the Third Estate's to eliminate it. There are also several specific rights for which there are more noble *cahiers* urging "maintain" than "abolish." There is strong support for continued symbolic distinction, an arena concerning which, as we have seen in Chapter 2, p. 47, the usually reticent nobility has

27. Saint Jacob, *Paysans de la Bourgogne du Nord,* 420–22.

28. In one Burgundian village, the existence of no fewer than forty-six ovens became the occasion of a bitter lawsuit between lord and community in 1781. See Hilton Root, *Peasants and King in Burgundy: Agrarian Foundations of French Absolutism* (Berkeley and Los Angeles: University of California Press, 1987), 189.

29. Jean Bastier, *La féodalité au siècle des lumierès dans la région de Toulouse, 1730–1790* (Paris: Bibliothèque Nationale), 169–72. Renauldon, in the earlier of his treatises on seigneurial rights (Joseph Renauldon, *Traité historique et pratique des droits seigneuriaux* [Paris: Despilly, 1765], 251), wondered rhetorically whether in light of the widespread sense that the monopolies are "odious," it might not be a good idea to permit small ovens some restricted uses. He responded to his own query by concluding that as desirable as liberty is, permitting such ovens would be contrary to the lord's interest, and would "give an excessive extension" to such liberty.

30. The noble propensity toward silence suggests examining institutions taken up in as few as five texts. From the point of view of statistical reliability this would normally be an unwise procedure, but the great thought that went into these documents suggests a more confident evaluation of reliability than does the analysis of a typical survey item.

much to say. And note the preponderance of "maintain" over "abolish" for the highly symbolic hunting rights[31] and for pigeon raising as well.[32]

Tocqueville, drawing on a reading of the *cahiers* of the nobility, argued that the nobles' commitment to their status honor coexisted with a willingness to abandon monetary advantage: "Generally speaking, the nobility, while abandoning many of their beneficial rights, cling with anxiety and warmth to those which are purely honorary. They want not only to preserve those which they possess, but also to invent new ones. So conscious were they that they were being dragged into the vortex of democracy: so terribly did they dread perishing there."[33]

Certainly Tocqueville might have found noble *cahiers* that claimed to value honor over material advantage. Upon examination, however, some of these claims are at once followed by clarifications. Consider the second estate of Carcassonne. Their *cahier* tells us forthrightly that "the nobility shall generously offer sacrifices to pay off the government debt and ease the sufferings of the people." However, they go on to tell us, in their province of Languedoc the most important direct tax, the *taille,* is "real" rather than "personal," following the legal terminology of the day. This meant that those exempt from the *taille,* in Languedoc, were those holding "noble land," rather than, as in northern France, those who were noble persons.[34] Therefore, these generous gentlemen reason, they, noble persons as they are, have no tax privileges to abolish. Moreover, they point out, seigneurial rights are assessed on land already taxed. It clearly follows that the revenues from *cens* and *champart* ought not to pay taxes. The peasants, after all, on receiving land from "the hand of the seigneur" have already agreed to bear all expenses. Having developed their argument to this point, the nobles of Carcassonne are now in a position to assert the proposition toward which this line of reasoning is heading: seigneurial rights are not to be taxed, for that would be an infringement of the sacred rights of property.[35]

31. Garaud's claim (*Révolution et propriété foncière,* 163) that the noble *cahiers* are "almost unanimously" attached to the hunting rights is an exaggerated simplification. It is true that a bare 3% of those expressing views call for abolition; and, as will be seen below, there is also no support for the option of indemnifying the seigneurs. But only 16% of the *cahiers* of the nobility discuss this right at all. (Garaud earlier had noted the frequent silence of the nobility [162].) Garaud also overlooks the important complexity that only 25% of noble *cahiers* expressing views want to maintain this privilege intact. As we shall show below, there were many reform proposals.

32. Only a handful of noble *cahiers* take up either the right to raise rabbits or the right to fish. Of these few, there is none that calls for abolishing either, and some support for maintenance.

33. Tocqueville, *Old Regime and Revolution,* 26.

34. Marcel Marion, *Les impôts directs sous l'Ancien Régime, principalement au XVIIIe siècle* (Geneva: Slatkine-Megariotis Reprints, 1974), 18–20.

35. What was this Carcassonne nobility prepared to sacrifice for the public interest? These nobles, with a tone of generosity, will not protest against the *vingtième* tax (one of the Old Regime's attempts to get the privileged to pay something). When imposed in 1749, their *cahier* contends, it was described as temporary. They, therefore, have every right to complain, but rather than argue

The invocation of property as an argument against uncompensated abolition was rather common, in the *cahiers* of the Third Estate as well as of the nobility (see Chapter 2, p. 34, and Chapter 9, p. 531). But the claim that property rights forbade taxing seigneurial income was unusual.[36] But for all its unusual features, this *cahier* teaches us to be hesitant about taking the altruistic protestations at face value. If the reasoning of the gentlemen of Carcassonne is unique, their fellows of Perche furnish a good example of a more common position: "The nobility declares that since its pecuniary privileges are those to which the order is the least attached, it shall sacrifice them painlessly. It shall reserve, however, those announced in the report to the Council by the Director General of Finances on Dec. 27 . . . and shall reserve, moreover, the sacred rights of property. It declares formally that it cannot nor ought not to consent to any change which will bring about any degradation to the person of its members or to the essence, the dignity and the prerogatives of its fiefs" (*AP* 5:323). Evidently this painless sacrifice of pecuniary advantage is achieved by avoiding those that are too painful. The advantages in access to government posts referred to in the Council's decree of December 27, 1788, are to be kept.[37] More strikingly, property rights are not to be infringed.[38] And if these aren't reservations enough, the nobles of Perche refuse any degradation of their persons. To a keen sense of honor, that could cover anything.

Tocqueville's reading of the *cahiers* is certainly borne out by many of the nobles' general formulations. It is less certain that it is an accurate summary when one takes the reservations, qualifications, distinctions, and definitions into account, particularly as these are often rather murky. The rhetorical style of sweeping and highly generalized renunciation followed by extensive qualification and careful definition that wholly altered the commonsense meaning of the initial generalization was an important noble contribution to a rhetorical style that blossomed in the revolutionary legislatures. In this way a portion of the nobility managed to participate in a rather radical language whose detailed working-out would be far less sweeping. They thus contributed simultaneously to the public expression of longing for rapid, sweeping,

about the *vingtièmes,* the nobility is "always ready to sacrifice its fortune and its life for the good of the State" (*AP* 2:530).

36. The relation of taxation and seigneurial rights is seen quite otherwise, for example, by the parish of Marly-la-ville in the *bailliage* of Paris-hor-les-murs. Inveighing against compensation for the holders of detested rights, this document argues that by bearing the full weight of taxation, the people have already adequately indemnified the nobles for any losses suffered through abolition (*AP* 4:678).

37. Jean Egret discusses the background of this decree in *La pré-révolution française, 1787–1788* (Paris: Presses Universitaires de France, 1962), 364–67.

38. As we shall show later, "property rights" were often construed very broadly by the nobility and might even cover virtually the entire seigneurial regime. See p. 86, as well as Chapter 4, p. 188, and Chapter 9, p. 531.

and total social transformation, in a word, to revolutionary maximalism and, at the same time, to the construction of minimalist reforms designed to change as little as possible and to constitute barriers to further change. Partisans of all political options could take heart or lose heart depending on the selectivity with which they assimilated this rhetoric. The language of revolutionary legislation on seigneurial rights from the famous session of August 4, 1789, well into 1792 was permeated with this ambiguity (see Chapter 9).

Trying to discover precisely which rights the gentlemen of Perche wished to shield under the umbrella of property rights or those which their colleagues of Limoges held to be "purely honorific" (*AP* 3:569) turns out to be a rather difficult matter. Indeed, the absence of specification permitted "honorific" to expand as needed to cover lucrative claims, all the while maintaining a language of sacrifice. Rather than search for explicit definitions of "property" and "honorific" for the nobility, we can more easily see in practice which rights the noble *cahiers* seek to defend and which to eliminate.

Let us return to Table 3.5. First of all noble commitment to honor is indeed quite evident. The strongest commitment to maintenance is precisely in the area of symbolization of status distinction. There are also a number of income-producing rights that attract more demands for abolition than maintenance: this is true for the dues on fairs and markets, the compulsory labor services, and the seigneurial tolls.[39] And the handful of noble *cahiers* that take up serfdom have a very strong abolitionist element. It is not the case, however, that the preponderance of noble sentiment—among those assemblies that took a public position, that is—favors abolishing all income-producing rights. Notice the hints of support for *champart* and mutation fees.[40] These were not merely income-producing but were among the more

39. Tocqueville wildly exaggerates when he asserts on the basis of his study of the noble *cahiers*: "All the *cahiers* demand that *corvées* be definitively abolished. A majority of bailiwicks desire the rights of banality and toll be made redeemable" (Tocqueville, *Old Regime and Revolution,* 265). Only a handful of noble *cahiers* even mention the *banalités* at all, to mention only the most striking error. Tocqueville seems to have completely missed the significance of the silence of the nobility. Inadequate attention to noble reticence also distorts the picture painted in the path-breaking work of Nikolai Karéiew, *Les Paysans et la question paysanne en France dans le dernier quart du XVIIIe siècle* (Paris: V. Giard and E. Brière, 1899). In his generally insightful discussion of the noble *cahiers,* he writes, for example, that "the nobility unanimously declares itself for the preservation of the right to hunt" (425); there is no indication to the reader of how unusual any discussions at all of this right actually were.

40. Our discussion of these rights as material exactions or symbolic distinctions does not imply that these categories are at all exclusive. As Pierre de Saint Jacob points out, even as lucrative a claim as the mutation fees has a significant symbolic aspect. It showed the domination of the seigneur well beyond his own domain land. As a restriction on the free alienability of land, one of the critical aspects of any modern notion of property, what could be a more powerful reminder of the incompleteness of peasant freedom than *lods et ventes*? (What, that is, other than the even more restrictive—and even more hated—*retrait*?) (Saint Jacob, *Paysans de la Bourgogne du Nord,* 65).

lucrative rights. Perhaps few noble *cahiers* dared in the atmosphere of the spring of 1789 to defend their naked interests, but the relatively lucrative rights seem more likely to be defended than renounced, when mentioned at all (and there are very few mentions). The nobles of Perche may painlessly sacrifice its "pecuniary privileges"; sacrificing something as specific as *champart* is another, and more painful, matter entirely.

More revealing, perhaps, is the strong support for the retention of the seigneurial courts, one of the rights that more than a handful of noble assemblies were willing to discuss. One might claim that the provision of a visible public service, sometimes accompanied by special marks of distinction[41] falls within the "symbolic" group.[42] The nobles of Limoges mount such a defense of the right of justice. They tell us that "the order of the nobility willingly renounces its pecuniary privileges." The "purely honorific," however, are to be conserved, for "it is essential that the nobles hold fast to the distinctions necessary for a monarchy." These distinctions, indeed, support "the liberty of the people, the respect due the sovereign and the authority of the laws." And what do the gentlemen have in mind as "purely honorific?" Among other claims, they insist "that seigneurial courts and other honorific rights of the *seigneurs* be conserved and augmented."[43] But the seigneur's court also served rather widely as the linchpin of the system, "the soul of the fief," in Saint Jacob's expression.[44] It provided an institutional mechanism for compelling peasant compliance.[45]

41. A seigneur with the right of "high justice," which once upon a time meant the right to try people for their lives, might erect a gallows on his land, a more elaborate gallows for a higher-ranking lord. See Joseph Renauldon, *Dictionnaire des fiefs et droits seigneuriaux utiles et honorifiques* (Paris: Delalain, 1788), 1:478.

42. Discussions of seigneurial courts tend to be found in noble *cahiers* that also devote proportionately more space to unambiguously honorific rights; there is no such association with unambiguously lucrative ones; see Chapter 4.

43. *AP* 3:570. The other "purely honorific" rights itemized: bearing arms, entry into military careers, being listed on a separate tax role for a specially named tax, a bit of land.

44. *Paysans de la Bourgogne du Nord,* 407.

45. But not everywhere. Bastier's exhaustive study of 55 seigneurial courts around Toulouse shows almost no cases in which the lord used them to enforce payment of dues (although they did serve as an arena to protect hunting rights). It appears to have been too easy for the defendants to appeal such judgments for it to have been worthwhile to bring the case before the lord's own court at all. And in the Vannes region, cases involving a local lord automatically went to a higher court in Brittany's unusual hierarchy of seigneurial courts. A seigneurial court, but not one's own, heard the lord's case (at least in cases involving Brittany's distinctive tenure arrangement, *domaine congéable*). The more usual judgment of historians has been well stated in Robert Forster's detailed studies of estate management. In Aunis he finds the courts to be "significant instruments for a family of domain-builders" by enforcing *retrait,* the collection of arrears, and the seizure of uncultivated land. Around Toulouse, unlike Bastier, he finds the seigneurial courts "a key institution in the maintenance of the noble's interests in general and of the seigneurial system in particular"; see Bastier, *Féodalité au siècle des lumières,* 123–25, 168–69; Timothy J. A. Le Goff, *Vannes and Its Region: A Study of Town and Country in Eighteenth-Century France* (Oxford: Clarendon Press, 1981), 279; Robert

If there were some material claims the nobles wished to defend (sometimes by cloaking them in honor), there were some symbolic ones they did not. There was no enthusiasm for defending those two ancient ritualized acknowledgments of entering into possession of a fief: "fealty and homage" and "avowal and enumeration." Status distinctions among lords were like serfdom in having no noble support whatsoever for unaltered preservation. The once elaborate and emotionally intense ceremony by which the vassal declared himself the man of another man and the detailed accounting of the feudal holding were weaker in the eighteenth century, when observed at all, and altogether devoid of their former moral intensity.[46] But it was not merely their institutional feebleness that made the nobles uninterested in their defense. We suggest, rather, that the eighteenth century's most celebrated critic of the entire seigneurial system, Boncerf, was on target. He pointed out that these rights were disliked by most of the seigneurs, because they themselves had to acknowledge the overlordship of their own suzerains.[47] Few noble assemblies took up (see Chapter 2, p. 61), and none supported, an elaborated hierarchy.[48] By contrast, the noble *cahiers* of 1614 were permeated with a vision of a society both corporate and elaborately stratified. In 1614, a typical document organized its grievances in articles that dealt with "clergy," "nobility," and so on. This corporate structure survived in some *cahiers* in 1789; in many others it had been displaced by "constitution," "agriculture," and other categories that cut across social hierarchies and within which reasoned programs were elaborated. The

---

Forster, *Merchants, Landlords, Magistrates: The Depont Family in Eighteenth Century France* (Baltimore: Johns Hopkins University Press, 1980), 88–89; and *The Nobility of Toulouse in the Eighteenth Century: A Social and Economic Study* (Baltimore: Johns Hopkins University Press, 1960), 29.

46. On eighteenth-century ideas of hierarchy, see Yves Durand, *Les fermiers généraux au XVIIIe siècle* (Paris: Presses Universitaires de France, 1971).

47. Pierre-François Boncerf, *Les inconvéniens des droits féodaux* (London: Valade, 1776), 67. The ecclesiastical corporations of Angers, for example, were appalled when the count of Provence insisted in 1774, that he be rendered *foi et hommage* and *aveu et dénombrement* and went to court to enforce his will. In the late 1780s, the advisers of the duke of Orléans successfully urged him to reassert his claim to demonstration of fealty from his vassals (so as not to be outshone by the king and his brothers). But the Revolution intervened, and the duke became Philippe-Egalité instead. See John McManners, *French Ecclesiastical Society under the Ancien Régime: A Study of Angers in the Eighteenth Century* (Manchester: Manchester University Press, 1960), 119–20; Beatrice F. Hyslop, *L'Apanage de Philippe Egalité, Duc d'Orléans (1785–1791)* (Paris: Société des Etudes Robespierristes, 1965), 62–63, 167–68.

48. What the nobility chose not to defend, the southwestern villagers of Castelferrus were willing to let them keep. In line with the pervasive peasant focus on material exactions, and relative indifference to the symbols of the seigneurial order, their *cahier* calls for the abolition of compulsory labor and monopolies and the right to buy out "the payments they owe annually to their lord, and shall only leave him the pre-eminence of his fief." Do we read this as generosity or as derisive Gascon wit? See Daniel Ligou, ed., *Cahiers de doléances du tiers état du pays et jugerie de Rivière-Verdun pour les états généraux de 1789* (Gap: Imprimerie Louis-Jean, 1961), 53–54.

sense of the monarch empowered by God was largely (but not totally) displaced by the executive whose powers derive from a contract. And the sense of gradation within the nobility has all but vanished.[49] We see here the lack of commitment to a truly hierarchical society, perhaps the consequence of the extensive representation of the lesser nobility in the assemblies that drafted the *cahiers*. Or perhaps this is a symptom of that penetration of democratic thought into the nobility which Tocqueville regarded as undermining their capacity to rule.[50] The nobles of Périgueux explicitly insist on "the essential equality of the nobility which may not be divided into several classes." They go on: "we are pleased to consider the princes of the blood as the first of our order and we recognize the functions of the peers in *parlement* but we shall never recognize their preeminence and still less their pretentions."[51]

Noble Defense and Third Estate Attack

How do the nobles justify the seigneurial regime when they propose to preserve it? Often, to be sure, they do not justify it but merely state their demand as when the nobles of Limoges assert their claims to honorific rights (*AP* 3:570). Unlike the other forms of noble reticence, this is not especially distinctive; the Third Estate and parishes often similarly omit any arguments

49. Ludmila Pimenova, "La noblesse à la veille de la Révolution," in *La grande Révolution française* (Moscow: Editions Naouka, 1989), 50–55. See also Gilbert Shapiro and John Markoff, *Revolutionary Demands: A Content Analysis of the Cahiers de Doléances of 1789* (Stanford: Stanford University Press, 1997), chap. 19.

50. The notion of a specifically noble egalitarianism can be occasionally glimpsed much earlier in the century. Insofar as the eighteenth-century nobility produced a coherent defense for privilege in a democratic world without a God fixing each in his place, it was Boulainvilliers's attempt to found present-day social distinctions in the barbarian conquest of Gaul. In his view, the free Germanic conquerors were profoundly egalitarian; the creation of distinctions within the nobility was a disgusting outcome of royal despotism. On the other hand, the effort to distinguish more genuine nobles from newcomers kept Boulainvilliers himself reinventing internal gradations, as shown in Harold Ellis's close survey of his political ideas. The rare moments when nobles spoke collectively outside of the usual institutions suggests some support for such ideas. In the absence of an Estates-General after 1614, nobles occasionally assembled themselves in moments of crisis, a practice that continued into the early eighteenth century. The last such mobilization in 1717 gave voice to an intra-noble fraternal egalitarianism; see Harold A. Ellis, *Boulainvilliers and the French Monarchy: Aristocratic Politics in Early Eighteenth-Century France* (Ithaca: Cornell University Press, 1988); Jean-Dominique Lassaigne, *Les assemblées de la noblesse de France aux dix-septième et dix-huitième siècles* (Paris: Cujas, 1965), 143–46. See also François Furet and Mona Ozouf, "Deux légitimations historiques de la société française au XVIIIe siècle: Mably et Boulainvilliers," *Annales: Economies, Sociétés, Civilisations* 34 (1979): 438–50.

51. *AP* 5:341. This *cahier* plainly embraces the vision of an internally fraternal nobility, nonetheless distinguished from the commoners, found in the thinking of Boulainvilliers, rather than the finely graded hierarchy whose pinnacle was the monarch that was championed by the princes of the blood.

in support of their insistence on abolition. When the nobles discuss the seigneurial rights as an aggregate, however, they do tend to put forth an explicit rationale. A study of these claims discerns two distinct lines of defense that assemblies of the nobility evidently held (or at least hoped) to be persuasive. First, the nobles may appeal to an image of a hierarchical and monarchical social order in which distinctions of status are vital matters of honor. The nobility of Limoges, for example, insist on "the distinctions necessary in a monarchy" and then go on to stress particularly the right to bear arms, seigneurial justice and other honorific seigneurial rights as well as appearing on a separate tax role (*AP* 3:569–70). This argument tends to conflate noble and seigneurial prerogatives. Past service, especially of a military variety, and sacrifice, especially of blood, may be invoked. Such language suffuses the introductory paragraphs of the *cahier* of the nobility of Villers-Cotterets, for example (*AP* 6:189). Much more commonly, the nobles may appeal to property as an ultimate value, not to be encroached on by the state nor usurped by the avaricious. The discourse of property occurs in contesting arbitrary state power to seize one's person in unmotivated imprisonment or one's goods in unconsented taxation. The nobility of Saintes enumerate several essential laws, the first of which "will assure our personal liberty and our properties." Such a law, in their view, simultaneously abolishes the royal practice of arbitrary imprisonment through *lettres de cachet* and protects seigneurial rights. The second basic law bars taxation without the free consent of the Estates-General (*AP* 5:665). The nobility sometimes defined property with some care to include seigneurial rights.[52] For the discourse of honor to cover the entire seigneurial regime, the category of specifically honorific rights had to expand and the income-generating aspects of particular rights ignored. For the discourse of property to cover the entire seigneurial regime, a contractual and voluntary aspect needed to be imputed to social relationships held by critics to be either inherently or historically coerced (see Chapter 9).

The Third Estate shows its own sense of a good case when it justifies its attacks. The seigneurial regime is sometimes attacked for its harm to the public interest, particularly in its injury to agriculture. The argument of utility—or rather disutility—sometimes runs quite deep. The Third Estate of Nemours adopted a document in which an extensive discussion of seigneurial rights is a subsection of a broad treatment "of the administration of agriculture," itself a section of a chapter on "laws bearing on the administration of labor" (*AP* 4:191–207). And if the nobles sometimes point to the needs of a monarchical system to align the lords with the forces of light, the Third Estate has its counterimage of darkness. The noble assertion of honor was countered by the Third's depiction of dishonor. In its reminis-

52. For example, nobles of Saintonge, *AP* 5:665.

cence of ancient servitude, the seigneurial system embodies the vestiges of barbarism.[53] And whatever there once might have been to say on behalf of these lordly prerogatives, these justifications have evaporated. Compulsory labor service was a particularly conspicuous example of barbarism to the Third Estate. In Gien it was held to be among the "odious remains of the tyranny of the powerful" (*AP* 3:285). The three orders of Villiers-la-Montagne agreed that it was "an intolerable vice" (*AP* 2:246).

The weight of these considerations varies with the nature of the particular right in question. With regard to its honorific distinctiveness, the nobility is especially apt to assert the requirements of a monarchical constitution,[54] thereby adhering to a central thesis of Montesquieu.[55] The nobles of Nivernais et Donzois add that being publicly singled out by virtue of clear and visible distinctions makes nobles feel they must live up to the qualities of their ancestors (*AP* 4:253). (The Third Estate of Etampes, as if replying tongue-in-cheek, suggest the possibility of a new and distinctive emblem for nobles to wear—nobility, however, being redefined as a nonhereditary reward for public service; *AP* 3:284). The Third Estate did not, any more than the nobility, reject a "monarchical constitution," but they did not with any frequency claim that seigneurial rights and especially honorific distinctions are essential in a monarchy.[56] For its part, the nobility did not mount a defense of barbarism—although as we shall argue below, their sense of themselves as warriors is implicit in many of their texts—but neither did they defend the seigneurial regime against this charge.

A defense couched in terms of honor was virtually an invitation to an attack couched in terms of scorn. The more common defense in terms of property appealed to the very same values being drawn on by some of the fiercest critics of the seigneurial regime. On the level of detailed debate on particular rights, however, the gulf in discourse is so great that attackers and defenders sometimes appear to be speaking of distinct institutions that happen to bear the same name. When the Third Estate demanded the abolition of the exclusive right to bear arms, it is clear they were concerned about the protection of crops and the claims of self-defense.[57] The Third Estate of the border area of Perpignan, for example, wanted its strong

53. Vitry-le-François, *AP* 6:219.

54. Arras, *AP* 2. The noble defense of status markers as property is not unknown, however (see, e.g., Nobles of Meaux, *AP* 3:726).

55. *De l'Esprit des Lois* (Paris: Société Les Belles Lettres, 1950), book 5, chapter 9.

56. The Third Estate of Digne does, however, argue atypically that "in a great State, it is necessary not to confound ranks. Distinctions must not be destroyed. The national assembly must abolish all servitude and everything that contrasts with the rights and the dignity of man and citizen. Ranks may and must be conserved without any element of humiliation." Note that the emphasis here is on the preservation of the dignity of subordinate strata within the necessary framework of rank. This was hardly a widespread noble concern; see *AP* 3:348.

57. Examples: Ponthieu, *AP* 5:441; Bailleul, *AP* 2:177.

tradition of self-protection reaffirmed (*AP* 5:376). The nobles were caught up with a different matter entirely: their sense of honor. The rich symbol that they insist should be exclusively theirs is the sword. Their documents are less inclined but not completely disinclined to talk of firearms.[58] But if the possession of firearms might not make the gentlemen of the era of Louis XVI feel themselves to be with Roland at Roncesvalles, swaggering with sword on hip was even less consequential to those who worried about wolves and birds and thieves. The "right to bear arms," then, hardly connoted the same "arms" to all participants in 1789.[59] Were the right to bear arms the only point at issue, it is not difficult to imagine a compromise—if one is willing to assume that the public discourse is the only reality.

That at least a part of the Third Estate was eager for a formula that might preserve the honor of the lords is suggested by the discussion of seigneurial justice on the part of the notables of Forcalquier. After proposing the abolition of the lord's courts in no uncertain terms, they reconsider. "If," they indicate, "someone proposes the means to conciliate the dignity of the fiefs and the tranquility of the vassals, the deputies must not refuse to adopt them." They then suggest consideration of several options, without urging adoption of any of them (*AP* 3:331). They are in short prepared to grant the lords their public esteem, if no one is thereby injured.

Indemnification

If neither "abolish" nor "maintain," what else might be proposed? One important intermediary position, commonly expressed by the verb *racheter,* was aimed at mollifying many parties. Under this proposal, a seigneurial right would be eliminated upon payment of a suitable indemnity to the lord. Such a suggestion responded to many desires: to relieve one social class of a burden without damaging the interests of another; to create the sense of change while delaying or perhaps blocking it; to rationalize rural France without damaging the present proprietors. Of course, it did not respond to the desire to hold fast expressed by a part of the nobility, nor the desire to clear the system away, expressed by a larger part of the Third Estate and an even larger part of the peasantry.

Although some historians, like Alfred Cobban, whose argument I consider

58. Nor, for that matter, did the Third Estate always insist on firearms. Avesnes, for example: "All proprietors shall be permitted to destroy game without firearms" (*AP* 2:153).

59. On August 7, 1789, the bishop of Chartres proposed amending the decree on abolishing feudal rights to the effect that game could only be destroyed with "innocent weapons." The bishop never elucidated this curious concept; his suggestion was greeted with laughter and he dropped out of the debate (*AP* 8:358).

below (see also Chapter 10, p. 594) have seen the indemnification proposal as little more than a smokescreen to conceal the preservation of seigneurial rights, it is important to see how radical, in the eyes of some, the notion appeared when it was advocated a dozen years before the Revolution. Boncerf's pamphlet of 1776 on "The Disadvantages of Feudal Rights" had argued for such an indemnification, at a high rate, considerably more generous to the lords than the legislation eventually adopted by the National Assembly proved to be.[60] Even this was far too radical for the Paris Parlement, which ordered the work publicly torn and burnt, an act that ensured the brochure's celebrity.[61] The parlementary decree left little doubt about how threatening was even such a generous indemnification: "One is tempted to the view that there is a secret party, an underground agent, who is trying to shake the foundations of the state through internal shocks. What is happening resembles those volcanos which, having announced themselves with subterranean noises and a sequence of tremors, end in a sudden eruption that covers everything around with a flaming torrent of ruins, ashes and lava thrust up from the furnace in the bowels of the earth."[62] The precise fear of the magistrates, the decree goes on to make clear, was that such a measure would provide a focus to mobilize peasants who might then go far beyond Boncerf's ostensibly limited purposes: "vassals will not hesitate to rise against their lords as will the people against their sovereign" (70).

Historians have often noted that the parish *cahiers* sometimes called for compensation to the lords for the loss of their rights and sometimes favored abolition pure and simple. There has been, however, no sustained exploration of whether it was only certain rights that tended to attract the more moderate demand. The proportion of parish and of Third Estate grievances calling for the abolition (in some fashion) of a seigneurial right was about the same, 44%; they differed in the proportion favoring a simple termination of the lord's claim as opposed to an indemnity (see Table 3.1).

The advocacy of indemnification has been understood in quite different ways. The core of Alfred Cobban's argument that the revolutionary legislatures were at one with the nobility in their resistance to the dismantling of the seigneurial regime (due to their sharing in the ownership of seigneurial

60. Boncerf proposed compensating the lords at 50 or 60 times the annual value of their rights. The indemnification rate established in May 1790 for regular annual dues was, depending on the particular right, set at 20 or 25 times the annual yield (Boncerf, *Les inconvéniens des droits féodaux,* 11; *AP* 15:365–66).

61. Douglas Dakin, *Turgot and the Ancien Régime in France* (New York: Octagon Books, 1965), 247–48.

62. *Arrêt de la cour de parlement qui condamne une brochure intitulée: Les inconvéniens des droits féodaux* (London: Valade, 1776), 66.

rights)[63] lies in his attempt to present their distinctive advocacy of indemnification as a smokescreen behind which they confidently expected to preserve the system they merely pretended to attack. Cobban sees indemnification as a fraud: since the peasants could not pay, indemnification would carry the rhetoric of abolition but the reality of conservation. Anatoly Ado, on the other hand, sees the indemnification option as a compromise many peasant communities were willing to accept, a compromise that would eliminate the seigneurial structures without rupturing the fragile unity of an "anti-feudal" coalition that included even relatively conservative sectors of the bourgeoisie.[64]

The statistical evidence suggests both views need considerable modification. If Cobban is correct that the essence of indemnification is an elite trick, there ought to be virtually no peasant support yet 27% of parish assemblies proposed indemnifying at least one right. The mere fact of significant, if minority, rural support shows that indemnification could be advocated for reasons other than sugarcoating an essentially conservative position. Whereas a few villagers, such as those employed in collecting them for the lord,[65] might have had a pocketbook motive for maintaining seigneurial rights, it is hard to see this group as obtaining a recognition of those interests by their fellows in more than one assembly in four. On the other hand, if three-quarters of villages had no indemnification demands whatsoever, what happens to Ado's consensus on a moderate compromise? If we examine grievances that take up the seigneurial rights as an aggregate, we are led to similar reservations. Of *cahiers* that discuss "the seigneurial rights" collectively, one in four calls for indemnification: too many by far to see indemnification as merely an elite fraud but rather short of a compromise consensus.

Further progress on understanding indemnification may come from going beyond the seigneurial rights as an inseparable aggregate and asking whether those villagers who sought compromise were equally likely to embrace indemnification regardless of the specific right. Table 3.6 shows that Third Estate enthusiasm was substantially greater than that of the parishes for almost every single right. But we also see that it was far more likely to be advocated with regard to certain seigneurial rights than others.[66]

63. Cobban's summary claim with regard to "the men who drew up the *cahiers* in the towns and the members of the *tiers état* in the National Assembly" is that "there can be no doubt of their opposition to the abolition of seigneurial dues and rights" (*Social Interpretation,* 43).

64. Anatoly V. Ado, *Krest'ianskoe dvizhenie vo Frantsii vo vremia velikoi burzhaznoi revoliutsii kontsa XVIII veka* (Moscow: Izdatel'stvo Moskovskovo Universiteta, 1971), 97.

65. Jacques Dupâquier, "Structures sociales et cahiers de doléances. L'exemple du Vexin français," *Annales historiques de la Révolution française* 40 (1968): 438.

66. Marcel Garaud's nonquantitative discussion of the *cahiers* is sensitive to the different treatment of different seigneurial rights, but he errs in asserting that "the Third Estate comes out very generally in favor of indemnification" (Garaud, *Révolution et propriété foncière,* 162). We see, in

It is almost nonexistent in connection with the right to bear arms and the seigneurial courts; it is quite unusual in connection with the recreational privileges. It is most commonly employed, by both the parishes and the Third Estate, in the area of periodic dues, and, for both groups, it is urged at an intermediate frequency in connection with seigneurial monopolies, dues on property transfers, compulsory labor services, and serfdom.

We often conceive of peasants as acting on their emotions, as rising in anger when not subdued by fear. I believe some fresh light may be shed on the entire indemnification question by the simple act of addressing a cognitive issue; instead of focusing on which rights were more or less hated, let us ask for which ones it was plausible to compute lump-sum monetary equivalents. If a monetary equivalent could be assigned with relatively little ambiguity then indemnification was at least a conceivable mechanism for compromise. To the extent that such a valuation would necessarily seem arbitrary, the plausibility of any figure proposed by way of compromise would be reduced. Table 3.6 shows quite clearly that some rights were not candidates for indemnification at all, while others were so seen by a significant rural segment, although generally a minority. Rural enthusiasm for indemnification varied enormously depending upon the particular seigneurial right in question, from a nearly two-thirds majority in the case of *cens* down to no support whatsoever with regard to the seigneurial courts or some of the recreational privileges. The mere fact of such selectivity in advocacy of indemnification would be hard to reconcile with Cobban's position at all and suggests some modification of Ado's.

The periodic dues were the class of rights most likely to attract peasant proposals for indemnification. Indeed, with the exception of "monopolies in general," no other right attracted so much support for the payment of an indemnity as the least enticing of the periodic dues. By virtue of being an annual payment, were not the periodic dues that class of rights whose value was most precisely determinable? We may go further: among periodic payments, surely those paid in cash were easier to assign a cash value than those paid as a portion of the crop. Note that the *cens*, a cash payment, was head and shoulders above the rest, while *champart*, a payment in kind,

fact, from Table 3.1 that "abolish" is generally more common for the Third Estate; and Tables 3.4 and 3.6 compared show it to be more common for 20 of the 26 institutions listed. "Abolish" is even about as common a demand for the seigneurial regime in general as is "indemnify." Garaud's error is far from uniquely his. A similar judgment of Third Estate opinion is common among historians. Certainly sentiment for indemnification was strong but, on the evidence of the *cahiers*, Georges Lefebvre goes too far when he suggests that "until July 14, the bourgeoisie had neither the time nor the taste to attack the tithe and the feudal rights" and that there was no intention of conceding to the peasants an abolition without compensation (an opinion in which he was joined by Alfred Cobban). See Lefebvre, "La Révolution française et les paysans," 343, 355; Cobban, *Social Interpretation*, 37.

Table 3.6. Parish and Third Estate Documents Demanding that Seigneurial Rights Be Ended with Compensation Paid to the Seigneur (%)

Right[a]	Parishes		Third Estate	
Periodic dues				
Cens	64%	(17)	57%	(28)
Champart	21	(92)	60	(61)
Cens et rentes	31	(86)	59	(37)
Periodic dues in general	25	(86)	55	(30)
Miscellaneous periodic dues	29	(38)	9	(22)
Seigneurial monopolies				
Monopoly on ovens	7	(39)	29	(50)
Monopoly on milling	2	(128)	25	(70)
Monopoly on wine press	7	(37)	31	(44)
Monopolies in general	21	(90)	43	(103)
Assessments on economic activity				
Seigneurial tolls	2	(61)	27	(117)
Dues on fairs and markets	14	(17)	33	(45)
Property Transfer rights				
Dues on property transfers *(lods et ventes)*	12	(60)	12	(49)
Retrait	14	(36)	0	(48)
Justice				
Seigneurial courts in general	0	(104)	10	(90)
Seigneurial courts, miscellaneous	0	(41)	0	(56)
Recreational privileges				
Hunting rights	4	(97)	2	(107)
Right to raise pigeons	0	(152)	0	(96)
Right to raise rabbits	0	(35)	0	(39)
Fishing rights	8	(17)	0	(24)
Symbolic deference				
Right to bear arms	0	(27)	0	(41)
Serfdom				
Mainmorte	0	(9)	30	(36)
Serfdom in general	2	(18)	15	(26)
Other				
Compulsory labor services	7	(102)	32	(109)
Miscellaneous right	9	(54)	27	(79)
Regime in general	25	(112)	22	(91)

[a]Rights discussed in at least 20 Parish or 20 Third Estate *cahiers* (and at least 5 of each).

trailed. Mixed categories (miscellaneous payments that could assume either form and periodic payments as a whole, which include both) were intermediary.

At the other extreme, consider the difficulties facing anyone who wished to estimate the monetary cost to the peasants or the monetary income to the lord represented by some of the rights. The right to raise pigeons or rabbits, to hunt, or to fish seem particularly difficult to assign a value to which all parties could assent. It is hard to imagine that the very attempt to set a price on such rights would not itself provoke endless conflict. The right to bear arms seems utterly hopeless: what did it cost the peasants—and how to reckon in quantitative terms the deprivation to the lord's pride of losing the exclusive prerogative to swagger, sword at side? It is telling that not a single peasant *cahier* of the 748 in our sample suggested indemnification here.

The costs to the peasants and the gains to the lord of seigneurial courts also seem quite difficult to summarize as a monetary figure. On the peasant side the costs included unfavorable decisions when the lord was an interested party—but there were benefits when justice was dispensed by someone with some knowledge of community life. The rural community might well weigh the costs of travel (and consequent lost time) that use of the more distant royal court entailed. The lord had to consider the possible value of the court in enforcing his other seigneurial claims against costs of legal personnel, courtroom, and perhaps a jail. Both sides had the esteem due the lord as provider of justice to weigh as well. If seen this way, there is little surprise in seeing that no one supported indemnification.

Now consider seigneurial claims that involved a payment, but one extracted at irregular intervals. One might imagine assessing the cost to the peasant and to the lord, but the variation in the annual burden might well make agreement difficult. Mutation fees and dues on fairs and markets had but a small body of rural support for indemnification. The value of the seigneurial monopolies seems calculable but with considerable difficulty; note that there was some support for the general notion of indemnifying monopolies but that there was only very slight support for indemnifying the holder of any particular monopoly. The idea of indemnification for monopolies may have seemed attractive to some, perhaps appealing to the spirit of compromise as Ado suggests; but when one tries to imagine, concretely, how to indemnify the holder of a specific monopoly, the intellectual difficulty appears formidable. By the same token, about one-fourth of those who take up the seigneurial rights in general suggested indemnification as the path to dismantling the whole structure; yet apart from the periodic dues, no specific rights seem to lend themselves so easily to this proposal.

For the most part, then, the data are consonant with the rather simple proposal that the plausibility of a monetary evaluation was critical for rural support for indemnification. But a few seigneurial rights do not seem to fit this pattern. *Retrait* permitted the lord to substitute himself for the purchaser when a member of the rural community sold land; it is hard to see why it should have attracted indemnification proposals about as frequently as mutation fees when it surely would have been harder to quantify. The ease of evaluation also does not explain why seigneurial tolls did not attract indemnification proposals when they seem about as easy to evaluate as some of the others; nor are the distinctions made among our monopoly categories clear.[67]

In spite of such reservations, however, the pattern of rural support for indemnification certainly suggests a compromise, but hardly one embraced with widespread passion. More than one-third of parish *cahiers* advocate this option only for the *cens*. Given any difficulty confronting the monetary valuation of a particular right, the support for indemnification fell precipitously. Peasant support for compromise may have been there, as Ado has argued, but on the evidence of the *cahiers* it was limited. But even a weak rural advocacy for compromise may have been an important straw at which a revolutionary leadership, hoping for civil peace, could grasp. The public positions taken in the assemblies of village France in the spring may well have encouraged the National Assembly to believe that it could get away with a detailed body of legislation on the seigneurial rights in which indemnification was a significant mainstay.

The urban notables were clearly more enthusiastic about indemnification than the country people. In 14 of the 25 categories, the Third Estate's proportion is larger, often much larger. Indeed, Table 3.1 showed it is in their support for indemnification that the Third Estate *cahiers* differ most sharply in their program from the parish texts. A country lawyer representing his parish at the *bailliage* assembly in Ploërmel recalled in his memoirs how he first gained and then lost the support of other rural delegates in the course of debating the *cahier*. An initial denunciation of privilege brought him considerable notice and made him a front-runner for election to the Estates-General; a later, judicious speech on behalf of indemnification as a compromise could not even be finished in the face of shouts, threats, and clenched fists.[68] The peasant-notable difference over indemnification was to have great consequence for the subsequent relationship of revolutionary legislature and revolutionary village (see Chapter 8). This difference is the obverse of the peasants' greater enthusiasm for abolition, pure and simple, discussed above. And why not? Some leading members of the Third Estate were themselves seigneurs,[69] for whom indemnification was a way to

67. Perhaps the urban notables differed a bit from the peasantry in their perceptions of the feasible. While generally paralleling the parishes, the Third Estate *cahiers* have moderate support for indemnifying tolls and none for *retrait,* thereby more closely approximating the ease of calculability than do the parishes. And perhaps they are more confident about indemnities for *champart.*

68. Roger Dupuy, "Les émeutes anti-féodales de Haute-Bretagne (janvier 1790 et janvier 1791): meneurs improvisés ou agitateurs politisés," in Jean Nicolas, ed., *Mouvements populaires et conscience sociale, XVIe–XIXe siècles* (Paris: Maloine, 1985), 452.

69. A point discussed with great vigor by Cobban, *Social Interpretation,* 27, 43–48. We shall consider his thesis shortly.

eliminate seigneurialism (and thereby march into the modern world) at minimal personal cost (or even gain if the indemnification terms were set high enough).[70] The urban notables, moreover, whose concern for the financial situation of the state was far greater than was the peasants',[71] were also, we suggest, far more likely to worry about the consequences of simply abolishing a portion of the crown's revenues, namely the king's own seigneurial dues,[72] at a time of crisis. To the extent that urban elites were among the burdened rather than among the beneficiaries of the seigneurial system, moreover, they would seem more likely to have been able to afford to indemnify their own lords. Studies of the actual operation of the law, indeed, show a greater urban proclivity to buy off the seigneurial rights than was true of the countryside.[73]

70. In the event, the rates of indemnification that came to be discussed did vary. The dramatic call of the duc d'Aiguillon for an end to feudalism on the night of August 4 proposed a rate of indemnification most profitable to the seigneurs and notably higher than that eventually enacted; see *AP* 8:344.

71. As may be seen, say, by examining their *cahiers* on the subject of government finances.

72. For those advocating a state takeover of church landholdings to alleviate the empty fisc, the seigneurial rights of ecclesiastical institutions would also be taken into account. As the legislative reconstruction of France proceeded, concern among the deputies for the continued collection of seigneurial rights on the former royal or church property was evident. When the departmental and district administrations, to whom the supervision of "national property" was originally entrusted, proved understandably lax in the collection of seigneurial rights, the National Assembly assigned this responsibility elsewhere. See J. N. Luc, "Le rachat des droits féodaux dans le département de la Charente-Inférieure (1789–1793)," in Albert Soboul, ed., *Contributions à l'histoire paysanne de la Révolution française* (Paris: Editions Sociales, 1977), 314–15.

73. The peasants rarely paid the indemnities. In some places very few took advantage of the indemnificatory aspects of the new laws; in others, some people did, but these were largely anything but peasants. In Charente-Inférieure, merchants, legal professionals, administrators, and urban seigneurs were the main users of the elaborate indemnification procedures. Similarly in the *département* of the Gironde, the indemnifications virtually all took place in Bordeaux and its suburbs. In the *département* of the Nord, most indemnifications were made by bourgeois proprietors or even nobles (including the duke of Orléans). In other *départements* studied in Brittany, Normandy, Franche-Comté, Champagne, and Limousin, indemnification seems hardly to have taken place at all. The *département* of Corrèze appears unusual in the extent of peasant utilization of the legal route (at least in the hill country—lowland Corrèze refused participation). See J. N. Luc, "Le rachat des droits féodaux," 332–33, 345; and *Paysans et droits féodaux en Charente-Inférieure pendant la Révolution française* (Paris: Commission d'Histoire de la Révolution Française, 1984), 125–59; André Ferradou, *Le rachat des droits féodaux dans la Gironde, 1790–1793* (Paris: Sirey, 1928), 210–12; Robert Garraud, *Le rachat des droits féodaux et des dîmes inféodées en Haute-Vienne* (Limoges: Imprimerie Dupuy-Moulinier, 1939); Jean Millot, *L'abolition des droits seigneuriaux dans le département du Doubs et la région comtoise* (Besançon: Imprimerie Millot Frères, 1941), 172–96; Georges Lefebvre, *Les paysans du Nord pendant la Révolution française* (Paris: Armand Colin, 1972), 387–90; Philippe Goujard, "L'abolition de la féodalité dans le district de Neuchâtel (Seine-Inférieure)," in Albert Soboul, ed., *Contributions à l'histoire paysanne de la Révolution française* (Paris: Editions Sociales, 1977), 366–73; Donald Sutherland, *The Chouans: The Social Origins of Popular Counter-Revolution in Upper Brittany, 1770–1796* (Oxford: Clarendon Press, 1982), 139–41; Jean-Jacques Clère, *Les paysans de la Haute-Marne et la Révolution française: Recherches sur les*

It is striking that the actual legislation of the early revolutionary period responds in a broad way to the pattern of demands. The political and intellectual histories of the legislation are taken up in Chapters 8 and 9, but it is useful at this point to jump ahead temporarily to show the broad correspondence of the eventual legislation and the *cahiers*. In a threatening atmosphere of peasant revolt, the National Assembly, on the night of August 4, 1789, was the scene of a combination of ideological fervor, careful calculation, and resignation to the inevitable in which one deputy after another called for an end to all sorts of privilege. The committee charged with drafting the detailed legislation to bring about the heralded end to feudalism skillfully managed the minimum conceivable, when they finally reported half a year later. The lawyers had drawn a distinction between seigneurial rights that were the results of an initial act of violent appropriation and those that derived from a consensual contract. The former, held illegitimate, were to be abolished outright. The latter were legitimate property, but no longer desirable under modern conditions, and were therefore to be eliminated upon payment of an indemnity (and still enforceable pending such payment). The distinction was historically precarious since no one really knew the mix of coercion and consent in the origins of most rights in what the French call the night of time; and it proved politically impossible since the peasants couldn't and wouldn't meet the detailed terms for indemnification.

What is impressive in the present context is that the intricate legalisms of the Committee on Feudal Rights distinguished among the various rights along the lines of the *cahiers*. Outright abolition was the declared fate of rights that rested on distinctions of status honor.[74] Such rights included the right to bear arms and the various recreational privileges for which indemnification found no support whatsoever in the *cahiers*. As for seigneurial justice, uncompensated abolition was also the order of the day; a decision on a variety of rights held to be part and parcel of the right of justice was deferred.[75] (Even in seven months, the committee couldn't deal with everything.) The periodic rental dues, on the other hand, were slated for indemnification,[76] the majority position on most of them for the Third Estate.

The categories intermediate in Third Estate support for indemnification

structures foncières de la communauté villageoise (1780–1825) (Paris: Editions de l'Histoire de la Révolution française, 1988), 189–91; Jean Boutier, *Campagnes en émoi: Révoltes et Révolution en bas-Limousin, 1789–1800* (Treignac: Editions "Les Monédières," 1987), 146–51.

74. See *AP* 12:172–77. On honorific distinctions, see Title I, Art. 1.

75. Title II, Art. 39.2 and *AP* 11:499. The relevant detailed legislation ending seigneurial courts was part of the general restructuring of the judicial system and therefore followed a different path than most seigneurial rights.

76. If it could be proven that a particular payment derived from coercion rather than contract, it would be abolished. Ibid., Title III, Arts. 1–2.

tended to receive a more complex and intermediate legislative determination. The seigneurial monopolies,[77] dues on fairs and markets,[78] seigneurial tolls,[79] and compulsory labor services[80] were to be abolished unless evidence of a contract could be produced, in which case they were to be maintained pending indemnification. Since such evidence could rarely be produced, this was not, in practice, far from abolition, but it was a powerful statement that the rights were not to be taken as necessarily and intrinsically illegitimate. While serfdom and associated practices, such as *mainmorte,* were to be abolished outright, dues paid by serfs that in the opinion of the subtle jurists, could have been assessed on free men or free land (and hence were not inherently servile), could continue to be assessed, subject to the free peasant's indemnity opportunities.[81] The mutation rights do not fit this neat picture of conformity to the *cahiers* quite so easily. *Retrait féodale* was indeed declared abolished, consistent with the views shown in Tables 3.4 and 3.6. But *lods et ventes* as well as other dues on property transfers were slated for indemnification although this was not a very strongly supported proposal in the spring of 1789.[82]

With the exception of such dues on property transfers the only rights made unconditionally subject to indemnification were those for which Third Estate support for that option was greater than for pure abolition. But notice the degree of peasant acquiescence in this program. If the Third Estate *cahiers* were consistently more welcoming to indemnification than the countryside, they were nonetheless broadly similar in which specific aspects of seigneurialism were appropriate for compensation. As far as periodic rentals were concerned there actually was more support in the parish *cahiers* for indemnification than for abolishing them outright (although the same cannot be said of dues on property transfers). In short, insofar as the *cahiers* represented peasant opinion or were at least believed to do so, the new politicians of the revolution had some grounds to think that the agrarian reform they favored as detailed in March 1790 would be acceptable to peasant France. Although the extremely important limitations to the abolition adopted by the National Assembly with respect to monopolies, tolls, labor services, and serfdom have no basis in the parish *cahiers,* those

77. Ibid., Title II, Arts. 23–26. In a display of concern for property, attacks on the mills, ovens, and winepresses were outlawed.

78. Ibid., Title II, Arts 17–21. The former seigneurs are allowed to keep the structures where the market takes place and to sell or rent them.

79. Ibid., Title II, Arts 13–15.

80. Title II, Art. 27.

81. Title II, Arts. 1–6. In a preliminary report to the National Assembly, the spokesman for the Committee on Feudal Rights reasoned: "You have considered *mainmorte* illicit and have happily the courage to ban it; but when, in whatever way, an illicit condition is joined to a proper one, does nullifying the first affect the second? You all know it does not" (*AP* 11:502).

82. Title III, Art. 2.

limitations were in the symbolic realm in which the parish *cahiers* generally took little interest. Few lords could actually prove a contractual basis for the labor services, for example, as the law demanded. The parish *cahiers,* moreover, had supported compensation for periodic payments and the Assembly had conceded outright abolition of the recreational privileges, the symbolic apparatus and, most critically, the courts. The peasants of the spring of 1789 were not pressing for much more than they were given in the spring of 1790. (Let us note the important corollary that they got little that they did not press for—a central theme to be dealt with at length below.) Certainly they had pressed for far less than the complete abolition of the seigneurial regime that August 4 appeared to promise. The Constituent Assembly had good reason to believe, mistakenly, that they could get away with defaulting on that promise. But the peasants of March 1790 were not those of March 1789. The indemnification plan foundered on massive peasant resistance and, indeed, triggered renewed and increasingly widespread rural insurrection.[83]

What Can be Reformed—and How?

There are assemblies that opted neither for maintaining the status quo nor the termination (with or without compensation) of such burdens. The burden, or at least one of its aspects, is to be relieved, rather than terminated or maintained intact. In considering the specific area of rural burdens, I include under "reform" demands that taxes, ecclesiastical payments, or seigneurial claims be reduced (but not that they be ended); demands that injustices in assessment or collection be eliminated; as well as demands for the provision of some legal remedy for nefarious abuses, the establishment of some supervisory authority, simplification or standardization of collection, elimination of arbitrariness in assessment or collection, removal of inequalities in the distribution of the burden and the institution of various forms of efficiency. We observed, toward the beginning of this chapter, that all three collections of documents contained substantial numbers of reformist grievances with regard to taxation, considerably fewer with regard to ecclesiastical payments, and fewer still concerning the seigneurial regime. Taxation was actually more likely to attract reform proposals than institutions other than burdens. The seigneurial rights were to be eliminated or, for a portion of the nobility, retained; it appeared difficult for many to imagine their improvement. Taxes, on the other hand, were to be improved. The pattern of demands to replace an institution by

83. For the dialogue of peasant insurrection and revolutionary legislation, see Chapter 8.

another was similar: it was proposed with any notable frequency only for taxation. Hardly anyone wanted a seigneurial right replaced.

The data suggest a certain level of acceptance of the central state, but it can by no means be maintained that the French were happy with their taxes. On the contrary, we have seen that taxes were the most common subject of grievance in the *cahiers* of all three groups (see Chapter 2, p. 36). What is equally clear is that all groups—including the peasant communities—did not propose to simply throw out taxes but to improve the tax system. No claim is made here that the state was regarded with enthusiasm, but it was at least regarded as an unavoidable reality. This is most definitely not the case for seigneurial domination. Those who did not want to keep the claims of the lords as they were (quite a rare outlook outside the nobility) tended toward abolition (although many, particularly among the urban notables, favored a protracted and indemnified process). Even among those for whom indemnification may have been embraced as a smokescreen, is it not significant that such a device was needed? From the village to the *château* the French held that the seigneurial rights could not, on the whole, be improved—but they certainly could be jettisoned altogether.

The state's claims on resources were quite another matter. Virtually no one wanted to keep these claims operating as at present; but reform and replacement outweighed outright elimination by a wide margin. The modern French state may have been an achievement of the Revolution, but the French people—not just the national elites but the inhabitants of the villages—appeared ready for its existence. This readiness may have been a grudging one, but it was already in place. Charles Tilly[84] has argued for a long-term shift in the nature of collective political action in Western Europe. The growth of the state and the intrusion of the market are at first, he contends, bitterly resisted by communities struggling to defend their sense of their traditional rights. As the state and market eventually stood undefeated and indeed emerged strengthened through the defeat of their enemies, there was a shift to demands for power within these structures. These newer demands might well take the form of laying claim to new rights never before enjoyed. The French Revolution, in our data, appears as a point at which the total opposition to the state as such had passed: what was now at issue was a better state.[85]

84. For one among many essays: "Collective Violence in European Perspective," in Hugh Davis Graham and Ted Robert Gurr, eds., *The History of Violence in America* (New York: Bantam Books, 1969), 4–44.

85. To be sure it would be foolish to identify one moment in a complex, long-term, ambiguous, contested, and hard-to-measure process as *the* instant of transformation. Tilly, for example, points to the continuity of collective action across the Revolution; in his view the mid-nineteenth century is more of a turning point than the great eighteenth-century upheaval; see *The Contentious French* (Cambridge: Belknap Press of Harvard University Press, 1986), 380–404. Recently, the portrait of

Taxation: Services and Equity

Since the most interesting, and perhaps surprising, contrast of the taxation proposals with those concerning seigneurial rights is the substantial support for reform that had found a home not just among elites but in rural communities, we shall examine those views of village France more closely. If we can understand what makes taxes worth reforming in the view of parish assemblies, we may get some clues as to what makes the seigneurial regime beyond reform. It is evident that there are two quite distinct groups of taxes. Demands for reform or replacement strongly outweigh demands for abolition for the *taille, vingtièmes, capitation,* the registration taxes, and the *corvée royale.* Demands for abolition, on the other hand, dominate with regard to the *aides,* town duties, *gabelle,* taxes on manufactured goods, and *franc-fief.* The customs duties occupy an ambiguous position depending on what one counts as "reform." Some of these taxes were defined earlier (see Chapter 2, p. 36 et seq.). The other principal taxes include the *traites,* an extensive network of tolls and custom duties; various assessments on merchandise entering or exiting towns (grouping together demands referring to *octrois* and *droits d'entrée et de sortie*); various fees collected on the registration of legal documents (including grievances addressing the *droit de contrôle, droit d'insinuation, droit de centième denier,* and *droits domaniaux*); and a variety of fees accompanying government inspection of manufactured goods (often referred to as *droits de marque*), particularly on iron, leather, soap, and oils (see Table 3.7).

Notice that the differences shown in Table 3.7 are quite substantial. For each tax or group of taxes, rural communities favored abolition or favored reform by a wide margin. What distinguishes the two groups of taxes from one another? Those slated for abolition are all among the Old Regime's indirect taxes. The reformable taxes include the three major direct taxes (*taille, capitation, vingtièmes*), the registration taxes, and the compulsory labor on the royal roads that was now on the way to replacement by a money tax.[86] The *traites* may also be held to be reformable, depending on

---

a traditional rural community besieged by state and market has been called into question. See Root, *Peasants and King in Burgundy.* For some of the proposals for reorganizing the state, see John Markoff, "Governmental Bureaucratization: General Processes and an Anomolous Case," *Comparative Studies in Society and History* 17 (1975): 479–503.

86. Various reforms had already been instituted in several provinces prior to the decrees of the late 1780s that were to replace it altogether by a money tax over the next several years. The uneven application of these decrees (Brittany, for example, maintained the *corvée* unaltered), their recency, the strength of local resistance to the new money tax, and perhaps a general distrust of the steadiness of official policy are reflected in those many *cahiers* that treat forced labor as very much a live issue. See Joseph Letaconnoux, *Le régime de la corvée en Bretagne au XVIIIe siècle* (Rennes: Plihon et Hommay, 1905), 100–106; Robert Werner, *Ponts et Chausées d'Alsace au dix-huitième siècle* (Strasbourg: Imprimerie Heitz, 1929), 58–86, 100–114; Marcel Marion, *Dictionnaire*

Table 3.7. Parish *Cahiers* Demanding Abolition or Reform of Specific Taxes (%)

Type of Tax	Abolish	Reform or Replace	(*N*)
Direct taxes			
Taille	13%	75%	(293)
Vingtièmes	24	56	(165)
Capitation	20	57	(122)
Indirect taxes			
Aides	66	29	(260)
Town duties *(droits d'entrée, droits de sortie, octrois)*	57	10	(87)
Gabelle	67	34	(325)
Taxes on manufactures	72	22	(166)
Franc-fief	90	11	(95)
Registration taxes *(droits domaniaux, droit de contrôle, droit d'insinuation, droit de centième denier)*	27	63	(247)
Customs duties *(traites)*			
1. Demands to abolish internal customs duties regarded as "reform"	25	63	(262)
2. Demands to abolish internal customs duties regarded as "abolish"	78	19	(262)
Compulsory labor			
Corvée royale	21	54	(364)

which aspect is under consideration, a point to which I shall return. If anything clearly distinguishes the two groups it is not the sheer size of the payments. The *taille* was often heavy but reformable; the *aides* and *gabelle,* often heavy as well, were not. Nor is there a clear relation to how frequently a tax is the subject of grievance. The *gabelle* is one of the most discussed taxes (see Table 2.1) and is slated for abolition by a two-to-one margin; although the *droit de contrôle* is also a front-runner in the quantity of complaints, the registration taxes generally are seen as objects of reform.

Let us explore the more extreme position generally taken on the indirect taxes; we shall return to the exceptional cases of the registration taxes and the customs duties below (see p. 107). Indirect taxes were, first of all,

des institutions de la France au XVIIe et XVIIIe siècles (Paris: Picard, 1969), 153–55 and *Impôts directs,* 113–19; Guy Arbellot and Bernard Lepetit, *Atlas de la Révolution française,* vol. 1, *Routes et communications* (Paris: Editions de l'Ecole des Hautes Etudes en Sciences Sociales, 1987), 32; Georges Weulersse, *La physiocratie à l'aube de la Révolution, 1781–1792* (Editions de l'Ecole des Hautes Etudes en Sciences Sociales, 1985), 109–12.

assessed on economic activities of one sort or another. The *aides,* say, were assessed on the sale of alcoholic beverages. Second, the indirect taxes, for much of their history, were not collected by government agencies but by the agents of tax farms, notably the Royal General Farms, the complex collection apparatus for many major taxes, which was leased on a periodically renegotiated basis to a syndicate of financiers.[87]

It was rather widely recognized that the inefficacy of the tax system involved its administrative structure and not merely the capacity of potential taxpayers to protect their incomes through personal or regional privilege. The administrative critique, however, was usually aimed at the indirect taxes. The leasing of the tax collection apparatus to the corporation of Royal General Farmers raised many questions: to what degree was the state getting the full benefits of its collection and to what degree was a syndicate of the rich ripping off the treasury? To what degree were those whose motivation was private profit resisting tax reforms that might ultimately increase the wealth of the state by eliminating obstacles to economic development (by reducing or eliminating, for example, the internal tolls collected by the General Farms)? To what degree could the crown even penetrate the maze of financial contracts within which the tax system was enmeshed so that rational planning would be possible? When a leading historian of Old Regime finances writes of indirect taxation, he cites Necker's remark that hardly one or two people in each generation could make sense of the system.[88] Such observations might equally well have been made of the world of the direct taxes[89] but the visibility of the corporation of General Farmers and the open negotiation of the terms on which they leased the tax farms made evident that the collection of the indirect taxes was a speculative business venture.

The appearance of linkage with private profit rather than state enterprise and public function would seem to be a major pole attracting a more intransigent form of discontent here.[90] Indeed, the central government's occasional but harsh judicial assaults on its own financiers, a tradition culminating in the revolutionary execution of the tax-farmers, may have

87. George T. Matthews, *The Royal General Farms in Eighteenth-Century France* (New York: Columbia University Press, 1958).

88. Marcel Marion, *Histoire financière de la France depuis 1715* (Paris: Rousseau, 1914), 1:27.

89. John Bosher has demonstrated how little effective bureaucratic control existed in the direct tax system; but the vivid visibility of the General Farms was lacking. See Bosher, *French Finances, 1770–1795: From Business to Bureaucracy* (Cambridge: Cambridge University Press, 1970), 67–110.

90. For a village near Rouen, those associated with the General Farms are "the state's leeches. They are vermin who devour it; they are a plague that infects it. There are as many places where they are loathed as there are places where they exist." See Marc Bouloiseau, ed., *Cahiers de doléances du tiers état du bailliage de Rouen pour les états généraux de 1789* (Rouen: Imprimerie Administrative de la Seine-Maritime, 1960), 308.

contributed to the image of thievery that hung over the whole tax system but especially over the General Farms.[91] While a sense of burden is central to the rural world's expression of grievance in the spring of 1789, the sheer weight of the burden is not the only issue: the burdens of participating in French life are to be made tolerable, but the burdens of contributing to either seigneurial revenues or the multimillionaires of the Royal General Farms are to be eliminated.[92] Payments for public purposes may be reformed; payments for private purposes are to be abolished. Hence taxes are more reformable than seigneurial rights; and among taxes those associated with private parties—the indirect taxes—are less reformable than those not so tainted. (We shall ask below whether the reverse holds: are those seigneurial or ecclesiastical payments that might be seen as supporting a public purpose relatively prone to attract reform demands?)

The direct tax sector, moreover, however odd, haphazard, or unfair in appearance, at least had the potential of being converted into (or being replaced by) taxes keyed to ability to pay whereas taxes on economic transactions are almost inherently regressive. The attempts to reform the principles of assessment of the *taille,* or to supplement it with taxes initially intended to be levied more universally and more equitably like the *capitation* and the various *vingtièmes,*[93] however distorted in ultimate actual practice, testify to the recurrent hope that such taxes were capable of revision. But what sort of reform? To refashion a burden might mean a reduction in its weight, an assurance that it be directed toward a good use, that its costs be fairly shared or that its collection be as efficient as possible. All these may play a role, but the public attention to privilege in the late eighteenth century suggests an examination of proposals for reform through an alteration in who bears the burden.

We can rather crudely measure the weight that considerations of equity had among reform proposals by examining demands that privileges or exemptions in the allocation of burdens be eliminated; that the burden be borne equally by all who hold land, or by all households, or by all who live in France (or by some other definition of the body of taxpayers); or that the burden be proportional to means (whether understood as the value of land, the potential for earnings, or some unspecified sense of capacity). We wish to know the degree to which the *cahiers* respond to equity considerations when they are advocating reform. Table 3.8 presents the percentage of

91. James Riley makes a good case that perceptions of the profits of tax-farming far outstripped the reality, substantial as that reality was; see *The Seven Years War and the Old Regime in France: The Economic and Financial Toll* (Princeton: Princeton University Press, 1986), 62–67.

92. It may be that the sense of private profit at the expense of the suddenly impoverished that tainted the court-sponsored auctioneers underlies the extent of peasant attention to them (see Table 2.1).

93. Marion, *Impôts directs.*

reform grievances that urge a more equitable sharing of the burden. We see quite clearly the very distinctive nature of taxation. Equity considerations in all three groups of documents are strongly focused on taxation. By contrast, whatever other reform measures might be proposed with regard to the seigneurial regime, an equitable distribution of the burden is pertinent for but a miniscule number of noble and Third Estate assemblies and of no interest whatsoever to the country people who pay.

The most general grievances about taxes are also quite revealing. Examining all documents that speak of taxation in general rather than—or in addition to—discussing any specific tax, an impressive 79% of rural communities raise some issue of equity.[94] The contrast with general discussion of the tithe or of the seigneurial rights is sharp. A scant 4% of *cahiers* that discuss seigneurial rights as an aggregate speak of a fairer or better distribution of the burden. The figure for the tithe is close to identical. That the burden be borne by more and stronger shoulders is characteristic of proposals about tax reform and no other exaction. This suggests a closer look, tax by tax, as it were. The data for the parish *cahiers* are displayed in Table 3.9. A glance suffices to show how insignificant such concerns were for most of the indirect taxes and how weighty a component of proposals to change those burdens that were seen as directly imposed by the state. Note that the weight of a particular tax or its peculiar noxiousness does not seem to be the issue here. Forced labor struck many of the enlightened as barbaric[95] whereas the registration fees were merely a (major) nuisance; yet equity occupies one-third of the parish documents that do not call for outright abolition of the former and very few of those that take up the latter.

The special salience of equity issues in discussions of the direct taxes

Table 3.8. Reform Grievances Showing Concerns for Equity (%)

Type of Burden	Parishes	Third Estate	Nobility
Taxation	52%	46%	51%
Ecclesiastical payments	8	7	4
Seigneurial rights	0	3	3

Note: This table refers to demands concerning privileges and exemptions (whether attached to individuals, groups, or regions); demands advocating equalization of burdens or making them proportional to wealth. These percentages are based on all reform grievances.

94. If we are at all persuaded by C. B. A. Behrens's argument that the extent of taxation privilege has been much exaggerated or by James Riley's contention that the consequences of the structure of privilege were far less irrational and socially inefficient than often assumed, the extent to which the privilege issue infused thinking about taxation is all the more striking; see C. B. A. Behrens, "Nobles, Privileges and Taxes in France at the End of the Ancien Régime," *Economic History Review,* ser. 2, 15 (1963): 451–75; and Riley, *Seven Years War,* 44–45, 54–55, 68, 71.

95. Royal and seigneurial *corvées* alike are characterized by the Third Estate of Rustaing as "humiliating remains of ancient servitude" (*AP* 2:368).

Table 3.9. Tax Equity Concerns in Parish *Cahiers*: Reform Grievances Demanding a Redistribution of Tax Burden (%)

Tax	Percentage of Reform Grievances	(*N*)[a]
Direct taxes		
Taille	46%	(216)
Vingtièmes	51	(92)
Capitation	70	(67)
Indirect taxes		
Aides	26	(58)
Town duties (*droits d'entrée, droits de sortie, octrois*)	37	(24)
Gabelle	8	(102)
Taxes on manufactures	3	(44)
Franc-fief	6	(20)
Registration taxes (*droits domaniaux, droit de contrôle, droit d'insinuation, droit de centième denier*)	3	(173)
Customs duties		
1. (Demands to abolish internal customs duties regarded as "reform")	2	(161)
2. (Demands to abolish internal customs duties regarded as "abolish")	6	(57)
Compulsory labor		
Corvée royale	32	(203)

This table refers to demands concerning privileges and exemptions (whether attached to individuals, groups, or regions); demands advocating equalization of burdens or making them proportional to wealth. Excluded: demands for abolition (with or without compensation); demands for maintenance.
[a]This is the number of *cahiers* which demand tax reform (and thereby excludes those calling for abolition or maintaining a tax unchanged).

may derive in part from their distinctive character and the debates brought on in the collection process itself. One pictures, for example, the controller-general wearily negotiating with the *intendants*—the chief royal administrators in the provinces—the burdens of next year's *taille* to be borne by each *généralité* (the region under their jurisdiction). The *intendants* protest the unfairness of their own burden and the lightness of the others'; all are conscious of those towns and provinces that by treaty have achieved a reduced or fixed assessment. The *intendant* in turn engages in a dialogue with his subordinates over the regional allocation of the burden within his *généralité*. Then, at the parish level, finally, the share of each household remains to be determined; and all, concealing their wealth, decry the injustice of their own assessment and resent the privileged persons who need not pay at all (unless we are in the *pays de taille réelle* in which property carried fixed portions of the total tax and privilege went with property not persons). Once taxes were levied at last, there is still the possibility of endless litigation: one's sense of the injustice of it all could be brought before the judges, who are never very keen on royal taxation. Long before 1789, in short, the language of equity was constantly on the lips of those who staffed the apparatus that allocated and collected the *taille*.

A series of frustrated reform efforts, in which the central government's ceaseless quest for revenue took the form of schemes to tax the insufficiently taxed, kept equity issues salient from top to bottom of the direct tax system. There was to be the *taille tarifée,* which would more precisely assess land revenues; there was the *capitation,* intended to be a tax with no exemptions; there was a string of taxes—of which only the *vingtièmes* survived to the late eighteenth century—that were to be uniform taxes on revenues. These taxes either became so saddled with privileges on the model of the *taille* as to be assimilated to it in practice like the *capitation,* or abandoned altogether like the precursors of the *vingtièmes,* or so widely resisted as to yield far less than their apparent value like the *vingtièmes* themselves.[96]

Demands concerning the *corvée* had a higher stress on equity than most indirect taxes. It was perhaps more evident to many peasant communities that roads provide a service than that many other state activities did. As they put it in Esves-le Moutier: "Abolish the privileges of the order of the nobility and of the clergy in the payment of the *corvée.* Subject them to it just like members of the Third Estate since they share in the advantages and convenience of the roads."[97] While the service was unproblematic,[98] the issue of the distribution of the burden does stand out. Like the direct taxes, moreover, the *corvée* was the subject of considerable recent public discussion.[99] The commutation into a money tax that would pay the wages of road laborers was pushed by the central government and resisted by the courts with great vigor at the end of the Old Regime. Among partisans of a reformed *corvée,* moreover, there were significant differences that emphasized issues of fairness. If forced labor were to be replaced by a money tax, ought that tax to fall on those near the roads who previously were drafted into road gangs? Ought it to fall more widely (on all who paid the *vingtièmes,* for example)? Ought it to fall on those who used the roads?[100] Perhaps the

96. Marion, *Impôts directs.*

97. T. Massereau, *Recueil des cahiers de doléances des bailliages de Tours et de Loches et cahier general du bailliage de Chinon aux états généreaux de 1789* (Orléans: Imprimerie Moderne, 1918), 555.

98. The *corvée* was earmarked for roads, after all, whereas what was purchased with the *aides* or *gabelle* was considerably less evident.

99. For a local study of conflicting views on *corvée* reform, see Anne Zink, "Parlementaires et entrepreneurs: A propos des événements à Bascoms (1776–1782)," in *La France d'Ancien Régime: Etudes réunies en l'honneur de Pierre Goubert* (Toulouse: Privat, 1984), 2:715–24.

100. *Cahiers* coping with these issues include the Third Estates of Auxerre, Avesnes, and Rustaing; see *AP* 2:125, 152, 368. The Third Estate of Etampes offers the unusual proposal to

unusually great attention to equity issues evoked by the *corvée* was due to the degree to which rural communities in most of France had recently experienced one or another major alteration in that burden.

Finally, the two anomolous indirect taxes—the registration taxes and the customs duties—resemble the other indirect taxes in the low salience of equity issues but are like the direct taxes in the importance of some sort of reform. As for the *droit de contrôle* and the like, I would suggest that rural communities, whose members were continually involved in transactions, disputes, and agreements, recognized the value of some form of registration and therefore regarded such taxes, although tainted by their historical tie to the General Farms, as reformable.[101] But the reform issues here concern issues quite different from the distribution of the burden. The parish of Beaulieu-en-Argonne enumerates some: "For the *contrôle,* we ask a fixed and invariable schedule of rates that may not be extended at the whim of clerks; that these agents do not continually harass poor people who do not know what taxes one demands of them and who therefore are subject to fines; that the *contrôle* is surely necessary to establish the date of contracts; that this tax be moderate and that other taxes not be added on; that, from time to time, let there be displayed an announcement of the taxes to which one is subject, so that an accidental slip of memory not be punished as fraud."[102]

The frequency with which the parishes discuss these registration taxes (see Chapter 2) and the reformist flavor of these demands (see Table 3.7) is yet another sign of a rural acceptance of a rationalizing state engaged in the record-keeping that permits a world of freely negotiated contracts to operate. France was ready for the bureaucratic state and the contractual society. Was it ready as well for the legally trained professionals who draw up proper contracts and staff the state's recording and regulating agencies? These grievances on the registration taxes are probably themselves a sign of the long habituation of peasant communities to legal practice and practitioners. We shall see many other signs.

As is the case for those seigneurial rights that attract reform demands, the main reform issues for the *contrôle* and *insinuation* taxes are not issues of equity. The customs duties, too, seem capable of reform (and with equity

---

have peacetime soldiers build roads that would not only save money but get the soldiers "used to work and fatigue" (*AP* 3:287).

101. An example: The villagers of Lassay in the *bailliage* of Romorantin recognize the value of a public repository of public acts but want the tax reduced to the amount needed to provide for those who perform the service; see Bernard Edeine, ed., *Les assemblées préliminaires et la rédaction des cahiers de doléances dans le bailliage secondaire de Romorantin* (Blois: Imprimerie Raymond Sille, 1949), 46.

102. Gustave Laurent, ed., *Cahiers de doléances pour les états-généraux de 1789,* vol. 1, *Bailliage de Châlons-sur-Marne* (Epernay: Imprimerie Henri Villers, 1906), 70–71.

issues also beside the point). Many reform proposals in this case are frequently quite specific to this tax: it is proposed that internal customs be eliminated so that duties would only be collected at the frontiers of France. This viewpoint is reflected in the first row for *traites* in Table 3.7. In light of our discussion of other taxes, it seems a reasonable supposition that many held customs duties to have a useful function and merely wished the eradication of internal nuisances. If one wished to include demands for eliminating the internal duties under "abolish," one would have the second row, which looks like the basic pattern for the other indirect taxes. In short the internal *traites* are valueless, but the external trade barriers are to be kept. If rural communities distinguish customs duties within the kingdom from those at its frontiers, are they perhaps implicitly distinguishing a national French community for whom justice is sought? Movement of goods within France is no longer to be the occasion for enriching the General Farmers; but payments by foreign commercial interests to the General Farmers are eminently acceptable. We will see shortly further evidence that their taxation grievances reveal a sense of a France beyond the local community (see p. 137).

One sees here, I think, an emerging concept of citizenship at work; individuals, equal in their moral worth, are all to be assessed in accord with some principle of equity[103] and directly by the state. When it is a payment to a lord, to the church or, we now see, to the manifestly private structure of intermediaries that operated the indirect tax system, citizenly equality is irrelevant and such reform issues as might arise (and fewer arise to begin with) are concerned with rather different issues.[104] The thirty-five households of Heming (near Sarrebourg) were represented by a *cahier* in which these distinctions are clear. The main taxation concern is that the clergy pay their fair share on the model of Jesus who, like all the rest, paid Caesar. "Aren't ecclesiastics subjects like us?" the villagers ask. And they go on: "Let them join our ranks following the example of our divine Master and pay the king" like their "co-citizens." When this same document arrives at seigneurial rights, the main issue is the failure of the current lord to live up to his part of the engagement entered into by lord and community in

103. The *cahiers* are not uniform on the specific principle. Indeed they do not always even invoke one. The primary issue is that all are morally bound to participate; the precise quantitative formula to assure this participation is simply less significant than the eradication of distinctions of quality. On ideas about tax equity see Jean-Pierre Gross, "Progressive Taxation and Social Justice in Eighteenth-Century France," *Past and Present,* no. 140 (1993): 79–126.

104. Bryant Ragan's research on peasant petitions in the early revolutionary years in the *département* of the Somme shows a continuing pattern of demanding equity in direct tax assessment but abolition of indirect taxes. See Bryant T. Ragan Jr., "Rural Political Activism and Fiscal Equality in the Revolutionary Somme," in Bryant T. Ragan Jr., and Elizabeth A. Williams, eds., *Recreating Authority in Revolutionary France* (New Brunswick, N.J.: Rutgers University Press, 1992), 36–56.

1529. Since the lord has defaulted on his contractual obligations, the villagers believe themselves released from their own obligations even though a court ruled against them a dozen years earlier when they carried this belief into refusal of payment.[105]

Lord and Church: The Irrelevance of Equity

If a significant thrust of taxation reform is the satisfaction of a sense of equity through a proper, fairer, juster distribution of the burden, what considerations come into play when village communities consider reforming other exactions? A glance at Table 3.10 is revealing. The *casuels,* it is clear, are seen quite differently than the tithe. The tithe is seen as intimately linked to an absolutely essential social role. The pastoral activities of the priest must be paid for in some way by someone and such support must provide, surely, for his material well-being and the physical upkeep of the local church. I am suggesting then that it is the sense that this particular payment purchases an indispensable service that energizes the reformist side of rural France. Perhaps this may explain why the Third Estate *cahiers* are more prone to abolish than the countryside (reversing the pattern for the seigneurial rights). The urban notables are less likely to value the country priests than their parishioners. Many parish grievances are focused on getting their payments out of the hands of the tithe-holders and into the hands of the priests; or on making sure the tithes are not spent on maintaining the lifestyle of a local lord but on maintaining the local church.[106] A few parishes are even sympathetic to indemnifying the current tithe-holders as part of a reform (see Table 3.1). In these gaps between country people and urban elites we can see the bases for some of the Revolution's most difficult dramas: the persistent peasant antiseigneurial action in a countryside stimulated by but not satisfied with legislated reform and the rallying around the local priest in defense against urban and national pressures that gave so much energy to peasant counterrevolution.

And once the tithe is suitably reformed, why pay extra in the form of the *casuels?*[107] As a village near Romorantin sees it: "The tithes . . . falling by

105. P. Lesprand and L. Bour, *Cahiers de doléances des prevôtés bailliagères de Sarrebourg et Phalsbourg et du bailliage de Lixheim pour les états généraux de 1789* (Metz: Imprimerie P. Even, 1938), 94–96.

106. The Third Estate *cahiers* sometimes concur. A succinct example is provided by the Third Estate of Château-Thierry: "The tithes, in their initial intention, had three purposes: first, providing for the priests; second, the upkeep of the temples; and third, poor relief. The Third demands that they be brought once again to these ends" (*AP* 2:674).

107. Analogously one finds demands for a single registration tax. If one separates the *droit de contrôle,* the *insinuation,* and the *centième denier* (unlike Tables 3.7 and 3.9, which aggregate them), one sees a preponderance of rural villages actually favor abolition of the last of these. Was this specific registration tax singled out for abolition due to its having become tainted by the seigneurial

Table 3.10. Parish *Cahiers* Demanding That Ecclesiastical Payments Be Abolished, Reformed, or Maintained (%)

	Abolish	Reform	Maintain	(*N*)
Casuels	80%	6%	2%	(95)
Tithe	29	39	0	(102)

their nature principally on the class of cultivators, it would be more advantageous to free them by indemnifying the proprietors and assigning the *curés* and others responsible for souls a reasonable revenue drawn on either public or ecclesiastical sources. . . . Finally, and as a consequence of the above, the suppression of the obligatory *casuels* that pastors demand for marriages and burial services—the last of the taxes still to be paid after life—which so often afflict the most indigent and numerous class of society."[108] In both the case of ecclesiastical burdens and the case of seigneurial rights the central issue for reformers is obtaining an appropriate service commensurate with what is exacted. Let the tithe be appropriately used; let the lords do their job (when there is one). The equity issues, so important when the service can be assumed (as in some taxes) does not arise.

Against the background of reformism in taxation and ecclesiastical exaction, we now return seigneurial rights to center stage. I present the detailed evidence on reform proposals for seigneurial rights in Table 3.11. Peasant reformism always involves a minority of communities—never many more than one-third—and varies greatly from one right to the next. The differences in support for reform of the seigneurial rights also suggest that those rights that are seen as linked to essential functions (someone has to hunt, dispense justice, supervise markets) are more likely to receive reform proposals than are those that do not serve the village community (no one has to build and stock a fishpond). Not many parishes are concerned with dues on fairs and markets, but to those who take up these rights, are not fairs and markets vital institutions that must be initiated and operated by someone? If so, why not the seigneur—but in an improved fashion? Why is milling the most reformable seigneurial monopoly? It may be a recognition of the public function performed. Consider a comparison with the monopoly on bake-ovens: even a community prosperous enough for several peasants to afford their own small ovens[109] would still be a most improbable base for

property with which it was associated? In distinguishing the tithe from the *casuels* and the *droit de centième denier* from other similar fees, the country people show a judicious quality not always evident in accounts of rural chaos; and they show a sense of an interconnected social system not always evident in accounts of angry and ignorant villagers.

108. Edeine, *Cahiers de Romorantin,* 47. Notice that this parish proposes to deal with the titheholders by indemnifying them.

109. Renauldon's article on the monopoly on bake-ovens expresses a concern over such small

more than one mill. Even well-off peasants might easily think of a mill as inherently more communal than an oven.[110] Why are some periodic payments seen by minorities as reformable? Perhaps we see here the influential role of fairly substantial peasants in rural France: they were villagers who could look forward to collecting rents themselves and are keen to protect property rights. They hope to remove the ills of rentlike exactions but not to abolish them.[111]

On Seigneurial Courts (and Other Objects of Rural Reform)

We may go beyond the statistical patterns by attending to what France's villagers say when they propose reforms. Let us consider first and foremost the seigneurial courts, which vie with rights over fairs and markets for the distinction of attracting the highest proportion of peasant reform proposals, but stand utterly alone when one takes into account how frequently seigneurial courts are discussed in the first place (see Table 2.5). The seigneurial courts are, I suggest, reformable to the degree that there was a living function to be carried out in some fashion. Table 3.11 shows that the enthusiasm of the peasants for reforming the lord's courts exceeds that of the Third Estate by almost as much as the Third Estate's desire to ameliorate the hunting rights exceeded that of the peasants. The Third Estate, more confident in the royal courts, are less likely to see much virtue in doing anything other than simply abolishing the seigneurial component of the judicial system; just as the parish *cahiers* are more comfortable than the urban notables in simply abolishing the restrictions on hunting, with all that implied for an armed rural population.

If rural France in some measure accepted the continued existence of

individual ovens that appears to acknowledge an empirical reality. See Renauldon, *Dictionnaire des fiefs,* 1:477.

110. Cl. Gindin, "Aperçu sur les conditions de la mouture des grains en France, fin du XVIIIe siècle," in Albert Soboul, ed., *Contributions à l'histoire paysanne de la Révolution française* (Paris: Editions Sociales, 1977), 159–88.

111. The efforts to reclaim what was seen as common land encroached upon by the lords included pressures by some to divide the commons and by others to preserve them. Attempts to purchase the lands of church, king, and émigrés were frequent enough, but movements for a general redistribution of land, the seizure of large properties, or the occupation of land other than the commons were most uncharacteristic of the entire revolutionary period. The extensive support for either indemnifying or reforming periodic payments seems to foreshadow the respect for property that is in comparative perspective one of the striking features of France's rural revolution. On the role of peasant actions over land within the rural insurrections as a whole, see Chapter 5, p. 250, and Chapter 8, p. 482.

Table 3.11. Parish and Third Estate Documents Demanding That Seigneurial Rights Be Reformed (%)

Right[a]	Parishes		Third Estate	
Periodic dues				
Cens	3%	(17)	32%	(28)
Champart	24	(92)	26	(61)
Cens et rentes	29	(86)	35	(37)
Periodic dues in general	34	(86)	23	(30)
Miscellaneous periodic dues	21	(38)	36	(22)
Seigneurial monopolies				
Monopoly on ovens	1	(39)	8	(50)
Monopoly on milling	19	(128)	13	(70)
Monopoly on wine press	11	(37)	5	(44)
Monopolies in general	2	(90)	15	(103)
Assessments on economic activity				
Seigneurial tolls	20	(61)	9	(117)
Dues on fairs and markets	36	(17)	16	(45)
Property transfer rights				
Dues on property transfers (*lods et ventes*)	15	(60)	39	(49)
Retrait	2	(36)	25	(48)
Justice				
Seigneurial courts in general	36	(104)	19	(90)
Seigneurial courts, miscellaneous	17	(41)	18	(56)
Recreational privileges				
Hunting rights	15	(97)	39	(107)
Right to raise pigeons	13	(152)	18	(96)
Right to raise rabbits	8	(35)	13	(39)
Fishing rights	2	(17)	21	(24)
Symbolic deference patterns				
Right to bear arms	7	(27)	5	(41)
Serfdom				
Mainmorte	23	(9)	17	(36)
Serfdom in general	2	(18)	4	(26)
Other				
Compulsory labor services	11	(102)	14	(109)
Miscellaneous right	16	(54)	9	(79)
Regime in general	18	(112)	18	(91)

[a]Rights discussed in at least 20 Parish or 20 Third Estate *cahiers* (and at least 5 of each).

judicial activity, suitably reformed, the ways in which the seigneurial courts might be altered to carry out their legitimate tasks are spelled out clearly in two *cahiers* from the *bailliage* of Troyes that, between them, enumerate most of the principal reforms being urged. The parish of Buisson makes it clear that its preference is for abolition. If that prove impossible, however, improvements are easy to see. To begin with, the judges should be named by the king "and totally independent of the lords." "For," this text continues, "who is the official with a sense of self-preservation who will find against the lord—unless he be animated by bitter resentment—and who is the attorney who will act with vigor and without fear?" The notaries, too, must be independent. As things stand, legal records have a way of getting lost or of being seized by the lord. Finally, the court officers are not only dependent but are poorly trained. Why, the assembly of Buisson asks, would a competent person make a career in a small seigneurial court?[112]

Buisson's demands are complemented by those of Bucey-en-Othe. The former parish wanted to ensure judicial independence by preventing the lord from appointing officials; the latter insists that, once appointed, those officials be irremovable (unless properly convicted of embezzlement). As an added precaution the lord is not to be permitted to bring cases regarding himself or his lands before his own judge. The former addressed itself to the training of court officials; the latter demands that the court have a full complement of legal personnel so that all roles in the judicial process can be properly carried out. In the same vein they insist on adequate physical facilities: a proper courtroom and a proper jail. Until such measures are in place, a higher court is to be used.[113]

Other parish *cahiers* propose other mechanisms for ensuring judicial independence or direct their attention to clarifying the sphere of competence of the seigneurial courts.[114] What is common to all these reform proposals is that they do not challenge the legitimacy of some sort of judicial activity. They are, sometimes only grudgingly, willing to let something called a seigneurial court remain in existence, so long as it judges with impartiality, skill, and efficiency. If these aims can be achieved, the seigneur may keep the honorary aspect of having justice done in his name. We have seen that the parishes are not particularly concerned about the patterns of symbolic deference. Under their reform proposals the honorific symbolism of seigneurial justice will rest in force, but the material benefits to the seigneur and burdens to the rural community will be eliminated. It is almost as if these proposals take the noble *cahiers* at their word when they insist that they will renounce their material advantages but wish to continue their honorific distinctiveness. "If you are willing to bear the costs of community service," one almost hears many a parish telling its lord, "we are willing to honor you." (Does one also hear a whisper among the villagers: "They claim to want honor, not income: very well, now we have them"?)

112. Jules-Joseph Vernier, *Cahiers de doléances du bailliage de Troyes (principal et secondaires) et du bailliage de Bar-sur-Seine pour les états généraux de 1789* (Troyes: P. Nouel, 1909), 480–81.

113. Ibid., 466–67.

114. In the *bailliage* of Toulouse, for example, see the *cahiers* of Saint-Jory and Bruguières: Félix Pasquier and François Galabert, *Cahiers paroissiaux des sénéchausées de Toulouse et de Comminges en 1789* (Toulouse: E. Privat, 1925–28), 26, 61.

But why were the peasants more likely to grant that the seigneurial courts had some legitimate function than they were for most of the rest of the seigneurial regime? Several recent studies suggest an answer. Donald Sutherland's work on upper Brittany[115] takes the earlier work of André Giffard[116] to task for too readily accepting the charge that the seigneurial courts did nothing but enforce the lords' claims. In fact, Sutherland shows, the majority of cases that came before them had nothing whatsoever to do with the seigneur's interests. All sorts of property disputes among their dependents, a wide variety of family affairs, declarations of pregnancy, the verification of weights and measures, the regulation of the grain trade, and the control of popular festivals formed the bulk of their activities. One Breton court had a considerable role in supervising uncontentious transactions, regulating local medical practice and diffusing judicial rulings on abandoned infants; the same court also had a significant role as a bulwark of seigneurial power.[117] Olwen Hufton's survey of research on local justice concludes that not only were seigneurial courts dying because lords found them unprofitable, but that even when viable, France's lords did not find it worthwhile pressing their own disputes in these courts: fines levied on peasants were trivial compared to judicial salaries. When seigneurial advisers on feudal law proclaimed "justice is only honorific," Hufton urges us to take them at their word. Honor and duty were the only reasons, in her view, for a lord to maintain a court.[118] Bataillon's judgment is that hostility to the lord's courts sprang more from seigneurial neglect than greed.[119] Jonathan Dewald's research on the history of seigneurial justice in a Norman barony shows a clear pattern of decay: the number of court sessions declined from 48 per year in the late sixteenth century to 15 in the 1780s; the number of questions considered per session fell from 40 to 9; the value of the leases negotiated by those who took on the court clerkship (a position in which they were paid by litigants for court documents) declined by more than four-fifths. In 1735 the marquis sold the building that had served as courtroom and jail.[120] Other scholars, however, argue for the continuing role of the

115. *The Chouans,* 182–84.

116. André Giffard, *Les justices seigneuriales en Bretagne aux XVIIe et XVIIIe siècles (1661–1791)* (Brionne: Montfort, 1903).

117. Jean-François Noël, "Une justice seigneuriale de haute Bretagne à la fin de l'Ancien Régime: la châtellenie de la Motte-Gennes," *Annales de Bretagne* 83 (1976): 127–67.

118. Olwen Hufton, "Le paysan et la loi en France au XVIIIe siècle," *Annales: Economies, Sociétés, Civilisations* 38 (1983): 682.

119. Jacques-Henri Bataillon, *Les justices seigneuriales du bailliage de Pontoise à la fin de l'Ancien Régime* (Paris: Sirey, 1942), 152; see also Robert Forster, *The House of Saulx-Tavanes. Versailles and Burgundy, 1700–1800* (Baltimore: Johns Hopkins University Press, 1971), 85–86.

120. Jonathan Dewald, *Pont-St.-Pierre, 1398–1789: Lordship, Community and Capitalism in Early Modern France* (Berkeley and Los Angeles: University of California Press, 1987), 254–55.

lords' courts in pressing (or even expanding) the lords' claims,[121] or for a continuing vigor generally.[122] Abel Poitrineau finds great variety within a single province: in the lower Auvergne one seigneurial court handled two cases a year and another took on ninety-two.[123] And in Burgundy, the Dijon Parlement in 1768 seems to have revived seigneurial courts that, while functioning as judicial bodies in lesser cases, provided a framework for convening the rural community under seigneurial control.[124]

Peasant communities have their transactions to be validated, their quarrels to be adjudicated, their rule-breakers to be controlled. Not one peasant *cahier* in our sample proposes the abolition of all judicial institutions; the issue confronting France's villagers was whether to count on the royal or on the seigneurial courts and how to make the one or the other (or both) work better. For many villagers, the advantages of a nearby magistrate who knew local needs was an attractive option and one whose restructuring was easier to imagine than the more distant (and perhaps more mysterious) royal courts. Restif de la Bretonne's idealized portrait of his father, a prosperous peasant become seigneurial judge, makes the case for the superior benefits of local experience over "the quill-driving strangers,"[125] as well as providing a vivid portrait of a far-from-moribund institution.

Clearly the actual practice of seigneurial justice varied enormously. In Aunis it enforced the seigneurial regime, around Vannes it did not, and in the Sarthe it was being abandoned by the lords.[126] Bastier concluded that the judges were competent and honest in the region of Toulouse but

121. Serge Dontenwill, *Une Seigneurie sous l'Ancien Régime: L' "Etoile" en Brionnais du XVIe au XVIIIe siècle (1575–1778)* (Roanne: Editions Diffusion Horvath, 1972), 76–77. Anthony Crubaugh's research on seigneuries near St. Jean d'Angély shows, in some detail, a vigorous enforcement of seigneurial claims in their courts. See also Jean-Pierre Gutton, *La sociabilité villageoise dans l'ancienne France* (Paris: Hachette, 1979), 172–84, and *Villages du Lyonnais sous la monarchie (XVIe–XVIIIe siècles)* (Lyon: Presses Universitaires de Lyon, 1978), 90–97.

122. Nicole Castan, *Justice et répression en Languedoc à l'époque des lumières* (Paris: Flammarion, 1980), 149–55.

123. Abel Poitrineau, *La Vie rurale en Basse-Auvergne au XVIIIe siècle, 1726–1789* (Paris: Presses Universitaires de France, 1965), 636.

124. O. Morel, "Les Assises ou Grands Jours dans les justices seigneuriales de Bresse à la fin de l'Ancien Régime (1768–1789)," *Annales de la Société d'Emulation et de l'Agriculture de l'Ain* (1934): 230–84, 311–44.

125. Nicolas-Edmé Restif de la Bretonne, *My Father's Life* (Gloucester: Sutton, 1986), 71–74, 103–8.

126. Forster, *Merchants, Landlords, Magistrates,* 88–89, 101; LeGoff, *Vannes and its Region,* 279; Bois, *Paysans de l'Ouest: Des Structures économiques et sociales aux options politiques depuis l'époque révolutionnaire dans la Sarthe* (Le Mans: Imprimerie M. Vilaire, 1960), 402–3. The seigneurial court near La Rochelle that Forster studied was clung to tenaciously by the local lord in the face of revolution and in spite of its minimal revenues (Forster, *Merchants, Landlords, Magistrates,* 218–19).

Poitrineau finds the case quite otherwise in Auvergne.[127] Nicole Castan finds in Languedoc a great diversity: some lords couldn't afford to support a court while others held it their civic duty.[128] Around Sarlat seigneurial courts were actually increasing their initiation of criminal prosecutions.[129] Pierre Villard's detailed study of La Marche shows that while a still active seigneurial justice was significant in enforcing the seigneurial rights (especially monopolies and mutation fees), peasants made far more frequent use of this institution for civil litigation than did the lords, no doubt attracted by the relatively low costs and ready access that Villard can document.[130]

To whatever degree a national summary would find the courts to be moribund (or alive but merely a prop for the lord's pocketbook), Sutherland's work is persuasive that there were places where there was a life of quite a different kind in this institution.[131] The courts of the spectacularly wealthy house of Bourbon-Penthièvre—the duke's fortune was evaluated at over one hundred million livres in 1794—were vigorously active throughout the eighteenth century.[132] It is for this reason, we suggest, that a substantial group of parishes did not join the majority of their fellows in insisting on abolition, but saw some sense to demanding improvement.

The *cahier* of Dolving in the *bailliage* of Lixheim beautifully epitomizes the majority outlook in a detailed and bitter case for abolition when it observes that "under such justice the people can never be anything but a hopeless victim of the most disastrous rapacity and pillage." The seigneurial courts are a "sad residue of the feudal regime" and utterly useless.[133] If the people of Dolving, like those of many other parishes, thought seigneurial justice

127. Bastier, *Féodalité au siècle des lumières,* 120–25; Abel Poitrineau, "Aspects de la crise des justices seigneuriales dans l'Auvergne," *Revue Historique de Droit Français et Etranger* (1961): 552.

128. Nicole Castan, *Justice et répression en Languedoc,* 103–21.

129. Steven G. Reinhardt, *Justice in the Sarladais, 1770–1790* (Baton Rouge: Louisiana State University Press, 1991), 239. Increased court activity near Sarlat followed royal edicts of 1771 and 1772 which provided powerful inducements: under its terms, if a seigneurial court initiated criminal actions, the royal courts would take the case—and its expenses—over; if the royal court moved first, however, the seigneurial court became responsible for the costs (62–63). It is likely that these edicts were only spottily enforced; it is, therefore, an interesting question whether they gave a boost to seigneurial justice in other places.

130. Pierre Villard, *Les justices seigneuriales dans la Marche* (Paris: Librairie Générale de Droit et de Jurisprudence, 1969), 181–235.

131. The major attempt at a national survey suggests that seigneurial courts were vigorous in parts of Normandy and the Seine valley, Flanders, parts of Burgundy, Alsace, Franche-Comté, and coastal Languedoc but withering away in central France as well as Provence and parts of Ile-de-France. But where they were alive, they were focused on communal issues rather than seigneurial exploitation; see Hufton, "Paysan et loi," 681–83.

132. Jean Duma, "Place de l'élément féodal et seigneurial dans la fortune d'un 'grand': L'exemple des Bourbon-Penthièvre," *La Révolution française et le monde rural* (Paris: Comité des Travaux Historiques et Scientifiques, 1989), 58, 63–64.

133. Lesprand and Bour, *Cahiers de Sarrebourg et Phalsbourg,* 187.

badly wounded but still dangerous, and only wanted to administer the coup de grâce, there was yet a significant minority for whom this was a live institution that deserved a future (or for which some tolerable future was at least imaginable).

The rural reform proposals for seigneurial justice may have had an official inspiration. Most of the parish reformism we have observed restated the principles of the ill-fated Lamoignon reforms of 1788.[134] At a relatively calm moment in the crisis that eventually forced the calling of the Estates-General, the government issued a sweeping set of changes in judicial organization. A small part of this complex package dealt with seigneurial justice. Had the country people been influenced by the recent elite controversy? If one's starting point is an image of an unthinking rural mass into which ideas are from time to time injected by external forces, one might see here an instance of peasants getting their ideas from the educated. If one is persuaded that the *cahiers* are generally showing a village world of fine distinction and careful reasoning, however, one might then wonder whether many villagers in the spring of 1789 merely looked to the abandoned Lamoignon reforms as a statement of the maximum to be achieved for the moment: here was a project with some elite support (after all, it had royal authority behind it), yet that went too far to withstand the intra-elite counterattack. On this model, rather than simple-minded rustics blindly taking up some cast-off notions from their betters, we have politically thoughtful villagers finding a balance of daring and caution in aligning with a proposal that just might fly under the more favorable circumstances presented by the deepening crisis. And on this model, too, we ought not to be surprised that, when favorable opportunity beckoned, peasants pushed even further. It also suggests that we see the *cahiers* not as so many utterances of opinion *in vacuo* but as pieces of an intricate dialogue. In the spring of 1789 the peasant-elite dialogue was carried on in the *cahiers;* in the years that followed insurrection and legislation were important vehicles for communication (see Chapter 8).

If we have correctly characterized the reformism of rural France in 1789, is not its underlying emphasis the curtailment of the lords' opportunities for income and power coupled with the preservation of their public claims to esteem? Indeed, by curtailing the material interests in seigneurial courts, in fairs and markets, in tolls, and less commonly, in the seigneurial mill, are

134. On the seigneurial aspects of the Lamoignon edicts see Marcel Marion, *La Garde des Sceaux Lamoignon et la réforme judiciaire de 1788* (Paris: Hachette, 1905) and John Q. C. Mackrell, "Criticism of Seigneurial Justice in Eighteenth-Century France," in J. F. Bosher, ed., *French Government and Society, 1500–1850* (London: Athlone, 1973), 127–28. The political background and the overall judicial changes are covered in Egret, *Pré-Révolution,* 246–306; and Dawson, *Provincial Magistrates and Revolutionary Politics in France, 1789–1795* (Cambridge: Harvard University Press, 1972), 135–49.

not the lords being offered a new opportunity for earning public admiration? The lords are being asked in effect to shoulder the costs of carrying on vital public functions.

Did those parish assemblies making such proposals have any basis for even dreaming that the seigneurs would actually accept such terms? Would the lords not simply let their courts sink deeper into ignorance and incompetence than even the most hostile *cahiers* charged? Why operate the mill at all if not at a profit? Certainly there is some evidence that lords whose remuneration was inadequate were already abandoning some of their rights. But there are also instances of at least some lords carrying on, for their honor, at a loss.[135] With the proper example in mind the rural proponents of reform might well have held their plans realistic. More strikingly, we have the noble *cahiers*. In their repeated assertions of concern for honor and indifference to pecuniary advantage, in their repeated claims of willingness to sacrifice their material advantages for the public interest, were they not inviting such reforms? Their very reticence on the seigneurial regime may have contributed to a climate in which others might mistakenly see acquiescence where there was only silence. Such is the price of abstention.

How to Reform the Lord's Amusements

The Third Estate *cahiers* have their largest reform minorities in two areas: first, the hunting rights, but not the other recreational privileges; and second, the broad range of dues, both annual payments in cash and kind as well as the mutation fees.

Hunting Rights

We shall treat these two areas in turn. Peasants find the hunting rights more worthy targets of reform than they do other seigneurial recreations. On the other hand, they find all the lords' games less reformable than does the Third Estate. In exploring how the *cahiers* discuss how the lords play, we shall seek to understand the distinction drawn between hunting and the rest as well as the gap between country people and urban elites. Proposals to

135. Although he used his judicial prerogatives with some effectiveness to enforce his seigneurial rights, the expenses of the duke de Saulx-Tavanes in maintaining an impressive court and prison seem to Robert Forster to indicate "that not money but prestige and local pre-eminence were the duke's principal motives" (Forster, *Saulx-Tavanes,* 100). Around Toulouse the honor of naming officers to exercise justice in their names was so coveted that the *parlement* felt compelled to try to halt the tendency to wasteful multiplication of judicial personnel (Bastier, *Féodalité au siècle des lumières,* 105).

reform the hunting rights generally have one of several objectives, which we will examine in turn.

1. *Restrict the season, place, or circumstances of the hunt or limit those who may exercise the right.* Among restrictions on the conduct of the hunt we find demands that the use of dogs be carefully controlled,[136] that peasants' dogs may not be killed,[137] that hunting on horseback in seeded land be forbidden,[138] that birds that kill insect pests not be hunted,[139] that enclosed gardens adjoining dwellings be off limits,[140] that only lords with large estates hunt[141] and that hunting rights not be transferred by the seigneur to another party.[142] Such demands for limiting the place and nature of the hunt are more characteristic of the urban notables than of the country people.

2. *Peasants (or other non-lords), under suitable restrictions, shall be allowed to kill game.* This second group of proposals address themselves not to the damage wrought by the hunt, but to the damage wrought by the hunt's quarry. The nobles and Third Estate of Péronne jointly urge, for example, that when the quantity of game exceeds the capacity or desire of the lords to control it, the peasants, upon petition to the Administration of Waters and Forests, may be permitted to hunt (under proper supervision) (*AP* 5:360). The Third Estate of Melun asks for the right to destroy all rabbits not killed by the lords, using all means short of firearms, a restriction they accept (*AP* 3:746).

3. *Limit the harshness of repression by seigneur or state.* A group of reform proposals protest the harshness of the current sanctions against offenders, whether the brutality of the lord and his game wardens or the criminal penalties of the state, without necessarily challenging the monopolistic right to hunt itself. The Third Estate of Melun, for example, demands that seigneurial violence and unjustifiable imprisonment be prevented (*AP* 3:746), while their colleagues of Chaumont-en-Bassigny want an alleviation of the harsh penalties for infractions (*AP* 2:727).

4. *Facilitate legal defense of peasants.* Here we find a group of proposals that, grudgingly or otherwise, acknowledge the continued existence of hunting rights but insist that seigneurs be liable for damage caused. As the

136. Third Estate, Alençon, *AP* 1:714.

137. Third Estate, Chalon-sur-Saône, *AP* 2:609.

138. Third Estate, Blois, Frédéric Lesueur and Alfred Cauchie, *Cahiers de doléances du bailliage de Blois et du bailliage secondaire de Romorantin pour les états généraux de 1789* (Blois: Imprimerie Emanuel Rivière, 1907), 2:453.

139. Third Estate, Digne, *AP* 3:356.

140. Joint *cahier* of Nobles and Third Estate of Péronne, *AP* 5:360.

141. Third Estate, Orléans, Camille Bloch, ed., *Cahiers de doléances du bailliage d'Orléans pour les états généraux de 1789* (Orléans: Imprimerie Orléannaise, 1906), 2:332.

142. Third Estate, Clermont-en-Beauvaisis, *AP* 2:755.

Third Estate of Orléans puts it, there must be penalties for the powerful who abuse their rights as well as the powerless with no rights.[143] The Third Estate of Auxerre, for example, insists on the legal responsibility of the lords for the actions of their game wardens (*AP* 2:123) while the Third Estate and nobility of Péronne jointly demand that peasants must find it easier to sue lords for damages; in particular they must be able to get a hearing at a nearby royal—not seigneurial—court (*AP* 5:360).

5. Finally and most interesting of all, we find demands *that seigneurs fill the responsibilities that alone justify these rights*. Hunting rights are seen not merely (and in some documents not at all) as a seigneurial amusement but as a vital public trust. The clearing of game is necessary and those lords who fail in their duty are to be responsible for the damage wrought, not merely by their hounds and horses in hunting, but by the game animals they failed to exterminate. The urban notables of Belfort et Huningue, for example, insist that the royal courts ought to have jurisdiction, in a text in which it is particularly clear that the lords' monopoly is granted for the fulfillment of a public duty. The lord is not entitled, he is *required* to kill game—or else pay up (*AP* 2:318). The Third Estate of Château-Thierry, for their part, find the target of reform in the current complexity, expense, and uncertainty of legal procedures. They demand a drastic simplification to make it possible to hold the lords accountable, in actual practice as well as legal principle, so that it no longer will be the case that "agriculture suffers immense losses, through the ravages of too abundant game. Hunting rights may not be the right to ruin the hard-working cultivator by permitting excessive multiplication of game" (*AP* 2:675).

The idea of reforming seigneurial hunting along these lines plainly appeals less to the villagers than to the non-noble well-to-do (see Table 3.11); among village-sponsored reforms, restricting the circumstances of the hunt and forcing lords to kill damaging animals are prominent. The community of Norroy, in the *bailliage* of Pont-à-Mousson, for example, wants to defend late summer's ripening crops. Although, they claim, hunting is forbidden until August 15 to prevent the extermination of game, existing legislation fails to protect the fields covered with their riches. They appeal rather plaintively for stronger laws, for they are too timid to risk opposing the incursions of "grown men carried away by their passion for hunting."[144] The peasants of Molitard, in the *bailliage* of Blois, concede the honorific distinction involved in a hunting monopoly, but strongly demand that the lords do not exploit this right as a source of profit: "One sees . . . with indignation

143. Bloch, *Cahiers d'Orléans,* 2:332–33.

144. Zoltan-Etienne Harsany, ed., *Cahiers de doléances des bailliages des généralités de Metz et de Nancy pour les états généraux de 1789,* ser. 1, vol. 5, *Cahiers de Bailliage de Pont-à-Mousson* (Paris: Librairie Paul Hartmann, 1946), 127, 128.

the ravages of game; for five or six months we have watered our fields with our sweat, and just at the moment when our greatest hopes are excited, our harvests are utterly destroyed. . . . We are nonetheless far from wishing to strip the nobility and the gentlemen of the right to hunt which, it seems, ought to belong to them exclusively. But let there no longer be any souls low enough to make an object of gain out of what ought only to be an honor. Let them have the sole right to hunt, let this right be regarded as their property, but let greed no longer carry them to try to sell game for 12 to 15,000 *livres*. This speculation is iniquitous."[145] The peasants of Saint-Cloud-en-Beauce, in the *bailliage* of Blois insist that if the right cannot be abolished, the lords must pay for damages: "since it is not just that the harvests be an unconstrained pasture for game which serves nothing but the pleasure of the lords."[146]

Pigeons, Rabbits, Fish

Reform proposals are less commonly enunciated by parishes and Third Estate in regard to the other recreational privileges. When we examine these proposals, however, we find some broad similarities to those we have discussed. We also find a dramatic and highly significant difference. Peasants and urban notables propose that there be restrictions on pigeons during sowing, harvesting, or other critical periods (sometimes offered as the next best thing to outright abolition);[147] that dovecotes or warrens be enclosed;[148] that the right to raise pigeons or rabbits be restricted (to those with proper titles, to those with the right of high justice, to those with at least one

145. One takes the enormous sum of money mentioned as a measure of the anger of the country people rather than a statement of how much actually changed hands. See Lesueur and Cauchie, *Cahiers de Blois,* 1:369–70.

146. Lesueur and Cauchie, *Cahiers de Blois,* 1:318.

147. *Parishes:* Kuntzig in Thionville, N. Dorvaux and P. Lesprand, eds., *Cahiers de doléances des bailliages des généralités de Metz et de Nancy pour les états généraux de 1789,* ser. 2, vol. 7, *Cahiers du bailliage de Thionville* (Bar-le Duc and Paris, 1922), 197; Châteauneuf in Rennes, Henri Sée and André Lesort, eds., *Cahiers de doléances de la sénéchausée de Rennes pour les états généraux de 1789* (Rennes: Imprimerie Oberthur, 1911), 3:130; Third Estate, Dieuze, Charles Etienne, ed., *Cahiers de doléances des bailliages des généralités de Metz et de Nancy pour les états généraux de 1789,* ser. 1, vol. 2, *Cahiers du bailliage de Dieuze* (Nancy: Imprimerie Berger-Levrault, 1912), 420; Etain, Beatrice F. Hyslop, *A Guide to the General Cahiers of 1789, with the Texts of Unedited Cahiers* (New York: Octagon Books, 1968), 299.

148. Parishes, St. André-sur-Cailly in Rouen, Bouloiseau, *Cahiers de Rouen,* 2:248; Gemonville in Vézelise, Charles Etienne, *Cahiers de doléances des bailliages des généralités de Metz et de Nancy pour les états généraux de 1789: Cahiers du bailliage de Vézelize* (Nancy: Imprimerie Berger-Levrault, 1930), ser. 1, 3:163; Third Estate, Autun, Anatole de Charmasse, ed., *Cahiers des paroisses et communautés du bailliage d'Autun pour les états généraux de 1789* (Autun: Imprimerie Dujussieu, 1895); Meaux, *AP* 3:731.

hundred arpents of land);[149] that the numbers of pigeons be limited.[150] Other documents demand, should these measures prove inadequate, that fields and crops may be defended by killing pigeons and rabbits.[151] Still others insist that the lord be responsible for damage.[152]

While reform demands concerning rabbit-raising are quite similar, if far less numerous than those dealing with pigeons, the monopoly on fishing and the associated right of construction of fishponds are quite different in detail. Although fish don't eat crops, these demands tend to fit into the same broad categories already sketched. It is demanded, for example, that the permissible locations of fishponds be restricted to avoid flooding;[153] it is proposed that moderate fines for infraction be set in a predictable fashion;[154] it is demanded that standards of proof in cases of infraction be tightened.[155]

Hunting Rights and Other Seigneurial Pleasures

We are now in a position to set reform proposals for hunting rights side by side with the less frequent demands to modify other privileged amusements. Common to all are proposals to limit damages and to reduce the harshness with which these rights are enforced. But it is almost only in regard to the hunting rights that there is any attempt to compel the seigneur to perform a duty. It is almost only with regard to the hunting rights that there is even the barest acknowledgment that there is a public function carried out, even if inadequately, by the lord. Only the hunting rights are regarded as having some purpose other than the amusement of the lord or the maintenance of a status marker. An occasional *cahier* of peasants or urban notables might acknowledge grudgingly some value in the raising of pigeons,[156] say, or

149. Parishes, Teilly-le-Peneux in Orléans, Bloch, *Cahiers d'Orléans,* 123; Han-devant-Pierrepont in Longuyon, P. d'Arbois de Jubainville, *Cahiers de doléances des bailliages des Longuyon, de Longwy et de Villers-la-Montagne pour les états généraux de 1789* (Nancy: Société d'Impressions Typographiques, 1952), 26; Third Estate, Gien, *AP* 3:409; Châlons-sur-Marne, Laurent, *Cahiers de Châlons-sur-Marne* (Epernay: Imprimerie Henri Villers, 1906), 862. The Third Estate of Metz, curiously, would bar general staff officers from having dovecotes (*AP* 3:767).

150. Parishes, Grostenquin in Vic, Charles Etienne, ed., *Cahiers de doléances des bailliages des généralités de Metz et de Nancy,* vol. 1, *Cahiers du bailliage de Vic* (Nancy: Imprimerie Berger-Levrault), 283; Third Estate, Douai, *AP* 3:182.

151. Third Estate, Châtillon-sur-Seine, *AP* 2:714.

152. Third Estate, Boulogne-sur-Mer, *AP* 2:441. The parish of Saint-Denis-Les-Ponts in the *bailliage* of Blois offers an option: either everyone should be free to kill rabbits and pigeons or the lord must be compelled to destroy game on pain of being liable for damages (Lesueur and Cauchie, *Cahiers de Blois,* 267).

153. Third Estate, Chartres, *AP* 2:631.

154. Third Estate, Dijon, *AP* 3:135.

155. Third Estate, Chartres, *AP* 2:631.

156. Pigeons, in the view of the Third Estate of Château-Thierry, have "a usefulness too widely recognized to demand their total destruction." So widely recognized, indeed, that they do not bother to tell us what that usefulness might be (*AP* 2:675).

insist on the performance of some riverine responsibility they associate with fishing rights.[157] Their numbers pale before those who recognize the control of destructive animals as a vital public responsibility and demand that it be carried out. We find, in short, that the *cahiers* distinguish between seigneurial rights that are merely a burden and those that, while burdensome, have some point to them.

While hunting rights stand out among the lord's amusements for their reformability, it is the Third Estate, far more than the peasants, who make these reform proposals. We find, indeed, Third Estate documents which insist that, in some particulars, the hunting rights of the lords actually be extended. The seigneur's hunting rights, which restricted those of everyone else, had in turn been limited by certain prerogatives of the king. The royal *capitaineries* were preserves within which even the lords could not hunt without special dispensation. A lord so unfortunate as to have his seigneurie within one of these preserves could find his right to hunt quite obliterated. Deer, moreover, as royal animals, were under special protection in and out of *capitaineries.* The desire to control animal damage sometimes led to the demand that the royal hunting privileges be abolished or modified and that those of the lords be expanded. The Third Estate of Crépy-en-Valois, for example, announces that it is fed up with endless discussions of precisely which animals cause crop destruction. Let fief-holders kill deer as well as other game, at least away from the *capitaineries,* and let these royal preserves themselves be drastically reformed (*AP* 3:178).

So vivid, at the beginning of the Revolution, was the idea that hunting was a public duty, that even *cahiers* that argued that the seigneurial monopoly be ended might take note of its rationale. The Third Estate of Château-Salins, for example, concedes that the "destruction of game is truly necessary." "But," they continue, "it is far from the case that this is the motive of the *seigneurs,* who do everything they can to multiply [game]."[158]

We began this section by noting the high propensity for reform proposals to be advocated for the hunting rights (but not for the other recreational privileges) by the Third Estate (to a greater extent than the rural parishes). The extermination of game was held to be a present need and not merely an outworn relic of the past. One conceivable reform, the imposition of constraints on the lords, to compel them to hunt enough as well as not to hunt in a destructive fashion, required a confidence that the judicial system could actually be used to coerce the seigneurs. The lawyers and judges who

157. The parish of Lay-St.-Christophe (*bailliage* of Nancy) insists that those who claim the right to fish have an associated duty of bridge repair; see Jean Godfrin, *Cahiers de doléances des bailliages des généralités de Metz et de Nancy pour les états généraux de 1789,* ser. 1, vol. 4, *Cahiers du bailliage de Nancy* (Paris: Librairie Ernest Leroux, 1934), 4:230.

158. "Doléances, plaintes et remontrances du tiers état du bailliage Royal de Château-Salins en Lorraine," *Annuaire de la Société Historique et Archéologique Lorraine* 16 (1904): 226.

were so important a component of the Third Estate[159] may well have had such confidence. It was this confidence that the peasants, whose experience of legal procedures was far more frustrating, altogether lacked.

Their confidence in legality was probably not the only element in the greater enthusiasm for cleaning up the lord's games on the part of the Third Estate than the villagers. As substantial landholders themselves—or if not landholders, aspirants to such a state, or related to one, or whose friends were one, etc.—it surely was easier for members of the urban notability to imagine themselves sharing in similar diversions. If seigneurial hunts were a model of forbidden pleasures, would not many well-off landholders and would-be landholders look to the day when they could invite those they sought to impress to their own hunting party? A properly enlightened hunt (or, in lesser degree, other once-lordly diversions)—which still carried social exclusion with it—was more appealing to the well-off than to the peasants, who, while more likely to want hunting reformed than rabbit-raising, were nonetheless even more inclined to abolition (see Table 3.4).

Periodic Payments and Mutation Rights

With regard to both periodic payments and mutation rights the Third Estate's reformist bent was so much more evident than the parishes'. Is this because a good number of those in the upper reaches of the Third Estate could see themselves as lords? The reformist bent here, in any event, shows a desire to curb seigneurial "abuses" while preserving property, a position that was to infuse the debates on legislation in the months ahead. Reform proposals aim at limiting the lord's capacity to use these payments as a vehicle for forcing peasants to sell out, sometimes by insisting on measures assuring a more scrupulous adhesion to individually negotiated contracts. For example, the period in which arrears may be collected is to be limited, say, to five years.[160] Such a measure would inhibit the seigneurial practice of letting arrears accumulate for up to 29 years, demanding payment

159. By Lemay's count, 60% of those elected to the Estates-General by the Third Estate were legal professionals of some sort: judges, lawyers, notaries. Judges from the *bailliage* courts alone made up one-fifth of the deputies. Forty-eight Third Estate *cahiers* were actually drafted by assemblies that had elected a *bailliage* magistrate to preside over their deliberations. See Edna Hindie Lemay, "Les Révélations d'un dictionnaire: du nouveau sur la composition de l'Assemblée Nationale Constituante (1789–1791)," *Annales historiques de la Révolution française*, no. 284 (1981): 179, for the summary figures. Timothy Tackett suggests an even higher count in *Becoming a Revolutionary: The Deputies of the French National Assembly and the Emergence of a Revolutionary Culture (1789–1790)* (Princeton: Princeton University Press, 1996). See also Dawson, *Provincial Magistrates*, 186–87.

160. Ploërmel, *AP* 5:379; Annonay, *AP* 2:52.

and then accepting the peasant's holding as settlement of unpayable debt.[161] Collective communal responsibility for each individual's obligations is to be curtailed.[162] Payments are to be more carefully recorded to avoid paying twice.[163]

Other proposals are specific to certain forms of payment. Of a heavy payment in kind it was demanded that it be commuted into a cash payment;[164] that the lord collect it at the peasant's fields rather than have the peasant deliver it to the lord;[165] and that its relationship to the tithe or to royal taxes be regulated to avoid ruin.[166] The Third proposes exemptions to *lods et ventes*[167] as well as rate reductions.[168] As for *retrait,* the notables of Agen propose all the major reforms: that the seigneur cannot assign the right to another; that *retrait* cannot be exercised past a certain date; and that the collection of *lods et ventes* bars the exercise of *retrait.*[169]

It appears, however, that these complex projects had little appeal in the parishes, even when those proposals would seem clearly to have met rural concerns. The greater hold of reformism in the Third Estate *cahiers* than among the parishes for both regular and occasional payments seems explicable in the same fashion as the similar pattern with regard to recreational privileges. The urban notables are proposing more complex legal procedures backed up by access to judicial safeguards. The same remarks apply to the greater confidence in such processes on the part of urban elites (among whom legal professionals were a weighty component) and their greater sense of themselves as lords or would-be lords.

A Note on the Ideological Rationale for Reform

It is noteworthy that these reform proposals, for the most part, were appropriations of current and available claims of how the system was

161. The Third Estate of Ploërmel characterizes this practice as "the perfidious negligence of the seigneurs" (*AP* 5:379).

162. Châtellerault, *AP* 2:696; Bellême, *AP* 5:328.

163. Châtellerault, *AP* 2:696.

164. Dourdan, *AP* 3:253; Etampes, *AP* 3:285.

165. Clermont-en-Beauvasis, *AP* 2:756.

166. Avesnes, *AP* 2:153.

167. Hennebont, P. Thomas-Lacroix, *Les cahiers de doléances de la sénéchausée d'Hennebont (Extrait de Mémoires de la Société d'Histoire et d'Archéologie de Bretagne,* vol. 25) (Rennes: Imprimerie Bretonne, 1955), 89; Auray, *AP* 6:116.

168. Calais, *AP* 2:512; Toul, *AP* 6:13.

169. Agen, *AP* 1:668.

supposed to work: claims found in compilations of customary law, claims found in judicial rulings, claims found in the manuals of the *feudistes*. If actual practice deviated from legalistic principle, if the principles of one province differed from those of another, if the restraints and restrictions that limited seigneurial burdens in the idealistic world of lawyers' documents diverged from a more dreary reality, the urban notables and, to a lesser extent, the country people could find ammunition for reforming without destroying the seigneurial regime. Customary law frequently limited hunting rights to fief-holders or lords with the right of high justice; in Burgundy, the seigneurs were held to be forbidden to hunt in the enclosed fields of their dependents; an edict of 1780 ruled, against the regulations of the comte d'Artois, that the dogs of their dependents could not be killed; a royal ordinance of 1669 forbade hunting during growing season; hunting rights, widely regarded as honorific, were not, in a widespread lawyer's view, to be farmed out for cash; dovecotes were barred for those in possession of too little land to support them.[170] Such idealized portraits of the system constituted a source to be drawn upon in the search for reform.

Reforming Nobles: How Elite Reforms Differ

Tables 3.11 and 3.12 show that the nobles were every bit as likely to propose reforms in those rights as were the others, yet a reading of their documents finds a shading that slips through the statistical analysis. Their reforms were different. It is not so much that they proposed changes which were in no way advocated by the peasants or urban notables; indeed, their reforms drew on the same fund of ideas. But if the nobles' theme was common, it was nonetheless a theme with variations. The nobles of Sens, for example, would have restricted pigeon-raising to those whose claims to dovecotes could be validated by proper titles.[171] The nobility of Aix embraced the common Third Estate demand that hunting rights not be rented out (*AP* 1:694). These are common enough demands of the Third Estate, but was not a part of their special appeal to the nobility their embrace of the symbolic trappings of the seigneurial regime? The point of these proposals for the many parish and Third Estate assemblies advocating them was clearly to limit destruction. But when taken up by a noble assembly, one suspects the appeal of the gratifications of exclusivity, to maintain an airborne status marker that functioned like the wearing of a sword, or the

170. See Garaud, *Révolution et propriété foncière*, 87–101.

171. Charles Porée, *Cahiers de doléances du bailliage de Sens pour les états généraux de 1789* (Auxerre: Imprimerie Coopérative Ouvrière "L'Universelle," 1906), 820.

Table 3.12. Noble Documents Demanding That Seigneurial Rights Be Reformed (%)

Right[a]	Nobility	
Periodic dues		
Cens	29%	(7)
Champart	22	(9)
Periodic dues in general	40	(5)
Seigneurial monopolies		
Monopolies in general	27	(15)
Assessments on economic activity		
Seigneurial tolls	10	(39)
Dues on fairs and markets	17	(6)
Property transfer rights		
Dues on property transfers *(lods et ventes)*	33	(6)
Justice		
Seigneurial courts in general	22	(27)
Seigneurial courts, miscellaneous	18	(17)
Recreational privileges		
Hunting rights	37	(27)
Right to raise pigeons	17	(12)
Symbolic deference patterns		
Right to bear arms	13	(30)
Honorific rights	10	(21)
Fealty and homage *(Foi et hommage)*	33	(9)
Avowal and enumeration *(Aveu et dénombrement)*	33	(9)
Symbolic deference patterns in general	0	(27)
Serfdom		
Mainmorte	60	(5)
Serfdom in general	14	(7)
Other		
Compulsory labor services	15	(13)
Miscellaneous right	10	(20)
Regime in general	12	(34)

[a]Rights discussed in at least 5 Noble *cahiers*.

construction of a gallows, or the display of a weathervane. The same demand appealed to a peasant wish for damage control, a Third Estate ideal of fostering economic development, and a noble concern for honor.

Consider now the nobles of Laon, who accepted that the lords have a duty as well as a right to hunt and who accepted as well that damage caused by the hunt or by failure to hunt ought to be made good. But in accepting these principles, they add something of their own:

> The right to hunt is to be reserved as the property of the seigneur on his lands. The bearing of arms is to be prohibited in view of the

> abuses and the dangers, both civil and political. But at the slightest complaint addressed by the tillers to the Provincial Estates concerning the ravages of game and the indiscretion of the hunters, the Estates shall immediately name as agents an equal number of gentlemen and tillers. These agents shall verify the damage and they shall not only determine the compensation to award, but shall even order the destruction of overabundant game. Their judgment shall be executed without appeal; and by the same token they shall have the power to pronounce a fine—to be turned over to the administration of poor relief—against anyone who brought a frivolous complaint. (*AP* 6:143)

The gentlemen of Laon stressed their monopolies on hunting and on guns. That they have a duty to hunt is clearly implicit. Where the peasants spoke of the catastrophic destructiveness of the hunt, these nobles acknowledged "indiscretion." The widespread demand that seigneurs be liable for damage was conceded, but seriously weakened. The Provincial Estates—often repositories of privilege—shall name a commission half of whom are nobles;[172] and the commission is to fine peasants who complain with no good reason. Given the long experience of fruitless legal struggle over seigneurial rights, how many peasant communities would have felt protected by such a procedure? Perhaps Laon's privileged expected their inferiors to be gratified that the fines were to go to charity rather than into their own pockets.

If the nobles of Laon were lucid on the reasons for keeping access to weapons within social boundaries but spoke delicately of "indiscretions," other nobles adopted a stance of vagueness. The nobles of Châteauneuf-en-Thymerais boldly described game as "one of the most terrible scourges of agriculture." They then observed that "powerful considerations appear to oppose the proposition that hunting be freely available for all classes of society" without specifying what these "powerful considerations" were (*AP* 2:643). A different form of reticence was exhibited by the nobles of Amiens. They instructed their deputies to consent to all ordinances that restrict the number of pigeons without, however, actually proposing any (*AP* 1:741). What was explicitly embraced in Amiens was implicitly characteristic of the nobles' reform proposals taken as a whole: they were reacting to an agenda set by others. Even when their deputies were told to vote for some of the same measures advocated by the Third Estate, the nobles were going along; they were trying to limit their damage, they were attempting to reassert their claims to honor while under fire, and they sound evasive. It is not their agenda.

One of the options permitted in drafting *cahiers* occasionally allows a

172. This *cahier* demands that Provincial Estates exist throughout France (*AP* 6:140).

unique glimpse into the intense national dialogue taking place in 1789. The clergy, nobility, and Third Estate were allowed to choose to draft *cahiers* in common, an opportunity of which a small number of assemblies availed themselves. Sometimes two, sometimes all three, orders collaborated on a text. Some of these attempts at a unified document, however, failed in whole or in part and left us a fascinating record of the points of disagreement. In Bourg-en-Bresse, the clergy, nobility, and Third Estate acknowledged their differences. The Third Estate proposes: "that every landowner be permitted to kill wild animals that he finds among his crops without incurring a fine. To this effect, every inhabitant shall be allowed to have fire-arms at home." The nobles respond to these not unusual proposals: "Preserve in its entirety the right of hunting. . . . Maintain the laws of the realm that restrict the bearing of arms, and solicit a regulation that will prevent the crop damage caused by the large number of wild animals" (*AP* 2:460). In this *bailliage* the noble response to a challenge to seigneurial prerogatives is to assert the claims of privilege, and to wish for a "regulation"—they propose none themselves—to solve the problem.[173] The specific demand of the Third Estate of Bourg-en-Bresse and the vagueness of the nobility in response are both reform proposals—but how different they are.[174]

Peasants and Nobles Protect Themselves; The Third Estate Opts for Lawsuits

We see that the parishes, Third Estate, and nobility are remarkably similar in the proportion of reform proposals put forward (Table 3.1); we also see that this similarity conceals great differences in the spirit moving the reforms: a peasantry concerned with paying less, a nobility concerned with conserving its position, an urban upper stratum concerned with legal remedies. One finds regions of agreement and possibilities of future cooperation among these groups; and possibilities of future division as well.

The peasant lack of interest in seeking amelioration through mechanisms

173. If it is not putting too fine a point on it, the structure of the nobles' prose seems to urge something even weaker. Since "solicit" is used parallel to "preserve" and "maintain," they seem to be urging not an unspecified regulation, but merely that such a regulation be solicited. The clergy, for their part, responded by consenting to the proposal of the Third, but insisting that the permission for private possession of firearms be stricken from the grievance. Since they don't propose an alternate method of killing animal nuisances, one wonders whether the clerics of Bourg-en-Bresse pictured the peasants attacking rabbits with hoes or catching birds with their hands.

174. Once again the evidence is inconsistent with Cobban's picture of a Third Estate virtually indistinguishable from the nobility on seigneurial rights. Had Cobban actually examined the *cahiers* of the nobility, he might have seen how different were the views of the urban notables.

of legal enforcement and their desire for rate reduction are not independent facets of their mentality. A distrust of their capacity to utilize the judicial apparatus[175] to compel the lords to do something or to compel them not to do something is quite compatible with the form of relief they do seek. If rate reduction is the rule, then legal relief would frequently become the problem of the lords. If the lord is unhappy about the reduced rate at which the peasants propose to pay, the invocation of legal procedures would be his problem, not theirs. The peasants in short are reluctant, compared to the Third, among whom legal professionals were so significant, to modify the seigneurial regime in directions whose realization would depend on legal initiatives on their part. The Third is, by contrast, relatively enthusiastic about such procedures. They are more likely to trust the abstract power of the Law; they have more confidence that judicial procedures can constrain the lords; and, let us not forget, some of the lawyers and judges among them are hardly averse to the creation of litigation. Many of the Third Estate reforms would promote peasant suits against seigneurs; these might, as the proposals suggest, benefit the peasants, but they would be sure to benefit their urban attorneys.[176] "Let's you and him fight" might be a good maxim for lawyers. If we look ahead from the spring of 1789 to the ensuing history of revolutionary legislation on seigneurial rights, we shall see how large a role was played by one or another enactment empowering peasants to sue for their claims—and how limited was peasant assent to such a framework (see Chapters 8 and 9).

A National Dialogue

In understanding the positions taken (or the subjects avoided) by the assemblies that gathered in the spring of 1789, I have often treated these statements (and silences) as strategically conceived, delivered in particular circumstances, for particular audiences, to attain particular ends. The nobles' reform notions, for example, were described as reactive. The nobility of Soule were not very appreciative of the contributions of others to the debate: "The Third Estate, exalted by circumstances, disregarding our sacrifices and contemptuous of the sacred rights of property, demands the

175. The people of Etiolles (in Paris-hors-les-murs) describe their experience of administrative and judicial protection. When one protests, they write, "one is told there are rules to take care of it, the rules must be followed." (They have been complaining of the prohibition on mowing hay before June 24 in order to protect often nonexistent partridge eggs.) See *AP* 4:541.

176. To the extent that we see, with Cobban, the Third Estate as themselves seigneurs, we might also suppose that some support for such measures lay in the hope that they wouldn't work, that the country people would be unable to mount a judicial defense.

suppression of this right" (*AP* 5:779). More generally, the assemblies were responding to their sense of the positions of others, crucial data in considering what it would be shrewd and what it would be prudent to say oneself. The making of the *cahiers* took place against a background of ministerial reform, parlementary pronouncement, an avalanche of pamphlets, the intense campaign to influence the content of the *cahiers,*[177] and finally the debates of the tens of thousands of assemblies themselves. Some of the broad characteristics of the interactive quality of the grievance-generating process shows up in a few simple statistical tabulations.

- The correlation of the proportion of parish documents urging abolition without compensation and the number of Third Estate *cahiers* treating a seigneurial right is .44.[178] That is to say, the Third Estate is likely to discuss precisely those rights concerning whose elimination the parishes are most vociferous. When the parishes are most adamant, the Third Estate feels it has to say something, even if only to offer a different proposal.
- The nobility demands anything other than maintenance when the Third Estate discusses a right with some frequency. The correlation of the proportion of noble documents insisting on maintenance and the number of Third Estate *cahiers* discussing a seigneurial subject is -.69;[179] the correlations of the proportions advocating virtually anything else and the extent of Third Estate discussion are positive and significant: abolition without compensation (.50), indemnification (.61) and reform (.56).[180]

The urban notables, then, appear to be careful to say something about institutions to which rural France is markedly hostile while the nobles are most reluctant to advocate preserving unchanged the institutions widely attacked by others. It is this diffidence, I suggest, rather than indifference that underlies the silence of the Second Estate. This may add something to our understanding of the nobles' attachment to their symbolic prerogatives: it was perhaps in this realm, of relatively little interest to the Third Estate and of next to no interest to the parishes that the nobles dared to express their wishes.

177. It has sometimes been suggested that seigneurial rights were not so much discussed in the pre-electoral explosion of opinion. (See Garaud, *Révolution et propriété foncière,* 159–60.) Our data, however, suggest that the parishes, Third Estate, and nobles had some knowledge of and sensitivity to one another's concerns.

178. Computed for the 27 institutions discussed in at least 10 parish *cahiers* ($p < .05$).

179. Computed for the 12 institutions discussed in at least 10 noble *cahiers* ($p < .01$).

180. For all three correlations, $p < .05$.

Peasants Assess Their Burdens

That utility is a significant criterion for the evaluation of their burdens permits us to throw some more light on the vexing subject of indemnification. I tried to show above that the ease with which a monetary equivalent may be associated with a seigneurial right helps explain why the village assemblies preferred indemnifying some rights to others. Whether or not it is easy to arrive at a quantitative determination, however, one wonders whether all rights were seen as morally worthy of compensation. If the French countryside clearly distinguished rights that were tied to genuine services from those that were not, is it conceivable that they also distinguished rights that deserved indemnification from those that did not? If so, the choice of indemnification is not only a technical question of the feasibility of calculating a cash value but a moral question of the legitimacy of the seigneurial claim. Consider these observations of a community in Bigorre: "Some charges and new rights were introduced solely by the force and authority of the lord over the weakness and ignorance of their vassals. We insist that the former establishment of these rights must be justified as the concession of some advantage, because one cannot establish charges on one side except in consideration of a payment or advantageous concession on the other. In the case of such concessions, the inhabitants may redeem these charges by returning the capital."[181]

Indemnification is reserved for rights that are worthy of respect.[182] In the case of this particular community, what makes them worthy is the existence of some genuine service. The broad rural position on seigneurial rights that emerges from this study of the *cahiers* is complex. When those rights are seen as payments in return for nothing they were to be abolished. Rights that were once attached to services were more worthy of indemnification than those that were always coerced, but the question of indemnification also depended on whether a monetary equivalent was plausible. Those rights that might still be linked to services in the eighteenth century, however, also attracted some reform proposals intended to make those services real.

Reform proposals about ecclesiastical payments or seigneurial rights, then, were focused on rights seen bound to the performance of vital public services; one distinctive thrust of many of these proposals was to assure that the service was actually carried out. The problematic aspect in the cases of ecclesiastical payments and seigneurial rights was not the distribution of

181. Balencie, *Cahiers de doléances de la sénéchausée de Bigorre pour les états généraux de 1789* (Tarbes: Imprimerie Lesbordes, 1925), 580–81.

182. The National Assembly similarly distinguished legitimate from illegitimate seigneurial rights; see Chapter 8.

the burden at all, but rather the assurance of getting what one pays for. For those for whom traditional modes of financing services by payments to a local individual or corporate body are no longer to be trusted at all or for those to whom the advancing capacity of the central authority suggests alternate means of provision, one might as well do away with the prevailing modes altogether. Justice can be provided by the state and financed by some centralized body, perhaps out of taxes as well.

But taxes themselves are different: we find fewer proposals to abolish them and the equity issues center on who will pay the unavoidable. In the tense and expectant spring of 1789, as the steeply rising price of bread made all other payments unusually difficult to contemplate, the rural communities nonetheless clearly differentiate the state's due from the church's and the lord's. To what degree may one see this distinction as the successful accumulation of a certain measure of legitimacy by the modern state in which its claims on resources are experienced as so many more or less justified means to support vital services? In such a view, the lords' entire position may be held to have been radically undermined by the successful seizure by the state of the role of provider of such services.[183] To what

183. The classic argument for this position is that of Alexis de Tocqueville (*Old Regime and Revolution*). The geographic patterning of antiseigneurial revolts permits a test of Tocqueville's argument in Chapter 7. For recent evidence that increasing state tutelage over rural communities was not only undermining the lord's position but actively encouraging peasant resistance to seigneurial rights through the medium of lawsuits, a resistance moreover increasingly assuming the form of an attack on an abstract conception of "seigneurial rights" as illegitimate (rather than quarrels about specific claims), see Root, *Peasants and King,* 155–204. Although the assertion that peasant communities were increasingly pronc to sue their lords seems to have become an accepted fact among historians, a fact which no longer needs to be bolstered by citing evidence, there are few studies that, like Root's, have actually deployed such evidence, and these few do not always clearly distinguish suits initiated by peasants from those initiated by lords, generally present no tabulations to support what is surely a quantitative claim, and do not always compare the frequency of the lawsuits late in the century with some earlier period. Nonetheless, these studies are at least suggestive, and do converge on the same conclusion. See Yves Castan, "Attitudes et motivations dans les conflits entre seigneurs et communautés devant le Parlement de Toulouse au XVIIIe siècle," in *Villes de l'Europe méditerranéenne et de l'Europe occidentale du Moyen Age au XIXe siècle. Actes du Colloque de Nice (27–28 Mai 1969)* (Nice: Centre de la Mediterranée Moderne et Contemporaine, 1969), 233–39; L. Trénard, "Communication de M. Trénard," in *L'abolition de la féodalité dans le monde occidental* (Paris: Editions du Centre National de la Recherche Scientifique, 1971), 589–605; Gutton, *Villages du Lyonnais,* 88–90; Wolfgang Schmale, *Bäuerlicher Widerstand, Gerichte und Rechtsentwicklung in Frankreich: Untersuchungen zu Prozessen zwischen Bauern und Seigneurs vor dem Parlament von Paris (16.–18. Jahrhundert)* (Frankfurt am Main: Klostermann, 1986). For some evidence on an increase in anti-tithe litigation as well, see Georges Frêche, *Toulouse et la région Midi-Pyrénées au siècle des lumières vers 1670–1789* (Paris: Cujas, 1976), 539–40. Finally, peasant communities in Languedoc sometimes successfully sued to have "noble" land reclassified as "common" land, and thereby subject to the major direct tax, the *taille;* see Emile Appolis, *Le diocèse civil de Lodève: Etude administrative et économique* (Albi: Imprimerie Coopérative du Sud-ouest, 1951), 90–92. Although evidence of peasant litigation on tithes and tax privileges does not directly bear on the existence of a legal front in an antiseigneural struggle, it does at least

degree may one see this as the sense of hopelessness that makes the state seem merely inevitable, after the bloody defeats of the great antifiscal risings of the seventeenth century? The statistical tabulations presented here pose that question, but they do not answer it.

François Hincker has argued that prior to the eighteenth century when the lord and the priest were known figures of the rural world, and figures from whom some services were expected, seigneurial dues and church tithes were less intolerable than taxes. The state was too abstract, too distant, not concretized in a living provider for community needs.[184] If so, our data show a radical shift in outlook. It is unfortunately not possible to compare the parish *cahiers* of 1789 in any systematic way to their closest analogues from earlier Estates-General. But Roger Chartier's research makes it possible to do so at least for the *bailliage* of Troyes in 1614. If one compares shifts in the proportion of demands falling under Chartier's various rubrics it is striking that the largest rise in demands is under "seigneurial rights," which (counting them together with "tithes") climb from a scant 3% in 1614 to 11% in 1789 (175 years later). All his combined tax categories fall from 48% to 33%.[185] So concerns with seigneurial exactions were up, and with state exactions, down, between France's penultimate and its final Estates-General. My data suggest, moreover, that far more striking than any shift in how frequently seigneurial rights are discussed—taxation is still far more widely taken up than seigneurial rights in 1789—is a new way of dealing with them: they are to be reformed.[186]

As for the tithes, they are not very significant in Chartier's counts for the grievances of 1614, in spite of a measurably rising burden. The key issue, then, was peasant demand for a greater and more orderly presence of the church in the countryside. The early seventeenth-century church was too sparse and scattered as well as too poorly controlled (an organizational failure that shows up in demands that the ill-educated and dissolute clerics fill their proper roles). To get the service, Chartier's villagers of 1614 were willing to pay. By 1789 village France had much more contact with an internally reformed church (now it was the clerics who complained of the state of peasant morality); the rural issues turned to the efficiency with which payments got what they should.[187]

---

show rural communities capable of mounting legal challenges to extractors of resources, that sometimes, one should think, included the lords.

184. Hincker, *Les français devant l'impôt sous l'Ancien Régime* (Paris: Flammarion, 1971), 17–18.

185. Roger Chartier, "De 1614 à 1789: le déplacement des attentes," in Roger Chartier and Denis Richet, eds., *Représentation et vouloir politiques: Autour des états-généraux de 1614* (Paris: Editions de l'Ecole des Hautes Etudes en Sciences Sociales, 1982), 110.

186. The degree to which the brunt of anti-tax hostility is borne by the indirect taxes is another feature in which the *cahiers* of 1789 appear to differ from their predecessors of 1614. The greater acceptability of the direct taxes is a sign of the increased acceptance of the state. See Chartier, "De 1614 à 1789."

187. Chartier, "De 1614 à 1789," 104.

We may summarize the lesson of these calls for reform: for those who favor an improvement in taxation, a frequent critical issue is to assure that all pay as equal citizens;[188] for those who favor an improvement in seigneurial or ecclesiastical assessments, a critical issue is to assure the performance of a service. In a justly famous essay, Frederic Lane characterized certain state activities as a protection racket.[189] What one obtained in return for payment of taxes was merely to be spared state coercion. The French villages in 1789 were calling for dismantling the racket, but they accepted payments that purchased genuine protection. The *droit de contrôle,* for example, paid for the validity of legal documents. And even where protection was seen as having turned into a racket, as with some of the lord's claims, some villagers still wanted the service back. The indirect taxes resembled the payments to the lord in their permeation by private interest rather than public service. Yet, where public service was recognized, even indirect taxes could attract reform proposals.

Is the acceptance of the state that one finds in the parish assemblies no more than strategically calibrated public discourse, given the unchallengeable power now in the hands of the state's servitors? Or do the peasants even in private see the state as the locus of valued actions, valued enough so that, suitably reformed, a taxation system is actually now accepted? When parish assemblies treat state exactions differently from the claims of church and lord, do we need to be careful to distinguish the public transcript from the hidden one?[190] The insurrectionary actions of French peasants in the breakdown of authority when taxes, tithes, and seigneurial rights could all be defied may give us some clues in the chapters ahead (see Chapters 5 and 6).

Unstructured Resentment

An assembly sometimes complains of an institution without telling us whether it should be abolished, replaced, reformed; indeed, without any specific proposal at all. We count such grievances under the heading "unfavorable." Glancing back at Table 3.1 we see that these amorphous

188. There has been some interesting theoretical work on taxation systems that also sees conceptions of citizenship emerging out of the conflict of rulers and taxpayers. See Margaret Levi, *Of Rule and Revenue* (Berkeley and Los Angeles: University of California Press, 1988) and Robert H. Bates and Da-Hsiang Donald Lien, "A Note on Taxation, Development and Representative Government," *Politics and Society* 14 (1985): 53–70.

189. Frederic Lane, "Economic Consequences of Organized Violence," *Venice and History: The Collected Papers of Frederic C. Lane* (Baltimore: Johns Hopkins University Press, 1966), 412–28.

190. James Scott, *Domination and the Arts of Resistance* (New Haven: Yale University Press, 1990).

expressions of hostility are most characteristic of the peasantry and somewhat more so with regard to their burdens than for other institutions. Vague expressions of approval of an institution also occur, but much less commonly; when the subject is their burdens, these diffuse expressions of approval ("favorable") are virtually nonexistent in the countryside. There is no rural reserve of goodwill to be tapped or shaped by the conservative forces in the struggles to come: those who do not already favor preservation are not likely to come to do so.[191]

On the other hand, there was a substantial reservoir of ill will toward Old Regime burdens that had not yet been transformed into a vision for specific action. The struggle for the political allegiance of the countryside was not over in the spring of 1789. Especially when it came to their burdens, then, not all rural communities had formulated specific actions by the spring of 1789, even though they had far more ill-will than benevolence. One sees here how more moderate and more radical revolutionaries might both have seen the possibility of appealing to the countryside. I have tried to show that their *cahiers* reveal a peasantry that has thought far more carefully about just what they want done and precisely about which burden than has always been recognized, although we also see here a significant infusion of complaining that was not fully thought through. On this point, the present evidence supports Taylor in stressing the degree to which popular sentiment was in flux, and that it was not fixed and frozen when the Estates-General was convoked. But the range of options had its limits: the unformed sentiment is on the hostile side.

The revolutionary leadership could well have imagined the possibility of appeasing the countryside short of outright and immediate abolition of the seigneurial rights. If one hopes that the sentiment behind "unfavorable" might settle for indemnification and adds those who wanted it from the beginning as well as those favoring reform, one might imagine a substantial counterweight to the more radical peasants. This was a terribly mistaken calculation: the great increase in rural risings after 1789 suggests that the undecided but hostile element moved toward the extreme.

Parochialism

We have been treating the *cahiers* as if the geographic scope of all demands is the same and as if all refer to the entire territory of France, yet a significant minority quite explicitly restrict themselves to their town, village,

191. Amorphous demands that someone do some utterly unspecified action are not only less uncommon for the nobility but also quite scarce.

or province. Table 3.1 shows that the country people were the most likely to state that they were addressing some local concern. One might see this as another indication of the absence of a fully articulated political position among the parishes in the spring of 1789. Yet this localization is quite selective.

Comparing their views of the three burdens, the parishes were considerably less likely to see taxes as a purely local matter. They did not live in a morally isolated rural world. This again suggests that there has been a (possibly bitter) acceptance that the French state was here to stay. The peasants, moreover, were the least likely to have a provincial orientation when they lack a local one—and particularly so when they speak of their burdens. The days when regional nobles and peasants united in broad movements against royal claims, especially financial ones (so striking in some of the great risings of the seventeenth century) seem hopelessly archaic, even in the environment of 1789 made favorable by the regime's collapse. Not only were tax grievances, widespread though they may have been, shot through with reformism in the villages, but rural communities that did not think of their grievances in a local context may have been thinking in a national, not a regional, one.[192] The defense of regional privilege is not (no longer? not yet?) a part of their idiom of grievance.[193]

To the extent that the parishes did articulate the local demands bounded by the horizons of the village, they were surely on a different plane than the

192. Only 33% of parish *cahiers* have any grievances about "this province," as compared to 78% of the documents of the nobles. On the other hand, 66% of the rural assemblies have at least one grievance in which a national question is discussed only at the local level ("abolish the *gabelle* in our village") and 21% contain at least one strictly local complaint ("the next village rings its church bells too loudly"). Alan Forrest also has some pertinent observations on the absence of a peasant provincial identity in "Regionalism and Counter-Revolution in France," in Colin Lucas, ed., *Rewriting the French Revolution* (Oxford: Clarendon Press, 1991), 157–59, 165–67. See also Albert Soboul, "De l'Ancien Régime à la Révolution: Problème régional et réalités sociales," in Christian Gras and Georges Livet, eds., *Régions et regionalisme en France du dix-huitième siècle à nos jours* (Paris: Presses Universitaires de France, 1977) and Fernand Braudel, *L'identité de la France* (Paris: Flammarion, 1986), 1:40. The evidence presented here is not consistent with claims in the literature to the effect that "most Frenchmen, especially those who lived in *pays d'états,*" thought "of themselves as belonging to a province rather than to some abstraction known as France," a proposition for which the author presents no evidence; see Norman Hampson, "The Idea of the Nation in Revolutionary France," in Alan Forrest and Peter Jones, *Reshaping France: Town, Country and Region during the French Revolution* (Manchester: Manchester University Press, 1991), 13.

193. It is only the nobility who evince a regional perspective to any significant degree, although they are less provincial in this literal sense than the rural communities are parochial. The restriction of regional consciousness to elites perhaps helps explain the weakness of separatist and autonomist movements under the Revolution even though much conflict was structured in regional terms. By way of comparison consider the Russian Revolution of 1917, which led to the secession of Finland, Poland, and the Baltic states and defeated separatist movements in Ukraine, Transcaucasia, and the Muslim regions; the Soviet upheaval that began in the 1980s is proving to be even more spectacular from this point of view.

nobility who emerge as the least locally oriented grouping. If the seigneurial regime is experienced locally by the rural community, the nobility on the edge of revolution are not, in their public language, open to talking of the concrete, specific village at all. Peasants do not join in noble regionalism and nobles do not join in peasant parochialism.[194] If we think of the degree to which many a noble fortune still rested on land, the nobles appear, in relation to their historic roots, not merely alocal but delocalized. It is in this context that we can fully appreciate Timothy Tackett's discovery that nearly 40% of noble deputies to the National Assembly were actually Parisian residents, elected by their fellows in some electoral jurisdiction where they or their kin held property.[195] In their *cahiers* as in their choice of deputies the collective sense of their own identity of France's nobility toward the onset of the slide into the revolutionary chasm found little place for the everyday concreteness of a specific rural place.

While a majority of parish assemblies sometimes explicitly restricted their vision to their own local world, they did not express most of their grievances in this restrictive vein; still less did they speak of their province. The geographic scope of most grievances (and of all grievances in a significant minority of *cahiers*) is unstated. Were they thinking of France as a whole? What we may assert at a minimum is that they use language that might well have a national scope when they have shown themselves quite capable of narrowly delimiting their complaints. And we saw above how many villages sharply distinguished customs duties on transit goods within France from those duties collected at the frontiers. There is room to debate how truly national an orientation may be attributed to them, but we are surely observing an awareness beyond the village that was largely indifferent to the province.

Tocqueville's summary of his reading of the parish *cahiers* almost anticipates our data—but not quite:

> When the peasants came to ask each other what their complaints should be about they cared not for the balance of powers, for the guarantees of political liberty, for the abstract rights of man and citizen. They dwelt at once on objects close to themselves, on burdens which each of them had had to endure. One thought of the feudal dues which had taken half of his last year's crops; another of

194. Since the electoral process forced the urban notables to deal with rural delegates at the *bailliage* level, it is not possible to use our data to tell whether town lawyers, city officials, and guild-masters would have otherwise been more receptive to the country people on this score than the nobility.

195. Only some 20% actually lived in their *châteaux*. See Timothy Tackett, "Nobles and Third Estate in the Revolutionary Dynamic of the National Assembly, 1789–1790," *American Historical Review* 94 (1989): 276.

> the days he had been compelled to work for his landowner without pay. One spoke of the lord's pigeons which had picked his seed from the ground before it sprouted; another of the rabbits which had nibbled his green corn. As their excitement rose with the common recitation of their miseries, to them all these evils seemed to proceed not so much from institutions as from a particular single person who still called them his subjects though he had long ceased to govern them. . . . And to see in him the common enemy was the passionate agreement that grew.[196]

Yes, the data show peasant preoccupation with their burdens in their concrete everyday reality. But no, they do not show a peasantry carried away by emotion, blind to institutions, focusing on the local lord. A far more reasoned evaluation of the seigneurial system is what we have seen, and one grounded in notions of justice and equity. If it was the local lord whom rural militants attack, the parish *cahiers* show us not so much a personalized enemy, but a generally malignant social system, with the lord merely the occupant of a social role to be redefined by ending its diseased aspects and strengthening its few healthy ones. If we are not carried away by Tocqueville's eloquence, let us note how rare is the parish *cahier* that actually named the local lord. On this Tocqueville got it almost exactly backward: it was not so much a particular single person as a social institution from which evils proceded.[197] Notice that Tocqueville's vivid language has the peasants as individuals thinking their grievances through individually and then discovering that their fellows think alike. He does not see them as social beings, as members of a community well aware of each other's positions prior to assembling to thrash out a collective, political, strategic statement; still less does his language, in this passage, suggest a community with experience of lawyers and tax-collectors, and a long, close experience of seigneurial rights.

Seigneurial Rights and Public Service

For Tocqueville, the legitimacy of seigneurial authority in the past had rested upon the provision of vital services. As the greedy central state gathered public responsibility to itself, the weakened lords were no longer able to

196. Alexis de Tocqueville, *The European Revolution and Correspondence with Gobineau* (Garden City, N.Y.: Doubleday, 1959), 82.

197. For corroborating evidence from a study of the targets of antiseigneurial actions, see Chapter 5, p. 228.

justify their privileges. Both the envious class of the well-off but unprivileged as well as the angry peasants burdened with seigneurial obligations alike found morally outrageous what their ancestors found tolerable. I have shown in this chapter how significant some sense of public service was in the French countryside. Peasant communities who hoped that the lords might still be held to perform such services were inclined to demand them rather than simply abolish seigneurial claims; for the most part, however, as Tocqueville argued, it was to the state that peasants looked and, therefore, while the lord's claims were to be eliminated, the state's were to be made fairer. Renauldon's *Dictionary of Fiefs and Seigneurial Rights,* whose second edition appeared in 1788 with the crisis already under way, reveals both the claims of service on which the seigneurial rights were held to rest as well as the limited degree to which such service was in actuality a vital component of the world of the lords on the eve of the Revolution. In his very definition of "seigneur," Renauldon presents an impressive picture of the lord's duties: "to see that crimes are punished, to protect their vassals and subjects, to maintain peace among them to the extent possible, to see that official regulations are observed, to supervise proper functioning of churches, hospitals, poor relief, food for foundlings, to prevent injustice by their officials and injuries by their various agents."[198]

The lords, he goes on, are not only obligated to see justice done on their lands, but "they are even more strongly to do no injustice themselves" (2:393). When he is considering certain specific rights, Renauldon stresses the corresponding obligation. Of the right of lords to collect a fee in return for providing a ferry-service at river-crossings (*droit de bac*) he sternly comments that this right never exists "without imposing responsibilities on the lord." The lord must keep the boat in good repair, keep the docking facilities safe, maintain the stretch of road leading up to the crossing and have an adequate number of properly trained crewmen (he spells out details of the requisite training and experience) who must operate the service throughout the day (but are forbidden to operate at night to avoid giving passage to lawbreakers going about their business). He even insists on the satisfaction of impatient commuters: during busy seasons, services must be adequate and prices cannot be raised.[199]

When it comes to previewing his treatise by way of enticing prospective purchasers, however, Renauldon's preface stresses the thoroughness of its coverage: as the eighth of a list of topics to be covered, for example, we learn that: "Finally, we instruct the lords concerning the rights they have in village community properties, over communal assemblies . . . the naming of municipal officers, the access to the accounts of the local church, the

198. Renauldon, *Dictionnaire des fiefs,* 2:393.

199. Ibid., 1:94–95. See also his discussion of the monopoly on baking, 1:475–76.

appointment and removal of judicial officials, etc." (1:5). The point of the manual is to tell the lords what their peasants owe them, a subject on which "this volume will be highly informative." If the lords, however, "are curious" to learn something of their own duties, they are referred to another author's work, one that appeared 120 years previously (2:393). What up-to-date lords really need is to know what they can claim. Acknowledging critics of the seigneurial regime in his earlier treatise of 1765, Renauldon does not even attempt to justify seigneurial rights as payments for present services. He falls back on the claim that they are compensations for the relaxation of an initially violent usurpation.[200]

Conclusions

While recognizing the variety of viewpoints, the dominant rural sentiment emerges. For the seigneurial rights and the ecclesiastical payments, abolition is the most likely response, although some would urge indemnification for the former. For taxes, it is reform and replacement that are favored. Residents of rural France can also make distinctions. Among seigneurial rights and ecclesiastical payments, those that are tied to a service to the rural community are held, at least by a significant minority, to be reformable. Among taxes, those most closely linking the state and the citizen are the targets of reform proposals grounded in a vision of a more egalitarian future; taxes linked to private intermediaries are open to the attacks that fall on payments to the lord and church and, are, like them, candidates for abolition. Does this pattern not suggest a certain acceptance, however resignedly, to the existence of the state? Richard Pipes, commenting on the outlook of the countryside as another revolution approached, asserts that Russian peasants were anarchists in their hearts.[201] Our evidence from France suggests something rather different. While the heavy hand of the royal tax-collector drew more comment in the countryside in the late eighteenth century, it is the exactions of lord and church that were hopelessly illegitimate.

The antipathy of the French toward their taxes is much celebrated. James Riley takes this aversion to be the bedrock upon which all the apparent quirks of the Old Regime's finances hinge: "The French loathed their tax

200. Thus Renauldon could protest in 1765 against the critics: "I hear it said every day that the seigneurial rights are odious. For my part, I say that this is the language of prejudice and ignorance—even ingratitude. Whoever pays a seigneurial due thinks it a needless and whimsical charge that has been imposed upon him. If, however, he goes to the origin of things, he will see that this seigneurial due that seems so odious is only a light indication of a great liberality" (*Traité,* iii).

201. Richard Pipes, *Russia Under the Old Regime* (New York: Scribner, 1974), 162.

system in the first place with a great primeval loathing."[202] Gabriel Ardant's magisterial study looks beyond France as it dramatically begins with the observation: "Of all institutions, taxation has the distinction of having always been and of continuing to be the most detested."[203] The *cahiers* do reveal taxation as the issue occupying the most attention of the people of the French countryside, but they also reveal that an attempt at achieving a new structure of taxation that would enjoy at least the grudging toleration of substantial sectors of rural opinion would be an easier project than would any effort at reorganizing the payments to church and lord.

Our data also suggest some of the complexity of the continuing discussion of the integration of its rural people into the French nation. Documenting the continuing multifarious character of this country, a recent sociological tour de force speaks of "the invention of France."[204] Eugen Weber has eloquently argued that whether one explores the diversity of peasant cultures, the extent of interchanges with the rest of the country or the existence of a sense of shared fate, one must date the period of most significant transformation as the late nineteenth and early twentieth centuries.[205] In light of such arguments, it is the national orientation of the demands of rural communities that is striking. Yes, they are more inclined to localism than are the elites; but even so, the great majority of their demands, if more tersely expressed than in the *cahiers* of the nobility and Third Estate, are not especially local.

To be sure, as Taylor forcefully points out, the parishes do not embrace demands concerning the constitutional order; yet the rural *cahiers* have their own striking characteristics: an orientation to reforming the state's fiscal machinery and eliminating private revenue collectors; a markedly extralocal expression for the great majority of grievances; a strong sense of equity; an insistence on getting the public goods for which the villagers paid; an implicit yet thoughtful concern for public finance that is capable of reasoned discriminations among claims on resources. The liberal movement bidding for power in 1789 sometimes expressed in epigrammatic fashion the inseparability of taxation and citizenship. Thus the statement of the Third Estate of Nemours: "He is not a citizen who does not pay taxes" (*AP* 14:173). Thus the Revolution turns taxes from "impositions" to "contributions." Their *cahiers* reveal France's rural communities to share something of this

202. Riley, *Seven Years War,* 39.

203. Ardant, *Théorie sociologique de l'impôt* (Paris: Service d'Edition et de Vente des Publications de l'Education Nationale, 1965), 1:7.

204. Hervé Le Bras and Emmanuel Todd, *L'invention de la France: Atlas anthropologique et politique* (Paris: Livre de Poche, 1981).

205. Eugen Weber, *Peasants into Frenchmen: The Modernization of Rural France, 1870–1914* (Stanford: Stanford University Press, 1976).

outlook. It may be going too far to see in their grievances a sense of citizenship already rooted in the countryside,[206] but surely it is a basis on which a citizen's identity could build. Let us call it proto-citizenship.

Is the relatively high degree of national orientation—not only but particularly on taxes—the result of slow change, the heritage of defeat in the seventeenth century, or the circumstances of the moment? As to this latter possibility, consider the degree to which some 40,000 communities around France were more or less simultaneously meeting and drafting their grievances, choosing their representatives, and experiencing themselves as part of a countryside in ferment. What was achieved on a regional basis in the great uprisings of the seventeenth century, was perhaps for the first time in French history organized on a national scale by none other than the central government itself: a broad, sustained, thoughtful peasant movement. It was not a movement whose local units were structured into a translocal hierarchy with national spokesmen at the apex, but if initiative and vitality were centered on the local community, the consciousness was more than parochial. Perhaps we may see in the *cahiers*-drafting process one of the wellsprings of the extraordinary capacity for independent initiative in simultaneous action without external structures of authority that was to characterize the pattern of peasant insurrection in the summer of 1789 and into the 1790s.[207]

As we ponder the degree to which the *cahiers* express long-held positions as opposed to responses to the current situation, we can at least say with some certainty that the documents demonstrate a considerable capacity for subtle and sophisticated judgments among the people of the French countryside. Such a capacity could be drawn on again during the great Revolution and beyond, but not necessarily in support of precisely the same positions. The *cahiers,* after all, provide us with a snapshot of claims asserted at one moment; with the rapid changes in constraints and opportunities, we would not expect the rural views of March 1790 to be what they were a year earlier. It would be an error to try to predict the forms of rural

206. Two other studies converge here. Régine Robin's close analyses of the language of the *cahiers* of Semur-en-Auxois leads her to the view that there is a virtual identity between the concept of the taxpayer and of the citizen. Approaching the issue of the social role of the peasants through a study of a great lord, Robert Forster observes that they were "vassals" to the lords but sometimes "citizens" to the king. See Régine Robin, *La société française en 1789: Semur-en-Auxois* (Paris: Plon, 1970), 306–7, 330–33; Forster, *Saulx-Tavanes,* 207–8.

207. Only the Western counterrevolution seems exceptional in its tendency to develop "armies"; that is, somewhat more hierarchical coordination across communities (and even this statement does not apply to the counterrevolution north of the Loire whose autonomous bands recall the usual structures of peasant action). See Maurice Hutt, *Chouannerie and Counter-Revolution: Puisaye, the Princes and the British Government in the 1790s* (Cambridge: Cambridge University Press, 1983), 3–5; Sutherland, *Chouans,* 282–85.

activism of the 1790s from the *cahiers* alone,[208] but the snapshot the *cahiers* give us is an important starting point.

Eugen Weber writes that the "transition from traditional local politics took place when individuals and groups shifted from indifference to participation because they perceived that they were involved in the nation."[209] He adds that in regard to taxation, there was a sense of a government, but that otherwise politics until one hundred years after the Revolution was largely conceived of in local terms. But the *cahiers* indicate that at least for a moment in the spring of 1789, the people of rural France had a different sort of consciousness. If the world of the rural community was a world of burdens, it was those burdens most often held to be essentially local—the payments to lord and church—that were to be abolished; the burdens that bound the village to the state were to be set right.

208. I try to demonstrate this in detail in John Markoff, "Peasant Grievances and Peasant Insurrection: France in 1789," *Journal of Modern History* 62 (1990): 445–76; see also Chapters 5 and 6.

209. Weber, *Peasants into Frenchmen,* 242.

CHAPTER

4

ON THE IDEOLOGICAL CONSTRUCTION OF THE SEIGNEURIAL REGIME BY THE THIRD ESTATE (AND OF TWO SEIGNEURIAL REGIMES BY THE NOBILITY)

The meaning of any social institution to those who support it or oppose it must lie in part in its transactions with other institutions. The seigneurial rights in particular have, from the eighteenth century to the present, been discussed in conjunction with "feudalism." Yet there are few terms on which scholars so intensely insist on the necessity of proper usage and on which there is so little actual consensus as to what that proper usage might be.[1]

For those who were to sit in the Revolution's legislatures, this and related terms were part of their everyday vocabulary and, as such, constituted important elements of their tools for understanding the waves of rural insurrection as well as the terms in which their actions to regenerate France

1. When the papers of the important 1968 Toulouse colloquium on "the abolition of feudalism in the Western world" were published, this discomfort was betrayed in a cover format that featured "féodalité" within quotation marks that don't appear on the title page. See *L'Abolition de la féodalité dans le monde occidental* (Paris: Editions du Centre National de la Recherche Scientifique, 1971). I have tried to explore why this term has so successfully resisted consensual definition in John

were framed. What I propose to do here is to establish something of the conceptual map of the seigneurial regime in the minds of the Third Estate and nobility in 1789. We cannot directly enter the heads of the future legislators to investigate how they saw the seigneurial rights within the fabric of French institutions. But we can use the *cahiers* to explore what the assemblies that adopted them understood to be the role of those rights in relation to their concerns about state finances, economic development, religious institutions. Were the seigneurial rights seen as a group of isolated institutions or were they seen as some sort of unity? And to the extent that the seigneurial rights formed a structure, was there a web of associations that appeared to bind these institutions to other arenas of French society? We shall direct our attention first to the Third Estate and shall then consider the contrast presented by the nobility. In this way we can explore the conceptual enmeshment of the seigneurial regime with other institutional arenas in the language of the assemblies that chose the delegates to what became the National Assembly.[2]

The discussion to follow will repeatedly refer to several broad aspects of the treatment of the seigneurial rights in the *cahiers*. First of all we shall frequently be interested in the number of distinct seigneurial rights discussed by a *cahier;* this tells us something of how wide-ranging a document is in its consideration of the seigneurial regime. It does not tell us, however,

Markoff, "¿Cuál es la cuestión? Algunos comentarios sobre la transición hacia el capitalismo," *AREAS* 11 (1989): 37–46.

2. While the absence of the *cahiers* of the clergy denies us the opportunity to develop a parallel study of the discourse of the assemblies selecting an important group of delegates, the gravity of this gap in our data is reduced by virtue of the relatively low participation of the deputies of the First Estate. Although they played a major role in the events leading up to the merger of the three estates as the National Assembly, they tended to be far less active than the other delegates thereafter: they participated far less than their numbers would warrant as speakers in the debates, in the rotating positions of chair or secretary of the assembly or in the activities of the assembly's 34 committees. (See Edna Hindie Lemay, "Les révélations d'un dictionnaire: du nouveau sur la composition de l'Assemblée Nationale Constituante (1789–1791)," *Annales historiques de la Révolution française,* no. 284 [1992]: 159–89.) Along the same lines, note that in the selection made by François Furet and Ran Halévi of major orators of the Constituent Assembly, there are eight who had been delegates of the Third Estate, seven of the nobility and three of the clergy; see *Orateurs de la Révolution française,* vol. 1, *Les constituants* (Paris: Gallimard, 1989). Of course we're losing something in not having coded the clerical *cahiers:* many ecclesiastics were members of corporate bodies that enjoyed seigneurial rights; the tithe—so often coupled with seigneurial rights in the debates of 1789—was a significant component of the income of many others; clerical delegates were an important part of the events of August 4–11; and over the next two years one of the major speakers of the right (Maury) and a significant voice on the left (Grégoire) were in this group; see Timothy Tackett, *Becoming a Revolutionary: The Deputies of the French National Assembly and the Emergence of a Revolutionary Culture (1789–1790)* (Princeton: Princeton University Press, 1996). Some of the complexity of the conceptions of the seigneurial regime the deputies carried to Versailles is missed in omitting the clerical element.

how salient the seigneurial regime is among the multitude of institutions and practices about which one might complain. Some documents have much to say on seigneurial rights—and on everything else as well. To assess the importance of the seigneurial regime compared to other institutions, I computed the proportion of a *cahier's* grievances devoted to the seigneurial rights. The distinction between these two measures—the number and the proportion of grievances about seigneurial rights—may be seen in a comparison of the *cahiers* of the parishes and of the Third Estate. The first of these measures would show that the peasants commonly address fewer seigneurial rights than does the Third Estate; but the second measure would show that the seigneurial rights are the subject of a larger proportion of peasant grievances (see Chapter 2).

The distinction between these measures is of methodological as well as substantive importance. Since the *cahiers* differ so greatly in their length, one sometimes wonders whether the large number of demands on, say, the seigneurial regime in a particular group of documents is a facet of a propensity to have a large number of demands on any subject whatsoever, or, on the contrary, is an indication of a greater focus on the seigneurial regime as compared to other institutions.[3] Particularly troublesome in this regard is the interpretation of the degree to which demands are associated with one another. Consider two grievances in whose relationship we take an interest. They will both tend to occur in longer documents; they will both tend not to occur in shorter ones. Two randomly selected grievances will, therefore tend to be positively associated, in the sense that they are likely to be present (or absent) in the same documents.

It is the first of our measures that is the more problematic for those *cahiers* having any particular grievance (for example, demands about church revenues) will also tend to discuss a relatively large number of seigneurial rights. We shall have two means of evading this difficulty. First of all we shall avoid focusing our attention on the size of the relationship between discussions of an institution and the number of seigneurial rights mentioned in the *cahiers* in isolation. We shall look instead for the pattern of such associations. Second, we shall also be exploring the relationship between discussion of an institution and the proportion of all grievances that concern the seigneurial system. This second measure, of the *salience* of the seigneurial regime, is not subject to the same problems as the first, the *extensiveness* of the discussion.

3. Since the variability of the number of demands is not merely a methodological nuisance but also a critical variable in its own right, a simple statistical elimination of the effect of size might well be a cure that is worse than the disease.

The Unity of the Seigneurial Regime

The very first matter to be addressed is whether or not the various seigneurial rights have a coherence for those who have adopted the *cahiers* in the spring of 1789. Let us first ask whether there is some explicitly conceptualized totality embodied in such phrases as "the feudal and seigneurial rights," "the feudal regime," and the like. Nearly half of those Third Estate *cahiers* that treat the seigneurial regime (which itself is almost all of them) have some such notion. The corresponding figures for parishes and nobles respectively are 24% and 26% (and only about three-fourths of each of these groups take up seigneurial rights at all; see Tables 2.3 and 2.4).

Such explicit conceptualization is an important step toward the revolutionary definition of "the feudal regime" that has been abolished and whose abolition in turn defines the revolution. But there is an implicit conceptualization to look for as well. Does discussion of one seigneurial right suggest discussing others? Table 4.1 shows the tendency for Third Estate documents that take up virtually any seigneurial right to discuss others as well. The table considers two classes of documents: those that do not and those that do discuss the right in question. For each class of documents, the table displays the mean number of other seigneurial rights treated within each class.[4] Consider the right to raise pigeons, as an example. Those documents that discuss this right discuss, on the average, 8.7 other rights as well, while those that do not take up the lord's avian amusements consider, on the average, 5.6. Examining Table 4.1 as a whole, we can see that the discussion of any seigneurial right is associated with the discussion of others, almost always at a high level of statistical significance.[5] Yet Table 4.1 is not fully persuasive since, as pointed out above, *cahiers* that have *any* particular grievance will tend to have many others. We need to ask, additionally, whether a Third Estate assembly that discusses a particular right also has a higher *proportion* of its demands focused on other seigneurial rights. Table 4.2 presents the appropriate data. To pursue the previous example, in documents taking up the right to raise pigeons, 7.3% of demands concern other seigneurial rights, 2.1% more than in *cahiers* that do not mention pigeon-raising. The overall conclusion is that there is a very strong implicit unity to the seigneurial regime in the Third Estate *cahiers*. Documents that discuss one right discuss others as well.

4. The tables are limited to those rights mentioned with sufficient frequency to have figured in our previous discussions. See Table 3.4.

5. The level of statistical significance is presented only in order to give some sense of whether these differences are of a size comparable to those sociologists conventionally think worthy of discussion. Since the sample of Third Estate *cahiers* consists of the quasi-totality of surviving *cahiers*, itself a large but not a probabilistic sample of all that were produced, there is no process of statistical inference involved.

Table 4.1. Other Seigneurial Rights Discussed by Third Estate *Cahiers* that Do or Do Not Discuss a Particular Right (mean number)

Seigneurial Right	*Cahier* Does Not Discuss Particular Right	*Cahier* Does Discuss Particular Right	Difference
Periodic dues			
Cens	7.0	9.8	2.8***
Champart	6.3	9.4	3.2***
Cens et rentes	6.9	9.6	2.8***
Periodic dues in general	7.2	8.8	1.6*
Miscellaneous periodic dues	7.2	9.5	2.3**
Seigneurial monopolies			
Monopoly on ovens	6.4	10.1	3.7***
Monopoly on milling	6.2	9.1	2.9***
Monopoly on winepress	6.6	10.0	3.4***
Monopolies in general	6.6	7.5	0.9
Assessments on economic activity			
Seigneurial tolls	6.1	7.6	1.5**
Dues on fairs and markets	6.9	9.0	2.2***
Property transfer rights			
Dues on property transfers *(lods et ventes)*	6.6	9.4	2.7***
Retrait	6.8	9.0	2.2**
Justice			
Seigneurial courts in general	6.1	8.3	2.2***
Seigneurial courts, miscellaneous	6.6	9.1	2.5***
Recreational privileges			
Hunting rights	5.3	8.5	3.2***
Right to raise pigeons	5.6	8.7	3.1***
Right to raise rabbits	6.8	9.8	3.0***
Fishing rights	7.0	10.9	3.9***
Symbolic Deference Patterns			
Right to bear arms	7.0	8.7	1.7*
Serfdom			
Mainmorte	6.8	9.9	3.1***
Serfdom in general	7.1	9.8	2.7**
Other			
Compulsory labor services	5.4	8.4	3.0***
Miscellaneous right	5.8	9.2	3.3***
Regime in general	6.0	8.5	2.5***

*$p < .05$ (1-tailed t-test).
**$p < .01$ (1-tailed t-test).
***$p < .001$ (1-tailed t-test).

Table 4.2. Demands Dealing with Other Seigneurial Rights in Third Estate *Cahiers* that Do or Do Not Discuss a Particular Right (mean %)

Right	*Cahier* Does Not Discuss Particular Right	*Cahier* Does Discuss Particular Right	Difference
Periodic dues			
Cens	6.2%	7.8%	1.6%**
Champart	5.7	7.9	2.2***
Cens et rentes	6.0	8.4	2.4***
Periodic dues in general	6.4	6.7	0.3
Miscellaneous periodic dues	6.3	8.2	1.9**
Seigneurial monopolies			
Monopoly on ovens	5.7	8.4	2.7***
Monopoly on milling	5.7	7.5	1.8***
Monopoly on winepress	6.0	8.1	2.1***
Monopolies in general	5.7	6.7	1.0*
Assessments on economic activity			
Seigneurial tolls	5.8	6.4	0.6
Dues on fairs and markets	6.2	7.2	1.0*
Property transfer rights			
Dues on property transfers *(lods et ventes)*	6.0	7.8	1.8***
Retrait	6.1	7.2	1.1*
Justice			
Seigneurial courts in general	5.7	6.8	1.1*
Seigneurial courts, miscellaneous	5.9	7.6	1.8***
Recreational privileges			
Hunting rights	5.4	6.7	1.3**
Right to raise pigeons	5.2	7.3	2.1***
Right to raise rabbits	6.2	7.5	1.2*
Fishing rights	6.2	8.5	2.2*
Symbolic deference patterns			
Right to bear arms	6.3	6.9	0.6
Serfdom			
Mainmorte	6.1	7.9	1.8**
Serfdom in general	6.2	8.5	2.3***
Other			
Compulsory labor services	4.8	7.4	2.6***
Miscellaneous right	5.6	7.2	1.6***
Regime in general	5.2	7.3	2.1***

*$p < .05$ (1-tailed t-test).
**$p < .01$ (1-tailed t-test).
***$p < .001$ (1-tailed t-test).

Is it also the case that those which make specific proposals about one of these rights also tend to make the *same* proposals about many of them? Table 4.3 presents such an analysis. Pursuing our pigeon-raising example, are those *cahiers* that demand its abolition without compensation more likely to pose similar demands of the other rights discussed than do those *cahiers* that, while taking up pigeon-raising, fail to demand abolition without compensation? (For this analysis to be based on stable numbers we included only those rights for which at least 15 documents did and 15 did not make such a demand.) The results are clear: for most seigneurial rights there is a marked tendency for those assemblies that wanted abolition without compensation to desire the same for other rights as well. A similar study of demands for indemnification (which I shall not present here), moreover, shows the same pattern. Thus there is not only a global propensity to discuss seigneurial rights but to view them as calling for the same general sort of treatment as one another. And this propensity coexists with a capacity to differentiate among seigneurial rights that we have extensively discussed in the previous chapters.

If the seigneurial rights have a structure for the authors of the Third Estate *cahiers,* it is a loose structure. The number of distinct rights mentioned in the *cahiers* of the Third Estate ranges from a low of 0 to a high of 18; the presence of a particular right is typically associated with the discussion of an additional two or three others as well. This is a strong association, but it also leaves a considerable distinctiveness in the discussion of particular rights. There is no single right so strongly tied to the others that it carries them all along with it. Similarly, if Table 4.3 showed a clear tendency for abolition to be a demand that is generalized across the seigneurial regime, it also shows that different rights are hardly thought of indistinctly. It is far from the case that documents either propose to abolish all rights they discuss or to abolish none.

Even such a loose unity, however, stands in contrast to the *cahiers* of the nobility. The format of Table 4.4 differs from Tables 4.1 to 4.3 in that we will only present the relevant *differences,* that is to say, the analogues to column 3 in those earlier tables. This and subsequent tables using this format always indicate how much greater are the mean number and percentage of demands on seigneurial subjects for *cahiers* with specified grievances over *cahiers* without those grievances. Looking at the entries in Table 4.4, for example, we see that those noble *cahiers* which discuss the *cens,* take up, on the average, 3.8 more distinct seigneurial rights than those that do not and that 2.7% more of all their grievances deal with the seigneurial regime. We go through the details here because many subsequent tables in this chapter are to be read in the same fashion. Turning to the substance of Table 4.4 shows that about half the seigneurial rights are not, for the nobles, associated with discussions of other rights. The unity seen implicitly by the

Table 4.3. Among Third Estate *Cahiers* Discussing a Particular Seigneurial Right, Demands for the Abolition Without Compensation of Other Seigneurial Rights, for *Cahiers* That Do or Do Not Call for the Abolition of the Right in Question (mean %)

Seigneurial Right	*Cahier* Not Demanding Abolition	*Cahier* Demanding Abolition	Difference
Seigneurial monopolies			
Monopoly on ovens	26%	55%	29%***
Monopoly on milling	31	56	25***
Monopoly on winepress	20	54	35***
Monopolies in general	25	45	20***
Assessments on economic activity			
Seigneurial tolls	29	40	11*
Dues on fairs and markets	24	48	25**
Property transfer rights			
Dues on property transfers (*lods et ventes*)	35	51	16**
Retrait	33	34	1
Justice			
Seigneurial courts in general	32	35	4
Recreational privileges			
Hunting rights	37	50	13*
Right to raise pigeons	32	43	12*
Right to raise rabbits	19	42	22**
Serfdom			
Mainmorte	32	36	4
Other			
Compulsory labor services	25	45	20***
Miscellaneous right	36	52	15**
Regime in general	34	48	14*

*$p < .05$ (1-tailed t-test).
**$p < .01$ (1-tailed t-test).
***$p < .001$ (1-tailed t-test).

Note: excluded from this table are computations in which there were not at least 15 *cahiers* demanding abolition and 15 not demanding abolition.

Third Estate, therefore, is not to be taken for granted. We shall return to the nobility later in this chapter after a closer examination of the place of seigneurial rights in the *cahiers* of the Third Estate.

Table 4.4. Differences in Numbers of Distinct Seigneurial Rights Associated with Particular Rights in Noble *Cahiers*

Seigneurial Right	Number of Distinct Seigneurial Rights Discussed	Grievances Concerning Seigneurial Regime as a Percentage of All Demands
Periodic dues		
Cens	3.8*	2.7%
Champart	3.1	2.9*
Periodic dues in general	3.7*	3.0
Seigneurial monopolies		
Monopolies in general	1.8**	2.1**
Assessments on economic activity		
Seigneurial tolls	0.9*	1.1*
Dues on fairs and markets	2.6	4.0*
Property transfer rights		
Dues on property transfers (*lods et ventes*)	2.9	2.2
Justice		
Seigneurial courts in general	1.7***	1.2**
Seigneurial courts, miscellaneous	1.0†	1.9**
Recreational privileges		
Hunting rights	1.8**	1.7**
Right to raise pigeons	3.2***	3.1**
Symbolic deference patterns		
Right to bear arms	1.4**	0.8
Honorific rights	0.1	−0.3
Fealty and homage (*foi et hommage*)	1.9**	1.1
Avowal and enumeration (*aveu et dénombrement*)	2.4*	1.6
Symbolic deference patterns in general	0.3	0.3
Serfdom		
Mainmorte	2.8	3.9
Serfdom in general	1.8	1.9
Other		
Compulsory labor services	4.0***	3.5**
Miscellaneous right	1.2*	1.8*
Regime in general	1.6**	1.5**

*$p < .05$ (1-tailed t-test).
**$p < .01$ (1-tailed t-test).
***$p < .001$ (1-tailed t-test).

The Seigneurial Regime as a Financial Burden

In Chapter 2 we saw how much of the world seen through the parish *cahiers* was a world of burdens. In this section, we shall explore the extent to which the urban notables saw the seigneurial regime as a burden among others. In what ways was the seigneurial regime seen as separate and distinct? Did the *cahiers* join lord, church, and state as partners (or rivals) in the extraction of resources from the French people?

Church Exactions

Table 4.5 shows the degree to which discussion of the principal church exactions are associated with the seigneurial regime. This table and many of those that follow, will display the ways that *cahiers* that do or do not have some specified characteristic differ in their discussions of seigneurial rights. In Table 4.5, for example, we are concerned with the degree to which the seigneurial regime is treated differently in *cahiers* which do or do not discuss the tithe (or the *casuels*). As for the substance of Table 4.5, it is clear that both those *cahiers* with grievances concerning the tithe and those that discuss the more detested *casuels*[6] are also more concerned than other documents about the seigneurial regime.

Let us consider whether the association of church and seigneur is limited to an association of their burdens, or whether those documents that deal with seigneurial rights are also particularly prone to deal with ecclesiastical matters more generally. We shall first of all inquire whether or not discus-

Table 4.5. Differences in Discussions of Seigneurial Regime Associated with Discussions of Church's Financial Exactions in Third Estate *Cahiers*

	Number of Distinct Seigneurial Rights Discussed	Grievances Concerning Seigneurial Regime as a Percentage of All Demands
Tithe	2.4***	1.4%**
Casuels	1.9***	1.2*

*$p < .05$ (1-tailed t-test).
**$p < .01$ (1-tailed t-test).
***$p < .001$ (1-tailed t-test).

Note: The quantities shown are *differences;* they are the quantities by which those *cahiers* that take up the tithe (or the *casuels*) exceed the *cahiers* that do not in their discussions of the seigneurial regime.

6. On tithes and *casuels* see Chapter 3, p. 109.

sions of the seigneurial regime are more extensive and more salient in those *cahiers* that are most opposed to the religious institutions and practices of France other than the tithe and the *casuels*. We shall then ask if such discussions are more extensive and more salient in those *cahiers* giving most attention to religious matters, whether opposed or not. In Table 4.6 we explore antagonistic discussion of religious institutions (including among other topics the organization of the Catholic Church, church-state and church-Rome relations, the role of monastic orders, and the parish clergy). One sees that the more frequently a *cahier* demands the abolition of some feature of the church, the more extensive is its discussion of the seigneurial regime. It is striking that one finds this even without taking the tithe and *casuels* into account.

Table 4.7 shows, even more remarkably, that it is not only hostile references to religion that are implicitly linked to the seigneurial regime. The greater the proportion of all demands discussing religion—as before, excluding the tithes and the *casuels*—the more attention is given to the seigneurial rights as well. Why? At the local level the local seigneur was often honored by the local church as head of the community. Whatever the actual nature of political leadership—and this varied a great deal—the lord was often granted great public respect in local religious practice. Writing on Brittany, Sutherland observes:

> Any "haut et puissant seigneur" who was also "fondateur de la paroisse" had an impressive array of [honorific] rights. He had his armorial bearings over the church door, a reserved family pew, the right to be first to receive bread at Mass, to be buried in the church, to have a seat on the parish council, and to have public prayers said for the family's welfare. It is significant, too, that most of these rights were connected with the Church because it was through the

Table 4.6. Attention to Seigneurial Regime and Hostility to Religious Institutions or Practices (Other than the Tithe and *Casuels*) in Third Estate *Cahiers*

Numbers of Demands that a Religious Institution or Practice be Abolished[a]	Mean Number of Seigneurial Rights Discussed	Grievances Concerning Seigneurial Regime as a Percentage of All Grievances	Number of *Cahiers*
0	4.7	5.0%	48
1	5.7	6.1	31
2	7.3	6.9	37
3	8.8	6.9	26
4 or more	10.4	7.8	56

[a]All demands concerning religious matters other than the tithe and the *casuels* are included here

Table 4.7. Attention to Seigneurial Regime and Salience of Religious Institutions or Practices (Other than the Tithe and *Casuels*) in Third Estate Cahiers

Percentage of All Demands Devoted to Religion[a]	Mean Number of Seigneurial Rights Discussed	Grievances Concerning Seigneurial Regime as a Percentage of All Grievances
0–3.7%	4.2	3.6%
3.8–6.1%	6.7	6.3
6.2–9.9%	8.0	7.0
10% or greater	8.5	7.1

[a]All demands concerning religious matters other than the tithe and *casuels* are included here

> Church that the rural community defined itself in the scattered pattern of the Breton countryside.[7]

While this immersion of the lord in religious imagery at the parish level may have had a special potency in Brittany, it was hardly limited to that province. A Burgundian seigneurie is characterized by its historian as enveloped in religion.[8] Renauldon's discussion of honorific rights is remarkably revealing in this regard. The completeness of his coverage of these matters is one of his great points of pride and the list is fascinating. As pointed out earlier (see Chapter 2, p. 47n), almost every practice mentioned under the head "droits honorifiques" is religious in nature. Indeed, Renauldon tells us that strictly speaking, honorific rights mean "the honors that lords receive in the churches."[9] The honor of the lord, then, was to a large extent supported by church practice. These symbolic trappings established a relationship of lord and church and may have linked hostility to the one with hostility to the other. This lord-church nexus was largely unchallenged in the *cahiers,*[10] but it became a focus of peasant action as the Revolution continued to redefine the seigneurial regime. The church benches of many lords were ripped out and burned (see Chapter 5, p. 222).

7. Sutherland, *The Chouans: The Social Origins of Popular Counter-Revolution in Upper Brittany, 1770–1796* (Oxford: Clarendon Press, 1982), 182.

8. Dontenwill, *Une seigneurie sous l'Ancien Régime: L'"Etoile" en Brionnais, du XVIe au XVIIIe siècles (1575–1778)* (Roanne: Editions Horvath, 1973), 109.

9. Joseph Renauldon, *Dictionnaire des fiefs et des droits seigneuriaux utiles et honorifiques* (Paris: Delalain, 1788), 1:iii, 346, 355.

10. Religious honors for the lords might be carried a bit too far. The peasants of Montastruc-la-conseillère (in Toulouse) protested the practice of painting a black band on the local church at the lord's death. A black piece of cloth, easily removable, would do nicely. See Félix Pasquier and François Galabert, *Cahiers paroissiaux des sénéchausées de Toulouse et de Comminges en 1789* (Toulouse: Privat, 1925–28), 53.

Taxation

Table 4.8 shows that far from being linked to the seigneurial regime, taxation seems, if anything, antithetical. The more attention a document gives to taxation, the less does it take up the seigneurial rights. An analysis of hostility to taxation—as measured by the proportion of demands concerning taxation that call for the abolition of an existing tax or an aspect of the tax system—also fails to show a positive association. Taxation, then, unlike church exactions, is the pet topic (or the favorite target) of different *cahiers* than those that focus on the seigneurial system.

If ecclesiastical burdens were and state burdens were not so closely associated with the seigneurial regime, was this not in part due to an institutional structure in which church and seigneurial exactions were sometimes easy to confound? The tithe's acknowledged purpose was for support of the person and activities of the parish priest. Yet ecclesiastical corporations (monasteries, say) were often notorious possessors of the tithe. Though formally responsible for the support of the pastoral work of the parish clergy, such tithe-holders were hardly noted for their devotion to parish affairs.[11] The Third Estate of Castelmoron d'Albret, for example, reports the complaints of several parishes. One complains of an absent tithe-holder who neither resides locally nor supports a *vicaire;* another has a priest who only comes by for one religious service a year (*AP* 2:548); Melun wants a proper balance of clerical exactions and duties (*AP* 3:746) and Montreuil-sur-Mer wants tithe-holders to take responsibility for church upkeep and schoolmasters' wages (*AP* 4:71). These tithe-holding corporations were often seigneurs as well, devoted to collecting a broad range of seigneurial rights. Clerical corporations were but the most evident target of grievance for such practices; any ecclesiastic other than the priest might, if

Table 4.8. Attention to Seigneurial Regime and Salience of Tax Matters in Third Estate *Cahiers*

Percentage of All Demands Devoted to Taxation	Mean Number of Seigneurial Rights Discussed	Grievances Concerning Seigneurial Regime as a Percentage of All Grievances	Number of Third Estate *Cahiers*
0–11.4%	8.3	6.9%	49
11.5–14.0%	8.8	7.0	52
14.1–17.9%	7.3	6.7	48
18.0% or more	5.8	5.5	49

11. When the tithe-holder was not the parish priest, the priest was supported by the *portion congrue,* a frequently though not invariably small salary. Payment of the *portion congrue* was the responsibility of the tithe-holder, as were such parishional obligations as physical repair of the church; see Chapter 3.

tithe-holder, provoke such issues; and ecclesiastical persons as well as corporations might hold seigneurial rights. It was hardly obvious, when peasants attacked their clerical lords in 1789, whether it was as seigneurs or as tithe-holders that they were opposed.[12]

There were lay tithe-holders as well, since the tithe, in the course of the centuries, might have passed into anyone's hands. The revolutionary legislators had to deal with the *dîme inféodée* as such lay tithes were known, and in their remarkable confidence in the power of words to distinguish what was and what was not feudalism, they managed to outdo themselves in confusion.[13] If a monastery could collect *champart,* often known as the seigneurial tithe,[14] as well as the clerical tithe from which it was not readily distinguishable, while a lay seigneur could collect the *dîme inféodée,* any attempt at clarity was a guarantee of obscurity. The line between ecclesiastical and seigneurial exactions, then, could be hard to draw.[15] And beyond the confusion of exactions there was the whole church-lord nexus.

Are there perhaps specific taxes that might be less distant from the seigneurial regime? Table 4.9 shows that when the Third Estate discusses almost any particular tax, it also is prone to discuss more seigneurial rights. On the other hand, the stronger test of whether a greater proportion of demands concern those rights is only satisfied by four specific taxes. Evidently, discussion of specific taxes is often a sign of more verbose texts that contain more of just about everything. At the risk of throwing babies out with bathwater, we shall only consider closely those taxes that survive the more stringent test of salience.

The *droit de franc-fief* was a substantial payment every twenty years by commoners in possession of so-called noble land. The no longer plausible rationale for this payment was that it compensated the king for the loss of military resources when noble land passed out of the hands of the warrior class. This tax quite clearly derives from a feudal image of society, which may account for Alfred Cobban thinking of it as almost a seigneurial right.[16] Table 4.9 shows that the Third Estate in 1789 is with Cobban, quite strongly

12. For some examples in 1789, see Lefebvre's survey of the insurrections in Alsace, Franche-Comté and Mâconnais in *La Grande Peur de 1789* (Paris: Armand Colin, 1970), 125–26, 131, 136–37.

13. P. Herlihy, "L'abolition de la dîme inféodée (1789–1793)," in Soboul, ed., *Contributions à l'histoire paysanne de la Révolution française* (Paris: Editions Sociales, 1977), 377–99.

14. The Nobility of Soule speak of *their* "tithes" without adjectival qualification (*AP* 5:779).

15. After 1789 peasants might exploit this confusion by claiming that the revolutionary legislation on the tithe gave them the right not to pay what we—but not they—would call *champart.* For a good example, see Robert Forster, *The House of Saulx-Tavanes: Versailles and Burgundy, 1700–1830* (Baltimore: Johns Hopkins University Press, 1971), 149–54.

16. Alfred Cobban, *The Social Interpretation of the French Revolution* (Cambridge: Cambridge University Press, 1965), 38.

Table 4.9. Differences in Discussions of Seigneurial Regime Associated with Specific Taxes in Third Estate *Cahiers*

Tax	Number of Distinct Seigneurial Rights Discussed	Grievances Concerning Seigneurial Regime as a Percentage of All Demands
Capitation	2.0**	0.2%
Vingtième	1.5*	0.5
Taille	1.6**	0.3
Franc-fief	2.8***	1.5**
Droit de contrôle	1.7**	0.5
Droit d'insinuation	0.8	−0.2
Droit de centième denier	2.0***	0.9*
Gabelle	0.7	0.2
Aides	2.1***	1.2**
Taxes on manufactured goods	1.1*	−0.3
Octrois	1.2*	−0.4
Droits d'entrée et de sortie	0.5	0.0
Royal *corvée*	2.3***	1.2*
Traites	1.6*	0.4

*$p < .05$ (1 tailed t-test).
**$p < .01$ (1 tailed t-test).
***$p < .001$ (1 tailed t-test).

so, in fact, in the sense that it is the tax most strongly associated with the seigneurial regime.

The *droit de centième denier* was a tax on the registration of property transfers. This one-percent tax applied not merely to the ownership of land but to the ownership of seigneurial rights as well. The very similar *droit d'insinuation* applied to the registration of transfers of ownership of income-bearing resources other than real property and seigneurial rights (government annuities, say). It is, by contrast, not associated with the seigneurial regime at all.[17] The most general registry tax, the *droit de contrôle,* levied on all legal documents, including those paying *insinuation* or *centième denier* as well, is also not associated with an increased proportion of demands on the seigneurial regime. Of the three registry taxes, then, it is the one institutionally linked to seigneurial rights that is associated with those rights in the *cahiers*.

If the *droit de franc-fief* and the *droit de centième denier* were institutionally intertwined with the seigneurial regime, the same cannot be said of either the royal *corvée* or the *aides*. The government's exactions of compulsory

17. An unusually clear explanation of the various and extremely murky registration taxes is found in George T. Matthews, *The Royal General Farms of Eighteenth-Century France* (New York: Columbia University Press, 1958), 176–79.

labor services for the construction and maintenance of roads and bridges, levied upon peasants whose misfortune it was to reside near those roads and bridges, was if anything, an encroachment on the lord's capacity to claim similar services. But the direct constraint of human labor stood out from all the many other royal taxes; did it not appear to be just the sort of thing the lords did in the barbaric past, reducing "the king's subjects to the condition of serfs," as Lavoisier commented in the course of the debates of the late 1780s on reform?[18] The central government, in fact, seemed on occasion to have regarded the two *corvées* as close kin:[19] the royal demand for labor built on the seigneurial one. When Orry as controller-general decided on an elaborate road-building program, the government attempted to get the seigneurs to extract the labor from their peasants; when this approach failed, the royal *corvée* was substituted.[20]

The *aides* were an exceedingly complex group of taxes levied on alcoholic beverages. I am not certain why they seem more associated with the seigneurial regime than many other taxes. Perhaps it was because the structure of privilege largely exempted the first two estates.[21] Ecclesiastical and noble seigneurs, whose vineyards produced less heavily taxed wine, had thereby a competitive edge over their peasants in the marketplace, an edge sometimes augmented by the lord's right to control the date of harvesting of the grapes *(ban de vendange)* or the right to get his wine to market first *(banvin)*. But direct institutional linkages are certainly not the heart of this association. Although all of the handful of *cahiers* that discuss the *ban de vendange* also take up the *aides,* there is absolutely no relationship with the *banvin* (and only a feeble one with the monopoly on the winepress).

18. Henri Pigeonneau et Alfred de Foville, *L'Administration de l'agriculture au contrôle des finances (1785–1787): Procès-verbaux et rapports* (Paris: Guillaumin, 1882), 409. The Third Estate of Agen objects to the *corvée* that those in the Third Estate are no longer the slaves of the first two orders (*AP* 1:688).

19. *Cahiers* sometimes treat the two *corvées* together as in the common disgust expressed by the Third Estate of Rustaing (*AP* 2:368).

20. Douglas Dakin, *Turgot and the Ancien Régime in France* (New York: Octagon Books, 1965), 63. An alternative hypothesis: The commonality of royal *corvée* and seigneurial rights lies in the damage to agriculture, a point stressed in physiocratic writings on the *corvée*'s nefarious removal of control over their own labor power from those subject to it; see Georges Weulersse, *Le Mouvement physiocratique en France de 1756 à 1770* (Paris: Félix Alcan, 1910), 1:442–47. The Third Estate of Angers, for example, joins together as "terrible hindrances" the *gabelle,* the *corvées,* and seigneurial rights (*AP* 2:43).

21. A straw in the wind: The *cahier* of Lay-St.-Christophe in the *bailliage* of Nancy inserts a grievance about the *aides* into the midst of several dealing with seigneurial rights. The complete suppression of these taxes is demanded because they fall only on commoners. This parish opposes the *aides,* we are told, "in the same way" as the seigneurial monopolies and desires their abolition "equally"; see Jean Godfrin, *Cahiers de doléances des bailliages des généralités de Metz et de Nancy pour les états généraux de 1789,* vol. 4, *Cahiers du bailliage de Nancy* (Paris: Librairie Ernest Leroux, 1934), 4:230.

The relationship of this tax and the seigneurial regime, in short, whatever it may be, is not a spillover of the special concerns of wine-producers.

To parallel our earlier shift in focus from grievances about church burdens to grievances about religious matters we raise the question here of hostility to the central government. Consider the proportion of all grievances concerning the central government, apart from taxation, that demand the abolition of some institution or practice. Every Third Estate *cahier*, without exception, discusses some aspects of government. The proportion of such discussions that urge abolition of the specific institution or practice in question ranges from an apparently satisfied zero to a certainly angry two-fifths. Table 4.10 shows a clear relationship: attention to the seigneurial regime is sharply lower in documents with minimal hostility to the central government.[22] Among the urban elites, anger at the central government and concern about the seigneurial regime went hand in hand.

The seigneurial rights proper, then, are seen as closely related to the church exactions and to some though far from all taxes; grievances about the seigneurial regime are, moreover, more wide-ranging and more prominent in *cahiers* hostile to the conduct of religious affairs and in *cahiers* above a low threshold of hostility to the central government. The association with church burdens might be in part a matter of the blurriness of institutional outlines in which ecclesiastical lords collect *cens et rentes* and lay ones the *dîme inféodée;* and the link to the *droit de franc-fief* and the *droit de centième denier* may be one of institutional interconnectedness. But with the *aides* and the royal *corvées* we are dealing with an association of a different order; this is even clearer with regard to the broader grievances about church and state from which tithes and taxes were excluded.

If institutional confusion or institutional connection were all that mattered

Table 4.10. Grievances About Seigneurial Regime and Hostility to Central Government in Third Estate *Cahiers*

Percentage of demands for abolition among demands concerning central government[1]	Number of Distinct Seigneurial Rights Discussed	Grievances Concerning Seigneurial Regime as a Percentage of All Demands
0.0%	4.3	4.6%
0.1–3.9%	6.8	4.7
4.0–7.3%	8.7	7.2
7.4–10.7%	8.1	7.3
10.8% or greater	7.9	7.1

[1]Taxation excluded.

22. Taking 4.0% as the breakpoint, the differences in number of seigneurial rights and in proportion of grievances about the seigneurial system are both significant at $p < .001$.

surely we would find that the king or the monarchical system was associated with the seigneurial regime. The king, after all, held extensive seigneurial rights of his own, collected along with *aides, traites,* and *gabelles* by the Royal General Farms.[23] On occasion, complaints about royal claims to hunt could parallel complaints about seigneurial ones.[24] Yet our analysis of the presence or absence of favorable mentions of the king or discussions of the principle of monarchy, shows no relation whatsoever to discussion of seigneurial institutions. There is no spillover from the fact that the king was a seigneur to an association of the royal and the seigneurial in the *cahiers.* Institutional linkages then did not wholly control ideological ones. If the tithe is so strongly linked, is it only because of the institutional blurriness? No, there must be more at issue here. The seigneurial regime is not only a coherent entity for the Third Estate *cahiers* in which discussion of any right leads to discussion of others, but that whole is connected in a discriminating way to other entities. Does this add up to a conception of a larger whole of which the seigneurial regime is a part?

Looking Downstream: August 4, 1789

Since 1789 the seigneurial rights have been located within an unending discussion of feudalism. We are assured by some historians that the destruction of feudalism was the central accomplishment of the Revolution while others argue that feudalism did not exist in any meaningful form by the late eighteenth century. Still other writers urge us to discover what the revolutionaries meant when they used the term, as they did extensively. We shall consider this question at some length in Chapter 9. In this section, I examine the ways in which some broad notion of feudalism was already implicit in the *cahiers* of the spring. As a reference point, let us glance ahead at the primal document around which the whole complex pattern of subsequent revolutionary legislation evolved: the decree of August 4, 1789. The dramatic and animated discussions of the National Assembly were actually given three different formal versions: the rough-and-ready summary adopted in the small hours of August 5; a more careful summary officially enacted the next morning as a basis for further discussion; and, finally, the series of articles adopted in final form over the subsequent

23. The acquisition of these seigneurial rights (and those of the church) by the revolutionary state was a component of the durability of its support for the indemnification option.

24. Writing on hunting in general and on royal hunting in particular, the Third Estate of Mantes demands: "that individuals as well as the king, yes, the king himself—the first organ of the law cannot believe himself absolved from the obligation to be just—are to repair damages done by game" (*AP* 3:672).

days culminating on August 11. I shall take the first, rough summary as a statement of what the National Assembly thought belonged together with seigneurial rights.[25]

The articles enacted form a fascinating list. The seigneurial rights are mentioned first of all, with special attention to serfdom and *mainmorte,* seigneurial justice, and the recreational privileges: hunting and raising pigeons and rabbits. The tithe is to be turned into a money payment and its elimination through indemnification is to be permitted. Tax privileges are to be eliminated at once. All citizens are to be eligible for all positions. Justice is to be free. The purchase of office is to be done away with. Provincial and town privileges are ended. Church payments to Rome are to be ended. Many church benefices are to be suppressed. Improperly obtained government pensions are to go. Finally, the guilds are to be reformed. We may take this broad list to enumerate the institutions that were part and parcel of "feudalism" as it appeared to the revolutionaries of the summer of 1789. To what extent had these same institutions been, at least implicitly, tied together with the seigneurial regime for the authors of the *cahiers,* several months earlier?

Tithe, Benefice, Payments to Rome

Table 4.11 examines the associations with these institutions. The tithe we have already explored. We see here that the authors of the *cahiers* also coupled benefices with the seigneurial regime. One bitter complaint was the noble hold on the obtaining of benefices. We shall see shortly that this is a facet of a broad association of privileged career opportunities and the seigneurial regime. Although there is a general linkage with the church, as shown above, there is no strong association of the *annates* (a payment to Rome when certain benefices changed hands) with seigneurial rights as shown in the second column.

Tax Privileges

We failed to find any association with tax advantages, either in general or specifically, as mentioned in the decrees, for province or town. This demonstrates that seigneurial rights were not yet linked in the spring of 1789 to the Old Regime's full range of privilege, a point to which we shall return in this chapter.

25. See *AP* 8:350. One might, alternatively, have chosen either of the other two summaries, an amalgam of all three, or an inventory of all institutions mentioned in the debates, even if rejected for inclusion on all three lists (colonial slavery, for example). A fuller discussion of the decrees of August 4–11 is found in Chapters 8 and 9.

Table 4.11. Differences in Discussions of Seigneurial Regime in Third Estate *Cahiers* Associated with Other Institutions Cited in Summary of the Debate of August 4, 1789

Institution Cited in Decree of August 4, 1789	Number of Distinct Seigneurial Rights Discussed	Grievances Concerning Seigneurial Regime as a Percentage of All Grievances
Tithe	2.4***	1.4%**
Ecclesiastical benefices	3.5***	1.5*
Annates	2.7***	0.8
Tax advantages	0.4	−0.5
Tax advantages for nobility	0.7	0.4
Tax advantages for province	−1.6	−1.1
Tax advantages for towns	0.9	0.9
Guilds	0.8	−0.8
Pensions	2.7***	0.7
Venality of office	1.6**	0.4
Posts and careers in government service	1.7**	1.1*
Posts and careers in church	2.2***	1.2**
Posts and careers in judiciary	1.3*	1.1*
Posts and careers in military	2.8***	2.3***
All concerns about posts and careers	4.9***	3.3***
Judicial expense	0.5	0.2

*$p < .05$ (1 tailed t-test).
**$p < .01$ (1 tailed t-test).
***$p < .001$ (1 tailed t-test).

Guilds, Pensions, Venality of Office

If the guilds, the practice of government pensions, and the venality of office seemed part of "feudalism" on August 4, they did not have so clear an association several months before. Although venality and pensions do occur in documents that discuss a wider range of seigneurial institutions they are not associated with proportionally more attention to the seigneurial regime; the linkage with the guilds is even weaker. A plausible association with any of the three might have been possible. The pensions might have been viewed as a continuation of the taming of the once-dangerous feudal magnates. In this vein, these payments might have been taken as another survival of financial reward no longer accompanied by public function, and thereby subject to one of the central critiques of the seigneurial regime.[26] To the

26. As the Third Estate of Montpellier puts it, "Suppress all rights established by the lords over their vassals or commoner dependents in time of war or disorder for reasons that no longer exist" (*AP* 4:58). Might not such reasoning also embrace government payoffs to politically threatening lords? If those with armed force in the Middle Ages, in this view, had seized (or been freely given)

critics of venality, public affairs needed to be separated from private concerns. Venality of office might be seen as part of some sort of neo-feudal dispersal of public power,[27] a major barrier to the formation of an effective central bureaucracy, rather than as a step toward central authority as it might have been seen earlier. This would be particularly plausible in light of Necker's recent efforts to undo the stranglehold of venal officeholding on the tax system.[28] As for the guilds, they represented, as did the seigneurial regime, a corporate and stably hierarchical image of society. The free exercise of an individual's productive capacity and his gifts for imaginative innovation were as circumscribed in the artisans' associations as they were in the countryside; the freedom to undertake industrial activity as limited and as hedged in with restrictions as the market in land; the web of obligations, privileges, and immunities in which members participated as pervasive as in the seigneurie; the fixing of an individual in a scheme that defined one's place in society and which allocated social honor—all these were common to the world of the guilds and the seigneurial world alike.[29] One would think that the belief that the guilds "suffocate material industriousness"[30] was widely shared. But although the seigneurial regime was seen in such company by early August, it was not yet located there in the spring.

Career Opportunities

One facet of the society of privilege already linked to the world of the lords was the question of access to careers. A great deal has been written on the hold of the nobility on the heights of power, whether in the central administration, the judiciary, the church, or the military. The extent and nature of the noble monopoly on posts and careers, the degree to which that monopoly was (or was not) becoming tighter, the mechanisms by which commoners might be ennobled, and the possible consequences of blocked mobility for Third Estate radicalism have all received much scholarly attention.[31] This was an arena of significant concern to the Third Estate: there

seigneurial rights, might not one similarly see the great rebels of the seventeenth century as being put on the government payroll?

27. On the use of some such concept in the analysis of the venal officers on the part of recent historians, see Ralph E. Giesey, "State-Building in Early Modern France: The Role of Royal Officialdom," *Journal of Modern History* 55 (1983): 191–207.

28. J. F. Bosher, *French Finances, 1770–1795: From Business to Bureaucracy* (Cambridge: Cambridge University Press, 1970), 125–65.

29. William H. Sewell Jr., *Work and Revolution in France: The Language of Labor From the Old Regime to 1848* (Cambridge: Cambridge University Press, 1980), 25–37.

30. Third Estate *cahier* of St.-Pierre-le-Moutier, *AP* 5:638.

31. Elinore G. Barber, *The Bourgeoisie in 18th-Century France* (Princeton: Princeton University Press, 1955); Gilbert Shapiro and John Markoff, *Revolutionary Demands: A Content Analysis of the*

are many demands that only technical qualifications and achievement, not birth, be considered; that members of the Third Estate be permitted access to this or that career (or to careers in general); that, as one reads repeatedly in the *cahiers,* careers must be open to talent. Some 27% of Third Estate *cahiers* concern themselves with administrative posts in the central government, 42% with ecclesiastical careers, 43% with judicial appointments, and a rather spectacular 77% with the military. Indeed only a scant 9% evince no such concerns. This was not only an important subject to the Third Estate but the very subject on which their differences with the nobility were most sharp.[32]

Returning to Table 4.11, we see how consistently these matters are discussed by the same documents that focus on the seigneurial rights. (Perhaps, as suggested above, the association with benefices is symptomatic of similar concerns.) Indeed the eighteen documents with no interest at all in mobility issues are also dramatically different than the vast majority. They take up almost 5 fewer seigneurial rights and devote 3% fewer of their grievances to the seigneurial regime. We have found no other feature of the *cahiers* of the Third Estate that so sharply distinguishes the documents that focus on seigneurial rights.

Among the specific career channels that we have distinguished, the military stands out for the strength of its association with the seigneurial regime as well as for the sheer number of concerned Third Estate documents. Perhaps this is due to the recent intense public attention given to the 1781 ordinance that barred from the officer corps, not merely commoners, but those without four generations of nobility on the father's side. With a few exceptions—the artillery, those already officers—the new law insisted that future generals or even lieutenants would not merely be noble but very noble indeed. David Bien has shown persuasively that this contraction of opportunity was not so much directed against the aspirations of a bourgeoisie that was largely excluded to begin with as it was a triumph for the old military families against the upstarts rooted in the venal officialdom of the judiciary and the royal administration.[33] The "nobility of the sword," to use the social terminology of the day, had won one of its rare victories over the "nobility of the robe." Nevertheless, it does not follow that it was perceived by the urban notables of the time as a mere intra-nobility dispute;[34] and the

Cahiers de Doléances of 1789 (Stanford: Stanford University Press, 1997), chap. 18; David D. Bien, "La réaction aristocratique avant 1789: L'Exemple de l'armée," *Annales: Economies, Sociétés, Civilisations* 29 (1974): 23–48, 505–34.

32. Markoff and Shapiro, "Consensus and Conflict at the Onset of Revolution," 44–46.

33. David D. Bien, "La réaction aristocratique avant 1789: L'exemple de l'armée," *Annales: Economies, Sociétés, Civilisations* 29 (1974): 515–16.

34. Following the resonant image of an increasing constriction of opportunity for a talented commoner elite that flourished on the eve of revolution, many have seen the Ségur law as a significant moment in a shutting down of previously open channels. See Barber, *Bourgeoisie,* 122–23.

Ségur law, moreover, certainly called attention in a dramatic way to military careers. But what we suspect is more significant, is that the issues dramatized by the 1781 ordinance shared in some of the mythology of seigneurial rights. The assertion of a monopoly on military skills and service was a basis on which a claim to general deference and financial compensation might once have helped sustain the seigneurial regime. This assertion had now to some extent been transferred to the defense of jobs in the army of the French state. The defense was now, in the modern eighteenth century, articulated as a professional concern.[35] The claim of the lords to a monopoly on the right to strut in public with swords on their hips and of the nobility of the sword to a monopoly on military careers drew on a common symbolic heritage.[36]

The nobles of Laon beautifully articulated the intimacy with which the very idea of a distinctive nobility was fused with the profession of arms: "No public office or employment may confer nobility, unless a subject of the Third Estate is so deserving that the Estates of his province ask such an honor for him. But all brilliant feats of arms in war shall be rewarded by titles of hereditary nobility—even for a common soldier" (*AP* 6:140). For their part, the nobles of Limoges demand: "That the bearing of arms may only be tolerated for military personnel in uniform and for nobles dressed in any manner whatsoever."[37] The bearing of arms is held to be essentially a noble status marker whereas soldiers must dress in a manner to show themselves worthy of their weapons. The fusion of a mystique of honor with a claim on income and power that characterized the defense of seigneurial rights was shared with noble claims on high office, and nowhere more than in the armed forces.

Judicial Expense

Turning now to the last item gleaned from the August 4 identification of feudalism we see no association whatsoever between the seigneurial regime and the expense of judicial procedure. Such an association, however, is by no means unimaginable, and, of course, was imagined on August 4. The existence of a profusion of overlapping jurisdictions, uncertain judicial

35. How could those not brought up with military values hope to acquire the skills of a modern officer? asked the spokesmen of the nobles of the sword. A magical transmission of noble prowess through blood had been transformed into the creation of an appropriate environment for professional socialization. See Bien, "La réaction aristocratique," 521–26.

36. Note that artillery officers whose competence was measurable by an all too unambiguous reality test—whether or not they could point a cannon at something and hit it—were excluded from such symbolic baggage.

37. *AP* 3:569. Quite consistent with the view that nobles are in some essential sense bearers of arms, this document insists that all nobles shall have the right to enter military service. In this conception, military service appears as an extension and expression of nobility.

spheres of competence, and a complex, confusing, uncertain, and exhausting appeals process were all grievances sometimes aimed at the seigneurial courts.[38] We find indeed, as Table 4.12 shows, quite a consistent association of discussions of the seigneurial courts and the royal courts in the spring of 1789. The seigneurial courts, in short, were seen as courts as well as seigneurial.[39] What the *cahiers* failed to exhibit, however, was a clear association of the specific feature of the judicial system mentioned in the August 4 decree, with the seigneurial rights as a whole.

Conclusions

The debate and discussion surrounding the proclamation of the complete destruction of feudalism shows us what the seigneurial regime seemed a part of in the summer of 1789. Pierre Goubert, not implausibly, can read their decrees as the revolutionaries' own definition in practice of feudalism.[40] An examination of the grievances composed several months earlier shows

Table 4.12. Discussions of Seigneurial Courts in Third Estate *Cahiers* by Extent of Discussion of Other Courts

Number of Grievances Concerning Courts (Other than Seigneurial Courts)	Percentage of Documents Discussing Seigneurial Justice in General	*N*
0–6	24%	50
7–12	48	58
13–18	57	44
19 or greater	54	46

38. While this judgment seems a commonplace in the historical literature, some *cahiers* see the seigneurial courts, locally accessible as they were, as a mechanism to keep court costs down. Sutherland has recently stressed this facet of seigneurial justice in Brittany (*Chouans,* 183). Even in the same region, opinion could easily differ. The Third Estate of Beauvais reports that some local villagers want to maintain seigneurial courts while others are opposed; the Third Estate *cahier* merely reports the division, taking no position of its own (*AP* 2:301). See also Chapter 3.

39. Based on his reading of the parish *cahiers* of the Sarthe, Paul Bois has contended that, in the villages, the seigneurial courts were not seen as seigneurial at all. Complaints about seigneurial justice, he suggests, were part of a program of judicial reform and have little to do with social conflict between lords and peasants. To whatever degree one may generalize Bois's analysis to rural France as a whole (as Mackrell appears to do), it is clearly inappropriate for the Third Estate. See Paul Bois, *Les paysans de l'Ouest: Des structures économiques et sociales aux options politiques depuis l'époque révolutionnaire dans la Sarthe* (Le Mans: Imprimerie M. Vilaire, 1960), 167; John Q. C. Mackrell, *The Attack on "Feudalism" in Eighteenth-Century France* (London: Routledge and Kegan Paul, 1973), 172.

40. Pierre Goubert, *The Ancien Régime: French Society, 1600–1750* (New York: Harper, 1969), 5–7.

that only part of this formulation was then clearly in place. The ecclesiastical institutions singled out on August 4 as well as restrictions on mobility opportunities were already clearly associated with the seigneurial regime. But tax privileges were not, nor were the guilds, nor were the pensions, nor was venality of office, nor were court costs. We see here a stage in the formation of a conception of the seigneurial regime by the revolutionary conquerors. By the summer a broad, some might say amorphous, conception of feudalism was elaborated, to the dismay of historians debating their own ideas of feudalism ever since. The seigneurial rights were a central part of this conception and indeed of the revolutionaries' conception of the Old Regime, which having been killed could be named and perhaps imagined.[41] The web of associations in the *cahiers* advanced this vision a significant distance, but was as yet far short of the ideological construction of the Revolution.

The Society of Privilege

Let us extract from the protean sense of "feudalism" emerging in 1789, the more specific notion of privilege. Jerome Blum has made a forceful case that the seigneurial regime in France can be seen as part of a larger structure of dependence, social distinction, and privilege. In much of Europe in the eighteenth century peasants owed servile obligations (whose weight varied greatly) to lords who were most often members of a legally distinct nobility marked out by a large variety of rights and immunities.[42] Blum attempts to treat the liberation of the peasants of Europe and the erosion of the hierarchy of orders as a single, if complex, movement. In his view the emancipation of rural Europe is part and parcel of a generalized shift from traditional orders to modern classes as the central set of significant social distinctions (418–44). The unparalleled condemnatory power of the notion of privilege was recognized by a no less eminent observer of the political crisis than Louis XVI when he attempted to order a halt to the current designation of the clergy and nobility as "the privileged."[43] To what degree

41. Diego Venturino, "La naissance de l'Ancien Régime," in Colin Lucas, ed., *The French Revolution and the Creation of Modern Political Culture,* vol. 2, *The Political Culture of the French Revolution* (Oxford: Pergamon Press, 1988), 11–40.

42. Jerome Blum, *The End of the Old Order in Rural Europe* (Princeton: Princeton University Press, 1978), 11–28.

43. In a letter from mid-June 1789, Louis wrote: "I disapprove of the repetition of the expression *privileged classes* that the Third Estate is using to indicate the first two orders. These novel expressions are good only to perpetuate a spirit of divisiveness" (*AP* 8:129). See also Philippe Roger, "The French Revolution as 'Logomachy,' " in John Renwick, ed., *Language and Rhetoric of the Revolution* (Edinburgh: Edinburgh University Press, 1990), 11. On the powerful equation of

were the seigneurial rights, as Blum's work suggests, seen as part of the structure of privilege in the spring of 1789? We have already seen in Table 4.11 that privileged claims to careers in government service and church, in the judiciary, and in the military were, but tax privileges were not, associated with the seigneurial rights. The guilds, exemplars of a vision of a corporate order, were also a wholly separate matter in our texts.

Table 4.13 explores several arenas of noble privilege that we have not yet covered. We see that, for the Third Estate at least, there does not seem to be much more support for this tempting hypothesis that the critique of the seigneurial regime was a part of a multistranded critique of privilege than we have already seen. Explicit attacks on privilege in diverse institutional areas occur in four Third Estate *cahiers* out of five. There is no question that this is a highly significant area of complaint for the urban notables; but it is not significantly related to the seigneurial regime. Nor is the right of *committimus,* the nobles' highly visible privilege of immediate appearance before a high court without struggling one's way up the exhausting ladder of judicial appeal. Nor is the fundamental principle of the distinction of noble and commoner. What, in 1789, could better stand for the entire society of orders than the traditional vote by order of the Estates-General? Yet those many *cahiers* of the Third Estate that endorsed, in some measure, the principle of vote by head are not more prone to discuss the seigneurial

Table 4.13. Differences in Discussions of Seigneurial Regime in Third Estate *Cahiers* Associated with Discussions of Distinctions among the Orders

Distinctions Among Orders	Number of Distinct Seigneurial Rights Discussed	Grievances Concerning Seigneurial Regime as a Percentage of All Grievances
Attack on privilege, all institutional contexts	1.2	−0.1%
Single tax roll (proposal that all—nobles and commoners alike—appear on same list)	2.6***	1.4**
Noble right to be heard by high court in first instance (*committimus*)	1.0	0.2
Nobility	1.0	−0.2
Vote by head in Estates-General	0.9	0.6

**$p < .01$ (1 tailed t-test).
***$p < .001$ (1 tailed t-test).

"privilege" and "nobility" by Sieyès, see William H. Sewell Jr., *A Rhetoric of Bourgeois Revolution: The Abbé Sieyes and What Is the Third Estate?* (Durham: Duke University Press, 1994).

regime than the small minority that are silent. (Third Estate support for vote by order is virtually nonexistent.)

Although tax privileges generally are not related to seigneurial rights, we find, however, that it is otherwise for the specific question of tax rolls. The privileged insisted, and had largely obtained, that when taxed at all, they would be listed in rolls distinct from those for commoners. Since every tax tended to be separately administered, this added a substantial administrative burden to an already complex tax system. For the nobles, the wish to avoid having their names contaminated by residing on the same piece of paper with those of commoners was joined to the benefits of obfuscating their relatively low rates of assessment. (This is another instance of a claim of honor in the service of interest.) That tax rolls but not the differential assessments themselves are taken up in those *cahiers* that are particularly concerned with the seigneurial regime, is just another indication of how limited was the link, in the spring of 1789, with a broader sense of a society of privilege. That sense would grow with the Revolution.

Communal Rights

In rejecting a corporate and hierarchical society in the spring of 1789, the Third Estate did not yet speak of the seigneurial rights and the guilds as two aspects of a single structure as their representatives were to do a few months later. But much closer to the seigneurial regime in concrete everyday life were the corporate claims of the rural community. Even if the corporate structure of urban life was not seen as connected to the lords of the countryside, the corporate structure of rural France may have seemed intertwined with seigneurial authority. If artisans and shopkeepers were members of an industrial or commercial community in which they had rights and which had rights over them, the communal rights[44] of rural France were at least equally powerful. Decisions about what to plant, how to work the soil, when to harvest or what sort of tools to use were all highly constrained by a variety of collective claims. The seigneur, like the individual peasants, lived with or struggled against these communal rights. By virtue of likeness and by virtue of opposition seigneurial and communal authority may have been linked for the Third Estate in 1789.

Likeness: In their analyses of French economic life, the physiocrats argued that the seigneur and the community both restricted the unfettered

44. The classic works of Marc Bloch are still the principal touchstones for the study of the multifaceted interrelations of seigneurs and peasant communities. See *Les caractères originaux de l'histoire rurale française* (Paris: Armand Colin, 1964) and "La lutte pour l'individualisme agraire dans la France du XVIIIe siècle." *Annales d'Histoire Economique et Sociale* 2 (1930): 329–81, 511–56.

development of the market.[45] The "direct rights" of the lords restricted the freedom to dispose of one's property at will; to mill one's grain, press one's grapes, bake one's bread where one wished; to labor free of judicial and political constraint; to choose one's crops (since holders of *champart*—and tithe—resisted juridically uncertain innovations); and, should the lord have the right of *ban de vendange, moisson,* or *fauchaison,* the freedom to decide when to harvest was restricted as well. The communal rights dictated work rhythms, impeded risky adoption of new crops, dictated limits in seeking individual advantage, and regulated common patterns of grazing.

Opposition: The seigneur as an individual often found it was his own interest that was shackled by the communal rights. If animals could wander freely, could the seigneur enclose his land and remove himself from the collectively dictated work rhythms? Should he desire to rationalize his agricultural activity, he might run up against communal protections for the impoverished.

The rights of the community and the rights of the seigneur were so intertwined, in short, that they may well have been experienced as aspects of a single, communal rural world. We shall ask whether this was in fact the case. Table 4.14 shows that some 70% of Third Estate assemblies had something to say about communal rights. The single most widely discussed issue was the rights on woods. As a place of uncultivated land where animals could wander, as a source of food fallen to the forest floor (acorns, say), as a living warehouse of wood itself (which could be used domestically for fuel, building, or artisanal shaping, as well as sold for cash), the question of who owned these lands was of the greatest significance. The related questions of common land, pasturage rights, and enclosures also received their share of attention. Animals might feed unfenced on the commons; they might graze on land left fallow by community obligation *(vaine pâture);* they might munch on the stubble that one was required to leave, rather than cut one's crops to the ground; and several communities might have mutual and reciprocal grazing rights *(parcours).* The seigneurs might assert a claim on a portion of the commons of one-third or even two-thirds; and, by the right of "separate herd" *(troupeau à part)* claim an exemption from an obligation to join his animals to the common grazing herd, a right he might profitably sell to stock-raising interests. There were, then, seigneurial aspects to the complex of communal rights. On the other hand, much conflict in rural France in the eighteenth century involved the lord's attempt to erode those rights that hindered him and the rural community's attempt at defense, a pattern of conflict that Saint Jacob has described magnificently for Bur-

45. See Georges Weulersse, *La physiocratie à l'aube de la Révolution, 1781–1792* (Paris: Editions de l'Ecole des Hautes Etudes en Sciences Sociales, 1985), 86–105.

gundy.[46] The general climate of uncertainty as to who had what rights over land encouraged endless litigation, not only costly in itself, but very discouraging to any potential investor in expensive projects for increasing agricultural yields, such as drainage or irrigation.[47]

Table 4.15 shows the associations for those aspects of the communal claims that occur with sufficient frequency to make these tabulations meaningful. Some of the collective rights the Third Estate cared about are indeed linked to the seigneurial regime. Most strongly associated was an arena of conflict. The communities' claims for the use of forested areas conflicted with the lords' desire to expand the area under cultivation and, perhaps more important, with the desire to profit from the sharply rising price of wood. This conflict was greatly exacerbated in the eighteenth century by other claims: of merchants hoping to furnish a growing urban population with the raw materials for building and carpentry, of royal officials' inadequate attempts at long-term conservation of an essential naval resource. A climate of individual evasion of the laws and collective resistance flourished: The woods became a focus of contestation between peasants and seigneurs.[48] It is understandable, then, that when the urban notables wrote of

Table 4.14. Third Estate *Cahiers* Discussing Communal Rights (%)

Miscellaneous right	36%
Communal rights in general	10
Rights on woods	39
Common land	26
Seigneur's claim to portion of commons	18
Enclosures	26
Gleaning (*glanage*)	4
Pasturing rights (*pacage*)	22
Obligation to leave land fallow (*vaine pâture*)	11
Mutual grazing rights between two communities (*parcours*)	18
Seigneur's right to separate pasturing (*troupeau à part*)	4
Seigneurial encroachments	4
Any discussion of communal rights	70

46. Pierre de Saint Jacob, *Les paysans de la Bourgogne du Nord au dernier siècle de l'Ancien Régime* (Paris: Société Les Belles Lettres, 1960), 377–86, 488–89.

47. Jean-Laurent Rosenthal's study is quite compelling on the adverse impact for investment of the legal climate surrounding property rights; see *The Fruits of Revolution: Property Rights, Litigation and French Agriculture, 1700–1860* (Cambridge: Cambridge University Press, 1992).

48. Andrée Corvol, "Forêt et communautés en Basse Bourgogne au dix-huitième siècle," *Revue Historique* 256 (1976): 15–36; and "Les délinquances forestières en Basse-Bourgogne depuis la réformation de 1711–1718," *Revue Historique* 259 (1978): 345–88; Christian Desplat, "La forêt béarnaise au XVIIIe siècle," *Annales du Midi* 85 (1973): 147–71; Saint Jacob, *Paysans de la Bourgogne du Nord,* 488–90 and passim; Denis Woronoff, "Les châteaux, entreprises forestières et industrielles aux XVIIe et XVIIIe siècles," in André Chastel, ed., *Le château, la chasse et la forêt* (Bordeaux: Editions Sud-Ouest, 1990), 115–26. See also Chapter 5.

the community's rights on woodland, they were likely to also write of a wider variety of seigneurial rights and focus more of their attention on the seigneurial regime.

Issues of pasturing also raised questions of seigneurial rights. On the other hand, the related questions of the commons and of enclosures did not. I suggest that in conflicts of lord and community over the commons and over enclosure, the Third Estate would have been likely to favor individual proprietorship and enclosure rights. These are part of the agricultural program of physiocracy, for example. On this particular issue, in other words, the lord's side in lord-community conflicts is seen, by the Third Estate, as the side of the angels. In the construction of an image of a retrogressive seigneurial regime, part and parcel of a wide variety of social ills, seigneurial attempts to rationalize market-oriented production have no place. It is only detested elements in rural life that are to be admitted into the conception of the seigneurial. Recall how we saw in Chapter 2 that it was precisely those elements of the seigneurial order that constituted impediments to the market on which the Third Estate placed greatest stress. On the other hand, the specific notion that lords have a claim to a portion of the commons is viewed with ill-favor: surely the presence of such a claim would discourage peasants from seeking to divide their lands.

Table 4.15. Differences in Discussions of Seigneurial Regime Associated with Discussions of Communal Rights in Third Estate *Cahiers*

Communal Rights[a]	Number of Distinct Seigneurial Rights Discussed	Grievances Concerning Seigneurial Regime as a Percentage of All Grievances
Miscellaneous communal rights	1.4*	0.2%
Communal rights in general	2.1	0
Rights on woods	2.4***	1.8***
Common land	0.9	0.3
Seigneur's claim on portion of common land	2.3**	1.5*
Enclosures	1.2	1.2
Pasturing *(pacage)*	1.7*	1.3*
Obligation to leave land fallow *(vaine pâture)*	0.9	0
Mutual grazing rights between two communities *(parcours)*	2.5**	1.3*
Any communal right	2.8***	1.8***

*$p < .05$ (1 tailed t-test).
**$p < .01$ (1 tailed t-test).
***$p < .001$ (1 tailed t-test).

[a]Includes communal rights discussed in at least ten Third Estate *cahiers*

Consider, in sum, that the urban notables were concerned far more than the others with issues of economic development.[49] Were they not likely to endorse enclosures and individual innovation themselves—and thereby not regard this matter as especially connected with the world of the seigneurs at all?

Economic Development

In considering the proposition that the seigneurial regime was seen to be intimately linked to the collective rights of the rural community, we had to consider the commitment to economic development of Third Estate assemblies. It seems plausible that seigneurial rights would earn the hostile attention of the followers of the new and prestigious economic doctrines that aimed at the advancement of wealth through the release of individual energies from social constraint. Mackrell has suggested that the economic thinkers of the eighteenth century "defined the State in terms which left no room for the justification of privilege on grounds of military prowess"[50] and so presumably undermined the defense of seigneurial rights. Their vision posited a world in which the claims of the lords were largely irrelevant. They did not, Mackrell asserts, directly challenge the lords, but "deprived of nourishment in the form of controversy and attention, political and social claims which were based on an imaginary feudal past tended to perish from inanition" (77).

There is, however, a body of economic thought in the eighteenth century that went well beyond the inattention to the seigneurial regime that characterizes the champions of commercial enterprise taken up by Mackrell. The physiocrats were insistent in their opposition to barriers to the movement of goods, to taxation levied on the gross product of agriculture, to monopolistic economic privilege; to a dispersion of property rights that discouraged investment in agriculture; to direct claims on labor that detracted from cultivation, and to barriers to free sale and purchase of grain. The agricultural developmentalism of these thinkers, then, constituted a vigorous intellectual challenge to seigneurial tolls, to the *champart,* to *mainmorte,* mutation fees and *retrait,* to seigneurial hunting rights, to compulsory labor services, to claims over fairs and markets, in a word, to much of the

49. Ninety-nine percent of the *cahiers* of the Third Estate discuss commerce as compared to 89% of the Nobility and 49% of the parishes. For industry and manufacturing, the percentages are 79%, 48%, 13%; for finance, 71%, 55%, 8%; for transportation, 89%, 64%, 68%; for agriculture, 98%, 81%, 79%.

50. Mackrell, *The Attack on Feudalism,* 77.

seigneurial system.[51] As the Old Regime drifted toward its crisis, then, a powerful body of thought was developing a critique of the seigneurial regime as a barrier to economic development. Did this critique enter into the Third Estate's attack on seigneurial rights in 1789?

Agriculture

Almost every Third Estate *cahier* had something to say concerning France's agriculture, as shown in Table 4.16. We may identify several distinct areas of concern for the French rural economy.

- *Encouragements to agriculture* are proposals to offer financial subsidies to those who would adopt new agricultural products or practices, such as forage crops or artificial meadows *(prairies artificielles)*.
- *Rewards for achievement in agriculture* are proposals that the state reward conspicuous success or fruitful innovation either symbolically (medals, citations, proclamations, membership in honorary orders) or financially (prizes, pensions).
- *Protective measures for crops and lands* include discussions of a variety of sources of damage against which remedies are required. These include: livestock disease; destructive animals, ranging from wolves to partridges; erosion; floods; and industrial wastes.
- *Developing new lands for cultivation* covers discussions of draining marshes and clearing forests.
- *Developing new products* includes both new or improved sources of

Table 4.16. Third Estate *Cahiers* Dealing with Aspects of the Development of French Agriculture (%)

Encouragements to agriculture	40%
Protective measures for crops	40
Developing new land for cultivation	28
Developing new crops	4
Agricultural methods	16
Production of alcoholic beverages	18
Grain	43
Animal raising	17
Any discussion of agricultural improvement	97

51. Weulersse, *Mouvement physiocratique,* 1:270–73, 419–22, 434–37, 442–47, 449, 510–13. Mackrell also treats the physiocrats in *The Attack on Feudalism,* 138–50. Some of the social criticism of the physiocrats was directed more at the royal rather than the seigneurial version of an institution (as in the case of the *corvées*), but the principles documented by Weulersse unquestionably cover the seigneurial rights as well.

human food such as potatoes, and discussions of the as yet limited use of forage crops for animals (clover, corn, alfalfa).

- *Agricultural methods* for the increase and improvement of products includes discussions of fertilizer, irrigation, meadows, cultivation, and crop rotation.
- *Alcoholic beverages*
- *Animal raising*
- *Grain*

The striking thing about this list and Table 4.17 is that not one of these subjects is associated with greater attention paid to the seigneurial regime although many of these concerns are part and parcel of the physiocratic program. To the extent that *cahiers* discussing these matters tend to take up a larger number of seigneurial rights, this seems largely a function of both subjects being more likely in longer documents.

But this hardly means that the social life of rural France is not seen as intimately tied to the seigneurial regime. Turn now from economic development to questions of land tenure. Our global land-tenure category deals with leaseholds and sharecropping; with questions of ease of land purchase and with landless rural laborers; with modes of recruitment of a workforce and

Table 4.17. Differences in Discussions of Seigneurial Regime Associated with Discussions of the Development of French Agriculture in Third Estate *Cahiers*

Aspects of Agricultural Development[a]	Number of Distinct Seigneurial Rights Discussed	Grievances Concerning Seigneurial Regime as a Percentage of All Grievances
Encouragements to agriculture	1.0*	−0.2%
Rewards for achievement in agriculture	2.2**	0.6
Protective measures for crops	2.2***	0.5
Developing new land for cultivation	1.4*	0
Agricultural methods	1.5*	0.1
Production of alcoholic beverages	−0.1	−0.6
Animal raising	1.3	−0.1
Any discussion of agricultural improvement	1.9**	0.6

*$p < .05$ (1 tailed t-test).
**$p < .01$ (1 tailed t-test).
***$p < .001$ (1 tailed t-test).

[a]Includes aspects of agricultural development discussed in at least ten Third Estate *cahiers*

with social conflict over ownership.[52] Table 4.18 shows a clear association between concern with such matters and the seigneurial regime. For the Third Estate in the spring of 1789, the seigneurial regime was, then, most definitely located in a region of concern for rural claims on resources: claims of peasant communities and claims of property holders.[53] But whether the resources were used effectively or squandered, whether French agriculture prospered or stagnated appears to have been, for the urban notables, an unrelated matter. The seigneurial regime was seen as part of a structure of local power; it was not, however, seen as tied to particular economic strategies—or to any strategies for the rural economy at all. Does this suggest a limit to the physiocrats' campaign? Perhaps, but it seems to follow from the extent to which the physiocrats were more concerned with showing the irrationalities of government policy than the more diffuse seigneurial institutions.

Industry, Commerce, Finance

In Table 4.19 we examine the association between developmental concerns that are not specifically agricultural and fail to find any association with seigneurial rights. Under the heading of "Industry" we include proposals about weaving or spinning, about metallurgy, about governmental controls and governmental promotion, about the state-licensed enterprises for the production of luxury goods such as tapestries or porcelain, about coal. We have excluded demands dealing with the guilds, since the absence of a relationship has already been documented. Under "Finance" we include discussions of banks and banking, of credit instruments (such as the *lettre de change*), of interest loans (and usury), of state annuities *(rentes perpetuelles* and *rentes viagères),* and of financiers. Under "Commerce" we include such

Table 4.18. Differences in Discussions of Seigneurial Regime Associated with Discussions of Nonseigneurial Aspects of Land Tenure in Third Estate *Cahiers*

Number of Distinct Seigneurial Rights Discussed	Grievances Concerning Seigneurial Regime as a Percentage of All Grievances
3.4***	1.1%*

*$p < .05$ (1 tailed t-test).
***$p < .001$ (1 tailed t-test).

52. We exclude explicitly seigneurial matters here such as seigneurial forms of property.

53. The critique of communal rights was also part of the physiocrats' project. See Weulersse, *Mouvement physiocratique,* 1:408–19.

matters as tolls[54] and customs duties; government controls and government promotion of wholesale commerce, fairs, markets[55] and merchants, colonial trade, commercial treaties, and discussions of obstacles to free circulation of merchandise within France.

It is striking that these matters seem altogether unrelated to the seigneurial system. In J. Q. C. Mackrell's *The Attack on Feudalism in Eighteenth-Century France,* there is an extended argument to the effect that the economic theorists of the time, in effect, delegitimated the social structure of rural France by proposing a concept of a modern state and society in which seigneurial rights could no longer be justified. Mackrell pays particular attention to the barriers to noble commercial activity. That the status of noble could be lost through participation in demeaning endeavors, it was held, seriously inhibited the vitality of the French economy. First of all, some wealthy and talented nobles were barred from bringing their resources to bear on economically fruitful activities. Perhaps more important, the legal principle of *dérogeance* helped to define certain activities as demeaning and thereby discouraged well-to-do commoners (as well as nobles) from

Table 4.19. Differences in Discussions of Seigneurial Regime Associated with Concern with Industry, Finance, or Commerce in Third Estate *Cahiers*

Discussion of Industry, Commerce, or Finance	Number of Distinct Seigneurial Rights Discussed	Grievances Concerning Seigneurial Regime as a Percentage of All Grievances
Any grievances concerning industry[a]	0.4	−0.7%
Any grievances concerning finance	1.8**	−0.7
Commerce: freedom of grain trade	1.0	−0.1
Commerce: any demand dealing with freedom of commerce	1.1*	−0.5
Commerce: demands dealing with loss of noble status *(dérogeance)* for commercial activities	0.7	−1.3
Any three (or more) grievances dealing with commerce	2.0*	−0.2
Private property	0.7	−0.6

[a]Excludes guilds.

*$p < .05$ (1 tailed t-test).
**$p < .01$ (1 tailed t-test).

54. But not seigneurial tolls (so as not to inflate the relationship misleadingly).
55. But not seigneurial rights over fairs and markets.

continuing to engage in them.[56] But whether or not *dérogeance* was a significant component of the pattern of low-risk but high-prestige investment that George Taylor has identified as central to the Old Regime,[57] we see absolutely no sign in Table 4.19 that the authors of the *cahiers* held it, even implicitly, to have any relation to the seigneurial regime whatsoever.

Mackrell is far from the first to have asserted that the requirements of a new economic order contributed to the critique of feudalism. Most famously, Marx wrote: "We see then: The means of production and of exchange on whose foundation the bourgeoisie built itself up, were generated in feudal society. At a certain stage in the development of these means of production and of exchange, the conditions under which feudal society produced and exchanged, the feudal organisation of agriculture and manufacturing industry, in one word, the feudal relations of property became no longer compatible with the already developed productive forces; they became so many fetters. They had to be burst asunder; they were burst asunder."[58]

The most forceful recent exponent of this view of the Revolution has been Albert Soboul: "The French Revolution took 'the truly revolutionary way' from feudalism to capitalism. By wiping out every surviving feudal relic, by setting the peasant free from every seigneurial right and church tithe—and to a certain extent from most communal dues—by destroying corporative monopolies and unifying trade on a national basis, the French Revolution marked a decisive stage in the development of capitalism. The suppression of feudal estates set free small direct producers. . . . Henceforth, with the entirely new relations of production, capital was removed from the stresses and strains of feudalism . . . [which] finally ensured the autonomy of capitalist production both in the agricultural and in the industrial sectors. . . . The agrarian question occupies a crucial position in the bourgeois revolution."[59]

At least one eighteenth-century commentator, the lawyer and revolutionary Barnave, expounded a view which has some striking resemblances to this position. For Barnave, European feudalism was intimately linked to the dominance of landed property. The irretrievably opposed claims of commercial and industrial property have time and again, in his view, fueled risings

56. The Third Estate of Lyon, for example, wishes to encourage commercial activity by making it more honorable, proposing ennoblement for merchants distinguished by their "probity and worth"; that those who follow their fathers into commerce be honored; that the merchant marine be a career route into the royal navy and that commercial activity not remove someone from the nobility (*AP* 3:613).

57. George V. Taylor, "Noncapitalist Wealth and the Origins of the French Revolution," *American Historical Review* 72 (1967): 469–96.

58. Karl Marx and Frederick Engels, "Manifesto of the Communist Party," in *Selected Works* (Moscow: Foreign Languages Publishing House, 1955), 1:39.

59. Albert Soboul, *The French Revolution, 1787–1799. From the Storming of the Bastille to Napoleon* (New York: Vintage Books, 1975), 8.

against aristocratic rule: in the challenge of the medieval urban communes to the territorial lords, in the Reformation's defiance of the pope, and most recently, in the political revolutions of modern Europe, first in England and currently in France. If the physiocratic critique of the seigneurial regime was structured around an inefficient and blocked agriculture, for Barnave what was central to the Revolution in which he was a most prominent participant, was the assertion of new forms of wealth against agriculture.[60]

Other individual observers, may, like Barnave, have held some such view. We see, however, that in the spring of 1789, the Third Estate, while commenting frequently on the seigneurial regime and strongly concerned for the French economy, does not, on the whole seem to have connected the two in any general way. The formulation, central to contemporary historical debate, of a new economic order forcing the displacement of an older social structure was not a universally held part of the outlook of the urban notables at the outbreak of the Revolution. Nor are discussions of private property associated with the seigneurial regime. If the physiocrats were unhappy about privileges that clouded the claims of an individual to own a parcel of land,[61] there is no connection between the two concepts in the *cahiers*. In short, the economic institutions of a developing capitalism and the structures of domination of rural France did not, in general, enter into the same framework at the outbreak of the Revolution.

Further Explorations

In light of all that has been said on this subject from Barnave to the current day, the complete and consistent rejection of any relationship shown in Tables 4.17 and 4.19 is startling. Is it perhaps misleading? Certainly one can find *cahiers* that exhibit explicit economic rationales for their positions on seigneurial rights. The peasants of Molitard in the *bailliage* of Blois, for example, oppose the *champart* because it impoverishes the land and discourages agriculture,[62] a reasonable complaint about the payment of a portion of the crop.[63] Or consider the Third Estate of Hennebont whose

60. Antoine-Pierre-Marie Barnave, *Power, Property and History: Barnave's Introduction to the French Revolution and Other Writings* (New York: Harper and Row, 1971).

61. Weulersse, *Mouvement physiocratique,* 2:3–4; Elizabeth Fox-Genovese, *The Origins of Physiocracy: Economic Revolution and Social Order in Eighteenth-Century France* (Ithaca: Cornell University Press, 1976).

62. Fréderic Lesueur and Alfred Cauchie, *Cahiers de doléances du bailliage de Blois et du bailliage secondaire de Romorantin pour les états généraux de 1789* (Blois: Imprimerie Emmanuel Rivière, 1907), 1:369.

63. Payment of a fixed portion of the harvest may drastically cut into profit margins or even exceed them (a critique that infuses the physiocrats' call for taxation on the "net product"). There are also serious collection costs. Finally, the formal embodiment of rights to such revenues in edicts and judicial decisions that specify claims on particular portions of particular crops, creates a powerful

proposal for restricting mutation fees to certain kinds of transactions (at, moreover, a reduced rate) is put forward with the avowed aim of facilitating the sale of property.[64]

There are, indeed, many such arguments in the *cahiers*. But if the authors of the *cahiers de doléances* explicitly relate the seigneurial regime to their economic concerns, why don't the tables that we have examined show a co-occurrence of grievances? Let us look more closely at the two documents just cited. The peasant of Molitard argue that the *champart* injures French agriculture and the notables of Hennebont contend that mutation fees hinder the operation of the market; but neither these peasants nor those urban notables claim that the seigneurial regime, taken as a whole, is an obstacle to economic advance. Could it be that although the seigneurial regime as a whole does not seem to come up for discussion to any marked degree in *cahiers* marked by developmental concerns, nevertheless, there are *particular* seigneurial rights that are most definitely seen as economically critical institutions? Tables 4.20 and 4.21 show this indeed to be very much the case. In these tables we take the same variables that entered into Tables 4.17 and 4.19. Instead of exploring the mean differences in extensiveness and salience of discussions of seigneurial rights, we cross-tabulate these variables with the presence or absence of discussions of particular seigneurial rights. Of the large number of possible coefficients available to summarize the strength of associations in such cross-tabulations, I present Goodman and Kruskal's gamma.

In examining the tables we are at once struck by how often hunting rights, pigeon-raising and rabbit-raising are associated with concerns for agriculture. A link with protective measures is transparently obvious, but the link to concern with methods of working the land and with the development of new land (as well as with proposals to free commerce from restrictions) show that there is some more abstract sense of agricultural productivity at work here. Note that the lord's right to amuse himself by constructing and stocking fishponds, far less destructive of agriculture, simply has none of the same associations for the Third Estate in 1789, although it is a commonplace for historians' discussions to group it with the other recreational privileges.

The only other right so frequently highly associated with the state of French agriculture is the right to dues on property transfers, which, as the notables of Hennebont just reminded us, were a striking interference with

group of revenue-collectors with a strong interest in blocking the introduction of new crops on which their claims are legally uncertain. See Gabriel Ardant, *Théorie sociologique de l'impôt* (Paris: Service d'Edition et de Vente des Publications de l'Education Nationale, 1965), 1:207–15, 407–12.

64. P. Thomas-Lacroix, *Les cahiers de doléances de la sénéchausée d'Hennebont (Extrait de Mémoires de la Société d'Histoire et d'Archéologie de Bretagne,* vol. 25 (Rennes: Imprimerie Bretonne, 1955), 89.

the market. Like the recreational privileges, this right, too, is prone to be treated by *cahiers* concerned with freedom of commerce as well. As for the other large associations in these tables, most are with rights that, to one degree or another, constitute market hindrances. The monopoly of the winepress, quite understandably a concern of those *cahiers* concerned with wine-growing, is also important to those proposing subsidies for agricultural development; the monopoly on milling is rather reasonably associated with the freedom of the grain trade. *Retrait,* like mutation fees, disrupts land sales and has its share of associations (although we find the particular associations baffling). In fact, six of our eight agricultural categories are associated with either the dues on property transfers or *retrait* or both. Compulsory labor services, rights over fairs and markets, and seigneurial tolls account for several other of the associations here.

Most of the associations in Table 4.20 are either organized around the ravages of the lord's amusements or the hindrances to the market. But there are a few others. *Champart,* as the country people of Molitard pointed out, stood out among periodic dues for its restraint of production and is the only such payment to have any large associations with agriculture. What we are, perhaps, surprised by is that it is not more frequently tied to developmental concerns. If the reasons that *champart* is linked to protective measures in particular are mysterious, that the lord's monopoly on arms is so linked is far less so. The disarmed peasantry was rendered helpless against game and against the lord's own rabbits and pigeons. (Might the lord's claim to a portion of the crop be experienced as a form of parasitism alongside other forms—the lord's rabbits and pigeons, livestock disease, wolves, and partridges—that threatened the fruits of peasant labor?)

In sum, particular seigneurial rights are linked to economic concerns. Yet these connections are weak. They are not generalized to the aggregate of seigneurial rights as a collectivity, to recall our discussion above. And there is not a single significant association in Tables 4.20 and 4.21 between *any* of our fourteen categories and general discussions of the seigneurial regime. We do not see, then, that the Third Estate had embraced an elaborated developmentalist ideology in which the regime was grasped as a whole and taken as a barrier to progress.

But there are other limitations to the ways in which the seigneurial rights are tied to developmental concerns. Property-transfer dues apart, the most consistent associations are with the recreational privileges, which account for one-third of all the associations in this table. There is a heavy emphasis, then, on the direct physical destruction of crops at the hands of the lords and their servitors. The restrictions on the market (again excepting mutation fees) are far less frequently implicated by developmental thinking. And *champart,* so clear an obstacle to growth for contemporary economic historians and the peasants of Molitard alike, has only one significant

Table 4.20. Measures of Association (Gamma) Between Third Estate Discussions of Individual Seigneurial Rights and the Development of French Agriculture

Seigneurial Right	(1) Encouragements to Agriculture	(1a) Rewards for Achievement in Agriculture	(2) Protective Measures	(3) Developing New Land	(4) Agricultural Methods	(5) Production of Alcoholic Beverages	(6) Animal Raising	(7) Any Discussion of Agricultural Improvement
Miscellaneous right	.42**	.23	.11	.06	.20	.00	.28	.38*
Regime in general	.05	.27	.20	−.01	.21	−.15	−.31	.07
Monopolies in general	−.07	−.05	.08	.17	.07	−.01	−.01	.05
Monopoly on ovens	.15	.35*	.11	−.06	.02	.02	.24	.05
Monopoly on milling	.17	.17	.18	.09	.24	−.03	−.05	.14
Monopoly on wine press	.36*	.15	.26	−.02	.22	.36*	.07	.19
Right to bear arms	.03	.08	.34*	.12	.07	−.03	.31	.44*
Dues on fairs and markets	.28	.50**	.23	.24	−.01	a	a	.21
Compulsory labor services	−.04	.15	.27*	.19	.15	a	a	.13
Miscellaneous periodic dues	.12	a	.13	.11	a	−.04	a	.12
Periodic dues in general	.10	a	.16	.32	.18	−.04	a	.11
Cens	.30	a	.07	.30	a	a	a	.33

Champart	−.03	a	.36**	−.06	−.05	.17	.15	.37*
Cens et rentes	−.21	a	.09	.06	.34	.05	−.61	−.13
Lods et ventes	.18	.52**	.08	.38**	−.18	.42*	.53**	.45*
Retrait féodal	.10	.53**	.37**	.18	.05	.05	.59***	.35
Hunting rights	.16	.18	.42**	.36*	.40*	.01	.16	.43**
Right to raise pigeons	−.12	.05	.50***	.26*	.51**	.34*	.07	.57***
Right to raise rabbits	.08	.34	.55***	.30*	.46**	−.36	.27	.52*
Fishing rights	.31	a	.14	.04	*	a	a	.23
Serfdom in general	.22	a	.06	.44*	*	a	a	.01
Mainmorte	.10	a	.31*	−.18	.44*	−.17	−.13	.04
Seigneurial tolls	.29*	.25	.23	.08	−.10	−.12	.19	.07
Seigneurial courts, miscellaneous	.02	.07	.19	.09	.02	−.27	−.22	.07
Seigneurial courts in general	.07	.28	.05	.15	.07	−.06	.29	.05

[a]Distributions prevent meaningful computations

*$p < .05$
**$p < .01$.
***$p < .001$.

Table 4.21. Measures of Association (Gamma) Between Third Estate Discussions of Individual Seigneurial Rights and Concern with Industry, Finance, or Commerce

Seigneurial Right	(1) Any Grievances Concerning Industry	(2) Any Grievances Concerning Finance	(3) Freedom of Grain Trade	(4) Two (or more) Demands Dealing with Freedom of Commerce	(5) Any Three (or more) Grievances Dealing with Commerce	(6) Private Property
Miscellaneous right	−.07	.30*	.19	.39*	.45*	−.08
Regime in general	−.12	.21	−.02	.11	.08	.08
Monopolies in general	−.13	.23	.01	.09	.15	.04
Monopoly on ovens	.33*	.03	.29	.07	−.02	.20
Monopoly on milling	.13	.06	.31*	.12	.03	.16
Monopoly on wine press	.22	−.02	.26	.07	.19	.16
Right to bear arms	−.19	.22	.24	.22	.39	.02
Dues on fairs and markets	.10	.45*	−.01	−.14	−.19	.35*
Compulsory labor services	.01	.31*	.06	−.03	.29	.08
Miscellaneous periodic dues	−.21	.04	a	.16	a	−.01
Periodic dues in general	.26	.16	.39*	.51**	.76*	−.09

Cens	.20	.46*	.04	−.02	a	.15
Champart	−.22	.09	.12	.14	.07	.24
Cens et rentes	.15	−.25	−.05	.16	−.05	.02
Dues on property transfers (*lods et ventes*)	.12	.07	.01	.30*	.16	.23
Retrait féodal	.03	.34*	−.06	.01	.25	−.07
Hunting rights	.17	.23	.34*	.29*	.40*	.20
Right to raise pigeons	.32*	−.02	.22	.37**	.41*	.06
Right to raise rabbits	−.03	.10	.11	.40**	.66*	.15
Fishing rights	.20	.24	a	−.13	a	−.01
Serfdom in general	−.16	.56*	−.04	−.30	a	−.19
Mainmorte	−.03	.30	−.26	−.01	.17	−.15
Seigneurial tolls	−.11	.33*	−.17	.14	.32*	.12
Seigneurial courts, miscellaneous	.01	.39*	.13	−.08	.17	−.01
Seigneurial courts in general	.19	.24	.18	.17	.21	.02

[a]Distributions prevent meaningful computations

*$p < .05$.
**$p < .01$.
***$p < .001$.

association. The people of Molitard are not typical of the countryside at that moment. In short, the pattern of linkages of seigneurial rights and broad economic concerns shows a limited vision and is only clear in visible collisions of animals and grain; it does not (yet?) extend to more abstract clashes of legal structures and investment.

In this same vein, note that a central concept of the capitalist economy in the making, private property, is almost untainted by any relationship (positive or negative) with discussions of seigneurial rights. This was, we suggest, because this sacred catchword was serviceable not merely as a justification for eliminating the old order, but as a justification for barring its elimination as well. Recall the frequency with which property is invoked by noble defenders of their prerogatives (see Chapter 2, p. 34). We are likely to associate the modern idea of property with the physiocrats' defense of it, with their attempt to conceive of an absolute property, unburdened by other claims than the will of an owner.[65] The *cahier* Dupont wrote for the Third Estate of Nemours has something of this spirit: "For there is something beautiful, noble and pleasing in the status of landowner, above all in the status of landowner of the Third Estate. . . . This class of citizens has not a single concern which opposes those of their fellow citizens. The better they pursue their own affairs, the more food is created, and raw materials, goods and riches for all men, prosperity for the country and power for the state" (*AP* 4:197). Yes, he goes on, seigneurial revenue is property, too. But the power to vex another and to trouble his labor cannot be anyone's property (*AP* 4:197). On these grounds, then, seigneurial dues must be subject to indemnification.

Now consider the nobles of Saintonge. They, like the Third Estate of Nemours, uphold the claims of liberty and of property with the greatest determination. Their *cahier* begins by forcefully forbidding their deputies to agree to any taxes, borrowing, or spending whatsoever without obtaining a series of laws, the very first of which would "assure our personal liberty and our properties." They go on to explain that "as for the significance of the word property, the order of the nobility understands it to mean all mobile and immobile possessions of each individual, notably all rights inherent in fiefs, such as the right to hunt (except in prohibited times), the right to fish, the monopolies, the labor dues, pigeon and rabbit-raising, mutation fees, *cens,* regular cash payments, *champarts, retraits,* infeudated tithes: in short all property, whether real or fictive, for which a claim may be justified either by inheritance or by titles, or by possession, or finally by legal disposition" (*AP* 5:665). No wonder those who speak of private property were no more nor less likely than others to discuss the seigneurial regime. This use of

65. For an interesting recent exposition, see Fox-Genovese, *Origins of Physiocracy,* 200–201, 228.

"property" as the standard under which marched both opponents and defenders of the seigneurial regime came to be an important element of the legislative debates (see Chapter 9, p. 531).

If, then, some developmental concerns were tied to specific seigneurial rights, this was not yet the vision of the feudal shackles to be broken. The outlook of Barnave (written down in 1792 or 1793) has a coherence that is only partly in place for the urban notables of 1789. Why, then, were the seigneurial regime and the necessities of economic progress not more forcefully, consistently, and generally seen as part of a single discussion at the outbreak of the Revolution? It has, after all, seemed to many scholars that a modern economy is necessarily antithetical to feudal anachronisms. But lords in the eighteenth century were often able to use their seigneurial rights as the very vehicles for modernization. If, on the one hand, *retrait,* say, interfered with the market in land, it was also a central mechanism in the lord's drive to expand and consolidate his holdings to take advantage of commercial opportunity. A stricter enforcement of seigneurial dues could be a mechanism to break the rural community. Saint Jacob has shown in practice how the same concerns that undergirded the thought of the physiocrats, promoted an intensification of the seigneurial system in Burgundy.[66] The very concept of private property was appropriated by those defending the past as well as by those advancing into the future; indeed, nobles, more than urban notables, invoke property rights (see Chapter 2, p. 34).

The notion that the seigneurial regime, as it existed in 1789, was unambiguously and totally irreconcilable with capitalist economic practice was vigorously challenged by Georges Lefebvre. The scrupulous (and thoroughly bourgeois) patterns of estate management of noble lords has been documented in detail by Robert Forster; the degree to which the conceptual apparatus with which the lord's legal advisers defended the claims was already using the language of property and contract has been shown by Régine Robin. Considered as an aggregate of individual claims, seigneurial rights could be instruments of economic change as well as obstacles. If those committed to believe themselves in the forefront of human advance were to identify "feudalism" with the retrograde institutions to be eliminated, that feudalism could not be coextensive with the rights of the lords. There might be a narrow concept, a subset of the seigneurial rights that would be held to exhaust a category of "feudal rights" to be rigorously defined; there might be a broader concept, grouping some of the seigneurial rights and much else besides as constituting what needed to be destroyed in order to liberate France. But "feudal and seigneurial rights," a generic term in so many Third Estate *cahiers* in the spring of 1789, would

66. Saint Jacob, *Paysans de la Bourgogne du Nord,* esp. 405–34.

have to cease being used as virtually synonymous. Under the tremendous pressures of the Revolution, both a narrower and a broader notion of "feudalism" were eventually forged.[67] What was grouped together in the discussion of "feudalism" on August 4 had been partly, but only partly, brought together in the *cahiers* of the spring.

Honor and Income: The Two Seigneurial Regimes of the Nobility

Two Kinds of Rights

By way of contrast let us consider the *cahiers* of the nobility. To examine the web of associations of the seigneurial regime in the texts of the nobility is to do something quite different than merely to parallel this chapter's earlier analyses. That analytic strategy rested on the degree to which the Third Estate implicitly conceived of the seigneurial regime as having some sort of unity. It then became possible to develop some simple quantitative measures for the extensiveness with which that unity was discussed and the salience of that unity compared to other subjects. This in turn permitted an analysis of the degree to which the presence or absence of other subjects was associated with the extensiveness and salience of discussions of the seigneurial regime.

It would be convenient although it might be monotonous if a similar strategy were a reasonable one for the nobility. This strategy is inappropriate, however, for the nobles' seigneurial regime does not exhibit the unity of the Third Estate's. For the Third Estate, to review Tables 4.1 and 4.2, *cahiers* that discuss any particular seigneurial right are, with few exceptions, prone to discuss others as well. But for the nobility, as Table 4.4 showed, discussions of about half the seigneurial rights treated are not associated with discussions of other rights.

The distinction between the honorific and the income-producing aspects of the seigneurial regime has appeared so frequently in our earlier analyses, has been invoked so frequently in the *cahiers* themselves, and has played such a large role in the historical literature, that it seems worth exploring whether these two classes of rights are conceived of quite independently by the nobles. Although, as remarked earlier, many rights have both aspects to some degree, it is not too difficult to classify most of the 21 categories discussed in 5 or more noble *cahiers* as primarily lucrative (the eighteenth-

67. The points made in this paragraph are elaborated upon in Chapter 9. The relevant references to Lefebvre, Forster, and Robin are in that chapter's footnotes.

century euphemism was "useful") or primarily honorific. Anything that involved a payment in cash, kind, or labor to the lord we classified as lucrative even if the payment was small as the *cens* or *corvée* usually were. An exploration of the "miscellaneous" category revealed that these are usually rather obscure payments and not obscure recognitions of honor and so this category, too was counted as lucrative. Serfdom and *mainmorte* are more difficult, since it is not a particular payment that is at issue but rather restrictions on the mobility of the local labor force. Since this conferred material advantage, we counted these here as well. Honorific rights, then, were those that did not involve such economic advantage, even though hunting and pigeon-raising have culinary consequences. Three of our categories we failed to classify either way. Seigneurial rights in general could only be classified if we knew a priori whether the 34 noble *cahiers* that explicitly speak of these rights as a collectivity have in mind honor or income or both. The two categories that deal with seigneurial justice were also not assigned to one group or the other because of the developing debate over the economic value of the lords' courts.[68]

Table 4.22 shows how discussions of particular seigneurial rights are associated with discussions of lucrative rights generally and Table 4.23 does the same for the honorific rights. We see in Table 4.22, for example, that *cahiers* which take up compulsory labor services take up two more from among the other lucrative rights than those which do not, that these make up a difference of 1.3% of all demands and that both these differences are statistically significant. Documents dealing with symbolic deference patterns, on the other hand, are only barely more likely to take up lucrative rights than those that do not. Examining both tables together we see that consideration of an honorific right is rarely associated with greater attention to those that produce income (see the honorific group in Table 4.22); consideration of a lucrative right is rarely associated with greater attention to honor (see the lucrative group in Table 4.23); while consideration of rights of either group are often, although far from always, associated with more extensive treatment of and greater salience to rights of the same kind (see the lucrative group in Table 4.22 and the honorific group in Table 4.23).

The lucrative and the honorific appear to be fairly distinct categories for the nobility—at least to the extent to which they are categories at all. While these categories appear to have some internal coherence, it certainly is less than the unity the class of *all* seigneurial rights possessed for the Third Estate. Nor are the two groups wholly disjoint. The rights to hunt and raise

68. Olwen Hufton, "Le paysan et la loi en France au XVIIIe siècle," *Annales: Economies, Sociétés, Civilisations* 38 (1983); Peter M. Jones, "Parish, Seigneurie and the Community of Inhabitants in Southern Central France During the Eighteenth and Nineteenth Centuries," *Past and Present*, no. 91 (1981): 90–96; and Chapter 3.

Table 4.22. Differences in Numbers of Distinct Lucrative Rights Associated with Particular Lucrative Rights, with Particular Honorific Rights, and with Other Rights in Noble *Cahiers*

Seigneurial Rights	Number of Distinct Lucrative Rights Discussed	Grievances Concerning Lucrative Rights as a Percentage of All Demands
Lucrative[a]		
Miscellaneous right	0.8*	0.6%*
Monopolies in general	0.8*	0.8**
Dues on fairs and markets	1.5	2.0
Compulsory labor services	2.0***	1.3*
Periodic dues in general	2.1***	0.7*
Cens	2.3*	1.6
Champart	2.0**	1.6*
Dues on property transfers (*lods et ventes*)	2.2	1.5
Serfdom in general	0.7	0.4
Mainmorte	2.1	2.1
Seigneurial tolls	0.6**	0.7**
Honorific		
Symbolic deference patterns in general	0.1	0.1
Honorific rights	−0.2	−0.4
Right to bear arms	0.4	0.1
Avowal and enumeration	0.9	0.6
Fealty and homage	0.1	−0.2
Hunting rights	0.9*	0.7*
Right to raise pigeons	1.6**	1.0*
Other		
Seigneurial regime in general	0.7*	0.4
Seigneurial courts, miscellaneous	0.4	0.3
Seigneurial courts in general	0.9**	0.4

[a]The seigneurial right indicated in the left-hand column is excluded from the computations presented here.

*$p < .05$ (1-tailed t-test).
**$p < .01$ (1-tailed t-test).
***$p < .001$ (1-tailed t-test).

pigeons, honorific in our rough-and-ready classification, are the only such rights, Table 4.22 shows, to be associated with the lucrative group as well. Were these additions to the lord's dinner table experienced as a sort of income supplement? As for our efforts at identifying the lucrative, note that the lord's power to compel use of his resources or to command labor on his lands or *château* are equally noteworthy in their honorific aspect.

The unclassified categories ("other" in the tables) are also noteworthy.

Table 4.23. Differences in Numbers of Distinct Honorific Rights Associated with Particular Honorific Rights, with Particular Lucrative Rights, and with Other Rights in Noble *Cahiers*

Seigneurial Rights	Number of Distinct Honorific Rights Discussed	Grievances Concerning Honorific Rights as a Percentage of All Demands
Honorific[a]		
Symbolic deference patterns in general		
Honorific rights	0.2	0.2
Right to bear arms	0.6**	0.4*
Avowal and enumeration	1.2*	0.3
Fealty and homage	1.3	0.7**
Hunting rights	0.7***	0.3*
Right to raise pigeons	1.0**	0.8**
Lucrative		
Miscellaneous	0.2	0.1
Monopolies in general	0.7*	0.9*
Dues on fairs and markets	0.4	0.0
Compulsory labor services	1.2***	1.0**
Periodic dues in general	0.8	1.2
Cens	0.6	0.2
Champart	0.4	0.0
Mutation fees	0.5	0.0
Serfdom in general	0.5	0.7
Mainmorte	0.6	0.2
Seigneurial tolls	0.2	0.3
Other		
Regime in general	0.6***	0.6*
Seigneurial courts, miscellaneous	0.3	0.4
Seigneurial courts in general	0.6**	0.5*

[a]The seigneurial right indicated in the left-hand column is excluded from the computations presented here.

*$p < .05$ (1-tailed t-test).
**$p < .01$ (1-tailed t-test).
***$p < .001$ (1-tailed t-test).

Discussions of the seigneurial regime in general occur in *cahiers* with more extensive discussions of honor, but are not particularly linked to questions of income. When the nobles speak of the seigneurial regime as a whole, perhaps by using "the seigneurial rights" or some equivalent as a global category, the concrete rights they are apt to have in mind concern their status distinctions and not their pocketbooks.[69] "Seigneurial courts in gen-

69. On the nobles' distinctive concern for honor, see Chapter 2.

eral" is also associated with the honorific and not the lucrative category. The French nobility did not see (or at least publicly claimed not to see) their rights of justice as importantly income-producing, thus taking the view of some of the recent scholars of this institution.[70]

That the nobles see something like two seigneurial regimes where the Third Estate sees one can be emphasized in a somewhat different fashion. Table 4.24 classifies the noble *cahiers* into those that do or do not have grievances concerning any of the lucrative rights and that do or do not have grievances concerning any of the honorific rights. This table again underscores the role of honor for the nobility in that rather more documents discuss matters of honor than income (79 vs. 68). What is even more striking is that there is little relationship between discussing the two classes of rights at all; the low gamma of .22 is not significant. By way of rather dramatic contrast, the corresponding gamma for the Third Estate is .70 and that relationship is significant at the .001 level.[71] Quite clearly, honorific rights and income-producing rights are barely, if at all, spoken of in the same context by the French nobility; quite the contrary is the thinking of the Third Estate. For the Third Estate, there is a seigneurial regime, one seigneurial regime.

Two Webs of Association

To explore the institutional associations of the seigneurial rights for the nobility, we must proceed in a somewhat different manner than for the Third Estate. Conceptually, we should take into account the bifurcated sense of those rights for the nobles; methodologically, we need to be sensitive to a

Table 4.24. Co-occurrence of Lucrative and Honorific Rights in Noble *Cahiers*

		Cahier Discusses At Least One Lucrative Right		
		No	Yes	Total
Cahier discusses at least one honorific right	No	57	30	87
	Yes	41	38	79
Total		98	68	166

Note: Gamma = .22 (not significant).

70. See, for example, Hufton, "Paysan et loi," 682.

71. If one objects that the Third Estate's discussions of lucrative and honorific rights ought not to be divided into "none" and "one or more" because the frequency of mention is so much greater than for the nobility, one might alternately dichotomize both groups of rights at the median number discussed. By this procedure, such a cross-tabulation produces a gamma of .41; the relationship is significant at less than the .005 level.

much greater scarcity of noble discussions of any of these rights than was true for the Third Estate. We shall proceed by exploring the distinction between documents that do or do not have discussions of any honorific or lucrative right, rather than, as for the Third Estate, examine the numbers of such rights discussed and the proportions of such demands among all grievances. While this runs the methodological risks discussed above to the effect that phenomena of real interest may be obscured by the propensity of *cahiers* that are merely longer to be talking of all sorts of subjects, there are some safeguards. By comparing the associations of honorific as opposed to lucrative rights and by comparing the presence or absence of such associations with different demands, we are protected from the possible errors of interpretation of a single association in isolation. We shall look for such associations with the institutions that figured in the earlier discussions in this chapter. Institutions associated with the lucrative but not the honorific rights are shown in Table 4.25, listed in descending order of the size of the association; Table 4.26 is the equivalent for the honorific rights; and Table 4.27 shows those institutions associated with both classes of seigneurial rights (in descending order of association with the honorific). I show only statistically significant relationships in any of these tables.

There are few surprises here. There are some developmental concerns that are related to the seigneurial regime as was the case for the Third Estate. Questions of industrial production, however, are in no way tied to

Table 4.25. Institutions Associated Only with Lucrative Rights in Noble *Cahiers*

Institutions Whose Discussion in *Cahiers* Is Significantly Associated with Discussion of Any Lucrative Seigneurial Rights (But Not with Honorific Rights)	Association (Gamma)
Torture in judicial procedure	.56*
Casuels	.51**
Any discussion of communal rights	.49***
Taxes on manufactured goods	.46**
Guilds	.45**
Annates	.44**
Any demand concerning industry (other than guilds)	.42**
Any demand concerning religion (other than tithe or *casuels*)	.40**
Tithe	.34*
Droit d'insinuation	.34*
Any demand to abolish religious institution or practice (other than tithe or *casuels*)	.32*
Any demand showing hostility to central government	.32*

*$p < .05$.
**$p < .01$.
***$p < .001$.

Table 4.26. Institutions Associated Only with Honorific Rights in Noble *Cahiers*

Institutions Whose Discussion in *Cahiers* Is Significantly Associated with Discussion of Any Honorific Seigneurial Rights (But Not with Lucrative Rights)	Association (Gamma)
Rewards for military achievement	.64***
Titles of nobility	.57**
Private property	.37**
Ennoblement	.30*
Vote by order in Estates-General	.29*
Tax advantages for nobility	.28*
Ecclesiastical benefices	.26*

*p < .05.
**p < .01.
***p < .001.

Table 4.27. Institutions Associated with Both Lucrative and Honorific Rights in Noble *Cahiers*

Institutions Whose Discussion in *Cahiers* Is Significantly Associated Both With Discussion of Any Lucrative Seigneurial Rights and Any Honorific Seigneurial Rights	Associations (Gamma)	
	Lucrative Rights	Honorific Rights
Any demands concerning military affairs	.63**	.71***
Four or more demands concerning agriculture	.53***	.30*
Five or more demands concerning military affairs	.51**	.39**
Franc-fief	.50**	.52***
Two or more demands regarding commerce	.48**	.29*
Salt tax	.42**	.33*
Intendants	.41*	.81***
Taxes on alcoholic beverages	.32*	.30*
Tax advantages	.30*	.46**

*p < .05.
**p < .01.
***p < .001.

the lord's claims on honor: thus demands concerning both guilds and other aspects of manufacturing are associated only with the income-producing rights, as is "taxes on manufactured goods." The *droit d'insinuation,* in principle a tax on transfers on movable property rather than on real estate, perhaps belongs in this group as well. Questions of commerce and agriculture, on the other hand, are implicitly experienced as linked to both clusters of seigneurial rights; their linkage to the honorific group is probably more specifically a link to the rights to hunt and to raise pigeons so widely excoriated for crop damage. The contrast between the honorable character of agrarian activity and the (at best) neutral character of manufacturing bears out the standard view of how the ideology of nobility evaluated different arenas of economic enterprise.

Some of the visible social distinctions of the Old Regime are associated with the honorific rights. We are not surprised that the nobility understood these rights as part and parcel of a hierarchical vision of society. What is perhaps most worthy of note in this regard is the *absence* of an association. Little in the half-year before the Estates-General met was so bitterly debated as the very structure of that body. The Parlement of Paris had generated a political explosion when it pronounced for what was understood to be an Estates-General organized in the customary way: namely as three autonomous bodies. If each order were to vote separately, of course, the privileged would feel confident in their capacity to dominate.

This is one of the handful of issues over which the noble and Third Estate *cahiers* were most sharply polarized;[72] and when the Estates met it proved to be the impasse that led frustrated deputies to announce themselves to constitute a new body, the National Assembly, thereby self-consciously abandoning the Old Regime. What is striking about noble discussions of the issue, is that it is the public honor and not the incomes of the lords that appear associated for them with this debate. It is as if the symbolic distinctions inherent in the division of representatives of the Three Estates gathering at the center of national power—the prescribed differences in dress and behavior toward the king, the ceremonial entrances that clearly demarcated three distinct bodies, in short the theatrical aspect of the Estates-General of old—are held to be of a piece with the local symbols of differential status. But the obvious material consequences of the voting rule is not translated into an equally clear link with the material benefits of the seigneurial regime. The absence of even an implicit association here is one of the strongest indicators of the seriousness of the lords' frequently repeated claim of indifference to material but not prestigious distinctions. Indeed, the entire list of institutions that are only linked to honor is of great interest. The nobles, it appears, can only defend their tax advantages or their bid for control of the Estates-General as matters of honor. Their public discourse stays away from coupling their prerogatives with anyone's material interests, including their own.

Note too that discussions of "private property" are, in the nobles' texts, associated with honorific but not with income-bearing rights. It is in the defense of those claims that are the hardest to conceive as property, that the French nobility was most zealous in pressing its arguments in such terms. To argue that claims on periodic payments in cash or in kind

72. Shapiro and Markoff, *Revolutionary Demands*, chap. 15.

constituted property would be to argue what even the critics of the seigneurial regime might readily concede (as the physiocratic *cahier* of the Third Estate of Nemours, for example, shows clearly; *AP* 4:197). It was of less moment, then, even for those nobles with some interest in retaining them, to defend such rights as property, since much of the Third Estate already would have granted the point. It was precisely the claims that were least plausible that most reliably evoked this defense. In this opportunistic stretching of "property," did the nobles contribute to vitiating the later attempts of the new government to remind the peasants of the respect owed property rights?

Like the Third Estate, the nobility were prone to write of a variety of other payments, to church or state, when they wrote of the seigneurial regime. While many of these are associated with the lucrative rights alone, it is noteworthy that several of them are associated with the honorific as well. Perhaps it is, again, the very concept of privilege that underlies this link. Certainly for *franc-fief,* the most strongly associated tax, the very distinction made between noble and common land is a fundamental premise on which that tax rested. We see, too, that the broad category of "tax advantages" is even more strongly associated with honorific rights than it is with lucrative ones. The more specific "tax advantages of nobility" is also only associated with the lords' claims to honor.

Some of the very strongest associations with the lords' honor (and the lords' claims on income for that matter) have nothing to do with taxation at all, but are discussions of military affairs. We see again the intimate moral association in which the military service of the lords of the past or of the noble officers of the present was an essential justification for privileges. And if the growing central power had largely, as Tocqueville held, destroyed the rationale on which that privilege rested, we are struck that the very largest association of any institution with the honorific rights is the *intendants,* the most visible agents of the centralized despotism that had gnawed away at autonomous authority.

The Third Estate Considers the Seigneurial Regime

Alfred Cobban, in his attempt to debunk the relevance of feudalism for the understanding of the Revolution, commented: "Whatever qualifications or limitations we have to introduce, however, the close association, almost equal to an identification, between the attack on seigneurial rights and the attack on 'feudalism' must remain the basic fact on which all discussion of the latter must centre. If 'feudalism' in 1789 did not mean seigneurial rights, it meant nothing."[73] But if "feudalism" meant at least the seigneurial rights, it does not follow that it meant nothing else.[74] We have explored the other institutions that the Third Estate closely associated with those rights, to discover something of the structure of the institutions of the Old Regime as experienced at the beginning of the Revolution. We have not tried to discern what they said they meant by feudalism, but what they meant in practice, whether they said they meant it or not. We have glimpsed a moment in the elaboration of a web of associations. Or, rather, several webs.

For the upper reaches of the Third Estate, in the spring of 1789, some of the seigneurial rights were quite clearly seen as economic nuisances. Here in embryo is the conception of a past whose central institutions are so many barriers to economic growth: whose obligations fetter an idea of progress identified with material advance; and in which hindrances to the operation of the market are the legacies of darkness. For Barnave and still later for many Marxists the sweeping away of such a past was the heart of the Revolution. We see this meaning of feudalism in the *cahiers* in embryo; but only in embryo.

We have also seen a partial realization of the shaky consensus of August 4, in which "feudalism" was taken as the core of an Old Regime in which seigneurial rights and the reign of privilege were of a piece, a conception recently elaborated upon by Jerome Blum. For Tocqueville, the center of the Revolution was a clearing away of outworn privilege no longer justified by current social responsibilities; the Revolution destroyed rights that had cast off the moorings of duty. Indeed, for Tocqueville, the legitimacy of all differential claims to honor had become problematic before the power of the idea of democracy. If August 4 was a step toward an image of the past as the locus of outworn privilege and of the seigneurial rights as a constituent part of such an image, then several months earlier, the authors of the *cahiers* had taken a step toward that step.

We may now suggest the great significance to be found in the association of the very limited anticlericalism of the *cahiers* with the seigneurial regime—and the association, indeed, of discussions of religion of whatever stripe. This link may represent the pervasiveness of a view that linked church and lord as representatives of a benighted past. We may refer to this as the Voltairean identification of the forces of reaction. This great and tireless publicist portrayed a dying world of ignorance, greed, and inhumanity in his depiction of the evils of serfdom in which he was able to bring about a fusion

73. Cobban, *Social Interpretation,* 34–35.

74. By August 1789, "feudalism" was also used in a narrow as well as in the broad way considered at this point; the narrow way meant something well short of the entire bundle of seigneurial rights (see Chapter 9).

of his animosity against the feudal past and his ecclesiastical enemies.[75] The serf-holding monasteries of eastern France became the perfect target. Voltaire was far from alone, toward the end of the Old Regime, in identifying as a single entity the worst in both seigneurial and ecclesiastical life, an outlook that seemed an inexhaustible source of lurid or learned fantasy.[76] This anticlericalism had only limited reign in the *cahiers,* apart from the critiques of tithe and *casuels;* but the association of religion and the seigneurial regime ran deeper.

The sense of rupture is essential to the felt experience of revolution. Nowhere did the revolutionaries create for themselves this sense of discontinuity with greater deliberation than in breaking with the calendar of the Christian world and starting time from zero again. But this dramatic gesture was soon effaced. More enduring was the definition of a past now dead and gone, a past from which we are hopelessly separated by revolution. For the urban notables, the seigneurial regime was an essential element of this rejected world. But this lost world, which stands as a dead benchmark by which we find superior the living present, was elaborated upon in more than one way. Several of the more influential such images are found, not fully grown, in the *cahiers* of the Third Estate. The association of the seigneurial regime and religious institutions and practices looks ahead to the liberal and secular nineteenth-century rejection of the ignorant and superstitious past. But we do have yet the full flowering of liberal republicanism; king and monarchy (in March 1789) are as yet untainted by association with the lord.

We see as well the germ of an image of the dead world of the past which, when elaborated in the nineteenth century and beyond became an unparalleled frame of reference within which the experience of change could be assimilated to a sense of orderly, if violent, progress. But the association of the seigneurial regime with economic backwardness is even farther from Marxism than its association with religion is from republicanism. Only aspects of the seigneurial regime are so associated. And these associations are as likely to recall the theories of agricultural blockage of the physiocrats as they are the sense of the flowering of new forms of wealth expressed by Barnave.

And we have seen, again in embryo, the seigneurial regime as part of that doomed world of outworn privilege that for Tocqueville so eloquently defined an Old Regime unable to stand against the modern democratic tide. Privileged access to high posts tended to be discussed in the same *cahiers* that wrote at length of seigneurial rights; the same was true of the charged

75. Among his improbably many diatribes, see, for example, his attacks on "des moines bénédictins devenus chanoines de Saint Claude en Franche Comté," in *Oeuvres complètes* (Paris: Garnier Frères, 1879), 28:353–60.

76. This is nicely treated by Mackrell, *The Attack on Feudalism,* 31–34, 119–20.

question of placing noble and common families on the same tax role. But tax privileges generally had little connection to seigneurial rights in the *cahiers,* nor did noble privilege in access to the courts nor did other elements of corporate legal distinctiveness.

At the beginning of the Revolution the seigneurial rights were seen as part of several larger structures. The shape of these structures would become clearer, and more elaborate, as the Revolution wore on (see Chapter 9) and as the thoughtful continued, in the nineteenth century, to define their modern world by reference to a revolutionary break. We have glimpsed a moment in the assignment of meaning to the seigneurial regime by the Third Estate. We have examined, across three chapters and many tables, the way that the seigneurial regime appeared to the energetic and educated who got their views to prevail in the assemblies of the Third Estate and the nobility. We have seen the positions they had developed by the spring of 1789, the positions with which they would face the mounting rhythms of rural revolt. The Third Estate had an antiseigneurial agenda, particularly focused on barriers to the perfecting of the market. The most distinctive element of their program was its stress on indemnification of the lords, a proposal that would accomplish many ends: it would, if carried through, phase out the seigneurial rights with minimal injury to the lords; it offered the pleasures of regarding oneself as holding to the reasonable and enlightened middle ground between immobilism and anarchy; its inherent complexities would provide intellectual activity for legal theorists, assure lawyers a significant role in the revolutionary state, and provide endless clients in endless lawsuits for legal practitioners throughout the kingdom. By adjusting the terms of indemnification one could fine-tune the general proposal down the line, in light of political, economic, or ideological needs. Thus indemnification could bring together a broad array ranging from those who would rather keep seigneurial rights but dared not say so to those who would like a radical abolition and dared not say so. If we may look ahead to the summer, we shall, perhaps, find a few among the Third Estate deputies prepared for something avowedly more radical and a larger number who felt that the initial decrees of the National Assembly went too far (see Chapter 8, p. 444).

Among the nobility, a substantial number of assemblies were not prepared to accept indemnification—let alone uncompensated abolition—but many were. What is at least as striking, however, as the streak of avowed noble conservatism is the propensity toward utter silence. Many a noble assembly could find nothing it was prepared to say at all (not in public, at any rate). If the silence of some is one element of the absence of an independent noble discourse, what was said by those who spoke was another. Much of the language of defense of seigneurial rights accepted the central elements of the language of attack. For those nobles not content with the language of honor, these rights were justified, if at all, as "property." Nobles were even more prone to adhere to "property" as an ultimate value than the Third Estate.

Finally, we saw that seigneurial rights mattered a great deal to the elites. They had their coherence for the Third Estate assemblies and were part of larger discussions as well. As Third Estate assemblies drafted and debated their *cahiers* and elaborated their critiques of France's present and their hopes for its future, their thoughts kept coming back to seigneurial rights. Assemblies that addressed the barriers to economic development found that certain seigneurial rights came into their texts; assemblies that took up issues of privilege (and in particular their sense of access to posts and careers) found themselves addressing seigneurial rights as well; assemblies that addressed the role of the church in France likewise were prone to consider seigneurial rights.

The nobility, by contrast, took pains to distinguish two kinds of seigneurial rights, did not connect them with each other (as shown in the lack of any tendency for the nobles to discuss them jointly) and, sometimes, held fast to the one while relinquishing the other. The nobles insisted on their honor but not their incomes, so they said. Yet they did not defend a society organized around God-given hierarchies but one created in freely negotiated contracts. Honor was defended in the language of property and contract. And, on the other hand, income-bearing rights, if defended, were sometimes defended by an expensive notion of honor.

Such were the public positions of urban notables and nobles in the spring of 1789 as the antiseigneurial movement of the countryside was just beginning to gather steam. I shall show how the deputies at the National Assembly, Legislative Assembly, and Convention coped with the insurrections of late July and beyond. But we need, first, to turn from the web of interconnections of institutions in the agendas and programs of the elites early in the revolutionary process, to the ebb and flow of rural revolt in time and space.

CHAPTER

5

FORMS OF REVOLT: THE FRENCH COUNTRYSIDE, 1788–1793

As the Old Regime collapsed in France, the countryside rose. The rural rebellions took many forms and were directed against many targets. As the parish assemblies began meeting to formulate grievances and elect deputies to *bailliage* assemblies the as yet scattered acts of peasant self-assertion testified to the potential storms and formed a significant part of the context within which the elections took place. By the time the parish deputies met with the town deputies to adopt a Third Estate *cahier* for the entire *bailliage* as noble and clerical assemblies met nearby, the rural turmoil had reached new heights.

Dramatic as the spring events were, they were but a prelude to the summer disturbances ahead. The continuing rural turbulence, both demonstrating and aggravating the incapacity of the existing political order, made a major contribution to the sense of crisis that led the representatives of the Third Estate in June to abandon the concept of the Estates-General to which they had been duly elected, and in an act of revolutionary self-assertion, declare themselves the nucleus of a National Assembly. The great wave of rural mobilization that started in the middle of July, together with the turbulence of the towns, formed the backdrop to the National Assembly's ringing declarations of a break with the past and the inauguration of a new social order. The announcement of the total destruction of the "feudal regime" of August 11 and the enactment of the Declaration of the Rights of Man and Citizen of August 26 are the touchstones. A central goal of the revolutionary legislature in that turbulent summer was the demobilization of the countryside, a goal that proved elusive for years to come.

Over the course of the next several chapters we shall track the insurrectionary movements across time and space. At what points in time and at what places were country people particularly unruly? And at what times and at what places was their unruliness directed against seigneurial rights, directed toward subsistence questions, or manifest in land invasions? We shall be able to make use of these variations, particularly the geographic patterns, to examine a wide variety of hypotheses about the social roots of insurrection. We shall also be able to use these variations, particularly the temporal patterns, to explore the dialogue of peasants and power-holders. In this chapter we shall chart the major types of insurrectionary actions; Chapters 6 and 7 will examine their temporal rhythms and spatial patterning. But we must first consider the sources to be utilized.

In exploring the ways in which rural insurrection and revolutionary legislation shaped one another, we may say that on the legislative side the relevant evidence is relatively unproblematic. We have the laws enacted, we have preliminary reports of the relevant legislative committees, we have debates on the floor of the legislatures, and we have a good number of letters and memoirs of the legislators to ponder. On the peasant side, however, we do not have anything close to an enumeration of the time, place, and nature of rural actions on a national scale. There are excellent and invaluable monographic studies of particular regions, particular forms of conflict and particular time periods,[1] but nothing that approximated what I was after. The archival exploration of rural conflict on a nationwide scale from 1661 to spring 1789 carried out by a team directed by Jean Nicolas and

1. For a few instances among many, see Jean Boutier, *Campagnes en émoi: Révoltes et Révolution en bas-Limousin, 1789–1800* (Treignac: Editions "Les Monédières, 1987); Jean-Jacques Clère, *Les paysans de la Haute-Marne et la Révolution française: Recherches sur les structures foncières de la communauté villageoise (1780–1815)* (Paris: Editions du Comité des Travaux Historiques et Scientifiques, 1988); Hubert C. Johnson, *The Midi in Revolution: A Study of Regional Political Diversity, 1789–1793* (Princeton: Princeton University Press, 1986); Michel Vovelle, "Les campagnes à l'assaut des villes sous la révolution," in Michel Vovelle, ed., *Ville et campagne au 18e siècle: Chartres et la Beauce* (Paris: Editions Sociales, 1980), 227–76; Anatoly V. Ado, *Krest'ianskoe divizhenie vo Frantsii vo vremia velikoi burzhuaznoi revoliutsii kontsa XVIII veka* (Moscow: Izdatel'stvo Moskovskovo Universiteta, 1971).

Guy Lemarchand[2] was an inspiring but also daunting model. I opted for the relatively limited task of attempting to assemble as complete a set of data as could be done from already published accounts. Such a data set carries with it the limitations and the biases imposed by the selective interests of historians of France; on the other hand, it also has the considerable virtue of being a far more modest undertaking than the multiyear transatlantic archival search to be carried out by a research team requiring training and supervision.

Defining an Event

By an "event," I meant an instance of twenty or more people of the countryside, acting publicly and as a group, directly engaged in seizing or damaging the resources of another party or defending themselves against another party's claims upon them. I required, moreover, that if there was a party that could clearly be regarded as the initiator of the event (and there might not be) *and* if there were any clearly defined leadership roles (and there might not be) those roles must be filled by local people for the party that initiates the event. Finally, two narratives were taken to describe the same incident if they took place in the same location within an interval of twenty-four hours and did not differ in the participating groups. (Thus two accounts, drawn from separate sources, of "peasants" stopping a grain convoy in the same parish one day apart were regarded as aspects of a single event.)[3]

Such a definition is designed in the first place to provide guidelines so as to delimit the range of events to enter into one's data set. By being explicit about just what one intends to count, one makes clear the sorts of things not counted (which is not always clear when one works with heterogeneous compilations produced by others—in the forms of official statistics of one sort or another, say.) The point of this particular definition is not to approximate some theoretically ideal notion of conflict, but rather to delimit a subset of all conceivable conflictual events that one might hope to count in

2. See Nicolas, "Les émotions dans l'ordinateur: premiers résultats d'une enquête collective," paper presented at the University of Paris VII, October 1986, and Lemarchand, "Troubles populaires au XVIIIe siècle et conscience de classe: Une préface à la Révolution française," *Annales Historiques de la Révolution Française*, no. 279 (1990): 32–48. This research is discussed later in this chapter and also in Chapter 6.

3. This working definition of a codable event, like those used by other recent researchers, is a variant of Tilly's. See, for example, Charles Tilly, "Contentious Repertoires in Great Britain, 1758–1834," *Social Science History* 17 (1993): 270–71.

a reasonably uniform way, given the sources to be used. By excluding events below a certain size, one hopes to omit events so small that their mention should be taken as haphazard; by insisting on public and collective events, one hopes to avoid including such stray instances of furtive and individual acts that happen, in a very unrepresentative fashion, to have caught the notice of some worthy chronicler. Opting for direct claims upon or damage to another's resources includes such things as peasant seizures of land but excludes peasant petitions for land; it also includes peasants' slaughter of the lord's animals, but excludes peasant petitions calling for an end to the monopolistic right to raise animals. Including actions taken in light of threats against one's own resources includes the Great Fear and lesser incidents of rural panic, even when the feared party was largely imaginary. Excluding actions in which an initiating party acts under extra-local leadership excludes actions in which agents acting on behalf of the government attempt to arrest or attack peasants (but does not exclude actions in which peasants attack police in order to rescue a fellow who has fallen into their clutches); it also excludes many of the events of the civil warfare of the western counterrevolution,[4] but not the incidents that led up to its outbreak (provided those incidents were initiated by country people). The restriction to incidents involving country people as actors was of a different character; it was not dictated by the hope of avoiding incidents whose inclusion would be completely haphazard, but by the nature of my research interests and the finitude of resources (especially time).

Now these various conditions and distinctions do not always come neatly packaged in available accounts. However desirable a uniform threshold ("at least twenty people") might be, precise information about size is often, indeed generally, not present. Every one of the distinctions pointed to above, therefore, demanded some rough-and-ready rules of thumb, if they were actually to be applied. An event was regarded as involving rural people as actors, for example, if (a) it took place in the countryside and there was no *explicit claim* that the actors were townspeople (so that all attacks on rural *châteaux* were counted); or (b) it took place in a town but the source *explicitly* indicated significant rural participation (as in many, but far from all, market disturbances). (Instances in which townsfolk ransacked nearby farmsteads looking for grain, however, were excluded.) To take another example, an event was regarded as having twenty people if either (a) there was an explicit number of the proper magnitude given, (b) some other appropriate indicator of magnitude was present (such as adjectives like

4. Although the largest group of such excluded events are part of the counterrevolution in the West, concentrated from March 1793 on, another important although smaller cluster arise from the various attempts to organize and coordinate large-scale counterrevolutionary activity in the South, particularly in the *départements* of Gard, Ardèche, and Hérault from the summer of 1790 into 1792.

"enormous," "large," "many"), or (c) there were indications that the participants came from more than one parish *and* there was no explicit statement that fewer than twenty people were involved.

Temporal Boundaries

I wanted as temporal boundaries a period long enough for there to have been many significant alterations in the national political context within which country people acted—but not so long that data collection would be interminable. I opted to begin with the summer of 1788 when the political crisis between the monarchy and the sovereign courts came to a head in the desperate attempt to abolish the courts in May, an event soon followed by a call for a nationwide process of research, reflection, and advice on the rules to be followed in convening the first Estates-General in 175 years. I took as an endpoint the flurry of laws on land purchase, division of the commons, and seigneurial rights that the radicalized Convention enacted in the immediate wake of the Parisian insurrections of May 31 and June 2, 1793, that drove the Girondins from the legislature. (For precise dates I selected June 1, 1788, through June 30, 1793.)

Sources

The choice of sources in such research, like the choice of definitions, is a compromise between an ideal and the constraints of finite resources. Initially hoping for a relatively speedy although still acceptable substitute for an archival search on a vast scale, I turned to the extensive documentation of rural insurrection in Anatoly Ado's dissertation *Krest'ianskoe dvizhenie* ("The peasant movement in France during the great bourgeois revolution of the late eighteenth century"). Ado's ambitious work attempted to survey in some detail "the peasant movement" as a whole, by synthesizing the research of historians as well as exploring administrative correspondence, reports of committees of the revolutionary legislatures, letters from local government officials, and petitions. Sources in the National Archives were explored and some departmental archives looked into (particularly through printed inventories). Ado makes no claim to having achieved completeness; although this work is the closest thing there is to an attempt at a comprehensive enumeration, Ado makes clear that his intentions have certain clear boundaries (16–17, 77). He does not cover the famous rural panic (the Great Fear) of the summer of 1789 in any detail because Georges Lefebvre's magnificent book already has done the job. (Were this the only lacuna, one could simply supplement Ado with Lefebvre.) Additionally, however, Ado informs us that he is not interested in the counterrevolution (16); that is left for some other scholar. Finally, Ado's account of many incidents is too sketchy for my purposes.

Ado's survey, then, could only be taken as the starting point.[5] One must search further in the historical literature, or still face the daunting prospect of a major search through the archives. Given the vast literature on the Revolution, how could this search for relevant scholarship be narrowed? To read through everything written on the Revolution in the countryside in order to find accounts of rural conflict, after all, would not only have the frustrations of a vast "dross rate"[6] but would very likely take on the dimensions of the national archival search that I was hoping to avoid in the first place. I adopted, therefore, the following rules for exploring the literature so as to complete Ado's survey:

1. For the Great Fear, I went back to Lefebvre's classic account,[7] supplemented by a search for two categories of literature: (a) anything written on the Great Fear since Lefebvre and (b) an examination of sources prior to Lefebvre (for which his own bibliography was an important start) when Lefebvre's own account seemed too sketchy.
2. For the conflicts in the western departments that led up to the great counterrevolutionary battles of 1793 and beyond, I searched through the indefatigable chroniclers of those events.
3. I explored all titles that I could obtain that were published since Ado's work (but before March 1991) that seemed likely to deal with rural insurrection.[8]
4. When Ado's account was sketchy, I went back to his sources, often finding more detailed accounts than he summarized. Sometimes the more detailed account made clear that the incident in question did not meet my criteria for inclusion.

5. The data are provided in the form of maps, narrative accounts, and a supplementary listing of incidents. I used the first edition of 1971. The more recent second edition is enriched theoretically by Ado's situating his study in relation to some of the important recent research, but this new edition does not present all the detailed accounts of insurrection that were included in an appendix in the earlier version. See Anatoly V. Ado, *Krest'iane i velikaia frantsuzskaia revoliutsiia: Krest'ianskoe dvizhenie v 1789–1794 godu* (Moscow: Izdatel'stvo Moskovskovo Universiteta, 1987).

6. I appropriate this term from Eugene J. Webb, Donald T. Campbell, Richard Schwartz, and Lee Sechrest, *Unobtrusive Measures: Nonreactive Research in the Social Sciences* (Chicago: Rand-McNally, 1966), 32–33.

7. Georges Lefebvre, *La Grande Peur de 1789* (Paris: Armand Colin, 1970).

8. The March 1991 cutoff date was simply the point at which I felt it was time to shift from data collection to tabulation and writing. There is some important new work that has been done since that date and there will be more. I explore the implications of this below.

When I found an incident that did meet my criteria for inclusion, I recorded the information about that incident in which I was interested. When it was unclear whether or not an incident met my criteria or when an appropriate incident was inadequately described, I attempted to identify sources that might have more information (an effort far more successful with larger confrontations than smaller ones). Ultimately, some 110 sources proved to have information on at least one incident of conflict that I had not found elsewhere; see the Appendix. (A larger number of potential sources were consulted, many of which had no information that I had not already found; over time this search procedure encountered radically diminishing returns.)

Actions, Events, Types of Events

An "event" is understood to be composed of a set of "actions" undertaken by one or more identifiable groups against one or more targets with no break of more than one day between actions. An event, then, has a varying number of actions. If a group of villagers breaks into the *château,* seizes food, and demands that the lord give them some documents, we have an event with three actions. Events may be grouped into "types" that seem analytically useful. In this and the next two chapters I shall make considerable use of a small number of very broad classifications. Events will be classed as "antiseigneurial," for example, or "having a religious aspect." These categories are intended to give a very broad sense of the ebb and flow of conflict. Let it be noted that these broad categories—I use nine in Table 5.1—are hardly mutually exclusive. First of all, an event may have actions of more than one type. (Consider an event in which peasants first seize food from the *château* and then do the same at the local monastery. Its two actions made this event both "antiseigneurial" and "religious.") Second, an individual action may fall into more than one broad grouping: tearing out the lord's church bench is in itself both "antiseigneurial" and "religious."

One motive for the detailed code that I used, in fact, was to go beyond the limits of the simple and rigid scheme that I had used in previous studies of the countryside in the spring and summer of 1789.[9] I had originally classified events into one of six types that it most closely fit. I felt that my initial six categories (antiseigneurial, antichurch, antistate, subsistence, Great Fear, other) were both too crude to capture some very significant

9. See, for example, John Markoff, "The Social Geography of Rural Revolt at the Beginning of the French Revolution," *American Sociological Review* 50 (1985): 761–81.

distinctions (do they attack specific features of the seigneurial system, say, or do they attempt to destroy the capacity of the lords to claim any rights?) and too rigid in insisting that an event could fall into only one category.

I shall enlarge on this latter point. An action described in detail might fit in more than one place. If a group of country people invade the lord's *château* and menacingly insist that he feed them, are we to see this primarily as an invocation of a norm of hospitality, now to be mockingly parodied in order thereby to represent a world in which the lord's former dependents are now the enforcers of the rules? Or do we see this essentially as hungry people seeking food? Is it an "antiseigneurial" or a "subsistence" action? We usually cannot reconstruct the state of mind of the participants terribly well but it seems reasonable to observe that there are no doubt diverse motives within the group insisting that the lord feed them, there may well have been a mixture of motives within some (or all) of the participants and it is, in any event, most improbable that we can discover the precise mix in any particular crowd. Nor are the attributions of motive by participants and observers necessarily more credible than those of historians. It is doubtful that one ought to take a frightened lord's testimony or the hastily penned letter of a local official as authoritative on such a matter, even when that reporter comments on motive. Claims of rioters in police custody as to their motives also need to be taken with many grains of salt. Rather than attempt, then, to decide whether to regard such an event as essentially antiseigneurial or essentially subsistence in character, we regard it as both.[10]

Of some 4,700 incidents ("events") identified from the summer of 1788 to the summer of 1793, there was considerable variation in the level of detail in which I had some confidence. Sometimes all I knew was that there had been some sort of clash; at other times I may have learned that a group of peasants entered the lord's *château* but had no idea of what they did there; in still other instances I had a very rich account. While I often knew the exact day a particular event took place, sometimes the ultimate source of the account (a local official writing to request military help, say) was less precise than that. Sometimes indeed I could date an event only very roughly (as in an anxious report to the National Assembly on food riots over the last few months, for example). In general, the published literature on which I relied is a great deal clearer about when a conflict commenced than when it

10. From a methodological point of view, it may be noted that the attempt to insist that our categories be mutually exclusive ones (that is, that a particular event be either antiseigneurial or subsistence-oriented but most definitely not both at the same time) would surely have produced many highly unreliable codings; this discrimination calls for a nuanced judgment that cannot be made with any confidence on the basis of available sources. In fact, it is often doubtful if such a judgment could be made with any confidence on the basis of any conceivable sources whatsoever. The more concrete and manifest judgment, namely, that rural people did enter a *château* and did indeed coerce a meal is a coding decision that can be made far more reliably.

ended, to the degree, indeed, that I abandoned the attempt to analyze the duration of actions altogether. Nor did I find these sources at all usable for the reconstruction of sequences of action within a single event: I was far more likely to get a catalogue of the various things the invaders did in the *château,* monastery, or tax-office than I was to have any clear sense of the order in which they did those things; still less often did I get a clear picture of the process that brought them to the *château* (Did they assemble elsewhere? Did they come from church or parish assembly? Had they been working in the fields or chatting in the tavern? Did they converge individually before the lord's dwelling?) or what happened next (Did they disperse to their homes? Did they plan another attack?). I often had little but the vaguest indication of which elements in the rural community participated (Were they landless laborers, sharecroppers, rural textile-workers, small-holders?) and only quite rarely had any indication of the gender makeup of the group. I attempted to record the level of detail I did have concerning the character of the event, and in the case of dates, the approximate level of precision. Indications of size were generally very vague when they existed at all. While I was sure a "very large" group was at least twenty and therefore fit my definition, I was often far less sure if two hundred or two thousand was closer to the mark.[11] Far more successful, however, was the discovery of the targets of the action: that one gathering stormed a monastery while another looted a household's grain was generally clear enough. Given these limitations my analyses must focus on places, dates, targets, and tactics.

Biases

The biases of my data set are those of the body of literature on the French Revolution as a whole.[12] Evaluating those biases is a complex matter, for there are many. We shall consider four here.

1. *Urban Bias.* The historical profession has disproportionately focused on the rural zones around large cities. First of all, the town is likely to have the resources in the form of archival facilities, funds, and trained personnel

11. It is an interesting symptom of the continuing vitality of corporate images of society that one fairly frequently finds claims about which parishes had participants in an event. If multiple parishes were involved I always assumed there were at least twenty participants, unless explicitly informed otherwise.

12. In some ways they do, and in some ways do not, resemble the biases in the use of newspaper sources for sequences of conflict, a practice reviewed by Roberto Franzosi, "The Press as a Source of Sociohistorical Data: Issues in the Methodology of Data Collection from Newspapers," *Historical Methods* 20 (1987): 5–16.

that facilitate research. Second, and not necessarily less important, university-educated historians are likely to prefer the amenities of living in a large town while they carry on their research. (I recall Richard Cobb observing at a conference once something to the effect that Clio may not be any closer in Paris than in the middle of the Auvergne but that everything else was a lot closer.)

2. *Dramatic Bias.* Second, one strongly suspects a tendency to publish more where something dramatic happened during the revolutionary years. If one assumes that such a propensity carries over into the study of insurrectionary activities themselves, one is led to the conclusion that it is likely that regions known to have promoted dramatic rural clashes have had those clashes more thoroughly researched than such clashes as actually took place in quieter zones. The gap between regions that appear relatively peaceful and those that appear relatively turbulent according to the data are very likely valid but are exaggerations of reality: the true gap is not so great.

We may be almost certain that the same mechanism operates in the temporal as well as the spatial dimension of the data set. A plot of the total number of electoral districts involved in insurrections by month, for example, reveals July 1789 to have an enormous spike and March 1790 a striking trough (see Chapter 6). No doubt there was such a peak and such a trough, but the data exaggerate the difference: a historian may spend a lifetime studying the July events; I doubt if many would care to make a career out of the following March. The reputation of July for turbulence attracts armies of diligent graduate students to the archives in search of still more turbulence to discover—and discover they have; the very scarcity of rural disturbances the following March no doubt discourages students of disorderly politics from investing too much energy.

3. *Size Threshold Bias and the Dilemma of Unorganized Actions.* Events involving large number of persons, open challenges to some other party, and explicit formulation of grievances are undoubtedly far better covered than actions undertaken by a few persons or a solitary individual in the dead of night and with no explicit formulation of grievance. The crowd that marches at noon to the gate of the *château* and demands that the lord renounce his rights is far more likely to have its deeds enter the historical literature than a few friends who carry out a midnight act of arson . . . or the nonconfrontational nonpayment of some traditional obligation, a matter of the greatest significance. While overt resistance to the military draft in March 1793, for example, was rare in the *département* of Corrèze, draft-dodging was widespread and significant.[13] Through the years of revolution draft evasion was as significant as—if not more significant than—draft resistance, tax evasion as tax resistance, and so on.

13. Boutier, *Campagnes en émoi,* 211–19.

Now this is hardly a unique feature of this data set but I wish to consider this problem at some length because its implications are rather serious. It is the collective and virtually unanimous wisdom of researchers on conflict events that whatever sources we are working with (newspapers, official statistics, archives of one sort or another) understate the occurrence of smaller, less dramatic, and less openly confrontational events. It has become a part of the standard wisdom that one tends to have a more valid sample to the extent that one establishes a threshold for the scale of the event, below which one does not incorporate that event into one's data set.[14] Some of this research claims a theoretical rationale, in happy conjunction with the lacunae in the data, that downplays the damage done by the methodological problem, indeed, that makes a virtue of necessity. If one has as one's theoretical focus the interaction of popular protest and elite action, then surely it is the forms of protest that are noticed on high that one ought to study.[15] The small group or individual action, the surreptitious expression of rage in the dark of night, the act of sabotage that keeps its motives hidden—these simply do not carry the weightiness of protest that is collective, disruptive, and that openly and explicitly challenges the prevailing order. It may be true, as James Scott[16] has eloquently argued, that the normal forms of peasant resistance (and of underclasses more generally) are furtive, individual, anonymous, and inexplicit. But counterbalancing the severe, and usually impossible, obstacles to the systematic study of such everyday resistance, is their lesser significance in historical processes. It is the collective, open, and explicit challenge that gets the elite to sit up and take notice.

To whatever extent this argument genuinely suits other historical situations (as opposed to comfortingly soothing researchers' anxiety over unavoidable error), it probably does not accord terribly well with the French Revolutionary period. The methodological difficulty is as pertinent as ever: it is far harder to assess the passive noncompliance with seigneurial dues than the *château* burnings. The *theoretical* rationale for omitting the study of such phenomena, however, is rather weak. The Revolution began with a severe financial crisis whose attempted solution obsessed the leadership in

14. David Snyder and William R. Kelly, "Conflict Intensity, Media Sensitivity and the Validity of Newspaper Data," *American Sociological Review* 42 (1977): 108–21. There is no consensus on the threshold: Tilly's French data set, for example, required a minimum of fifty persons, his British data, 10.

15. For a compelling statement of this position, see Sidney Tarrow, *Democracy and Disorder: Protest and Politics in Italy, 1965–1975* (Oxford: Oxford University Press, 1989), 9; and "Political Opportunities, Cycles of Protest and Collective Action: Theoretical Perspectives," paper presented at Workshop on Collective Action Events and Cycles of Protest, Cornell University, 1990.

16. James C. Scott, *Weapons of the Weak. Everyday Forms of Peasant Resistance* (New York: Vintage Books, 1985).

Paris for years. The mere nonpayment of taxes, without overt challenge, without explicit demands, without collective gatherings, was, under these circumstances, something that was very much noticed. The same applied to other forms of nonconfrontational noncompliance. The central item in the initial strategy for replenishing the empty treasury was to seize and sell land (of king and church first of all, and later of émigrés). A significant component of the value of that land was the various seigneurial rights attached thereto; and thus the revolutionary regime, avowedly "antifeudal" though it proclaimed itself to be, found itself attempting to enforce the collection of seigneurial rights on "national land" as well as enforcing seigneurial payments elsewhere.

But even before the Revolution, the people of the French countryside had honed the skills of hidden noncompliance with the lords' demands to a fine art. A recent survey of the difficulties of collection by Gérard Aubin points up such simple devices as delayed and partial payments, which might be more trouble for the lord to challenge than to live with; such awkward ones as avoiding mutation fees by concealing land transfers—frequent enough that many lords reduced their claims by one-fourth to one-half to encourage payments rather than concealment; and such a subtle one as claiming one didn't know what one owed or even who the lord was, thereby imposing on lords the burden of documenting their lordship before judges who in a rationalistic age might want nonexistent documentary proof.[17] (This last technique had the additional virtue of adding to the peasant reputation for general ignorance.) In the face of such practices the lord's legally defensible claims were rather larger than his actual revenues; the lord's claims were, in effect, the starting point for protracted but tacit negotiation. With so much experience behind them, nonpayment surely enlarged with Revolution. But under the Revolution's straitened financial circumstances, such widespread nonpayment was surely noticed.

The French Revolution, I am suggesting, was a moment when the usual hidden weapons of the weak did not go overlooked; they contributed to the government's sense of what it was up against in the countryside every bit as much as the more visible, dramatic, collective, and often violent confrontations. And yet how much harder measurement is. On those rare moments of overt invasion of forests, the startled, frightened, and angry landowners, police, and judiciary produce written descriptions that we may look for. Of those many moments when acts of poaching, illicit tree-felling, or pilfering of forest products occurred, only a relatively haphazard selection

17. Gérard Aubin, "La crise du prélèvement seigneurial à la fin de l'Ancien Régime" in Robert Chagny, ed., *Aux origines provinciales de la Révolution* (Grenoble: Presses Universitaires de Grenoble, 1990), 23–33. For a survey of similar practices surrounding the tithe, see James C. Scott, "Resistance without Protest and without Organization: Peasant Opposition to the Islamic *Zakat* and the Christian Tithe," *Comparative Studies in Society and History* 29 (1987): 417–452.

enters the ken of the overworked rural police, the courts, and the world of the administrators.

In the interpretation of trends in conflict from 1788 to 1793, therefore, it will be essential to pay attention to the possibility that events excluded for absolutely sound methodological principle, nonetheless play an important role as an alternative form of conflict and, therefore, affect our understanding of the events that are included. The rise and fall of overt antiseigneurial violence, for example, may be due not merely to changing perceptions of opportunity for collective mobilization and assessments of the probabilities of repression, although, of course, these played critical roles. It may also be due to shifts among forms of struggle some of which are impossible to track within the same data series. A fall in measured incidents of antiseigneurial conflict may not only indicate either the success of repression or the satisfaction of desires; it may signal a shift to nonconfrontational avoidance of payment as a preferred tactic.

4. *Axe-grinding Bias*. Finally, we need to consider the biases in the literature that bear on the *type* of event represented. By virtue of the concern of some historians with locating the revolutionary actions of the peasantry, some, like Anatoly Ado, have been most diligent in the enumeration of the sort of "antifeudal" events widely held to have been a central key to what the Revolution is all about; still others, in admiration or revulsion, have meticulously chronicled the conflicts in western France that form the background to the great counterrevolutionary explosions of 1793; still others have been fascinated by the subsistence events so crucial to recent debates over the relationship of the rural community to the developing market. By way of contrast, relatively few historians have paid much attention to the Revolution's antitax rebellions. The specific scholarly axes being ground have varied: some, especially on the left, have a theoretical axe and wish to show up the antifeudal character of the Revolution or the peasant resistance to the market, thereby looking for attacks on *châteaux* or grain convoys. Others of the left (or right) have historical axes: to show up the barbarous (or heroic) actions of the western peasantry confronted with the revolutionary state.

When tabulations reveal the data set to contain relatively few anti-tax incidents (see Table 5.1), one must at once pose three rival hypotheses, each with its own plausibility: (1) the country people were less profoundly hostile to taxation than to their other burdens;[18] (2) nonconfrontational avoidance of taxes, possible under the institutional breakdown of the Revolution, was a more cost-effective tactic than insurrection (since gallows or guillotines were always possible outcomes); and (3) historians have

18. See Chapter 3 for evidence on how frequently taxes were to be reformed, seigneurial rights and tithes abolished.

systematically failed to give taxation issues their full significance, by virtue of their preoccupation with other forms of struggle that seemed more to the point given prevailing interpretations of the Revolution.

Moving Beyond the Biases of the Sample

Given the problematic character of the evidence,[19] the only justification for such an enterprise is the expectation that even a very rough tracing of the flow of insurrection as it unfolds in time and across space and as its targets and tactics change will permit a fuller appreciation of the richness of rural political action. It should also help fill in an important context for the behavior of other parties to revolutionary struggles, particularly the legislatures.

What is fundamental is recognizing first of all that the aggregate number of all incidents identified and counted is in no sense a sample from some clearly defined universe; and second, that variations in the relative frequencies of different types of incidents are not nearly so prone to the sorts of invalidity I have been discussing. To enlarge on the first half of this statement: the difficulty in unambiguously defining the conflicts to be included; the uncertainty over the recording practices of the police, judges, annalists, journalists, and historians that one takes for sources; the certainty that as the scope, intensity, and scale of conflict grow smaller the less likely is a particular event to enter one's sources combined with one's uncertainty as to the extent of this size bias at different sizes (does it matter, to cite numbers actually used in recent studies, if one sets the threshold at fifty, twenty, ten, or four?); the difficulties in assessing the relative extent of bias in incidents of different sorts (just how much less likely is an anti-tax insurrection than an antiseigneurial insurrection to enter the historical

19. For all the problems inherent in working with published accounts, it is not, however, to be taken for granted that the exclusive use of archival materials, while vastly more costly, would necessarily produce a superior sample. It surely would have more incidents, but would not thereby necessarily have a more representative selection or even one whose biases were easier to assess. Indeed, occasionally the deliberate efforts of historians to represent reality adequately might actually improve on what's in the archives. The French government's official project of publishing *cahiers* has actually produced a more representative sample than the very much larger collection of all surviving manuscripts in the archives. For a national picture of grievances one is better off with the published documents; see Gilbert Shapiro, John Markoff, and Silvio Duncan Baretta, "The Selective Transmission of Historical Documents: The Case of the Parish Cahiers of 1789," *Histoire et Mesure* 2 (1987): 115–72. The collection of seventeenth- and eighteenth-century French rural disturbances collected by Jean Nicolas and Guy Lemarchand is a model of such an exhaustive archival search for conflict-events, yet it has its biases, too. Not all disturbances were reported; not all judicial or police investigations were equally thorough; not all archives have been equally well inventoried. See Jean Nicolas, "Un chantier toujours neuf," in Jean Nicolas, ed., *Mouvements populaires et conscience sociale, XVIe–XIXe siècles* (Paris: Maloine, 1985), 16.

record?)—all these processes guarantee that the aggregated count of incidents of all sorts will be a very crude measure indeed.

What can be done rather more confidently is to compare the distributions of different classes of events with one another across time and space. While the extent of relative undercounting of tax rebellions is unknown (and therefore the overall proportion of tax incidents in the sample is not especially informative) the *shifts* over time (or space) in the proportion of events that concern taxes (or of districts that have tax rebellions) is far more useful. Along these lines, for example, the variations in time or space in the proportion of all incidents of an antiseigneurial character or the proportion of antiseigneurial events of a particular sort is far more credible than any aggregate proportion. Why? Because a tendency of historians to overcount antiseigneurial events relative to some other sort of incident is irrelevant to the temporal or spatial variations in proportions; a tendency of historians to overcount incidents in some periods relative to others is similarly irrelevant to such comparisons of proportions.[20]

To take up another instance: the data set is clearly biased toward the inclusion of violent events. The peaceful assemblies of claim-making groups (the countless acts of petitioning, for example) are virtually excluded by the definition's insistence on a group's direct seizure of or damage to another's resources. This means that the overall proportion of incidents of a violent character is of only limited use from the point of view of the continuing discussion of the place of violence in disorderly politics. What is perfectly possible, however, is to chart the *variations* in violence: variations by target, tactics, time, and place. Are certain types of targets more prone to involve violence than others (attacks on the claims of the lord rather than the state, for example)? Are certain tactics inherently violence-prone (demanding the lord's own documents rather than demanding that the lord make a public renunciation of his rights, for example)? Does the tendency to violence shift with time? Are certain regions prone to violence independently of the targets of their attacks? While it is not, then, very useful to bring the aggregate data alone to bear on the recent and sometimes lurid discussion by historians of the violence of the Revolution,[21] comparing the propensities to personal injury in antiseigneurial events with events that have, say, a religious element may prove more revealing (see below, p. 230).

20. While one can abstractly conceive of complex 2- or 3-way interactions of bias, time, and space, it is hard to imagine a plausible concrete process that might really produce such complexly structured biases in actual conflict data.

21. See Brian Singer, "Violence in the French Revolution: Forms of Ingestion/Forms of Expulsion," in Ferenc Fehér, ed., *The French Revolution and the Birth of Modernity* (Berkeley and Los Angeles: University of California Press, 1990), 201–18; Simon Schama, *Citizens: A Chronicle of the French Revolution* (New York: Vintage Books, 1990).

Forms of Revolt

If we examine the targets of our actions, aggregating together all events from June 1788 through June 1793 that meet our criteria, we get a first, crude sense of the multifarious nature of rural mobilizations during the revolutionary crisis. Table 5.1 gives a rough distribution of those events in broad categories to be explored further. There are three sets of figures. The first column indicates how common a particular class of events is in our data; the second and third indicate how widespread such events are.[22] We see, for example, that while antiseigneurial events are the most common, they are not as widespread as subsistence events or panics.

Some 83% of *baillages* experienced at least one event of some sort. But what sort? Under each broad category in this table, I have counted every event any of whose component actions fit under that head. *Antiseigneurial* events involved any attack on the lord's person, property, rights, or anything that symbolized the lord. Events were classified as *religious* if they in any way had a religious referent: they, therefore, include challenges to the perogatives of some ecclesiastical body, actions over church organization or personnel and conflicts involving religiously defined minorities. *Subsistence events* were struggles over the availability or the price of food and were the second most widespread form of conflict. *Land conflicts* involved struggles

Table 5.1. Frequency of Events

Type of Event (Broad Categories)	Percentage of All Events	Percentage of All *Bailliages* with Events	Percentage of All *Bailliages*
Antiseigneurial	36%	49%	41%
Religious	16	39	33
Subsistence	26	67	56
Land conflict	8	26	21
Wage conflict	1	5	4
Panics	13	73	61
Anti-tax	3	23	19
Anti-authority (excluding tax agents)	5	27	22
Counterrevolution	9	15	12
(*N*)*	(4,689)	(344)	(412)

*Excludes nonconfrontational actions and questionable cases.

22. The data were tabulated by *bailliages*. Unless some other figure is specified, this and subsequent tabulations are for all *bailliages* of metropolitan France that have rural parishes. *Bailliages* that participated in the elections for the Estates-General but do not enter these tabulations include Corsica, overseas colonies, and purely urban *bailliages* (such as Paris-within-the-walls).

over the possession or use of land and may or may not have involved a seigneurial or ecclesiastical landholder. *Wage conflicts* pitted rural workers against their employers and are the scarcest of the forms distinguished here. *Panics* were incidents in which collective action was oriented to an imaginary enemy, whether fleeing or marching to an expected encounter. *Anti-tax events* were challenges to claims on resources of the central government, both Old Regime and revolutionary. *Anti-authority events* were attacks on agents of governing authority at national, provincial, departmental, or local levels. Finally, *counterrevolution* involved an overt challenge to a specifically revolutionary authority, most often, as we shall see below, in conjunction with either certain forms of religious conflict or in resistance to conscription. A more detailed specification of these broad labels will follow. With all due reservation about the data at this level of aggregation, we find that if the turbulent countryside was concerned about one arena it would have to be said to be the seigneurial arena. Nonetheless, nearly two-thirds of all events do not have an antiseigneurial component. If, like Ado, we develop an "antifeudal" category by adding to the antiseigneurial group appropriate actions against ecclesiastical bodies, we still cover no more than 40% of all events.[23] If we consider the geographic extent of the various classes of actions, we find that both subsistence events and panics actually surpass antiseigneurial movements.

To consider the likely direction of distortions in our data set, I would estimate that the anti-tax events are surely undercounted and that the apparently rare wage events probably are: anti-tax events because the historians whose accounts I used are relatively uninterested (relative to antiseigneurial events, subsistance events, and counterrevolution); wage events because they didn't easily fit into the contemporary vocabulary of social conflict. If we imagine inflating the figures for wage events a bit and anti-tax events substantially, we would thereby shrink the antiseigneurial share. Antiseigneurial events cannot be equated with the peasant movement (although they are its largest single element); the question before us, then, is to find the place of antiseigneurial actions within a much broader spectrum of rural turbulence.[24]

23. One may create a subcategory of religious events consisting of conflicts with ecclesiastical authorities that have close analogues in antiseigneurial events. These would include attacks on ecclesiastical lords, of course, but also conflicts over the tithe (often very difficult to distinguish from *champart* when there is an ecclesiastical lord), and over communal rights to pastures or woodland. Such events can then be included together with antiseigneurial events in a broader *antifeudal* category conceived of the way Ado does. Such antifeudal incidents amount to 40% of all our events and took place in some 52% of those *bailliages* where some conflict occurred.

24. Anatoly Ado opened this question by entitling his work "The Peasant Movement" and by carefully enumerating both antifeudal (understood in much the same way as I have done here) and subsistence events. But although he intriguingly suggests that the anti-tax actions of the Old Regime provided a stock of experience drawn on for other goals in the Revolution (*Krest'ianskoe dvizhenie,*

Antiseigneurial Events

The great diversity of these numerous actions, is depicted in Table 5.2. This table presents data on the frequencies of forms of antiseigneurial events in two ways. The left column gives the percentages of all antiseigneurial events of a particular class. The right column presents the proportion of all *bailliages* that had one or more antiseigneurial events (= "antiseigneurial *bailliages*") in which one or more events of that same particular class took place. (The tables that follow for other sorts of events follow the same format.) These categories are by no means exclusive. Some are subcategories of others ("violence against persons" includes "violence against lords"). In addition, an event can have multiple actions, so that the same event could be counted under several rubrics because several things happened. Thus percentages can total more than 100%. Peasants invaded the lord's fields, destroyed his crops, felled his trees, pastured communal animals on his property (or on what he—but not they—took to be his property), destroyed his fences, and attempted to redraw the boundaries of communal and seigneurial holdings (often insisting that improperly usurped land was being reclaimed). The lord's *château* might be broken into, and, once entered, a variety of actions might be undertaken: furniture might be seized or damaged, the lord's archives might be ransacked in search of seigneurial titles or—particularly if the search was resisted—the documents might be set alight. The invaders might demand food or drink or, in a tense parody of some old norm of hospitality, compel the lord to have them served a feast right then and there.[25]

Even without entering the interior of the building, there was plenty of damage to be done. While remaining outside, the attackers had other means of challenging the lord's rights and other means of punishment; and such actions might also proceed or follow indoor actions. The lord might be dragged outside and forced to make a public renunciation of his rights, often transcribed by a notary (himself perhaps under compulsion). The lord's

58–60, 114) and although he regards wage events as a significant form of conflict, he does not collect anti-tax events, nor panics, nor counterrevolution, nor wage events. Nor does he convincingly find any organic connection of subsistence and antifeudal events, leaving a certain sense of arbitrariness, and a certain puzzlement over what to make of his maps. See the discussion, "Table Ronde: Autour des travaux d'Anatoli Ado sur les soulèvements paysans pendant la Révolution française," in *La Révolution française et le monde rural* (Paris: Editions du Comité des Travaux Historiques et Scientifiques, 1989), 521–47.

25. Under the now rare rights to lodging, lords could demand that their subjects put them up; under similarly rare requisition rights, lords could seize needed supplies at a price they held appropriate. See Joseph Renauldon, *Dictionnaire des fiefs et droits seigneuriaux utiles et honorifiques* (Paris: Delalain, 1788), 1:4; Garaud, *Histoire générale du droit privé français,* vol. 2, *La Révolution et la propriété foncière* (Paris: Recueil Sirey, 1958), 64.

Table 5.2. Types of Antiseigneurial Events

Type of Event (Fine Categories)	Percentage of Antiseigneurial Events	Percentage of Antiseigneurial *Bailliages*
Violence		
Violence against persons or property	54%	72%
Violence against persons	5	23
Violence against lord	3	16
Château penetrated and interior invaded, with varying degrees of damage	27	48
Château a target; interior penetrated or exterior damaged	53	68
Destruction (rather than seizure) of food sources; killing in lord's game reserve; killing pigeons, fish, or rabbits; destruction of lord's crop; destruction of lord's trees	5	19
Titles vs. renunciation		
Coerced renunciation of rights	8	20
Searches, seizures, and demands for documents (at *château* or at notary's office)	16	35
Subsistence		
Search for food stores; seizure of goods in wine cellar; compelling lord to feed the invaders	7	28
Recreational		
Attacks on lords' game reserves or game; attacks on raising of pigeons, rabbits, or fishpond (includes both acts of seizure and of destruction); open defiance of hunting restrictions	9	22
Attacks on game reserves or hunting only; open defiance of hunting prohibition only	3	10
Lord-church nexus		
Destruction of church benches; damage to family tomb; disruption of religious ritual honoring lord	4	17
Dues		
Collective and public statement of refusal to pay	10	23
Collective and public refusals to pay; demands for restitution; attacks on scales	18	31
Coerced restitution only	9	16
Land conflict		
All land conflicts	11	31
Conflicts over ownership or use-rights in woods	5	17
Monopolies		
Collective and open violation of monopolistic restrictions; damage to seigneurial mills, oven, winepress	1	3
Agents		
Attacks on persons or property of seigneurial judges, dues-collectors, stewards, notaries, legal advisers	4	16
King as lord		
Any antiseigneurial action directed at royal holdings	1	4
Symbolics		
Attacks on honorific symbols of seigneurial status (weathervanes, coats-of-arms, gallows, turrets, battlements)	12	28

amusements might be targets: his rabbits or pigeons slain (or sometimes seized for food) and their habitations trashed; his fishpond emptied or fouled; his compulsory mill or oven destroyed. Sometimes the focus was quite specifically the lord's collection of dues: he might be forced to make restitution of such dues; the scales used to measure his portion of the crops might be smashed; or the community might openly announce its solidarity in future nonpayment, sometimes backed by coercive measures taken (or at least threatened) against any who might choose to continue paying. At times, the agents of the lord were the target: perhaps his judge, perhaps his notary, perhaps his rent-collector, perhaps the guard who had often engaged in a battle of wits with would-be poachers and violators of hunting rights; sometimes the lord himself was beaten, an action usually (but not always) halted short of his death.

An interesting group of actions were the attacks on the lord-church nexus: the lord's family bench in the local church might be dramatically torn out and unceremoniously (or very ceremoniously) dumped outside, and sometimes smashed or set afire; more rarely but even more dramatically the family tombs in the church might be desecrated.[26] Only 4% of antiseigneurial events thus challenged the religious warrant for seigneurial authority, but a much larger number of events included actions that had some religious aspect: 15%. The seigneurial rights at issue might be those of an ecclesiastical body: a local monastery, say, might be the lord under attack. Or, in a more complex action, a group challenging annual payments in kind to the lord *(champart)* might well go on to challenge annual payments in kind to a nearby monastery (generally a tithe, but sometimes *champart* as well).

In all these ways, the lord's prerogatives were challenged; his material accumulations reclaimed, damaged, or desecrated; the legal basis of his authority seized from his archives as a text or from his mouth as a sworn renunciation; his connection with the sacred grounding of the community severed as the family tomb or family bench was torn from the local church.[27]

26. Such actions, it may be worth pointing out, are hardly inherently antichurch, but might be experienced as cleansing the true Church of an intruder. Some priests, therefore, may well have encouraged some of these acts, even by example. Jean Bart has found a number of Old Regime instances from Burgundy's judicial archives in which priests were convicted of inciting friends to remove and damage a lord's bench, of smearing oil on it, of defacing (with grafitti) the tombstone of the local lord's uncle. See Jean Bart, "Encore un mot sur les curés de campagne . . . ," in Robert Chagny, ed., *Aux origines provinciales de la Révolution* (Grenoble: Presses Universitaires de Grenoble, 1990), 159. For similar incidents near Toulouse, see Jean Bastier, *La féodalité au siècle des lumières dans la région de Toulouse (1730–1790)* (Paris: Bibliothèque Nationale, 1975), 286–87.

27. The smashing, tearing-out, or burning of churchbenches seem lifted out of centuries of religious struggle. On Catholic-Protestant attacks on church benches two centuries earlier, see Natalie Zemon Davis, "The Rites of Violence" in her *Society and Culture in Early Modern France* (Stanford: Stanford University Press, 1975), 173. The same action is sometimes used in struggles over the Civil Constitution of the Clergy: Chassin reports several such from the spring of 1791; see

In late 1790, peasants in the impoverished countryside around Sarlat were heard to explain this last action by the commandment that all, equally, should kneel on the church floor before God.[28] (Villagers near Nevers went a step further and compelled the well-off to join them in attending Mass on their knees.)[29] And then there were the simple assaults on the symbols of seigneuralism that made the lord more than another man. The weathervane was one such likely target, as were turrets and battlements. Although the advance of the central state had long since rendered the fortress aspect of the medieval castle thoroughly out of date, many a lord maintained reminders of a warrior identity in the form of architectural motifs of a thoroughly decorative sort in their elegant lodgings, only to have these pretty turrets and graceful battlements attract the rage of peasant communities. Any display of the family coat-of-arms was a tempting target as well. If some had justified the lord's position by claiming a contract[30] and others had invoked God's design or the blessings of time,[31] still others had pointed to the social utility of a warrior class whose privileges were but just repayments for blood shed on behalf of community or king.[32] Just as some communities reappropriated the contract and others signaled the withdrawal of divine sanction in assaulting the lord-church nexus, still others eliminated the archaic military symbolism: with its turrets knocked down and its coat-of-arms destroyed the *château* was just a house.[33] The lord's home was to be no better than anyone else's. As the Revolution radicalized, in one of the many inversions of the old order by which the Revolution continually demonstrated its reality, the lord's dwelling might be searched for firearms or hidden counterrevolutionaries, just as the lords once sometimes joined

Charles-Louis Chassin, *La préparation de la guerre de Vendée, 1789–1793* (Paris: Paul Dupont, 1892), 1:244.

28. Pierre Caron, "Le mouvement antiseigneurial de 1790 dans le Sarladais et le Quercy," *Bulletin d'Histoire Economique de la Révolution* (1912): 357.

29. Nancy Fitch, "Whose Violence? Insurrection and the Negotiation of Democratic Politics in Central France, 1789–1851," paper presented at the Conference on Violence and the Democratic Tradition in France, University of California, Irvine, 1994, 11.

30. The joint *cahier* of the clergy and nobility of Sarrelouis, for example, denies the legitimacy of any restriction on seigneurial rights that are given in return for earlier concessions (Hyslop, *Guide*, 398).

31. The nobility of Soule defends seigneurial dues "consecrated by so many centuries" (*AP* 5:779).

32. For surveys of attacks on feudal symbolism in several regions, see Simone Bernard-Griffiths, Marie-Claude Chemin, and Jean Ehrard, *Révolution française et vandalisme révolutionnaire* (Paris: Universitas, 1992).

33. In March 1792, agents of the *département* of Ardèche reported to their superiors the peasant belief "that there is a decree which orders the demolition of all the towers of the *châteaux* because they are no longer regarded as anything but houses"; see Anatoly V. Ado, "Le mouvement paysan et le problème de l'égalité, 1789–1794," in Albert Soboul, ed., *Contributions à l'histoire paysanne de la Révolution française* (Paris: Editions Sociales, 1977), 124.

the state in searching peasant homes for forbidden weapons or concealed criminals. In a parish in Périgord a group of peasants compelled a lord to kiss them as a sign of fundamental equality.[34]

And, finally, there was a striking bit of byplay around the meaning of a wooden pole. Lords who had proudly demonstrated their claims to possess the rights of "high justice" often decorated their lawns with gallows, functionless in practice now that capital decisions were in the hands of the king.[35] Even Voltaire, it appears, acquired the right to an elaborate gallows when he climbed his way to the proper status.[36] Their practical inutility, however, did not spare them destruction in some parishes—and their replacement by a different pole by which rural communities indicated their own power and their newly seized freedoms. In early 1790 antiseigneurial events in Périgord and Quercy began to include the installation of a long pole or the trimmed trunk of a very straight tree, often decorated with antiseigneurial mockery and warnings, in place of the front-lawn gallows. Sometimes, indeed, the new pole was itself conceived as a gallows, but now it was the peasants' gibbet rather than the lord's. Eventually these became known as "trees of liberty" but to the peasants of the southwest they were just "mais."[37] The seeming symbolic arbitrariness with which some country people tore down gallows and others erected them should not be seen as indecision on how to symbolize the fall of one order and the creation of another: rather, in that very arbitrariness the community represented itself as the source of justice. For a brief moment, it was not the balance of forces between would-be state-aggrandizing kings and would-be autonomous lords that would determine who built gallows and where; it was the will of the sovereign popular community. The trees of liberty carried so many meanings that the authorities continued to worry about the intentions of those who planted them, a circumstance that itself constituted a peasant rejection of

34. Georges Bussière, *Etudes historiques sur la Révolution en Périgord* (Paris: Librairie Historique des Provinces, 1903), 3:265–66. Anatoly Ado sees this simply as among the "picturesque details of the revolts." It seems a very rich image. On the one hand it can be taken without irony as an application of the egalitarian "fraternal kiss" so common among the revolutionaries (and on which Robert Darnton has commented so interestingly). But it also seems an inversion of the symbolic center of the overturned feudal world. The freely given vassal-lord kiss had marked and cemented entry into the relations of unequals; in Sarladais in 1790 the coerced lord-peasant kiss marked and cemented the entry into the era of equality. See Ado, "Mouvement paysan," 123; Robert Darnton, *The Kiss of Lamourette* (New York: Norton, 1990), 3–20.

35. While no one may have hung from them for some time, a graded complexity of gallows architecture permitted an instantaneous recognition of status. Having the right of high justice, but no fancier title, got a lord the basic two-post model, a baron got four, a duke got six or the top-of-the-line eight. The lord who only had the right of low justice did not get a gallows at all. (Renauldon, *Dictionnaire des fiefs,* 1:478–79).

36. Fernand Caussy, *Voltaire, seigneur de village* (Paris: Hachette, 1912), 3.

37. Mona Ozouf, *La fête révolutionnaire, 1789–1799* (Paris: Gallimard, 1976), 280–316.

elite claims to control meanings. Among the likely meanings was a reference to the sheltering tree on the village green before the church, the most common meeting place for Old Regime village communities, in Jean-Pierre Gutton's estimation.[38] Now the community extended its dominion to the seigneurial lawn.

In considering the relative frequency of the different modalities of challenging the seigneurial regime, we must remember that the nature of our sources makes it certain that many incidents are not fully described and that, therefore, all the figures for the percentage of events with particular characteristics err on the low side. Nonetheless, some of these figures seem noteworthy. While more than half of incidents involved some overt violence (by which I mean here physical injuries to persons or property) as opposed to public declarations, invasions of fields without damage, penetration of the *château* (without smashing furniture, manhandling the lord, etc.), seizing animals but not harming them, demands or threats—almost all of that violence is property damage.[39] While lords may have been quite terrified by these events (and some *were* hurt or even killed and many threatened) revenge on the person of the lord played a fairly small role.

Since the data are undoubtedly skewed to underrepresent less violent forms of making claims, one must be skittish about using such data to attempt to assess the centrality of violence in the Revolution. But, in this light, it is worth observing that the direction of bias almost certainly means that the proportion of incidents with severe personal injury or major property destruction was actually *less* than my figures indicate. Of course there was violence against persons and that violence dominated the ways some recalled the great antiseigneurial risings. The lynching of two royal officials in the streets of Paris a week after the taking of Bastille plainly shocked many deputies as their discussion of the grim events makes evident (*AP* 8:263–67). As Timothy Tackett puts it: "The Rousseauist conception of the Common Man as repository of goodness and truth was frequently replaced, or at least strongly modified, by the image of the violent, unpredictable, and dangerous classes of July and August."[40]

An important recent literature is developing that places violence at the center of the revolutionary experience. Among the many debate-provoking elements of Simon Schama's *Citizens,* none occasioned more comment than

38. Jean-Pierre Gutton, *La sociabilité villageoise dans l'Ancienne France: Solidarités et voisinages du XVIe au XVIIIe siècle* (Paris: Hachette, 1979), 74; see also Henry Babeau, *Les assemblées générales des communautés d'habitants en France du XVIIIe siècle à la Révolution* (Paris: Rousseau, 1893), 21–22.

39. A broader definition of violence would still find the preponderance of such violence directed against property.

40. Timothy Tackett, "Nobles and Third Estate in the Revolutionary Dynamic of The National Assembly, 1789–1790," *American Historical Review* 94 (1989): 279.

his insistence that violence was at the very core of the Revolution.[41] Brian Singer, in prose less vivid but more analytic, similarly urges us to see the violence as far more than a mere by-product of rational actions.[42] I shall merely observe here that the multiple forms of antiseigneurial violence seem to be far more commonly directed at obliterating what distinguishes the lords from other human beings, that is to say, annihilating a social role, rather than the occupants of that role:[43] the *château* is to be stripped of what makes it seigneurial from its archives to its warrior symbols; the lord's animals are to be shared or slaughtered; dues are not to be paid.

One extremely interesting cluster of actions involve the destruction of food sources. While some peasant communities obtained meat while defying the lord's exclusive rights by hunting on the lord's preserves,[44] others appear to have killed the game and left the carcasses;[45] while some forced the lord to feed them, others destroyed the lord's crop;[46] while some made use of the products of the lord's forests, others appear to have primarily damaged the trees;[47] while some seized the creatures the lord was privileged to raise (pigeons, rabbits, fish), others seemed to have been primarily concerned with destroying dovecotes, warrens, and ponds (and their feath-

41. ". . . it [violence] was not merely an unfortunate byproduct of politics, or the disagreeable instrument by which other more virtuous ends were accomplished or vicious ones thwarted. In some depressingly unavoidable sense, violence *was* the Revolution itself." See Schama, *Citizens,* xv. See also Schama's remarks, 445–47.

42. For his important statement of the issues, see Singer, "Violence in the French Revolution."

43. For a similar observation on low levels of personal antiseigneurial violence, see Iain A. Cameron, *Crime and Repression in the Auvergne and the Guyenne, 1720–1790* (Cambridge: Cambridge University Press, 1981), 241.

44. A long tradition of solitary poaching and of communal sheltering of poachers lies behind such acts, to be sure; but probably a more immediate ancestor is to be found in dramatic instances of flagrant and insubordinate defiance of the lord's claims. Anne-Marie Cocula-Vaillières, who has studied such events in Guyenne, thinks them often the work of those whose relative prosperity or experience of urban life provided the resources for openly challenging the lords. See "La contestation des privilèges seigneuriaux dans le fonds des Eaux et Forêts. L'exemple acquitain dans la seconde moitié du XVIIIe siècle," in Jean Nicolas, *Mouvements populaires et conscience sociale, XVIe–XIXe siècles* (Paris: Maloine, 1985), 211–12 and "Les seigneurs et la forêt en Périgord aux temps modernes," in André Chastel, ed., *Le château, la chasse et la forêt* (Bordeaux: Editions du Sud-Ouest, 1990), 101–4.

45. At the same time that neighboring villages in Cambrésis were breaking into local abbeys to seize grain, in early May 1789, a dozen communities around Oisy exterminated a lord's game; see Georges Lefebvre, *Les Paysans du Nord pendant la Révolution française* (Paris: Armand Colin, 1972), 356.

46. On March 26, 1789, for example, the holdings of Count de Gallifet near Draguignan were attacked by peasants who drove their livestock on his sown fields, ruining them; see Jules Viguier, *La convocation des états-généraux en Provence* (Paris: Lenoir, 1896), 269–70.

47. Local officials reported on November 25, 1790, that fruit trees of the abbey of Beaubec in Normandy were cut down, a rather late date for collecting fruit; see Philippe Goujard, *L'Abolition de la "féodalité" dans le pays de Bray, 1789–1793* (Paris: Bibliothèque Nationale, 1979), 99.

ered, furry, or finny inhabitants).[48] It is striking that these acts of destruction are scarcely less numerous in our data than are seizures of food from the lord (5% versus 7% of events) although rather more restricted geographically (occurring in 19% vs. 28% of antiseigneurial *bailliages*).

Should we see such actions as merely the blind anger of those for whom adequate diets were an uncertain but always serious undertaking but among whom lived lords who made of provisioning a form of play? Viewed in this light, such actions would be the "irrational" destructiveness of the envious. But perhaps one might see such actions as an assertion of a claim to a social order in which peasants, like lords, can now defend their productive labors against pests. The lords' special rights in food production had permitted the rabbits, pigeons, ponds, and hunts to damage the lands and crops of their disarmed country neighbors, thereby placing the lords' definition of worthwhile activity over the peasants' (in fact, obliterating it).[49] Now the peasants, asserting claims to adequate weapons, were protecting their own crops by defining their activities as valuable and redefining the lords' game—and games—as so many pests in a way that actually eating the rabbits or fish could not do. If communities like Norroy (see above, p. 120) in March 1789 could express their fear that when their grain ripened in the summer, the lords, carried away by the hunt, could again trample it, it was now the turn of other villagers to decide where and when to hunt and whose fields to trample or spare. In this light, the destructive violence looks far less blind; rather, it appears a constituent part of contesting whose definition of value is to claim pride of place. In this light such actions would be of a piece with the erection/destruction of gallows as part of contesting the sources of the authority to render justice. In reflecting on the two actions, the consumption or the destruction of the lord's game, we have two quite different theses: in the first the distinction in action corresponds to a distinction of a rational search for food on the one hand as opposed to a destructive violence on the other; in the second we have the distinction between the actions of those moved by hunger and of those moved by dignity.[50]

48. In the spring of 1791 peasant communities around Uzerche, Tulle, and Brive fought what Jean Boutier calls "the war against the ponds" in which large numbers of peasants seized their fish and, in the process, destroyed them, a point seen favorably by local urban radicals who regarded the ponds as environmentally damaging. See Boutier, *Campagnes en émoi,* 118–24.

49. Rabbits, pigeons, hunting were often, in principle, activities constrained by customary legal codes, a set of principles often violated. A typical such rule might be that all lords in the province could have "closed" warrens (surrounded by walls or water-filled moats) but "open" warrens were only permitted those with enough land so that neighbors' crops were not ravaged; see Garaud, *Révolution et propriété foncière,* 92.

50. In a somewhat similar vein, Jean-Pierre Hirsch distinguishes among those for whom hunting in the summer of 1789 was "a pleasure long forbidden," those who experienced "the sensation of at last achieving the dignity of bearing arms" and those "moved simply by hunger"; see Jean-Pierre

It is also worth pausing over the relatively small number of incidents in which seigneurial agents are targets. Historians have commonly asserted that the lord's agents, by interposing themselves as intermediaries—whether as dues-collectors, judges, estate managers, or legal advisers—became for the peasants with whom they dealt, the personifications of the ills inflicted by the seigneurial regime. These agents thereby warded off hostility that might have been directed at the more distant lord.[51] The evidence of the actual insurrections as well as the evidence presented earlier from the *cahiers* suggest that on a national scale (see Chapter 2, p. 53) these intermediaries, this world between the lord and the peasant, were in fact relatively minor concerns to the country people. While the French peasants may not have loved the lord's agents, these agents were hardly significant enough to constitute a major target of either grievance or rebellion.[52] The peasants' target seems to have been a social institution and not, primarily, its human beneficiaries.[53] The country people were not, as some of the literature has it, sidetracked by the lord's agents nor were they blinded by the search for revenge on the lord himself. Our evidence confirms the observation of Ado on the scarcity of punitive actions undertaken in

Hirsch, *La Nuit du 4 août* (Paris: Gallimard/Julliard, 1978), 234. Jean-Sylvain Bailly, first mayor of revolutionary Paris, thought that the "disastrous" outpouring of hunting that first summer spared the lands of "patriot princes" like the duke of Orléans. If this claim could be confirmed, it also would assign hunger a reduced place as motive. See *Mémoires de Bailly* (Paris: Baudouin, 1821), 2:244.

51. See, for example, Saint-Jacob, *Paysans de la Bourgogne du Nord,* 428–34; Cobban, *The Social Interpretation of the French Revolution* (Cambridge: Cambridge University Press, 1965), 47–49.

52. Indeed, in some places the agents may have turned into the local leadership once the lord was pushed aside. That, at any rate, is what Jean-Pierre Jessenne found in what is the most detailed study to date of the Revolution's transformation of village politics. In Artois, those whose power had been conferred by the lords before 1789 did well in the municipal elections of 1790, unless the particular local community was at legal loggerheads with the lord—a situation that identified the agent too closely, Jessenne contends, with his master. The lord's appointed *lieutenant* became the Revolution's elected mayor. The 1790 elections were no fluke; the same group did well in 1791. While the 1792 upheaval brought in midsized landowners, urbanites, and artisans, these newcomers continued the same policies locally; and the post-Thermidor era saw the triumphant and long-lived return of the village elite. Is the success of the former seigneurial agents of Artois duplicated elsewhere—especially in the staunch zones of early antiseigneurial activism such as around Mâcon, in Franche-Comté, Dauphiné, and coastal Provence or in later antiseigneurial epicenters like Quercy, Périgord, and upper Brittany? Without the replications that one hopes will be inspired by Jessenne's marvelous study one does not know; but Nancy Fitch has found that insurrectionary actions in a sharecropping region of central France in 1790 sometimes involved the forceable exclusion of this rural stratum between lord and peasant from political life. See Fitch, "Whose Violence?" 12–13; Jessenne, *Pouvoir au village et révolution: Artois, 1760–1848* (Lille: Presses Universitaires de Lille, 1987).

53. For similar judgments, see Jessenne, *Pouvoir au village,* 59; Georges Fournier, "Société paysanne et pouvoir local en Languedoc pendant la Révolution," in *La Révolution française et le monde rural* (Paris: Editions du Comité des Travaux Historiques et Scientifiques, 1989), 388; Steven G. Reinhardt, *Justice in the Sarladais, 1770–1790* (Baton Rouge: Louisiana State University Press, 1991), 231.

1789 against the lords and their servitors, which he contrasts with the murderous insurrectionary practice of the risings of the fourteenth and seventeenth centuries.[54] Our data show an altered peasantry. The pattern of violent action, like the pattern of expressed grievances, suggests a peasantry with an abstract conception of a social system, not fooled by its personification in intermediaries at all.[55] Their actions are violent, to be sure, and often inherently violent, not merely by-products of resistance to peaceable grieving (although resistance might well augment the violence and, let us not forget, my data certainly underrepresents peaceful events). But to be angry does not mean that one must be blinded by anger and to be violent does not mean that one's actions are unguided by reason.

Incidents with a Religious Aspect

Table 5.1 shows incidents with a religious aspect to have been rather less than half as common as antiseigneurial events (although some such events took place in about three-fourths as many *bailliages* as saw antiseigneurial events). Indeed, the two categories are far from totally distinct: some of the events designated "religious" were attacks on the seigneurial rights of ecclesiastical institutions, often monastic establishments, and are counted under the antiseigneurial rubric as well. Table 5.3 shows the range of such "religious" events. The demands for titles, the looting and destruction of documents, the coerced renunciations of claims all marked the struggle against ecclesiastical lords as well as their lay fellows; so did land invasion, fence destruction, forest damage, and the like. Monasteries were a good target of food searches, just as *châteaux* were. But it was not merely through the existence of ecclesiastical lords that the antiseigneurial risings overlapped with conflicts concerning the church. The various forms of resistance to the tithe were also those familiar from the antiseigneurial movement: destruction of scales for determining the ecclesiastical portion of the grain, forceful public and collective avowals of determined refusal, attacks on tithe-collectors, destruction of relevant documents, not to men-

54. Ado, *Krest'ianskoe dvizhenie,* 119.

55. In a close study of rural contestation in Vivarais, Gérard Sabatier shows how violence against persons disappears between "Roure's revolt" in 1670 and the revolt of the "armed masks" of 1783, this last characterized as "the incineration of the material possessions and the instruments of oppression without the extermination of the oppressors." One wonders whether this shift can be generalized to other regions. See Gérard Sabatier, "De la révolte de Roure (1670) aux Masques Armés (1783): La mutation du phénomène contestataire en Vivarais," in Jean Nicolas, ed., *Mouvements populaires et conscience sociale, XVIe–XIXe siècles* (Paris: Maloine, 1985), 130.

tion the diversified array of techniques of surreptitious evasion.[56] Indeed, it is frequently quite difficult to discover from the accounts of the revolts whether the jurists of the day would have regarded the particular exaction that occasioned a rising as tithe or *champart* since the forms of relevant action were indistinguishable. If peasants challenged with force the collection of some of their grain by an ecclesiastical body, it is not always clear whether it was as in its capacity as lord or as tithe-holder that such a body was attacked. But then the tithe-*champart* confusion is one of many key points that associated the ecclesiastical and the seigneurial (see Chapter 4, p. 157). This suggests that it might be useful to conceive of a broader category of antifeudal actions by which I mean here antiseigneurial actions plus those actions against the church in its capacity as lord, as proprietor, or as tithe-collector. Defined in this way, antifeudal actions make up two-fifths of all rural actions in the half-decade under scrutiny and took place in rather more than half of all *bailliages* that saw some form of rural revolt (see Table 5.1).

The antifeudal element, however, hardly exhausts all actions with some religious dimension, for the revolutionary reorganization of the church polarized the rural world. When the revolutionary state insisted that the reorganized church was a church of the Revolution and that the clergy were now civil servants, expected like other civil servants to take an oath to the new regime, the stage was set for some of the most passionately felt bitterness in the French countryside in the entire decade.[57] The "constitutional" priest, who had accepted the Revolution's demands, was threatened, was spit on, was cursed, was stoned, in many a village; while in other peasant communities, it was the "non-juror," the "refractory" priest who refused to go along, who found himself beaten, who found his lodgings burned, who was driven away.

As Table 5.3 shows, incidents involving the Civil Constitution of the Clergy actually are a bit more numerous than the antifeudal share of religiously tinged events. But they also have a strikingly different character, which is revealed in their particular pattern of personal violence. Table 5.3 shows that "religious" events are far more likely to be characterized by

56. Henri Marion, *La dîme ecclésiastique en France au XVIIIe siècle et sa suppression* (Bordeaux: Imprimerie de l'Université, 1912); Marie-Thérèse Lorcin, "Un musée imaginaire de la ruse paysanne: La fraude des décimables du XIVe au XVIIIe siècle dans la région lyonnaise," *Etudes rurales,* no. 51 (1973), 112–24; Jean Nicolas, "La dîme: Contrats d'affermage et autres documents décimaux," in Roger Devos et al., *La pratique des documents anciens: Actes publics et notariés, documents administratifs et comptables* (Annecey: Archives Départementales de la Haute-Savoie, 1978), 173–94; Jean Rives, *Dîme et société dans l'archevêché d'Auch au XVIIIe siècle* (Paris: Bibliothèque Nationale, 1976), esp. 145–62; Georges Frêche, *Toulouse et la région Midi-Pyrénées au siècle des lumières (vers 1670–1789)* (Paris: Cujas, 1976), 536–43.

57. Timothy Tackett, *Religion, Revolution and Regional Culture in France: The Ecclesiastical Oath of 1791* (Princeton: Princeton University Press, 1986).

Table 5.3. Types of Religious Events

Type of Event (Fine Categories)	Percentage of Religious Events	Percentage of *Bailliages* with Religious Events
Violence		
Violence against clerics	47%	58%
(1) Old Regime roles (priest, bishop, canon, monk)	7	18
(2) Nonjurors	14	34
(3) Constitutionals	26	20
Monastery penetrated or trashed	18	36
Monastery or its holdings trashed	24	46
Monastery badly damaged or destroyed	6	12
Titles vs. renunciation		
Coerced renunciation	7	10
Searches, seizures, and demands for documents (monastery and notary)	4	10
Subsistence		
Search for food stores; seizure of goods in wine cellar; compelling monastics to feed the invaders	3	13
Tithe		
All challenges to tithe	8	20
Coerced restitution or other seizures of cash or exactions	3	11
Lord-church nexus		
Destruction of church benches; damage to family tomb; disruption of religious ritual honoring lord	9	21
Land		
All land conflicts (including woods)	5	16
Conflicts over ownership or use-rights in woods	3	9
Destruction of woods or orchards	1	6
Agents		
Attacks on persons or property of seigneurial judges (of ecclesiastical lords), dues-collectors, stewards, notaries, legal advisers	1	3
Civil constitution		
Attacks on anything associated with issues arising from constitutional church (includes attacks on both jurors and nonjurors and buildings used by them)	42	49
"Antifeudal": events with antiseigneurial analogues	39	49

violence against persons than are antiseigneurial events. Somewhat less than half of all religious events include some anti-person violence—ten times the comparable tendency in antiseigneurial events. Among these violent acts, we may distinguish those directed against occupants of roles in the Catholic clergy as such—roles that had existed in the Old Regime and that exist today—from those directed against those who had chosen one or the other side in the great divide opened up by the oath. Violence directed against pre-oath roles accounts for 7% of all "religious" incidents while the violence against nonjurors or jurors, social categories that only existed by virtue of revolutionary legislation, contributed respectively double and more than triple that number of violent events. Notice that violence against pro-revolutionary constitutional clerics was both markedly more numerous (26% vs. 14% of all religious events) and markedly more restricted geographically (20% vs. 34% of *bailliages* with "religious" events). Those who opposed the pro-revolutionary priesthood with violence, although more confined to particular regions than those who violently attacked the clergy who dissented, were also more intensively aggressive. Unlike the antiseigneurial movement, then, both the constitutional church and the illegal church of the nonjurors were attacked in their personified form, the local priest.

While the conflicts over the Civil Constitution were unusually prone to take the form of personal violence, to a reduced extent such a tendency permeated other forms of religious contestation. Even if we remove from the religious category all incidents arising out of the Civil Constitution we still have a rate of personal injury of 12%, more than double the antiseigneurial figure. While the specific issue of the Civil Constitution seems to have been largely experienced in French villages as a question of who is the rightful priest[58] a personalizing tendency seems to have inhered in religious conflict as such. Among the less common forms of religiously tinged conflict were instances of attacks on members of religiously defined groups: Jews in Alsace[59] and, more frequently, Protestants in the countryside around Nîmes.[60] Might such incidents also be held to exhibit the personification of conflict that seems to mark religiously tinged events elsewhere?

58. A smaller number of incidents involved the redefinition of diocesan or parish boundaries that were part of the new religious order. There were a number of attacks on the buildings used by the fraction of the clergy one opposed. And defenders of the nonjurors had some routines other than attacking the constitutional clergy. For example, they often held religious processions of an openly political character. (I found no incidents in which pro-constitutional peasants demonstrated their stand with such a religious procession.)

59. Jean-Claude Richez, "Emeutes antisémites et Révolution en Alsace," in Fabienne Gambrelle and Michel Tribitsch, eds., *Révolte et société* (Paris: Histoire au Présent, 1988), 1:114–21; Rodolphe Reuss, "L'antisémitisme dans le bas-Rhin pendant la Révolution (1790–1793)," in *Revue des Etudes Juives* 68 (1914): 246–63.

60. For some examples, see Gwynne Lewis, *The Second Vendée: The Continuity of Counterrevolution in the Department of the Gard, 1789–1815* (Oxford: Clarendon Press, 1978), 24–25. Peasants

Although the tendency to invest persons with great symbolic power was a common trait of religiously oriented events, the source of energy (defined by antagonists as benevolent or malevolent) might be found in some other concrete location as well. After a series of incidents beginning on Easter Sunday 1792, in which peasant groups that may have numbered in the thousands assembled by an oak where they saw the Virgin, local supporters of the Revolution cut the old tree down.[61] One thinks of Natalie Zemon Davis's discussion of Catholic-Protestant differences in the violence each worked upon the other two centuries and more before the Revolution. The distinctive (but not exclusive) Catholic element was the physical destruction of persons harboring pollution, Protestants being inclined (but not uniquely so) to see pollution in material objects. One wonders, however, whether the Protestant drive to create a newly structured religious community might not be the key to acts that dismantled structures, but left persons intact and, presumably, available to be reintegrated into a reformed church. If one looks for traditional sources of rural conflict patterns in the revolutionary years, a "Protestant" pattern seems pervasive: the objects that make a man a lord are destroyed, the man is spared. But when the source of conflict is the Civil Constitution of the Clergy, both sides cleanse the community by drawing on "Catholic" patterns of assaulting the person of the defiler.[62]

The pattern of peasant action against the lords when considered in contrast with religiously oriented events, suggests that with regard to the seigneurial rights a restructuring of social relations was in order, not the extermination of enemies.

Anti-tax Events

Although no topic so preoccupies the *cahiers* of the countryside nearly as much as the financial demands of the state (see Chapter 2), anti-tax revolts are a relatively scant 3% of all events. They are, however, fairly widespread: our sources identified at least one such event in one-fifth of the *bailliages* of France. Table 5.4 displays the principal forms and targets of tax revolts. In challenging the state's tax-collection apparatus, rural communities might attack the physical manifestations of the tax administration (the barriers at which goods had to be unloaded and inspected for a multiplicity of tolls, the salt-warehouses, the administrative headquarters); they might go after the

were also involved in Protestant-Catholic clashes in—as well as near—southern towns like Nîmes; such incidents are surely underrepresented in the data.

61. Célesin Port, *La Vendée angevine: Les origines—l'insurrection (janvier 1789–mars 1793)* (Paris: Hachette, 1888), 1:323–31.

62. See Davis, "The Rites of Violence," 173–75.

persons or property of the administrative personnel of the tax system; they might assemble in force to openly and massively resist attempts at collection; they might seize and destroy the tax records, a form of action closely analogous to attacks on the records of lord or monastery that indicated who was to pay what.

The rather small number of anti-tax revolts found raises intertwined methodological and substantive issues. At least three quite different hypotheses may be suggested to account for this low incidence. First of all, it is conceivable that rural hostility toward the exactions of lord and church were far more bitterly resented than those of the state. This would be particularly noteworthy in that tax grievances in the *cahiers* are considerably more numerous than grievances concerning the seigneurial regime and the ecclesiastical exactions (see Chapter 2). But, as I have shown in Chapter 3 (see Table 3.1), payments to church and lord drew especially bitter complaints. While such complaints are considerably fewer than tax grievances, the people of the countryside were a good deal more likely to call for the outright abolition of seigneurial rights and ecclesiastical payments while they tended to urge the reform of taxation. It is, then, imaginable that at the very onset of revolution, taxation was far less likely to be experienced as an appropriate target for collective resistance. It is particularly striking that Philippe Goujard has called our attention to rural petitioners during the Revolution who explicitly say that they respect the laws on taxation but not

Table 5.4. Types of Anti-tax Events

Type of Event (Fine Categories)	Percentage of Anti-tax Events	Percentage of Anti-tax *Bailliages*
Forms		
Attacks on tax facilities	25%	40%
Attacks on persons or property of tax officials	30	41
Collective and public statements of resistance	46	55
Attacks on tax records	10	16
Targets		
Tax on salt *(gabelle)*	18	23
Taxes on alcoholic beverages *(aides)*	30	41
Town duties *(octrois)*	8	14
Tax on tobacco *(tabacs)*	4	8
Principal direct tax *(taille)*	3	6
Indirect taxes in general	13	16
Direct taxes in general	3	4
All attacks on indirect taxes	61	66
All attacks on direct taxes	6	10

the continued enforcement of seigneurial rights.[63] If there is anything to such a hypothesis, it is all the more noteworthy when we recall that the great revolts of the previous century were so strongly focused on state revenues. In this regard the insurrectionary pattern of the late eighteenth century marked a great break with past traditions of rebellion.

There is a second conceivable explanation of the data, at once substantive and methodological. Our sources, as we have indicated, are undoubtedly far richer and more thorough in their recording of conflict to the extent that such conflict was open, collective, and aggressive. We exacerbated such a distortion of reality by deliberately not recording events we encountered that did not meet these criteria. Yet we know that the weak deploy a considerable range of hidden, furtive, and anonymous forms of resistance. It is conceivable that passive noncompliance with taxation demands were powerfully effective in the climate of 1789 and beyond, effective enough that the risky work of open, explicit, and forceful challenge in public was a game hardly worth the candle.

Now revolutionary France would seem to have been a tax-evader's paradise. Alison Patrick,[64] commenting on the serious revenue shortfalls in the early 1790s, tellingly points out how much of a mess the new tax situation was with its mix of new taxes, reformed old taxes, and still mandated arrears from the past. Local officials, often with no experience in administering anything and with little guidance from an official hierarchy in process of formation, learning to hire clerks and keep files, found themselves dealing with six different tax rolls (one for the ex-privileged, supposed to cough up their share for half of 1789; one for everyone (no more privileges) for 1790 but still using pre-revolutionary taxes; and four for the Revolution's various new taxes). As Patrick points out, it is a testimony to their seriousness of purpose that these officials managed to collect anything. The steady and ultimately drastic fall in the recovery of indirect taxes shows that the reform sentiments of the *cahiers* gradually yielded, for many peasants, to the possibility of avoidance. The most recent estimates indicate, for example, that in 1791–92 only 45% of what was hoped for in 1791 was collected, down to 27% the following year, then 20% and ultimately a pitiful 9% in 1794–95.[65] When we realize, however, that these goals set for 1791

63. Philippe Goujard, "Les pétitions au commité féodal: Loi contre loi," in *La Révolution française et le monde rural* (Paris: Editions du Comité des Travaux Historiques et Scientifiques), 72.

64. Alison Patrick, "French Revolutionary Local Government, 1789–1792," in Colin Lucas, ed. *The French Revolution and the Creation of Modern Political Culture,* vol. 2, *The Political Culture of the French Revolution* (Oxford: Pergamon Press, 1988), 399–420.

65. J. A. Le Goff and D. M. G. Sutherland, "The Revolution and the Rural Economy," in Alan Forrest and Peter Jones, *Reshaping France: Town, Country and Region during the French Revolution* (Manchester: Manchester University Press, 1991), 70.

were, as Le Goff and Sutherland put it, "astronomic" (72), one will incline to agree as well that "a surprising amount of tax was collected" (73). All of this indicates, I would suggest, that a widespread willingness to pay coexisted with a widespread willingness to resist, and is consistent with the more moderate tones with which taxation—at least direct taxation—was treated in the *cahiers* (see Chapter 3, pp. 100–109).

For those who would avoid payment as chaos enveloped the tax system, why fight head on what one could easily sidestep? If one could avoid loathed taxes by mere nonpayment, better to risk one's neck in attacking the lords than for goals achievable in safer ways. R. B. Rose, one of the few historians to have treated the tax revolts in any detail, argues that an initial burst of attacks on the facilities and personnel of tax collection was succeeded by widespread civil disobedience. A return to open and direct attack would take place whenever the authorities actually attempted to run the risks of seriously attempting collection.[66]

There is yet a third possibility to be grappled with, this time a purely methodological one. Perhaps the research of historians has understressed tax revolt relative to other kinds of events. Both antiseigneurial events and counterrevolutionary ones have found obsessive chroniclers because these sorts of actions are deemed important by significant schools of interpretation. Antiseigneurial events are close to the concerns of Marxists eager to demonstrate the antifeudal character of the Revolution, while enemies (or champions) of the counterrevolution have invested much energy in depicting the nefarious (or heroic) struggles waged by western peasants that led up to the full-scale revolt of 1793. Taxation, however, has rarely been seen as central to any school of interpretation or any post hoc declaration of political allegiance. The result of this neglect is a scarcity of detailed research on tax payment and tax resistance under the Revolution. The country people's extremely strong concern with taxation—recall again that Chapter 2 showed it first and foremost among rural concerns in the *cahiers*—suggests that more attention be paid by historians to insurrections with an anti-taxation thrust.

The purely methodological hypothesis of undercounting may be circumvented by methodological means. Instead of restricting our focus to the overall extent

66. R. B. Rose, "Tax Revolt and Popular Organization in Picardy, 1789–1791," *Past and Present* 43 (1969): 92. Donald Sutherland, drawing on anecdotal evidence, advances the conjecture that anti-tax actions were much more common a few years beyond our time-frame here; as the ease of nonconfrontational avoidance evaporated with the successfully reorganized fiscal system, those who did not want to pay, now, had to fight—and they lost. No one has done any systematic enumeration of anti-tax actions in the 1790s, but the suggestion of an increase later in the decade is plausible, especially if we complement Sutherland's thesis with the observation that the antiseigneurial war was over and peasant discontent, if transmuted into collective action, would have been directed against new opportune targets. See Donald Sutherland, "Violence and the Revolutionary State," paper presented at the Conference on Violence and the Democratic Tradition in France, University of California, Irvine, 1994.

of antiseigneurial and anti-tax uprisings, we shall explore how the relative preponderances changed in the course of the Revolution (as they do). We shall not limit ourselves in other words to the relatively problematic aggregate indications of a great antiseigneurial predominance among forms of revolt, but shall show the rapid growth in this predominance with the Revolution, thereby making the case that something about the Revolution itself played a major role in attracting peasant violence to the seigneurial regime (see Chapter 6). Methodologically, we shall be comparing comparisons and thereby sidestepping the issue of whether historians have wildly underreported on anti-tax movements in the Revolution generally. Perhaps they did, but we shall ask *when* during the Revolution do our data indicate that the relative salience of antiseigneurial movements (as compared, among other things, with anti-tax movements) was especially heavy, a quantity far less subject to challenge as to the unreliability of the aggregate data.

One last possibility to be considered is that there might be something to all three hypotheses. Antiseigneurial movements, in this view, drew on a greater fund of rural hostility to begin with. They also drew on a greater payoff for overt challenges. Divisions among government agents and officials on seigneurial rights meant that such open confrontations mobilized highly placed allies as well as opponents. Finally, the growing antiseigneurial character of the countryside was itself what led to such anti-taxation events as took place to have been understudied.

In light of such considerations, it is interesting to note that of anti-tax actions that entered our data file, a considerable number were only minimally confrontational statements of refusal, rather than offensive attacks on the persons or facilities of the collection system; a collective impeding of the local web of tax collection rather than an attempt to dismantle it or intimidate its directors. Why are such actions so much more salient than analogous actions against the seigneurial regime or the tithe? Perhaps the relative costs of other measures is to the point. To seize the archives of lord or monastery, to attack the person or property of the lord or the local religious establishment, to wreck the scales used in assessment, often required only a little travel time: the lord's *château* or the relevant monastery were often nearby. The tax administration's records, however, were kept in administrative headquarters, and were located in a town—as were the homes of tax officials.

The thinness of Old Regime tax administration meant that it did not reach inside the village. For the major direct tax, the *taille,* in large parts of France, village collectors were appointed from a list of eligible villagers, a task so unrewarding that to be listed was a mark of low status indeed.[67] In

67. Marcel Marion, *Les impôts directs sous l'Ancien Régime, principalement au XVIIIe siècle* (Geneva: Slatkine-Megariotis Reprints, 1974), 5–8.

many parishes, then, there was no tax system to attack: one had to go to town. Marching into town, however, was not only probably a longer walk for many peasants, but might raise issues of public order for the municipal authorities. If this conjecture is accurate, mobilizations against national taxes would have tended to involve peasants in confrontation with local authorities, who were not keen on ceding the streets to country people come to break into a salt depot or tax court. This might help explain why so many conflicts brought in these authorities (look ahead to Table 5.5). Apart from the town leadership, peasants might have feared the attitudes of municipal populations more generally.

Much of peasant participation in anti-tax incidents, moreover, involved them in events in which urban populations also took part, often the predominant part. On July 18, 1789, for example, the town council of Péronne in Picardy reported that "a large number of country people and some workers and apprentices from town" wrecked the tax office and drove out the employees.[68] The sense of rural-urban solidarity against taxes produced by such events over the next year in Picardy was evident in a report on the dismal tax-collection situation there that the controller-general delivered to the National Assembly on June 30, 1790. He described, for example, an incident on April 30, 1790, in the town of Ham in which innkeepers and butchers subject to the *aides* were ordered to pay; he reported that most of the assembled shopkeepers responded that they would refuse as long as others did and that, in nearby towns and even more so in the countryside, innkeepers and others were refusing to submit (*AP* 16:584). One will not find many accounts of country-dwellers storming into town to burn down tax headquarters that suggest that such events took place against a background of a passive urban population. In short, I am suggesting that much of the open anti-tax actions of peasants required urban allies. If these suggestions are accepted, it follows that publicly announcing a collective intention not to pay, or physically impeding the collector (or higher authority) in the performance of his duties, became more common in the taxation arena because the more aggressive descent on a town was a more difficult project than invading an ecclesiastical institution or seigneurial home.

This series of surmises also suggests that rural-urban divisions, which have achieved much prominence of late,[69] need to be rethought. Country people and urban elites (including revolutionary elites) often viewed one another with hostility; some country people and some among the urban

68. See G. Ramon, *La Révolution à Péronne: Troisième série (1789–1791)* (Péronne: J. Quentin, n.d.), 11–12.

69. The recent discussion seems to have been initiated by Tilly, *The Vendée* (Cambridge: Harvard University Press, 1964), Bois, *Paysans de l'Ouest: Des structures économiques et sociales aux options politiques depuis l'époque révolutionnaire dans la Sarthe* (Le Mans: Imprimerie M. Vilaire, 1960), and Cobban, *Social Interpretation*.

lower strata may have differed sharply and antagonistically on all manner of policies—food policy, first and foremost. Yet the evidence of urban riots with urban and rural participant-mixes, at least in anti-tax and subsistence events, shows some capacity for cooperation, too.

As for the target of the anti-tax actions, we note how much more significant were the indirect than the direct taxes, in parallel with the substantially greater hostility shown in the *cahiers* (see Chapter 3). This is in accord with the data of Marcel Marion, which show a severe decline in collection of direct taxes, but an even more severe falloff for the indirect.[70] The bitter sense of many *cahiers* that the indirect taxes, like the seigneurial rights, were destined for private hands rather than public purposes is sometimes clear in the insurrectionary milieu. Controller-General Lambert was struck by a statement of some innkeepers of Roye on their resistance to the *aides:* "We will die before yielding to nourishing with the fruit of our labors the revolting idleness of the vampires who prey upon the people" (*AP* 16:583). Peasant petitions to the National Assembly, in Bryant Ragan's analysis of rural Picardy, also urged reform of direct taxation, in contrast with the fundamentally illegitimate character of the indirect, which were challenged instead by collective violence.[71]

This focus on the indirect taxes in insurrectionary action and in demand-making alike is all the more noteworthy when one considers that the major target of the great anti-tax risings of the previous century were the new direct taxes imposed by the newly vigorous state fiscal bureaucracy. Indeed, Le Roy Ladurie has cogently argued that one of the postrevolt mechanisms by which the state made peace in the countryside was to back away from the direct taxes in favor of the indirect (a history to be repeated by the revolutionary regimes—and the contemporary Fifth Republic, for that matter). Indirect taxes accounted for 24% of revenues in the 1640s and 17% in the 1650s, but averaged between 42% and 50% in the eighteenth century.[72]

The indirect taxes were not only hated but pervasive: there were greater efforts needed for their surreptitious avoidance. The direct taxes tended to be collected by particular agents of the state or, as in the case of the *taille,* by unfortunate villagers dragooned into a tax-collector role at periodic

70. Marcel Marion, "Le Recouvrement des impôts en 1790," *Revue Historique* 121 (1916): 1–47. This, incidentally, constitutes some welcome evidence for the validity of our anti-tax category, one of the more problematic of our types of insurrection from the point of view of data quality.

71. Bryant T. Ragan Jr., "Rural Political Activism and Fiscal Equality in the Revolutionary Somme," in Bryant T. Ragan Jr. and Elizabeth Williams, eds., *Recreating Authority in Revolutionary France* (New Brunswick, N.J.: Rutgers University Press, 1992), 40.

72. Emmanuel Le Roy Ladurie, "Révoltes et contestations rurales en France de 1675 à 1788," *Annales: Economies, Sociétés, Civilisations* 29 (1974), 8; Yves Durand, *Les fermiers-généraux au XVIIIe siècle* (Paris: Presses Universitaires de France, 1971), 57.

intervals. The collection act, then, came to the village from the outside and at infrequent and predictable intervals. If one hid oneself or one's valuables at those times, perhaps the direct tax system would leave one in peace for a while, especially under the confusions and hesitations of the Revolution. The indirect system, on the other hand, pervaded daily life: one paid when one married; when one acquired or disposed of land; when one brought goods across the innumerable customs barriers; when one purchased all manner of things, starting with alcoholic beverages.

And the indirect system didn't chase after one; a person entered its clutches in the course of pursuing other activities to which it had attached itself. To be sure, evasion was possible as widespread salt-smuggling shows; but the risks were continual and had to be continually re-embraced. Even under revolutionary circumstances, simple evasion may have seemed a less definitive tactic than it was for the direct taxes. Generations of successful salt-smuggling had not brought the government to abandon the *gabelle*. The indirect tax system's very pervasiveness, then, meant innumerable opportunities at which those caught up in the sense of possibility opened by the Revolution were continually redrawn by their everyday activities into the world of indirect taxes: an explosive potential, that, it appears, frequently exploded.[73]

Attacks on Authorities

Our data include other challenges to state authority. With a bit of generosity, one might include virtually every event. I include here under the notion of "attacks on authorit*ies*" only events in which the persons or property of officials of national, regional, or local governments are injured. If villagers storm into town and sack the headquarters of the administration of the *aides* it doesn't count here; if they sack the home of the director, it does. Such movements were often by-products of other sorts of conflict: a prisoner

73. Babeuf's career as a champion of a radical conception of the rights of the people was launched in the struggle over the tax on alcoholic drink, the *aides*, in Picardy in 1790. In explaining Babeuf's arrest to the National Assembly, the controller-general felt he need do no more than present an excerpt from a speech of Babeuf's against the *aides* to the effect that "if the entire National Assembly were oppressive, it would be necessary to resist that oppression, that is one of the rights of man . . . that the right of veto belongs to the people alone" (*AP* 16:583). See R. B. Rose, *Gracchus Babeuf: The First Revolutionary Communist* (Stanford: Stanford University Press, 1978), 54–71.

seized for antiseigneurial action—or antichurch or subsistence or anti-tax action—might trigger a massive assault on the local jail, police, military forces, or even the local government; late in our period, a significant wave of anticonscription actions developed, with a very significant component contributed by peasants with little inclination to fight far away. And, then, of course, there were subsistence actions in which local, departmental, or even national authorities might be assailed to try to force them to do something about the food situation. Table 5.5 shows that a substantial proportion of these events involved clashes with the forces of order. For only a minority of such incidents was I able to classify the authorities under attack as "national," "local," or something in between. Of such incidents, however, it seems worthy of note that the local level of authority bore the brunt of the attacks.[74]

Does this suggest a certain boundedness to the political horizons of the people of the countryside, rather along the lines proposed by Eugen Weber? Weber argued, in *Peasants into Frenchmen,*[75] that it was not until the late nineteenth century that peasants began to acquire a genuine sense of involvement in the nation beyond their parish. We have argued, however, that the *cahiers* already showed a broader view (see Chapter 3). Perhaps the resolution lies in the degree to which local officials were ultimately those responsible for carrying out nationally decided policies. It was local officials who bent to the will of the crowd in hard times to avert a food riot or who stuck to the principles on which physiocratic theorists advised controllers-general and shaped the views of revolutionary legislators; it was local officials who let pass a priest's qualified yes in response to the demand for an oath on the Civil Constitution of the Clergy or who upheld the letter of

74. An example: On March 25, 1789, a large group of peasants in town for several of the assemblies being convened in Aix as part of the elections for the Estates-General, joined townspeople in demanding reduced prices on grain and bread as well as decrying the taxes the town levied on such foodstuffs. When a high town official tried to get them to go back to their proper electoral activities, throwing them some coins, insults, and threats, the crowd responded with shouts and stones. The arrival of some fifty soldiers, far from restoring order, enlarged the battle, which lasted long into the night, left several dead and wounded and saw the public granaries ransacked (as well as the stocks of local merchants) after which the military commander set prices and suspended taxes on foodstuffs as the town officials had not. The longer-term fallout included a number of arrests with one death sentence (the other arrestees were amnestied in August); and the formation of a sizable anti-riot town militia large enough that one official claimed an unbelievable four thousand recruits (the entire population of Aix was twenty-five thousand). Two days after the violence began a group of nobles, who like the country people were involved in the elections, announced their advocacy of an end to their own tax privileges. See Monique Cubells, "L'émeute du 25 mars 1789 à Aix-en-Provence," in Jean Nicolas, ed., *Mouvements populaires et conscience sociale, XVIe–XIXe siècles* (Paris: Maloine, 1985), 401–8.

75. Eugen Weber, *Peasants into Frenchmen: The Modernization of Rural France, 1870–1914* (Stanford: Stanford University Press, 1976).

Table 5.5. Types of Anti-authority Events

Type of Event (Fine Categories)	Proportion of Events	Proportion of *Bailliages*
Attacks on persons or property:		
By sphere of competence		
Taxation officials	18	31
Officials (other than taxation)	61	69
Officials concerned with subsistence	14	26
Forces of order (police, military, National Guard)	29	48
By geographic span		
Local officials	21	26
District or department officials	4	8
National officials	12	17

Note: Authority = administrative agents of central, regional, or local government and judges (including police and military forces).

the law and called that a no.[76] In this environment, a forceful figure like Babeuf could use anti-tax sentiment as a basis on which to mobilize people against local governments.[77]

Subsistence Events

These are a major category in themselves. Issues over food supply were a staple form of conflict all over Western Europe.[78] In our data such events constitute one-fourth of all events and are actually more widespread than antiseigneurial events (or even than the broader antifeudal category). Two-thirds of tumultuous *bailliages* saw some form of conflict over food (and more than half of all *bailliages* in the country). Indeed, if we were to regard the subsistence disturbances of 1788–93 as an aggregate, they would probably constitute the largest wave of food riots up to that moment in French history (and in Western European history, for that matter).[79] And

76. On local variation in refusing to accept anything short of an unconditional yes, see Timothy Tackett, "The West in France in 1789: The Religious Factor in the Origins of the Counter-Revolution," *Journal of Modern History* 32 (1990): 413–54. See also Bernard Plongeron, *Conscience religieuse en Révolution. Regards sur l'historiographie religieuse de la Révolution française* (Paris: Picard, 1969), 30–31.

77. R. B. Rose, "Tax Revolt and Popular Organization."

78. Charles Tilly, "Food Supply and Public Order in Modern Europe," in Charles Tilly, ed., *The Formation of National States in Western Europe* (Princeton: Princeton University Press, 1975), 380–455.

79. The results of a comparative enumeration of early modern food riots by John Bohstedt, Cynthia Bouton, and Manfred Gailus show that eighteenth-century French events outnumber

when we consider that the economic liberalism that dismantled the Old Regime's controls in 1789–91 was succeeded by the most systematic price controls in the country's history, we might well see this greatest of subsistence movements as uniquely effective—if only temporarily—in obtaining policy shifts.

Subsistence actions existed in many traditional forms, some highly ritualized. Our data suggest these traditions were doing quite well in the Revolution. Table 5.6 shows that the transportation of grain was a very traditional locus of conflict that was thriving under the Revolution. For the hungry to see grain transported through their turf to somewhere else was well-nigh intolerable and therefore socially explosive (in grim counterpoint to the equally hungry off the beaten track who perhaps quietly starved).[80] When we are considering rural participants and grain of local origin, we may have the added poignancy of the sight of the very grain they helped plant and harvest going elsewhere, but our data do not lend themselves to distinguishing the pillage of grain convoys of local origin from assaults on shipments just passing through. Reason could well add to anger: the involvement of distant claimants on scarce grain, the profit-seeking search of merchants for more lucrative and sometimes distant markets and the efforts of the state to feed soldiers and dangerous urban populations could easily be understood to be the very sources of local scarcity. The very effort of the government to control the flow of grain in order to limit the threat of scarcities associated the government with those scarcities.[81] This process was sometimes reflected in rumors that government officials, along with merchants or large grain-growers, were deliberately hoarding grain to drive prices up.[82] Champions of laissez-faire and of paternalistic regulation

English ones and that German food rioting hardly began before the tail end of the century. While the comparison of enumerations using distinct methodologies is hazardous, our figures here for the revolutionary period dwarf other French riot waves. (See Cynthia Bouton, "Regions and Regionalism: The Case of France," paper presented to the meetings of the American Historical Association, San Francisco, 1994.)

80. This argument has been well developed by Louise Tilly, "The Food Riot as a Form of Political Conflict in France," *Journal of Interdisciplinary History* 3 (1971): 23–57. For some statistical support from the period of the Old Regime's collapse, see John Markoff, "Contexts and Forms of Rural Revolt: France in 1789," *Journal of Conflict Resolution* 30 (1986): 253–90.

81. Steven L. Kaplan, *The Famine Plot Persuasion in Eighteenth-Century France* (Philadelphia: American Philosophical Society, 1982).

82. The usual approach to these rumors is to take them at face value; that is, as statements actually believed by the French (although often doubted or denied by the historian). Since the existence of such rumors could be assimilated to the image of an unenlightened peasantry led astray by a malicious minority, it was surely safer for ignorant peasants to riot on behalf of such a rumor than for clear-thinking peasants to riot on behalf of an openly expressed and rationally developed critique of government policy. The authories' greatest moral condemnation could then be reserved for those who sowed rumors (who could never be found) rather than those held to believe them. When irrational rumors may serve to ward off charges of sedition, one may wonder whether every

alike tended to see scarcities as socially caused and therefore remediable by appropriate legislation;[83] the hungry also experienced hunger as socially rooted rather than an act of God, but engaged in direct action rather than in lobbying legislators.[84]

Such events, around major roads, navigable river and canals, or towns at the junction of transportation arteries, occasioned the massive blockage of the convoy, the seizure of the grain, and pitched battles with the convoys' armed escorts.[85] The marketplace was another classical locale for subsistence disturbances, bringing together as it did many conflicting interests that were profoundly exaggerated in hard times. Market disturbances, indeed, are even more common than attacks on transported grain.[86] Is this

---

one of those rioters who proclaims a belief in such stories actually gives them an unreserved credence. When the existence of such rumors leads the policeman, like the historian, to see peasant unreason, it becomes the height of rationality to claim to act on the rumor.

83. This is a central theme in the great work of Steven Kaplan, *Bread, Politics and Political Economy in the Reign of Louis XV* (The Hague: Martinis Nijhoff, 1976); *Famine Plot Persuasion; Provisioning Paris* (Ithaca: Cornell University Press, 1984).

84. Anyone who writes on subsistence events is indebted to a recent and rich literature. Apart from work already cited, this literature includes: R. B. Rose, "Eighteenth-Century Price Riots, the French Revolution and the Jacobin Maximum," *International Review of Social History* 4 (1959): 432–41; George Rudé, "La Taxation populaire de mai 1775 à Paris et dans la région parisienne," *Annales Historiques de la Révolution Française* 28 (1956); E. P. Thompson, "The Moral Economy of the English Crowd in the Eighteenth Century," *Past and Present* 50 (1971): 71–136; Hilton Root, "Politiques frumentaires et violence collective en Europe au XVIIIe siècle," *Annales: Economies, Sociétés, Civilisations* 45 (1990): 167–89; Cynthia A. Bouton, "Les victimes de la violence populaire pendant la guerre des farines (1775)," in Jean Nicolas, ed., *Mouvements populaires et conscience sociale, XVIe–XIXe siècles* (Paris: Maloine, 1985), 391–99; Guy Lemarchand, "Les troubles de subsistances dans la généralité de Rouen (seconde moitié du XVIIIe siècle)," *Annales Historiques de la Révolution Française* 35 (1963): 401–27; William M. Reddy, "The Textile Trade and the Language of the Crowd at Rouen, 1752–1871," *Past and Present* 74 (1977): 62–89.

85. An anxious report to the Legislative Assembly on February 18, 1792, speaks of towns surrounded by gatherings of country people (= "brigands") threatening to block the movement of goods. The speaker is particularly worried because now, with war threatening, so many troops are needed at the frontiers that the only force available to keep open the grain market is "the national guards, that is to say, the people themselves" (*AP* 38:620).

86. If the secondary literature on which Louise Tilly based her account of the history of subsistence events is to be credited, the blockage of transported grain seemed to have become the most numerous form of such events, a pattern that still held good on the eve of the Revolution. Why, then, does my data give pride of place to market disturbances? Assuming her data and mine are both reasonably reliable on the relative frequencies of blockages and market disturbances, I offer a hypothesis: The general breakdown of authority in the countryside made the transregional shipment of grain an extremely hazardous proposition. Consider the analogy of Anglo-American naval efforts to supply Britain and Russia in World War II. These efforts led to the escorted convoy to counter U-boats. Is it possible that town governments and Parisian *commissaires* fought their own version of the battle of the Atlantic by organizing fewer but larger grain shipments, optimizing the use of such protective military force as they could spare? If so, the result would be fewer occasions for blockage and a higher proportion of these occasions made more risky by virtue of adequate armed escort. (I concede this is the purest speculation.) See Louise Tilly, "The Food Riot

Table 5.6. Types of Subsistence Events

Type of Event (Fine Categories)	Percentage of Events	Percentage of *Bailliages*
Action directed at strategic points in market process		
Transportation of grain blocked; land or river convoys attacked; grain purchases prevented; grain in transit seized (sometimes accompanied by price-setting)	18%	38%
Marketplace invaded; grain, bread, or flour seized; coerced price control in marketplace	29	49
Authorities asked to intervene in provisioning or pricing of food; authorities, persons or property attacked for failing to do so	6	15
Searches and seizures of stocks		
Lord's stock of food or drink seized; lord compelled to feed crowd; lord's game hunted, his privileged animals (rabbits, pigeons, fish) seized; lord's fruit seized	10	20
Monastery's stocks of food or drink seized; crowd feasts at monastery; fruit from monastic orchard seized	2	7
Food sought or seized from source other than lord or monastery; public warehouses broken into; domiciliary visits; raids on noble or bourgeois stocks; seizure of harvested grain (including seizures from prosperous peasants)	10	22
All searches and seizures	22	38
Retribution against the culpable		
Violence against persons or property of those held responsible for shortages: government officials, hoarders, merchants, grain speculators, millers, peasants withholding grain from market, peasants resisting price controls	8	25

because the market was a fixed rather than a moving target?[87] Markets were held on fixed days at fixed sites while transported grain required advance intelligence or lucky sightings as well as rapid mobilization to constitute a promising opportunity. (The frequency of attacks on moving

as Political Conflict," 50. It is worth noting that the largest wave of prerevolutionary subsistence disturbances, the Flour War of 1775, also had an atypically low proportion of blockages compared to market disturbances; see Cynthia Bouton, *The Flour War: Gender, Class and Community in Late Ancien Régime Society* (University Park: Pennsylvania State University Press, 1993), 141.

87. A spectacular cluster of such events took place in November and December 1792 as enormous bands (from several hundred to several thousand strong) went from one marketplace to another, recruiting participants to join them for a day's march as they traveled across some eight departments around Maine. See Michel Vovelle, *Ville et campagne au XVIIIe siècle: Chartres et la Beauce* (Paris: Editions Sociales, 1980), 245–53.

convoys is eloquent testimony to the rapidity with which French peasants could mobilize.)

In these urban marketplaces we find crowds (often including rural participants and even rural invaders) who seized grain or flour or bread; who insisted that the authorities control the price; who, the authorities in default, imposed that price themselves (meaning in practice that millers, bakers, well-off peasant sellers were threatened with injury—or worse—if they attempted to charge more than the crowd demanded). Searches and seizures were another time-honored response: crowds might break into municipal granaries and warehouses[88] or might carry out a dreaded "visit"—the invasion of the homes of the well-off by poor people seeking food. Such domiciliary visits troubled many a noble or bourgeois home in town and many a farmhome of a well-to-do peasant proprietor. In a related tactic, harvested grain was at risk from hungry people, however and wherever stored.

Some of these actions were quite likely to generate violence, particularly if resisted, but that is only a portion of the violence that hung over such events. In a moral climate in which hunger was understood as a social creation, the persons held responsible might well be the targets of anger: perhaps a peasant who was believed (sometimes accurately) to be withholding grain from the market, perhaps a speculative (or a merely cautious) hoarder, perhaps a baker or a miller or a merchant might find himself in great danger, all the more so if such a person was resisting a movement for controlling prices. And, perhaps particularly attractive in a climate of growing assaults on the attributes of the lords, lay and clerical alike, the local *château* or monastery was a good spot to visit if one sought food,[89] or sought those suspected of withholding from the marketplace until prices rose still further.

Rural visits unconnected to market disturbances or blockages, however, seem a tradition of very recent vintage, according to Cynthia Bouton's meticulous dissection of the changing structure of subsistence conflicts. She sees the Flour War of 1775, in which such events were (atraditionally)

88. A tempting target in towns at the center of regional export networks was the private storage room rented by a grain exporter prior to forming the export convoy; see Bouton, *Flour War,* chap. 4.

89. As I have only considered measures to secure food as subsistence events, Table 5.6 includes the seizure of the lord's stocks but not their destruction, a class of actions that I discussed under the general antiseigneurial category above (ditto for monastic or other stocks). It may well be that the scattering of grain on the ground, while sometimes genuinely one such destructive act, was at other times intended to make some food available for those too poor to pay at even the coerced just price that so many accounts report those seizing food stocks to opt for. At a time of acute social conflict, such an act has perhaps the added appeal of pointing up the failure of lord, monastery, or wealthy landholder to provide for the poor. Cynthia Bouton noted actions of this sort in the "flour war" of 1775; see her "L'économie morale et la guerre des farines de 1775," in Florence Gauthier and Guy-Robert Ikni, eds., *La Guerre du Blé au XVIIIe siècle: La critique populaire contre le libéralisme économique au XVIIIe siècle* (Paris: Les Editions de la Passion, 1988), 99.

numerous as a step toward going beyond the structure of distribution—in which the state was implicated—to the structure of production, in which the *château* and even the storage facilities of larger landowners of all varieties were targets.[90]

Her research on the great Flour War that followed the government's decontrol of the grain trade in 1775 offers the intriguing suggestion that an enhanced participation of rural people in seizing grain at likely rural sites in the later eighteenth century—whether monastery, wealthy peasant's place, or *château*—was a sort of contestatory bridge between what we may call the traditional forms of subsistence action and the antiseigneurial storms ahead. Bouton points out that from the point that developing state controls began to systematically trigger subsistence events[91] the usual forms were the market invasion and the blockage: the first essentially urban, the second often so; the participants were often women, gathered for market activity. By the late eighteenth century, however, a more rural and more male practice was developing in which grain was seized in the countryside before it got to market, a shift that brought an antiseigneurial (but also antimonastic and anti-prosperous-peasant) element into play. These rural men were largely wage-workers in domestic industries or agricultural day-laborers. Bouton's suggestion is that the new form of subsistence event was the outgrowth of the social polarization that was part of the general syndrome of rising urban and rural populations, rising grain prices, and falling real wages for laborers but rising profits for large grain-producers. This shift was reflected by adding a new cluster of actions to the classical forms of subsistence struggle. The traditional attacks on various intermediaries (millers, merchants, market-vendors, police, judges) was now joined by the direct attack by the losers on the winners in the class polarizations at the village level. From the classic struggle to force the state to live up to (or to bring back) effective paternalism, the subsistence events were taking on, by 1775, the lines of open and unmediated class conflict.[92] The newer forms of conflict that Bouton found in the Flour War anticipate some of the clashes of the Revolution.

During the Revolution, our data show that antiseigneurial (and religious) events were not only sometimes subsistence events. Even when the targets

90. Bouton, "Gendered Behavior in Subsistence Riots: The Flour War of 1775," *Journal of Social History* 23 (1990): 735–54. Ado and Lemarchand also see the subsistence conflicts after midcentury as steps toward taking on the lords and the church. See Ado, *Krest'ianskoe dvizhenie,* 72, and Lemarchand, "Troubles de subsistances," 412–13.

91. Since market disturbances of varying scales are quite old, a precise date is difficult. Louise Tilly suggests the 1690s as the time when "widespread food riots, involving large numbers of people" began; see "The Food Riot as Political Conflict," 24.

92. Bouton, "Gendered Behavior in Subsistence Riots," and "Economie morale et guerre des farines," 93–110.

could be clearly differentiated, there might be a common language of contention. The people who set up a gallows in the marketplace at Chemillé, presumably to deter hoarders, late in August 1790 made use of an idiom more commonly deployed before the *château.*[93] If subsistence disturbances could borrow an antiseigneurial language, the reverse was true as well. Some of the peasant participants in the Flour War were breaking into homes and interrupting their search for grain long enough to drink their victim's wine,[94] a mockingly coerced invocation of hospitality (and a mocking sacrament as well?) that was widely taken up in antiseigneurial actions in the 1790s.

For all their grip on people's minds in the eighteenth century, however, notice how the number of subsistence events involving vengeance upon personifications of the shortages—specific hoarders, profiteers, etc.—is hardly enormous (8%).[95] And much of the violence toward persons arises not out of a crowd's rough justice, but from the resistance of this miller, that merchant, or thus-and-such official to crowd demands about availability or price. However often some among the country people repeated rumors of personal and deliberate profiteering by business interests with the collusion of government officials, these country people nonetheless directed most of their actions toward very plausible sources of food. Venting anger upon the culpable is, by comparison, a relatively small part of the agenda of contentious gatherings (although hardly a small matter to the targets). Note the similarity with the low frequency of personal violence in antiseigneurial events and the profound contrast with the clashes surrounding the revolutionary reorganization of the church.

Colin Lucas has recently emphasized the theme of personal violence in an important new interpretation of revolutionary crowds.[96] He takes the personification of the bad as an element of a "traditional" sense of the crowd. This traditional crowd may fill in for a government derelict in its responsibility for provisioning towns[97] or for providing justice: a crowd that

93. See Port, *Vendée angevine,* 1:99.

94. Bouton, "Les victimes de la violence populaire," 393.

95. By way of confirmation, note that Cynthia Bouton finds violence against persons relatively rare in food riots generally. In the Flour War of 1775 only 2% of those arrested were accused of violence against another person (*Flour War,* chap. 4). Iain Cameron also finds violence against persons in subsistence events to be remarkably low in pre-Revolutionary Périgord (*Crime and Repression,* 240–41).

96. Colin Lucas, "The Crowd and Politics," in Colin Lucas, ed., *The French Revolution and the Creation of Modern Political Culture,* vol. 2, *The Political Culture of the French Revolution* (Oxford: Pergamon Press, 1988), 259–85.

97. Thus Louise Tilly has argued that it is only from late in the seventeenth century that the classical forms of subsistence events flourished in France. As the government backed off from blocking exports, the popular blockages multiplied; as the government began to deregulate prices,

may punish individual wrongdoers and even resist unjust officials. Yet the traditional crowd is one that experiences its own occupation of public space, whether the village square or the Place de Grève in Paris, as temporary. The crowd will soon enough, it knows, disperse; the king's power will again flow back into its usual abodes. Lucas finds it particularly significant that such personalized antiseigneurial violence was highly selective and cites a number of instances of lords in the Rhône valley who combined extreme abuse of their peasants before 1789 with imprudent action thereafter.[98] In the same vein one could refer to Georges Lefebvre's great account of "the murder of the count of Dampierre." This count for some years not only had particularly acrimonious dealings with his peasants, but was also visibly a supporter of the king as the unfortunate monarch was being dragged back to Paris following the flight to Varennes.[99] The selectivity in such violence persuades Lucas that the crowd action is not random frenzy, but follows a code of justice. This is persuasive, but Lucas only explores crowd selectivity in its choice of whom to lynch. The study of antiseigneurial events, of subsistence disturbances, of antitax risings shows quite a different sort of selectivity as well, one in which a personalized approach to conflict turns out to characterize only a small minority of events.[100] (Indeed it seems to be the case in Lucas's own evidence; the few dramatic cases of retribution against his Rhône valley lords stand out against a background of a different pattern in most antiseigneurial events.) The overall pattern of events suggests a crowd with a much more abstract conception of social structures than even Lucas allows. Nor did it take the revolutionary mobilization to educate or modernize the country people, at least not in these ways. The parish *cahiers,* we may recall, show us a peasantry at the very beginning of the Revolution, already imbued with a sense of unjust institutions and not just unjust individuals (see Chapter 3). Their views of seigneurial rights and taxation showed us a sense of a socially instituted and therefore socially modifiable system; not a collection of individually oppressive lords and tax collectors. In terms of our insurrection data, what stands out as unusual, in fact, is precisely the personification of the great religious conflicts, particularly once the Civil Constitution becomes the issue.

---

so coercively imposed popular price-setting arose. See Louise Tilly, "Food Riot as Political Conflict," 47–52.

98. Ibid., 269.

99. Georges Lefebvre, "Le meurtre du comte de Dampierre (22 juin 1791)" in *Etudes sur la Révolution française* (Paris: Presses Universitaires de France, 1963), 393–405.

100. Simon Schama notices this selectivity for the summer of 1789 ("there were remarkably few fatalities"), but doesn't pause in his depiction of horrors to try to explain the remarkable (Schama, *Citizens,* 433).

Wage Conflicts

If prices were the spur to economic conflict in premodern Europe, wages are that spur in the proletarianized world of the present. Anatoly Ado suggested that wage conflicts were already significant in the French countryside of the revolutionary epoch.[101] Preliminary results of the Nicolas-Lemarchand study show that such conflicts constituted a small but noticeable proportion of rural events in the century preceding the Revolution.[102]

In some areas wage conflict between harvest workers and rural employers had become a well-institutionalized annual drama, in which plans were developed and news communicated at the local cabaret; organized bands of workers then recruited others to join them and frightened still others into refusing to work. Clashes with the rural police often followed. The bands of strikers grew out of the work-gangs with which one often had to affiliate to get hired; work-gangs in turn were often formed around migrant laborers, linked by kinship or sharing a common regional dialect. The work-gang chiefs seem to have been country people with some experience of a world away from the village, acquired in town or military service.[103] A worried revolutionary government, as early as September 1791, forbade rural laborers to organize to press for higher wages.[104]

I found some 42 such wage events in my data, but as a proportion of all forms of rural conflict they account for under 1% of all events and only occur in a small number of *bailliages*. The significance of price issues compared to wage issues suggests the Revolution to be a period in which the major outlines of class struggle were traditional.

Land Conflicts

While rural class conflict only rarely took the form of wage disputes, however, more traditional struggles over land were far more numerous and

101. Ado, *Krest'ianskoe dvizhenie,* 17.

102. Nicolas finds 5% of his incidents from 1661 to 1789 to be "labor conflicts," a category very close in practice to the "wage conflict" used here ("Les émotions dans l'ordinateur"). Guy Lemarchand shows the proportions of disturbances that involve wages to be growing in the eighteenth century—it rises to about 6% of all incidents in the Nicolas-Lemarchand data set—but this data includes urban incidents. See Lemarchand, "Troubles populaires au XVIIIe," 37.

103. Jean-Marc Moriceau, "Les 'Baccanals' ou grèves de moissoneurs en pays de France (seconde moitié du XVIIIe siècle)" in Jean Nicolas, ed., *Mouvements populaires et conscience sociale, XVIe–XIXe siècles* (Paris: Maloine, 1985), 421–34.

104. True to its principled freeing of the market, proprietors were forbidden to join together to try to push wages downward. See Fernand Gerbaux and Charles Schmidt, *Procès verbaux des comités d'agriculture et de commerce de la Constituante, de la Législative et de la Convention* (Paris: Imprimerie Nationale, 1906–10), 2:549.

took on many forms. Many of these battles involved communal invasions of disputed turf: a field held to be communal property that had been illicitly usurped by lord, monastery, wealthy urbanite, or even prosperous peasant (a far rarer target) might be occupied, with peasants showing up to work the land (if arable) or driving their animals to graze upon it if not. Associated actions included the breaking of fences (also appropriate when a relatively prosperous landholder attempted to remove his own holding from communal constraints even if possession of the land was not in itself seen as illicit). Pastures were one notable locale for such clashes and forests were a very notable and much more numerous second.

Rights in the wooded areas of France were often the scenes of complex and many-sided disputes.[105] A peasant community might have long-standing rights there: rights to graze animals, rights to collect fallen wood, rights to acorns (a valuable stopgap in hard times). Lords who wished to clear more land for planting and lords who wished to hunt without competition from poachers might over the years have worked out some form of shaky accommodation with their peasants. In the late eighteenth century, however, wood prices were rising steeply as multiple uses for forest products grew explosively. Urban growth meant tremendous use of wood for the construction boom and urban building entrepreneurs could pay top prices. The developing metal industries (all industry for that matter) depended heavily on wood for fuel. The rural ironworks of Alsace, for example, consumed charcoal, not coal. But if construction and forges bid up the price of wood, so did the world struggle for imperial dominion. A French government obsessed with competing with Britain on the seas devoured timber for ship construction. Government technocrats, indeed, attempted to insist on a rational exploitation of French woodlands to prevent the depletion of an essential strategic material. With all this interest, prices soared: and secular lords, urban proprietors, and monastic landlords alike strained to break their traditional deals with peasant communities in order to fully appropriate the wooded areas. Nor did country people limit themselves to the defense of traditional claims. The location of conflict, Andrée Corvol has shown, was shifting during the eighteenth century from communal woods to royal forests and the infractions of the country people were becoming less oriented to domestic provision and more to market opportuni-

105. Andrée Corvol, "Forêt et communautés en basse Bourgogne au dix-huitième siècle," *Revue Historique* 256 (1976): 15–36; "Les délinquences forestières en basse-Bourgogne depuis la réformation de 1711–1718," *Revue Historique* 259 (1978): 345–88; and *L'homme au bois: Histoire des relations de l'homme et de la forêt (XVIIe–XXe siècles)* (Paris: Fayard, 1987); Christian Desplat, "La forêt béarnaise du XVIIIe siècle," *Annales de Midi* 85 (1973): 147–71; Saint-Jacob, *Paysans de la Bourgogne du Nord,* 488–90 and passim; Guy Lemarchand, "Vols de bois et braconnage dans la généralité de Rouen au XVIIIe siècle," in Jean Nicolas, ed., *Mouvements populaires et conscience sociale, XVIe–XIXe siècles* (Paris: Maloine, 1985), 229–39.

ties.[106] As a result the government's forestry program increasingly allocated resources to control illegal grazing, pilfering, and other violations of law.[107]

Grazing land competed with the forests as a location for conflict. In the struggle for pasture, a large stockraiser could profit by producing meat for growing urban and military populations, leather and horses for the military, and animal fat for a variety of industrial uses—but only if a more absolute claim to that pasture could win out over the claims of peasant smallholders and the landless to traditional rights to glean and to have their animals graze. In the eighteenth century, enterprising lords sometimes concocted newly profitable traditions in which their fellows in regional judiciaries supported them. One finds, for example, lords renting out land still claimed by peasant communities to commercial stock-raisers, almost everywhere a violation of traditional understandings that the land was for the small and the great of the local community alone.[108] Similarly, the lords were attempting, more and more, to seize the forests, in this case somewhat restrained by intermittent royal support for conservationist measures. And just as the peasants used the opportunity presented by the general collapse of effective repression to assert and reassert[109] their claims to the pastures, they let their animals loose in the forests, flamboyantly organized mass cuttings of wood and, when that was too dangerous, carried on massive and virtually unstoppable surreptitious pilferings at night. Cutting down the trees the lord

106. Andrée Corvol, *L'homme et l'arbre sous l'Ancien Régime* (Paris: Economica, 1984), 664–65.

107. Andrée Corvol, "La coercition en milieu forestier," in Jean Nicolas, ed., *Mouvements populaires et conscience sociale, XVIe–XIXe siècles* (Paris: Maloine, 1985), 199–207.

108. In its *cahier,* the parish of Dolving in the *bailliage* of Lixheim complains of the commercial stock-raisers to whom "contrary to the formal dispositions of the customary law of Lorraine and contrary to the public good" the local lords have leased their grazing rights. The peasants argue that as outsiders to the community these stock-raisers have no interest in caring for the land. In the cause of transforming a traditionally defensible claim claim to one-third of communal resources into an illegitimate source of rental income, the stock-raisers act with "inhumanity": they insist that the peasants make no more than double their own use of the grazing areas ("counting a horse or an ox or a cow as four sheep") and thereby force members of the community to get rid of either their draft animals or their pigs. (P. Lesprand and L. Bour, *Cahiers de doléances des prévôtés bailliagères de Sarrebourg et Phalsbourg et du baillage de Lixheim pour les états généraux de 1789* (Metz: Imprimerie Paul Even, 1938), 186.

109. Certainly the *cahiers* often speak of restoring a right encroached upon by a lord, by a monastery—or by the Water and Forest Administration. Thus one community refers to the permission granted to "his poor subjects" by a count 650 years ago to pasture their animals in the forest, now forbidden by the local viscount. ("Our monarch is no less generous and compassionate than Count Renaud was in similar circumstances; they therefore hope for the same grace."). See Zoltan-Etienne Harsany, *Cahiers des bailliages des généralités de Metz et de Nancy pour les états généraux de 1789,* ser. 1, vol. 5, *Cahiers du bailliage de Pont-à-Mousson* (Paris: Librairie Paul Hartmann, 1946), 120. The demand that something be *re*established or restored is far more common with regard to communal rights than most other institutions. Of all grievances on other subjects a minuscule 1% are calls to reestablish; when the subject is communal rights, however, 10% of demands are in this vein.

claimed as his own, even without hauling them off, was a conspicuous act of defiance.[110]

In disputes over ownership and use rights, moreover, whether the setting was pasture or forest, rural communities endowed with patience and access to legal advice could press their claims in court; the legal route may not have yielded much satisfaction (and was beyond the reach of poor communities) but the encounter of lawyer and peasants in taking on the lords may have been a major focus for the formation of an antiseigneurial discourse melded out of the lawyer's search for abstract principles of law and the villagers' knowledge of detail. When, to take up an Alpine example, the Commission Intermédiaire of the Provincial Estates in Dauphiné surveyed social issues in early 1789, it found, within the present boundaries of the *département* of Drôme, some half-dozen villages locked in legal combat with their lords over land use.[111]

But disputes between peasant communities and the well-endowed over land use hardly exhausts the forms of land conflict under the Revolution. Peasant communities divided internally in complex ways on issues of agrarian individualism. Were communal rights to fix the date of the harvest, to regulate technology, or to limit ownership resources to be preserved—or were they fetters to be destroyed? There has been a long-standing debate on whether communal rights of various sorts (rights of gleaning, of pasturage, of common proprietorship, of restrictions on technology) are to be understood as primarily benefitting the richer or the poorer members of the community.[112] Whatever the precise way the rural community threatened to fragment over such questions, illegal divisions of common land became one of the noteworthy forms of rural land struggle under the Revolution, amounting to one-fourth of our incidents of land conflict. Sometimes this might be combined with communal action against a large proprietor: a field worked by the lord's wage laborers, say, might be communally seized, a

110. Marc Bloch, "La lutte pour l'individualisme agraire dans la France du XVIIIe siècle," *Annales d'Histoire Economique et Sociale* 2 (1930): 329–81, 511–56; *Les caractères originaux de l'histoire rurale française* (Paris: Armand Colin, 1968).

111. Jean Sauvageon, "Les cadres de la société rurale dans la Drôme à la fin de l'Ancien Régime: survivances communautaires, survivances féodales et régime seigneurial," in Robert Chagny, *Aux origines provinciales de la Révolution,* 39–40. See also Cl. Wolikow, "Communauté et féodalité: Mouvements anti-féodaux dans le vignoble de Bar-sur-Seine, fin de l'Ancien Régime," in Albert Soboul, ed., *Contributions à l'histoire paysanne de la Révolution française* (Paris: Editions Sociales, 1977), 283–308.

112. Georges Lefebvre, "La Révolution française et les paysans," in his *Etudes sur la Révolution française* (Paris: Presses Universitaires de France, 1963), 338–67; Albert Soboul, *La Révolution française* (Paris: Gallimard, 1962), 1:61–63; Florence Gauthier, *La voie paysanne dans la Révolution française: L'exemple de la Picardie* (Paris: Maspero, 1977); Cobban, *Social Interpretation;* Ado, *Krest'ianskoe dvizhenie,* 192–93; Hilton Root, *Peasants and King in Burgundy: Agrarian Foundations of French Absolutism* (Berkeley and Los Angeles: University of California Press, 1987).

traditional enough sort of claim, particularly if it could be asserted that the field in question really, authentically, was communal land to begin with that had at some identifiable point been usurped by the lord (or his father or grandfather . . .). But when, as sometimes happened, the occupying peasants divided up that land, they were doing something that appears a good deal less traditional. And sometimes, the illegal division took place without being part and parcel of collective action against an outsider. There are intracommunal disputes here, too.[113] (There are also a small number of intercommunal land disputes).[114]

Table 5.7 shows the distributions of these various ways in which land was contested.[115] Of the incidents we found, the lion's share goes to conflicts between the lord and the peasant community. If we join anti-ecclesiastical land conflicts to antiseigneurial ones in an antifeudal category we get almost three-fifths of our land conflicts. That land issues and the seigneurial regime were intertwined would hardly have surprised France's elites. We may recall that we saw that Third Estate *cahiers* taking up issues of land arrangements not explicitly seigneurial—lease terms, condition of purchase, landlessness—were also prone to consider the seigneurial regime at greater length (see Chapter 4, p. 178). Among "non-feudal" targets, the bulk are conflicts among groups of peasants themselves, generally within but, occasionally, between communities. A surprisingly small number are over land owned by

113. Intracommunal struggles might be generated by revolutionary opportunities. In the Alpine parish of Baronnies, for example, the sale of church land generated a struggle between what appears to be a larger group committed to equal division of the property of the local priory and a smaller group of the apparently better-off who got the land at auction. A long period of threats, window-breaking, stolen seedlings, slaughtered animals, felled trees, fifes and drums, arrests and military force followed. See Jean Nicolas, *La Révolution française dans les Alpes. Dauphiné et Savoie, 1789–1799* (Toulouse: Privat, 1989), 141–42.

114. Intercommunal conflicts, sometimes of long standing, could become entangled with positions in revolutionary politics. For some examples from a frontier region, see Michel Brunet, *Le Roussillon face à la Révolution française* (Perpignan: Trabucaire, 1989), 96–98.

115. A striking aspect of land conflict is the virtual absence throughout the Revolution of seizures of land as such, that is, as principled redistributions of property regarded as a self-justifying measure. This absence is particularly striking when the actions of peasantries in other revolutionary contexts is explored by way of searching for comparative benchmarks. It is impossible to think of the countryside in the Russian, Mexican, or Chinese Revolutions without thinking of widespread land seizures. But in France it is only *usurped* land that is seized; it is property that is already communal that is targeted for illegal division and distribution. Indeed, often it is not even full ownership that is seized. When smallholders' animals are driven over the just-destroyed fences around land that the lord had defended against traditional village rights, we have the assertion of communal claims to shared usage. If we turn from peasant action to legislative action, we find that only the land of church and king (to which émigré land was later added) was to be redistributed. There is no revolutionary legislation that aims to break up large estates as such and turn France's microfundistas into minifundistas, just as there is only the most limited move from below for generalized land seizures. Even so, the fear that such a movement might emerge haunted the revolutionary legislatures as the Revolution radicalized generally; see Chapter 8, p. 485.

urbanites. The land administered by the revolutionary state itself, however, seized from church and king and destined for sale, was a rather more significant, if still relatively small, object of dispute. (Perhaps it doesn't fully belong under the "non-feudal" rubric since much of this land had belonged to the church.) What is striking overall is the absence of a grassroots movement for breaking up large estates. It is the lord's usurped land (lay and ecclesiastic) that is to be seized (or perhaps reseized from the state) or it is communal land (whether usurped by a lord or not) that is to be divided or differently used. In this respect, at any rate, the land movement does not seem to fit very well within the rubric of a rearguard action against a nascent capitalism.[116]

So many attempts to seize food or control its price, so many land invasions, so much tax resistance, and so little wage conflict. Such a picture is one of a tremendous recrudescence of traditional targets and strategies of conflict rather than the discovery of new ones. Charles Tilly argues that the dominant modalities of popular conflict in France remained within the traditional forms well into the 1840s. It is only in that fifth decade of the nineteenth century, Tilly argues, that newer forms of struggle begin to eclipse the venerable patterns of past centuries.[117] There was, in fact, an

Table 5.7. Types of Land Conflict

Type of Event (Fine Categories)	Percentage of Events	Percentage of *Bailliages*
Possessor of disputed land:		
"Feudal"		
Seigneurial	49%	58%
Ecclesiastical	10	24
Total feudal	59	67
"Nonfeudal"		
State	6	14
Urban bourgeois	1	2
Peasant (includes intracommunal and intercommunal conflicts)	37	44
Total nonfeudal	43	50
Issue		
Enclosures, fences	9	24
Rights in the forests	36	50
Division of the commons	27	30

116. On the mix of "antifeudal" and "anticapitalist" elements in the peasant movement, see Chapter 7.

117. Charles Tilly, "How Protest Modernized in France, 1845–1855," in William O. Aydelotte, Allan G. Bogue, and Robert William Fogel, *The Dimensions of Quantitative Research in History* (Princeton: Princeton University Press, 1972), 192–255.

innovative side of the Revolution's contention, Tilly writes elsewhere, but the revolutionary governments achieved remarkable success in harnessing, controlling, channeling, and ultimately taming these popular energies—so that the Revolution failed to leave an innovative legacy as far as the forms of struggle are concerned.[118] Our data on the Revolution certainly show the vitality of traditional targets and tactics. But there is nothing very traditional about the weight of antiseigneurial actions.

Counterrevolution

It was hardly the case that all rural events had targets identifiable as the beneficiaries of the Old Regime. Often, indeed, it was the newer revolutionary authorities who were under fire. Donald Sutherland has stressed the polarizing aspect of the Revolution, arguing that it divided French society in two right from the beginning.[119] In his treatment of the background to the explosion of open and armed peasant counterrevolution that began in 1793, Sutherland urges us to see the *chouannerie* first and foremost as a civil war within the countryside.[120] We can trace the rivulets of tension that ultimately flowed into the flood sparked by the embattled state's attempt to conscript unwilling peasants to die far from home in defense of the new order. When our time-frame ends in June 1793 the military campaigns of the counterrevolution were still running strong, so we cannot trace the aftermath. (And much of the military action is excluded by the way we have defined our events.) Nonetheless, there is a good deal that we can count.

Arguably, any form of opposition to any governing authority from the summer of 1789 on might be labeled counterrevolutionary in the sense that it constituted an actual or potential threat to the capacity of the regime to mobilize resources to defend itself. The government of the moment might well agree with such a categorization. However, many of the most intense sources of opposition to the various governments came from groups plainly committed to advancing the Revolution (at least the Revolution as they, rather than the new elites, defined it). I do not want to confuse angry peasants who feel their demands have not yet been met (and therefore

118. See Charles Tilly, *The Contentious French* (Cambridge: Belknap Press of Harvard University Press, 1986), 388–89.

119. "The history of the entire period can be understood as the struggle against a counterrevolution that was not so much aristocratic as it was massive, extensive, durable and popular"; see Donald M. G. Sutherland, *France, 1789–1815: Revolution and Counterrevolution* (New York: Oxford University Press, 1986), 10.

120. Donald M. G. Sutherland, *The Chouans: The Social Origins of Popular Counter-Revolution in Upper Brittany, 1770–1796* (Oxford: Clarendon Press, 1982), 10.

demand a more genuine abolition of seigneurialism than has yet occurred) with equally angry peasants who oppose the Revolution as such. When Michel Vovelle, very sensibly, speaks of the "impossible map of the counterrevolution,"[121] he has in mind not so much the empirical difficulties of establishing a map of any specific sort of events, formidible though these difficulties may be, but rather the conceptual problem of what sorts of event one ought to count. With an eye on the range of popular resistance that took place without any linkage to avowedly counterrevolutionary elites, some scholars now offer the term "antirevolution."[122] What I shall mean here by rural counterrevolutionary events will be those events that are either accompanied by open counterrevolutionary sloganeering or that are directed against central institutions that are distinctively revolutionary. I also regarded as counterrevolutionary, events in which the word was not used, if adhesion to counterrevolution was otherwise clearly symbolized. I have, therefore, included among counterrevolutionary actions here those that explicitly announced themselves as such; actions in defense of the nonjuring clergy or hostile to the constitutional church; politicized religious processions that challenged the revolutionary state's authority;[123] and public and collective resistance to the conscription that was announced in late February 1793.[124] I do not, however, include actions of resistance against taxes, even

121. Michel Vovelle, *La découverte de la politique: Géopolitique de la Révolution française* (Paris: Editions de la Découverte, 1993), 275.

122. Vovelle, *La découverte de la politique,* 335–38; Roger Dupuy, *De la Révolution à la Chouannerie: Paysans en Bretagne, 1788–1794* (Paris: Flammarion, 1989), 335–36; Colin Lucas, "Résistances populaires à la Révolution dans le sud-est," in Jean Nicolas, ed., *Mouvements populaires et conscience sociale, XVIe–XIXe siècles* (Paris: Maloine, 1985), 473–85.

123. A small chapel in the countryside near Cholet, for example, locally celebrated for its miracle-working image of the Virgin, became, in the summer of 1791, the center of large and continual processions of pilgrims, whose bare feet and hand-held candles were to the authorities so many emblems of their "fanaticism." These processions and the local National Guard units became adept at locating each other's movements and blocking or dispersing the other in what, in retrospect, looks like practice for the coming hide-and-seek of guerrilla warfare. On August 28, 1791, for example, a National Guard unit operating between Chemillé and Cholet found its way blocked by a suddenly appearing group of eight hundred carrying arms and singing hymns before a locally well-known cross. See Port, *Vendée angevine,* 1:249.

124. I also include here earlier protest very closely related to conscription. I have in mind, in particular, the organized resistance that broke out in response to the call for volunteers for the military issued in the summer of 1792 a half-year before the more threatening full-blown conscription was launched. Conscientious local administrators were probably preparing for conscription before it was nationally organized; in maritime areas, for example, mounting tensions with England led mayors to do preconscription paperwork (for an example from the Vendée, see Chassin, *La préparation de la Vendée,* 3:270). By 1792 the pool of volunteers in some genuine sense was down—uncompelled volunteers had already joined up in 1791—and the war was on. Although the government called for "volunteers," local communities had to resort to coercion to fill their quotas. Even at the high point of genuine volunteering in 1791, volunteering was largely an urban phenomenon; by one count, only 15% of the volunteers were rural. See Alan Forrest, *Conscripts*

when those taxes were the new creations of the regime rather than holdovers of the old order; nor do I include challenges to the new authorities over food issues. Clearly, the latter two forms of resistance to the revolutionary state had the consequence of weakening its capacity to defend itself, but unless self-advertised as in principle antagonistic to the new order[125] they were not considered here. This amounts to taking a refusal to serve in the revolutionary state's wars as defying the new order more overtly than refusing to pay its taxes. When a group of country people demands the abrogation of new laws in favor of the traditional customary law of the region at the same time that they want their old priest back (and are busy making life as miserable as possible for the new one) it seems reasonable to accept their self-description as equivalent to "counterrevolutionary," although they themselves don't use the term.[126] The constitutional church was a newfangled (and in some regions a widely detested) innovation, identifiable with the Revolution and no other regime; the new conscription was not for some generic warfare against an unknown territory but rather for revolutionary France in its life-and-death struggle with the crowned tyrants of Europe.

In avoiding lumping all opponents of the forces of order of the moment together, I am avoiding lumping together the ultra-revolutionaries and the cis-revolutionaries (unlike the Committee of Public Safety during the Terror). It is therefore a bit difficult for an event to get labeled counterrevolutionary here: unless it is attacking the recruiting sergeant in 1793 or trying to lynch a constitutional priest, a group has to identify itself explicitly as in opposition to the new state. Almost 8% of incidents we found fit the bill. Counterrevolution as understood here occurred in a geographically narrow range of rural France, in about one *bailliage* in eight. Table 5.8 shows that nearly half of the counterrevolutionary events involve some action oriented to the polarized church; while substantially fewer events involve military recruitment, they occurred in about the same number of *bailliages*. Resistance to the new religious order, in regions where it occurred, was, it

and Deserters: The Army and French Society During the Revolution and Empire (New York: Oxford University Press, 1989), 20–26; and Jean-Paul Bertaud, *The Army of the French Revolution: From Citizen-Soldiers to Instrument of Power* (Princeton: Princeton University Press, 1988), 51, 54, 70.

125. At an evening meeting on June 19, 1791, for example, peasants from two communities near Chemillé applauded a tenant-farmer who praised the old order (Port, *Vendée angevine,* 1:212).

126. Some other instances of a self-proclaimed counterrevolutionary identity (even without use of the term): adopting a white flag (the Bourbon color) rather than the tricolor, especially after the overthrow of the king; attacks on bearers of tricolor insignia; pejorative use of terminology denoting adherents of the Revolution, as in the use of *démocrate* as a term of invective; breaking up the electoral procedures introduced by the Revolution; protest over formation of local pro-revolutionary clubs; attacks on local, district, or departmental officials attempting to enforce specifically revolutionary policies (inventorying church property for sale, for instance). (For instances of these see Port, *Vendée angevine,* 1:211, 212, 316, 322; Chassin, *La préparation de la Vendée,* 1:249 et seq., 323, 3:4–5; Dupuy, *De la Révolution à la Chouannerie,* 219–39).

appears, far more intense than resistance to the draft (even if, in March 1793, it was the draft that ignited the explosion).

Counterrevolutionary events might well utilize actions that appear to draw on the same collective repertoire as other events. Consider a group of country people around La Caillère (near Fontenay) who seized a list of potential conscripts for coastal defense on February 24, 1793.[127] They were attempting to defy an oppressor engaged in something far more systematic than random predation—in developing a capacity for rationalized seizures of resources—just as other peasant communities had seized or burned the records of the tax system, the lords, and the monasteries. When peasants supporting their good priest rip out the church benches of "patriots"[128] they draw on the same act of cleansing the house of God as do other peasants in destroying the places in church reserved for the lord's family.[129]

Panics

Panic appeared in the great work of Georges Lefebvre on *The Great Fear* as a remarkable form of rural mobilization all its own. Lefebvre documents, for the first summer of the Revolution, the rapid spread, from a small number of distinct epicenters, yielding a nearly simultaneous chain of panics through much of the countryside. The background is the confluence of social (and natural) forces that imbued that moment with a remarkable combination of hope and desperation. A period of economic hardship was capped off by a disastrous harvest; threatening strangers were everywhere as the unemployed and the hungry sought the means of survival at precisely the moment

Table 5.8. Types of Counterrevolutionary Events

Type of Event (Fine Categories)	Percentage of Events	Percentage of *Bailliages*
Defense of nonjuring clergy; attacks on civil constitution (including juring clergy)	48%	54%
Resistance to conscription or voluntary recruitment	15	52

127. Chassin, *La préparation de la Vendée,* 3:270.

128. Ibid., 1:244–45.

129. One wonders whether, in this new world of revolution, the antipatriot bench destruction doesn't also carry the power of inversion. Is the attack on the church benches of supporters of the Revolution a reappropriation that gathers ironic force when seen against a background of anti-seigneurial events? I know of no evidence that would permit one to know if western peasants ripping out benches are (or aren't) making a statement about their fellows attacking their lords.

when the political impasses of the elites paralyzed the repressive capacities normally deployed against vagabondage, capacities inadequate even in good times; the unprecedented summoning of the Estates-General roused hopes even as assembling in their forty thousand communities to draft *cahiers* involved large numbers of country people in the experience of formulating their grievances and of banding together for the common expression of those grievances; insurrections in the towns and in the countryside had begun and were understood in peasant villages both as models and as threats. In this climate, rumors spread fast and far, and in late July and early August rural France was convulsed by a belief in an invading force bent on stopping the revolutionary process. While some held the invaders to be aristocrats, others knew them as Savoyards or Germans or English (or even Moors) and everywhere villagers acted; some fled into the forests, but other sought arms, roused the local lord out of bed to lead them, marched off to fight the imaginary enemy. Lefebvre tells us, moreover, that the Great Fear was not the only panic. There were earlier and later fears as well, less widely diffused but not necessarily less intensely felt where they occurred. Covering the entire half-decade spanned by our data, the figures in Table 5.1 identify 13% of all incidents as panics. Remarkably (and unexpectedly) by one measure, at any rate, panics were the most widespread of all the forms we have tabulated, occurring in two-thirds of the *bailliages* of the country (and in nearly three-quarters of all *bailliages* in which disturbances of one sort or another took place). If there was a single common mobilizational language in which Norman, Alsatian, Alpine, and Provençal country people all spoke, one would almost say it was panic.

Recapitulation

Most disturbances between 1788 and 1793 fit into one (or more) of these categories: jointly, antiseigneurial events, religiously tinged events, antitax events, panics, land conflicts, wage conflicts, anti-authority events, subsistence events, and counterrevolution constitute some 91% of the events that I identified.[130] Let us recall that we think of an event as a

130. A few haphazard examples of less common events that fit none of the major categories: seizures of transported goods other than food (for example, on August 23 and again on November 21, 1792, wagonloads of cotton were seized by people from a dozen villages around Maromme in Normandy (Guy Lemarchand, *La fin du féodalisme dans le pays de Caux* [Paris: Editions du Comité des Travaux Historiques et Scientifiques, 1989], 447); attacks on people identified as "nobles" (but not also clearly "lords") or the taking of positions other than those so far enumerated (the two combined, for example, in the summer of 1789 at Montdidier where peasants forced nobles to wear revolutionary insignia and cry "Long live the Third Estate") (Lefebvre, *La Grande Peur,* 238); movements over prices other than food as in coerced price reductions on wood and iron such as enforced on March 3, 1792, at an ironworks at Conches (Vovelle, *Ville et Campagne,* 240).

sequence of discrete actions. A single multiaction event might have actions that place it simultaneously in more than one of these nine categories. A demand for the documentation on the basis of which a monastery lays claim to seigneurial rights is an event that is counted under both the "antiseigneurial" and "religiously tinged" rubrics, for example. It follows, then, that many actions that fall outside of our categories may be attached to events whose other actions place them within one (or more such category). If a group of peasants invades the fields of large, local landholders some of whom are seigneurs, some of whom are well-to-do urbanites, and some of whom are wealthy peasants themselves we have an entry in our antiseigneurial group, a fairly rare entry under "land conflict" as well as an action that fits under none of our rubrics. The 91% figure just cited refers to events all of whose actions are contained within our nine categories. An additional 5% of events have some actions that could not be so classified. Finally, 4% either fall wholly outside these nine or are events whose nature is unknown.[131]

Rural Revolt, 1788–1793

The forms of peasant action, we see, are varied. But they are variations within known patterns. There are a number of motifs ("routines" in the language of students of contestation) that regularly recur:

- Seizure or destruction of power-giving documents (the titles of lords, the tax rolls, the conscription lists)
- Sacking the residence of wrongdoers (the lord, the tax official, the official in charge of food supply, the merchant, the peasant withholding grain from the market)
- The rescue of one's fellow (seized in the wake of antiseigneurial, anti-tax, or subsistence event; conscripted)
- The reappropriation (of land: the invasion of field or forest; of exactions: the counterexaction of cash from lord or monastery; of the source of justice: erection/destruction of gallows; of one's fellow: the rescue)
- Severing the enemy's sacred tie (the destruction of the church benches of lords or of opposing sides in the church split of 1791; assaults on opponents' priests by pro- and counterrevolutionaries)
- Redistribution (of grain; of money taken from lord or cleric)
- Imposing costs on violators of communal solidarity (by threatening or

131. Occasionally a source tells us no more than that there was a disturbance, with little information as to its character.

attacking peasants who might make payments to church or lord despite a boycott; who might work as laborers at unacceptable wages; who might be hauling grain to market at unacceptable prices; who remove themselves from collectively decided agricultural routines; who attend religious services conducted by the wrong priest)

Most of these elements were familiar to villagers and authorities alike, a circumstance permitting their rapid diffusion. Of course there were numerous innovations in detail: such as self-identification by revolutionary tricolor or Bourbon white; or identifying clerical deviation with position taken on the ecclesiastical oath of 1791. And there were occasional irruptions of peasant actions the authorities did not understand (the maypoles in the Southwest; see Chapter 8). But taken individually, there was much about most of the actions that would have been familiar in the pre-1789 countryside. Even such a specific trigger of action as revolutionary legislation on religion was challenged in large part by peasants rejecting a newly assigned priest or defying the authority of an old one with well-known gestures.[132] The attacks were generally made by local people in their own localities (although some events, like the great market invasions of the spring and late autumn of 1792 in the plains between the Seine and the Loire, involved traveling bands sometimes of vast size);[133] they are in large part direct assertions of justice, seizures or reseizures of resources or, more rarely, punitive actions rather than appeals to national authorities. (We have seen, indeed, that anti-tax events apart, whatever officials are attacked tend to be local.) And they often borrow the repertoire of the authorities themselves: the crowd fixes the food prices where the authorities have neglected their duty; they make the lord live up to his claims as protector by compelling him to feed them. The borrowing may be straight or it may be malicious parody: if the lords had hunted when and where they chose, now it is their pigeons, rabbits, or fish that are slaughtered; now it is the peasant community that erects gallows. In the turbulent seventeenth century, when many a local lord went his own way, often joining one or another murderous military contingent, the reassertion of royal authority sometimes punished mutinous lords by demolishing their *châteaux* or felling their trees. In the late eighteenth century, with a state unequal to the effort, the country people took up the

132. In a village in Rouergue in 1736, for example, parishioners tumultuously prevented a priest from reading a statement that the local lord had given him (the local women tore his clerical garb); a half-dozen years later, women from a nearby village as well as men dressed as women greeted a new priest with stones. See Jacques Frayssenge and Nicole Lemaître, "Les Emotions populaires en Rouergue au XVIIIe siècle," in Jean Nicolas, ed., *Mouvements populaires et conscience sociale, XVIe–XIXe siècles* (Paris: Maloine, 1985), 378.

133. Vovelle, *Ville et campagne,* 230–31.

task.[134] All of this approximates Charles Tilly's summary sketch of traditional forms of European collective action.[135] Tilly suggests a marvelous checklist of the characteristics whereby we might summarize the traditional patterns of popular contestation that had developed in the formative period of Western European statemaking (let us say, sixteenth through eighteenth centuries); these patterns may be contrasted with a more recent repertoire of contention that crystallized in the nineteenth century and continues to the present day.[136]

The most important way in which the revolutionary events in the data studied here deviate from Tilly's generic portrait is not in his approximate listing of forms of action but in his overall summary of "local" and "patronized." Local these events certainly are; patronized they just as certainly are not. These actions are neither made on behalf of nor rarely with the support of some powerful patron external to the community; and only rarely do they appeal to any such patron. They are usually direct attacks. And yet they betray something beyond an exclusive focus on everyday events in their full concreteness. With the very significant exception of events with a religious element, it is only infrequently that they are centrally focused on harming persons, vengefully or otherwise. It is usually not the person of the lord but the symbols that make a person a lord that are destroyed.[137]

The appropriation, parodistic or otherwise, of the action of the authorities, the quasi-legalistic strain in crowd action (sometimes paying for seized grain—at a below-market just price) brings to mind Colin Lucas's stress on the crowd as flowing into a void left by authorities who have failed in their duties. The crowd substitutes in effect for the absent authority; rather than having a fundamentally defiant character, the crowd in this characterization is a sort of pinch-hitter filing in for the derelict, misguided, overburdened,

134. On an extraordinary royal tribunal in 1665 see Arlette Lebigre, *Les Grands Jours d'Auvergne. Désordres et répression au XVIIe siècle* (Paris: Hachette, 1976).

135. Charles Tilly, "Speaking Your Mind Without Elections, Surveys or Social Movements," *Public Opinion Quarterly* 47 (1983): 461–78.

136. William Sewell has criticized Tilly for neglecting the ways in which the Revolution opened the path for popular mobilization of an "associational" rather than a "communal" character; that is, for organizing for struggle in special-purpose associations like clubs, parties, or unions rather than in multipurpose corporate groupings like villages. I take up some indirect evidence for the development of such associational structures in Chapter 6. See William Sewell Jr., "Collective Violence and Collective Loyalties in France: Why the French Revolution Made a Difference," *Politics and Society* 18 (1990): 527–52.

137. This is in no way to dispute Brian Singer's quite brilliant discussion of the ferocity of the Parisian events in which someone was lynched, few in number until the late summer of 1792, but spectacular—in the literal sense of constituting a spectacle. I do not believe my sources are adequate to determine whether rural acts of exemplary vengeance share the characteristics Singer describes for Paris. See Singer, "Violence in the French Revolution."

or nearsighted agents of a social order that is not at bottom challenged.[138] The crowd is temporary, the authority will return, the crowd desires nothing more than this return, perhaps even, by its action, provokes it. I believe Lucas is compelling and insightful in his description of the behavior of prerevolutionary crowds; with the breakdown of the Old Regime, it is less obvious that mobilized forms of popular struggle were merely filling in until royal (or legislative) authority took matters in hand. In large part they employed the older vocabulary of action, but I am not sure that the grammar hadn't changed. If peasants riot occasionally over a lord's actions and withdraw from the field when the courts step in, we have the situation that Lucas is describing. If peasants rise again and again over a half-decade until they get the laws they want concerning the seigneurial regime, it seems no longer adequate to speak of a temporary filling-in for absent authority. The peasants are learning how to influence authority, how to alter authority. And if the actions have an immediate local target—Tilly's point about traditional actions—I shall show in what follows that there was a distant, national agent of power already held as an audience as well. I shall show in Chapter 8 that these local peasant actions were part of a dialogue with the legislatures. The forms of action may have been, still, very traditional for the most part; but they were deployed for newer ends. Tactically, one might say, the targets are still local; but strategically, there is another element, and a national one: the peasants are shaping the Revolution.

Traditional forms of contention, but untraditional utilization of those forms: one might say the same with regard to targets. The greatest target, we have seen, is the seigneurial regime. Now there is nothing traditional about that whatsoever. Emmanuel Le Roy Ladurie, noting the shift from the central anti-tax thrust of rural insurrection in the seventeenth century to the strongly antiseigneurial actions of the Revolution, has suggested that some great mutation must have taken place in the intervening century to produce such an outcome, and sees the understanding of that process by which the lords supplanted the state as Peasant Enemy Number One as a central agenda for French rural history.[139] The question is all the more intriguing when we study the patterns of rural insurrection in the relatively peaceful century between the two great explosions. Jean Nicolas and Guy Lemarchand have been engaged in an extensive project of data collection from 1661 into the spring of 1789. Their preliminary results[140] show the

138. A very fine study of an eighteenth-century crowd replacing an errant, even criminal, authority set in a quintessentially urban milieu is Arlette Farge and Jacques Revel, *Logiques de la foule* (Paris: Hachette, 1988).

139. Le Roy Ladurie, "Révoltes et contestations rurales."

140. Nicolas, "Les émotions dans l'ordinateur"; Lemarchand, "Troubles populaires au XVIIIe siècle."

continuing predominance of state over lord as a target down to the brink of revolution (although antiseigneurial events were on the rise).

Indeed, looking at the entire century and a quarter that they cover, one sees that subsistence events and anti-tax events were running neck and neck, each with about 22% of the incidents they have identified. Also right up there, contributing another 22%, are clashes with police, military, or judicial authority (rather like our anti-authority category in fact). This in turn is followed by a miscellaneous group of "youth" events (a category I was unable to use): youth groups involved in a variety of brawls, conscription resistance, inter- and intracommunal battles (about 9%). Only then does one get to antiseigneurial events (a relatively paltry 7% of the total). Thus the countryside after the long period of *croquants, nu-pieds,* and *Fronde* was not only relatively quiet but had not yet turned away from what we may call a "traditional" focus on taxes and food supply, taxation being the great focus of the major seventeenth-century risings, subsistence growing to prominence around century's end. One of the great things about the Nicolas-Lemarchand data is the clarity of its overall temporal pattern. From low levels during much of the century, apart from a spike around the great famine of 1709, one sees clearly that the curve of conflict starts to rise in the 1760s. There is a sharp peak, the highest in the century so far, at the Flour War of 1775 and although the trajectory falls back afterward, it remains above its pre-1760s level and then begins a new, accelerating, dizzy ascent in the late 1780s. It is clear that the term "prerevolution," widely used for the elite conflicts and crises of the last years of the Old Regime, had a plebeian counterpart, largely neglected in current accounts of revolutionary origins. Equally striking to us must be the growth in antiseigneurial actions. Not only do the total number of rural clashes tracked by Nicolas and Lemarchand rise from the 1760s on, but the antiseigneurial emphasis of those clashes rises as well. For the entire 1661–1789 stretch, the number of anti-tax events exceeds antiseigneurial events by 3 to 1; in the last five years of the Old Regime, however the ratio has fallen to 2 to 1. If antiseigneurial events are beginning to grow,[141] however, they are still, on the verge of revolution, far from dominant. And in the eighteenth century as a whole, they are, to reiterate, considerably outweighed by both anti-tax and subsistence events. In this conclusion, Nicolas and Lemarchand have been seconded by a number of regional studies that converge on finding eighteenth-century antiseigneurial actions outnumbered in some places by anti-tax events, in others by subsistence events, in still others by a diverse

141. For some confirmation of a rise in antiseigneurial actions late in the Old Regime, see Nicole Castan, *Les criminels de Languedoc: Les exigences d'ordre et les voies du ressentiment dans une société pré-révolutionnaire (1750–1790)* (Toulouse: Association des Publications de l'Université de Toulouse-Mirail, 1980), 103–11.

array of insurrectionary forms.[142] So antiseigneurial events may have been on the rise, but down to the breakdown of the Old Regime, they were not the dominant mode of rural resistance.[143]

This survey of the general pattern of eighteenth-century insurrection and of the limited but real shifts in targets late in the Old Regime, may be paralleled by more limited, but nonetheless important, data on shifts in patterns of grievance-making. It would be marvelous were we able to go back before that spring of 1789 to see how the pattern of grieving in the parishes had been changing. We cannot do this for all of France, but Roger Chartier's work on the Estates-General of 1614 at least permits us to do it for a single *bailliage,* Troyes.[144] There is much to be garnered from this comparison, and we will reiterate our discussion from Chapter 3.

According to Chartier, in 1614 an impressive 48% of grievances addressed taxation; indeed, in his view a good deal of other grievances implicitly bore on the states' newly increased hunger for revenue, bringing the quantity of early seventeenth-century grievances that focused on taxes to some two-thirds of the total. By contrast, a mere 3% of grievances addressed the seigneurial regime. Rather than compare this with our own national totals for 1789 or even our own figures for the *bailliage* of Troyes, let us use Chartier's own data for Troyes at the onset of revolution so that there is no question of the consistency of categories. His taxation category has now fallen considerably to a still impressive 33% and his seigneurial category is up strikingly to 11%[145] (note that this is roughly similar to our own national picture; see Chapter 2, p. 40).

What this adds up to is as simple to state as it is significant in its implications. Long-run processes had increased peasant attacks on their lords, whether one measures the structure of grievances or the nature of insurrectionary actions between the seventeenth century and the collapse of the Old Regime. The search for a long-run process that might effect such

142. See three of the essays in Jean Nicolas, ed., *Mouvements populaires et conscience sociale, XVIe–XIXe siècles* (Paris: Maloine, 1985); René Pillorget, "Les mouvements insurrectionels de Provence (1715–1788)," 351–60; Frayssenge and Lemaître, "Les émotions populaires en Rouergue"; and Abel Poitrineau, "Le détonateur économico-fiscal et la charge des rancoeurs catégorielles profondes, lors des explosions de la colère populaire en Auvergne, au XVIIIe siècle," 361–70. (I have included Poitrineau on Auvergne here even though he gives no figures, because of the general tenor of his essay.)

143. The area around Sarlat seems unusual in the degree to which collective actions at the end of the Old Regime were directed at lords or their agents (Reinhardt, *Justice in the Sarladais,* 227). Future research might reveal more such localities.

144. Roger Chartier et Jean Nagle, "Paroisses et châtellenies en 1614" and Roger Chartier, "De 1614 à 1789: le déplacement des attentes," in Roger Chartier and Denis Richet, *Représentation et vouloir politiques: Autour des états-généraux de 1614* (Paris: Ecole des Hautes Etudes en Sciences Sociales, 1982), 89–100 and 101–12.

145. Chartier, "De 1614 à 1789," 108–9.

a change is therefore an important enterprise. We are led to affirm the good sense of Tilly's observation that major shifts in the nature of contention are not just outgrowths of the contingencies of the moment. There are deep, long-run processes that realign interests and that create or destroy capacities for action. We must, Tilly writes, "look beyond narrowly political explanations."[146] Something was happening in the century that preceded the Revolution to turn the French countryside away from its sometimes violent rejection of the claims of the state and toward a focus on the seigneurial regime. One must consider changes in the state, in the seigneurial regime and in the social world of the French countryside itself. We must consider a possible Marxian transformation in the form of a linking of local economies with regional, national, or international ones. In this linking, considerations of commercial advantage in distant markets came to shape the social world that moved in local arenas, a process rife with conflict. And we must consider as well a possible Tocquevillean process in which an increasingly present and increasingly rationalizing central authority was expanding its own tasks, encouraging a political culture of standardization and uniformity, sucking the vitality out of regionally rooted elites by luring their talents to Paris and by establishing a sense that the future would see the submerging of regional distinctions in national power. This centralization, for Tocqueville, meant the concomitant erosion of deference toward what remained of local relations of domination.[147]

But we also must see that such long-term processes take us only part of the way and no farther. The increase in prerevolutionary antiseigneuralism, either as grievances openly expressed when rare opportunities offered or as insurrectionary direct action when more common opportunities offered, are still inadequate to explain the degree to which antiseigneuralism was the dominant mode of action of a countryside in revolution. Whatever shifts toward antiseigneurial targets there may have been in prerevolutionary actions or grievances, such shifts are only a step toward the predominantly antiseigneurial countryside of France in revolution that appears in Table 5.1. Or rather, such long-term processes only get us to the starting gate: they do not by any means explain what happened *within* the Revolution to give the antiseigneurial risings the role they had.

We are led, then, to a version of a question Lynn Hunt posed at the outset of her *Politics, Culture and Class in the French Revolution.*[148] Her complaint was that the Marxist and Tocquevillean perspectives alike tend to jump from a set of prerevolutionary conditions to a set of postrevolutionary outcomes,

146. Tilly, *The Contentious French,* 9.

147. We shall attempt to assess these theses in Chapter 7.

148. Lynn A. Hunt, *Politics, Culture and Class in the French Revolution* (Berkeley and Los Angeles: University of California Press, 1984), 1–16.

as if nothing happened in the Revolution that was problematic, contingent, uncertain. The Revolution is merely the turbulent path from a given beginning to a known ending.

But after several chapters' worth of grievances at the onset of revolution, we must, I think, accept that the Revolution, or at least its rural aspect, should be considered as a process. Consider an imaginary reader in the spring of 1789 who miraculously has this book's first four chapters and a quiet evening. This is a reader who does not yet know that June 17, July 14, and August 4 are going to happen. Our reader, provided with the tabulations presented in those chapters, might well have surmised that, although antiseigneurial grieving in the countryside is up, the sheer amount of rural complaining about taxation is vastly greater; that taxation issues have been the trigger of rural contention not merely in the great insurrections of the seventeenth century but also in the more sporadic and smaller-scale struggles of the eighteenth (thus far) alongside subsistence concerns; and that, moreover, there was much consensus between the peasants and the well-to-do on tax issues. Such a reader, in fact, might find only the height of sense in a government whose reformers hoped that a good package of tax reforms could be enacted, simultaneously soothing the countryside and ending the treasury's ache.

Other readers, perhaps shrewder, noting the actual insurrectionary pattern in late 1788 and early 1789 (see Chapter 6), rather than extrapolating from the past and the *cahiers,* might have placed less stress on taxation and more on subsistence issues. This prediction would have been far closer to the mark, but still incomplete. That the countryside was going to rise again and again against the lords, that the legislature would define its break with the past as first and foremost a break with "feudalism" rather than a clear program of tax reform—these are not obvious features of either grievance or rebellion at the beginning of 1789 (although we can find in the *cahiers* the seeds from which they grow). The turn toward antiseigneuralism in the countryside, we shall see, was just that—a turn; the legislative actions on seigneurial rights were not just the drawing-out of the logical implications of some set of principles already present to the revolutionary elites. Legislators and peasants confronted one another and not in an empty room, but in a context; out of that confrontation and within that context (and the context itself changed) came the decisions in many peasant communities to run the risks of injury to others and to themselves in trying to throw off the domination of the lord; and the decisions to legislate an increasingly radical dismantlement came out of that confrontation as well.

If the relatively low proportions of anti-tax events in our data are credible, then, they must be set beside the tabulations of Nicolas and others that indicated that the transformation in the key target of peasant wrath that Le Roy Ladurie wants us to explore was not complete on the very eve of the

Revolution. Something must have happened in the course of the Revolution itself that made the lords rather than the state the prime target. But what?

We must ask again what it was that made rural conflict so focused on the seigneurial rights. If the great seventeenth-century struggles were centrally about taxes, if the eighteenth century's much-reduced turbulence sees taxes vie with food as the primary concerns (even after taking into account an increase in antiseigneurial events); if the grievances of the spring of 1789 still have a considerable preponderance of demands about taxation (although the antiseigneurial demands of the countryside are bitterer), if a comparison of the documents of 1789 with those of 1614 does show an increase in antiseigneurial sentiment and a decrease in anti-tax views, but also shows that these changes still leave the lion's share of grieving focused on taxes, how did the pattern of peasant action come to take on its antiseigneurial preponderance? The exploration of the deployment of rural action over time is our obvious next step.

CHAPTER

6

RHYTHMS OF CONTENTION

Peaks and Troughs

As a baseline for what follows, Figure 6.1 displays the overall ebb and flow of rural conflict from June 1788 through June 1793. Each point represents the total number of events in a one-month span. In addition to the number of events, it is often valuable to consider other facets of the intensity of conflict. I had no confidence in being able to assess the duration of more than a small minority of those cases that lasted beyond a day, themselves a minority of all events. The number of *bailliages* in which conflict took place over the course of a month was as easy to measure as the sheer number of incidents, and could serve to indicate the geographic range of conflict. The number of participants was rarely given very clearly but the number of parishes whose people joined the event was much more commonly indicated; one might think of this as a measure of size, Old Regime style, in which a corporate, rather than an individualistic, sense of representation prevailed. One might also hope to measure the destructiveness of particular events but consistent estimation of the extent of personal injury or property damage was not possible.

It turns out that both the number of *bailliages* in which events took place and the estimated number of parishes involved in events have trajectories very similar to the simple number of events. It follows, then, that other aspects of the intensity of conflict are either not available for any very large proportion of incidents (duration, size conceived of as the number of individual participants, extent of damage) or have shapes that differ little from the sheer number of events (number of *bailliages* or parishes with conflicts). I shall, therefore, usually only present data on the sheer number of events. Although it will be the comparative soundings of the ebb and flow of different sorts of conflict that will prove most revealing, this aggregated graph already displays some of the fundamental features that will appear, with variations, in all of the subsequent figures. The single most striking thing in this graph is its sawtooth character. Conflicts oscillate wildly from one month to the next. This is, we shall see as we proceed, no less true of most specific forms of conflict as it is of aggregate figures.

This seesaw pattern is telling us something quite fundamental about the nature of these clashes. The fundamental reason for this pattern is the quintessentially interactive character of social conflict. If we are willing to make the smallest gesture toward seeing participants in even the most

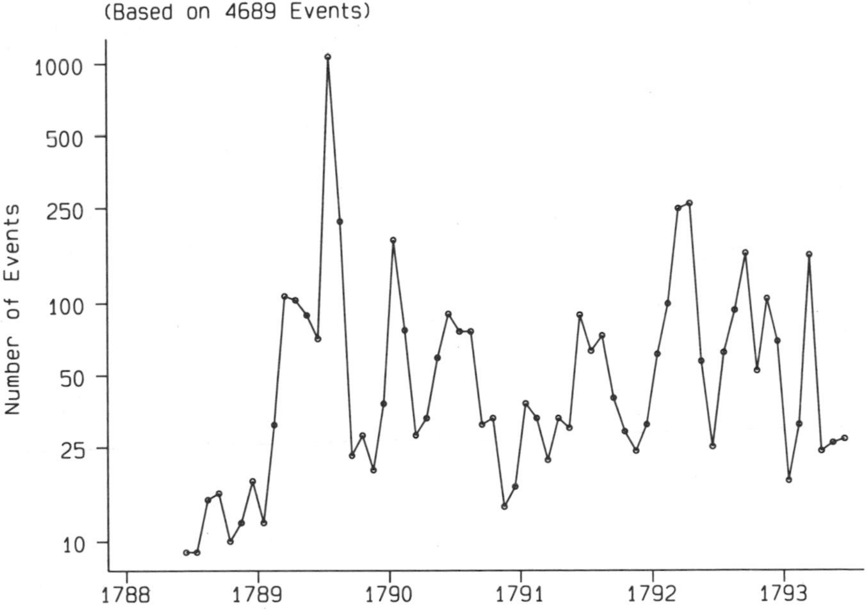

Fig. 6.1 Insurrectionary Events by Month

disorderly of politics as under the influence, if not necessarily the dictate, of reason, and if we bear in mind the profoundly interactive character of these clashes, the wild oscillations follow. (And all the more so if we see peasant communities as engaging in a good deal of reasoned evaluation of their situation, as the evidence of the *cahiers* strongly indicates that they do). The questions confronting these communities involve not merely the formulation of their needs, but a sense of the risks and benefits associated with alternative courses of action. Is attacking the seigneurial regime likely to result in any payoff? Is it likely to get one hanged or confined for years in a miserable galley? These calculations are themselves highly complex. What is the firmness of will of those in command of the forces of repression? And what is their repressive capacity in light of the number of similarly inclined peasants in my community and in similarly inclined communities across the province and across the kingdom? As information about what sorts of action one may safely get away with comes in, assessments of the risk probabilities shift; as information about the thinking of the revolutionary leadership (in Paris, in the main town of the local *département,* in the nearest market) comes in, there is a shift in the sense of what sorts of payoff may accrue to particular actions. As the Old Regime collapsed, all the old assessments of risk and of success were shattered and every new development had potential reverberations across France's forty thousand rural communities. It seems a reasonable speculation that news that a community got away with compelling a lord to make a written renunciation of his claims traveled far; so did the news the next month that the nearby urban National Guard hunted down insurrectionary peasants and hanged several. News that the National Assembly issued a favorable decree on the future of the tithe also traveled; so did assessments of the relationship of those in command of local armed forces to central governments.[1] In short, we have a continual pattern of assessment and reassessment of forms and targets of action, with an eye on their relative safety and relative efficacy. Relevant information continued to flow about the military, the local National Guards, local lords and clerics, national urban political groupings, the next village, and the generality of villages. The impulse to strike and to strike in particular directions and with particular means, all underwent continual revision.

The extreme oscillation of these and other graphs may make the statistical analysis of such data tricky, but it is of the greatest significance for historical and sociological understanding. It is not possible to appreciate conflict fully

1. We do not, alas, have many studies that permit one to evaluate these hypotheses, but detailed research on the diffusion of news of particularly striking events (the Great Fear or the royal flight to Varennes) shows how readily and swiftly important information traveled from one rural community to the next. See Lefebvre, *La Grande Peur de 1789* (Paris: Armand Colin, 1970) and Guy Arbellot and Bernard Lepetit, *Atlas de la Révolution française,* vol. 1, *Routes et communications* (Paris: Editions de l'Ecole des Hautes Etudes en Sciences Sociales, 1987), 70.

by considering only one side: that is what follows from grasping the interactive nature of conflict phenomena. Positing some peasant propensities, then, in themselves, can only be a part of the story. Theories of the sources of mobilization for action are many and their applicability to the revolutionary situation of the French countryside are equally many. Is it peasant hardship (as indicated, perhaps, by the level or the increase in food prices) that drives people in general and French peasants in the Revolution to rise? Is it a changed consciousness (as indicated perhaps by variations in levels of rural literacy)? Is it the erosion of traditional relationships with local patrons under the heavy hand of the bureaucratizing state (a thesis dear to Tocqueville that may be explored empirically by comparing provinces under the administrative control of the king's *intendants* with those in which Provincial Estates still held significant powers)? Is it the dynamism of the market economy that upsets older forms of stable accommodations (and it is easy enough to distinguish relatively commercialized from uncommercialized areas in the late eighteenth century by the urban presence, the density of road and river networks, or even the flow of marketable commodities)? The current fashion in the American literature on social movements places heavy stress on structural contexts and organizational capacities,[2] even to the exclusion of grievances altogether: again one can explore the strong regional differences in rural communal structures and look for those that might more readily nurture insurrection.

There may be something to one or some or all of these theses.[3] But what none of them, in themselves, can explain, is the sharp oscillatory pattern. For that we need to see that peasant communities, more or less hungry, more or less under the thumb of the state, more or less literate, more or less in the market, are looking at one another, at what happened last month, at the local National Guards, at the political situation in nearby towns and distant capitals, and are making judgments of danger and of opportunity.

If the spikiness of this (and other) graphs is to be expected on the basis of the social dynamics of insurrectionary waves, the particular points at which the country people experienced favorable opportunities, safety in action, and opportune targets are a function of the specificities of the historical moment. The social dynamics leads one to expect peaks and troughs but not any particular peak or trough. It is not the general social dynamics that explains the great spike of July 1789 and the lesser spikes of January 1790, June 1790, June 1791, April 1792, August 1792, and March

2. For example, Mayer Zald and John D. McCarthy, *The Dynamics of Social Movements: Resource Mobilization, Social Control and Tactics* (Cambridge, Mass., 1979) and *Social Movements in an Organizational Society* (New Brunswick, N.J.: Transaction Books, 1987); Anthony Oberschall, *Social Conflict and Social Movements* (Englewood Cliffs, N.J.: Prentice-Hall, 1973).

3. For the use of regional comparisons to weigh these and other theses about the social roots of rural revolt, see Chapter 7.

1793, nor the troughs of September–November 1789, March 1790, December 1790, March 1791, June 1792, or January 1793. Another way to point up the spikiness of the ebb and flow of events is to notice that the six most eventful months (among the sixty-one months covered) contain 50% of all incidents; July 1789 alone, the spike of spikes, accounts for some 25%. By contrast, the six quietest months (June, July, October, November, and December 1788 and December 1790) contain a mere 2%. (We shall investigate below whether the movements in the peak months differed from those of the troughs in character or only in quantity.)

Eight Trajectories

Up to this point we have only explored the very crude sum of all insurrectionary events. Let us now consider separately the major forms of rural action. Our first inquiry is into the general character of the peaks and troughs. Consider two rather extreme and opposed conceptions of rural action. In the first, the Revolution is, for the country people, merely a glorious series of opportunities to strike out at all enemies, as the coercive power of the state collapses. With such a proposition, the choice of a particular target is virtually a matter of happenstance; all forms of action, responding to pretty much the same opportunities should ebb and flow at the same rhythms as one another; the peaks and troughs of the aggregate trajectory of events should therefore be replicated in miniature in each particular type of action. The second, and quite different, image urges us to see each form of action as following its own rhythms. The peasants are seen as clearly distinguishing among various enemies; the opportune moments to strike and the perceived rewards for striking are different for various targets. The Revolution is not a single bloc but a kaleidoscope of different sorts of opportunity and constraint: indeed, perhaps in some ways it is better thought of as a series of revolution*s* in the plural.[4] (Or surely better still, we need to see it as both one and many.) In this image, the peaks and troughs of different forms of action need not coincide because favorable opportunities for one form of action may be distinct from the time for another.

We shall drop our "anti-authority" category here since these events almost always appear as a continuation of some other struggle and therefore rise and fall with them. When country people ambush a military patrol or seize the building that houses local authority it almost always is an attempt

4. Not yet having fully acquired its modern meaning, the term was, in 1789, at first used in the plural, as in the title of the journal that first appeared on July 18, 1789, *Révolutions de Paris*. But soon a conception of a series of "revolutions" gave way to a conception of a singular and unitary process, "the French Revolution." See Keith Michael Baker, "Inventing the French Revolution," in his *Essays on French Political Culture in the Eighteenth Century* (New York: Cambridge University Press, 1990), 203–23.

to free their fellows seized as a result of antiseigneurial or anti-tax actions, to release villagers conscripted by force, to prevent the enforcement of some edict on land use, or to get at the hated juring (or nonjuring) priest. From this point on we shall restrict ourselves to the eight other major categories.

Figures 6.2 (a)–(d) present a series of miniature graphlets showing the number of events each month in each of our major categories plotted against time. To permit ready comparison of the location of peaks and troughs, each graph has its own scale set so that the largest spike for each is about the same height. Thus the 6 struggles over wages that took place in March 1792 look as impressive, relative to other wage-conflict episodes, as the 323 antiseigneurial disturbances of July 1789. In other words, we are focused here on the rhythms rather than the amplitude of the conflict.

The comparison of the eight graphs reveals both common elements and particularities. To point up one common element in the trajectories: all the graphs, if to different degrees, exhibit considerable month-to-month oscillation. There is no stable form of conflict that serves as a sort of monotonous undertone to all the rest. On the other hand, it appears, there are circumstances favoring many (but not all) forms of rural conflict; there are other circumstances uniquely favorable to one or another particular form. The antiseigneurial movement exhibits three main peaks: a great one in July 1789 (323 events) that is trailing off but still substantial in August (78 events), a second peak in the spring of 1792 with 75 events in March and rising to 189 in April, and a third in January 1790 (159 events). There are also three lesser peaks (of 56 to 61 events apiece) in June 1790, June 1791, and September 1792. Five of the other seven forms of action also experience a high point in July 1789 but otherwise differ in varying degrees from the rhythms of the antiseigneurial challenges.

Religiously tinged events are the closest to the antiseigneurial pattern (although the April 1792 peak was almost equaled in March). Subsistence events follow a three-peak pattern clearly enough but the second peak is definitely a bit earlier (March rather than April 1792) and the third peak is in November 1792 (quite a low point for antiseigneurial actions), rather than in January 1790 when subsistence events only exhibit a small peaklet. The July 1789 spike for tax events comprises 52 incidents, utterly eclipsing even the nearest rival month of February 1790 with its mere eight. The most intense anti-tax stretch in 1792, moreover, is not April (not even in the running with its zero events) but July and August (each with a mere 3). Land conflicts are also highest in July 1789 with 43 events; the secondary peak is, like the antiseigneurial disturbances, in April 1792 (but relatively larger, amounting to some 77% of the main peak); and January 1790 is nothing much to speak of in the land-conflict arena (but there is a tertiary peak in November 1792, rather like the subsistence events). If the rhythm of land conflicts differs

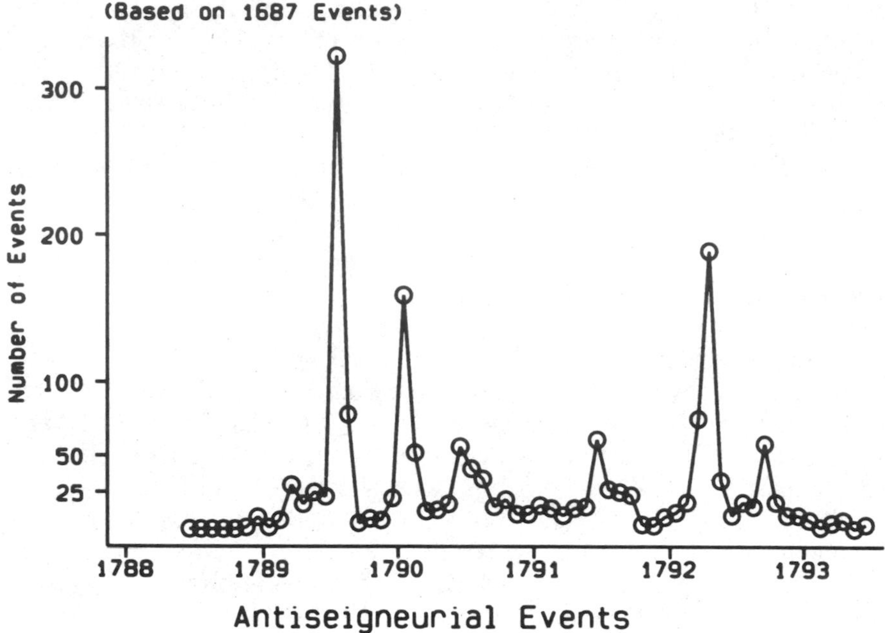

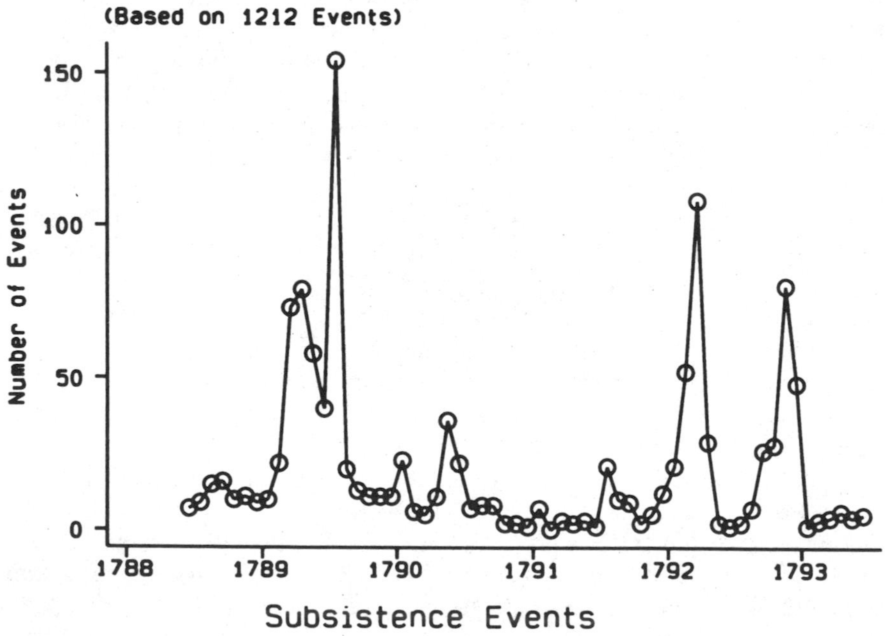

Fig. 6.2 (a) Incidence of Rural Insurrection by Date

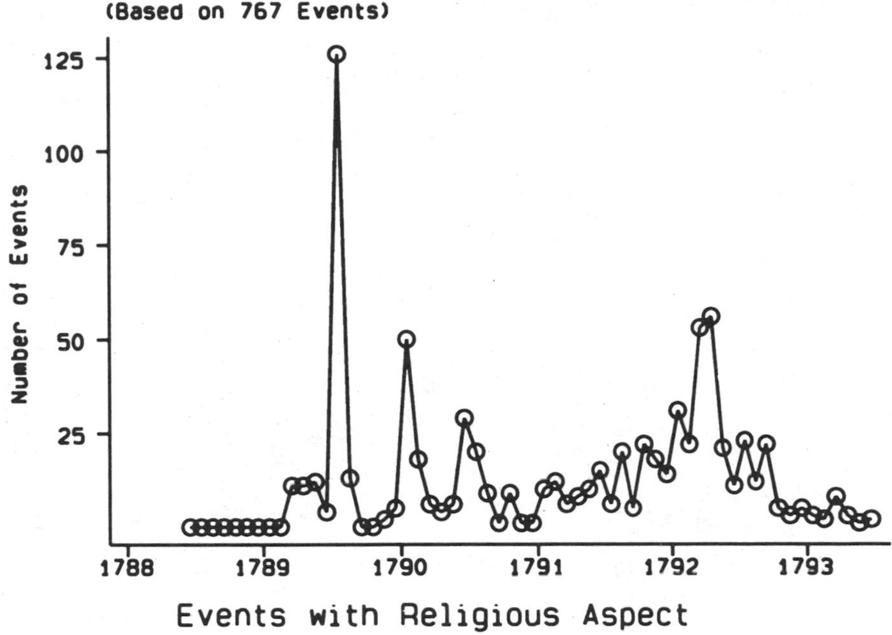

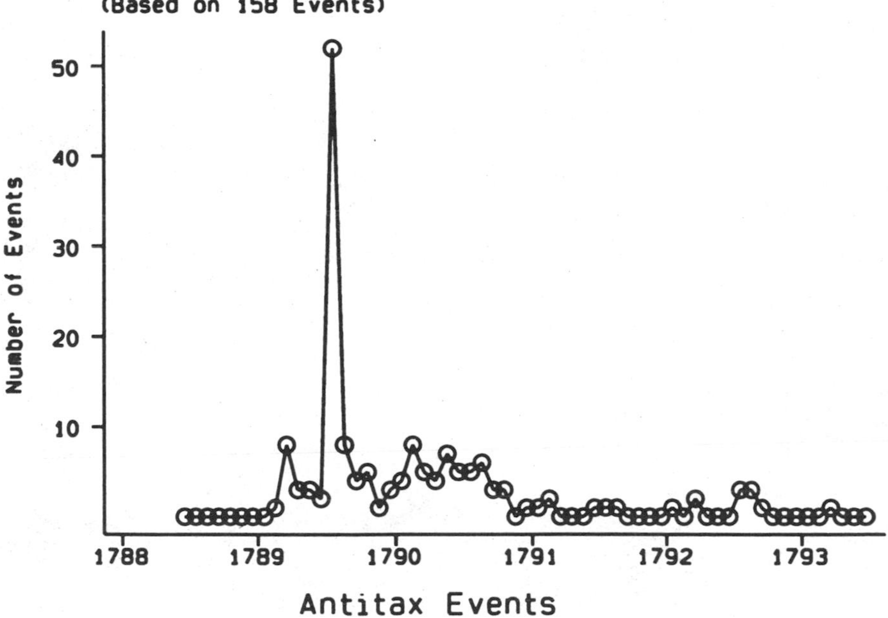

Fig. 6.2 (b) Incidence of Rural Insurrection by Date

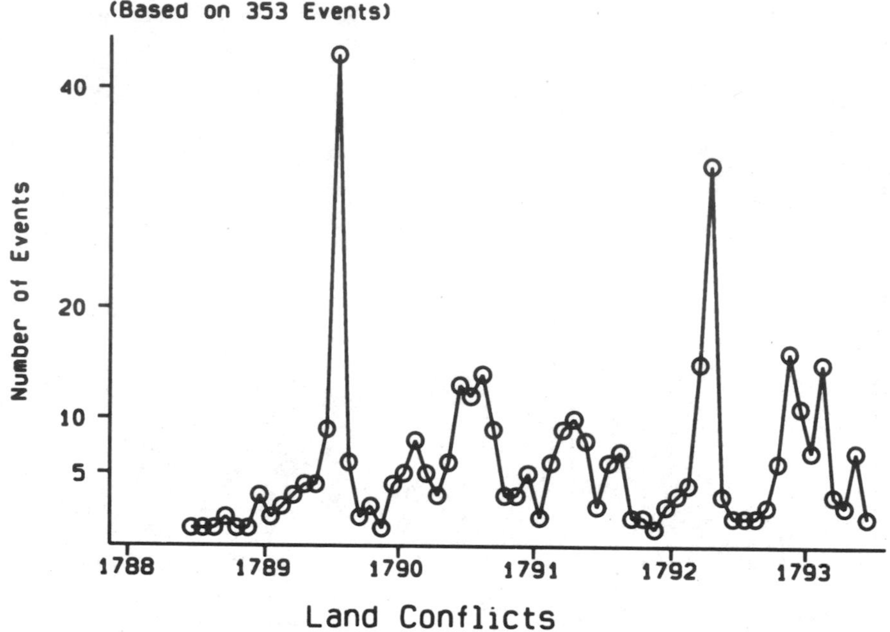

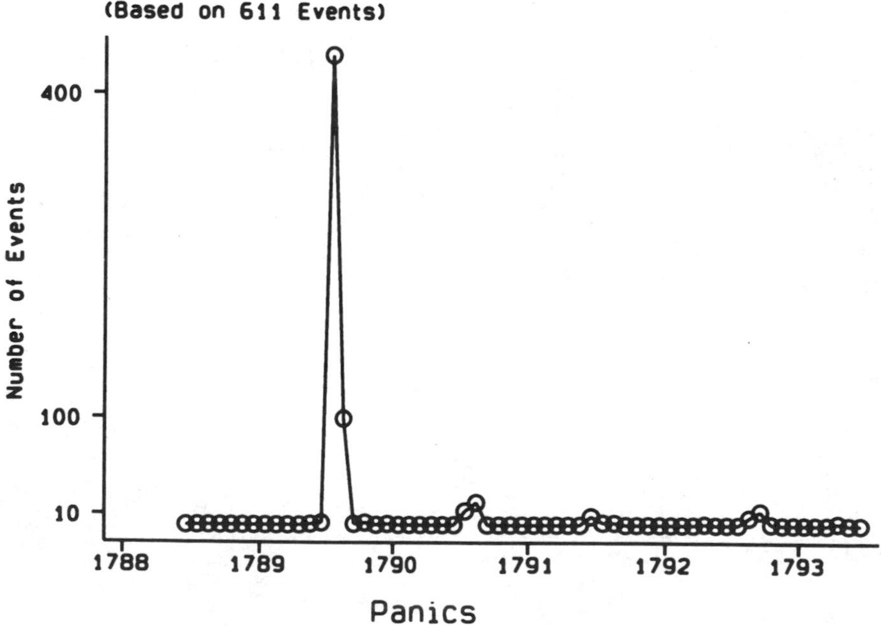

Fig. 6.2 (c) Incidence of Rural Insurrection by Date

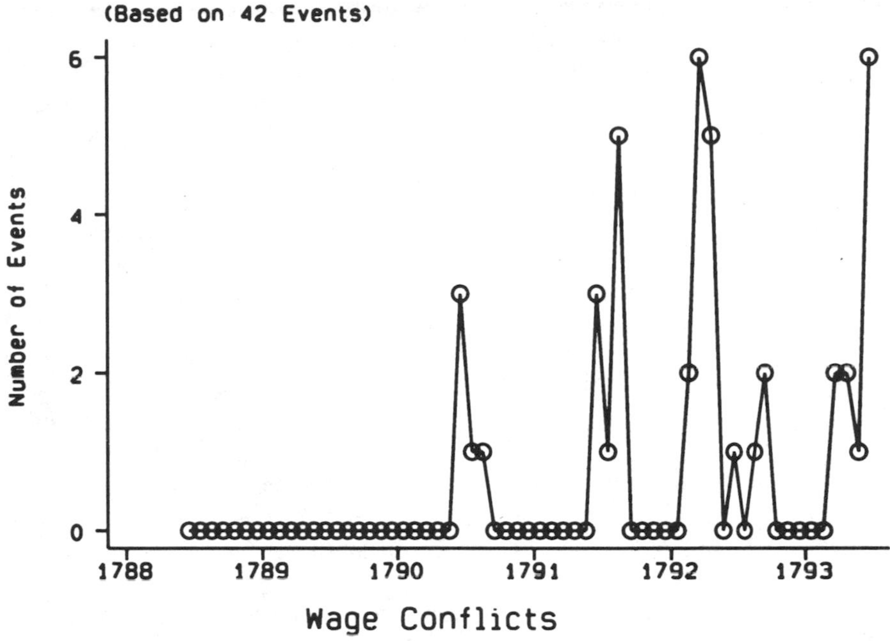

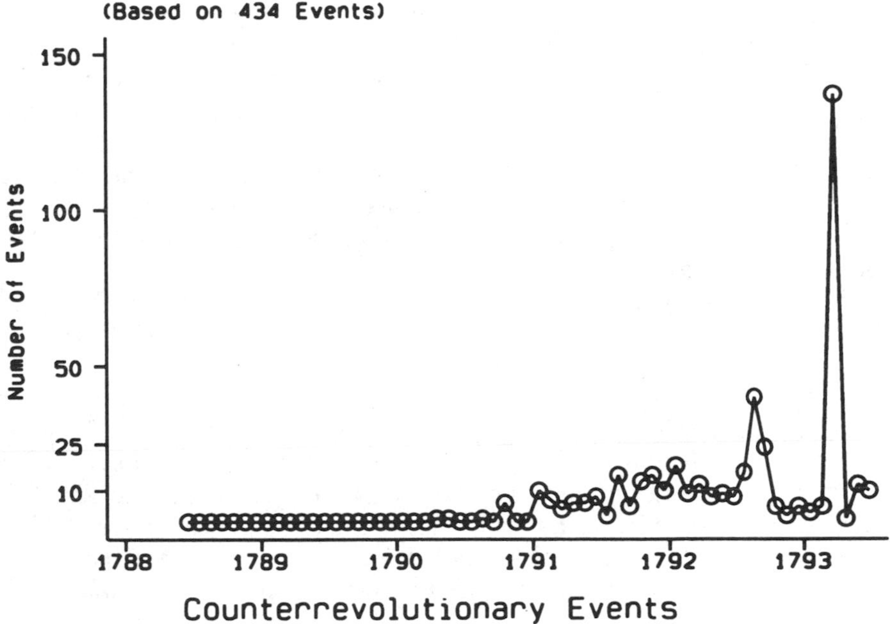

Fig. 6.2 (d) Incidence of Rural Insurrection by Date

from antiseigneurialism in how large the April 1792 peak is compared to the great spike of July 1789, the pattern for panics differs in precisely the opposite direction. The July 1789 spike utterly overwhelms the distribution of panics, although there are little spikelets (virtual flyspecks on the graph) a year later in the summer of 1790, again in June 1791, and August 1792. Summer is panic time in rural revolutionary France: the Great Fear of 1789 and the minifears of the next three summers.

If these half-dozen series all peak in the first summer of revolution and—anti-tax events and panics apart—are strong in the spring of 1792, they also share another rhythmic element as well. They are small or nonexistent in the early summer of 1788, rise rapidly by March 1789, and then, generally after a slight pause later in the spring, shoot way up in summer. Although they fall off later that summer they maintain an erratic but noticeable persistance until sometime late in 1792 or early in 1793 (there is a good deal of variety on the timing of this last turning point) and then fall to very low levels by late spring of '93. Thus for six of these eight major forms, the data exhibit a rapid rise, an erratic persistance, and then an equally rapid and radical fall. (The anti-tax events and panics deviate from this picture.)

Two of the insurrectionary forms move to a different rhythm altogether. Wage events and counterrevolution are virtually nonexistent in our sample well into 1790 and on the other hand remain notable well into 1793. Counterrevolutionary events begin to be felt late in 1790, grow slowly (and as usual erratically) until August 1792, after which they subside until their strong peak in March 1793. (They may be headed for another rise when we cut the story off at the end of June.) Wage events are scarce; but they totally fail to turn up in our sample before early in 1790. While their high time in March and April 1792 is also a strong time for many of the insurrectionary forms, wage conflicts, like counterrevolution but unlike other forms, are strong into 1793 (and perhaps are still rising at the end of our five-year period).

Why this web of similarities and differences? If it is easy enough to see July 1789 as a general crisis point in which most forms of conflict flourished, it is less obvious why April 1792 should be a second such point, more striking for some of our series than the following August. The rising of August 10, 1792, in the capital by Parisian militants and radicalized National Guards from the provinces overturned the constitutionalized ambiguity by which royal authority and revolutionary legislature coexisted; the Republic was inaugurated and, along with the Republic, the search for a new constitution. The crisis of the urban center had its rural and provincial counterpart in the steep rise in incidents from July through September. Yet in rural and provincial France, March and April were substantially more explosive both in the aggregate statistics and for antiseigneurial, religious, and land-conflict events (and, to a lesser degree, subsistence events as well).[5] If some, with an eye on the center, speak of August as the critical point in a "second revolution,"[6] what is April?

Table 6.1 summarizes some of this concentration by pointing up the degree to which one single month stands out for every kind of conflict—and for most, it is the same month. It is true that there is variation here: panics, followed by anti-tax events and then counterrevolution are more extremely concentrated in a single month than the other event-types, but even the least concentrated of these others has more than a tenth of all incidents in a single month. The analysis here confirms the observations on the trajectory of all events to the effect that the sense of opportunity and danger, altering with great rapidity, makes the incidence of conflict tantalizingly unstable.

We may look at the same data from another angle. Rather than scrutinizing the numbers of events of different sorts, let us take a look at the *salience* of different sorts of events. The overall proportion of events with an antiseigneurial aspect, for example, was seen (Table 5.1) to be somewhat more than one-third. But is this constant through time, or is the proportion of antiseigneurial events something that shifts with (and perhaps shifts) the Revolution? Figures 6.3 (a)–(d) present eight images of salience for our major insurrectionary modes. We see again, unsurprisingly, the rapid oscillations, as before. But this time, the eight trajectories are far more distinctive in appearance.

We may think of the rise and fall of contestation of various sorts as composed of two components—a general propensity for open conflict of all sorts, born out of a conjunction of opportunity and mobilizational capacity that nurtures a wide spectrum of actions (as in July 1789) and circumstances that favor specific forms of action but not others. By shifting from examining the numbers to examining the proportions of events of particular sorts, we are, in effect, removing the common element, thereby generating a more individualized set of graphs. In spite of the sawtooth pattern, the salience of antiseigneurial actions exhibits a fairly clear pattern of rise and fall. The proportion of events directed against the seigneurial rights is zero in the summer of 1788, then begins to rise in November and remains high until the late spring of 1792 (apart from a drastic fall in autumn 1791). From that point it falls, at first sharply, and then, after a brief September upsurge, more slowly and irregularly. Some of the high points of peasant action are

5. One hesitates to make too much of the data on the scarce wage conflicts, but the shape of their trajectory also stresses the spring rather than the summer of 1792.

6. See, for example, the concurrence of two scholars more often noted for their differences than their commonalities: Albert Soboul, *The French Revolution, 1787–1799: From the Storming of the Bastille to Napoleon* (New York: Vintage Books, 1975), 251; François Furet, *La Révolution de Turgot à Jules Ferry, 1770–1880* (Paris: Hachette, 1988), 123.

Table 6.1. Peak Months of Insurrection

Type of Event (Broad Categories)	Date of Principal Peak	Date of Secondary Peak	Ratio of Number of Events in Principal Peak to Secondary Peak	Ratio of Number of Events in Peak Month to All Events
Antiseigneurial	July 1789	April 1792	1.4	.18
Religious	July 1789	April 1792	2.2	.17
Subsistence	July 1789	March 1792	1.6	.13
Anti-tax	July 1789	February 1790	6.8	.35
Land conflict	July 1789	April 1792	1.9	.12
Wage conflict	March–April 1792	August 1791	1.6	.20
Panic	July 1789	August 1790	20.8	.86
Counterrevolution	March 1793	August 1792	3.0	.23

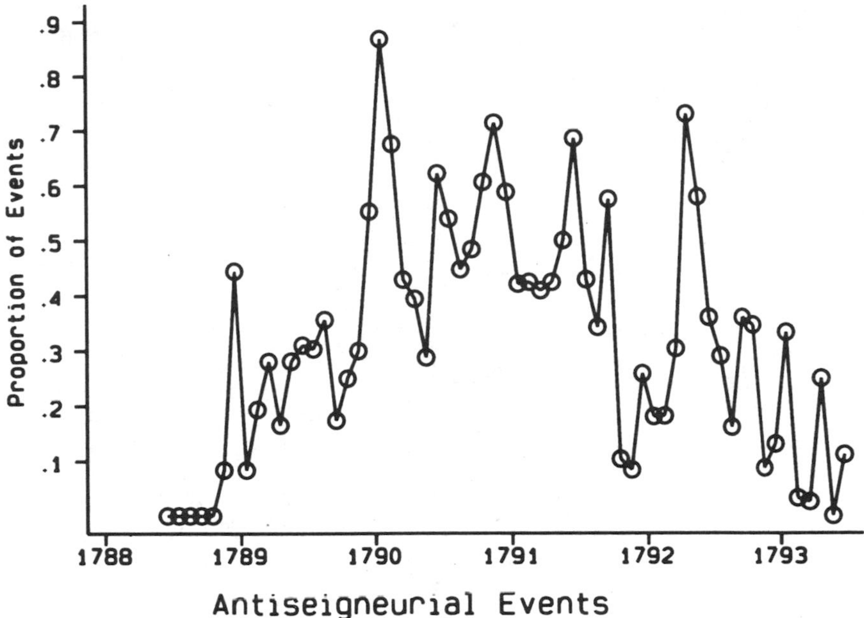

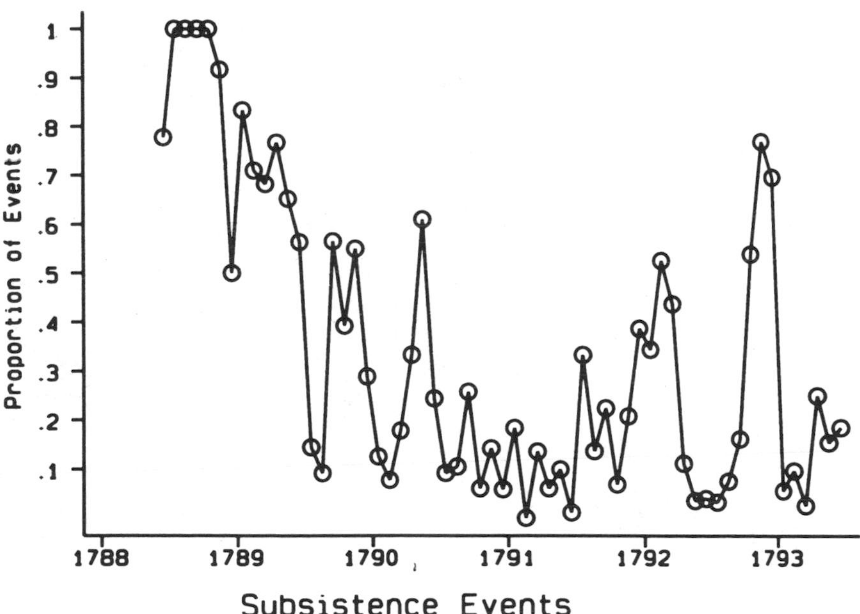

Fig. 6.3 (a) Proportions of Rural Insurrection by Date

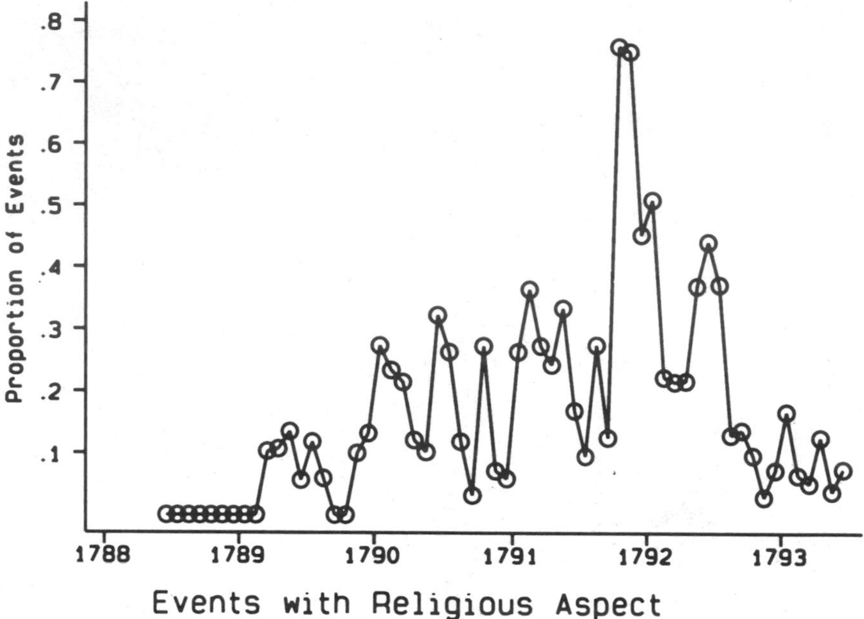

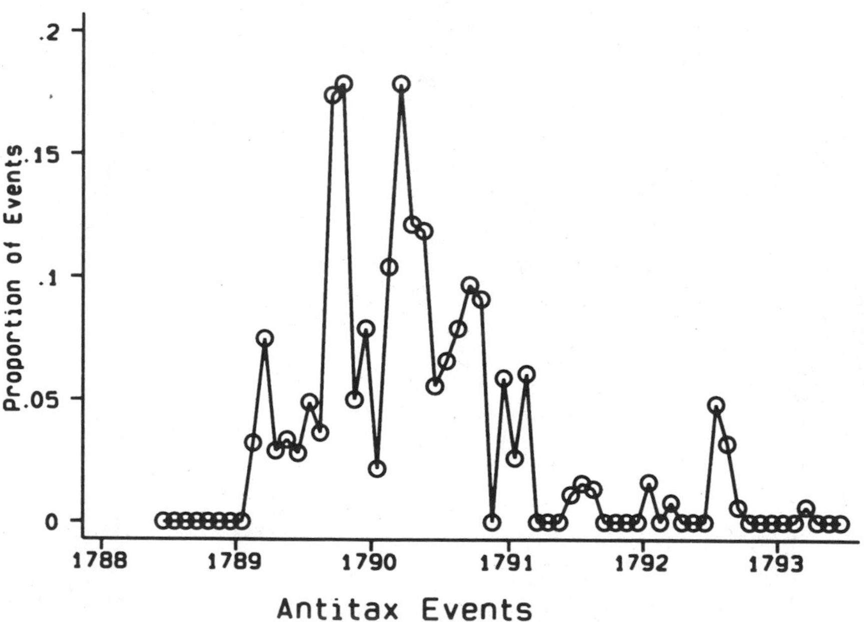

Fig. 6.3 (b) Proportions of Rural Insurrection by Date

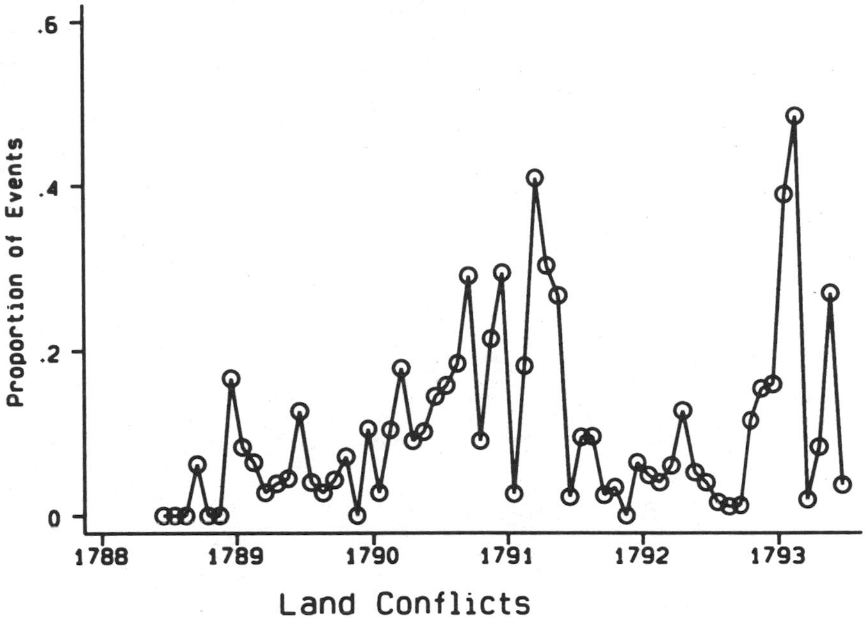

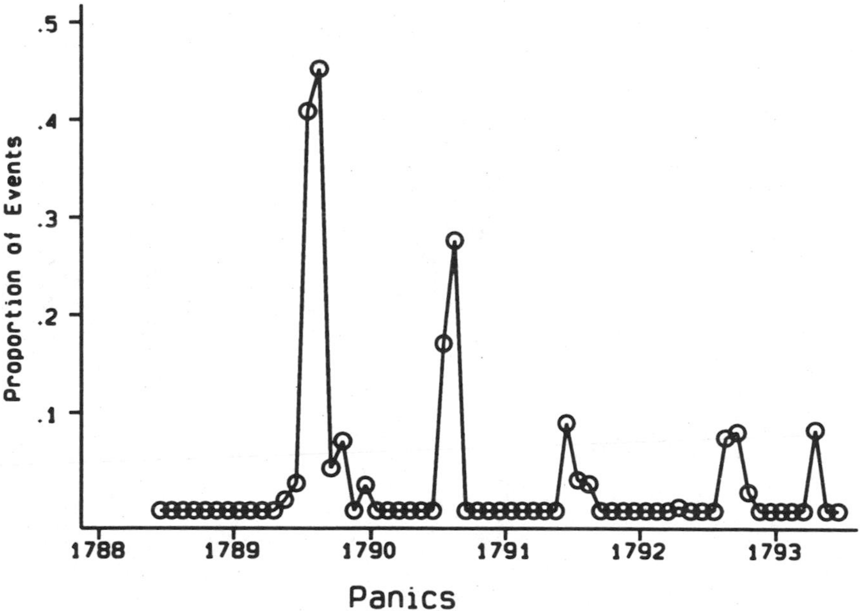

Fig. 6.3 (c) Proportions of Rural Insurrection by Date

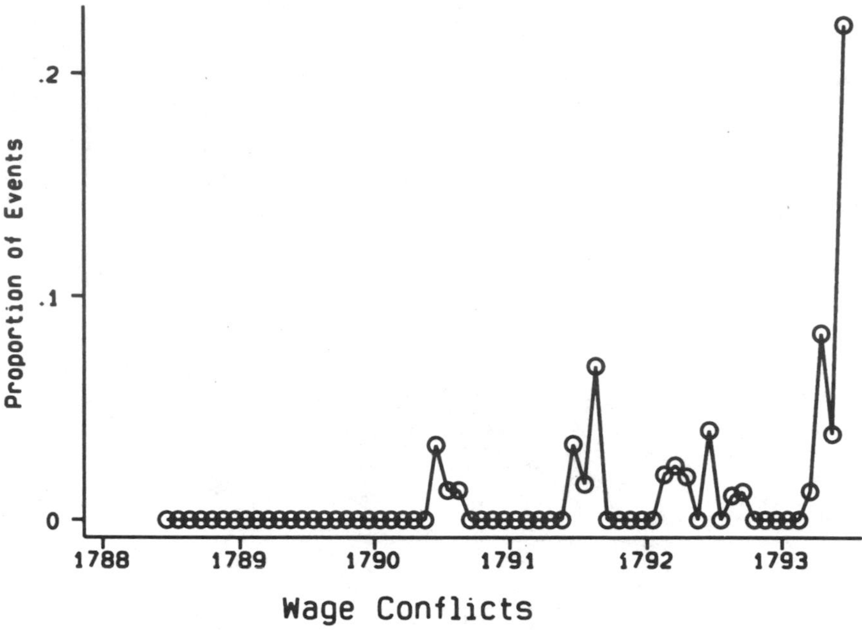

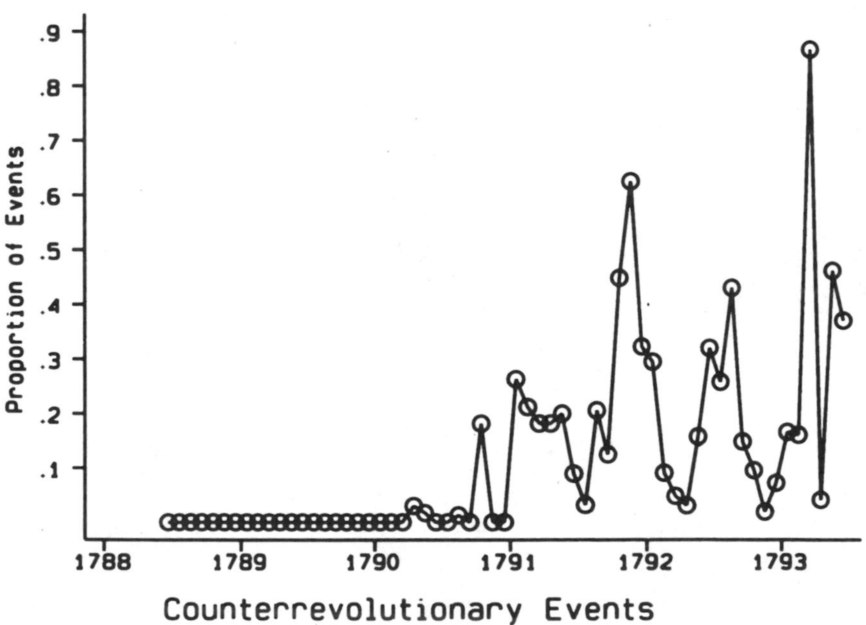

Fig. 6.3 (c) Proportions of Rural Insurrection by Date

overwhelmingly antiseigneurial. In January 1790, 87% of all events have an antiseigneurial character; in April 1792, 73%.

The gross trend in the salience of subsistence events resembles the inverse of the antiseigneurial pattern. Figures 6.3 (a)–(d) show that in the summer of 1788, almost all events were oriented to the provision or price of food. Subsistence issues began to share the spotlight in November; by the following March they had fallen to some 68% and in June they were still holding strong at 56%. The initial slow falloff in the salience of subsistence issues over the first 13 months of our sample then gave way to a precipitous decline, down in one month to 14%. Even after the dropoff at the beginning of the summer of 1789, there were still a number of months in which half or more of all events were over food issues: September 1789 (50%), May 1790 (60%), and a long autumn of 1792 with 60%, 73%, and even 79% in October, November, and December respectively. On the other hand, there were also a number of months with few or no subsistence events. Although rather less numerous overall than antiseigneurial events (see Table 5.1) there were nonetheless nineteen months in which they were at least half of all events and thereby constituted the dominant form of social struggle.

To pursue the significance of subsistence events for a moment, they not only outnumbered all other forms of conflict combined during a (discontinuous) year and a half of the Revolution but they were also, to recall Table 5.1 again, quite widespread, second only to panics in their geographic range. They were notably less restricted than antiseigneurial events in the number of *bailliages* in which they occurred. In their temporal sequencing for France as a whole, subsistence events seem virtually the forerunners of the entire rural explosion. They constituted a widely understood repository of forms of contentious action on which mobilizations directed against other targets might draw. They played a role in the unraveling of the Old Regime by demonstrating a national movement of opposition by popular forces at the very instant that the elite struggles led to the political stalemate and the desperate improvisations to break that stalemate that culminated in the convocation of the Estates-General.[7] In the context of that convocation, as

7. Not to exaggerate: the summer events of 1788 are not exclusively subsistence-oriented. A small number indeed show a considerable involvement in national politics through participation in the intra-elite conflicts that have come to be known as the "prerevolution." At the very beginning of our time-frame, for example, country people participated in the resistance to the last attempt of the monarchy to ride roughshod over what ministers who identified with some notion of state-promoted progress tended to see as judicial obstructionism. The desperate abolition of the powerful *parlements* in May 1788 triggered disturbances a month later, two of which entered our sample because of significant rural participation (even though the location of the struggle was the town that housed the court). Peasants from surrounding villages, in Grenoble for Saturday market on June 7, 1788, armed themselves with rocks, hatchets, pitchforks, and an occasional gun and joined together with townspeople in resisting the royal troops sent to enforce the letters that had arrived that morning ordering the judges into exile. In the Pyrenees a dozen days later, people from the

the reality of the Estates-General came to the fore, other forms of rural action begin to displace the subsistence event from its dominant role. Most dramatically, the antiseigneurial movement came into its own.

The rural insurrections were at once causes, symptoms, and consequences of the breakdown of the political and moral authority of the Old Regime: causes, in that it strained the resources of those on high to deploy either benefits or coercion (and thereby insurrections intensified the intra-elite conflict since strategies for dealing with popular upheaval differed); symptoms, in that the failure to contain popular violence through alleviation, distraction, appeals to morality, and fear of repression, demonstrated to the elites themselves that something new was essential; and consequences, in that elite division and elite innovation (themselves in part reactions to popular threat) provided both opportunity and encouragement for further grassroots mobilization. In this process, by which popular action helped crack the sinews of the Old Regime, the subsistence disturbances constituted the major element, if to a decreasing degree after the autumn of 1788. In changing the parameters within which they mobilized, the patterns of mobilization themselves changed and other forms of popular action began to flourish.

Different Targets, Different Rhythms

Let us return to the question of the shift in peasant insurrection from primarily antifiscal and subsistence-oriented to primarily antiseigneurial. Peasant action was not overwhelmingly antiseigneurial as the Revolution commenced; it became so. There are not only structures of action but processes. Explanation, then, will require more than explaining an inherently antiseigneurial countryside forged by long-term historical change; we need as well to identify processes by which the countryside came to choose antiseigneurial action. Long-term processes generating antiseigneurial grievances are essential—our entire analysis of the *cahiers* shows this (see Chapters 2 and 3)—but they are only a part of the story.

The predominantly antiseigneurial thrust of revolutionary French peasant insurrection was not achieved by the slow evolution of institutions during the eighteenth century and just waiting for the revolutionary opportunity to reveal itself. Nor did it emerge instantaneously and full-blown out of nothing.

countryside around Pau attempted to seize artillery pieces in order to force the reopening of the *parlement.* For Pau, see Anatoly V. Ado, *Krest'ianskoe dvizhenie vo Frantsii vo vremia velikoi burzhaznoi revoliutsii kontsa XVIII veka* (Moscow: Izdatel'stvo Moskovskovo Universiteta, 1971), 78; for Grenoble, see Viallet, "La journée des tuiles: Accident de l'histoire ou première manifestation politique populaire à la veille de 1789?" in Vital Chomel, ed., *Les débuts de la Révolution française en Dauphiné, 1788–1791* (Grenoble: Presses Universitaires de Grenoble, 1988), 72–85.

While absent until late in 1788, it grew. We need, then, to look for nurturant structures and processes, both. Antiseigneurial events moreover are far more characteristic of some regions than others (41% of *bailliages* according to Table 5.1). We shall ask which were the antiseigneurial regions (and which regions were antiseigneurial when?) and shall be able to use spatial variations to stand in for institutional ones (see Chapter 7). But however much some regions (at some times) were favorable soil and others were inhibiting, the antiseigneurial movement was not simply there, fully developed, not in even the most favorable soil. It grew and we need to try to identify the growth-promoting process.

The evidence presented thus far bears on another discussion among historians, one more marked, on the whole by statements of opinion than by deployment of evidence. What sort of consciousness of political process, if any, did the peasantry bring to the Revolution? Historians' opinion ranges from the view that the peasants harbored profound antipathy to seigneuralism in all its forms to a view that they endured it with utter apathy. For Georges Lefebvre, "that these obligations, far more than the royal taxes, were execrated unanimously by the whole peasantry cannot be doubted and was to be proved by experience."[8] For William Doyle, "even among the peasantry who bore most of the burden, feudal rights were scarcely questioned spontaneously."[9] In consequence, historians have differed deeply among themselves on what, if anything, the countryside contributed to the Revolution. For Georges Lefebvre, the peasants collectively were a major shaper of events: "Against the aristocracy the peasants had far more substantial grievances than did the people of the cities, and it is natural, therefore, that they took it upon themselves to deal the blow by which the aristocracy was laid low."[10] Donald Sutherland's summary of 1789, on the other hand, asserts that "the Revolution was largely an urban phenomenon."[11] In the long run, contends Sutherland, the peasantry were actually a brake on revolution: "In the end, therefore, the vast weight of ancient peasant France imposed itself upon the government at the expense of many of the ideals of 1789."[12] George Taylor sees the peasants as contributing next to nothing to revolutionary radicalism. When they express

8. See Georges Lefebvre, *The Coming of the French Revolution* (Princeton: Princeton University Press, 1967), 142.

9. William Doyle, *Origins of the French Revolution* (Oxford: Oxford University Press, 1980), 198.

10. Lefebvre, *Coming of the French Revolution,* 142.

11. Sutherland, *France, 1789–1815. Revolution and Counterrevolution* (New York: Oxford University Press, 1986), 439.

12. Ibid., 442. The Sutherland quotes are, I believe, fair summary statements of the tone of the concluding chapter of this survey of the Revolution from which I extracted them; however, the argument of the entire book assigns the peasantry a far more active and complex part than indicated in his own conclusions.

their views, he writes, one sees "docility." Wherever the Revolution's *ideas* came from, it surely was not, Taylor argues forcefully, the French countryside.[13] Alfred Cobban, on the other hand, sees the peasants as precisely the force that pushed a conservative revolutionary leadership into taking action.[14] Guy Lemarchand, addressing those subsistence events in which monasteries or *châteaux* were attacked, suggests that the radicalism of peasant doings outran their thoughts: "Thus," he writes, "these popular risings, intending first of all to seize grain wherever it was found, came to challenge the entire social system of the epoch without the rebels clearly realizing it."[15] So the peasants hated the regime or never questioned it. They delivered the Old Regime's death blow or they were docile. They received the blessings of the Revolution from the bourgeoisie and, indeed, were even a brake on urban radicalism or they forced the hand of a conservative governing elite. They knew what they were doing or they challenged the social order without realizing it. The various claims of what the peasants brought to the Revolution are thoroughly contradictory.

The changing pattern of peasant unrest that our data present suggests that this issue has not been well posed, for the peasants brought different things to the Revolution at different times (and places). Initially they brought subsistence concerns, which were increasingly displaced by antiseigneurial ones (although the insurrectionary calendar was still punctuated by months in which subsistence events dominated). The antiseigneurial events, I shall argue below, buttressed the critique of "feudalism" participated in by so many of the new national revolutionary elite. In this sense, the thinking of the peasantry—not just their empty bellies, traditional mentalities, emotional reactions—the *thinking* that underlies their analyses of the seigneurial regime that we have seen in the *cahiers* played a part in defining the Revolution.

This, in turn, brings us to a more general level of controversy that has raged for some time among comparative students of revolution. Is peasant participation understood to be creative, to embody projects and programs, to be consciously political? Or, on the other hand, is peasant action to be understood primarily, if perhaps significantly, as destructive, requiring either a revolutionary party to contain and channel it or an ideological reconstruction by strategically located intellectuals to give a revolution meaning and direction? In his important work, *Agrarian Revolution,*[16] for

13. George V. Taylor, "Revolutionary and Nonrevolutionary Content in the *Cahiers* of 1789," *French Historical Studies* 7 (1972): 495.

14. Alfred Cobban, *The Social Interpretation of the French Revolution* (Cambridge: Cambridge University Press, 1965), 53.

15. Guy Lemarchand, "Les troubles de subsistance dans la généralité de Caen (seconde moitié du XVIIIe siècle)," *Annales Historiques de la Révolution Française* 35 (1963): 413.

16. Jeffery M. Paige, *Agrarian Revolution: Social Movements and Export Agriculture in the Underdeveloped World* (New York: Free Press, 1975).

example, Jeffery Paige vigorously defended a notion of peasant revolutionaries as self-conscious adherents to a program of social change. By way of contrast, James Scott, in *The Moral Economy of the Peasant,*[17] urged us to see peasant action as overwhelmingly shaped by bedrock survival concerns and only marginally concerned with most of what preoccupies triumphant parties. Scott's peasants make revolution by constituting the armies that overcome the Old Regime; they thereby are the vehicle ridden by others to their own purposes, often to the bitter disappointment and sometimes the armed enmity of the very rural forces that overthrew the old order. Paige's peasant revolutionaries, on the other hand, do more than break the framework of the old order: they participate in framing the vision of the new. Our data suggest that, in the case of France, something of both may be at work. The subsistence revolts of the summer and fall of 1789 (and beyond) helped wreck the Old Regime, without providing a coherent image of a new order. (And, indeed, it would be hard to make out that the eventual new order, of unified national markets and substantial abandonment of Old Regime provisioning policy, would be seen by many as unambiguously in accord with rural popular desires.) But if all forms of peasant action contributed to cracking the old order, the shift toward antiseigneurial action suggests another role as well, a defining role.

Subsistence events were the initial point of departure for the national movement, by opening the way, on a national scale, to the emergence of other goals and other forms of action.[18] But how did the transition to other forms of action, especially antiseigneurial actions, come about? One possible vehicle was through the reactions of antagonists. As various authorities responded to rising subsistence disturbances with concessions, as repressive attempts proved unequal to the scale of the disturbances in light of the military weaknesses of the twilight of the Old Regime, it may well be the case that those with other goals in mind took heart and began to move into action.[19] There is a second possible path from subsistence events to other challenges. Did the experience, locally, of mounting food riots, market invasions, transportation blockages, and domiciliary visits in search of

17. James C. Scott, *The Moral Economy of the Peasant: Rebellion and Subsistence in Southeast Asia* (New Haven: Yale University Press, 1976).

18. Ado has pointed to the early subsistence struggles as the opening wedge for the antiseigneurial events to come. One of his sections is titled "From the Struggle for Bread to the Attack on the Bases of Feudalism." See *Krest'ianskoe dvizhenie,* 74, 87.

19. Divisions on appropriate government policy in the political crisis that opposed many to the monarchy in conjunction with the blocked careers within the military of many junior officers of commoner or provincial noble background was making the military an unreliable instrument in urban confrontations. Nonetheless the army continued to be generally reliable in subsistence disturbances and antiseigneurial events in the countryside. See Samuel F. Scott, *The Response of the Royal Army to the French Revolution: The Role and Development of the Line Army, 1787–1793* (Oxford: Clarendon Press, 1978), 78–79.

hoarded grain provide a significant seedbed in which further mobilization could grow? Differently put, did the subsistence action encourage mobilization for other ends largely through decreasing state coercion and bringing on a general revolution, within which various locally based communal mobilizations were facilitated? Or did a local subsistence action provide a local inspiration and a local experience out of which grew local mobilizations for other ends? Put yet another way: did subsistence actions merely open the way for other actions—or did they also *evolve* into other actions?

If the temporal patterning raises the possibility of subsistence events as a sort of grounding from which later events of various sorts may have sprung, a comparison of the anti-tax and counterrevolutionary events, returning now to Figures 6.3 (a)–(d), is also intriguing. The proportion of anti-tax events rises swiftly after March 1789 and after reaching its first peak in October attains its highest point—a bit under one-fifth of all events—in March 1790 and then, after passing through another peak late in the year remains small to nonexistent for almost the entire remainder of our period.[20] But it is just at the end of 1790 that recognizably counterrevolutionary events come into their own, attaining their apogee of 87% of all events in March 1793. Could it be the case that the anti-tax events were the forerunners of the recognizably counterrevolutionary mobilizations? In Chapter 7 I shall explore whether or not localities that at an early point experienced subsistence or anti-tax events are the localities in which other forms of conflict later flourished (see pp. 411–17).

The juxtaposition of the timing of the counterrevolutionary events and other forms of conflict casts an interesting light on another juxtaposition as well, perhaps surprisingly so. The timing of wage conflicts is rather similar to that of counterrevolution: virtually nothing until well into 1790, a drop in 1791, followed by a peak toward the end of that year; a drastic falloff early in 1792, followed by a midyear upsurge;[21] and finally a fall at the end of 1792 followed by a sharp rise in early 1793. Is this mere coincidence, perhaps a fluke due to the low numbers of wage conflicts? Or is there some interconnection? I pose the hypothesis that the connection is rooted in the similar causal matrix of the two. The counterrevolution was in part a reaction to

20. Note that anti-tax events drop off after a wave of suppressions of the indirect taxes in late 1790 and early 1791. This is an important and welcome sign of validity of our data. The indirect taxes were either radically reformed or slated for abolition through various enactments, culminating in the suppression of the General Farms by the laws of March 5 and March 20, 1791. See *AP* 23:292–93, 670–72; *AP* 24:222–23; George T. Matthews, *The Royal General Farms in Eighteenth-Century France* (New York: Columbia University Press, 1958), 278.

21. The rise in wage disputes in 1792 may in part be explicable by the deteriorating currency (the *assignat*) and concomitant price rises. But this would not explain the precise timing very well. See Yvonne Crebouw, "Les salariés agricoles face au maximum des salaires," in *La Révolution française et le monde rural* (Paris: Editions du Comité des Travaux Historiques et Scientifiques, 1989), 113–14.

the attempt of the endangered Republic to conscript young villagers into France's armies. The timing of counterrevolution responds with great sensitivity to the moments at which new and threatening steps are taken.

Not that France's wage laborers were the strike force of counterrevolutionary struggle. The wage-labor sector, often migratory, often foreign to the community in which they labored, often tied to urban entrepreneurs for part of the year, were not likely to be part of communal resistance to the new revolutionary order, were less likely to miss the old priests, less likely to be loyal to the old elites, and also less likely to be competitors with urban landgrabbers for the former church holdings now up for sale. (All of these propositions have been suggested by historians recently as part of the nexus of counterrevolution).[22] Nonetheless, precisely as outsiders, itinerant laborers may have been likely to have their names turned over to the government by solidary communities that could designate which of their sons would go to war. How tempting it was not to name their sons at all, but to list instead migrant workers, temporarily resident. And if they did name their sons, why not name those who in their turn had migrated elsewhere seeking employment, who, with a little luck, might never be picked up by the cops?[23] So thc threat of conscription may have cemented ties between draft evaders and their own communities, a staple of the literature on conscription; but, by the same token, conscription may have exacerbated the relations of solidary communities and marginalized laborers. (I know of no adequate study of this process.) Thus the same moments that triggered counterrevolution may also have decreased whatever tendencies might have emerged for laborers to tolerate low wages.

But conscription meant more than a rupture of social bonds between marginal workers and stable peasant employers.[24] Conscription decreased the labor force in the countryside both directly, by placing young men in the armies, and indirectly, by sending large numbers of young men into the forests and mountains to hide from the recruiting sergeants. That is to say,

22. See Paul Bois, *Paysans de l'Ouest: Des structures économiques et sociales aux options politiques depuis l'époque révolutionnaire dans la Sarthe* (Le Mans: Imprimerie M. Vilaire, 1960); Timothy Tackett, "The West in France in 1789. The Religious Factor in the Origins of the Counterrevolution," *Journal of Modern History* 54 (1982): 714–45; Charles Tilly, *The Vendée* (Cambridge: Harvard University Press, 1964).

23. In a part of Limousin known for exporting migratory stoneworkers, one finds communities that opted to elect the villagers to send in response to the levy of 300,000 of March 1793 and that then put together lists of young village men who were nowhere to be found. See Paul d'Hollander, "La levée des trois cent mille hommes en Haute-Vienne (mars 1793)," *Annales du Midi* 101 (1989): 78–79.

24. The pressure of conscription may also sometimes have hardened village class divisions rather than reinforced village solidarity against outsiders. The better-off or worse-off villagers seem to sometimes have feared that the other group would use the conscription rules against it. (See d'Hollander, "La levée des trois cent mille," 77–78, for several such incidents.)

the strike, not the easiest of tools to wield within the social structure of the French countryside,[25] suddenly became a far more profound threat and a far more potent social weapon. Thus, it is in the wake of the great counterrevolutionary explosion of March 1793 that wage disputes rise rapidly. Consider one community at the very tail end of our period, June 29, 1793. On that date, the agricultural laborers of the Alpine community of St. Hilaire-de-Brens demanded that meals be provided by their employers and that they be paid even when bad weather prevented work. They further announced that they would hang any newcomers who sought lower wages. Should the owners refuse, they went on, they would harvest the crops anyway and take their own pay. Surely Jean Nicolas is right when he reads this tough talk as the sudden confidence of workers made hard to replace by wartime labor shortages.[26] The capacity of agricultural workers to press wages upward is shown in the wage statistics summarized by LeGoff and Sutherland.[27]

One final comparison among the trajectories is suggestive. Ado contends that conflicts over food and land coincide. Ado sees land conflicts and subsistence events alike as forms of rural class struggle born in similar circumstances of want and opportunity.[28] Returning to Figures 6.2 (a)–(d) and Table 6.1 we can see that there is indeed much similarity, but not identity, in the timing of the three major spikes: Summer 1789, Spring 1792, and Autumn 1792. But some of this coincidence comes from these being generally favorable times for many forms of insurrection. When we explore the trajectories of proportions of events (Figs. 6.3 [a]–[d]) we see that the curves are quite different, with the proportion of land conflicts irregularly rising until early 1791 and the proportion of subsistence events even more irregularly falling. Halfway through 1792, however, the two curves do merge and are quite similar for the last year of our data set. This is, I suggest, because the nature of land conflicts shifted. At first, as will be developed in Chapter 8 (see p. 482) land conflicts had a very strong

25. Work-gangs of some half-dozen or so laborers, often formed around a common place of origin, seem to have had enough solidarity so that work-gang leaders could plan a work stoppage. To secure sufficient solidarity across separate work-gangs to persuade (or frighten) other laborers into halting work would seem quite difficult in a period of substantial population pressure and no legal recognition of any sort of rural laborers' associations. (The whole arena seems to be largely historical terra incognita.)

26. Jean Nicolas, *La Révolution française dans les alpes: Dauphiné et Savoie, 1789–1799* (Toulouse: Privat, 1989), 194. The government clearly worried about how to ameliorate the impact of war-induced labor shortages. See Octave Festy, *L'agriculture pendant la Révolution française: Les conditions de production et de récolte des céréales; Etude d'histoire économique, 1789–1795* (Paris: Gallimard, 1947), 164–268.

27. Timothy J. A. LeGoff and Donald M. G. Sutherland, "The Revolution and the Rural Economy," in Alan Forrest and Peter M. Jones, eds., *Reshaping France: Town, Country and Region During the French Revolution* (Manchester: Manchester University Press, 1991), 72.

28. Ado, *Krest'ianskoe dvizhenie,* 199–200.

antiseigneurial thrust, and as such were the work of fairly unified peasant communities; then as antiseigneurial actions began to fall after the spring of 1792, the antiseigneurial side of land conflicts falls away as well. The spurt of battles over land in fall 1792 were largely struggles within rural communities, pitting those without enough land against the better endowed; these later land battles probably had participant profiles very similar to those of food conflicts (see Chapter 5, p. 247) and, we see here, very similar temporal rhythms as well.

Peak Times and Quiet Times

A series of peaks, then: peasant action comes in waves. Do the events of the turbulent months differ from those of the peaceful times other than in their quantity? Let us consider as peak times those months with at least 75 events and as quiet times those with 28 or fewer. Table 6.2 shows that there are indeed some differences. Panics are almost completely confined to the peak periods. Since such a large proportion of all panic events took place in one single month—July 1789 (see Table 6.1)—this is perhaps not very informative about the pattern of peaks and troughs as a whole. More interesting is the comparison of antiseigneurial and subsistence events: the former rises in high times and the latter falls. This table suggests then, that to the extent that a peak is driven by a particular sort of event, overall, it will be the ebb and flow of antiseigneurial actions that we should watch for.

Such an aggregation may cover too much ground. Let us consider each peak episode separately. By a peak episode in Table 6.3, I mean a sequence of contiguous months each of which has at least 75 events. A peak month

Table 6.2. Forms of Insurrection in Periods of Peak Activity and in Quiet Periods (%)

Type of Event (Broad Categories)	Peak Periods[a]	Quiet Periods[b]
Antiseigneurial	38%	24%
Religious	15	14
Anti-tax	3	4
Subsistence	23	39
Land conflict	6	13
Wage conflict	1	3
Panic	18	1
Counterrevolution	7	13
(*N*)	(3,294)	(397)

[a]Months with 75 or more events.
[b]Months with 28 or fewer events.

and peak day will be the month and day within an episode with the largest number of events. For each peak episode, and for each peak month and peak day within that episode, we may compute the frequencies of the various forms of insurrection. Table 6.3 displays the percentages for all forms that reach 20% for at least one among the triad of episode, month, and day. The significance of antiseigneurial events stands out again. Of the nine peak episodes identified, antiseigneurial events were the dominant form in five; and they are a secondary focus of action in another two. Two of the peak periods (March–May 1789 and November 1792) were dominated by subsistence events, which were also a secondary component during the February–April 1792 wave. Panic, as we expected, was only a major force in the summer of 1789 (with a strong boost from antiseigneurial actions) and counterrevolution dominated the explosion of March 1793.

For some of these peak periods, narrowing the focus to a single month or even a single day, sharpens the picture. If we focus on the peak of peaks of the entire five-year span (July 27, 1789) we find that nearly two-thirds of the events on that day were panics. The peak day in the early 1790 wave (January 24, 1790), was one in which every event in the data collection had an antiseigneurial character; it was also a day on which an unusually large proportion of those antiseigneurial events involved actions directed against ecclesiastical targets (39%). The high day of the wave of June 1791 was also completely antiseigneurial. One other peak day, April 5, 1792, was also overwhelmingly antiseigneurial with a substantial group of ecclesiastical targets. Similarly, the peak days within the subsistence-dominated wave of November 1792 and the counterrevolution-dominated wave of March 1793 were even more subsistence-oriented or prone to counterrevolutionary events than those episodes as a whole.

One final table (Table 6.4) approaches the alternation in salience of different forms of contestation. If we consider each of the 61 months our data covers, we may ask how often did it happen that particular forms of rural action predominated? We again find that antiseigneurial actions were the leading form of turbulence in a bit under half the months covered and that subsistence conflicts constitute a close second, with religious conflicts, counterrevolution, land conflicts, and panics, in that order, trailing far behind. There is no single month in which wage conflicts dominate, bearing out again the often repeated contention that prices rather than wages were central to eighteenth-century collective mobilizations. Perhaps more surprisingly, there is not a single month in which the tone of insurrection was set by anti-tax actions.[29]

29. Although we have seen good reason to treat the anti-tax data with a certain reserve, it does seem very reasonable upon examination, that the combination of acceptance of the state (with whatever degree of resignation), support for the Revolution, and—for those who wished not to pay—the ease of evasion adequately account for the low number of events; see Chapter 5.

Table 6.3. Most Common Forms of Insurrection During Peak Episodes, Peak Months, and Peak Days (%)

Most Common Forms[a]	Peak Episode	Peak Month	Peak Day
	Mar.–May 1789	Mar. 1789	26 Mar. 1789
Subsistence	70%	68%	50%
Antiseigneurial	24	28	20
	July–Aug. 1789	July 1789	27 July 1789
Panic	42	41	65
Antiseigneurial	31	30	20
	Jan.–Feb. 1790	Jan. 1790	24 Jan. 1790
Antiseigneurial	81	87	100
Religious	26	27	39
	June–Aug. 1790	June 1790	1 June + 9 June 1790[b]
Antiseigneurial	54	62	45
Religious	24	32	0
Subsistence	15	24	20
	June 1791	June 1791	26 June 1791
Antiseigneurial	69	69	100
	Feb.–Apr. 1792	Apr. 1792	5 Apr. 1792
Antiseigneurial	47	73	91
Subsistence	31	11	9
Religious	22	22	22
	Aug.–Sept. 1792	Sept. 1792	9 Sept. 1792
Antiseigneurial	29	36	29
Counterrevolution	25	15	36
	Nov. 1792	Nov. 1792	24 Nov. 1792
Subsistence	77	77	90
	Mar. 1793	Mar. 1793	10 Mar. 1793
Counterrevolution	87	87	96

[a]Forms of insurrection characterizing at least 20% of the events of at least one among a peak episode, a month, or a day.

[b]1 June and 9 June 1790 were tied as peak day. I based the computations on aggregating the events of both days.

Table 6.4. Number of Months in Which a Type of Event Is Most Common

Type of Event (Broad Categories)	Number of Months as Most Common Event
Antiseigneurial	25
Religious	5
Anti-tax	0
Subsistence	22½
Land conflict	2½
Wage conflict	0
Counterrevolution	4
Panic	2

Note: If two categories are tied in a particular month, each gets ½.

We may summarize this survey of the changing targets of rural mobilization. A large number of months saw antiseigneurial actions in the ascendant and an almost equally large number were led by subsistence events. During the moments of most intense conflict, however, antiseigneurial events were the most generally characteristic feature of rural struggles. But the makeup of each particular peak is distinctive. The greatest peak of all is dominated by panics. The antiseigneurial aspect of some of the peaks is in part composed of assaults on ecclesiastical establishments but this is not the case of other strongly antiseigneurial months. Subsistence events are a secondary theme of some of the antiseigneurial waves, and they actually dominate antiseigneurialism in the spring of 1789 and totally eclipse it in November 1792; and, of course, counterrevolution is the source of the actions of the early spring of 1793.

We have, all in all, ebbs and flows here, not a monolithic movement. If we had to focus on one single element, we would get furthest by seeking to understand the surges of antiseigneurial action. But we would do better to notice the special features of each wave: the degree to which some of the peaks are dominated by other sorts of events, the degree to which the antiseigneurial waves share the stage with other forms of conflict and the degree to which antiseigneurial events at some points (but not others) are simultaneously directed at religiously defined targets. Perhaps this overall point can be made more sharply with an image. Figure 6.4 reiterates Figure 6.1, but this time displaying the types of action characteristic of the graph's spikes. If we think of each peak separately as constituting a research agenda, we can also suggest that the depth of historical research into these high points varies considerably. Georges Lefebvre's research on the panic-dominated spike of late July–early August 1789 still stands as a masterpiece, some six decades after its appearance.[30] The counterrevolutionary outbreak

30. Lefebvre, *La Grande Peur.*

of March 1793 is by now virtually a field of research all its own.[31] Other spikes lack a full synthetic treatment, although some have been covered in important regional research. Both the early winter wave of 1790 and the spring wave of 1792 have been marvelously analyzed in their Limousin manifestation by Jean Boutier,[32] for example. How to understand the pattern of ebb and flow as a whole, however, is a task still to be done: why do particular events assume the salient role they do at particular points in time and—to mention a subject not yet broached—space? (see Chapter 7).

Peak Episodes Day by Day

The month-by-month trajectories across five years of revolution that we have been exploring are vital tools for focusing the vision of scholarly hindsight; these trajectories are essential for revealing the way in which social structures and revolutionary events interacted to produce shifting patterns of confrontation. Those who lived through these events, who participated in popular challenge or who feared being the targets of this challenge, were surely responding on a different rhythm. When a villager joined his fellows after the Sunday sermon to plan some significant action, there was likely to be a specific day involved that very week—often, indeed, that very afternoon or evening. Those who followed the progress of insurrection were not collecting aggregated statistics, but hearing the hot news with anxiety or excitement, incident by incident, day by day. Let us see what these peak times were like from day to day. Let us start with the utterly unique peak of the summer of 1789 and chart the occurrence of events for July and August. Figure 6.5 shows that during the first half of July the number of events taking place each day was rising ever so gradually

31. Major recent work includes: Tilly, *The Vendée;* Bois, *Paysans de l'Ouest;* Sutherland, *The Chouans: The Social Origins of Popular Counter-Revolution in Upper Brittany, 1770–1796* (Oxford: Clarendon Press, 1982); Claude Petitfrère, *La Vendée et les vendéens* (Paris: Gallimard, 1981); Jean-Clément Martin, *La Vendée et la France* (Paris: Editions du Seuil, 1987); Roger Dupuy, *De la Révolution à la Chouannerie: Paysans en Bretagne, 1788–1794* (Paris: Flammarion, 1988); Timothy J. A. LeGoff, *Vannes and its Region: A Study of Town and Country in Eighteenth-Century France* (Oxford: Clarendon Press, 1981); Maurice Hutt, *Chouannerie and Counter-Revolution: Puisaye, the Princes and the British Government in the 1790s* (Cambridge: Cambridge University Press, 1983); Timothy Tackett, *Religion, Revolution and Regional Culture in Eighteenth-Century France: The Ecclesiastical Oath of 1791* (Princeton: Princeton University Press, 1986). An older, less thoughtfully analytic but more event-packed literature includes: Charles-Louis Chassin, *La préparation de la guerre de Vendée, 1789–1793* (Paris: Imprimerie Paul Dupont, 1892) and Célestin Port, *La Vendée angevine: Les origines—l'insurrection (janvier 1789–31 mars 1793)* (Paris: Hachette, 1888).

32. Jean Boutier, *Campagnes en émoi: Révoltes et Révolution en bas-Limousin, 1789–1800* (Treignac: Editions "Les Monédières," 1987).

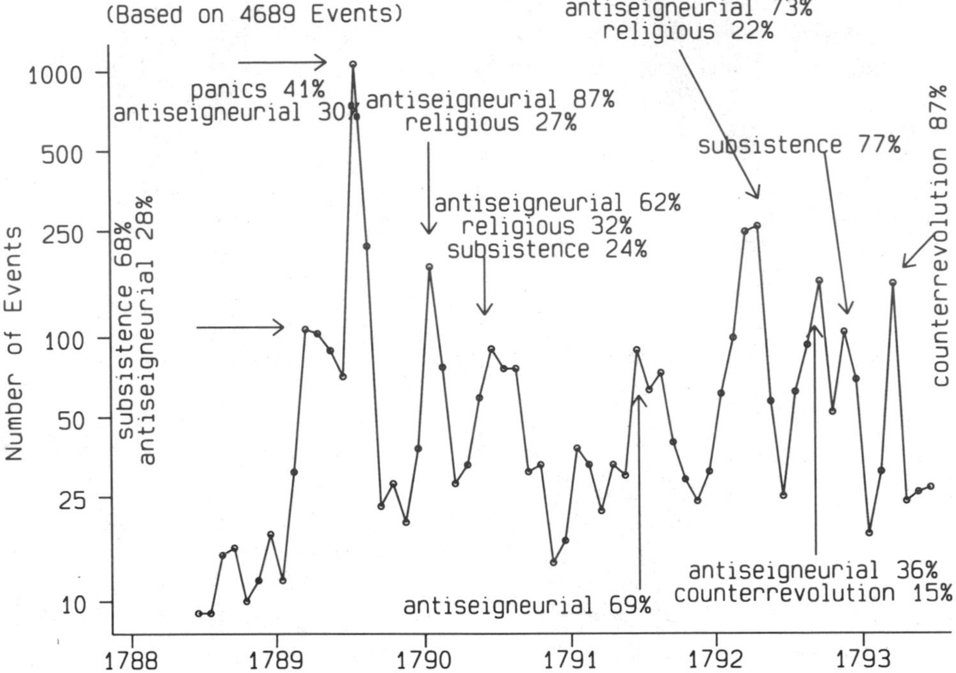

Fig. 6.4 Insurrectionary Events (by month) with Major Components of Peaks Indicated

until the middle of the month when it began to rise much more steeply, appearing to level off at quite a high level of turbulence around July 22 where it hovered for four days at the enormous level of about 60 events each day, and then precipitously rose to some 145 separate events on July 27, a height from which it dropped back over the next week to the pre-spike drumbeat of several incidents a day for the remainder of August. By the time the deputies resolved to announce the dismantling of the feudal regime on the famous night of August 4, the crisis had already passed. (Or, a bit more precisely, the crisis had returned to its normal level for the revolutionary epoch: the steady expectation of several incidents a day, while far less dramatic than the 145 incidents of July 27, still constituted a chronic pressure on those who sought the regeneration of the kingdom.) Is this simply an irony? We shall consider in Chapter 8 (see p. 437) the question of how and when the deputies at the National Assembly heard of the rural explosion.

The other peak periods do not have the same extreme spike that characterizes July 1789. Figures 6.6 (a)–(d) show that none of the other peak days towers so strongly over its month, nor do we have any rise quite so precipitous. Perhaps the sharpest rise shown in the other peak periods is the dramatic explosion of counterrevolution on March 10, 1793. Although,

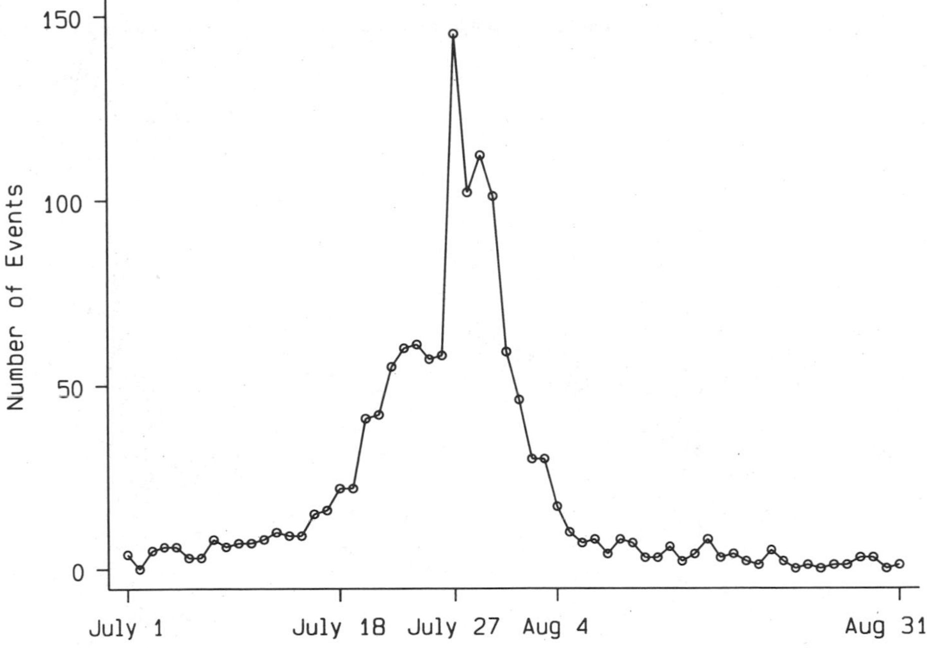

Fig. 6.5 Daily Incidence of Insurrection: July–August 1789

as we have just seen, what made the peak periods generally was a surge in antiseigneurial actions, the two most marked spikes, when considered on a daily basis, were in large part not antiseigneurial: the Great Fear of July 1789 and the counterrevolutionary explosion of March 1793. Once again, we are reminded that explaining peasant insurrection requires explaining a different mix of actions at different moments of the Revolution. And explaining the trajectory of peasant insurrections directed against one target requires considering a curve with a different shape than actions directed against another.

Rhythms

The ebb and flow of conflict is structured by the general rhythms of social life. In rural France, the interweaving of times of work, of play, and of rest could vary from year to year with the weather. Yet there was a clearly visible cycle of tasks that could be discerned through the variation in the precise dates of sowing, harvesting, marketing, and celebrating. The web of social institutions that sustained or that made demands upon rural

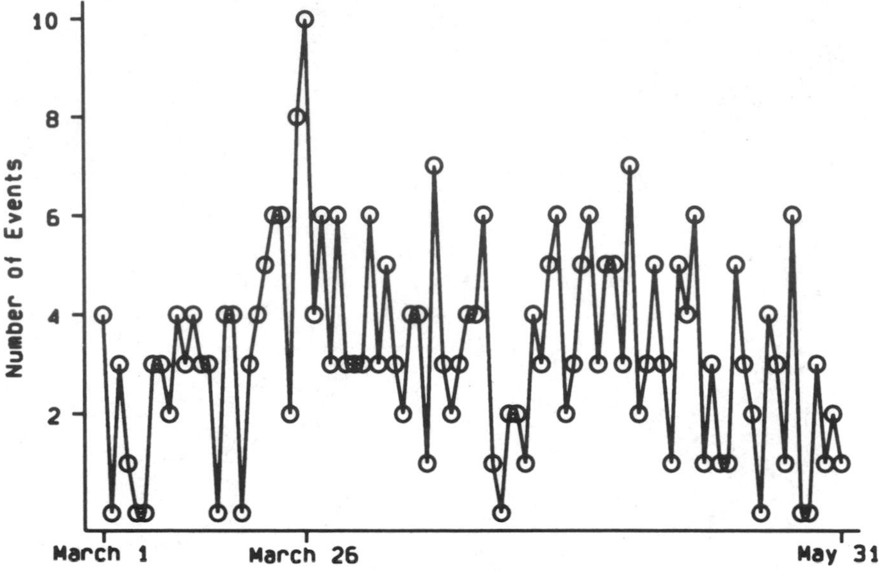

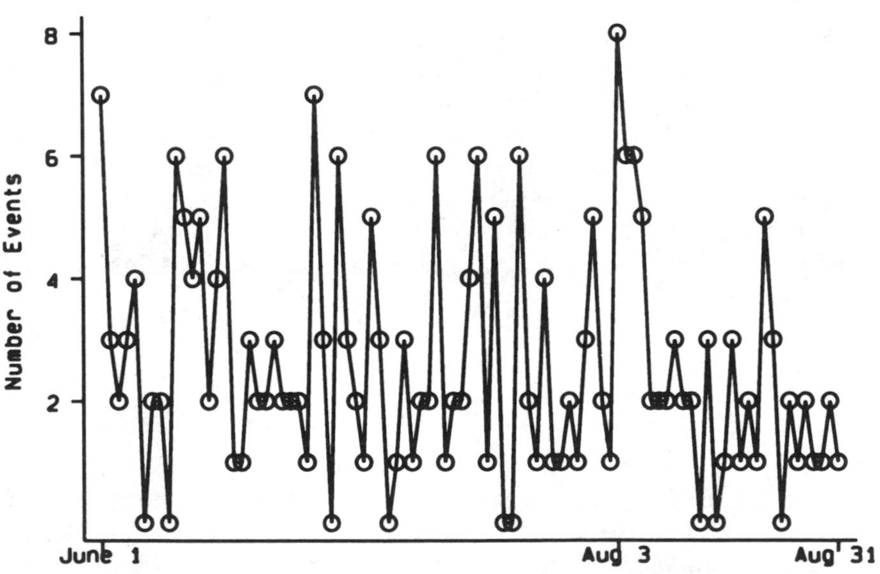

Fig. 6.6 (a) Peak Periods of Insurrection

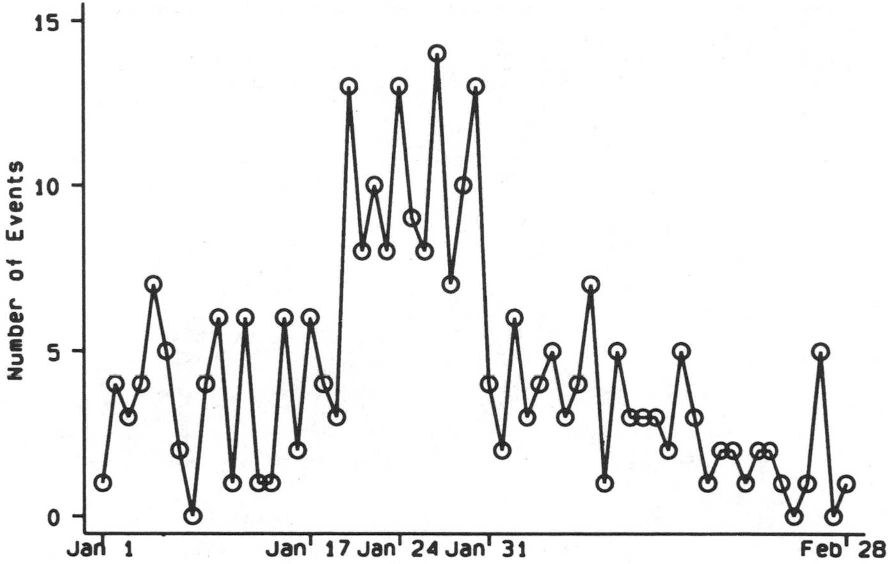

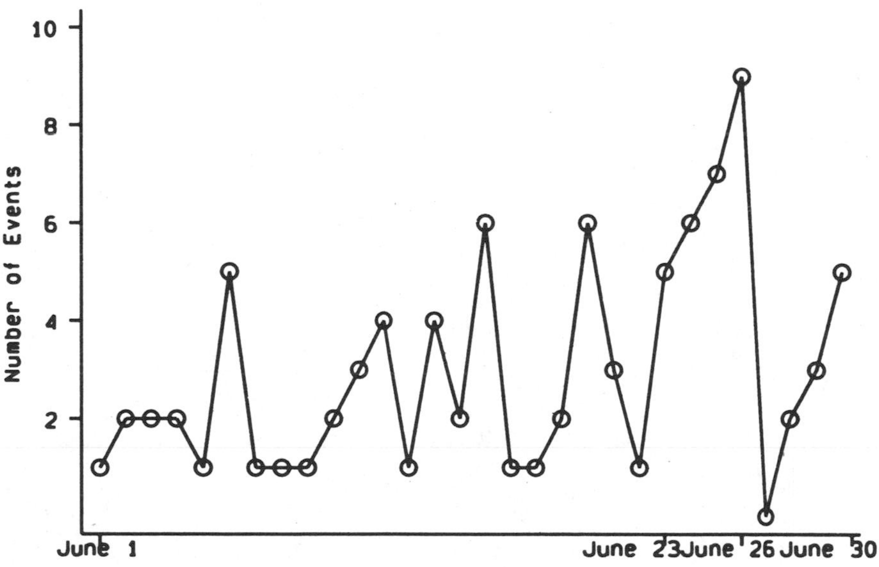

Fig. 6.6 (b) Peak Periods of Insurrection

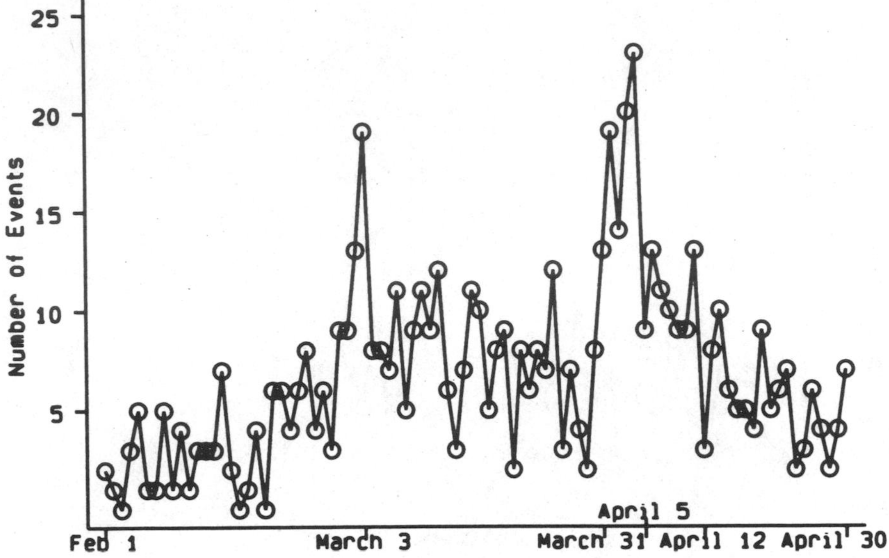

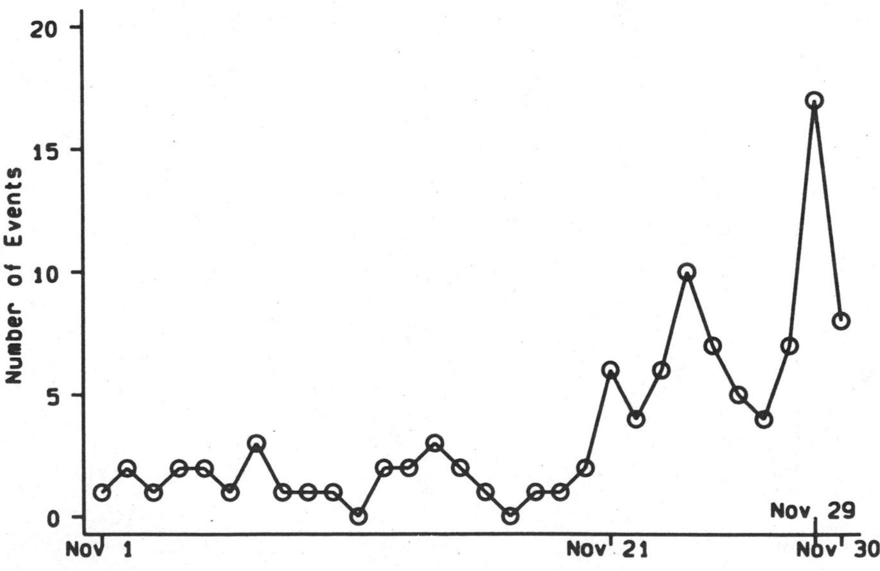

Fig. 6.6 (c) Peak Periods of Insurrection

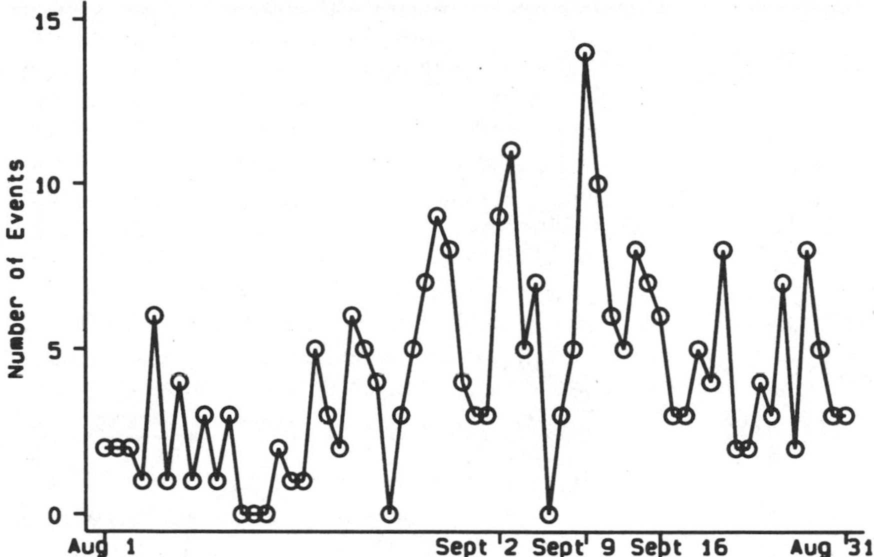

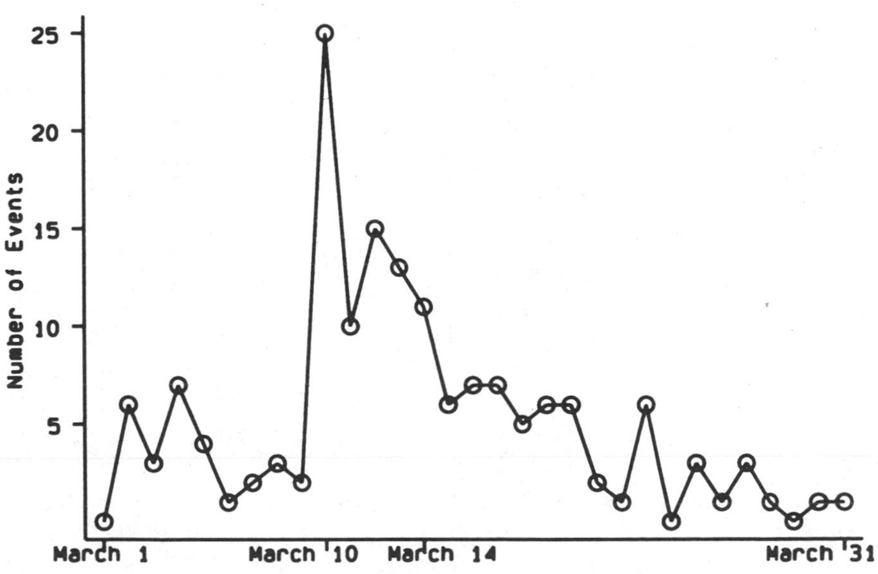

Fig. 6.6 (d) Peak Periods of Insurrection

communities operated on their own rhythms, too, the whole constituting, in its temporal dimension, a contrapuntal structure of tensions, constraints, and opportunities. Seigneurial payments in kind, the tithe, and to some extent the direct taxes had annual high points linked to harvest time: food scarcities, and hence prices, rose in the spring and summer, then fell with the availability of harvested crops; the cycle of festivals, generally with a marked religious component, was itself linked to the rhythms of agricultural work, and it provided opportunities for conviviality, drink, and mobilization for conflict (and thus the liturgical year helped frame the calendar of riot and rebellion); spring planting and summer reaping were occasions for a social truce. Of course, one year was not identical to the next: open conflict could be triggered by a particular change in the burden of taxation or the modalities of tax collection; by a particular action taken by a particular lord; by the specific misfortunes of this year's weather; by a reassignment of visible armed force altering the calculus of risk; by unusual signs of division among elites. But the particularities of specific moments of hardship or opportunity occured against a background of calendrical regularities in conflict-promoting circumstances. There is a structure in these affairs but *fortuna* also plays a considerable part.

To explore the rhythms of rural conflict in the revolutionary period, I shall first attempt to establish as a baseline the general patterns of rise and fall of open conflict through the annual cycle of months and the weekly cycle of days. Against a sense of this background pattern, we may attempt to gauge some of the specific features of the conflicts of the revolutionary years. To what degree were the temporal rhythms of rural insurrection during the Revolution a playing-out of long-standing patterns and to what degree did the shock of revolutionary events or the creativity of revolutionary participants in the countryside break with the usual seasonal and daily rhythms?

Microrhythms: The Weekly Cycle

Thanks to the herculean researches of a team directed by Jean Nicolas and Guy Lemarchand (see Chapter 5, p. 264) there is a great deal of invaluable information available on the patterns of rural contestation for well over a century preceding the Revolution. The published data to date include an inventory of the timing of disturbances involving youth groups, about 13% of the total incidents they are examining. These events include clashes of the young people of rival villages, confrontations arising from the role of enforcer of communal morality often assumed by organized youth groups, conflicts involving students or journeymen, and clashes with military recruiters. If we are willing to let youthful battles do duty for rural clashes as a whole,[33] we find in Figure 6.7 a clear depiction of the weekly cycle that plainly existed between 1661 and the outbreak of the Revolution. The height of each bar represents the proportion of conflicts that took place on a given day. The horizontal line shows what those heights would be if the same number of events fell on every day of the week.[34] Sunday plainly predominates: it may have been the day of rest and prayer but it was also the day of riot and rebellion in the traditional French countryside. During the five decades before the Revolution, more than twice as many events took place on Sunday as on Monday, the next most frequent day.

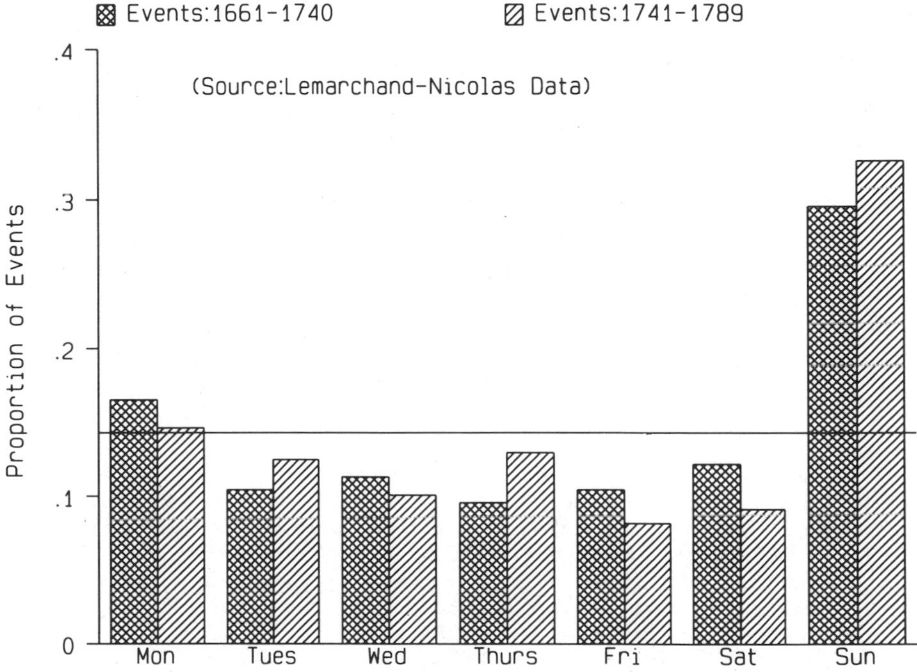

Fig. 6.7 Insurrectionary Events (1661–1789) by Day of Week

33. The results for the full data set are not yet available but I have been able to use their data on disturbances involving youth to trace weekly and annual rhythms. Since many significant forms of rural conflict do not involve youth as such, it is conceivable that their full data set might show some deviations from this picture. See Jean Nicolas, "Une jeunesse montée sur le plus grand ton d'insolence," in Robert Chagny, ed., *Aux origines provinciales de la Révolution* (Grenoble: Presses Universitaires de Grenoble, 1990), 147.

34. Subsequent graphs in this chapter differ in whether the temporal units are days or months (and if months, how many are included). They also differ in scale, so a reader needs to look carefully at the indications on the left side. But the horizontal lines always represent the height that the bars would have if all temporal units had equal numbers of events.

Few occasions rival the regular Sunday Mass for bringing together an eighteenth-century rural community. The weekly Mass was one of the few elements of a Christian identity that were observed with anything approaching unanimity[35] and had become the most common event by which the very existence of a community was made visible. After Mass, communal issues could be discussed, grievances aired, anger focused, plans hatched, and actions taken. From hearing the word of God in the morning to the often riotous expression of the voice of the people in the afternoon or evening was a short step.

If we return to Figure 6.7, we see that the preeminence of Sunday clashes was, if anything, even more marked in the five decades preceding the Revolution than in the eight decades before that. If we think of the Church's evolving position on celebrations we can see why this would be the case. Sundays were the preferred times for the festivals that punctuated the liturgical year; it is unlikely that the connection of Sunday and celebration was at all weakened during the eighteenth century. As a well-trained priesthood, increasingly inclined to disapprove of what it took to be paganism, was supported by modernizers disdainful of traditions inimical to economic advance, the taming of popular festivals became a standard weapon in the Catholic clergy's battle with popular religion.[36] One tactic in this battle was to eliminate festivals that fell on days other than Sunday (thereby eliminating an alternate day on which contestation was likely);[37] another tactic was to relocate festivals to Sundays (thereby eliminating a day of leisure).[38] For that rather large (and perhaps increasing) number of

35. Roger Chartier, *The Cultural Origins of the French Revolution* (Durham: Duke University Press, 1991), 93–96. Sometimes, even that unanimity was not to be found and peasants were noticed playing, drinking, or even working on Sundays. For an example, see Alain Molinier, *Une paroisse du bas Languedoc. Sérignan, 1650–1792* (Montpellier: Imprimerie Dehan, 1968), 130–35. Jean Quéniart stresses how far short of full participation was the weekly mass in *Les hommes, l'église et Dieu dans la France du XVIIIe siècle* (Paris: Hachette, 1978).

36. Yves-Marie Bercé, *Fête et révolte: Des mentalités populaires du XVIe au XVIIIe siècle* (Paris: Hachette, 1976), 127–87; Jean Delumeau, *Catholicism between Luther and Voltaire: A New View of the Counter-Reformation* (Philadelphia: Westminster, 1977).

37. Yves-Marie Bercé begins his monograph on the festival-revolt connection with the observation that any local official knew that festivals could be dangerous (Bercé, *Fête et révolte,* 13). The Third Estate of Château-Thierry urges a reduction in the number of festivals since "each of them involves the activation of a large number of people, carrying considerable danger to the State." The elimination of festivals will insure "the sanctification of Sunday" (*AP* 2:674).

38. For some examples from Provence, see Michel Vovelle, *Les métamorphoses de la fête en Provence de 1750 à 1820* (Paris: Aubier/Flammarion, 1976), 82. The bishop of Tarbes seems to have enjoyed complete success in ordering festivals shifted to Sundays in 1782. Although we lack a full and precise chronology of such events, one of the leading scholars of the Counter-Reformation French church reports that such was the general tendency since the mid-seventeenth century. See Dominique Julia, "La Réforme post-tridentine en France d'après les procès verbaux des visites pastorales: Ordre et résistances" in *La Società religiosa nell'età moderna* (Naples: Guido Editori, 1973), 385.

special Sundays[39] another element of ferment was now added.[40] Not that the reformers wished to increase Sunday's riotous element. As they strove to curtail the number of festivals and to tame them by relocating them to the day of rest, they also tried to clean up Sunday itself. While the reformers did make a start on purging Sunday of elements that contaminated the Lord's day, it proved easier to alter the festival calendar than to remove Sunday's more profane aspects. Dominique Julia speaks of an obsessive concern among the agents of clerical reform with the Sunday cabaret, for example, as well as with the use of the church building for such profane purposes as hiding one's money from state agents. Julia contrasts the clerical reformers' conception of "the consecrated place that holds in its tabernacle the Body of Christ" with the view of the faithful for whom "the church remains the common house where they come to find each other again"[41] The reform movement, then, may have moved festivals but did not tame Sunday, as the Nicolas-Lemarchand data show.

Why was Monday the second most tumultuous day? This seems due to the confluence of several causes: Monday actions may sometimes have been a consequence of some action initiated the day before continuing into the next day (the targets of action might fight back, for example), sometimes a consequence of a plan of action requiring a bit more organization and structure than could be mustered on the spot and sometimes, one may suggest, a consequence of errors in the sources (a late-night action on Sunday coming to the attention of the authorities the next morning.) Similarly, Tuesday through Thursday was a more tumultuous stretch than Friday and Saturday, again suggesting a continuing falloff as one moves away from Sunday.

There was also, it would seem, a negative counterside to the church-based communal organization of rural conflict: There was a relative paucity of other organizational vehicles for conflict. Let us not exaggerate: some pre-revolutionary conflict was not organized at Mass. In many villages unmarried young men constituted a strike force that routinely made life miserable for those who violated village norms. While sanctions were generally various forms of public humiliation and fines (a pot-and-pan serenade beneath an offender's window, for example, that continued until a fine

39. The association of festival and Sunday was so great that in Provence well into 1794, revolutionary festivals were celebrated to a disproportionate degree on Sundays. (See Vovelle, *Métamorphoses de la fête,* 164–65.)

40. The events of a traditional Provençal Sunday or other festival moved from the sacrality of the morning Mass through sports, dancing, and a communal meal in the afternoon—and all too often, in the view of clerical spoilsports, on into drinks and pitched battles with the next village in the evening (Vovelle, *Métamorphoses de la fête,* 62–63.) And were there, perhaps, sometimes other battles to be fought?

41. Julia, "La Réforme post-tridentine en France," 352.

was paid) and the targets generally such unfortunates as the widow who violated sexual norms, there was a structure in place that might be activated against other targets. Other rural communities, especially in the South, had their religious confraternities, often very active.[42] And there were the shadowy organized structures of wage laborers of which we know all too little (see Chapter 5, p. 250). But if even the relatively well organized youth groups[43] found Sunday the day of choice, the overall paucity of other mobilizational structures stands out.[44] One consequence, perhaps, was a great difficulty in undertaking unusual or nontraditional forms of action that might require some planning, coordination, or travel-time. Actions that followed familiar forms, that could therefore be put together on the spot, executed at once, and staged at locations within easy reach were the dominant ones.

With the traditional pattern in mind, we turn to the rural revolution. Figure 6.8 contrasts the weekly cycle in the revolutionary years with the pattern for the previous half-century (itself, we have seen, only slightly changed from that of the previous eight decades). The darker bars show the events of the revolutionary years, the lighter the previous half-century. As before, the horizontal line indicates what a perfectly even distribution of events would look like. While Sunday and Monday still have more events than the rest of the week, the differences are now slight. The Sunday share has fallen by half and is actually a bit lower than Monday's. Considering rural disturbances as a whole, then, the French countryside was erupting along lines that broke with the pattern of the past. If Sunday Mass had lost the position it had occupied in past centuries as the organizational nucleus of actions almost immediately carried out in the vicinity, there are several conceivable processes by which this change might have been effected. First of all, alternative organizational structures might have developed within the politicized world of the villages. The micropolitics of rural France in revolution is in many ways still largely unknown to us, but it is clear that new structures were being invented during the Revolution. From early on, Roger

42. Maurice Agulhon, *Pénitents et Francs-maçons de l'ancienne Provence* (Paris: Fayard, 1968).

43. Natalie Zemon Davis, "The Reasons of Misrule," in her *Society and Culture in Early Modern France* (Stanford: Stanford University Press, 1975), 97–123; Nicole Castan, "Contentieux sociale et utilisation variable du charivari à la fin de l'Ancien Régime en Languedoc" and E. P. Thompson, " 'Rough Music' et Charivari. Quelques réflexions complémentaires," both in Jacques Le Goff and Jean-Claude Schmitt, eds., *Le Charivari* (Paris: Ecole des Hautes Etudes en Sciences Sociales, 1981), 197–205 and 273–83.

44. One likely rival to the Mass as a mobilizational pole would be the market. Since the market brought together, on a single day, country people from several communities that did not necessarily have easy access to each other, it may well have provided an important setting for organizing multiparish actions as well as for recruiting peasants into events at more than a day's walk from home.

Dupuy's research has demonstrated, there was a proliferation of village-level units of the newly created National Guard, units that often participated in support of peasant communities.[45] Ultimately, more than five thousand rural communities formed political clubs of one sort or another.[46] And the levels of rural participation in the numerous electoral processes created by the Revolution, while extremely variable, were often high, in some places and some elections quite as high as in the towns[47]—and high electoral turnouts usually suggest some organizational life.[48] Of course, we don't want to push this further than the evidence will bear: we know little about rural National Guard units outside of Brittany; most communities never formed a political club;[49] and much of rural France had consistently low electoral participation.[50] Nonetheless, it is plausible that new organizational

45. Roger Dupuy, *La Garde Nationale et les débuts de la Révolution en Ille-et-Vilaine (1789–mars 1793)* (Rennes: Université de Haute Bretagne, 1972).

46. Jean Boutier and Philippe Boutry, "La diffusion des sociétés politiques en France (1789–an III). Une enquête nationale," *Annales Historiques de la Révolution Française,* no. 266 (1986): 365–98. Serge Aberdam and Marie-Claude al Hamchari have indicated the significance of support from the local "people's societies" for the developing movement of sharecroppers around Autun in 1793–94. See "Revendications métayères: du droit à l'égalité au droit du bénéfice," in *La Révolution française et le monde rural* (Paris: Editions du Comité des Travaux Historiques et Scientifiques, 1989), 144–45.

47. Comparing voting in a half-dozen major cities with their surrounding rural areas, Malcolm Crook shows a larger rural turnout early in the Revolution, but a significant rural falloff thereafter. See Crook, "'Aux urnes, citoyens!' Urban and Rural Electoral Behavior during the French Revolution," in Alan Forrest and Peter Jones, *Reshaping France: Town, Country and Region during the French Revolution* (Manchester: Manchester University Press, 1991), 152–67. See also Melvin Edelstein, "L'apprentissage de la citoyenneté: participation électorale des campagnards et citadins (1789–93)," in Michel Vovelle, ed., *L'image de la Révolution française: Communications presentées lors du Congrès Mondial pour le Bicentenaire de la Révolution* (Paris: Pergamon Press, 1989), 1:15–25 and "La place de la Révolution française dans la politisation des paysans," in *Annales Historiques de la Révolution Française,* no. 280 (1990): 135–49.

48. As early as the summer of 1790, Jacobin clubs were extremely active in mobilizing support for desired candidates for local and national office as well as in the elections for priests and bishops set up under the Civil Constitution of the Clergy. See Michael L. Kennedy, *The Jacobin Clubs in the French Revolution: The First Years* (Princeton: Princeton University Press, 1982), 174–77, 210–23. (Although Kennedy's examples are largely from fairly sizable urban centers, it is very likely that the smaller clubs of smaller places were engaged in similar behavior.) For other indications of urban involvement in rural mobilizations see Ado, *Krest'ianskoe dvizhenie,* 270, 272–73, 289.

49. The founding of rural clubs, moreover, often was as late as 1792 or even 1793. See Christine Peyrard, "Peut-on parler du jacobinisme dans l'Ouest? (Maine, bas Normandie)" in *La Révolution française et le monde rural* (Paris: Editions du Comité des Travaux Historiques et Scientifiques, 1989), 371; Jean Boutier, "Un autre midi. Note sur les sociétés populaires en Corse," *Annales Historiques de la Révolution Française,* no. 268 (1987): 169. On the other hand, in some places, especially in the South, many clubs were formed early (Boutier and Boutry, "Diffusion des sociétés politiques," 397).

50. The comparison with 1848 is striking: in August–September 1792 fewer than 20% of adult

structures that could sustain mobilization developed in quite a number of rural communities.[51]

A second likely source of a displacement of Sunday as the day of confrontation is the frequency of tension-producing shocks whose relationship to the weekly cycle was essentially random. Even in the century before the Revolution, two-thirds of the events were not on Sundays: the arrival of recruiting officers, the passage of grain-laden convoys in times of dearth, the dramatic words of a local leader, the decision by a new lord to increase exactions—all such shocks hardly waited for Sunday Mass. It seems a reasonable conjecture that the Revolution was a period unusually dense in such shocks that altered the configuration of opportunity, risk, and costs of inaction. The legislature in Paris continued to grind out complex laws that altered the terms of the seigneurial rights and the tithe; local administrators,

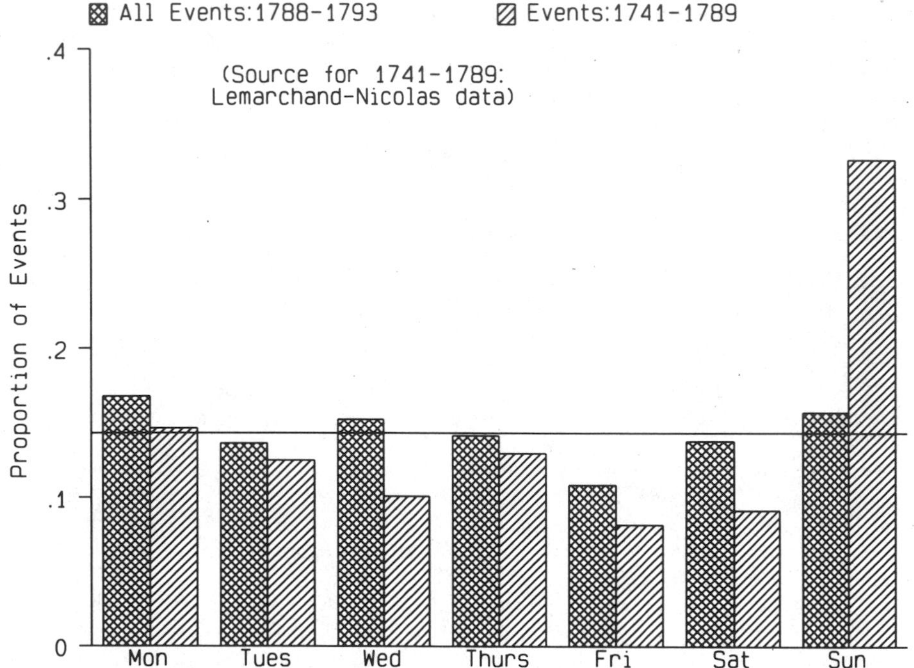

Fig. 6.8 Insurrectionary Events (1788–1793) by Day of Week

men voted; in April 1848, 84% did. See Peter McPhee, "Electoral Democracy and Direct Democracy in France, 1789–1851," *European History Quarterly* 16 (1986): 77–96.

51. For more on the development of the forms of revolutionary rural organization, see Chapter 7, pp. 419–22. For a very valuable overview of the many forms of organized activity, see Isser Woloch, *The New Regime: Transformations of the French Civic Order, 1789–1820s* (New York: Norton, 1994).

who changed with the frequent elections and the rapid shifts of revolutionary politics, were both struggling to master the new and changing laws and learning how to apply (or ignore) them on the job, one day at a time; the regulation of the grain supply as it existed in the Old Regime broke down; the capacity of central and local administrators to enforce tax-collection by force ebbed and flowed day by day; the judicial system, similarly, was subject to continual reorganization. On the assumption that such events were randomly distributed across the week, a weakening of Sunday dominance would be expected.

Third, and finally, let us consider communities for which Sunday remained the center of organizational life. To the extent that new forms of struggle were developed that would require some planning and some instruction in those plans for those not at the planning session, it might now take more than a few afternoon hours to launch an event. To the extent that some communities acquired a sense of effective participation in a national political struggle, one might well expect the concomitant development of less impulsive and longer-term orientation to conflict that also may have shifted events, even if first broached as usual on Sunday, to a later, more propitious moment. The Revolution's crash program in enlarging the field of participation, moreover, might have meant an enlargement in the geographic scope of concern. The actions contemplated on Sunday afternoon were more likely than before planned to take place at locales more than a few hours' walking distance. Consider for example the extensive terrain covered by enormous bands of price-controllers who invaded one market after another in November and December 1792 between the Seine and the Loire.[52] The need for greater preparation for newer forms of struggle, of greater care in selecting auspicious moments to strike in view of the sense of protracted struggle and the increased propensity to march to a more distant location—if these processes hypothetically suggested here actually took place—could certainly explain a part of the shift away from Sunday and might well explain, indeed, Monday's new prominence. While much of this must remain, for now, uncomfortably speculative, there is some evidence on the creation of new forms of contention, to which we shall return shortly.

With the evidence at hand, we can go rather further than our comparison of all events between June 1788 and June 1793 with the traditional weekly cycle of rural conflict. We can look at the distribution across the week of our separate forms of conflict. Figures 6.9 (a)–(d) present, side by side, the average daily patterns for our eight conflict forms. We see that different peasant actions differ in their propensity to focus on Sunday. Counterrevolutionary events are as fully concentrated on Sundays as in the prerevolution-

52. Michel Vovelle, *Ville et campagne au XVIIIe siècle. Chartres et la Beauce* (Paris: Editions Sociales, 1980), 230.

ary pattern, which I take as a sign of their rootedness in traditional structures. Wage conflicts, on the contrary, rarely commence on Sundays (and never on Mondays, for that matter). Antiseigneurial events are, in these terms, of an intermediate variety: rather more concentrated on Sundays than the horizontal baseline, but well below the traditional pattern.

I suggest a hypothesis to account for these differences. Conflicts pitting an entire community against a common enemy could be planned on a Sunday that brought the community together. Thus many land seizures, pitting the collectivity against the lord, could be planned after Mass; but wage disputes, pitting laborers against proprietors, were divisive and could hardly be planned in a gathering of the whole (and so much the worse if some of the laborers were seasonal migrants). Thus no work stoppages on Monday either. Subsistence disturbances pitted consumers against producers.[53] Thus other organizational structures, whatever they were, had to be created. That the antiseigneurial events occupy the intermediate position they do suggests that to a large extent they were still sustained by traditional communal structures, but were also coming to make use of newer structures that emerged in the Revolution (village units of the National Guard, village political clubs), thereby becoming less Sunday-oriented. To be sure, each of the forms of conflict that lacks a Sunday focus has its own special explanation. Of the Revolution's wage conflicts one observes that, at least in principle, labor was not taking place on the Lord's day anyway, thereby rendering inoperative the dramatic refusal to work. On the other hand, alternate actions were still conceivable, such as announcing that work would not be performed, threatening the employer, or seizing the fruits of labor. Hence a few wage conflicts were initiated on this day.

Many subsistence events clustered around market days, which could be any other day,[54] and therefore generate the appearance of essentially random groupings of events by day. But on the other hand, marketplace events are no more than 29% of all subsistence events (see Table 5.6). As for the provocative actions that could easily trigger subsistence events (a nearby town's seizure of grain, a state agent making a purchase or a provocative attempt to transport grain from place to place), these no doubt operated according to an administrative calculus unrelated to the sacred cycle of days, again producing an effectively random clustering of sparks

53. Cynthia Bouton shows that participants tended to be dependent on the market for their food but victims were those with marketable surpluses. See "Les victimes de la violence populaire pendant la guerre des farines (1775)," in Jean Nicolas, ed., *Mouvements populaires et conscience sociale, XVIe–XIXe siècles* (Paris: Maloine, 1985), 395; "Gendered Behavior in Subsistence Riots: The Flour War of 1775," *Journal of Social History* 23 (1990): 743.

54. The *Almanach Royal* for 1789 has a long list of places with weekly markets, as well as the less frequent fairs. The former are well represented on every day of the week except Sunday. See *Almanach Royal, Année Commune 1789* (Paris: Debure, 1789), 641–42.

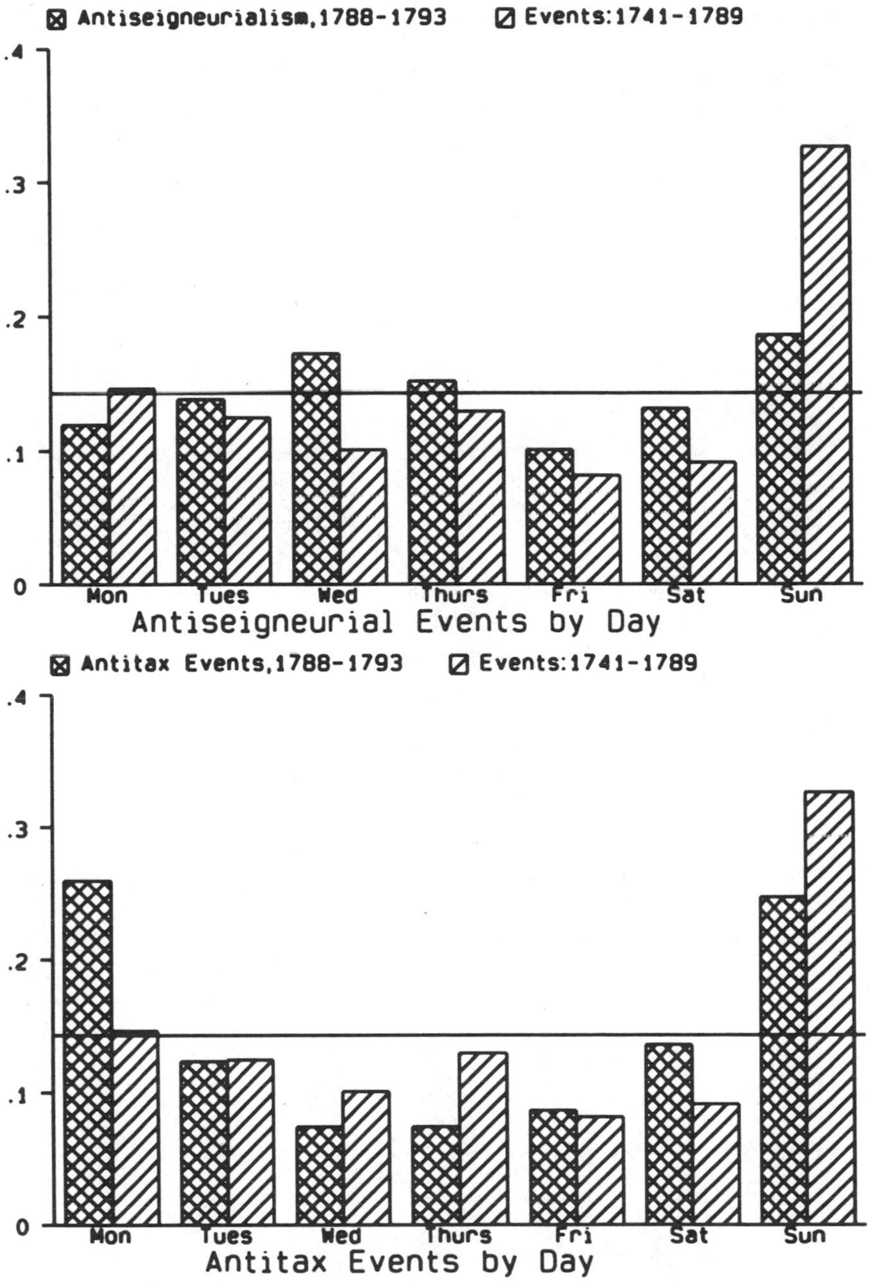

Fig. 6.9 (a) Types of Insurrectionary Events by Day of Week

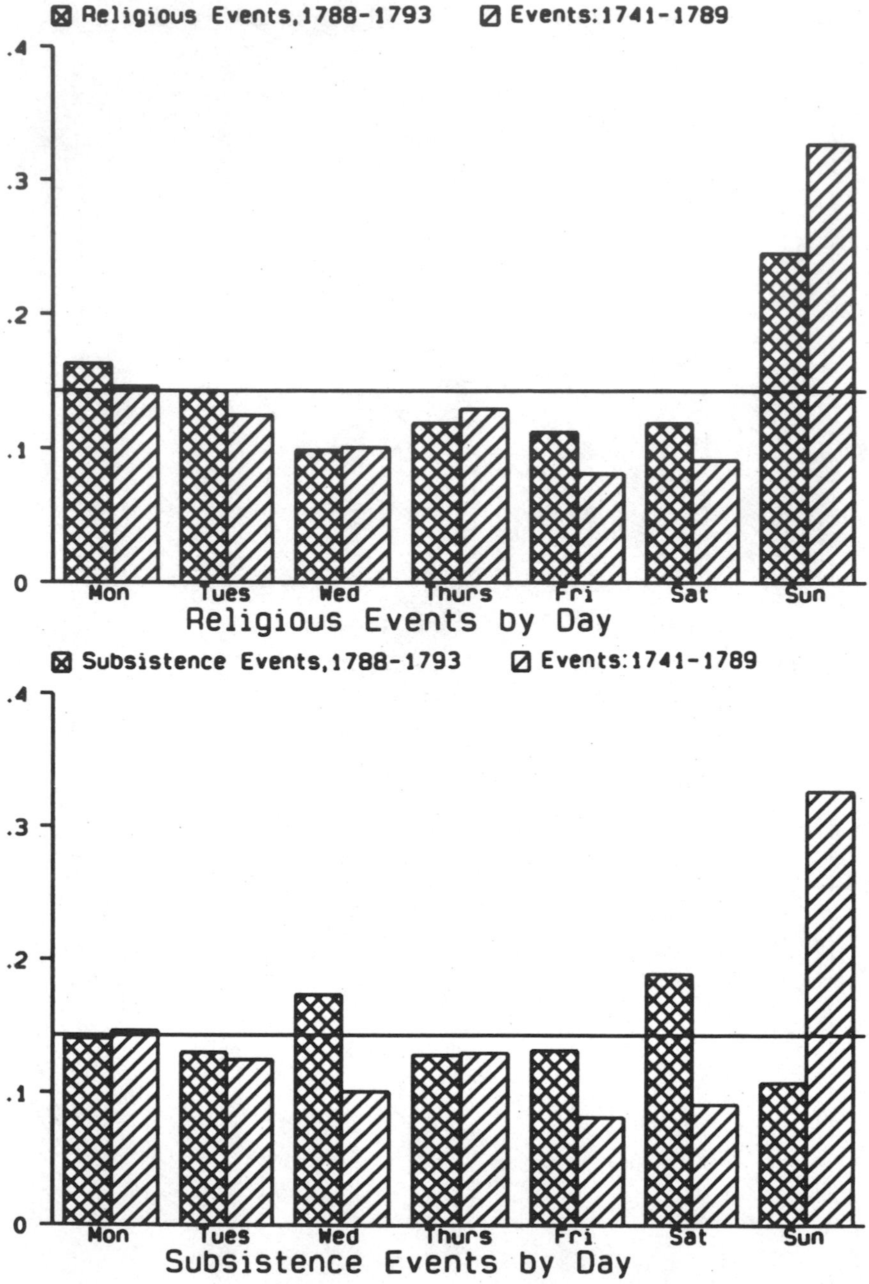

Fig. 6.9 (b) Types of Insurrectionary Events by Day of Week

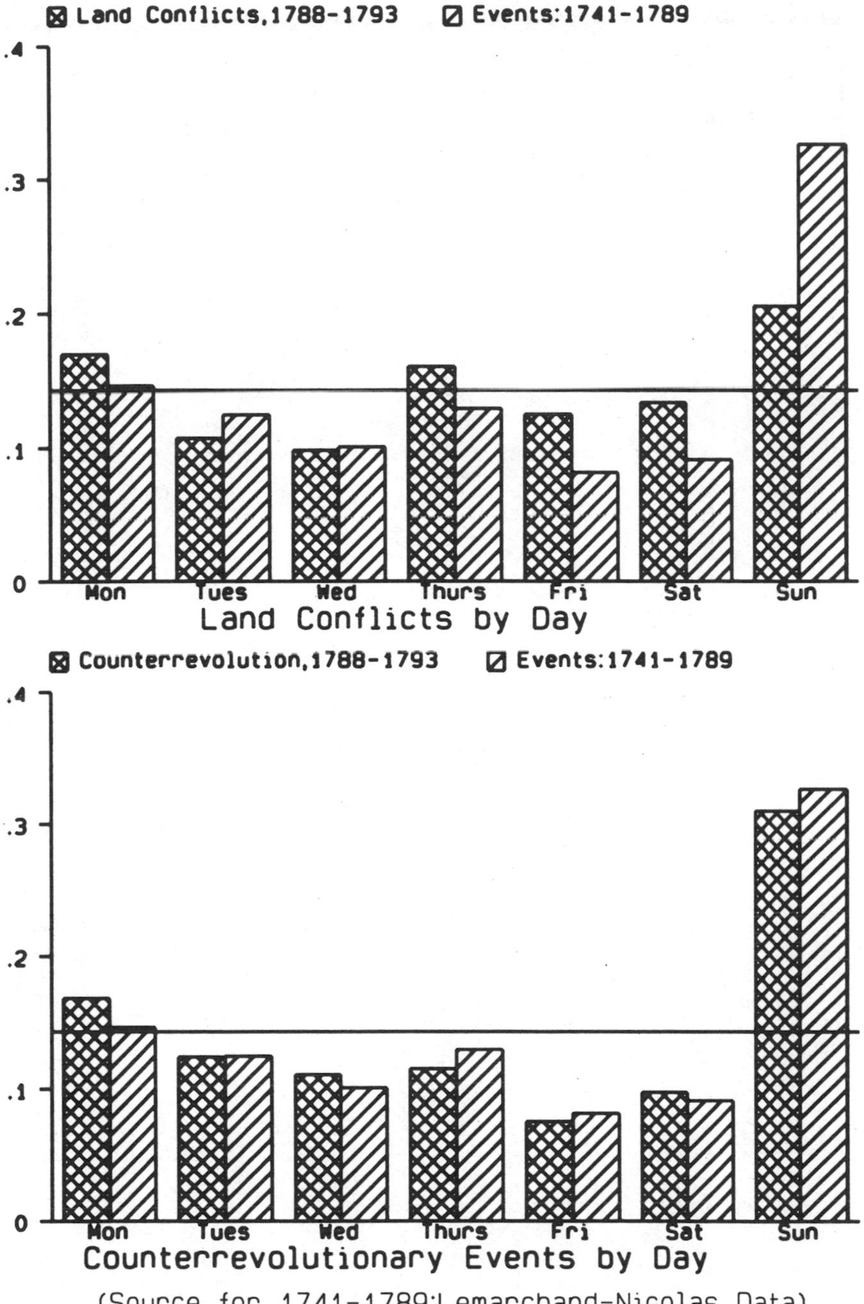

Fig. 6.9 (c) Types of Insurrectionary Events by Day of Week

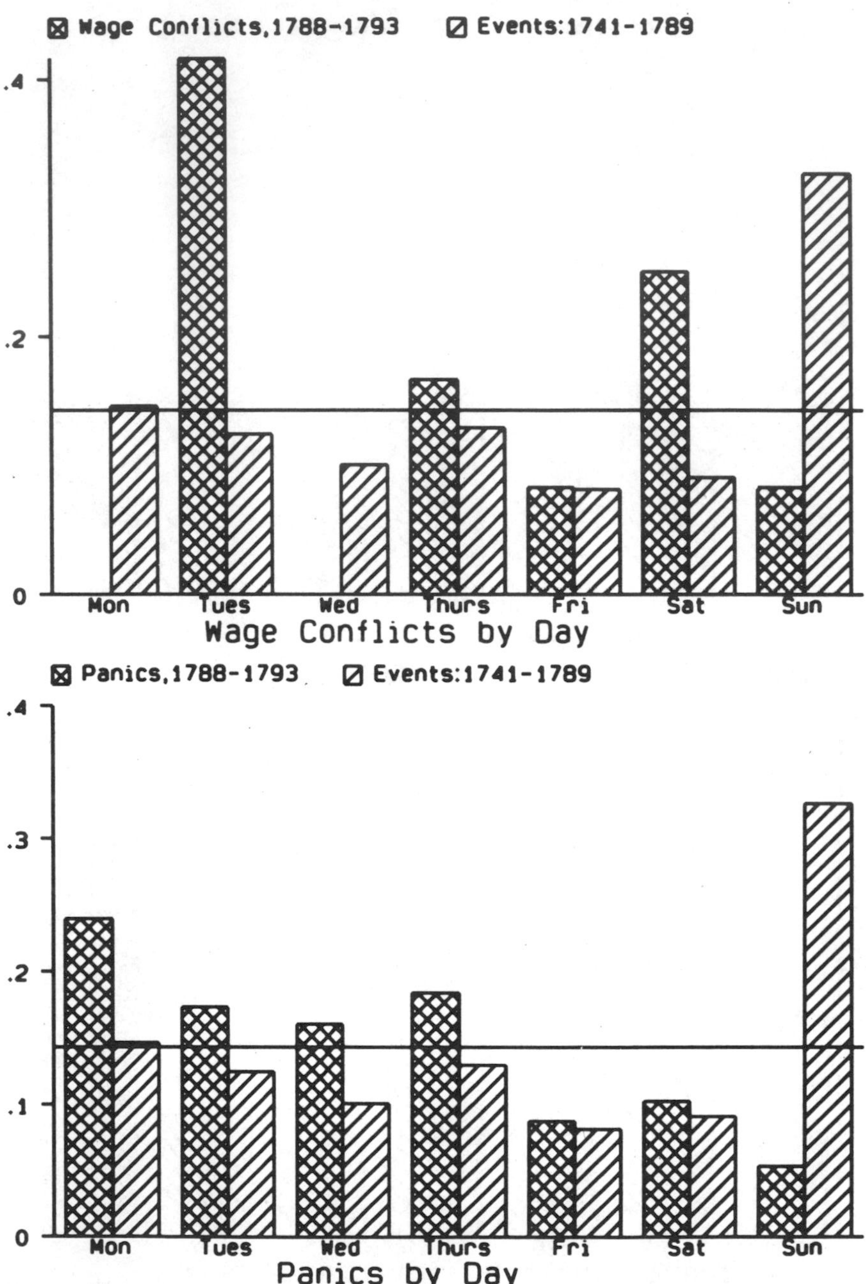

Fig. 6.9 (d) Types of Insurrectionary Events by Day of Week

that might strike the social dynamite created by scarcities—but such sparks could fall on Sundays as well.

What wage and subsistence conflicts have in common is their often divisive character, divisive in terms of French peasant communities. Wage conflicts took place within communities that included rural employers as members (and perhaps the most respected and influential members). Subsistence events are centrally the work of the village have-nots,[55] dependent on purchases in the market, seeking non-church-oriented bases for mobilization. It would seem likely that those who undertook to organize such events would do so away from the religious context, which favored a solidary sense of community.[56] We all know the nineteenth-century cliché of village politics: the socialist grouping of the rural poor and the schoolteacher against the village elite and the priest. Do we have here just a hint, perhaps, that the organizational base for mobilization of the rural proletariat in conflict against their local employers was, at least as early as the Revolution, already moving away from the church as the center of solidarity and organization?

Panics also seem to have avoided Sundays. Panics, like subsistence events were, no doubt, often triggered by events whose real or imagined occurance bore little relation to the rhythms of the week. Yet this would only explain the fact that Sunday was not especially characterized by such occurrences. The data show, however, an outright avoidance of Sunday; in fact, there is a Monday high that falls almost steadily through Sunday. I have no very compelling explanation to offer, except the possibility that the religious and secular structure of the day offered a certain measure of temporary immunity. The religious element may, perhaps, have generated a certain calm in the face of unknown danger, whether uncertain food shortages, seigneurial outrages, or ecclesiastical exactions. If religion was, to any extent at all, the people's opium, in a famous phrase, it was an opium only effective against anxious fantasy and, we have just seen, dulled actions against real targets not a whit. Moreover, the well-established Sunday traditions of mobilization may have channeled any anxious sensations into relatively well established directions. A community struck by scary tidings of threat may, on Sunday, have attacked the *château* or the tax-barrier, whereas, outside the structures that normally channeled their actions, they fled before or marched to meet the English, Savoyards, or Moors.

Antiseigneurial events and land conflicts occurred more frequently on Sundays than any other day, but Sunday's edge was slight and well short of

55. See Cynthia Bouton's evidence on participants in the Flour War a decade and a half prior to the Revolution in "Gendered Behavior in Subsistence Riots," *Journal of Social History* 23 (1990): 743. Flour War participants were wage laborers or wage-workers in small-scale domestic industry—a profile that no doubt resembles the participants in wage conflicts.

56. Does the absence of Monday wage conflicts mean that they were not even planned on Sunday?

its traditional leading position. Does this pattern suggest, perhaps, that traditional organizational forms were still serviceable for conflicts with lords and over land, but that newer structures, nonetheless, were emerging? This seems very likely. It is clear that rural National Guard units were often at the heart of antiseigneurial struggles. And Colin Lucas has some scattered evidence that, in the Southeast, political clubs tried to ally with the rural poor (but let us remember that Jacobins were often unhappy about any autonomous popular movement).[57]

In light of the foregoing, it will come as no great surprise that our broad class of religiously tinged events remain highly concentrated on Sundays (although not to the traditional degree). The causal processes probably ran in both directions: the religious auspices of the communal structures formed on Sundays probably tended to impart to such events a religious dimension; and those whose impulses to action carried a religious tinge were probably particularly drawn to Sunday events both as an appropriate organizational site and out of the spiritual needs for the religious service. In this light, it is interesting that even these events do not quite have the full Sunday salience that prevailed from the mid-seventeenth century to the dawn of revolution.

If anti-tax events, too, shared in a strong Sunday concentration (although also rather short of the traditional pattern) might it be because the long and virtually continuous tradition of Old Regime tax rebellion had evolved structures of contestation that continued to prove adequate into the revolutionary era? (Traditionally, we may note, again drawing on the work of the Nicolas-Lemarchand group, that anti-tax events constituted as many as 22% of all events between 1661 and 1789).[58] If so, is the increased salience of Monday a sign that anti-tax battlers were now seeking out the tax-collection apparatus at more than a few hours' distance from home? Such would seem to be likely. To attack the collection apparatus of the lords or the church, for example, one might burn the archives of the local *château* or monastery; to attack the collection apparatus of the state, one generally would have to march to an urban administrative center (see Chapter 5, p. 237). Many tax actions, planned near the village church on Sunday afternoon, may have led to peasant groups arriving in town the next day.

By comparison with the other major conflict categories, the pattern for counterrevolution stands out. Unlike the other seven categories, it is virtually identical to the Old Regime pattern. To merely note the religious element in counterrevolutionary protest is, however, by no means an adequate explanation, unless expanded: we have just seen that the "reli-

57. Colin Lucas, "Résistances populaires à la Révolution dans le sud-est," in Jean Nicolas, ed., *Mouvements populaires et conscience sociale, XVIe–XIXe siècles* (Paris: Maloine, 1985), 474.

58. Jean Nicolas, "Les émotions dans l'ordinateur," paper presented at Université Paris VII, 1986, 5.

gious" category of conflict, while stressing Sundays, still falls markedly short of the traditional frequency. Two complementary observations suggest themselves. First of all, a good deal of counterrevolutionary activity originated not in amorphous "religious" considerations but specifically around country-dwellers' attempts to protect their good priest against the urban intruders. In parts of France, large numbers of priests had refused to take the oath that the new regime insisted on for its priests, just as it insisted on oaths from other public functionaries (as priesthood was conceived as being under the new religious legislation).[59] The West not only had an unusual concentration of these nonjuring priests, as the oath-refusers were known, but they were far more likely to have been local boys than was the case elsewhere in France.[60] The revolutionary authorities, step by step, barred these refractory clerics from saying Mass. Ultimately, the authorities, declaring them outlaws, sent out search parties to run them down and bring them to justice (unless they went into exile, to be sure). Many country people began to acquire the habits of concealment, evasion, and clandestinity that were to provide the skills, experience, and culture of armed counterrevolution. Hiding priests in their homes, moving them about a step ahead of the authorities, hearing clandestine Mass in the woods, the nuclei of future armed rebel bands formed themselves. With the Mass providing a wonderful, if as yet peaceful, combination of filling a spiritual need, registering defiance of the alien revolutionary state and enjoying the fellowship in risk of co-worshipers, it is easy to understand that when the West exploded, it may frequently have been the illegal but unrepressible Mass at which the decision to strike at once was taken, leading to the many events of Sunday, March 13, and Sunday, March 20, 1793. But, more broadly, the data suggest that traditional organizational practices were, appropriately enough, embraced by those rising in defense of tradition.[61]

William Sewell has contended that the innovative character of the transformation of social struggles between the Old Regime and the mid-nineteenth century is best gauged by attending to the move away from "communal" bases of mobilization toward "associational" ones.[62] The traditional forms of tax resistance, subsistence disturbance, and land invasion are seen by him as profoundly communal.[63] The evidence we have reviewed above suggests

59. Tackett, *Religion, Revolution and Regional Culture.*

60. Tackett, "The West in France in 1789."

61. The western context of counterrevolution suggests considering the heightened significance of the Sunday gathering in this region of scattered farmsteads. Regional differences in the insurrectionary salience of Sunday will be explored in Chapter 7.

62. William H. Sewell Jr., "Collective Violence and Collective Loyalties in France: Why the French Revolution Made a Difference," *Politics and Society* 18 (1990): 527–52.

63. Ibid., 537. I think Sewell underrates the extent to which the latter two were, even traditionally, conflicts *within* rural communities.

the possibility that the uncommon wage conflicts and the quite common subsistence conflicts had gone rather far toward associational forms of organization; that the antiseigneurial events and land conflicts were developing new associational bases but still drew on communal traditions; and that counterrevolution was the work of communities.

Excursus on Innovation in Struggle

Our data suggest another way to get at the innovative character of peasant mobilization. If rising numbers of events mean more than simply a quantitative increase in the intensity of conflict but also signal a search for new forms of action, we would expect to see an increase in the numbers of multiaction events. The breakdown of the Old Regime, on this hypothesis, did more than present promising targets to those who would mobilize; it did more than decrease the costs of such mobilization as the repressive apparatus disintegrated (and as other rural communities revolted, multiplying the possible targets for repressive efforts, which were thereby diluted). The breakdown also encouraged rural communities to invent new forms of political action. On such a hypothesis, again, one would expect to see the opening of the rural struggle to show also an expansion in the numbers of actions undertaken per incident: rural communities experiment with new combinations of tactics and targets. In a comparative vein, let us note that those scholars of other "cycles of protest," to use Sidney Tarrow's expression,[64] whose data permitted them to undertake such an exploration report such results. In Tarrow's own impressive research into patterns of conflict in Italy in the 1960s and early 1970s, he finds that as the wave of conflict mounts in the streets, so does the complexity of the forms of that conflict.[65] Tarrow also finds a second element of patterning in his data: the early rise in complexity is followed by a simplification. The likely explanation for the second element of the story suggests a successful search: the participants in conflict, in the course of their initial innovative and experimental approach to struggle, come to discover which sorts of actions yield desired results against which sorts of targets and increasingly mobilize for more single-minded forms of action.

64. See, for example, Sidney Tarrow, "Political Opportunities, Cycles of Protest and Collective Action: Theoretical Perspectives," presented to Workshop on Collective Action Events, Cornell University, October 1990.

65. Sidney Tarrow, *Democracy and Disorder: Protest and Politics in Italy, 1965–1975* (Oxford: Clarendon Press, 1989). Charles Tilly's data on public contention in Britain from the mid-eighteenth century through 1834 has the richest density of detail on each incident that any researcher has yet achieved for such a long time period. For the period of popular mobilization that accompanied the Reform Bill of 1832, computations based on Tilly's data also show an initial rise in the number of actions per event and a subsequent decline; see Charles Tilly, *Popular Contention in Great Britain, 1758–1834* (Cambridge: Harvard University Press, 1995), p. 88.

Figure 6.10 shows the trend in the complexity of rural insurrectionary events. (We use three-month moving averages to smooth out an extremely spiky data series.) We find, very roughly, the rise-and-fall pattern, suggesting an early, if uneven, trend toward trying out more and more actions in the course of particular clashes and a later, if equally uneven, sloughing off of actions. If there is a sort of dialectic of innovation and routinization in the structure of conflict, the data suggest that innovation is far more likely to take the form of novel combinations of familiar elements than it is the invention of something wholly new. The 274 actions distinguished in the code that I utilized are modes of conflict that, for the most part, are not in themselves new.

Could one then reasonably conclude that were one to attempt to situate the rural upheaval within the great debate on the degree to which the Revolution is properly characterized by the participants' own sense of rupture or the more ironic sense of continuity with the past that observers since Tocqueville have displayed, one would have to stress continuity in the forms of struggle, even if, arguably, the intensity and the consequences of that struggle have little precedent? Such a formulation is a bit too quick. In the first place, it ignores the degree to which innovation in many other

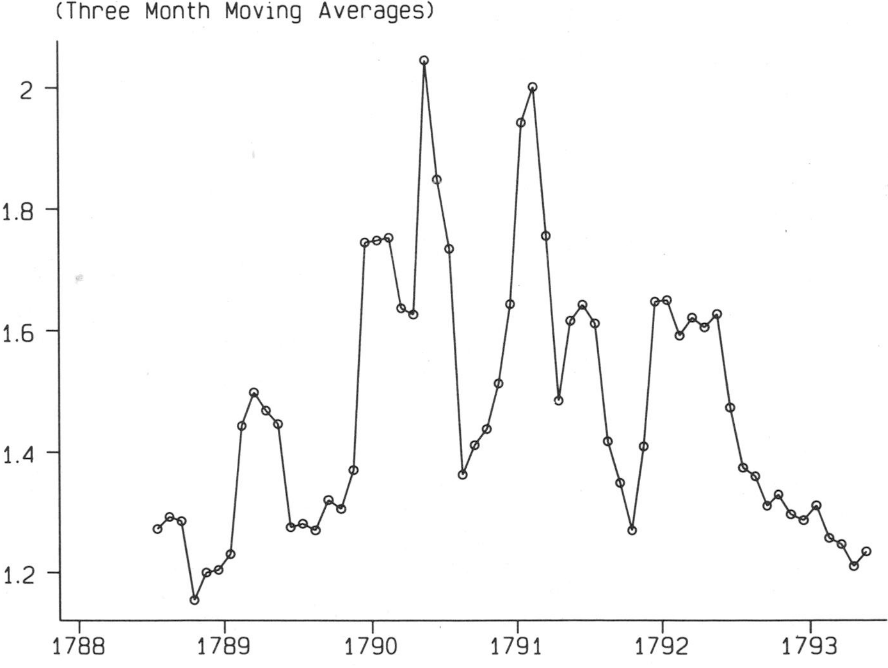

Fig. 6.10 Mean Actions per Event, June 1788–June 1793

contexts is often a rearrangement of the familiar.[66] And second, it ignores the new elements that were brought into the repertoire of revolutionary self-expression by these very country people (although, to be sure, these elements were brought *from* somewhere). Most famous among such innovations was the tree of liberty, a village maypole, whose implantation in a seigneurial lawn invested it with a meaning that expanded its traditional seasonal evocation of the awakening energies of springtime.[67] From its earliest reported defiant casting aside of the seigneurial winter in Périgord and Quercy in 1790[68] it became a standard part of the repertoire of rural action (and, for that matter, of festivals organized by urban elites; see Chapter 7, p. 418).

Annual Rhythms

Between the macrorhythms of peaks and troughs that structured rural disturbance from 1788 to 1793 and the microrhythms of the weekly cycle, there was an intermediary pattern, an annual periodicity (a mesorhythm?) in which the recurring events of the meteorological and liturgical years were significant contexts for contestation as they were for work, prayer, and leisure. Unlike the weekly microrhythms, the annual mesorhythms had undergone some significant mutations in the thirteen decades before the Revolution. Figure 6.11 shows that from the mid-eighteenth century on, summer was the highpoint of conflict mobilization, with a midsummer slackening in July, perhaps by way of a social truce for that season's extensive field labors.[69] (To aid in interpretation, I have once again drawn a line to indicate the value that all months would have if there were no month-to-month variation.) Disturbances fall off considerably by October and precipitously so by November, with an important December flareup. (The December flareup—relative to November and January—Nicolas suggests, may be due to the holiday season's provision of favorable opportunities by way of numerous social gatherings at which one may plan and organize some action.) The early new year is the off-season for tumult as well as for everything else, but in February the rate of disturbance tends to rise again.

The Nicolas data show this pattern to have supplanted a still older one in

66. See the important observations of Arthur Stinchcombe on the blurry boundary between innovation and routine administration in the management of factories (*Creating Efficient Industrial Organizations* [New York: Academic Press, 1974]).

67. The Constitutional Bishop Grégoire begins his essay on trees of liberty by pointing to the antiquity of "emblems of living nature, dying and being reborn." He then interprets the maypole as a spring ritual. See "Essai historique et patriotique sur les arbres de la liberté," in Henri Grégoire, *L'Abbé Grégoire, Evêque des Lumières* (Paris: Editions France-Empire, 1988), 192, 198.

68. Ozouf, *La fête révolutionnaire 1789–1799* (Paris: Gallimard, 1976), 281.

69. Nicolas, "Une jeunesse," 147.

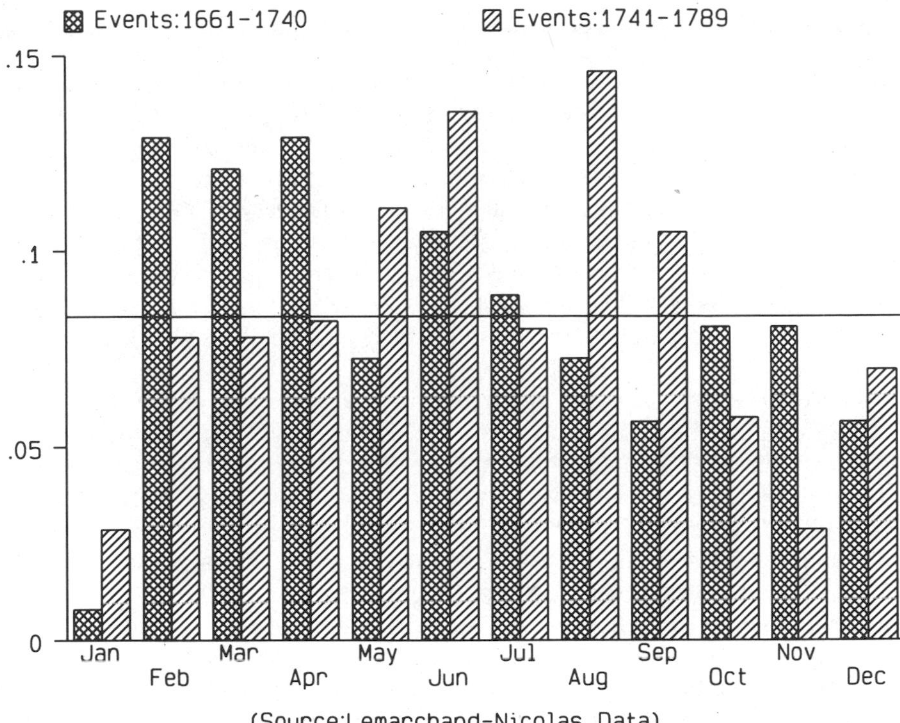

Fig. 6.11 Insurrectionary Events by Month

which February through April was the time of tensions. Both patterns suggest a certain observance of a social truce to protect the crops on which all depend. But it is a weak truce: the late seventeenth- and early eighteenth-century country people may have been avoiding destroying harvested crops by scaling back social struggles in August and September, but they extended the hotpoint of struggle from February into planting-time. And if planting-time is not an unusually conflictual moment after 1741, neither is it a low point. And, although the later eighteenth-century country people avoided destruction of harvested crops in the fall, conflict is still marked as late as September. One wonders, indeed, if the extent of conflict in August and September in the half-century before the Revolution may be taken precisely as an indicator of a breakdown of an older tradition of truce. One continuity throughout the era: conflict took a break in July and January was the lowest point in the year.

Those in power, in revolution as in earlier times, might well take such monthly rhythms into account. With his mind on the possibility that conflicts over food might serve the growing conservative challenge developing around recalcitrant Catholics, Thomas Lindet, himself a clerical deputy from Evreux, writes his brother on May 8, 1790, that "I won't conceal that I've always feared June and July." Lindet goes on to urge that the traditional prayers be reinstituted preemptively before a price rise forces an embarrassing revival in prayer to placate the faithful.[70] We note the imperfections of perception; July was normally much calmer than June. But then, we reflect, Lindet has just lived through the most unusual July in his country's history; after that summer one might well feel that one had always worried about July. (And perhaps Lindet's anxieties were exacerbated by the circumstance that the May in which he was writing was an unusually high point of food conflict in 1790 with more than one-fourth of all such events that year.)

There are many ways one might explore the seasonality of the insurrectionary countryside in the time of revolution. One might examine a monthly graph in which all incidents for the half-dozen years covered are represented; one might consider each type of incident separately over the six-year period; one might consider all incidents together for each of the six years individually; one might consider each type of event and each year in itself. The conclusion that emerges from a study of all these ways of attacking the question, however, is a simple one: the people of the countryside are very far indeed from the traditional seasonal rhythms. Like the weekly rhythm that approximated the traditional for only some forms of conflict, the rural insurrection in the years of revolution only occasionally resembled the traditional pattern, almost regardless of which type of conflict or which year we are examining. I shall present just one group of these graphs to point this up. Figure 6.12 sets side by side, for each year from 1789 to 1792, the monthly distributions of all insurrectionary events; Figure 6.13 presents the same information for 1788 and 1793, the two years for which our data only covers half the months. In 1788, only one of the two traditionally conflictual summer months approximates its usual character; and the autumnal falloff, which seems well launched with the typical October drop, doesn't take place but is replaced by a strong and steady rise after that month. July totally dominates 1789, of course, in striking violation of July's usual status as a relatively quiet place between the hot spots of June and August. In 1790, the overwhelming month for trouble is January, normally the low point of the year. By contrast, 1791 does approximate the typical Old Regime pattern, complete with a dip in July and a rise in December. We may note 1792 for its utter violation of any traditional tendency toward a springtime truce for planting; and, on the other hand, normally contentious June is the low point of the year. As for 1793, one's

70. Robert-Thomas Lindet, *Correspondence de Thomas Lindet pendant la Constituante et la Législative (1789–1792)* (Paris: Armand Montier, 1899), 158–59.

expectation of a middling level of conflict in March is thwarted by the surge of counterrevolution.

This last point may contain the germ of an understanding of the seasonally deviant nature of revolutionary peasant action. The Revolution was a time in which traditional forms of struggle were mobilized, as has been frequently stressed by historians and as our data reaffirms.[71] The Revolution was also a period in which new organizational possibilities emerged that complemented, but surely did not supplant, these traditional routes to mobilization. And the Revolution was a period of ceaseless challenges and opportunities that arose out of the political complexities of a French state and a French society in turmoil from the village to the legislature and from the Pyrenees to Flanders. The timing of these challenges and opportunities in no way obeyed the rhythms of the seasonal calendar of conflict to which the countryside was habituated. The work rhythms that were superimposed on the natural year, the rhythms of exaction by lord, church, and state superimposed upon both of these, the monthly cycle of prices similarly superimposed, and the liturgical calendar, again partly oriented to the cycle of sowing, ripening, and harvesting—all these had bound the local community in a complex and contrapuntal yet highly regular rhythm of conflict and peace to match the more fundamental cycles of work and rest.

But the great events of the Revolution were so many shocks that operated outside the constraints of this local world. The cyclical patterns of conflict, rooted in the rhythms of local, everyday life, were overwhelmed by the force of national events. France's villagers still acted locally, often in traditional ways, but the rhythms of contention were driven, not so much by the cyclical rhythms of work and prayer and rest, as by the unique shocks of unprecedented events felt throughout the country. If the summer of 1788 was succeeded by a quickening of the political crisis at the center over the structure of the coming Estates-General and a concomitant struggle around the country over the local preparations for the convocation, it is unremarkable that the rhythms of rural conflict joined in the ascending conflict of the national and provincial elites, rather than following the traditional autumnal cooling-down; if the great crisis of the self-declared National Assembly versus the king came to a head in July, that month's typical status as a hiatus between the storms of June and August was irrelevant; if the many, many forces pushing for war both in Paris and in hostile capitals were tightening

71. See Chapter 5; Colin Lucas, "The Crowd and Politics," in Colin Lucas, ed., *The French Revolution and the Creation of Modern Political Culture,* vol. 2, *The Political Culture of the French Revolution* (Oxford: Pergamon Press, 1988), 259–85. Peter Jones would seem to be summarizing a great deal of research in commenting on 1789 in the countryside: "The violence was directed against traditional enemies and by traditional means for the most part, and it seemed patterned on the *jacquerie* model of the seventeenth century"; see his *The Peasantry in the French Revolution* (Cambridge: Cambridge University Press, 1988), 60.

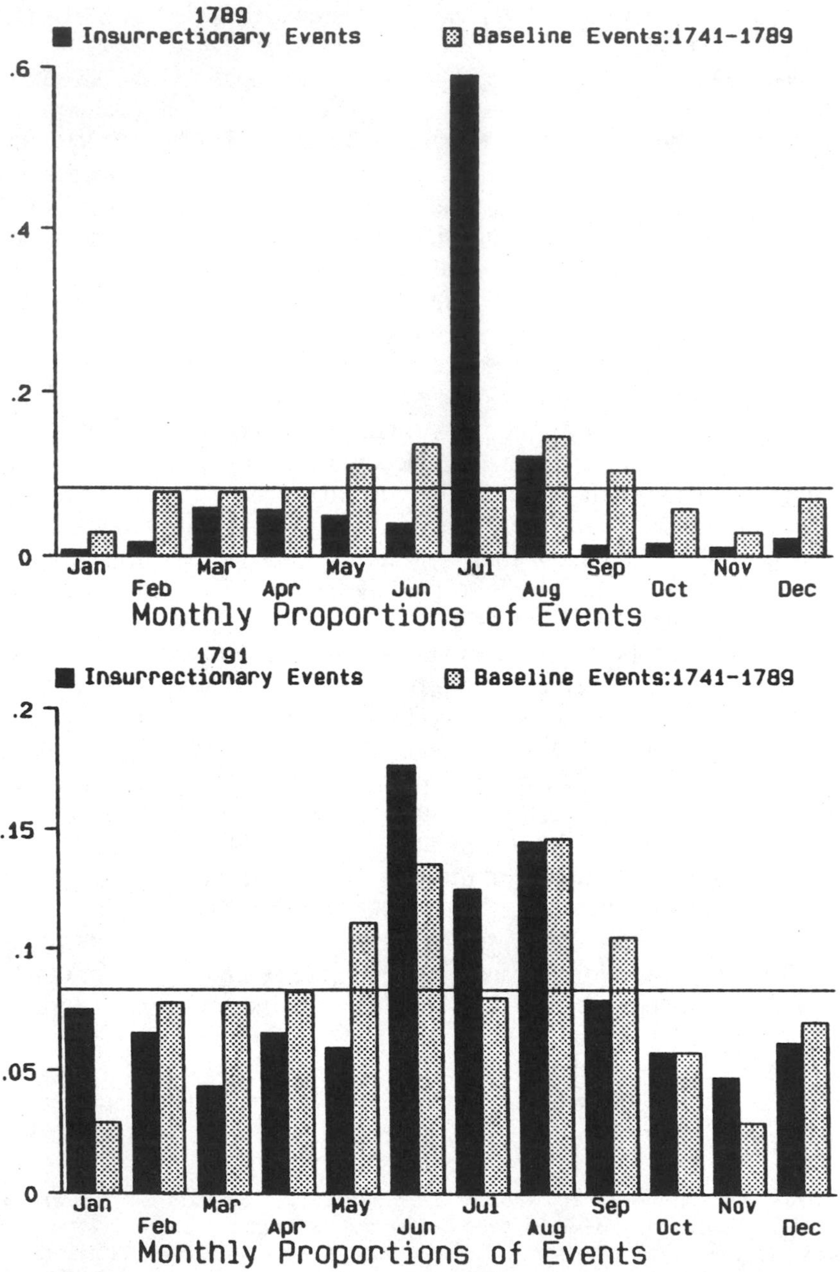

Fig. 6.12 (a) Monthly Proportions of Insurrections, 1789–1792

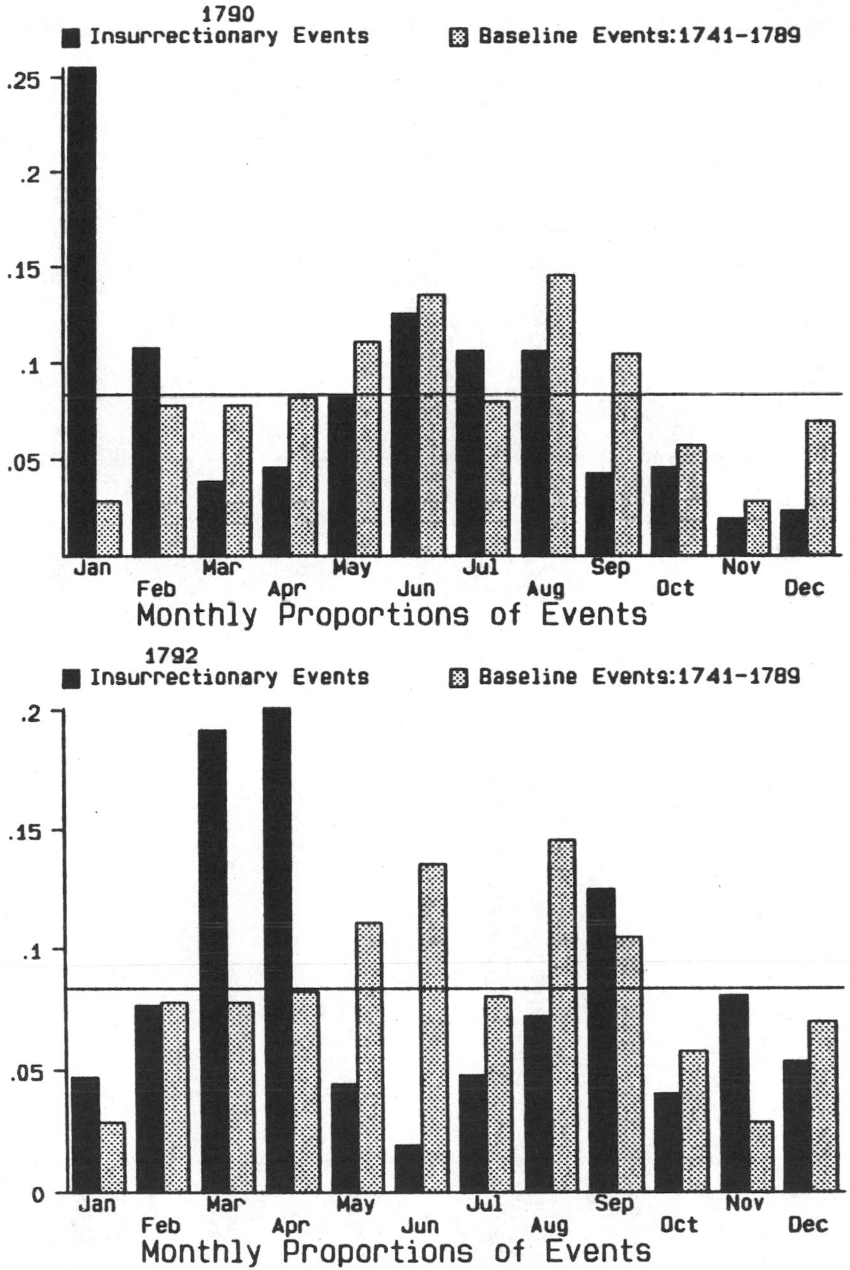

Fig. 6.12 (b) Monthly Proportions of Insurrections, 1789–1792

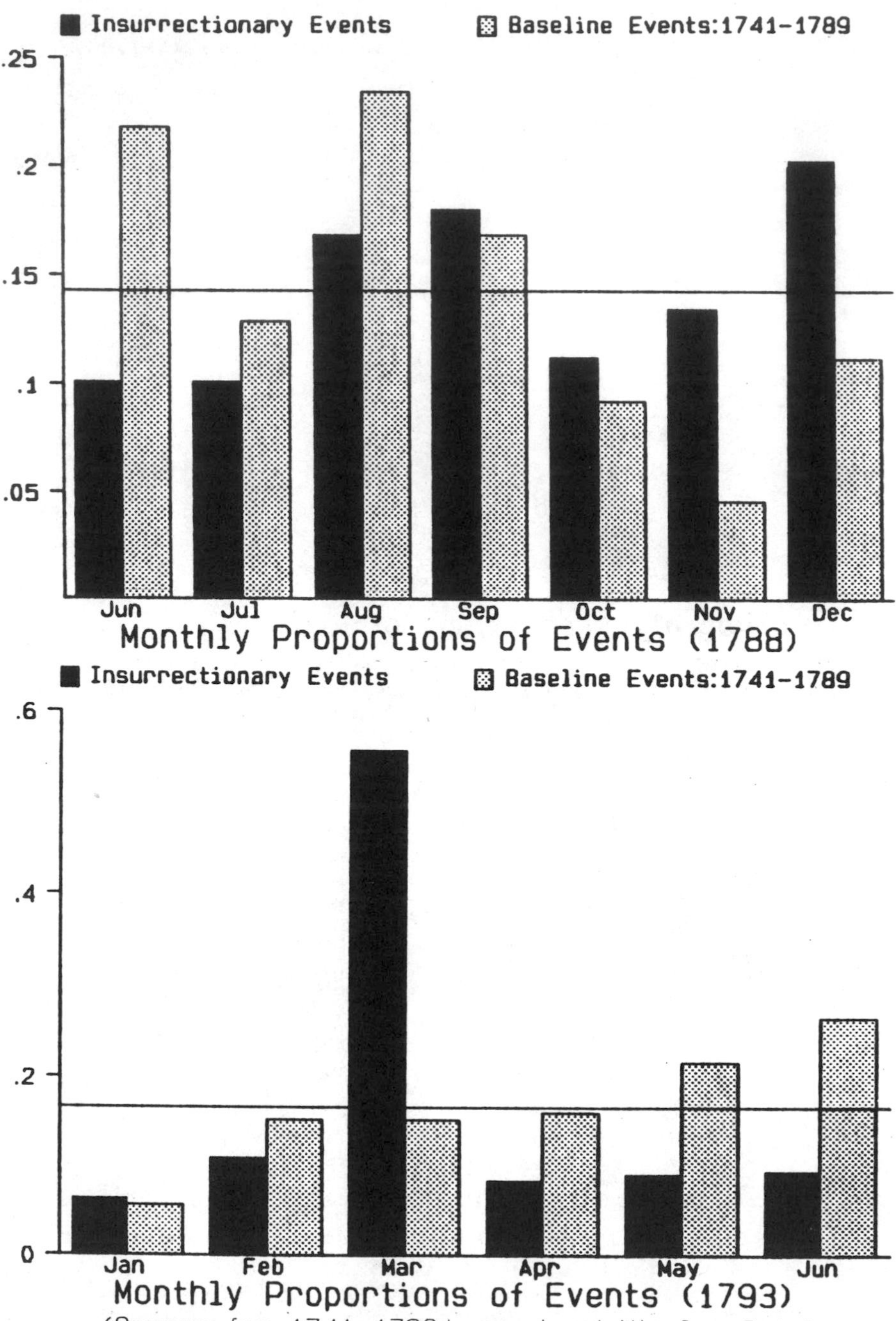

Fig. 6.13 Monthly Proportions of Insurrections, 1788 and 1793

interstate tension to the point that France's declaration of war on Austria of April 20, 1792, seems to be the playing-out of an inexorable logic of crisis, is it far-fetched to suggest that locally difficult situations were being invested with a tremendous freight, contributing in some areas to an extreme explosion in March and April?[72] If the war-forced rhythm of conscription hit the countryside in March 1793, why would a western countryside already activated and organized by the months of struggle over the Civil Constitution of the Clergy, already embittered by conflict for church holdings with urbanites, already disappointed in the irrelevance of revolutionary change to the particular concerns of local peasants, why would such a countryside await the usually more explosive summer months? Even in the least deviant year of 1791, distant events may have affected local actions. The king's attempted flight and subsequent humiliating capture in late June 1791 is an obvious exogenous source of tension that may have contributed to the somewhat higher number of disturbances than were usual for June and July.

What these reflections on the monthly statistics add up to is a strong indication that national politics were sending shock waves through rural France. Actions of legislature or king triggered actions in the villages. The targets of peasant actions may have been very much local ones but the causes of peasant actions, at least as reflected in the unusual monthly pattern of insurrection, included the decisions on national policies of revolutionary elites. We shall pursue below the mutual influence of legislature and village (see Chapter 8).

Further Observations

The weekly and annual rhythms enhance our understanding of the startling impact of rural insurrection. July 27, 1789, was not merely startling in the

72. The *département* of Gard and portions of its neighbors constituted a large powderkeg awaiting a spark. The Revolution provided an opportunity for Protestant and Catholic mobilization and countermobilization. The region was also an early site of attempts at organizing armed counterrevolutionary resistance and was thereby prey to armed preemptive measures undertaken by prorevolutionary forces, particularly National Guard detachments organized in Marseille. Like other areas near Avignon, moreover, Gard was drawn on for armed forces to participate in the assertion of French sovereignty in that papal territory, in what was to be a forerunner (and one of the minor causes) of the generalized interstate conflict which both France and the major Continental powers seemed by March 1792 to be bent on initiating. In such a climate the capsizing of an overloaded boatload of local troops on the Rhône became the occasion for a very large number of attacks on local *châteaux*. See Henri Mazel, "La Révolution dans le Midi: L'incendie des châteaux du bas Languedoc," *Revue de la Révolution* 8 (1886): 142–57, 307–19, 380–91, 456–69, and François Rouvière, *Histoire de la Révolution française dans le département du Gard* (Marseille: Lafitte Reprints, 1974), vol. 2.

number of insurrectionary events nor in their geographic dispersion. It was also a break with the patterns of rural insurrection that pointed to a new, unknown, and frightening future. Assumptions based on more than a century's experience of rural disturbance were violated in the choice of targets, the month they occurred, and the days of action. The fifth of the day's events (or the third of July's as a whole) with an antiseigneurial character pointed to a growing trend in peasant action to escape from the patterns enshrined in tradition. The movement not only failed to slack off in July, but accelerated. And far too many incidents got launched outside of the usual Sunday framework. Is it going too far to suggest that part of what made the Great Fear so uncanny to observers was that it so flamboyantly manifested itself in the wrong month and on the wrong days? Thus the rural movements of 1789 played a part in fixing the sense of a rupture with the past.

Both the persistence of the habitual rural cycles of conflict and the divergences from those habitual patterns tell us something of the nature of the revolutionary upheavals in the countryside and the articulation of village conflicts and national politics. But we have opened up, in this chapter, many more questions than we have answered. Why was one peak time of conflict primarily antiseigneurial, another focused on subsistence issues and a third structured around land? Why did antiseigneurial conflicts have a strong admixture of religiously tinged incidents at some points, but not at others? And, above all, why did battles over the seigneurial regime come to occupy the place they did among the many sources of contention in rural France? To deal with issues of temporal patterning, we will have to locate these conflicts in their social settings, which means, to a considerable extent, locating them more precisely in space (see Chapter 7).

We also see something of the mix of tradition and innovation in patterns of rural disturbance. There is of late an interesting bit of debate around this theme. Charles Tilly, attuned to the forms of contention, sees the Revolution as an incubator of new modes of contestation that withered soon after. For Tilly, the point at which there was a permanent sloughing-off of old forms and taking on of new is mid-nineteenth century. In the history of collective protest, Tilly provocatively urges, the Revolution of 1848 is much more of a turning point than the great Revolution of 1789.[73] William Sewell has responded with the argument that Tilly understates the significance of the emergence of associational forms of struggle, given currency by the powerful new model of the state itself as an association. A deliberately enacted written constitution that creates a structure, was a powerful model upon

73. Charles Tilly, *The Contentious French* (Cambridge: Belknap Press of Harvard University Press, 1986), 388–89.

which other, political associations might build.[74] Max Weber had contended that one of the major distinguishing characteristics of modern forms of authority ("rational-legal," in his terminology) is the claim that they are governed by rules that have been "intentionally established"[75] as opposed to rules that have been always there by virtue of being the eternal rules laid down by God or the unchanging order of the universe. Such "traditional" rules need to be *found.* Sewell is arguing that the revolutionary legislatures, in creating constitutions and laws, provided a culturally resonant model of rule-making and thereby legitimated the creation of new organizations for particular goals (= "associations") rather than diffuse organizations that seem part of the timeless fabric of existence (like the village).

Our data advance the discussion a bit, but only a bit. First of all, we saw in Chapter 5 that most forms of insurrectionary expression were variations on well-worn patterns. On the other hand, the mix of forms was new. Moreover, some of the actions were themselves new, at least on anything like this scale in France. (Thus the maypoles, while familiar enough to Americans, were initially quite mysterious to French elites when they appeared in the rural Southwest.) More strikingly, there is simply no recent precedent for such a focus on attacking the lords at all. Not only did the variety of seigneurial targets distinguish revolutionary insurrections from the upheavals of the seventeenth century; it distinguished them from previous events throughout the eighteenth century as well. When we look at the insurrectionary trajectories of different event-types, indeed, we see choices being made, not blind subservience to "tradition," even though the choices were made among largely traditional forms. And when we see just how scarce antiseigneurial events were in the early months of 1789, we see that it is the development of rural antiseigneurialism within the Revolution itself that needs to be explained. Defining the problem of peasant action as the conversion of the peasantry to an antiseigneurial outlook rooted in long-term transformations, an outlook that is solidly in place at the onset of the Old Regime's collapse, would be to misstate what needs to be explained. The antiseigneurial character of rural mobilizations was something that emerged between the summer of 1788 and the fall of 1789. It was not something already in place, just awaiting release. Of course that move toward antiseigneurialism may have precursors, as in the evolution of subsistence movements to embrace grain raids on lords' stocks by the time of the Flour War of 1775 (see Chapter 5, p. 246). And seigneurial rights may have been more loathed than in the past, as Chapter 3 has argued, at the onset of the Revolution. Yet peasants did not begin the Revolution primarily attacking the lords. In the disturbances of the spring of 1789, as

74. Sewell, "Collective Violence and Collective Loyalties," 540.
75. Max Weber, *Economy and Society* (New York: Bedminster, 1968), 1:217.

the *cahiers* were being written, the salience of seigneurial targets was higher than it had been the previous fall; it was to rise far higher by the following fall. It is not enough to explain how social structures shaped the villagers' complaints; we need to grasp the processes by which the seigneurial rights became the primary target of insurrectionary peasants.

Apart from creative deployment of older forms (rather than creative invention of the unprecedented) and creative focus on a relatively unusual target, the way the country people organized for conflict broke new ground. The traditional seasonal rhythms of contestion were utterly defied. If technological advance means defying the constraints of the natural world, the technology of insurrection took a great leap forward. The seasonal cycle seems to have hardly constrained insurrectionary peasants and their antagonists at all. The plaintive appeal of the leadership of the district of Sens in Burgundy to both peasants and lords at the beginning of August 1791 to collaborate in jointly examining seigneurial titles to avoid violence in the harvest just ahead,[76] seems to speak from a world thrown over. The social truce that avoids mutual ruin was not going to be observed. Social conflict was beginning to move to a social rhythm that was no longer more than minimally constrained by natural rhythms. If modernity has meant the partial emancipation of work and leisure from seasonality, the French Revolution appears as a point at which social conflict became similarly emancipated. This suggests the development of associational modes of organization that are geared to political struggle as such, rather than the overwhelming dominance of organizational structures primarily geared to the agrarian rhythms of nature and that engage in conflict only secondarily. The modern world has freed work-rhythms from nature so that factories run year-round, sexuality loses its seasonal character,[77] and, our data suggest, social conflict comes to be carried out with a life of its own, too. The weekly microrhythm with its hot Sunday was also blurred, but not effaced, again suggesting, as Sewell urges us to see, an organizational development of associational structures capable of mobilizing people for conflict in coexistence with communal ones. Indeed there was an imperfect split: religious conflict and, especially, counterrevolution remained structured by communal life, while the central focus of this book, the antiseigneurial events, seem likely to have been organized by both.[78]

76. Ado, *Krest'ianskoe dvizhenie,* 163.

77. For some evidence from one parish of the seasonal character of a sexuality linked to the liturgical calendar, see Serge Dontenwill, *Une Seigneurie sous l'Ancien Régime: L' "Etoile" en Brionnais du XVIe au XVIIIe siècle (1575–1778)* (Roanne: Editions Horvath, 1973), 112. For a general discussion, see Edward Shorter, *The Making of the Modern Family* (New York: Basic Books, 1975).

78. Might it be that one of the motivations behind the government's incredible attempt in the late 1790s to actually enforce the official effacement of Sunday in the ten-day week of the revolutionary

The country people thought about what they were doing, in choosing their insurrectionary actions from a repertoire of contention (in Tilly's felicitous phrase) as they thought about what they were doing in choosing which grievances to express in their *cahiers*. Ideas for insurrection were being tried out in the revolutionary years, accepted if they were relatively safe as well as effective, and rejected otherwise, as shown by the rise-and-fall pattern in the number of actions per event (see Fig. 6.10). Throughout the eighteenth century, the lords and their rights had not been prime targets, although there is a shift discernible by the 1760s that is also detectible even within the established arena of subsistence conflict. But these small shifts in the targets of insurrection and the corresponding shifts in the agenda of the *cahiers* (compared to 1614; see Chapter 5, p. 266) constitute no more than a rural *pre*revolution. As such it is significant enough; surely the term prerevolution, generally applied to intra-elite quarrels since the pioneering work of Jean Egret[79] has a long-neglected rural and plebeian component. But the emergence of the enormous antiseigneurial movement in the countryside demands, beyond explaining this rural pre-Revolution, beyond explaining the bitterness in the *cahiers* toward seigneurial rights, that we bridge what we can now plainly see as a gap between the grievances of the early spring and the growing insurrectionary momentum in the months beyond.

We shall proceed on two tracks in trying to understand where antiseigneurial actions came from. In the most literal sense we shall explore in Chapter 7 the regions of France that nurtured those events, which shall be especially valuable in understanding the long-term changes and enduring structures that favored one sort of rising over another. And we shall attempt in Chapter 8 to reconstruct the dialogue of French villagers and French legislators out of which emerged the intensity and durability of the insurrections and out of which also emerged the depth of the antifeudal legislation.

If we may hope to understand the way local structures and national politics shaped peasant action, nonetheless, we do not know very much about how these various forms of action were put together. All of the evidence presented in this chapter indicates that more than two hundred years after the Revolution, we may have made enormous strides in under-

---

calendar adopted in 1793, was to eliminate part of the organizational nexus of popular mobilization—a central theme of much governmental policy of the post-Thermidor moment? On the vigor of the government's anti-Sunday struggle, see Isser Woloch, "Republican Institutions, 1797–1799," in Colin Lucas, ed., *The French Revolution and the Creation of Modern Political Culture*, vol. 2, *The Political Culture of the French Revolution* (Oxford: Pergamon Press, 1988), 371–87.

79. Jean Egret, *La pré-révolution française, 1787–1788* (Paris: Presses Universitaires de France, 1962); "La prérévolution en Provence, 1787–1789," *Annales Historiques de la Révolution française* 26 (1954): 97–126; "Les origines de la Révolution en Bretagne (1788–1789)," *Revue Historique* 213 (1955): 189–215.

standing the organization, activities, and ideologies of the urban mobilizations but that there is a rural political universe, indeed there are forty thousand micro-universes, of whose inner workings we know very little. The path-breaking studies of Jessenne on local electoral politics, of Sutherland and Tilly on mobilization for counterrevolution, of Boutier and Boutry on local political organization, of Dupuy on Brittany's National Guards, throw a spotlight on one region or one form of political mobilization and, in so doing, emphasize the surrounding darkness where much remains to be discovered.

CHAPTER 7

TRACKING INSURRECTION THROUGH TIME AND SPACE

Up to this point, we have only examined the national picture of revolt. How did France's peasant communities, considered as a whole, resemble and how did they differ from, France's nobility and urban elites in the positions they asserted at the onset of revolution? What were the targets and tactics of rural rebels? How did these targets and tactics shift over time? France's forty thousand villages, however, were not engaged in nationwide coordinated action but in separate decisions and separate actions. A full account of local and regional differences would require a book at least the size of this one, if it is not altogether beyond the scope of any single book. But an exclusive focus on the national picture risks distorting that national picture; part of that national picture is precisely its shadings and contours as one travels across space as well as through time. Without some attention to the flow of insurrectionary events across space, we will not be able to appreciate the rural situation as it confronted the revolutionary legislators in the process of elaborating their own reorganization of rural institutions.

It is not only the search for a greater accuracy in assessing the context of revolutionary legislation that demands an exploration of insurrectionary geography: by taking methodological advantage of the covariation of differing regional trajectories of revolt with differing regional contexts, we may attempt to sift through many proposed explanations of the conditions that promoted those insurrections. It is precisely the decentralized character of rural rebellion, the separate decisions made in tens of thousands of rural communities, that makes it possible to speak of specific local or regional circumstances as associated with revolt (or as not associated). Do peasants rise more readily, or against distinctive targets, when prices are high? When a Paris-based semibureaucracy is in charge? When a village is integrated into a national market? When literacy is high? When communal institutions are strong?

Although I shall be presenting evidence that bears on a host of such classical and recent questions about the character of rural rebellion, my central concern is not so much the evaluation of a myriad of separate hypotheses and conjectures as it is the attempt to seize the relationship of long-term, structural elements in the genesis of revolution, on the one hand, and the immediate, shifting, negotiated character of the revolutionary process, on the other. We have a variety of explanations of revolution in general, or of the French Revolution in particular, that look to unchanging or slow-changing "structures" as powerful contexts that impel actions, in some accounts, or channel actions, in others. We might, for example, consider such a cluster of notions surrounding the political significance of literacy as the thesis that literacy increases the propensity to revolt (by increasing the capacity for critical thought), or that it decreases it (by increasing the capacity of state authorities to secure the assent of their population through long-term educational programs and short-term propaganda), or that it channels action against certain targets and away from others.[1] These are theories of slow-changing structural capacities. In addition to such structural notions, we also have hypotheses about the impact of immediately critical circumstances, particularly rapidly deteriorating economic conditions, on the breakdown of the Old Regime, a breakdown one of whose major components was rural insurrection.

The exploration of the covariation of the occurrence of insurrection, or of particular forms of insurrection, and such contextual circumstances, whose presence or severity often had considerable geographic variation, is an important vehicle for weighing such explanations. One of the principal conclusions to be drawn from the evidence in this chapter is that structural

1. For a survey of such theories in the context of a less-developed version of the sorts of data used here, see John Markoff, "Some Effects of Literacy in Eighteenth-Century France," *Journal of Interdisciplinary History* 17 (1986): 311–33 and "Literacy and Revolt: Some Empirical Notes on 1789 in France," *American Journal of Sociology* 92 (1986): 323–49.

explanations of the social tensions within France, while going some way toward explaining the occurrence of open revolt and some of the forms that revolt took, is nonetheless not nearly enough for understanding the rise and decline in antiseigneurial actions that we have seen in Chapter 6. Even adding the conjunctural circumstances of economic crisis, which, the data suggest, does take us somewhat further, is still not enough. Structural contexts and economic conjunctures are both a vital part of the story, but they are not the story; we shall still have to add something to understand the risky choices made by French villagers.

How France's Regions Had Different Rural Revolutions (and What They Had in Common)

Anatoly Ado's pioneering research revealed a significant spatial dimension to the rural conflicts of France in revolution; indeed, he pointed to a spatiotemporal component.[2] The locations of peasant actions change over time. An extended discussion of this study by Albert Soboul emphasized the geographic aspect of peasant revolt.[3] Ado's work has since been the focus of critical scrutiny[4] and has been utilized by other scholars trying to locate rural events within the Revolution as a whole.[5] I shall follow the lead of these scholars here, for the shifting locations of rural confrontation carries important clues both to the conditions that nurtured insurrection and to the character of the dialogue of those in the villages and those in the centers of power.

For this purpose, an act of analytic simplification is essential. We cannot usefully follow the trajectories of peasant action in hundreds of *bailliages*. Just as we grouped the great range and variety of targets of peasant

2. See maps of "antifeudal uprisings" and subsistence conflicts at various points in time in Anatoly V. Ado, *Krest'ianskoe dvizhenie vo Frantsii vo vremia velikoi burzhaznoi revoliutsii kontsa XVIII veka* (Moscow: Izdatel'stvo Moskovskovo Universiteta, 1971), 84, 104, 155, 238. I shall present some maps of my own data below (and I thank Gilbert Shapiro for developing a creative map-making computer program).

3. Albert Soboul, "Sur le mouvement paysan dans la Révolution française," *Annales Historiques de la Révolution Française* 45 (1973): 85–101.

4. "Table Ronde: Autour des travaux d'Anatoli Ado sur les soulèvements paysans pendant la Révolution française," in *La Révolution française et le monde rural* (Paris: Editions du Comité des Travaux Historiques et Scientifiques, 1989), 521–47.

5. Peter M. Jones, *The Peasantry in the French Revolution* (Cambridge: Cambridge University Press, 1988); Michel Vovelle, *La découverte de la politique: Géopolitique de la Révolution française* (Paris: Editions de la Découverte, 1993).

insurrection into eight or nine large "types" in Chapters 5 and 6, we now must provisionally reduce France's geographic kaleidoscope to a manageable number of broadly conceived regions within which we will track the ebb and flow of conflict. There is no standard division of the map of France for such a purpose. At the end of his own work on the Revolution's regional variety, in the course of which he examines dozens of maps, Michel Vovelle proposes thirteen regions "with the feeling of making too many or too few."[6] With too many regions, one risks losing a coherent picture; with too few one risks obscuring vital distinctions. For my rough sketch of the locations of insurrection, I divided France into nine broad regions.

In the rest of this chapter, "North" covers the area running north of the Paris region to the border of the Austrian Netherlands, roughly Picardy, Artois, and Flanders. The "Northeast" runs east of that area to the German and Swiss frontiers: it includes Alsace and Lorraine, and continues south through Franche-Comté; it also includes the broad plains of Champagne. Since one might well expect the vicinity of France's largest city by far to have some unique characteristics, I treated Ile-de-France as a zone to itself, the "Paris region." A broad horizontal strip made up the "North-Center" running from Burgundy on the east, moving westward through Orléanais and Berry and including Touraine. Further to the South, the "South-Center": Lyonnais, Auvergne, Bourbonnais, and Limousin. The "Southeast" is Dauphiné, Provence, and eastern Languedoc, while the "Southwest" (Pyrenees included) stretches west from the western half of Languedoc through Guyenne and Gascony along the Spanish frontier including Béarn, Foix, and Roussillon, and up the Atlantic coast past Bordeaux into southern Poitou. The "West" covers Brittany, Maine, Anjou, and northwest Poitou. Uncomfortable with dissolving Normandy into either "West" or "North," I counted it as a region apart. I shall sometimes group Normandy together with North, Northeast, North-Center, and Paris region into a broad "northern France" as contrasted with a grouped Southeast, Southwest, and South-Center ("the South"). To be able to specify precisely which events took place in which regions, I identified these nine areas in practice with Old Regime *généralités* and electoral *bailliages,* as specified in the first of this chapter's tables.

Of course all such classifications raise questions. It is easy to be uncomfortable with the cultural and topographical diversity of such a Southwest, with this (or any other) divide between Southeast and Southwest, with including Dauphiné in the Southeast (or, alternately, not separating the Southeast into the Mediterranean Coast and the hills and mountains to the north), and perhaps with adding Champagne to the Northeast frontier rather than grouping it with the North-Center. Nonetheless, I think the tables that follow show that these distinctions do capture important broad differences

6. Vovelle, *La découverte de la politique,* 327.

Map 7.1. Regions, Provinces, and Select Towns

in insurrectionary actions without being so fine-grained that all vanishes into the mists of microscopic detail.

Table 7.1 shows the regional distributions of all events over the entire five years and compares that with the area, population, and number of rural communities. The table also indicates for each region the percentage of all *bailliages* in which any events occurred (in column 3). All regions of the country were touched by the rural revolution. If there was nowhere in the vicinity of Paris that was far from some site of insurrection, the insurrections of the Southeast were almost as widespread and made up one-fifth the total. At the opposite extreme, the Northeast had many electoral circumscriptions where no insurrections at all turn up in our sample. Northern France generally was less at the center of things than one might have expected. Indeed, more than half our events occurred south and west of the famous line from Saint-Malo to Geneva that is often taken to roughly divide an "advanced" countryside of relative prosperity, open-field cereal agriculture, cash tenancy and smallholdings, heavy plows and good yields, the languages of states (French primarily, but also German and Flemish) and literacy from a South and West of poor yields, hills, zones of makeshift expedients, sharecropping, languages of no state (variants of Occitain but also Breton and Basque) and reduced literacy. The great majority of *bailliages* in the South and West had some form of contestation and enter our data set, the Southwest's experience being the most mixed.

Are any regions especially insurrection-prone? If we juxtapose the last three columns of Table 7.1 with the second column we can see whether insurrections are especially common anywhere compared to population, area, and the number of rural communities. This last comparison is particularly noteworthy if one sees the community as the social unit that organizes insurrectionary acts.[7] Several regions stand out. The Northeast has a bit fewer insurrections that one might expect on the basis of its population but markedly fewer in comparison to the number of distinct communities. Differently put, northeastern communities are by far the least likely to mobilize of any region. By contrast, the Southeast is the most disproportionately explosive, having twice as many insurrections as its share of population and even more than that in comparison to the numbers of its communities. The more prosperous agriculture of northern and eastern France did not, then, lend its peasants any greater proneness to revolt.

The West is not laggard either. While it is not dramatically more active than its share of the French population, it is in comparison to its portion of France's communities. Western France was an area of dispersed farmsteads,

7. This seems to have been the conception of contemporary chroniclers. As pointed out above in Chapter 5, the sources often identify those engaged in some action with one or more named parishes (and more often than not with precisely one parish).

Table 7.1. Regional Distribution of All Events (June 1788–June 1793), Area, Population, and Communities (%)

		Percentage of Region's			
Region[a]	Events	*Bailliages* with Events	Population[b]	Area[b]	Communities[c]
North	8%	89%	8%	6%	10%
Northeast	10	54	13	15	20
Paris region	8	100	7	4	5
North-Center	8	85	11	12	10
South-Center	8	93	10	10	8
Southeast	20	96	10	13	9
Southwest	14	79	18	20	19
West	15	86	15	13	8
Normandy	10	90	8	6	10
	(100)	(—)	(100)	(100)	(100)

[a]North: *généralités* of Amiens, Lille, Valenciennes, and Soissons.
Northeast: *généralités* of Metz, Nancy, Strasbourg, Châlons, and Besançon.
Paris region: *généralité* of Paris.
North-Center: *généralités* of Orléans, Dijon, and Bourges; eastern protion of *généralité* of Tours (*bailliages* of Tours, Loches, Châtillon-sur-Indre, Chinon, and Montrichard).
South-Center: *généralités* of Riom, Moulins, Lyon, and Limoges.
Southeast: *généralités* of Dauphiné, Aix; eastern Languedoc (*bailliages* of Mende, Le Puy-de-Velay, Annonay, Villeneuve-de-Berg, Nîmes, Montpellier, Béziers).
Southwest: *généralités* of La Rochelle, Bordeaux, Auch, Montauban, Perpignan; western Languedoc (*bailliages* of Toulouse, Castres, Carcassonne, Castelnaudary, Limoux, Conflans, and Cerdagne) and southern and eastern Poitou (*bailliages* of La Châtaigneraie, Châtellerault, Montmorillon, Civray, Niort, Lusignan, and St-Maixent).
West: *généralité* of Rennes, northwest Poitou (*bailliages* of Poitiers, Fontenay-le-comte, Marches Communes) and western portion of *généralité* of Tours (*bailliages* of Le Mans, Laval, Ste-Suzanne, Fresnay-le-Comte, Mamers, Beaumont-le-Vicomte, Château-Gontier, La Flèche, Baugé, Beaufort, Château-du-Loir, Loudun, Langeais, Angers, and Saumur).
Normandy: *généralités* of Caen, Alençon, and Rouen.

[b]*Source:* Jacques Necker, *De l'Administration des finances de la France* (Paris: n.p., 1784), 1:228–96 and inset table headed "Résumé de l'étendue & de la population de chaque Généralité."
[c]*Sources:* Brette, *Recueil de Documents relatifs à la Convocation des Etats Généraux de 1789* (Paris: Imprimerie Nationale, 1894–1915); various editors' introductions to series "Collection de documents inédits sur l'histoire économique de la Révolution française"; *Archives Nationales* (mainly in Div[bis] 43–46). Estimate for cases not covered in indicated sources is described in Gilbert Shapiro, John Markoff, and Silvio R. Duncan Baretta, "The Selective Transmission of Historical Documents: The Case of the Parish *Cahiers* of 1789," *Histoire et Mesure* 2 (1987): 121.

whose people came together for Sunday services, swelling, once a week, the population of its central places. The workday dispersion of its people seems to have been no hindrance to their organizing their fair share—or more—of riot and rebellion.

The generally southern character of revolt is even more marked for antiseigneurial events in particular. Table 7.2 shows that 62% of antiseigneurial events are in the South-Central, Southeastern, and Southwestern regions. But no region is immune: the famously counterrevolutionary West still has a substantial antiseigneurial element although at less than half the level of its share in all insurrections. And while the West was, indeed, most distinctive for counterrevolution, the Southwest and Southeast also had their share of such events, a rather less well appreciated and, until recently, understudied subject.[8] Religiously tinged events have a regional distribution rather like the antiseigneurial, although they are rather more common in the West and rather less in the South-Center and Southeast. Anti-tax activities are particularly striking in the North and Normandy and rather less concentrated in the Southeast. (It was in the northern area of anti-tax clashes that Babeuf got his start in revolutionary action.)[9] The three regions where counterrevolution was so strong are disproportionately low in the land conflicts that are disproportionately high in the Northeast. Did class conflict and counterrevolution avoid each other's proximity? Note that the Paris region and the North, the leaders, by far, in wage conflict, are nearly immune from counterrevolution (but Normandy, between North and West, has neither counterrevolution nor wage conflicts). Subsistence conflicts have a significant western concentration that extends into neighboring Normandy, a province also marked by its anti-tax events. Panics, finally, are unusually common near Paris and in North Central France and rarer in a broadly defined west that includes Normandy.

Some nuance may be added by Table 7.3, which indicates the geographic extent within each region of different forms of conflict. While the West is best known for its counterrevolution, the impressive extent of involvement

8. Michel Vovelle has pointed up the extent of rural resistance to the revolution in the South-Center and Southwest, but prefers not to use the term "counterrevolution" so broadly as I do here, favoring the recent term "antirevolution" for the villagers' rejection of state authority. See Vovelle, *La découverte de la politique,* 335–38 and Chapter 5. Urban counterrevolution in the South is better known: see, for example, Gwynne Lewis, *The Second Vendée: The Continuity of Revolution in the Department of the Gard, 1789–1815* (Oxford: Clarendon Press, 1978); J. N. Hood, "Revival and Mutation of Old Rivalries in Revolutionary France," *Past and Present* 82 (1979): 82–115. On rural events in the South, see Hubert C. Johnson, *The Midi in Revolution: A Study of Regional Political Diversity, 1789–1793* (Princeton: Princeton University Press, 1986); Peter M. Jones, *Politics and Rural Society: The Southern Massif Central, c. 1750–1880* (Cambridge: Cambridge University Press, 1985).

9. Rose, *Gracchus Babeuf: The First Revolutionary Communist* (Stanford: Stanford University Press, 1978), 55–71.

Table 7.2. Type of Events by Region, June 1788–June 1793 (%)

Region	Antiseigneurial	Religious	Subsistence	Anti-tax	Land	Wage	Panic	Counterrevolution
North	4%	7%	11%	26%	9%	24%	10%	1%
Northeast	12	11	4	11	20	—	12	1
Paris region	6	6	11	3	9	43	17	—
North-Center	4	6	14	6	3	10	16	1
South-Center	13	7	6	4	2	5	11	4
Southeast	28	22	10	12	31	12	10	17
Southwest	21	22	6	4	11	7	13	19
West	7	16	17	15	5	—	6	59
Normandy	5	4	21	21	10	—	5	—
	(100)	(100)	(100)	(100)	(100)	(100)	(100)	(100)

Note: Columns might not sum to 100% because of rounding error.

ought not to conceal the presence of the rather significant third of western *bailliages* where counterrevolutionary events did not happen. It is this western variety that makes possible the methodology of studies like those of Tilly and Bois that contrast loyal with defiant subregions as well as the interpretation of Sutherland who sees a rural civil war (with outside involvement).[10] The image of "blue" townsfolk in a sea of "white" peasants (that is, pro-revolutionary urbanites and counterrevolutionary country people) needs to be nuanced by noting urban counterrevolution (in towns like Tréguier or Guérande)[11] and pro-revolutionary rural zones (like much of the eastern half of the *département* of the Sarthe,[12] the Saumurois in Anjou,[13] and many parts of Brittany).[14] And some one-third of western *bailliages* had antiseigneurial events, recalling the question posed by Roger Dupuy and Michel Vovelle of the relation of this western antiseigneurialism and counterrevolution.[15] Are these the same third that do not have counterrevolutionary events? We shall look into this below (see p. 415). For the present we note that the antiseigneurial subregions of the West are more narrowly circumscribed than anywhere but the Northeast (this latter point a surprise). While the 257 western counterrevolutionary incidents that our sample unearthed are far more numerous than western antiseigneurial events (119) the latter surely deserve some notice; and western counterrevolution does not nearly so strongly dominate subsistence events, which weigh in with a hefty 205. The West's contribution to rural turbulence, in short, goes well beyond its eventual fostering of the most bitterly polarized and violent conflicts of the entire era.

Table 7.3 also reveals something impressive about southeastern antiseigneurialism: it is not only numerically impressive but touched at one point or another virtually the entire region. The Southeast, in this sense, is the most uniformly antiseigneurial part of the country,[16] followed, and none too closely, by South-Central France, in turn followed by the far less uniformly mobilized Southwest, which edges out the Paris area. To glance a moment

10. Sutherland, *The Chouans: The Social Origins of Popular Counterrevolution in Upper Brittany, 1770–1796* (Oxford: Clarendon Press, 1982), 12.

11. Dupuy, *De la Révolution à la Chouannerie: Paysans en Bretagne, 1788–1794* (Paris: Flammarion, 1988), 67–71.

12. Bois, *Les Paysans de l'Ouest: Des structures économiques et sociales aux options politiques depuis l'époque révolutionnaire dans la Sarthe* (Le Mans: Imprimerie M. Vilaire, 1960), 162.

13. Tilly, *The Vendée* (Cambridge: Harvard University Press, 1964), 303–4. For a very detailed study of opposition to the insurrectionary forces within the vendéen heartland, see Claude Petitfrère, *Blancs et bleus d'Anjou (1789–1793)* (Lille: Atelier Reproduction des Thèses, 1979).

14. Dupuy, *De la Révolution à la Chouannerie,* 197.

15. Dupuy, *De la Révolution à la Chouannerie*; Michel Vovelle, *La découverte de la politique: Géopolitique de la Révolution française* (Paris: Editions de la Découverte, 1993), 90, 283–84.

16. Clearly, if we used units of analysis smaller than the *bailliages,* southeastern areas without antiseigneurial events would be more visible.

Table 7.3. Extent of Regional Participation in Insurrection, June 1788–June 1793 (% of *Bailliages* with Events of Various Types)

Region	Antiseigneurial	Religious	Subsistence	Anti-tax	Land	Wage	Panic	Counterrevolution
North	37%	46%	67%	28%	26%	11%	61%	2%
Northeast	26	19	20	14	14	—	42	—
Paris region	44	16	64	8	40	20	96	—
North-Center	37	17	64	15	10	4	64	4
South-Center	68	46	61	18	21	7	89	29
Southeast	87	74	83	44	35	4	78	26
Southwest	45	40	39	7	21	3	63	8
West	33	42	67	26	12	—	49	65
Normandy	35	25	79	29	33	—	40	—

at the evidence on counterrevolution, we note that counterrevolutionary actions were rather widespread in the Southeast, but very confined geographically in the Southwest. These, and other, differences between the Southeast and Southwest show the inadequacy of any notion of a mere two Frances, north and south. We also see that the rural revolt against the lords is hardly the mere fallout of Parisian influence or the byproduct of the agricultural prosperity most easily found in the north.

The regional concentration of forms of revolt is striking. Returning to Table 7.2 we see that anti-tax events had a sharp geographic focus. Nearly half of our anti-tax events occurred in the North and Normandy. The affinity of northern and northwestern France for anti-tax actions can also be seen by comparing the proportions of anti-tax actions in those regions with their proportions of all actions: Normandy is more than twice as likely to have anti-tax events as one would expect from its proportion of all rural events, and the North more than three times. (One can see this by comparing Table 7.1 and Table 7.2.) Not only did the *aides* and *gabelles,* two of the most detested Old Regime taxes and the main fiscal targets of rural anger (see Table 5.4) run high in the North and part of Normandy, but especially explosive—so it would appear from the geography—was the proximity to the *gabelle*-free zones of Brittany to the west and Artois to the north as well as the very different rates for salt in lower and upper Normandy.[17] The proximity of the two differently taxed regions was famous for generating interzonal smuggling.[18] This same proximity, our data suggest, deserve an equal repute as the seedbed of insurrection.

One's first thought is to see this as evidence of the centrality of grievance in the genesis of contestation. In this view the sheer weight of burden was exacerbated by the visibility of freedom as the crucial element in grievance. Such an interpretation would have been very pleasing to those who used to

17. According to the map provided by Jacques Necker, the going price for salt in Artois in 1780 was a low seven to eight livres for a minot of salt and in Brittany an almost insignificant one livre ten sous to three livres. (Brittany and Artois were also part of "the provinces where the *aides* do not apply," as the administrative formula ran.) In lower Normandy, where it was permitted to extract salt from seawater, the price rose to thirteen livres. By contrast, in upper Normandy salt sold for over fifty-four livres, in Picardy (adjacent to Artois) fifty-seven to fifty-nine. (Lower Normandy and Picardy had the misfortune of being part of the "provinces of the Great Salt Tax.") See Jacques Necker, *Compte rendu au roi* (Paris: Imprimerie Royale, 1781), appended map ("carte des gabelles").

18. One catches a glimpse of these smuggling networks in Necker's observations on the annual arrest rates at the southeast border of Brittany in the 1780s. Some 23,000 men were employed at great expense to control salt smuggling and failed, as shown by, among other things, some 6,600 arrests of children each year around Laval and Angers. The children were held only briefly, then released to smuggle some more (*De l'administration des finances* [Paris: n.p., 1784], 1:195; 2:30–31, 57–58). Necker's report on the state of royal finances sketches this well-developed criminal world, beyond eradication, in his view, unless tax reform reduced the incentives to smuggling. See *Compte rendu,* 100–109.

argue for the revolt-generating significance of "relative deprivation" (the sense that compared to others one was inadequately rewarded).[19] Perhaps such resentments would explain the clustering of anti-tax revolt around the borders of Brittany and Artois as well as the divide between lower and upper Normandy, but there is an alternative hypothesis less oriented to affect and more to capacities. The extensive development of smuggling around those border areas, far more for contraband salt than contraband wine,[20] no doubt cultivated skills and experience in reading the police and gained considerable support and sympathy from the surrounding population. Might not such networks of organized resistance have seized the opportunity for open challenge that emerged in 1789? Salt-smuggling may have been a crime to the agents of tax-farmers but hardly to the ordinary people of Normandy or Picardy. The crowd that rescued a man seized for filling his home with contraband tobacco at Laon in November 1789 was just one of many such actions.[21] Certainly the moment would seem to have been a propitious one for tax revolt. For all the loathing the indirect taxes inspired in the *cahiers* (see Chapter 3, p. 100), the National Assembly at first opted to maintain them temporarily until a new taxation structure could be put in place.[22] The Assembly thereby created a situation in which aggrieved peasants knew well that the new legislators opposed these taxes, too, even while continuing them in force. Under these circumstances, what is remarkable is that there were not even more anti-tax risings than there were (see Chapter 5, pp. 233–37).

Were favorable opportunities for action seized by people already oriented to surreptitious struggles with police and courts over taxes or did those opportunities provide the channels into which an amorphous and previously unorganized resentment could flow? The data we have presented so far, aggregated to a large area like our "region," do not distinguish between our social-psychological account of burning anger and our structural-organizational account of capacities and networks. Let us consider a finer analysis, one that can explore more precisely just where within these broad regions

19. See James C. Davies, "The J-Curve of Rising and Declining Satisfactions as a Cause of Some Great Revolutions and a Contained Rebellion," in Hugh Davis Graham and Ted Robert Gurr, eds., *The History of Violence in America* (New York: Bantam, 1969), 415–36; Ted Robert Gurr, *Why Men Rebel* (Princeton: Princeton University Press, 1970); Ivo K. Feierabend and Rosalind L. Feierabend, "Aggressive Behavior within Polities, 1948–1962: A Cross-National Study," *Journal of Conflict Resolution* 10 (1966): 249–71.

20. Matthews, *The Royal General Farms in Eighteenth-Century France* (New York: Columbia University Press, 1958), 164.

21. See Ramsay, *The Ideology of the Great Fear: The Soissonnais in 1789* (Baltimore: Johns Hopkins University Press, 1992), 178. Ramsay reports several other incidents in which tax revolt appears to grow out of smuggling.

22. The *gabelle* was ended officially in March 1790, the *aides* one year later and the other indirect taxes at intermediate dates. See Matthews, *General Farms*, 278.

the anti-tax rebellions took place, with the goal of distinguishing the two theses. And once we are launched on such an analysis, let us recall that the third most insurrection-prone arena, as far as taxes were concerned, is the West. If we disaggregate "the West" so that we separate tax-free Brittany from neighboring (and heavily taxed) Maine and Anjou, could it be that it is along the western edge of Brittany where much of this western trouble is?

The "resentment thesis" suggests that when we examine the border between low and high *gabelle* zones in the three regions that account for 62% of all anti-tax events, we will find many troubles on the high-tax side, especially near the frontier, and few on the low-tax side at all. The "network of resistance thesis" suggests that we will find many troubles near the border on both sides, that is, where such smuggling networks operated. Do anti-tax incidents, then, cluster near the boundaries of *gabelle* zones, and, if so, do they cluster on one side or on both?

Let us now look at the data for the precise location of anti-tax events in the West, the North, and Normandy (are these events near the eastern border of Brittany, the southern border of Artois, and the southern boundary of lower Normandy?). There is a scattering of anti-tax troubles on the Breton side of the provincial border; there is also an outbreak deep in western Brittany in August 1792 with incidents around Concarneau, Gourin, and Quimperlé that are part of the buildup to counterrevolution;[23] the clear majority of western anti-tax events, however, are just outside of Brittany, across the border in the *bailliages* of Le Mans and Angers, supplemented by lesser numbers in the *bailliages* of Mamers and Poitiers.[24] If we set aside, then, the later protests against revolutionary taxation, perhaps especially bitterly received in previously privileged Brittany,[25] the preponderance of the remaining incidents are along the Old Regime taxation frontiers. If we look along the southern boundary of low-tax Artois, we see something quite similar: the *bailliages* of Abbeville, Amiens, and St. Quentin

23. See Dupuy, *De la Révolution à la Chouannerie,* 254. Among anti-tax incidents in my sample taking place from September 1791 on (by which time revolutionary taxation was being put in place), 82% were in the West.

24. As one instance: In December 1789 a large group from a village near Le Mans broke into the house of a former employee of the salt-tax agency, who was accused of still practicing his occupation despite the new legislation, smashed some of his furniture and insulted his wife, leaving only after she agreed to buy them drinks at the nearby cabaret. See Victor Duchemin and Robert Triger, *Les premières troubles de la Révolution dans la Mayenne: Etudes sur l'état des esprits dans les différentes régions de ce département* (Mamers: Fleury et Dangin, 1888), 53–54.

25. In parts of Brittany, revolutionary tax reform doubled the tax burden of the country people (Sutherland, *Chouans,* 134–38). And in the Vendée, Alain Gérard has shown that the Revolution rather drastically shifted the tax burden away from some places onto others; the regions losing out, one is hardly surprised to learn, became the center of the western counterrevolution. No wonder four-fifths of those among our anti-tax events that involve the new taxation are western. See Alain Gérard, *Pourquoi la Vendée?* (Paris: Armand Colin, 1990), 191–92.

are the centers of anti-tax events, seconded a bit to the south by Roye and Noyon. We are in Babeuf's country, for sure. This is to be compared to a mere sprinkling of insurrection north of the border. Here the low-tax zone, then, has few events. The Norman anti-tax theater is a bit different; the major centers are also clustered at the boundary between the fairly low-tax lower Normandy and the rest of the province, but the *bailliage* of Caen, where I have found eleven anti-tax events, is on one side of the line and Domfront, with nine, on the other. The Breton and Artesian frontiers, with the lion's share of events a bit to the expensive side of the provincial frontier, then, support the resentment hypothesis, while the Norman evidence suggests that it is the implantation of a network of tax evaders that counts. And there we must let this particular matter stand, as far as our statistical evidence is concerned. But we find the evidence, in its inconclusiveness, instructive: surely the Revolution was an opportunity both for preexisting networks to act in new ways and for those with grievances who had not yet organized to do so.

The small number of events that we have found focused on wages are also highly specific regionally. They are concentrated from the Paris region on northward, a prosperous area making extensive use of paid laborers in the fields, often in the form of seasonal migrants. A proletarianized Norman countryside supported subsistence events.[26] Struggles over land seem to have particularly characterized the Northeast (Was this the legacy of lord-community-state conflict over increasingly valued forest? See Chapter 5, p. 251), extending westward into the Paris region and the North, and also, if less sharply, down into the Southeast. This geographic pattern is close to that displayed in Peter Jones's mapping of the sources of petitions to the revolutionary government on land issues.[27] It appears that, at least on those land issues, legal appeal to distant authority and illegal assumptions of local initiative were taking place in the same general areas. Pestering the government and direct action were not opposed forms of action, but complementary.

Struggles over taxation, land, wages, food, and even more strikingly, counterrevolution, then, are all more concentrated regionally than antisei-

26. Why are there not wage actions mounted in Normandy's increasingly proletarianized countryside directed against the merchant-employers in textile production? Did the dispersed nature of an individual merchant's rural employees make collective action even more difficult than it was for laborers in the fields of nearby Picardy and Ile-de-France? Or did their actions take the form of a traditional convergence on the merchant's urban residence, perhaps thereby escaping my search for rural events?

27. Peter M. Jones, *Peasantry,* 146. Jones's map is based on the selection of correspondence received by the legislative committees dealing with the feudal regime published by Georges Bourgin, *Le partage des biens communaux: Documents sur la préparation de la loi du 10 juin 1793* (Paris: Imprimerie Nationale, 1908).

gneurial battles. This is seen clearly in Table 7.4 which presents, for each region, the quotient of the percentage of specific types of events by that region's percentage of all events. This figure shows how much more (or less) often one finds specific types of events in a region than its percentage of all events leads one to expect. A ratio of 1.00 (the West's anti-tax figure, as it happens) means that the propensity of that region to have that type of event is neither higher nor lower than for events generally. We may speak of the "relative proportion" of the West's events that are antiseigneurial, religiously tinged, etc. We see that most kinds of events have at least one region where they are at least twice as common as the generality of events, but that antiseigneurial events (as well as the religiously tinged) lack such a sharp geographic focus. Even the West, with proportionately fewer antiseigneurial events than the other regions—less than half of what one would expect if its share of France's antiseigneurial events were the same as its share of all insurrections—still has a substantial number of such conflicts. And the relative proportion of antiseigneurial events in much of northern France (North-Center, North, and Normandy) is only insignificantly greater than in the West. At the other extreme, the region whose insurrections were most disproportionately prone to antiseigneurial targets, the Southwest (followed closely by the South-Center and Southeast), is only about one and one-half times more likely to have antiseigneurial than other events.[28] (Compare the North's propensity to anti-tax actions, Normandy's to anti-tax or subsistence events, the Northeast's to land conflicts, the Paris region's to wage conflicts, and the West's to counterrevolution.)

Panics and subsistence struggles occurred in more *bailliages* than did overt challenges to the lord and his claims. If we take a broader, regional perspective, however, we see that panics and subsistence struggles are more clearly marked by their regional character than are antiseigneurial ones. Although widespread, they were also carriers of potential division (a "backward" countryside prey to irrational rumor vs. an "advanced" countryside of cool reason; a food-producing vs. a food-purchasing peasantry). Table 7.4 certainly shows variation in antiseigneurial intensity and, as we shall see, if we examine separately the different moments of the unfolding revolution, we will find very marked regional differences in the timing of antiseigneurial actions. But Table 7.4 also shows that compared to other forms of conflict, no region dominates, nor is any missing from, the

28. These overall regional patterns are inconsistent with the reputation the North has sometimes had as the heartland of the Revolution's revolt in general or of its antiseigneurial actions in particular. Perhaps the occasional image of a heroically antiseigneurial North is an extension of the particular moment when it was at the center of such actions; see, for example, William Brustein, "Regional Social Orders in France and the French Revolution," *Comparative Social Research* 9 (1986): 145–61, which has a very valuable and innovative discussion of the range of targets of peasant action, but assigns the North a uniformly antiseigneurial character that it only had briefly.

Table 7.4. Ratio of Percentages of Events of Specific Types to Percentages of All Events

Region	Antiseigneurial	Religious	Subsistence	Anti-tax	Land	Wage	Panic	Counterrevolution
North	0.54	0.83	1.38	3.19	1.13	2.98	1.28	0.06
Northeast	1.21	1.17	0.44	1.13	2.08	0.00	1.33	0.10
Paris region	0.75	0.74	1.43	0.33	1.15	5.50	2.14	0.00
North-Center	0.50	0.74	1.63	0.76	0.36	1.13	1.84	0.11
South-Center	1.51	0.87	0.76	0.46	0.23	0.57	1.34	0.47
Southeast	1.41	1.09	0.51	0.57	1.53	0.60	0.51	0.85
Southwest	1.53	1.58	0.43	0.28	0.81	0.52	0.91	1.34
West	0.48	1.06	1.16	1.00	0.35	0.00	0.43	4.05
Normandy	0.55	0.42	2.16	2.20	1.08	0.00	0.50	0.00

antiseigneurial battle. If there was one form of action that united rather than differentiated France's peasantries, it was the struggle against the lords.

For a revolutionary legislature seeking rural compliance (and at times rural mobilization; see Chapters 8 and 9), antifeudal language would be far more promising as a global summary of the meaning of the revolution, than would the language of tax equalization, land reform, wage protection, or even subsistence guarantees. Such projects would appeal to some peasants in some regions, but would be anathema to others. Tax equalization would be fine for peasants in high-tax zones but not for those across an administrative boundary that sheltered them. Land reform would please those disadvantaged by current land-tenure rules but not those favored. Wage relief would benefit migratory and other laborers but not those hiring them. Guaranteeing the staff of life, while keenly desired by consumers, was not likely to win support of those with marketable surpluses and storage capacities (and perhaps was so divisive an intracommunal issue as to be virtually suppressed as a subject for the *cahiers*).[29] The bitter rural division over religious policy is well known; the new regime's religious policies indeed are sometimes seen as its central political blunder.[30] The major rivals to antiseigneurial events for being truly national were panics, less common, but even more widely distributed, touching, at one point or another, three *bailliages* in five (see Table 5.1). But revolutionary legislators could hardly attempt to claim that panic was the central experience and meaning of the Revolution. To the extent that anything could, antifeudalism joined together sharecroppers and peasant smallholders, employees of seasonal labor and their laborers, those who liked protective communal rights and those who loathed constraining communal regulations, those who marketed their surplus grain and those who bought their food in the marketplace.

Time and Space

Table 7.1 conceals as it reveals. The previous chapter showed the rural revolution to be not so much a time of trouble as a sequence of times of

29. In light of the frequency of violence over the food supply, it is remarkable how few communities discuss subsistence issues in their *cahiers*. Those that do discuss them tend to be from regions with relatively little insurrectionary activity in 1789. This pattern suggests a widespread avoidance of a divisive subject in the communities' public and collective statements. Those communities that could not avoid raising contentious subjects may be demonstrating an incapacity to work as a united whole, an incapacity that may render them unable to mount insurrection as well—including subsistence conflicts. See John Markoff, "Peasant Grievances and Peasant Insurrection: France in 1789," *Journal of Modern History* 62 (1990): 445–76.

30. John McManners, *The French Revolution and the Church* (New York: Harper and Row, 1969), 38; François Furet and Denis Richet, *La Révolution française* (Paris: Fayard, 1973), 127–28.

troubles. We need to study the changing geography of revolt. Table 7.5 shows the geography of successive waves of insurrectionary events: it displays, separately, the regional distributions of events for the initial ascending trajectory of the summer of 1788 to the winter of 1789, the subsequent insurrectionary peaks (see Chapter 6, pp. 270–99) and the valleys between those peaks.[31] There are a number of surprises. The early prologue to the storms to come (the first row of the table), at least in this collection of data, is easily dominated by western France; as western-dominated, indeed, as is the counterrevolutionary explosion of March 1793. This western prelude was made up entirely of subsistence events without antiseigneurial or any other admixtures.

Roger Dupuy has suggested that the West, early on, shows a rural activism not obviously committed along the lines of the divisions to come.[32] In Brittany, starting in June 1788, crowds, with significant peasant participation, were stopping grain bound for England; such actions, first noted in the ports and then spreading inland, were sufficiently alarming that by August, the provincial intendant asked priests to read a calming announcement to the effect that such exports were lawful under the recently negotiated free-trade treaty. This may well have been the first of the many, many attempts (see Chapters 8 and 9) of those who saw themselves as reformers to calm the good people of the countryside by instructing them in the wisdom of the new legislation. The treaty contained, after all, a provision for state intervention if prices climbed above an intolerable threshold. The country people (and, in these subsistence events, their urban allies) were not apt pupils for this attempt at instruction in the law's benevolence: the violence continued into the fall, when the *intendant* asked for royal troops—and was turned down; by November 1788, with the Estates-General beginning to loom ahead, the royal officials did not judge it prudent to greet fears of hunger with force.[33] Over the next few years, the revolutionary government

---

Timothy Tackett has clearly established the great regional differences in Catholic practice on the eve of the Revolution that made revolutionary legislation in this area highly likely to run afoul of some region's deeply held tradition. Virtually any national reform would have violated some region's distinctive sense of the proper institutions for Christianity. See Tackett, *Religion, Revolution and Regional Culture in Eighteenth-Century France: The Ecclesiastical Oath of 1791* (Princeton: Princeton University Press, 1986).

31. A few brief intervals did not seem easily assignable to a peak or valley; I omitted them rather than muddy the waters. There were not, for example, enough events in May 1790 to subject that month to a scrutiny of its own yet it was not obvious to me whether to group May with the previous or the subsequent several months. I simply dropped May from the analysis presented here and later in this chapter.

32. Dupuy emphasizes the capacity of Breton communities both to loot *châteaux* in 1790 and rise against the conscription of 1793. He goes on to argue that "to revolt against the abuses of feudalism does not forever immunize you against all counter-revolutionary behavior" (*De la Révolution à la Chouannerie,* 330).

33. Dupuy, *De la Révolution à la Chouannerie,* 43–48.

Table 7.5. Geography of Events by Time Period (%)

Time Period	North	Northeast	Paris Region	North-Center	South-Center	Southeast	Southwest	West	Normandy	
June 1788–Jan. 1789	2	4	5	—	5	1	6	70	7	(100)
Mar. 1789–June 1789	21	8	11	3	1	28	6	11	11	(100)
July 1789–Aug. 1789	10	21	11	15	7	13	8	6	10	(100)
Sept. 1789–Dec. 1789	11	5	3	7	10	7	23	16	19	(100)
Jan. 1790–Feb. 1790	3	1	—	1	13	6	54	19	2	(100)
Mar. 1790–Apr. 1790	18	2	3	2	5	18	18	18	16	(100)
June 1790–Aug. 1790	8	18	18	9	10	10	17	5	5	(100)
Sept. 1790–May 1791	5	6	7	3	13	20	24	18	5	(100)
June 1791–Aug. 1791	11	3	5	5	14	9	19	19	14	(100)
Sept. 1791–Jan. 1792	15	7	4	3	13	17	20	16	5	(100)
Feb. 1792–Apr. 1792	3	1	11	6	11	43	8	5	13	(100)
May 1792–July 1792	6	5	2	1	2	38	31	10	6	(100)
Aug. 1792–Sept. 1792	1	6	4	6	8	29	12	28	1	(100)
Oct. 1792–Dec. 1792	1	6	3	30	3	19	8	18	12	(100)
Jan. 1793–Feb. 1793	8	27	4	—	2	51	—	8	—	(100)
March 1793	2	1	1	3	8	6	10	69	1	(100)
Apr. 1793–June 1793	5	13	4	—	—	35	1	18	23	(100)

intermittently assumed the role of tutor; France's villagers continued to be poor students.

From the West to the North and the Southeast: in the spring of 1789 (the second row of the table), northern France generates a rapidly rising number of events, a process especially marked in the North. Two-thirds of these northern spring events concern subsistence but one in four now focuses on the rights of the lords. The Southeast has also emerged as a major insurrectionary area and as a leader in antiseigneurial actions.[34] While more than half of southeastern events of the spring are also subsistence-focused, almost one-third have an antiseigneurial aspect. But the antiseigneurial propensity is even more marked around Paris where rather fewer than half the spring events involve the food supply and three-quarters are directed at the seigneurial regime.

The early mobilization in the West might be taken as bearing out Roger Dupuy's observation of a "precocious politicization" in the countryside there[35]—and an important indication that the insurrectionary politics of the countryside was keenly sensitive to the actions of men of wealth and power. The Breton elite scene was unusually polarized at an early date, and the prelude to the convocation of the Estates-General unusually bitter, with an increasing tension between a radicalizing urban commoner elite and an intransigent nobility and upper clergy, the latter ultimately refusing to participate in the elections when they failed to get them to proceed in the form they wanted. Jean Egret showed in a classic essay how the struggle over the Estates-General drew on urban collective actions, in the forms of pitched battles in major towns;[36] Dupuy now urges us to see the whole period leading up to the convocation as a fruitful opportunity for peasant action as well, as the old order came apart at the top. From the summer of 1788 on, in fact, the Breton nobility attempted to gain the support of peasants in their struggles with the king on the one hand and the non-noble urban elites on the other, by circulating a great deal of literature in Breton as well as French. The urban notables replied with their own pamphlet counterattack.[37] In the countryside, the rioting began.

Something of the same might be said of the spring events of Provence, which, if not quite so early as the Breton clashes, were distinguished for the degree to which they were beginning to shift to antiseigneurial actions.

34. The number, scale, diversity of targets, and violence of some of these events in Provence had a terrifying impact that is vividly conveyed in Monique Cubells, *Les horizons de la liberté: La naissance de la Révolution en Provence, 1787–1789* (Aix: Edisud, 1987), 92–110.

35. Roger Dupuy, *De la Révolution à la Chouannerie,* 19.

36. Jean Egret, "Les origines de la Révolution en Bretagne (1788–1789)," *Revue Historique* 213 (1955): 189–215.

37. Dupuy, *De la Révolution à la Chouannerie,* 24–32.

Again Egret has illuminated the conflicts over the political representation,[38] and that subject has been both greatly amplified and connected to popular mobilization by Monique Cubells.[39] Like Brittany, Provence had an intransigent noble elite hoping to use the weakening of the monarchy to reassert its claims of tradition, but in this case it was Provence's fief-holding nobles who had lost their exclusive right to speak for all the province's nobility in 1639 and now were demanding a Provincial Estates on the old model (and wished that Provincial Estates to choose Provence's delegates to the Estates-General). At the same time, elements of the urban elites who held themselves underrepresented in provincial affairs, in which Aix dominated, saw their chance. The result was an intensive campaign of petitions and counterpetitions reaching down into towns and villages as "general assemblies" of the heads of families met to pass resolutions. Cubells finds eleven villages of fewer than five hundred inhabitants demanding political representation in February 1789 (66). The provincial commandant, at one point, noting pamphlets circulating in Provençal, expressed his shock at the effort of the notables of Sisteron to "address the peasants and workers in their usual language in order to get them to take an interest in present affairs."[40]

Such efforts, it appears, not only produced an early mobilization, but one beginning to have an antiseigneurial content. Perhaps Cubells's work has a clue for us there as well. She suggests that the great division between a fief-holding group of nobles, on its way to setting a standard by which we could define the word "reactionary," and their non-fief-holding fellows, made the seigneurial regime an unusually salient element in the political struggles around the Estates-General in Provence. It is striking that Provence's spring upheavals were particularly intense during those March weeks in which rural communities were formulating their grievances, and that those grievances, to judge by Cubells's work on the extant *cahiers* of Provence, usually included the seigneurial regime, a datum we may contrast with the nationwide pattern of some quarter of parish *cahiers* not mentioning the lords.[41]

Without a regionally differentiated study of political rhetoric around the convocation that has not yet been done, it is hard to be sure if debate about the seigneurial regime really played an unusually large role in Provence's

38. Jean Egret, "La prérévolution en Provence," *Annales Historiques de la Révolution Française* (1954): 97–126.

39. Cubells, *Horizons de la liberté.*

40. Quoted in ibid., 68.

41. Eighty-eight percent of the *cahiers* Cubells found had antiseigneurial grievances. Since nearly two-thirds of the surviving documents are from a single *bailliage* (Aix), the cautions that apply to my attempts to use our own parish sample to characterize regions also apply to Cubells's study. See Table 2.2 and Cubells, *Horizons de la liberté,* 136.

elite squabbles. But it is certain that elite politics in Brittany and Provence were among the most polarized in France, perhaps the most polarized. All or a significant part of the nobility refused participation in the elections of the Estates-General in both Brittany and Provence, for example, and these were also among the most propitious provinces for early peasant action.[42] In Provence it also may be that a particular elite bitterness around fief-holding helped open the way for peasant antiseigneurialism. These are the sorts of things that some students of social movements like to call "political opportunity structure," by which they call attention to the degree to which elite activities favor grassroots actions.

But let us not push this point too far. First of all, there is an alternative explanation for Provence's early turn to antiseigneurial actions. Provence's countryside was probably unusually endowed with organizational capacities for popular mobilization, a matter I shall return to below (see p. 387). And no less important, in the spring of 1789, as we have just noted, the countryside around Paris was even more antiseigneurial than along the Mediterranean. Did being close to the center of things lead the peasants of the Ile-de-France, earlier than most, to begin to see the promise of moving against their lords? Or were longer-term forces at work here? A Tocquevillean might see, behind the spring insurrections, the heavy hand of the state apparatus, and nowhere in the countryside was it heavier than in the vicinity of the capital, destroying the moral basis for the seigneurial order. Others might see the corrosive effects of the marketplace, and nowhere in the French countryside did those effects on local structures of domination run so deep as in the vicinity of the capital. We shall take up such structural accounts of revolt below.

Let us move forward to the drama of the summer of 1789. In that greatest of peaks the action has shifted even more strongly toward the north. In the prelude of summer 1788 through early winter 1789, a mere 18% of events had taken place north and east of the Saint-Malo–Geneva line; in the hot spring 54% did; and in the hotter summer that cracked the Old Regime, 67%. As we move beyond the summer let us simplify our data to ease the intertemporal comparison of interregional comparisons. We shall be looking

42. It might be useful to contrast the situation of Brittany and, especially, Provence with Franche-Comté where a group of fief-holding nobles were similarly intransigent into the spring of 1789, holding out for a revived Provincial Estates in its seventeenth-century form as the body to name deputies to the Estates-General. But in Franche-Comté, a significant minority of fief-holding nobles rejected the intransigent actions (rather more than one-third at noble assemblies took a more accommodationist stance); the Third Estate leadership avoided alienating such moderates by soft-pedaling the seigneurial rights, a very touchy matter in this province of serfdom; and hardly anyone attempted to rouse the townsfolk, let alone the countryside. In this climate, there was very little peasant mobilization before July. See Jean Egret, "La Révolution aristocratique en Franche-Comté et son échec," *Revue d'Histoire Moderne et Contemporaine* 1 (1954): 245–71.

at those moments when particular regions were disproportionately engaged—and at what they at those moments were engaged in. We shall organize this discussion around Table 7.6, which shows the regions that are disproportionately higher in the occurrence of insurrections at particular moments. The table presents figures for only those locations in space-time in which the proportion of incidents was at least 1.25 times the overall proportion for a particular region. For example, the summer of 1789 shows a concentration of events in the area around Paris in the specific sense that during that summer its proportion of events was 1.35 times its usual proportion. We can then query our data as to the forms of action in that countryside near Paris that summer. Thus we can see the times and the ways a region was unusually active, region by region.

The summer of 1789 turns out to be the unique moment of "advanced" rural France; every northern region except Normandy disproportionately mobilized and nowhere else did. There are a number of other moments at which the Northeast or Paris region or even the usually quieter North-Center jumps forward and many at which the North is active, but at no other time are they all in the lead, with the rest of France playing a less prominent role. This northern explosion was significantly, but not predominantly, antiseigneurial. Thirty-eight percent of these northern summer events are incidents of the Great Fear; antiseigneurial events are in the second rank, now notably ahead of subsistence conflicts (30% to 13%).

By the fall of 1789 it is the Southwest that is at the cutting edge of rural action, joined a few months later by the South-Center (and the West); the Southwest and South-Center remain intensely active, most of the time, until the spring of 1792 (with a last, intense southwestern burst in the early summer). Over the 34 months from September 1789 through January 1792, 76% of these South-Central and Southwestern events were antiseigneurial.

As if a player in a southern relay team, the Southeast takes up the baton in the winter of 1792 and continues, a bit irregularly, in the forefront until the end of our period, only displaced in the fall of 1792 by the North-Central area (a burst of subsistence events)[43] and by the western counterrevolution

43. A vast movement of price control, whose epicenter was about halfway between Chartres and Le Mans was the terror of local officials in November and December 1792. A nucleus of foresters and workers from a large glassworks moved through the countryside, picking up large numbers of villagers (sometimes, it appears, coercively) and converged on the towns across some eight departments. The reported numbers are hard to believe (ten thousand assembling before Chartres on December 1, for example, a figure that, if true, must have been terrifying since the crowd would have outnumbered the townsfolk). National Guard units seem to have participated on both sides of the confrontations; local officials, no doubt with varying degrees of voluntary assent, often joined. It seems likely that previous experience was paying off in the development of an organizational capacity to mount such huge efforts whose size seems to have increased with practice. Villagers armed with axes and scythes, as in the disturbances of 1789, as Vovelle observes, now were flanked by the uniformed Guards, and were heralded by flags and drums. As if bearing portable maypoles

of March 1793. Sixty percent of southeastern events from February 1792 on are antiseigneurial; at the high point of winter 1792, 76%.

Varying combinations of northern regions intermittently join these largely southern mobilizations that followed the breakthrough of the first summer of revolution. The North and its western neighbor, Normandy, were active in the fall of 1789, as was the North in the spring of 1790, the Northeast and Paris region in the spurt of the summer of 1790, the North and Normandy again the following summer (with the North a continuing center of activity into the winter beyond that), the Paris region joining in the major wave of early 1792, an unusually intense period in the North-Center in the fall of 1792 (the subsistence actions mentioned above) and some northeastern activism in the quieter points of the first half of 1793 (joined by Normandy from April to June). The northern contributions at these moments, however, was not markedly antiseigneurial. If we only consider incidents in the northern regions and at the times just mentioned in this paragraph, a relatively scant 21% were antiseigneurial (and nearly half of this group of antiseigneurial events were from one region at one moment, the Paris area in the summer of 1790). But let us not forget that even this "scant" 21% is substantially higher than was typical of the prelude of rising rural action in the summer and fall of 1788.

Was the West a Different World?

The West[44] was relatively inactive in the wake of its very precocious leap into revolution in late 1788, but mobilized after the summer of 1789 at a steady, if lesser, level of intensity and like the South-Center, although a bit earlier, falls away in early 1792. Unlike the South-Center it makes a comeback in the late summer and maintains an engagement that, of course, peaks in March 1793. Table 7.7 displays the nature of the Western events compared to the rest of the country in the two long periods of western activism that lie between its initial, early outburst of subsistence events and the counterrevolutionary explosion. Because northern and southern France

as emblems of self-activation, the participants sported oak sprigs, especially the foresters among them. During those three weeks, the confrontations with the authorities unfolded everywhere in the same manner, but the price demanded varied, as if to suit local conditions. See Albert Mathiez, *La vie chère et le mouvement social sous la Terreur* (Paris: Payot, 1927), 104–6; and in much greater detail, Michel Vovelle, *Ville et campagne au dix-huitième siècle: Chartres et la Beauce* (Paris: Editions Sociales, 1980), 245–54. For the population of Chartres in 1789, see *Statistique de la France* (Paris: Imprimerie Royale, 1837), 270.

44. This Western trajectory is clearer in Table 7.5.

Table 7.6. Space-Time Zones Disproportionately High in Insurrections[a]

Time Period	North	Northeast	Paris Region	North-Center	South-Center	Southeast	Southwest	West	Normandy
June 1788–Jan. 1789	—	—	—	—	—	—	—	4.80	—
Mar. 1789–June 1789	2.64	—	1.46	—	—	1.38	—	—	—
July 1789–Aug. 1789	1.26	2.16	1.35	1.82	—	—	—	—	—
Sept. 1789–Dec. 1789	1.39	—	—	—	—	—	1.67	—	1.94
Jan. 1790–Feb. 1790	—	—	—	—	1.56	—	3.95	1.31	—
Mar. 1790–Apr. 1790	2.26	—	—	—	—	—	1.31	—	—
June 1790–July 1790	—	1.83	2.35	—	—	—	1.22	—	—
Sept. 1790–May 1791	—	—	—	—	1.52	—	1.77	—	—
June 1791–Aug. 1791	1.34	—	—	—	1.70	—	1.40	1.28	1.50
Sept. 1791–Jan. 1792	1.74	—	—	—	1.53	—	1.49	—	—
Feb. 1792–Apr. 1792	—	—	1.38	—	1.34	2.17	—	—	—
May 1792–July 1792	—	—	—	—	—	1.92	2.78	—	—
Aug. 1792–Sept. 1792	—	—	—	—	—	1.42	—	1.93	—
Oct. 1792–Dec. 1792	—	—	—	3.59	—	—	—	—	—
Jan. 1793–Feb. 1793	—	2.78	—	—	—	2.56	—	—	—
March 1793	—	—	—	—	—	—	—	4.74	—
Apr. 1793–June 1793	—	1.36	—	—	—	1.76	—	—	2.45

[a]Periods in which the proportion of events in a particular region was at least 1.25 times the proportion of events in that region for the entire period June 1788–June 1793. The entries in the table are such proportions.

are so different in our previous tables, I have grouped the data for the rest of France into these two very broadly conceived zones.[45]

In the period between the summer of 1789 and the spring of 1792 Westerners were less given to rise against the seigneurial regime than others were if those others are taken to be the rest of France as a whole. There is no surprise there, but if we separate those others into northerners and southerners we see that rural northern activists actually were targeting the lords even less than their western fellows. The true hard-core peasant antiseigneurialism was in the Midi. From the end of summer in 1792 antiseigneurialism was falling off nationally (see Figs. 6.3 (a)–(d)); and we now see that it falls considerably in West, North, and South alike, virtually disappearing in the West, to be sure, but not very marked in the North. Only the South was still bearing high the antiseigneurial torch—and less high than before.

In the wake of the summer breakthrough in 1789, western peasants, like those elsewhere in France, turned against the seigneurial regime.[46] Their risings were more likely to involve religious matters, but then, for this region of widely scattered farmsteads, the Sunday coming-together may well have been an almost unique moment of communal solidarity. On the other hand, conflicts that could pit the desperate against the relatively well-off over subsistence, land, or wages, were all about as common in the West as in the South up to the winter of 1792. The North, then and later, is the home of subsistence events, of panics, and of the relatively uncommon wage conflicts. And counterrevolutionary events were notably more frequent in the West well before March 1793.

So the West, like the South-Center and Southwest, takes up insurrection after the northern risings and the legislative breakthroughs of the summer of 1789, and participates in antiseigneurialism as does the rest of the country (largely in the extensive risings in eastern Brittany in the winters of 1790 and 1791).[47] But the West nonetheless has its points of distinction: these distinctive traits become only more marked in the late summer and fall of 1792. This is a period, we recall from Chapter 6 (see Figs. 6.3 (a)–(d) and 6.4), when antiseigneurialism enjoyed a final spurt, and then died away in the wake of the legislation brought about by the August overturning of the monarchy (see Chapter 8, p. 465). Land and wage events remain less characteristic of the West, and religious events more so, while subsistence

45. In Table 7.7, "North" aggregates North, Northeast, Paris Region, North-Central, and Normandy; and "South," South-Central, Southeast, and Southwest.

46. The western countryside also participated at high levels in the elections of 1790 (Melvin Edelstein, "La reception de la Révolution en Bretagne: étude électorale," paper presented at conference on Pouvoir Local et Révolution, Rennes, 1993).

47. Henri Sée, "Les troubles agraires en Haute-Bretagne, 1790–1791," *Bulletin d'Histoire Economique de la Révolution Française* (1920–21): 231–373.

Table 7.7. Western Participation in Revolution Compared to Rest of France: Insurrections of Various Types (%)

				September 1789–January 1792					
Broad Region[1]	Antiseigneurial	Religious	Subsistence	Anti-tax	Land	Wage	Panic	Counterrevolutionary	(*N*)
West	45%	34%	13%	3%	8%	0%	1%	29%	(205)
North	36	15	32	10	15	3	10	0	(442)
South	66	28	11	1	9	0	0	10	(682)
				August 1792–December 1792					
Broad Region[1]	Antiseigneurial	Religious	Subsistence	Anti-tax	Land	Wage	Panic	Counterrevolutionary	(*N*)
West	3%	14%	33%	3%	0%	0%	6%	47%	(113)
North	11	5	66	0	10	1	8	0	(166)
South	46	12	22	1	10	1	0	14	(189)

[1]For a definition of "North" and "South" in this table, see footnote 45.

events remain in between the northern and southern proportions. But western antiseigneurial action has almost completely ceased, replaced by a clear commitment to counterrevolution,[48] whose incidence continues virtually nonexistent in the North. Counterrevolution, present in the South, rises, as in the West, but only barely.

From the point of view of the prehistory of counterrevolutionary civil war historians are becoming increasingly sensitive to the degree to which actions of the revolutionary regime sparked peasant resistance. It is not always possible, indeed, to distinguish neatly between peasant violence intended to push the government to go further and peasant violence intended to push the government to go away.[49] Some historians, for example, now ask, "Why not the South also?" since some of the same circumstances that characterize the West also obtained in parts of that region as well, especially in the southern Massif Central.[50] The data we have been examining does not answer such questions but it does sharpen them. We see that West and South not only differ fairly early in their incidence of counterrevolutionary rebellion, but that the incidence rises in both—yet rises so much more steeply in western France. Western popular mobilizations against conscription, administrative reorganization, the new church of the Revolution, revolutionary taxation, and land purchase by urbanites increase sharply in an ascent as rapid as antiseigneurialism is in decline. The West's double shift—away from antiseigneurialism and toward counterrevolution—is part of the national trends,[51] yet the steepness of both shifts in the West is paralleled nowhere else.

48. An example: As late as the end of August 1792, National Guard units from two cantons burned a *château* east of Baugé at about the same time as panicky villagers nearby attacked suspected counterrevolutionaries. This was rather late for a western antiseigneurial action. A half-year later in the same vicinity, it was counterrevolutionary action that turns up in our data for March 1793. See Ado, *Krest'ianskoe dvizhenie,* 288.

49. The work of Colin Lucas on peasant "antirevolution" outside the West has been especially instructive. See Colin Lucas, "Aux sources du comportement politique de la paysannerie beaujolaise," in *La Révolution française et le monde rural* (Paris: Editions du Comité des Travaux Historiques et Scientifiques, 1989), 345–65; "Resistances populaires à la Révolution dans le sud-est," in Jean Nicolas, ed., *Mouvements populaires et conscience sociale, XVIe–XIXe siècles* (Paris: Maloine, 1985), 473–85; "The Problem of the Midi in the French Revolution," *Transactions of the Royal Historical Society* 28 (1978): 1–25.

50. See, for example, Peter Jones, *Peasantry,* 219–22. A part of the answer as to why there was no southern rural civil war amounts to a challenge to the question. In the southern Massif Central and in Provence there was, as our data confirm, a considerable number of "antirevolutionary" events as early as the summer of 1790, but local initiatives ranging from village strike forces in the departments of Lozère and Ardèche to the National Guard units of Marseille kept organized counterrevolution from securing control of the countryside. In other words, there was a rural civil war in the southern hill country, but the whites did not achieve the same successes as they were to have in, say, Anjou.

51. Melvin Edelstein's demonstration of widespread falloff in electoral participation by country people between early 1790 (when they were generally outvoting the urbanites) and mid-1791 may

There is yet another way we might attempt to look for western distinctiveness: did the western countryside differ in the extent of peasant antiseigneurialism in the *cahiers* of spring 1789? Our sample of parish documents, unfortunately, was designed for national statements, not regional ones,[52] and I have therefore made little use of these documents for interregional comparisons in this book. In the West, the sample includes some 79 parishes drawn from five *bailliages* (Quimper, Concarneau, Rennes, Angers, Château-du-Loir). There is no reason to see this as a sample well suited to characterize the West (not the purpose of its design), but it is our only way of even approaching the question, a question subject to some debate in previous research. Paul Bois's study of the *département* of the Sarthe anticipates Roger Dupuy in finding an initial antiseigneurialism to be by no means incompatible with a later support for counterrevolution. The subregions whose *cahiers* were more strongly hostile to the lords, he shows, were also generally those where counterrevolution took hold.[53] Bois is led to stress the unfolding of a political process: "It is not what the country people thought of the nobility and clergy in 1789 that is going to determine their attitude to the Revolution a few years later" (219). But further to the south, Charles Tilly, equally persuasively, shows that subregions producing the more antiseigneurial *cahiers* remained loyal to the Revolution when push came to shove in 1793, a finding he uses to attack, with some vigor, the notion that western peasants initially welcomed the Revolution, then turned on it.[54] Accepting as equally valid the data of both Bois and Tilly should, in itself, suggest that there probably is no general relationship at all of a collective position on seigneurial rights in the spring of 1789 in the *cahiers* and subsequent assumption of the risks of violent confrontation of one sort or another down the road.[55]

If we are willing, with however many grains of salt, to let the grievances of our five western *bailliages* represent the West early in the Revolution, this is the conclusion about the West that one comes to: neither the Bois nor the Tilly pattern are general. The data, for what they are worth, are not consistent with the picture of a western peasantry on a different course than

well, as he suggests, similarly indicate a widespread peasant disenchantment. See Melvin Edelstein, "Electoral Behavior During the Constitutional Monarchy (1790–1701): A 'Community' Interpretation," in Renée Waldinger, Philip Dawson, and Isser Woloch, *The French Revolution and the Meaning of Citizenship* (Westport, Conn.: Greenwood, 1993), 105–21. For a similar interpretation of rural voting, focused on the heartland of the coming counterrevolution, see Charles Tilly, "Some Problems in the History of the Vendée," *American Historical Review* 67 (1961): 29.

52. Gilbert Shapiro and John Markoff, *Revolutionary Demands: A Content Analysis of the Cahiers de Doléances of 1789* (Stanford: Stanford University Press, 1997), chap. 12.

53. Bois, *Paysans de l'Ouest,* 190–219.

54. Tilly, *Vendée,* 175–86.

55. For a more detailed exploration of the relationship of *cahiers* grievances and the revolts of spring and summer see Markoff, "Peasant Grievances and Peasant Insurrection."

the rest of the country from the very beginning. The western parishes in our sample appear no less focused on the seigneurial regime in their *cahiers:* 84% of our western parishes address the seigneurial regime as compared to 77% for France as a whole (see Table 2.2), the mean number of relevant demands among those *cahiers* treating the regime is 7 compared to 6 for France as a whole (see Table 2.3). The westerners also seem no less hostile to those seigneurial institutions discussed: 39% of their demands are calls for abolition without compensation as compared to 36% for the entire kingdom (see Table 3.1). While the uncertain character of the sample and the variation of the *bailliages* within it,[56] make any claim for great accuracy here unwarranted, the data are consonant with Dupuy's sense of a fluid situation, of a live western antiseigneurialism. At the onset of revolution, if we credit the data, the western countryside was not less antiseigneurial than anywhere else.

It appears that the West's course diverged from the rest not so much by being utterly different, but by going further and faster along a road followed elsewhere as well.[57] What happened in the West, then, was not simply just there from the beginning, but evolved as country people evaluated changing situations, including changes brought about by their own previous actions.[58]

Northern France Falls Quiet

Intense engagement of the northern and eastern countryside was far more episodic. The Northeast, the most intensely mobilized area in the summer of 1789 with 264 events, 140 of them antiseigneurial, became far less active, except for a few episodes, practically dropping out of the Revolution as Michel Vovelle remarks.[59] In the summer of 1790 there was a wave of panics, although nothing on the scale of the Great Fear, and a sprinkling of antiseigneurial events; at a number of points in 1793 it was the prime location of land conflicts, but the usual state of the Northeast compared to

56. The parishes we have sampled from Château-du-Loir are strikingly less prone to antiseigneurial grievances than the others.

57. Donald Sutherland's general history of the Revolution assigns a central place to just such a widespread and increasing tempo of plebeian resistance to revolutionary authority in counterpoint with growing revolutionary radicalism, as noted in his title: *France 1789–1815: Revolution and Counterrevolution* (New York: Oxford University Press, 1986). For an interpretation of the Vendée in such terms see Gérard, *Pourquoi la Vendée?*

58. A depiction of a Brittany where antiseigneurialism is succeeded by counterrevolution, rather than an inevitably counterrevolutionary province just needing a good occasion to reveal its essential nature, is a central theme of Roger Dupuy's *De la Révolution à la Chouannerie*.

59. Vovelle poses the "apparent docility" of parts of the Northeast as an unresolved question *(La découverte de la politique,* 90).

the rest of the country was relatively calm. Recall that I found no incidents at all in 46% of northeastern *bailliages* (see Table 7.1), a much greater rate than any other region. But North-Central France is hardly more engaged after that first summer, apart from a subsistence wave in the fall of 1792. And even the Paris region, intensely active through the spring and summer of 1789, yields pride of place to the South at most points thereafter. The North is more often active, although intermittently so, into early 1792.

The rural revolution differed in its intensity and its mix of actions at different times and places. If northern France was the prime location of the insurrectionary thrust of the summer of 1789, the same could hardly be said for the previous autumn in which the West had taken the lead or the spring in which the Paris area, alone in the North, vied with the Southeast.[60] And beyond that summer the South-Center and Southwest dominated until early 1792, succeeded by the Southeast and the Western counterrevolution with a sporadically, if significantly, engaged northern France. To be sure, for certain kinds of events, northern France was usually the center: the wage struggles around Paris and the North, land struggles in the Northeast, anti-tax battles in the North and Normandy, subsistence conflicts in Normandy (and stretching west to the North and south through the Paris region through north-central France). But the largest component of the rural revolution as a whole, the antiseigneurial movement, was not only not primarily a Paris-centric phenomenon, it was not even primarily northern, except at one crucial moment. After the summer of 1789, northern France struggled on over food supplies, over land, over wages on occasion, and mobilized in local panics. The antiseigneurial battle was largely elsewhere.

Local Contexts and Forms of Revolt in the Summer of 1789

France as a Laboratory

The shifting regional patterns of revolt posed many problems to those in Versailles and Paris who thought the Revolution an opportunity to remold France according to their own vision. But it constitutes an opportunity for later scholars. We may utilize the regional diversity in order to explore the plausibility of many hypotheses about the generation of revolt. Did long-

60. A reader who took to heart the only reference to "Peasants, revolt of" in the index to the classic history by Mathiez would be profoundly misled by the statement that the Paris region was the epicenter of the rural revolution. See Albert Mathiez, *The French Revolution* (New York: Grosset and Dunlap, 1964), 51.

term structural changes in the elaboration of the market or the development of the state so shape the interests and organizational possibilities of France's villagers as to motivate them to revolt and provide them the means to do so? We may look to regions where the market was more pervasive or where the hand of the growing state clutched more tightly and see if those are indeed the places of revolt. Did enduring patterns of social organization make it easier for some to organize revolt than others? We may see if the clustered settlements of the Northeast or the larger semi-autonomous communities in the South facilitated action. Did rising literacy reshape consciousness in the countryside? Was the extent of economic hardship decisive for mobilizations?

Such hypotheses, which abound in the literature on the French Revolution (as they do in the growing comparative literature), can be investigated, treating the great variety of local structures and circumstance as if France were a sort of laboratory for studying the effects of different situations, but with several important cautions. First of all, we have seen that rural contestation changes in form and in location as we move through the five years covered by our data. So we need to be careful in attempting to distinguish structures and circumstances that raise the likelihood of revolt generally from those that raise the likelihood of specific forms of insurrection. We also need to distinguish aspects of French social structure that nurture revolt throughout our period from those that only apply at some points in time but not others. Explanations of attacks on the lords that are based on the insurrectionary geography of the summer of 1789, for example, may be wildly misleading because the geography shifts so profoundly afterward, as we have just seen. Second, we need to consider the contagious aspect of insurrectionary waves: one revolt stimulates others as the repressive forces appear weaker than previously known, as those forces are actually weakened by failure, and as organizational possibilities and tactics are debated and knowledge of successful organizational models and tactics becomes widely diffused. That a group of nearby villages all engage in anti-tax revolt may not just be a sign that a particular region produces conditions conducive to anti-tax struggles but that an initial success is taken up by others who might have been initially inclined to attack the local monastery before they heard that taxes were a promising target. Or the news that the local National Guard helped the next parish's young men seize the nearby *château* might lead some villagers to see previously unexpected opportunities in forming their own Guards unit.

Regional structures, then, may channel actions one way rather than another but these effects may then be magnified locally or regionally or perhaps even nationally by example. If villagers near a large town follow the inspiring example of neighboring villages and burn the local *château,* the impact of that large town nearby on the propensity to revolt, while real, appears magnified in the data because some of those nearby *château* burnings are the work of peasants emulating others. On the other hand, if knowledge of *château* burnings sparks similar actions throughout France, the real impact of those big towns will appear attenuated in our data because distant villages in less urbanized areas may be following the lead of their more urbanized fellows. There are statistical techniques, none perfect, for attempting to separate such contagion processes from the effects of town size or other structural and conjunctural elements that have been developed, mostly by geographers, but I shall not present such a complex analysis here, and merely suggest a certain caution in interpreting the figures that follow. But we must bear in mind that the unfolding of revolution is a process, is a series of choices in which insurrection is significantly shaped by the responses of local lords, district and departmental officials, and Parisian legislators, and in which information on elite views and actions and on the fate of other villagers' actions changes daily. The processual side of revolution may make a judicious weighting of the role of local context quite difficult.

Let us take as our point of departure the period of most intense activity of the entire five years, the summer of 1789. (We shall look beyond that critical summer later.) Table 7.8 examines several indicators of the contexts within which the forms of rural mobilization were nurtured. For each of the indicators of France's political, economic, and social circumstances employed here, I present some indication of its relationship with each of the types of rural event other than the wage events, scarce that summer, and counterrevolution, which flourished later. I shall adopt the simplest possible mode of presentation: Each indicator shall be treated as a simple dichotomy. Continuous variables (such as the proportion of men signing marriage documents) have been dichotomized at the median. To continue the example of male literacy: *bailliages* are classified as "low" or "high" on this variable according to whether the proportion of men signing is below or above .51. Among those *bailliages* in the low and in the high groups, I compute the proportion that experienced each form of rising. Continuing the same example, we see that among *bailliages* of relatively low male literacy 63% experienced the Great Fear, whereas among the more literate districts, the frequency of events of this sort drops to 43% (a statistically significant decline).[61] Such significant differences may be positive or negative. While

61. These figures are based on a much more extensive body of data than I used in several earlier articles on the revolts of 1789: these figures, then, have more incidents of more varieties of insurrection in more places more finely classified than the earlier data. While most of the claims about the geography of revolt of the earlier research are confirmed by this more thorough data, I shall indicate a few points where my previous published results must be modified. See John Markoff, "The Social Geography of Rural Revolt at the Beginning of the French Revolution," *American Sociological Review* 50 (1985): 761–81; and "Contexts and Forms of Rural Revolt: France in 1789," in *Journal of Conflict Resolution* 30 (1986): 253–89.

literacy significantly depresses panics, male literacy significantly augments anti-tax events. The asterisks that indicate such statistically significant differences[62] may help pull the reader's eye toward those places in the table where something can be said most confidently. (But patterns in weaker relationships may be worth thinking about as well.)

For some of the variables used, dichotomization at the median is not meaningful because the variables are dichotomous by definition. Whether or not a *bailliage* was in the broad northern and eastern belt of openfield farming, for example, was coded as a simple dichotomy to begin with. In such instances, the high category in Table 7.8 indicates "presence" and the low, "absence." The data presented in this table and most later tables in this chapter have been computed for all *bailliages* of metropolitan France having rural parishes (as in Chapters 5 and 6).[63] The literacy variables, exceptionally, have some missing data.

The Misery Thesis

Let us now consider the plausible proposals for the roots of the rural upheaval. The sheer level of misery in 1789 has always received attention. C. E. Labrousse's path-breaking work[64] on the economic structure of the Old Regime set forth a particularly cogent version of this thesis. Labrousse presents a theoretical model and much empirical evidence for the central role of cereal prices in the economy of the Old Regime. Labrousse contended that in an economy of the "old type," a concept he magnificently elaborated, food prices were the key to popular well-being. When food prices rose, for example, the erosion of disposable income meant the collapse of industrial production. Artisans in urban workshops and rural producers in cottages were alike in their loss of livelihood. Moreover, Labrousse urges, since grains were the major item in diet and since other grain prices varied in tandem with the price of wheat,[65] we may take the reasonably good price series for wheat as a measure of aggregate misery. As for the Revolution

62. The statistical tests used were Fisher's Exact Test (two-tailed) when the numbers were very small and chi-square corrected for continuity (two-tailed) otherwise.

63. See above, Chapter 5. Some of the data were initially coded by *bailliage*. Other series were recorded for the postrevolutionary *départements;* in these latter cases, *bailliage* approximations were computed; see John Markoff and Gilbert Shapiro, "The Linkage of Data Describing Overlapping Geographical Units," *Historical Methods Newsletter* 7 (1973): 34–66. For the price data, *bailliages* were assigned the value of the *généralité* in which they are located.

64. Camille-Ernest Labrousse, *Esquisse du mouvement des prix et des revenus en France au XVIIIe siècle* (Paris: Librairie Dalloz, 1933).

65. If wheat prices rose, people shifted to rye, driving up that price as well—and so on for even less desirable grains. For data on the similar price trajectories of various cereal grains, see Labrousse, *Equisse*.

Table 7.8. Forms of Rural Mobilization by Social Contexts, July 1789–August 1789 (% of *Bailliages* with Particular Forms)

	Antiseigneurial		Religious		Anti-tax		Subsistence		Land		Panic	
Value of dichotomized variable listed below	Low	High	Low	High	Low	High	Low	High	Low	High	Low	High
Size of largest town	9%	18%*	3%	11%*	3%	11%*	10%	27%****	2%	6%	31%	62%****
Length of road	8	24****	6	12*	4	14***	14	32****	2	8*	44	64****
Number of road intersections	10	21**	5	12*	5	13**	14	31****	2	7*	52	54
Administrative centralization (*pays d'états/pays d'élections)*	15	16	14	5**	5	12*	16	27*	6	4	38	64****
Percentage of men signing marriage documents	16	16	9	9	5	13**	20	26	5	5	63	43****
Percentage of women signing marriage documents	15	16	7	11	7	12	19	27	4	6	64	42****
Proportion arable	21	13	12	7	7	10	11	28***	4	5	67	46****
Proportion grassland	6	18**	2	11*	8	9	35	19**	1	6	57	52
Proportion wasteland	14	18	8	9	11	6	28	14**	6	3	44	66****
Proportion planted in vines	18	14	8	9	11	8	30	18**	5	4	37	64****
Proportion woodland	16	15	7	10	10	8	27	18*	4	5	51	56
Wheat yield	16	15	8	10	9	9	19	25	4	5	61	46**
Rye yield	16	14	8	10	9	9	17	29**	4	5	59	46*

Openfield	21	10**	8	10	9	10	18	28*	5	5	61	44***
Plains other than openfield	15	20	9	7	9	9	24	10*	5	5	50	71**
Mountain	11	22**	7	11	8	10	24	19	5	5	50	59
Olives	16	15	9	8	9	4	23	12	4	8	52	65
Almonds	16	15	9	8	9	4	23	15	4	7	52	67
Nucleated villages: More than 60% live in central place	18	14	5	12*	9	9	23	23	4	5	59	50
Nucleated villages: More than 90% live in central place	17	3	9	7	9	10	24	14	5	3	57	28**
Migration	17	14	8	9	10	8	19	26	3	7	50	56
Price of wheat, 1789	18	13	9	8	10	8	20	24	4	5	40	64****
Increase in price of wheat over lowest value from 1784 to 1788	17	14	6	11	8	10	21	24	5	4	59	46**

Notes: All variables, except for ability to sign, are measured for 412 cases. Ability to sign is measured for 400.

Coding dichotomous variables: Administrative centralization: "High" = *Pays d'élections*; Openfield, Plains other than openfield, etc.: "High" = in region.

Migration: "High" indicates net emigration.

Sources of variables are given in the text and notes that follow.

*$p < .05$
**$p < .01$
***$p < .001$
****$p < .0001$

in particular, Labrousse lays great weight on the immediate economic circumstances: the *conjoncture.*[66]

It is certainly noteworthy that want does not seem strongly linked to any form of mobilization apart from the Great Fear (see the last two rows in Table 7.8).[67] Even the relationship with conflict over food supply is rather weak. Hunger or the fear of hunger may have nurtured the Great Fear; it does not seem a potent source of the attacks on the central human institutions of material exactions: the lord, the church, the state. On the other hand, price rises might have raised local fears of raids on ripening grain, thereby setting an anxious stage for talk of nonexistent raids in late July.[68]

What might be rather more surprising to some students of revolts are the associations of *increases* in the price of wheat or rather the lack of such associations. The view that sheer misery accounts for social upheaval has often been challenged as hopelessly naive. A variety of alternate proposals have been put forward that share the notion that past experience provides a basis for future expectations.[69] In this view, what we should examine is not so much difficult straits as deteriorating circumstances. This line of thought suggests attention not so much—perhaps, not at all—to prices in 1789, but rather to price increases.[70] The evidence gives absolutely no support to this

66. Data on wheat prices from 1756 to 1790 are presented in Labrousse (*Esquisse,* 106–13). The data were initially collected by the Bureau des Subsistances on a semiweekly or weekly basis for a county-size administrative district, the *subdélégation.* These data formed the basis for the computation of unweighted means for the larger *généralité,* the basic administrative division of the Old Regime; Labrousse presents a table of annual *généralité* averages dredged out of the archives in the course of the Convention's debates on food policies in 1792. Although the *bailliage* is a much smaller unit, I assigned a *bailliage* the mean price for its *généralité.* This is probably not a serious distortion, for Labrousse has shown that nearby areas had very similar price trajectories (no doubt a consequence of the extent of market integration). Restriction to annual means, however, is unfortunate; the best measure of the hardship of the summer of 1789 would use a seasonal, not an annual, figure. See Labrousse's painstaking evaluation of the quality of the data (*Esquisse,* 16–85). A few details: I ignore the data Labrousse's source gives for "Bayonne," which was not a *généralité,* and which was administratively reassigned several times in various reorganizations of the administrative structure of the Southwest; I assume that "Hainaut" refers to the *généralité* of Valenciennes, including Cambrésis as well as Hainaut; I treat "Lyon and Dombes" as if it describes the *généralité* of Lyon alone of which Dombes was not a part.

67. Since most rural people experienced want much of the time, a more precise, if cumbersome formulation would be that *variations* in the level of misery as indicated by prices do not seem to explain much of the *variation* in the outbreak of open conflict.

68. It is worth noting that fears over scarcity are assigned great importance in Clay Ramsay's recent study of the Great Fear around Soissons (Ramsay, *Ideology of the Great Fear,* 3–51).

69. See Davies, "J-curve," Gurr, *Why Men Rebel;* Feieraband and Feierband, "Aggressive Behavior."

70. Charles Tilly, "Reflections on the Revolutions of Paris: An Essay on Recent Historical Writing," *Social Problems* 12 (1964): 99–121, for a critique of the "misery thesis"; see also David Snyder and Charles Tilly, "Hardship and Collective Violence in France, 1830–1960," *American Sociological Review* (1972): 520–32.

view. On the contrary, the only significant relationship of price increase and mobilization is actually negative.[71] What appears to be happening is that the largest price increases are in those areas of generally lower prices, which remain relatively low in 1789. The level of shortage rather than its contrast with some prior state seems to be what accounts for such impact as there is.

Involvement in Markets and Struggles over Food Supply

The price of grain does not even have a statistically significant effect in directing mobilization toward securing food. This is strikingly consistent with Louise Tilly's observations of other waves of subsistence events.[72] She suggested that it was not so much starvation as it was the actual possibility of relief in the face of shortages that triggered food riots. Starving peasants, with no food in sight, one may suggest grimly, starve; but hungry peasants through whose parish passes a grain convoy may well attack it. This is borne out by Table 7.8. Examine the conditions associated with subsistence events. The major roads whose *length* and *number of intersections* were counted were traveled by the convoys. The grain, of foreign or French origin, required armed guards to escort it to its intended destination, the major towns (a presence likewise strongly associated with subsistence events).

Note also that grain-producing regions are likewise riot-producing ones. *Bailliages* with much arable land, or relatively prosperous and cereal-producing openfield farms, are prone to subsistence events; whereas districts with significant wine production or extensive stock-raising (indicated by grassland), with considerable wasteland, covered with forests or in the plains south and west of the openfield country are notably deficient in such disturbances. If local visibility of grain is critical for subsistence events, one might also expect subsistence events to be associated with high yields of wheat and rye. The association with rye does appear, but the effect of high wheat yields, if any, is not statistically significant. The absence of a significant relationship with wheat yields is the one element in the data not consistent with the general picture. In short, the areas torn by food riots are those in which there was food—because grain was shipped there, through there, or from there.

71. The particular measure of price increase was the percentage by which the price of wheat had increased in 1789 over its lowest value since 1784. I experimented with other price-increase measures selected on the basis of plausible reference points for contrasting the miserable present with a less miserable remembered past, which is the psychological mechanism invoked in much of the literature. The relationships differ in size but generally show the same negative sign as the one presented here.

72. Louise A. Tilly, "The Food Riot as a Form of Political Conflict in France," *Journal of Interdisciplinary History* 2 (1972): 23–57.

Some communities might be more sensitive to food supply issues than others. Two decades of research on English food riots suggests that in the countryside it was those who worked in rural industry who were especially sensitive to the market and hence especially prone to engage in collective action.[73] A growing western involvement in rural textile production, especially in Normandy, saw many families with a member or two involved in cottage industries. Part-time peasants, with some weaving in the off-season, had been shifting into full-time manufacturing and were struck a double blow in the economic crises of the 1780s. In one of the Old Regime's rare triumphs for those who would radically dismantle state controls of economic life, the commercial treaty of 1786 with Britain opened the French market to British textiles, taking effect the following year.[74] Rural purchasing power was almost at once dealt an even more devastating blow in the form of miserable harvests at the end of the 1780s. This catastrophe completed the shutting down of textile manufacture in northwestern France, with especially difficult consequences in Normandy. At the same time as employment fell, food prices skyrocketed in a Norman countryside increasingly populated by ex-peasants cut off from whatever protection might still be alive in agricultural communities.[75] Perhaps the special affinity of Normandy and subsistence events[76] is thereby explained.

Finally, we note that regions characterized by *administrative centralization* are also prone to subsistence disturbance. Let us consider that variable's import for conflicts over food supply in conjunction with the expansion of the national state and the national market.

State, Market, and Insurrection in Summer 1789

Tocqueville's is the classic argument to the effect that the Revolution was the culmination of a centuries-long struggle of the central authority against

73. John Bohstedt, "The Moral Economy and the Discipline of Historical Context," *Journal of Social History* 26 (1992): 265–84.

74. J. F. Bosher argues that this treaty was far less of a significant factor in the economic hardship than was believed at the time, but even in this view the treaty came to be an emblem of an uncaring state, wholly failing in its responsibilities to provide. See J. F. Bosher, *The Single Duty Project: A Study of the Movement for a French Customs Union in the Eighteenth Century* (London: Athlone, 1969), 82–83.

75. On the social transformation of the countryside around Rouen, see William Reddy, *The Rise of Market Culture: The Textile Trade and French Society, 1750–1900* (Cambridge: Cambridge University Press, 1984); and Gay Gullickson, *The Spinners and Weavers of Auffay: Rural Industry and the Sexual Division of Labor in a French Village, 1750–1850* (Cambridge: Cambridge University Press, 1986).

76. See above, Table 7.4. Cynthia Bouton's work shows Normandy to be the region most prone to subsistence disturbances throughout most of the history of this form of conflict from the late seventeenth century into the early nineteenth, which suggests a specific regional culture of revolt even more than it does a consistent outcome of environment on forms of conflict. See Cynthia

wielders of autonomous power. As the increasingly bureaucratized agencies of the Crown seized control of road building, taxation, and policing, as they acquired the capacity to raise and equip a centrally controlled military apparatus, as they nibbled away at the political and judicial authority of the lords, they destroyed the moral basis for whatever legitimacy local elites might once have possessed. The lords no longer had duties, and their privileges were thereby rendered intolerable. To pay seigneurial dues to someone who in turn provided military defense, poor relief, access to markets, maintenance of roads, and police activity had been one thing; for Tocqueville, the military and political erosion of the lord's role turned a servant of the common good into a legalized thief. By the late eighteenth century, the expansion of central authority had not only deprived the locally dominant strata of their own coercive resources but had removed from them as well any moral claims to the allegiance of the countryside. The local lords were now entirely dependent on the state; when the judicial and military structures of that central authority foundered in the political crisis of 1789, the peasants threw off the vestiges of a local social world whose vitality had been sapped by the Paris-centered bureaucracy.

Sasha Weitman's[77] exploration of Tocqueville's thesis suggests one way to measure the differential extent of central control. About one-third of France still had functioning provincial estates in which many public functions were carried out by regional authorities. Although these areas, the *pays d'états,* differed a good deal from one another in the extent of provincial self-rule, as well as in the composition of their Provincial Estates, they all retained some measure of autonomy. The *pays d'élections,* on the other hand, had an administrative structure dominated by a centrally appointed bureaucrat. The hypothesis to be examined here, then, is that the rural upheaval was nurtured by the pressures of the central administration, felt most heavily in the *pays d'élections.*[78]

Bouton, "Region and Regionalism: The Case of France," paper presented to the 1994 meetings of the American Historical Association, San Francisco.

77. Sasha Weitman, "Bureaucracy, Democracy and the French Revolution" (Ph.D. diss., Washington University, 1968).

78. For a few ambiguous cases my *pays d'états/pays d'élections* classification followed that of Weitman with one exception. He classifies as *pays d'états* several regions which properly speaking lacked Provincial Estates: Metz, Lorraine, and Alsace. These provinces—known as *pays conquis* or *pays d'impositions*—were relatively recent acquisitions of the French Crown and lacked the identifying institutions of both Estates and *élections.* I follow his argument that these regions preserved many of their forms of self-government and are therefore more like *pays d'états* than *pays d'élections* for the purposes of the present analysis (see Weitman, "Bureaucracy, Democracy and the French Revolution," 445). But I did not classify Dauphiné among the *pays d'états,* since its Provincial Estates were explicitly abolished in 1628. The defiant convocation of the Provincial Estates there in 1788 was a significant act in the movement toward revolution. On the other hand, although Provence also had its Provincial Estates suspended from 1639 to the crisis, it retained a rather differently constituted provincial administration under a different name. For a survey of the

Table 7.8 suggests a mixed evaluation of this hypothesis. On the one hand, anti-tax events, subsistence events, and the Great Fear are indeed more common in the regions where the hand of Paris fell most heavily. In the specific instance of disturbances over food, to return to this very important arena of conflict, this is especially easy to understand. The government's involvement in provisioning undoubtedly made the government a plausible target in the event of shortages. Louise Tilly has rather effectively shown the sense in which the food riots of the eighteenth century may even be seen as movements of resistance against the increasing authority of the central state apparatus.[79] More recently, the leading scholar of the government's provisioning policy has made a strong case that the very attempts of the government to intervene in the economy to avoid the likelihood of the dangerous social disorders that often followed in the wake of shortages were themselves a source of the widespread belief that the government itself was part and parcel of a plot by holders of grain to enrich themselves at the expense of the people—a cast of mind he calls "the famine plot persuasion."[80] In this light, it is not surprising that social disturbances over food were more probable where the hand of the state was most visible.

The Great Fear, too, is markedly more common in the *pays d'élections*. In the occurrence of those panics, perhaps we can see the consequences of a general loss of reassurance in the capacities of authority to provide: In the crisis of 1789 the national authorities were clearly lacking; and, if we follow Tocqueville, to the extent that Parisian tutelage had supplanted or undermined either the sense of responsibility of or the deference due to the locally dominant strata, there is little wonder at the upsurge of this most spectacular form of local action in self-defense improvised from below. At least, following Tocqueville again, one may conjecture that publicly active Provincial Estates provided some sense of reassurance that someone up there might know what to do. Georges Lefebvre has made the analogous suggestion that the relative freedom of Brittany from the Great Fear was due to the perceived efficacy of the municipal authorities, an efficacy demonstrated not so much in avoiding as in actively making the municipal revolution.[81]

---

evolution of the powers of the various Provincial-Estates, see Maurice Bordes, *L'administration provinciale et municipale en France au XVIIIe siècle* (Paris: Société d'Edition d'Enseignement Supérieur, 1972), 66–115.

79. "The Food Riot as Political Conflict."

80. S. L. Kaplan, *The Famine Plot Persuasion in Eighteenth-Century France* (Philadelphia: American Philosophical Society, 1982).

81. *La Grande Peur de 1789* (Paris: Armand Colin, 1970), 182. Lynn Hunt, however, doubts any relation of muncipal revolution and Great Fear; see her "Committees and Communes: Local Politics and National Revolution in 1789," *Comparative Studies in Society and History* 18 (1976): 333.

On the other hand, it is equally striking that the data appear to indicate that direct attacks on the representatives of the major social institutions of the Old Regime were no more likely in the *pays d'élections* than in the *pays d'états*—apart from the case of governmental institutions themselves, specifically in the form of anti-tax revolt. If we read Tocqueville's thesis not as asserting a general social malaise as the consequence of central bureaucratic encroachments upon traditional institutions, but rather as insisting upon a rather specific undermining of the legitimacy of the position of the local lords, we must admit that we see no evidence in the actions of the peasants in 1789. In the *pays d'élections* there is no special tendency to attack seigneurial institutions. As for invasions of monasteries and manhandling of bishops, such events were actually more characteristic of the *pays d'états.* I offer tentatively the speculation that this latter occurence may arise from the unusually heavy weight of the tithe relative to other material burdens in the extensive southern provinces of Provence and Languedoc that were endowed with Provincial Estates or the equivalent.

If we consider the payments due the tax authorities rather than the demands of lord or church, however, as we have just noted, the picture changes. There is a small but significant tendency for anti-tax actions to be more common in the *pays d'élections.* Perhaps this is nothing more than a consequence of the greater general taxation level that prevailed where Provincial Estates did not function to mitigate somewhat the insatiable cravings of the tax system. But we may recall that rather than a diffuse anti-tax mobilization throughout highly taxed regions, we were able to show above that anti-tax actions early in the Revolution clustered along the boundaries of very different taxed provinces (see pp. 348–51). Thus it is not the weight of taxes as such that explains the location of revolt, but either the resentments or the organization born of resentment and opportunity where low and high taxes are found together. (Is this why the difference in anti-tax events between the *pays d'états* and *pays d'élections* is not much greater than it is?)[82]

Whatever it was that impelled peasants to attack ecclesiastical institutions in the *pays d'états* and tax institutions in the *pays d'élections,* there is no significant effect of the heaviness of the hand of the state on antiseigneurial risings,[83] not, at any rate, in the summer of 1789. If any Tocquevillean

82. It would be interesting to see whether areas of Languedoc or Provence with similar tithe levels but different traditions of resistance are different in anti-tithe actions in 1789, but the microvariability of tithe assessments and the invisibility of much of the resistance makes an analysis that parallels the tax analysis here very difficult and I have not attempted it.

83. Since anti-tithe and anti-tax actions are so interestingly associated with the weight of tithes and taxation at the crisis point in the summer of 1789, it is unfortunate that the measurement of the weight of the seigneurialism proved recalcitrant. It is difficult to summarize the available research on a national scale. There are too many different sorts of seigneurial rights, some of which particular

process was discrediting the lords, it does not seem more marked, that summer, in the specific locales of greatest state direction.

From the state, we turn to the market. The presence of towns and roads does more than nurture subsistence events. The most consistently strong relationships for all forms of mobilization are with city size[84] and road length.[85] The propensity to rural mobilization of the *bailliages* with city size above the median is double (or more) that of those below for every type of event; the impact of road length is almost as marked. City size, like length of major roads, is a strong indication of market involvement. The growing towns of the eighteenth century were transforming rural life. Urban demand for food, clothing, fuel, and building materials had repercussions in the countryside. Food production was geared toward urban markets;[86] merchants turned from the urban guilds to an unorganized rural labor force whose agricultural income, moreover, facilitated lower wages;[87] and values rose, as urbanites sought land for commercial profit or for the prestige associated with "living nobly," as the eighteenth-century expression had it,

---

historians may attempt to measure in particular regions—if they have the documents; there is great variability from one seigneurie to another in the same province, or even one household to another in the same seigneurie; large areas with little relevant research (such as Alsace); large areas with very contradictory claims in the existing research (such as Brittany). It is surely the most important missing element in the analysis presented in this chapter.

84. *City Size:* The most complete list of city populations is "Populations des villes suivant les états envoyés par Messieurs les intendants de Province, années 1787–1789. Eléments ayant servi à la formation des Etats de Population du Royaume de France" (Archives Nationales, Série Div bis, Dossier 47). A second source, identical to the *Etats de Population* for those cities on both lists, is Ministère des Travaux Publics, de l'Agriculture et du Commerce, *Statistique de la France* (Paris: Imprimerie Royale, 1837). The population of several other towns or cities may be found in Gérard Walter, *Répertoire de l'histoire de la Révolution française (travaux publics de 1800 à 1940),* vol. 2, *Lieux* (Paris: Bibliothèque Nationale, 1951). For urban places of known location that do not appear in these sources, it was assumed that any estimate was better than an implicit assumption of zero population. Such places were assigned the mean value of those cases located in Walter but not given in either of the first two sources (taking the Walter group as representative of smaller places).

City Location: Brette's maps were used to locate towns in *bailliages.* The following works also helped in this: Beatrice F. Hyslop, *Répertoire critique des cahiers de doléances pour les états généraux de 1789* (Paris: Ministère de l'Education Nationale, 1933) and *Supplément au répertoire critique des cahiers de doléances pour les états généraux de 1789* (Paris: Ministère de l'Education Nationale, 1952); Paul Joanne, *Dictionnaire géographique et administratif de la France et de ses colonies* (Paris: Hachette, 1890); and Ludovic Lalanne, *Dictionnaire historique de la France* (Geneva: Slatkine-Megariotis Reprints, 1977).

85. Length of major road and number of intersections were coded from a map of *routes postales* from the Year Five reproduced in Pierre Vidal de la Blache, *Tableau de la géographie de la France* (Paris: Hachette, 1911), 379. A photographic enlargement was overlaid with a transparency with *bailliage* outlines and the length of the road was measured in arbitrary units.

86. Steven L. Kaplan, *Provisioning Paris* (Ithaca: Cornell University Press, 1984).

87. Peter Kriedte, Hans Medick, and Jürgen Schlumbohm, *Industrialization Before Industrialization: Rural Industry in the Genesis of Capitalism* (Cambridge: Cambridge University Press, 1981), 13–23.

now that commercial profits were already made. These transformations were experienced as pressures on rural communities as the powerful attempted to expand their holdings.

The lords had a variety of mechanisms at their disposal for responding to market opportunities. The seigneurial rights could be utilized not merely to increase the lords' revenues, but to force the peasants to sell. Obscure claims could be revived or invented with the advice of a class of legal specialists; arrears could be allowed to pile up in order to demand an unpayable sum; the right of option could be employed to compel a seller of land to sell to the lord.[88]

If these market-oriented regions were socially explosive it was because they were the location not of one particular conflict, but of many. Peasant communities attempted to defend themselves from profit-seeking secular lords and landholding monasteries; the hungry confronted the administrators of the urban-oriented grain supply system; former agriculturalists who had shifted into the growing rural industries had interests that were very different from those of prosperous peasants who produced a surplus; scarcities set the threatened inhabitants of the countryside against the threatened inhabitants of the towns. Exacerbated by severe hardship and the breakdown of authority, these multiple tensions bred not one, but many forms of collective mobilization.

Table 7.8 demonstrates the great significance of economic integration into larger structures. The most consistently efficacious promoters of the several forms of rural upheaval appear to be a large nearby town and a stretch of good road. Road length is the only variable in the entire table associated with all forms of conflict. A great deal passes over those roads of consequences to the country people. On those roads and near those towns market dependence had eroded anything resembling subsistence production; hard times were potential catastrophes. To return to our discussion of food supply: larger town size is noteworthy for the generation of subsistence events. Is this not a clear outcome of a provisioning apparatus in which the police authorities of larger towns dominated and were seen to dominate over their lesser satellites? To the extent that crowds set upon the millers, bakers, merchants, or officials concerned with provisioning, they did so more reliably the more that town was seen as accumulating stores while the people starved (or was even seen to be conspiring deliberately to profit from hunger).

The Great Fear, too, is extremely sensitive to a stretch of good road in the vicinity. Do we see here, perhaps, the significance of the road network in the oral transmission of rumor, as beautifully argued in Lefebvre's classic

88. Pierre de Saint Jacob documented the extent of such practices in northern Burgundy.

account?[89] The government's road-building policy may have aimed at uniting a modernizing France; in 1789 it provided the means for a rapid nationwide diffusion of often archaic fears. As for the role of the towns in the Great Fear: Apart from the general state of social vulnerability that integration into distant markets may have afforded,[90] the Great Fear was, in part, a reaction to the very real forms of urban mobilization simultaneously occurring on an extremely wide scale. Both urban insurrections and the rapid proliferation of pro- and anti-insurrectionary urban militias aroused fears in the countryside with a definite grounding in bitter realities. As a rather ominous indicator of one possible direction of urban-rural relations, the royal troops—who were likely to mutiny when ordered to fire upon the politicized crowds of the towns—were quite reliable in responding to rural unrest with disciplined brutality.[91]

Literacy

The presence of towns or roads may indicate something besides the pressures of the marketplace. By virtue of integration into commercial networks, the people of the French countryside may have become infused with values and ideas that were born in the urban centers as well. In particular, we might wonder whether rural communities penetrated by the market might also be influenced by the thinking of the eighteenth century's many social critics. From a methodological point of view, if our indicators of market involvement had to do double duty as a measure of a possible intellectual shift as well, we would find the interpretation of our data rather ambiguous. Perhaps the association of towns and roads with rural insurrection derives not so much from the marketplace as such but from the diffusion of urban ideas.

Let us now consider literacy. If towns and roads increased the pressures of the marketplace, did they not also increase the access of the countryside to the critical thought of the eighteenth century? In the vicinity of the cities and along the more accessible transportation arteries, were not the peasants more of a target in the struggle for the hearts and minds of the French that was waged with such energy by the pamphleteers in the weeks and months that proceeded the elections? Perhaps so, but rather than restrict ourselves to the physical accessibility of critical thought, we may more pointedly

89. Lefebvre, *Grande Peur.*

90. Yoichi Uriu has recently shown that in Dauphiné the Great Fear took place among villages connected to one another through the same market town. See Yoichi Uriu, "Espace et Révolution: enquête, Grande Peur et fédérations," *Annales Historiques de la Révolution Française* 62 (1990): 150–66.

91. Samuel F. Scott, *The Response of the Royal Army to the French Revolution: The Role and Development of the Army, 1789–1793* (Oxford: Clarendon Press, 1978), 79.

examine intellectual accessibility, namely, literacy. We take as measures of literacy the proportion of men and of women signing their marriage documents between 1786 and 1790.[92]

The development of literacy has rather frequently been credited with raising the insurrectionary potential of the socially subordinate. We may take as an instance Lawrence Stone's comments on the political significance of access to written communication: "Literate people are far harder to govern and exploit than illiterates."[93] Stone goes on to note the striking fact that the great revolutions of England, France, and Russia took place at moments when the proportion of men who were in some sense literate was between one-third and two-thirds (138). He suggests that rising literacy carries with it a developing impatience with the existing order.

But Table 7.8 does not reveal a pattern of free-floating alienation that might underlie any form of movement indiscriminately; nor does it show that more literate areas had a higher organizational capacity to act, however they defined the purposes of their action. Only anti-tax actions were especially characteristic of the literate countryside. What emerges clearly is that the main consequence of literacy that summer was to ward off the Great Fear.[94] It is as if the politics of mistaken rumor were weakened by the presence of people with access to the written word or with intellectual habits formed by contact with documents.

92. These data were gathered in a nationwide study begun in 1877 by Louis Maggiolo. There has been some controversy over the interpretation of signatures as a measure of literacy and over Maggiolo's data in particular; recent work that evaluates this data, however, suggests its validity as an indicator of regional variations. See Michel Fleury and Pierre Valmary, "Les progrès de l'instruction élémentaire de Louis XIV à Napoléon III d'après l'enquête de L. Maggiolo (1877–1879)," *Population* 12 (1957): 71–92; James Houdaille, "Les signatures au mariage de 1740 à 1829," *Population* 32 (1977): 65–90; Michel Vovelle, "Y a-t-il eu une révolution culturelle au XVIIIe siècle? A propos de l'éducation populaire en Provence," in Michel Vovelle, *De la cave au grenier: Un itinéraire en Provence au XVIIIe siècle. De l'histoire sociale à l'histoire des mentalités* (Quebec: Serge Fleury, 1980), 313–67; and François Furet and Jacques Ozouf, *Lire et écrire: L'alphabétisation des français de Calvin à Jules Ferry* (Paris: Les Editions de Minuit, 1977). The actual data are to be found in Ministère de l'Instruction Publique, *Statistique de l'instruction primaire* (Paris: Imprimerie Nationale, 1880), 2:156–73. Since Maggiolo's data are by *département, bailliage* literacy values must be estimated. This is done by weighting the literacy rates for the *départements* that intersect a *bailliage* by the proportion of the *bailliage's* area contained in those *départements*. Several *départements* lack data. *Départements* with missing data simply do not contribute to the estimated rates for those *bailliages* that they intersect. A *bailliage* is treated as a missing case only if its entire area lies in one or more *départements* with missing data. See Markoff and Shapiro, "Linkage of Data."

93. Lawrence Stone, "Literacy and Education in England, 1640–1900," *Past and Present* 2 (1969): 84–85.

94. This is the finding that differs most from earlier results reported in John Markoff, "Literacy and Revolt." In that article I treated the spring and summer of 1789 together, did not look beyond that summer, and thought my data showed not only a dampening effect of literacy on panicky reactions to fantasized enemies, but a channeling of mobilization against seigneurial targets as well. The latter, the present analysis makes clear, characterizes only a very early point in the unfolding of the Revolution; as a characterization of the breakthrough summer, it was erroneous (see p. 398).

Forms of Solidarity: Communal Ties and the Propensity to Revolt

And now let us consider the long-enduring structures that disposed people to act in particular ways and bent collective action in particular directions. The organizational capacity of rural people has been a classical concern of political sociology since Karl Marx vividly contrasted the amorphousness of smallholding peasants with the consciousness of modern factory workers in *The 18th Brumaire*. For Marx, the people who lived and worked on what he saw as separate and largely self-contained family farms in mid-nineteenth-century France constituted a revealing instance of a group unable to appreciate, define, or act upon a sense of shared interest: the worklives of these farm families did not bring them together but divided them.[95] Several American sociologists have recently brought such considerations to the exploration of the French rural communities in the Revolution. Theda Skocpol has found in the late eighteenth-century countryside the conditions for autonomous revolutionary action, independent of urban leadership; the countryside is both a central actor in the destruction of the Old Regime and a major problem for the Parisian-based task of political reconstruction.[96] If the capacity of the countryside to mobilize itself is seen by Skocpol as a central facet of revolution, Arthur Stinchcombe has argued that the conditions she holds to favor autonomous peasant action only existed in northern France.[97] Here Stinchcombe draws on a long and distinguished tradition of French historical geography. Ever since André Siegfried contended that the political conservatism of western France was rooted in its geographical distinctiveness,[98] the scholarly dissection of France's distinctive agrarian societies has flourished.

Does the structure of the local community affect the forms of revolt? Many scholars think so, but what is the relevant "structure"? For some, in a tradition that we might very approximately call "Marxian," the forging of local solidarities is grounded in the work patterns of everyday life in which wresting a livelihood in the struggle against nature on the one hand and the struggle against the claims of the dominant classes on the other forges patterns of cooperation in work and in political struggle alike. This line of thinking emerges in recent sociological reflection on a body of work in French historical geography very powerfully developed by Marc Bloch and

95. For the classic passage, see Karl Marx, "The Eighteenth Brumaire of Louis Bonaparte," in Karl Marx and Frederic Engels, *Selected Works* (Moscow: Foreign Languages Publishing House, 1955), 1:334–35. In the essay taken as a whole, Marx is at pains to contrast the world of these smallholders not only with that of factory workers but with other ways of rural life.

96. Theda Skocpol, *States and Social Revolutions: A Comparative Analysis of France, Russia and China* (Cambridge: Cambridge University Press, 1979), 118–26.

97. Arthur Stinchcombe, *Economic Sociology* (New York: Academic Press, 1983), 46–64.

98. André Siegfried, *Tableau politique de la France de l'Ouest sous la Troisième République* (Paris: Armand Colin, 1964).

Roger Dion. A second tradition looks to juridical definitions of community and autonomy and asks what responsibilities remained in village hands despite the growing seizure of power by the central state and its semibureaucratic agents in the provinces. We might call this second tradition, even more approximately than the first, "Tocquevillean," in recognition of the weight in that thinker's analyses that is played by the extent and social location of regions of autonomy from state power. Historians in this tradition are apt to consider the juridical responsibilities of communities, their rights to administer themselves (for example, to allocate taxes internally) and their capacities to engage in legally accepted collective action (for example, to file lawsuits). The first tradition looks to solidarities rooted in economic interdependencies in northern and eastern France; the second to solidarities rooted in juridically recognized autonomy and traditional communal responsibility in the south and especially along the Mediterranean coast of Provence and Languedoc.[99]

Since economic structures and political autonomy differed so much among France's regions, both accounts have a certain inherent plausibility. Certainly, the rhythms and routines of social life differed considerably across the French countryside. Cereal production in the northern plains was carried out in a social context that contrasted markedly with the polyculture of the Mediterranean coastal area, the wine-producing Southwest, or the desperate expedients of the impoverished Massif Central. And there has been especially great scholarly interest in the western pattern of dispersed farmsteads that shaped a way of life and whose Sunday gathering at church made the political community virtually indistinguishable from the ecclesiastical parish. What is needed is a basis for distinguishing on a broad regional basis among what Goubert has called "twenty contrasting peasantries."[100]

Consider first the nature of production. Anyone at all familiar with France is likely to think at once of the *openfield* agriculture of the North and East. The structure of economic activity and the pattern of settlement in this relatively prosperous grain-producing region were inseparable from a dense web of social relations.[101] Collectively negotiated communal self-regulation was part and parcel of the everyday activities of productive life. The village was surrounded by the holdings of its members, unfenced and intermingled.

99. Among recent writers, Michel Vovelle, whom many would usually associate with Marxians, turns up, on this matter, in the Tocquevillean camp.

100. Pierre Goubert, "Sociétés rurales françaises du 18e siècle: Vingt paysanneries contrastées. Quelques problèmes," in Pierre Goubert, ed., *Clio parmi les hommes: Recueil d'articles* (Paris and the Hague: Mouton, 1976), 63–74.

101. Marc Bloch, *Les caractères originaux de l'histoire rurale française* (Paris: Armand Colin, 1968); Roger Dion, *Essai sur la formation du paysage rural français* (Neuilly-Sur-Seine: Guy Durier, 1981); Etienne Juillard, *La vie rurale dans la plaine de Basse-Alsace* (Strasbourg: Le Roux, 1953).

Not only were the thin strips into which family holdings were divided scattered among the holdings of other families: the lord's holdings might also be mixed in among the peasants'. The unfenced and intermingled holdings required the development of a strong community to coordinate the productive activity and to deal with the lord. All activities required coordination: the dates of ploughing, sowing, or harvesting; the grazing of animals on the common and on the fallow; the guarding of crops. Effective coordination, not separation, protected community members' interests from one another;[102] effective coordination was also vital in the defense of members' interests against a predatory lord who might easily attempt to enlarge his claims, particularly in a period of expanded commercial opportunity. Living in close proximity in their villages, the members of an openfield community found respect and security in meeting obligations to the collectivity.

It is quite tempting to see in this tightly interdependent community a tradition of resistance to the lords that carries over into the drama of 1789. Generations of French geographers have developed the contrast of openfield and the Western *bocage*[103] with its tiny hamlets and scattered farms, its fields enclosed by hedges, its sunken roads with their restricted visibility, and its physical separation of grazing from cultivation. It would come as no great surprise to discover that such a human transformation of the French landscape nurtured actions that differed deeply from those of the northern plains.[104] I do not believe that any French geographer or historian has argued this case with greater imagination, clarity, and persuasiveness than an American sociologist has recently done. One can hardly fail to be convinced by Arthur Stinchcombe's account.[105] Despite its theoretical elegance, however, the data[106] suggest that this theory is mistaken.[107] It is not

102. "The distinctive feature of the agrarian regime in le Nord, distinguishing that region from others in France, was the power exercised by the village community in regulating farming." See Hugh Prince, "Regional Contrasts in Agrarian Structures," in Hugh D. Clout, ed., *Themes in the Historical Geography of France* (New York: Academic Press, 1977), 141.

103. The openfield-*bocage* contrast can be overemphasized as Pierre Goubert has protested: the communal herds that grazed on communal pastures in the *bocage* implied some level of communal structure. But the variety of interfamily negotiations and communal decision-making without which openfield farming was inconceivable is just not matched. See Goubert, *L'Ancien Régime,* vol. 1, *La Société* (Paris: Armand Colin, 1969), 78.

104. One historian has even raised the question of whether there was a rural community at all in the southern Massif Central whose communities bear some resemblances to the western pattern. While his answer is a compelling yes, such a question is far less likely in the openfield region. See Peter M. Jones, "Parish, Seigneurie and the Community of Inhabitants in Southern Central France During the Eighteenth and Early Nineteenth Centuries," *Past and Present* 91 (1981): 74–108.

105. Stinchcombe, *Economic Sociology,* 46–64.

106. For the boundary of *openfield* farming I follow the map of Roger Dion, derived from the descriptions of Arthur Young: Roger Dion, *Paysage rural français,* 10; Arthur Young, *Voyages en France en 1787, 1788 et 1789* (Paris: Armand Colin, 1976).

107. See the tenth row from the bottom of Table 7.8.

antiseigneurial revolts that characterize the openfield, but the actions of those going after available grain. The struggle against the lords has its own ecological context, but it was not in this region.

The role of openfield settlement was actually to inhibit mobilization against the lords. The openfield's reputation for solidarity rested on an analysis of work rhythms. But there is another region sometimes noted for an intensely organized life: the Mediterranean South. Is that reputation deserved? Michel Vovelle seems to think so, calling attention to the intensive southern "sociability," as the French put it, that Maurice Agulhon showed to be characteristic of Provence.[108] In these little village republics, to borrow another expression of Agulhon's,[109] a semidemocratic politics sometimes enabled the well-to-do village leaderships to earn the unified support of their communities in decades of legal struggles against the customary exactions and the recent encroachments of lord and church.

It was common in Provence, for example, for a council that was at least nominally an elected body to have considerable financial discretion in the management of communal funds, to supervise local markets and local industrial production, to employ specialists to evaluate crop damage due to natural disasters, wild animals, or thieves, to maintain the local roads, to appoint specialized officers for a variety of purposes, to maintain legal records, and to apportion royal taxes and seigneurial dues among members of the community. Such functions, particularly the last one, gave the village elites the habit of negotiation with powerful outsiders on behalf of their constituents, and gave them the habit of adjudicating the internal politics of village life as well.[110] This long tradition of responsible political existence for the Mediterranean rural community strongly indicates the experience and resources for organized collective action. Collective action to what ends? To whatever ends local circumstances suggested—and local circumstances varied a great deal in this region in which the mix of crops and animals differed greatly from one area to the next. But taking the presence of olives or almonds as indicating the region's distinct ecology, we find that hypothesis

108. Vovelle, *La découverte de la politique,* 148–50; Maurice Agulhon, *La vie sociale en Provence intérieure au lendemain de la Révolution* (Paris: Société des Etudes Robespierristes, 1970), 202–35.

109. See *La République au village: Les populations du Var de la Révolution à la Deuxième République* (Paris: Seuil, 1979).

110. Bordes, *Administration provinciale et municipale,* 188–91. Jacques Godechot's introductory essay to a number of *Annales du Midi* devoted to southern self-government is especially insistent on the vigor of the elected councils of southern villages compared to what he regards as moribund general assemblies in the North. The essays that follow his provide important exemplifications. See Jacques Godechot, "Les municipalités du Midi avant et après la Révolution," *Annales du Midi* 84 (1972): 363–67. For a thoughtful survey of the varieties of pre-revolutionary village government see Jean-Pierre Gutton, *La sociabilité villageoise dans l'ancienne France: Solidarités et voisinages du XVIe au XVIIIe siècle* (Paris: Hachette, 1979).

is only successful, that summer, in predicting the Great Fear (and even that prediction only if we are not fussy about statistical significance).[111]

We have sketched an implicit debate: a theory of solidarity rooted in work rhythms that suggests a northeastern center of political action and a theory of solidarity rooted in juridical autonomy that suggests a Mediterranean center. We have associated the former with the name of Marx and the latter with Tocqueville. Perhaps there is a sort of synthesis that, if it need any ancestral totem, might be assigned to Durkheim. We may look for the density of social contact as indicated by the density of human settlement. Empirically both the openfield Northeast and the Mediterranean South had nucleated villages: clusters of dwellings surrounded by fields, rather than the dispersed farmsteads characteristic of the West and much of the South-Center.[112] The hypothesis: a critical mass of people, living in close continuity, develop a capacity for collective action that is not true for more dispersed habitations. As it happens, then, the Durkheiman thesis of moral density points to both the Northeast and the Mediterranean South, well into the nineteenth century.

There is a severe measurement problem here. If we are willing to use data on settlement patterns from a century after the Revolution,[113] there is a government survey that indicates where various percentages of the inhabitants of a commune lived in a central place. The geographic distribution of nucleated settlement in 1891 shows several distinctive clusters: a large northeastern one (roughly the old openfield), a Mediterranean coastal one, a smaller Southwestern area around Bordeaux and a small, isolated zone in central France. For all the likelihood that the boundaries of these zones differed to an unknown extent a century earlier (Did the nineteenth century's rural-urban migration increase or decrease the concentration of the remaining country people?), the theoretical importance of this variable makes it worth studying, even poorly measured. Were both the "economic" and "political" hypotheses of action-promoting solidarity borne out, we would be tempted by the more parsimonious "moral" hypothesis that subsumes both. However, when we look at the tables, we see that this more general notion of superior organizational resources accruing to particular settlement patterns does not fare very well. The region of nucleated villages (at least if one is willing to use this nineteenth-century evidence as the best available) has no very clear relationship to revolt other than considerably reducing the Great Fear. Could it be that the pattern of information-diffusion in a densely clustered village provided a reality check as one or another neighbor might

111. Source: Maps in Hugh Prince, "Regional Contrasts in Agrarian Structures," and André Fel, "Petite culture," 142, 223.

112. See maps in Dion, *Paysage rural français,* 111.

113. See map in Prince, "Regional Contrasts in Agrarian Structures," 140.

well have doubted the fantastic rumors? This is surely how Marx thought the social world of the nineteenth-century factory would facilitate rational collective action (and what he thought missing in large parts of rural France at midcentury). Whatever the explanation, the case that settlement density provides organizational resources for all forms of action is hard to square with the evidence.

We may tackle the question of the forms of solidarity in another way. The West is famous for its isolated farmsteads, and some have argued that Sunday's religious services were therefore absolutely central for local solidarities. This, we suggested above, was likely to impart a religious element to communal mobilizations (and we saw above that Western conflicts, well before the great burst of counterrevolution, did have an extra religious flavor).[114] Parts of the South-Center have similar settlement patterns.[115] Are the West and South-Center, in fact, distinctive in having a disproportionate share of events launched after Sunday Mass? We can explore differing regional propensities for Sunday to be the day of riot. The clear evidence of Table 7.9 both confirms and surprises. The West and South-Center are, as surmised, prone to have a disproportionate share of Sunday events and the Southwest and Southeast also have Sunday concentrations. But the largest Sunday concentration of all turns out to be the Northeast. Indeed, only the Northeast has retained the traditional degree of Sunday concentration that seems to be typical of contestation since the mid-seventeenth century (see Fig. 6.7).

By contrast, the rest of northern France's contestation takes place any time but Sunday. If we recall (see Figs. 6.9 [a]–[d]) that Sunday concentration is greater for some forms of conflict than others, one simple explanation comes to hand: northern France, specializing in conflicts over land and wages as well as panics, may have had the sorts of struggles that, by dividing the well-off from the destitute, did not lend themselves so well to actions organized at or after the weekly reconnection of the whole community and God. But now consider likely alternative settings for collective sharing of grievances and initiatives: we have the marketplace, the traditional assembly of the community, and the new organizational facilities born of revolution (the National Guards and the political clubs). The political clubs, especially relatively early, were especially dense in the South, perhaps making a contribution to reducing, but not eliminating, the centrality of Sunday. As for communal assemblies, there is considerable division in the literature on their vitality in northern France. Is it possible that the literature is divided because they actually varied greatly and that the Northeast was

114. See above, p. 363; Sutherland, *Chouans,* 215–18; Maurice Bordes, *Administration provinciale et municipale,* 188–91; Maurice Agulhon, *La vie sociale en Provence,* 59–61, 203–35.
115. Jones, *Politics and Rural Society.*

Table 7.9. Events on Sunday by Region (%)

North	10%
Northeast	31
Paris region	8
North-Center	15
South-Center	20
Southeast	19
Southwest	22
West	29
Normandy	11
All France	19
Percentage if all days had equal numbers of events	14
(*N*)[a]	(2,144)

[a]Excludes events if day was not known precisely.

singularly deficient in Old Regime organizational nuclei? This would explain why northeastern actions—and these, in most periods, were few—remained Sunday-centered. In this hypothesis the Sunday-centered character of western and south-central insurrection, taken in conjunction with those regions' considerable insurrectionary propensities, was a sign of the strength of a religious-centered community; the Sunday-centered character of the Northeast, on the other hand, taken in conjunction with that region's usual relative inactivity, may, on the contrary, merely indicate the weakness of other organizing foci. Only comparative work on local communal organization could confirm (or refute) this. The present evidence, then, gives us something to speculate about, but leaves fundamentally mysterious the northeastern countryside's revolution. In any event, villages seem to have been developing a secularized style of protest, shorn of religiously permeated organization, a process particularly advanced in much of northern France.[116]

Land-use: Cereals, Pasturage, Viticulture, Woodlands, Waste

Having considered the role we might have expected to be played by the cereal-growing north and olive-growing Mediterranean in fostering revolt in

116. The northern countryside may have been taking the lead in the disconnecting of violent conflict from religious concerns that Claude Langlois sees as a central theme of nineteenth-century political evolution. See Claude Langlois, "La fin des guerres de religion: La disparition de la violence religieuse en France au 19e siècle," presented at the conference on "Violence and the Democratic Tradition in France 1789–1914" at the University of California, Irvine, February 1994.

1789, the role of *grasslands*[117] displayed in Table 7.8, is a genuine surprise. Surrounding the cereal-producing openfield of the Paris basin lies a belt of pasture land; no doubt such an arrangement enabled agriculturalists to exchange some of their grain for the draft animals needed to pull their heavy ploughs. In the south, there is another zone of grassland that supported extensive herds of sheep.

Stock-raising presented significant commercial opportunities as the growing towns purchased meat, leather, wool, and animal fat;[118] as the military required horses; and perhaps as an increasingly commercialized agriculture required animals for transport as well. No doubt the attempt to expand commercial stock-raising conflicted seriously with other claims, whether those of marginal subsistence farming or of market-oriented agriculture. Some lords, for example, held or invented the right of "separate herd" *(troupeau à part),* which exempted their own livestock from communal regulations.[119] Quite apart from their own personal use, lords were taking to renting such a right to commercial livestock interests, a practice generally forbidden by customary law, but often tolerated in practice by the courts. For the lord this might be quite a rewarding proposition; for the peasants it was an unmitigated disaster.[120] Near the Pyrenees, by way of example, the lords were increasingly in the habit of renting out grazing rights, in utter disregard for traditional communal restraints, to shepherds moving their herds.[121] The commercial exploitation of such a traditional or newly fabricated seigneurial right was hardly a practice that could be justified by any claim to some form of patrimonial responsibility for communal welfare.

The attack on the peasant community might well follow a different route, that of fencing in one's fields, and thereby breaking with the collectivity. Marc Bloch's classic study of the fate of the enclosure movement before the Revolution concludes that it was where "grass was on its way to pushing out grain"[122] that the balance of social forces favored enclosure. But not, I suggest, without a residue of tension that boiled over in the summer of 1789. The villagers involved with pasturage, Table 7.8 shows, are less likely

117. André Fel, "Petite culture, 1750–1850," in Hugh D. Clout, ed., *Themes in the Historical Geography of France* (New York: Academic Press, 1977), 221–22.

118. Paris, admittedly an exceptional case, was purchasing livestock from as far away as Limousin. See Nicole Lemaître, *Un Horizon Bloqué: Ussel et la montagne limousine au XVIIe et XVIIIe siècles* (Ussel: Musée du Pays d'Ussel, 1978), 109.

119. For the response to these and related issues in the *cahiers,* see above, p. 172.

120. Marc Bloch, *French Rural History: An Essay on its Basic Characteristics* (Berkeley and Los Angeles: University of California Press, 1966), 133, 225; "La lutte pour l'individualisme agraire dans la France du XVIIIe siècle," *Annales d'Histoire Economique et Sociale* 2 (1930): 366, 378, 517–19.

121. Bloch, "Individualisme agraire," 366.

122. Ibid., 532.

than others to engage in subsistence action that summer but are notably more prone to taking on the lords.

Although the data suggest that, at that moment, the tensions around stock-raising were particularly likely to generate open antiseigneurial conflict, it is far from obvious that stock-raising should prove to be the most conflict-inducing form of enterprise throughout the revolutionary era. After all, viticulture and woodlands had their own tensions. So did the central land use of rural France: cereals. Jeffery Paige has shown that distinctive crops in the twentieth century are embedded in distinctive social relations whose conflicts engender very distinctive sorts of social movements.[123] It seems worth inquiring whether the distinctive practices of France's various peasantries nurtured distinctive patterns of revolt.

Perhaps different sources of tension played their part at different moments. We shall consider this possibility below when we look past that dramatic summer. But let us pause a moment here to survey the sorts of tensions surrounding other uses of the land and see whether they joined grassland as a specific locale for summer's battles. Central to the lives of rural communities were the patterns of land use. Communities engaged in the cultivation of grapes, those with access to forests, those producing grain, those with extensive uncultivated land, as well as those caring for livestock had their own characteristic patterns of cooperation and division and were involved with the state and the market in particular ways. The association of grassland and revolt in the summer of 1789 is so striking, that we should consider the distinctive potentials for conflict in communities formed around other uses of the land as well. The significance of local production seems worth exploring as best we can; it is only "as best we can" because the national data that I use here dates from a government survey of the later 1830s,[124] a half-century after the revolutionary crisis. French historians are sometimes fond of stressing the broad continuities of daily life, workday routines, and economic structures across the revolutionary period. But land-use patterns were not identical a half-century downstream, although the geographic pattern in the locations of more and less arable, say, had probably not shifted so much as to invalidate the analysis presented here of the covariation of that pattern and revolt.

Was the land given over to *wine production?* If so, one might argue, the small producers were doubly vulnerable to the poor harvests on the eve of the Revolution in something of the same manner as the proletarian textile workers of rural Normandy; while small grain-producers may have had their

123. Jeffery Paige, *Agrarian Revolution: Social Movements and Export Agriculture in the Underdeveloped World* (New York: Free Press, 1975).

124. Departmental maps of the extent of woodland, vines, arable, grassland, and wasteland are presented in Fel, "Petite Culture," 221–22. The data derive from a government study of 1836–38.

marketable surplus wiped out, wine-producers could not even fall back on consuming their own unsold output.[125] Michel Vovelle, for example, suggests that its viticulture was one of the roots of the special proclivity to violent upheaval in Provence.[126] If one follows Marcel Lachiver, moreover, one might find our wine-producers to have their own special claim to solidarity. Lachiver argues, at least for the area around Paris, that wine-producing families develop a powerful bond around their own grape-stock that can be transmitted through the generations. Viticultural communities cement their sense of distinctiveness through such a strong culture of marrying both locally and within the wine-growing community that petitions for the waiver of the church's marital barriers among close kin were routine.[127]

The presence of *woodland* suggests another source of unrest. There were few locations in which the boundaries between the rights of peasant communities and the prerogatives of the lords were so contested as in wooded areas. Peasants claimed rights to graze their animals, to gather acorns or other dietary supplements (especially in hard times), and to gather wood for construction and fuel. During the eighteenth century, the value of wood and woodland was rising fast as urban construction boomed; as the royal authorities attempted to procure the raw materials for their ambitious shipbuilding program in their vain hope of rivaling England at sea; and as developing industries demanded charcoal or tannin. The incentive for the lords to reassert (or assert for the first time) their claims on the new profitable forests ran directly counter to custom (and perhaps rural population growth made customary peasant claims more precious).[128] Did these particular tensions play a role in the upheavals of 1789?

We may also measure the proportion of *arable* land. To provision the growing towns, it was to the grainlands first and foremost that urban administrators in search of tranquillity and urban merchants in search of profits turned. Were regions of extensive *arable* the scenes of intense conflict as landholders attempted to expand their control over the production

125. Camille-Ernest Labrousse, *La crise de l'économie française à la fin de l'Ancien Régime et au début de la Révolution* (Paris: Presses Universitaires de France, 1944).

126. Michel Vovelle, "Les troubles sociaux en Provence de 1750 à 1792," in Michel Vovelle, *De la cave au grenier: Un itinéraire en Provence au XVIIIe siècle. De l'histoire sociale à l'histoire des mentalités* (Quebec: Serge Fleury, 1980), 230.

127. Marcel Lachiver, *Vin, vigne et vignerons en région parisienne du XVIIe au XIXe siècle* (Pontoise: Société Historique et Archéologique de Pontoise, du Val d'Oise et du Vexin, 1982), 427–34.

128. Andrée Corvol, "Forêt et communautés en Basse-Bourgogne au dix-huitième siècle," *Revue Historique* 256 (1976): 15–36, and "Les délinquances forestières en Basse-Bourgogne depuis la réformation de 1711–1718," *Revue Historique* 259 (1978): 345–88; Christian Desplat, "La forêt béarnaise au XVIIIe siècle," *Annales du Midi* 85 (1973): 141–71; Pierre de Saint Jacob, *Les paysans de la Bourgogne du Nord au dernier siècle de l'Ancien Régime* (Paris: Société Les Belles Lettres, 1966), 488–90 and passim.

of cereals? In part this expansion meant the physical extension of their holdings, but it also meant attempting to extricate themselves from the constraints of communal obligations that blocked enclosures, prohibited the cutting of ripened grain to the ground (assuring the stubble for the poor) and dictated the precise crop to be grown or the date of the harvest. We may also measure the success of grain production from nineteenth-century data on *wheat* and *rye yields.*[129] A region characterized by extensive *wasteland,* finally, should typically be one in which there is considerable land that from the point of view of commercial opportunities is marginal (whatever the critical role such land may play in the local ecology).

As for the role of the conflicts endemic to these various land uses in the social explosion, we have already considered the grasslands. Regions of extensive arable, as also noted earlier, were prone to the subsistence conflicts that avoided the grasslands, but tended not to experience the Great Fear. Any land use other than cereals made subsistence conflict less likely but wasteland and grapes attracted the Great Fear. And, perhaps a surprise, none of the patterns of rural life, other than those characteristic of pasture land, significantly raised or impeded attacks on the seigneurial regime. Was this a peculiarity of the specific mobilization of the summer of 1789, or does it characterize our entire period?

Labor Migration

Finally, let us consider the general level of rural well-being. Much has been made of standards of living in the comparative study of peasant revolt, although much of the discussion is quite contradictory. In these terms, it has often been asked whether it is poorer peasants who rebel (out of their great need) or the more well-to-do (drawing on their greater resources). Eric Wolf has imaginatively put forth the "middle" peasant as the protagonist of rural upheaval:[130] the person with an adequate supply of both grievances and resources. It is not hard to see why the literature is so contradictory and why Wolf has been led to propose such an ingenious resolution: general discussions of the alleged consequences of extreme rural poverty or of relative ease lend themselves to the most diverse expectations. Are the most miserably destitute intrinsically

129. The data, derived from the study of the 1830s, are presented in the form of departmental maps in Hugh D. Clout, "Agricultural Change in the Eighteenth and Nineteenth Centuries," in Hugh D. Clout, ed., *Themes in the Historical Geography of France* (New York: Academic Press, 1977), 420. More complex, composite measures of land productivity are not explored here; see Hugh D. Clout, *Agriculture in France on the Eve of the Railway Age* (London: Croom Helm, 1980), 214–21; Thomas D. Beck, *French Legislators, 1800–1834: A Study in Quantitative History* (Berkeley and Los Angeles: University of California Press, 1974), 16, 155–57.

130. Eric Wolf, *Peasant Wars of the Twentieth Century* (New York: Harper and Row, 1973), 290–93.

radical because they suffer most grievously from the existing state of affairs, because they have the least to lose by risky action, and because the slightest further deterioration in their circumstances at the hands of landlord, tax collector, tithe-holder, or nature may threaten survival? Or are they politically immobilized (or only mobilizable for preservation of the status quo) by virtue of their utter dependence on one or another protector, by their lack of resources to sustain any collective action on their own behalf, and by utter aversion to any extra risk whatsoever? Alternatively, are the relatively well-off inherently conservative because they evaluate their own positions favorably and have something to lose should political action fail? Or are they a politically sensitive and savvy group with the resources to sustain a fight, the knowledge to see a favorable opportunity and the habits of active leadership in local affairs?

What sustains this debate, no doubt, is that there is something to both arguments (and to the Wolfian resolution as well). There will never be a satisfactory generalization here; what is possible is a series of specifications: identifications of contexts within which poorer or richer or in-between peasants rebel (or in which cross-class coalitions are formed, to use the currently fashionable language). In specific social settings, rural well-being and rural destitution have specific meanings as they bring country people into particular sorts of relations with one another, with urbanites, with administrators.

We hope to measure, if crudely, the gradations of prosperity or misery in the French countryside in general (as opposed to the specific disasters of the late 1780s). In a rough way we may approximate the depth of poverty by the patterns of seasonal internal migration. Year after year, large numbers left their homes seeking employment. The regions where work was not to be had sent agricultural laborers to the prosperous parts of the kingdom as harvesters and grapepickers; construction workers (like the stonecutters of Limousin) traveled far in search of employment; peddlers traveled everywhere; itinerant schoolteachers descended from the Alps. The Parisian basin, the lands along the Rhône, the plains of Languedoc, and other areas with paid work to be done received this migratory population. A survey carried out rather carefully under Napoleon is our source.[131] We distinguish regions of high *emigration*, too poor to support their own populations, from the richer regions which received these huge seasonal influxes. (The higher figures indicate *e*migration.) As it happens, regions of immigration and emigration do not differ significantly in their propensities to rebel.

What Sorts of Places Had Revolts in the Summer of 1789?

Out of the haze of numbers, several important lessons emerge. First, notions of "organizational capacity" and the like need to be set in specific

131. Data from Roger Béteille, "Les migrations saisonnières sous le Premier Empire: Essai de synthèse," *Revue d'Histoire Moderne et Contemporaine* 17 (1970): 424–41.

historical moments. The claim that the dense cooperative networks of northeastern villages or the political experience of self-rule of Mediterranean ones produce an unusual propensity to revolt appear more or less plausible in relation to different kinds of events.[132] The West with its dispersed habitations, is hardly short of peasant mobilization. We have also seen how the evidence qualifies the idea that in the summer of 1789, the openfield north and east as well as Mediterranean France were the prime loci of revolt. And if we look back at our earlier discussion of the shifting regional character of rural revolution from 1788 into 1793, we will recall that the great, national insurrectionary movement of the summer of 1789 is the only point at which the risings take place throughout the northeastern plain. Before that summer, the role of the Southeast stood out; after that summer came the turn of South-Center and Southwest, and then the Southeast yet again. If the breakthrough summer was the Northeast's moment, the Mediterranean coast, by contrast, stands out more at many other points in our tumultuous half-decade.

A second important lesson of all these numbers is that there are both commonalities and differences in the contexts that nurture different forms: market impact seems high for all forms, but literacy has more of a negative impact on panic than it has an impact of any sort on anything else. Third, the relationship of environment and action is an intricate one: catastrophically high prices rises were more likely to raise the likelihood of the Great Fear than of subsistence conflicts, which, as many have been insisting since Louise Tilly, seem to have been triggered by the visibility of nearby grain (at least, to take to heart the first lesson, in that particular two-month span). And fourth, the impact of market and state: the market looks very promising as a source of all sorts of fault lines in the social ecology, the state partially so. In that crucial summer, all manner of conflicts were more likely near a town or good road. And the heavy hand of the state may have created its own lines of fracture, as Tocqueville argued—but perhaps not quite where he saw those incipient fissures; the peasants of the *pays d'élections* are no more prone to attack the lords than those of the *pays d'états*. At least in that summer, one hastens to add: perhaps the story is different earlier or later.

Beyond the Breakdown

We need to move beyond the moment of breakdown of the old order, to set the rural revolution in motion—the only way to set it in dialogue with those in Paris who claimed to define the Revolution—and to see how the sorts of

132. We will see below that such claims also appear more or less plausible at different times.

places that sponsored antiseigneurial revolts through the whole turbulent era were like and were distinct from those that sponsored other forms of peasant action. It would be tedious as well as impossibly confusing simply to repeat the previous sort of analysis for all time periods and all event-types.

Antiseigneurialism: Changing Contexts

I shall proceed in two ways. First, in this section, I shall look at where antiseigneurial events took place throughout the whole period and then, in the next section, at how the aggregate pattern of antiseigneurial revolts compared to others across the entire five years. The contexts of antiseigneurial actions are displayed in Table 7.10. I shall use the same variables as before, apart from omitting the price data for 1789 as irrelevant to the flow of events beyond that time. Rather than present the full array of numbers, as in Table 7.8, I shall display a pared-down version that only shows where there is a statistically significant difference between the "low" and "high" *bailliages*. When there is such a difference I shall express the size of the difference as a percent. A negative figure means that the "low" *bailliages* have the larger percentage that are insurrectionary. Thus the second, "antiseigneurial," columns in Table 7.8 are used to construct the fifth column of Table 7.10. The "length of road" row gets a value of 16% since 24% of *bailliages* with more than the median length of royal road had antiseigneurial insurrection while 8% of those under the median did. On the other hand, "openfield" gets −11% because those areas not in the openfield were more prone, in that time period, to rise against the lords.

Finally, the second column, "Overall," needs some comment. To the extent that we are very concerned with how different contexts promoted antiseigneurial events at different times, it is the comparison among the various columns that is of interest. Occasionally, however, it is useful to ask whether, on the whole, antiseigneurial actions were favored by some particular context; we are especially likely to want to know this in comparing the contexts of antiseigneurial and other actions. The second column, which does not distinguish among our various periods but considers all antiseigneurial events from the summer of 1788 into the summer of 1793, is the place to look.

Let us now examine the table. Not one single indicator is invariably associated with such events. Wasteland tends to be associated with antiseigneurial events and arable with their absence after the first summer of revolution, as are low cereal yields, especially of wheat, as antiseigneurial movements shift to the south. And openfield is generally negatively associated. We simply have to abandon the whole notion of a specifically antiseigneurial openfield area, indeed of an intensely solidary peasantry, bound by intravillage solidarities forged in their intermixed fields, and involved in endless battles with the lord over the boundaries of their collective rights and his individual ones, taking the lead in the French rural struggle. Even in the spring and summer of 1789, which were exceptional in the level of northern participation, the openfield's only associations with antiseigneurial actions are negative. (The openfield's contribution that summer, to recall Table 7.8, was in subsistence conflicts.)

But perhaps the thesis of the solidary community as the seedbed of struggle against the lords does have something to it and it is the identification of such communities as lying in the northern plains that is off. Certainly this hypothesis works better than the openfield proposal. The Mediterranean coast specifically (defined in practice here as the region of olives and almonds) was especially active in the spring of 1789, the winter of 1790, and then almost continually from early 1792 on. And the associations, as measured by percentage differences, are quite substantial. Yet even here one must see that coastal Languedoc and Provence are not always the nurturers of antiseigneurial actions.

The general notion that nucleated communities developed a special solidarity that made them easy to mobilize against whatever targets they chose—including the lords—appears wholly improbable. The few associations with antiseigneurial actions are negative. Even taking into consideration the questionable measurements of these settlement patterns, the thesis of quotidian solidarity as the key to revolutionary mobilization seems very dubious.

Literacy is almost perverse as a context. The more literate zones are among the first to move against the lords in the fall of 1788. As peasant unrest grows, literacy ceases to play any special role for about three-fourths of a year. But in the large wave of early 1790 and the smaller one of June, literacy reemerges as important, but it is now largely villagers from the less literate areas who struggle over seigneurial rights. Even in the large wave of early 1792—and beyond—it is almost consistently unlettered France that is in action. Perhaps the more literate areas were quicker to see the dying Old Regime as ripe for claiming their rights against the lords; perhaps they were more in touch with the views of the urban elites and were, therefore, quicker to change their sense of the possibilities for collective action; perhaps their very reading generated a greater realism that helped inoculate them against the Great Fear (which was far more extensive among the unlettered; see Table 7.8). By the spring of 1789, however, any distinctive antiseigneurial propensity of the literate countryside had evaporated. Once the less literate rose, they turned on the lords, too, especially in the Southwest and South-Center (see Table 7.6). While the more precocious northern villagers stayed calmer after that first summer, once those who depended on a public reading of letters to acquaint them with the political scene entered upon the Revolution's stage, they stayed on it for years.

As for the powerful contexts of structural change, the penetration of both market and state appear to play a role but in different ways. In almost every time period antiseigneurial events are more likely near a big town or a stretch of good road or both; the only exception is the initial half-year beginning in the summer of 1788. Whatever the role of administrative centralization as a long-run cause of antiseigneurial risings, however, it appears in only a few of our time periods and in none of the peak times except the relatively small peak of summer 1791. Thus towns and roads appear as very powerful contexts overall: *bailliages* with a larger town had a 32% greater likelihood of having an antiseigneurial rising sometime in the five-year span than other *bailliages*. But the *pays d'élections,* while a bit more prone to such risings, do not have enough of an impact to rise to statistical significance overall and therefore do not even get noted in that second column of Table 7.10. (The difference is 7%.)

On the other hand, it could also be said that the earliest locales to rise against the lords, in small numbers, even before the spring of 1789, tended to be in regions under the administrative thrall of centrally appointed bureaucrats and that at several other moments, though not at the times of peak rural explosiveness, this element mattered. The point of this pattern is both the relevance and the limits of Tocqueville's analysis. If the data do suggest that an antiseigneurial cast of mind was being fostered where the king's powers supplanted the lord's responsibilities, and which may have made pioneers in antiseigneurial actions out of peasants in the *pays d'élections,* the data also show how peasants from elsewhere generally joined in the fray; in the summer of 1789, to take one especially important moment, there is no special antiseigneurial edge at all where Tocqueville leads us to expect it.

Five Years of Rural Revolt

Arriving at some consideration of overall propensities across the five-year span, brings us to Table 7.11. Columns 3–9 show the percentage difference, when significant, associated with the usual set of variables and column 2 shows the differences when we lump together all risings indiscriminately. If we want to know whether, on the whole, one or another local context favors "risings," without being fussy about what sort of rising, or when, column 2 provides an answer. This column is therefore both a helpful summary and misleading about particular forms of conflict at particular moments.

This table helps clarify the previous analyses. Town size and road length emerge as powerful indicators once again, promoting all forms of conflict other than those over wages. Even counterrevolution is similar to other forms of mobilization insofar as its broadly structural contexts are conceived. Location in the *pays d'élections* also has a strong effect overall, exerting a

Table 7.10. Antiseigneurial Risings by Social Contexts at Different Time Periods (% Difference between Low and High Values of Variable at Left)

Indicators of social context	Overall June 1788–June 1793	June 1788–January 1789	March 1789–June 1789	July 1789–August 1789	September 1789–December 1789	January 1790–February 1790
Size of largest town	32%****		7%*	9%*	5%*	8%**
Length of road	28****		6*	16****		6*
Number of road intersections	15**			11**		
Administrative centralization (*pays d'états/pays d'élections)*		3%*			5*	
Percentage of men signing marriage documents	−17***	4*				−8***
Percentage of women signing marriage documents	−17***	4*				−7**
Proportion arable	−28****				−6*	−16****
Proportion grassland			−8*	12**		
Proportion wasteland	25****					13****
Proportion planted in vines	13*					
Proportion woodland						
Wheat yield	−19***					−9***
Rye yield	−16**					−6*
Openfield	−23****			−11**		−10****
Plains other than openfield						
Mountain	17**			12**		9***
Olives	47****		30****			9****
Almonds	48****		28****			13****
Nucleated villages: more than 60% live in central place	−13*					−7*
Nucleated villages: more than 90% live in central place	−30**					
Migration			5*			

Indicators of social context	March 1790–April 1790	June 1790–August 1790	September 1790–May 1791	June 1791–August 1791	September 1791–January 1792	February 1792–April 1792
Size of largest town		11%**	10%**	11%**		9%**
Length of road		12****	11***	14****		
Number of road intersections	4%*	7*		7*		
Administrative centralization (*pays d'états/pays d'élections*)			7*	10**		
Percentage of men signing marriage documents						–14****
Percentage of women signing marriage documents		–8*				–14****
Proportion arable		–8*	–10***		–6%*	–16****
Proportion grassland	–6**			–8*		
Proportion wasteland		8*	9**	6*	5*	17****
Proportion planted in vines		7*				
Proportion woodland						
Wheat yield		–7*	–7*		–5*	–15****
Rye yield					–4*	–12****
Openfield						–13****
Plains other than openfield				11**	5*	9**
Mountain			8*			39****
Olives						41****
Almonds	20***					
	19***					
Nucleated villages: more than 60% live in central place						–9**
Nucleated villages: more than 90% live in central place						
Migration				7*		

Table 7.10. *(Continued)*

Indicators of social context	May 1792–July 1792	August 1792–September 1792	October 1792–December 1792	January 1793–February 1793	March 1793[a]	April 1793–June 1793
Size of largest town	−6%*		6%*			
Length of road		5%*	6*	3%*		3%*
Number of road intersections						2*
Administrative centralization (*pays d'états/pays d'élections*)						
Percentage of men signing marriage documents						
Percentage of women signing marriage documents	−6*	−7**	−6**			
Proportion arable	−9***	−8**	−7**			−3*
Proportion grassland			−6*			
Proportion wasteland	8***	8***	6**			
Proportion planted in vines		7**	6*			
Proportion woodland						
Wheat yield	−7**	−7**	−6**			
Rye yield	−6**	−7**				
Openfield	−7**	−5*	−5*			
Plains other than openfield	−7**					
Mountain						
Olives	36****	20***	32****			15****
Almonds	34****	19***	35****	6*		15****
Nucleated villages: more than 60% live in central place						
Nucleated villages: more than 90% live in central place						
Migration	−5*					

[a]Too few events to permit calculations. *$p < .05$ **$p < .01$ ***$p < .001$ ****$p < .0001$

Note: Only statistically significant percentage differences are shown in this table.

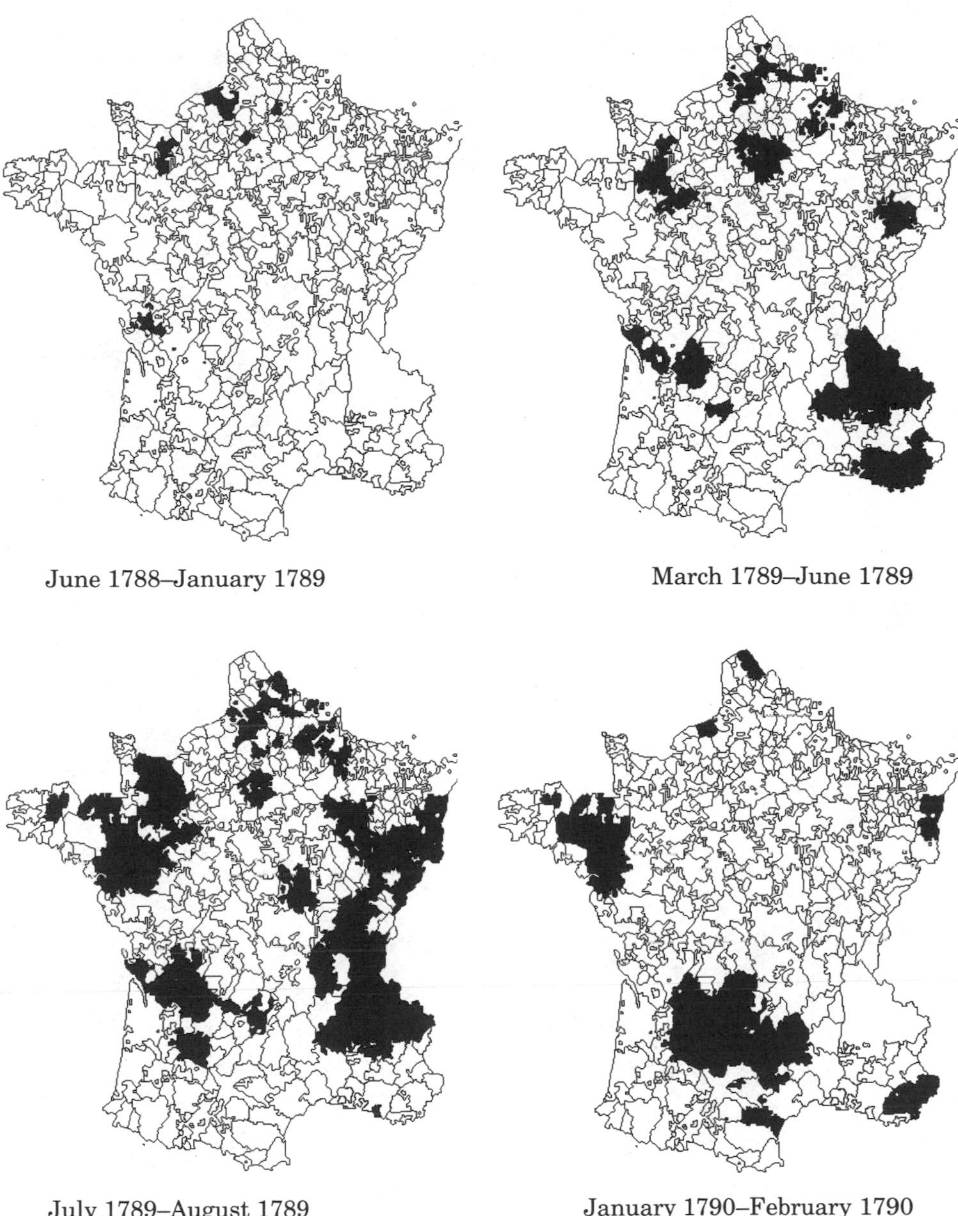

Map 7.2. Bailliages with Antiseigneurial Events: Early Months and Peak Episodes of Antiseigneurial Activity

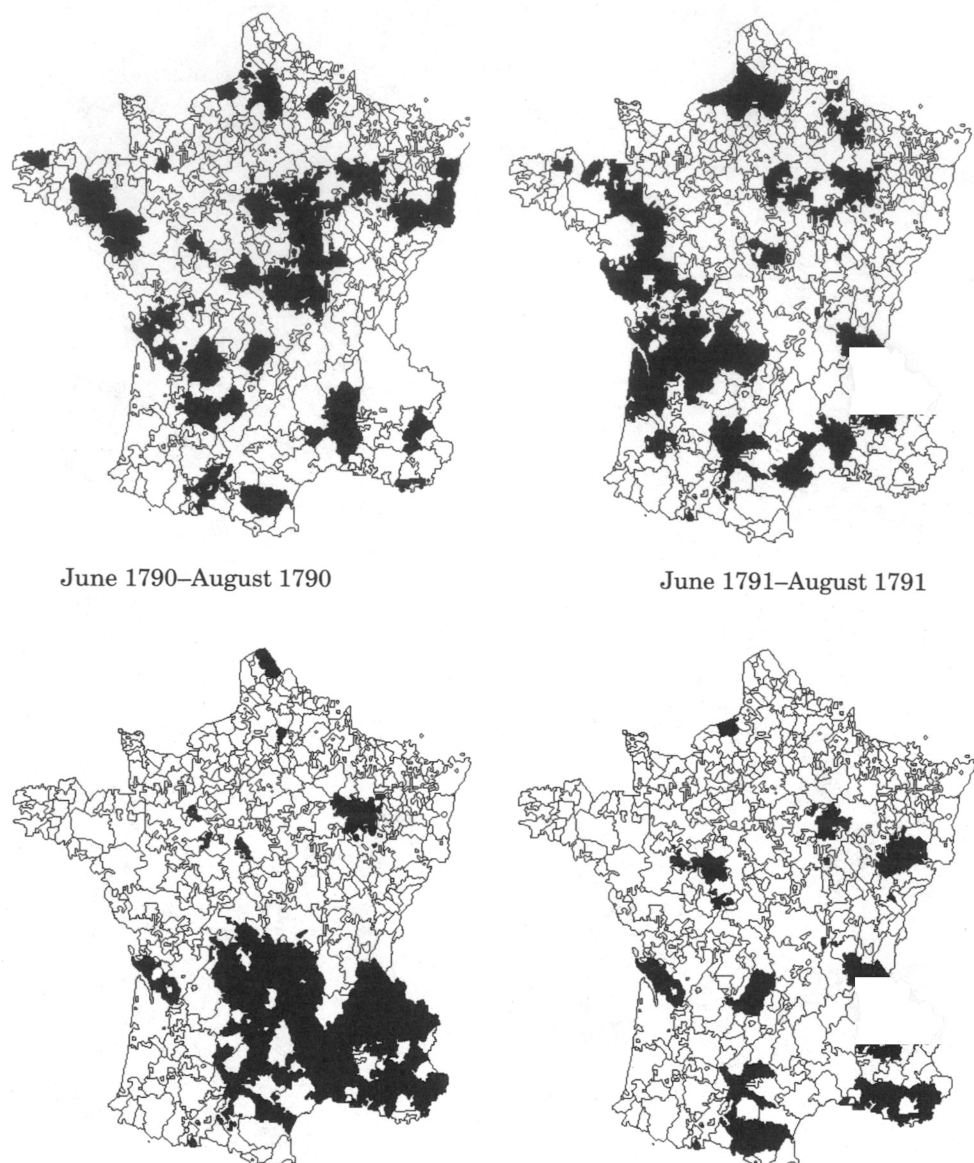

June 1790–August 1790

June 1791–August 1791

February 1792–April 1792

August 1792–September 1792

NOTE: The darkened *billiages* are those with at least one antiseigneurial event.

Table 7.11. Types of Rising by Social Contexts, June 1788–June 1793 (% Difference between Low and High Values of Variable at Left)

Indicators of social context	All Events	Antiseigneurial	Religious	Anti-tax	Subsistence	Land	Wage	Panic	Counterrevolution
Size of largest town	12**	32****	29****	18****	37****	14**		35****	
Length of road	21****	28****	22****	15****	34****	27****		25****	10**
Number of road intersections		15**		14***	12*	17****			
Administrative centralization (*pays d'états/pays d'élections)*	14**				22****	9*	5*	22****	
Percentage of men signing marriage documents	−16****	−17***	−21****		−12*	9*		−15**	−23****
Percentage of women signing marriage documents	−13**	−17***	−15**		−9*			−18***	−23****
Proportion arable	−11*	−28****	−23****					−14*	−14****
Proportion grassland					−25****				11*
Proportion wasteland	12**	25****	25****					17***	24****
Proportion planted in vines	10*	13*					5*	28****	
Proportion woodland					−13**		6**		−18****
Wheat yield		−19***	−12*					−12*	−9*
Rye yield		−16**						−12*	
Openfield	−13**	−23****	−13***					−11*	−21****
Plains other than openfield									
Mountain	10*	17**	19***						21***
Olives		47****	39***	24**	28**				
Almonds		48	40****	23**	29**				
Nucleated villages: more than 60% live in central place									−21****
Nucleated villages: more than 90% live in central place	−25**	−13*	−21*		−30**				−13*
Migration		−30**				11**			

*$p < .05$ **$p < .01$ ***$p < .001$ ****$p < .0001$

Note: Only statistically significant percentage differences are shown in this table.

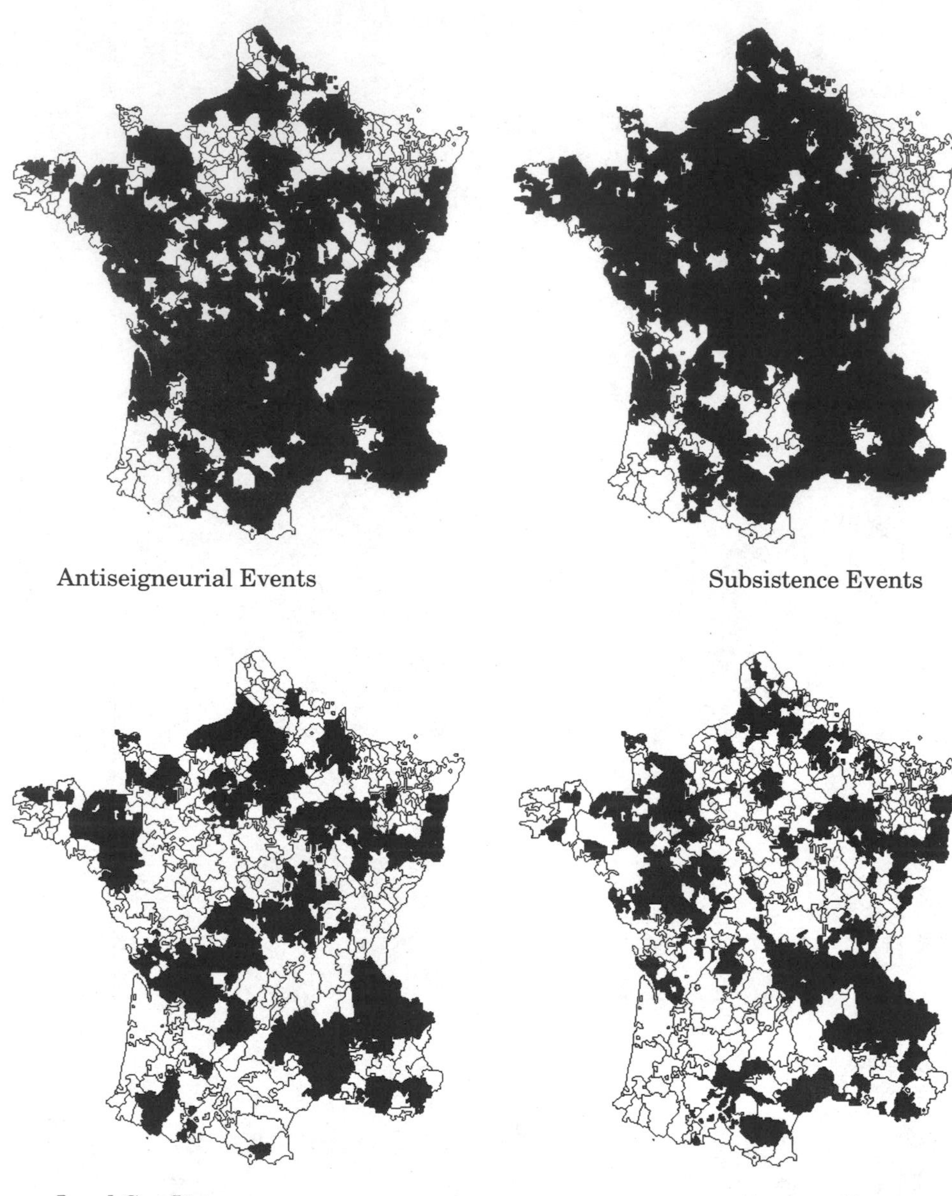

Map 7.3. Bailliages with Selected Forms of Insurrection, June 1788–June 1793

NOTE: The darkened *bailliages* are those with at least one event

discernable impact on conflicts over food, land, and wages as well as panics. Yet it is not an important context for counterrevolution nor for antiseigneurial events considered over the entire five-year span (as opposed to certain specific moments). On the whole, rural insurrection stays away from openfield and arable and gravitates toward wine country, terrain with extensive wasteland and mountain. Antiseigneurial actions eschew as well areas of good cereal yields, just as the Great Fear and other panics do. Could this in part be due to antiseigneurial action after the summer of 1789 moving along a path opened up by that summer's panic? We shall return to this hypothesis below.

We have to abandon completely the claim that the dense social web of nucleated villages provided the basis for concerted action, since high-density patterns of rural settlement, if they do anything, turn out to inhibit rather than enhance disruptive collective action. Not only is counterrevolution negatively related to concentrated settlement patterns—hardly a historical surprise, although profoundly disconfirming the sociological hypothesis[133]—so are antiseigneurial and subsistence events, and religious events as well. On the very important other hand, the South generally and the Mediterranean coast in particular (as defined by the cultivation of olives or almonds) are powerful contexts indeed. The presence of olives or almonds produces the most dramatic percentage differences in antiseigneurial insurrection in the entire table as well as promoting most other forms of insurrection. The Mediterranean coastal area is the most generally turbulent, although not notable for its counterrevolutionary action. Literacy's overwhelmingly negative effect when we considered the entire five-year span as a whole may surprise some (but it is less remarkable in light of the previous tables).[134] Although actions over land are engaged in by peasants from more literate areas, virtually all other forms of action, overall, are not.

Migration, finally, appears associated with almost no form of action, taken overall. But it appears that regions of extensive emigration also tended to land conflict, both emigration and conflict, perhaps, being responses to land scarcity. Some fled, some fought.

Market and State as Contexts of Revolt: Summing Up

There matters must stand insofar as geographic variation in the penetration of the market is indicated by towns and roads (no doubt quite well) and the replacement of local authority by distant, impersonal, rationalizing

133. Michel Vovelle comments on the surprising solidarity of dispersed western peasants, beyond what one would have expected from settlement patterns (*La découverte de la politique,* 293).

134. Perhaps the author was especially likely to be surprised since his earlier studies of the risings of spring–summer 1789 alone showed literacy in a different light. See "Literacy and Revolt."

bureaucrats indicated by the absence of Provincial Estates (less well).[135] Both were conflict-promoting contexts. Market expansion, by creating so many fault lines—well-off versus destitute, town versus country, consumers versus producers, communities versus individual enterprisers, state agents versus commercial interests, landowners versus leaseholders, long-standing communities versus migratory work-seekers, those wedded to traditional techniques of production versus those seeking the benefits of innovation—made likely many kinds of conflict in the collapse of the old order. The hand of the state drew frustration upon itself (probably what is happening in the subsistence arena) and wrecked the old assurances without providing, yet (if ever), any new ones (perhaps the reason for the Great Fear); yet as a force directly impelling a specifically antiseigneurial revolt, it appears weaker than Tocqueville thought, although notable at moments.

Methodological Autocritique

Before leaving our data on the spatial location of rural insurrection, let us reconsider the limits of this data that we set out in Chapter 5 and the appropriate cautions that apply in the present analysis. The small number of wage events in our sample taken together with the very limited research on such forms of conflict, make the regional claims above extremely vulnerable to the possibility that future research will refute the very tentative picture sketched here; the much larger number of antiseigneurial or subsistence events and the much greater tradition of research on such forms of conflict, especially the former, make the claims offered above a good deal less vulnerable and make my own hypotheses rather less tentative. (Land conflicts and anti-tax insurrections have an intermediary status.)

We must also be on our guard against slipping into the assumption that regional (or other) patterns of conflict on particular issues are fully represented by open, self-proclaimed, dramatic, violent, or assertive actions or by those that frighten judicial, police, or administrative authorities to take note of them in the written forms that enter the archival record. Open, collective wage actions are rare during the Revolution, but this hardly means that landowners and laborers only rarely negotiated about wages (for example, were meals in the fields to be provided?); that disgruntled workers had no weapons but collective strikes (individuals voting with their feet could sometimes do very well, at least when there was work to be had elsewhere); or that landowners never engaged in preemptive violence or recourse to authority (getting a potential agitator carted off by the police for vagrancy,

135. There were great differences in the autonomy of different Provincial Estates; the authority of royal agents in the *pays d'élections* was checked by the semiautonomous courts, differentially resistant. The actual rationalization of the royal administration was quite variable, notable at some moments and locations, not at others.

for example) before collective withholding of work got organized. The data tell us a great deal, but we must be careful not to think it tells us even more than it does. It is worth being especially cautious, as evolving revolutionary legislation was creating new legal channels for peaceful disputation. If the land legislation (see Chapter 8, p. 485) was sponsoring communal referenda on the future of the commons, might not many disputants try out those new channels rather than, say, land invasions? (Perhaps, but in this case it seems likely that legal and illegal channels were tried in the same places, as indicated above, p. 351).

A Collection of Explanations and How to Sort Through Them

We have been testing the impact of specific variables on revolutionary mobilizations in the French countryside. This has largely been an empirical exploration.[136] We need a conceptual exploration as well. How are different kinds of explanations related to each other? What sorts of things could a particular thesis explain—and what are its limits? Let us review the major sorts of explanations of the Revolution's origins and see what each purports to explain. One very fruitful endeavor has been the search for long-term structural changes that altered social relations in ways that redefined group interests, leading, in turn, to redefinitions of desirable social arrangements. Such desires might not even be expressed, not openly at any rate, while opportunities were lacking, but under favorable circumstances they might energize social movements and thereby radically transform institutions.

136. New research will undoubtedly uncover more events, raising the possibility that some of the spatiotemporal patterns found in this chapter will be called into question as our knowledge expands. The broad patterns identified for a numerous class of events, like the antiseigneurial, are less likely to be radically altered than our map of wage conflicts, which are scarce enough that a fairly small number found elsewhere could alter the picture or anti-tax events (which have been very much understudied); but nonetheless some concern is warranted, and some level of reservation is justified. At least three important investigations have recently uncovered rural conflicts that would have entered my data set if I'd had them in time. Monique Cubells has enriched our picture of insurrectionary Provence in the spring of 1789, Peter McPhee has found a large number of confrontations over seigneurial dues and tithes in the *département* of Aude only some of which have been previously discussed in the literature and Nancy Fitch has found a previously unknown antiseigneurial struggle in central France. Cubell's data, if included, would slightly emphasize further the early prominence of rural Provence in insurrection; McPhee's data would augment the already pronounced antiseigneurialism of our southwestern region as well as its propensity to produce conflict with a religious aspect. In neither case is the broad portrait altered, although McPhee's data would seriously alter one's sense of a more finely localized insurrectionary geography within Languedoc. Fitch's data would make the North-Center appear somewhat more turbulent than it does in this chapter, and more inclined to antiseigneurial actions in particular. See Cubells, *Horizons de la Liberté;* Fitch, "Whose Violence?"; and Peter McPhee, "Peasant Revolution, Winegrowing, and the Environment: The Corbières Region of Languedoc, 1780–1830," *Australian Journal of French Studies* 29 (1992): 153–69.

Theories about such structures might be poor at explaining what those appropriate circumstances are and worthless at predicting their occurrence, but may nonetheless be rather powerful in explaining the conflicts those circumstances unleash, rather in the manner of current understandings of earthquakes that can explain how the earth moves in response to the buildup of unrelieved pressures but that are nearly worthless at predicting their occurrence. (The day San Francisco crumbles we will all know why, but no one can foresee when). To follow the geological analogy, we might see such theories as explaining the developing fault lines around which open conflict will rage, without necessarily any notion of the trigger. The two major geological theories of the Revolution of this sort are associated with Marx and Tocqueville. Movement toward an integrated capitalist economy on the one hand or a rationalized central state on the other are held to have generated major stresses in local and national structures of domination. In this chapter it is primarily the local structures, the world of action of France's villagers, that has concerned us.[137]

For the eighteenth century, we may use the penetration of the regional and national market into the village community to stand for the strength of the forces significant in the Marxian model and the extent of central control by the royal bureaucracy for the Tocquevillean.

The notion of slow-changing structures, whose slow change insidiously lays down new fault lines, is only one approach to explaining social revolution. There are several other conceptions of what an explanation might involve. First, as an alternative to change, some direct our attention to motivating attributes that exert their powerful effect almost regardless of other, historically contigent, elements (and some sociologists are more comfortable when they can dispense with the "almost"). Virtually timeless claims about the consequences of such attributes cannot possibly explain the moment of crisis, but might explain subsequent actions if we see these attributes as powerful forces shaping the course of actions at critical junctures. Such a notion as "the better-off (or the worse-off) are always the rebels because they always have the resources (or the grievances)" are of this sort. They do not tell us under what banners rich (or poor) will march; still less do they tell us when (but they may, perhaps, tell us who does the marching). A second alternative to long-term structural change is a cultural one, conceived of as at least semi-autonomous from a change in structures, that leads people to evaluate their positions in new ways. Tocqueville's explanation has some elements of this, in its stress on a reevaluation (or a devaluation) of seigneurial legitimacy, although he roots these cultural changes, ultimately, in structures. Claims that the Enlightenment altered

137. For the bearing of our data on other aspects of the Marxian and Tocquevillean theses, see Chapter 10.

public discourse (or that spinoffs of Jansenist theology did so) are also of this sort. With rural France in mind, and more particularly, the participation of rural people in rebellion, the growth of literacy seems the place to look. Yet a third alternative to a focus on the slow buildup of social fault lines, is to look for short-term shocks, to shift from a focus on the structural to a focus on the conjunctural, the specific circumstances that precipitate the explosion. Here the "Labrousse thesis" of the catastrophic impact of food scarcity on the outbreak of revolutions has achieved the status of a classic.

The broad conclusion from the data is that explanations of these various sorts (other than the timelessly generalizable powerful causal force) do help us understand something. The high price of food helped explain the Great Fear of 1789, the advance of the state helped explain subsistence disturbances at certain points, literacy helped ward off the Great Fear and perhaps made a few rural communities more likely to develop an early movement against the lords, and so on. Yet, plainly, nothing we have looked at fully accounts for the extent of a *shift* to antiseigneurialism, let alone the timing of that shift. There is at least one missing piece to the puzzle here. We have been searching for the contexts of popular action. Is something inevitably left out of all such searches that employ the method of looking at the variety of local contexts? What is left out, I believe, is the interactive, dialogic, processual character of the situation of the countryside. A part of the context of village action was the consequence of the history of previous action (not just the structural, cultural, and conjunctural context). And not just their own previous action, but those of other villagers, whose aggregate impact on national institutions altered the situation. Peasants in village *X* had to deal with legislative actions, in part aimed at an ensemble of forty thousand peasant communities. The local context matters; the blizzard of numbers we have plowed through shows that. But the local contexts do not account adequately for the shifts in peasant targets and tactics.

Unity and Diversity in Revolt

Even a casual glance at rural revolts leads one to wonder at their extraordinary diversity: We find differences in organization and patterns of recruitment, in alliances forged, in enemies sought (and unsought). An important recent comparative literature puts such differences in the spotlight. Jeffery Paige addresses the differences in the goals and targets of squatters in the Peruvian highlands, nationalists in Angola, and social revolutionaries in Vietnam.[138] James Scott's case for the role of a threat to subsistence as the

138. Paige, *Agrarian Revolution.*

driving force behind peasant uprisings is made all the more vivid by the ideological gulf that separates the Burmese and Vietnamese instances on which he focuses.[139] Theda Skocpol finds that differences in the patterns of their rural upheavals placed different constraints upon urban revolutionary leaderships in France, Russia, and China (and offered different opportunities as well): in France and Russia, the holders of state power confronted a countryside that had made an autonomous revolution without them, whereas in China, the Communist party and the rural movement had supported one another symbiotically.[140]

If we go beyond these comparative treatments to examine rural upheavals in a single country, we find that narrowing the geography of the investigation does not necessarily narrow the diversity of rural movements. Students of the Mexican Revolution, say, are unfailingly struck by the contrasts between the *zapatista* movement of central Mexico with its overwhelming land-reform thrust and the diversity of movements, such as the *villistas* of the North, whose land-reform pressures were weak to minimal (not to mention the *cristeros,* who rose in defense of the church or the virtually enslaved people of the southern plantations to whom the revolution came from the outside).[141] The Brazilian Northeast had its spectacular messianic movements but was in the 1960s the location of fierce confrontations over landownership with significant participation by a variety of feuding leftists and in the 1980s saw a renewed wave of conflict largely led by Catholic radicals.[142]

In its rural aspect, the French Revolution is a case in point with its many forms of conflict. These separate forms of contestation were not nationally coordinated and certainly the specific actions engaged in differed greatly. To what degree do these diverse struggles have common sources? One common source, surely, is the very breakdown of the Old Regime, of which the risings are themselves a constituent part. In Chapter 6 we explored several sorts of cyclical time, the daily and monthly rhythms of the revolutionary tide. Perhaps we see here, in the common release in action opened up by regime collapse, a different sort of time, the moment that divides the world

139. James Scott, *The Moral Economy of the Peasant: Rebellion and Subsistence in Southeast Asia* (New Haven: Yale University Press, 1976).

140. Skocpol, *States and Social Revolutions.*

141. Alan Knight, *The Mexican Revolution* (New York: Cambridge University Press, 1986).

142. Robert M. Levine, *Vale of Tears: Revisiting the Canudos Massacre in Northeastern Brazil, 1893–1897* (Berkeley and Los Angeles: University of California Press, 1992); Rui Facó, *Cangaceiros e Fanáticos: Gênese e lutas* (Rio de Janeiro: Editora Civilização Brasileira, 1972); Joseph A. Page, *The Revolution That Never Was. The Brazilian Northeast, 1955–1964* (New York: Grossman, 1972); Vanilda Paiva, ed., *Igreja et questão agrária* (São Paulo: Edicões Loyola, 1985); Thomas E. Skidmore, *The Politics of Military Rule in Brazil, 1964–85* (New York: Oxford University Press, 1988), 298–303.

into before and after, the *kairos,* the moment of which "momentous" is the adjectival form, the moment when all forms of conflict were open.

The commonality is more than temporal coincidence, the common effect of breakdown; we see that a number of important social contexts nurtured multiple forms of revolt. Counterrevolution, in its connection with a very distinctive counterelite, might seem the cluster of rural actions most divergent from the others yet we have seen it resembles other forms of rural activism in being born near towns, away from openfield and arable, in the hills, among the less literate. Of all our forms of action, in fact, it is the wage conflicts that are the most distinctive in contrasting with other kinds of conflict in their association with good cereal yields and wooded areas.

Beyond such general considerations of the common impact of the historic moment and the common facilitating role of the nearby towns, we may inquire whether the act of engagement in one insurrectionary mode retarded or facilitated the engagement in others. The literature suggests now the one, now the other. Counterrevolution may seem simply antithetical to the antifeudal thrust; Lefebvre argued that the Great Fear, sometimes, although not always, bypassed the insurrectionary locales of the spring and summer, but mobilized peasants for the future, especially the antiseigneurial future;[143] Ado, speaking primarily of Old Regime rebellious traditions, sees the experience of anti-tax events as the seedbed of later, and different, revolutionary mobilizations; Ado also argued that mobilizations for the constitutional church or against refractory priests spilled over into antiseigneurial action;[144] and Vovelle has recently pointed to the intermittent subsistence conflicts of the revolutionary years as a continual source of turbulent mobilization that could readily shift into antifeudal forms.[145]

We can approach these issues more closely by inquiring, not about broad regional patterns, but narrowly local ones. We have our hundreds of *bailliages*. Do *bailliages* specialize in a single form of action? Do *bailliages* with one form of rural engagement have all others? Or some others? Table 7.12 presents some simple quantitative evidence on whether *bailliages* with insurrectionary actions at some point tend to be the same that have such at other points as well. For each of some half-dozen moments I identified those *bailliages* that had already had at least one rising and those that would have at least one later on. I then measured the degree to which these were the

143. Lefebvre, *Grande Peur,* 247. More recently, Clay Ramsay's study of the area around Soissons stresses the geographic disjunction of early antiseigneurialism and Great Fear. See Clay Ramsay, *Ideology of the Great Fear,* 242, 254.

144. Ado, *Krest'ianskoe dvizhenie,* 58, 239.

145. Vovelle, *La découverte de la politique,* 59. Cynthia Bouton's work on the Flour War of the 1770s shows subsistence events beginning to shade off into antifeudal actions. See *The Flour War: Gender, Class and Community in Late Ancien Régime French Society* (University Park: Pennsylvania State University Press, 1993).

Table 7.12. Occurrence of Insurrections in Same *Bailliage* Before and After Selected Dates (Q-coefficients)

Dates	Association of Insurrection Before Date and Insurrection After Date
January 31, 1789	.79*
June 30, 1789	.72****
August 31, 1789	.71****
December 31, 1789	.69****
February 28, 1790	.70****

*$p < .05$.
****$p < .0001$.

same *bailliages*. The table is quite clear that *bailliages*[146] that already had events are more likely to have them again. Those that have already had events by early 1789, for example, tend to have others later on, and so forth.

But does an insurrection of one sort lead only to a repeated action of the same type, to the occurrence of all types, or of some types? This question needs a more complex presentation, based on a much larger collection of figures. Consider Table 7.13. This table is devoted to the discovery of whether *bailliages* that had had incidents of various types by late summer of 1789 had incidents of the same or other kinds later on. (Wage events and counterrevolution are only considered here with regard to their later occurrence.) *Mirabile dictu*, the data are consistent with most claims in the literature. Where the Great Fear touched a *bailliage* (see the last row of the table), antiseigneurial and other actions followed; subsistence events opened the way to other forms of action, as did anti-tax events. Subsistence events early in the Revolution, indeed, are associated later on with both antiseigneurial and counterrevolutionary events, bearing out Vovelle's interpretation of the generative but indeterminative role of conflicts over food. Where the Great Fear occurred, similarly, a broad spectrum of other actions followed. On the other hand, the Great Fear seems a vaccine against panics down the road; the only significant negative relation in the table, in fact, is between the Great Fear and later panics.[147]

146. I examined a number of similar tables using different points to divide before and after and will only summarize the results in this discussion.

147. One claim not borne out concerns the way antiseigneurial action is held to have warded off the Great Fear, a matter that requires data not in this table. Despite frequent claims to the contrary, starting with Lefebvre (*Grande Peur,* 247), the Great Fear was not averted by the prior occurrence of nearby antiseigneurial events. Among 32 *bailliages* with antiseigneurial events prior to July 1789, 28 had instances of the Great Fear; among 64 with antiseigneurial events in July and August, 44 knew the Great Fear. Not only did a clear majority of such *bailliages* have the Great Fear, but that proportion is larger than the proportion of *bailliages* without antiseigneurial events that had the Fear. The Great Fear may have stayed away from the very community that had attacked its

Even the counterrevolutionary events do not altogether stand apart, associated as they are with the prior occurrences of food riots and panics. But matters are not so simple. If we were to examine an analogous table, but one that was based on events that occur before and after the end of February 1790, we would find a positive association of antiseigneurial events before that date and counterrevolution after. In other words, the locations of the antiseigneurial wave of early 1790, but not earlier, saw counterrevolution down the line. Western Brittany, we may recall, made a major contribution to that antiseigneurial wave. Let us also recall our earlier observations on the West generally (see Table 7.3) where we saw that some third of that region's *bailliages* had antiseigneurial events at some point while some third were spared counterrevolution. Were these the same third?

Table 7.14 displays, for the forty-three western *bailliages,* the occurrence or nonoccurrence of antiseigneurial and counterrevolutionary events. There is a very strong association of the two. The one-third of Western *bailliages* with antiseigneurial events are by no means the same as those without counterrevolution. Of the fourteen antiseigneurial *bailliages,* a remarkable thirteen went on to participate in counterrevolution as well; and nearly half the counterrevolutionary *bailliages* had had antiseigneurial events. The early mobilizations, as Roger Dupuy has insisted,[148] are signs of a political engagement that can turn against the Revolution. Where western peasants fought the lords early in the Revolution, they or their neighbors[149] turned on the regime, and were joined by other peasants as well. The western countryside was not diametrically opposed to a revolutionary France, but merely went further and faster in a progressive rural disenchantment (see also Table 7.7).

To sum up, the occurrence of most forms of conflict seem to make most other forms of conflict probable nearby. (Only wage conflicts stand apart from this generalization.) To what degree do we have here a direct effect in which one insurrectionary experience facilitates others? By virtue of

lord—my data, organized by *bailliage* rather than community, do not permit me to resolve this—but, in that case, it must be that the Fear was actually attracted to villages that were near antiseigneurial ones. (This is perfectly plausible if the Fear is sometimes an anxious reaction to antiseigneurial actions by one's neighbors.)

148. See, for example, Roger Dupuy, *La Garde Nationale et les débuts de la Révolution en Ille-et-Vilaine (1789–mars 1793)* (Rennes: Université de Haute Bretagne, 1972), 262.

149. I blur Dupuy's formulation a bit here since he insists that precisely the same villages, not just the same general regions, shift from antiseigneurialism to counterrevolution. It is a rather different micropicture if it is the neighbors of an antiseigneurial village who mobilize for counterrevolution, suggesting a fear and hatred of rural blues by rural whites and giving us an image of a rural civil war, perhaps closer to Donald Sutherland's model than Roger Dupuy's. At the *bailliage* level, my data do not distinguish between the two; an unpublished study by Sutherland shows that not a single person named in Henri Sée's important work as involved in antiseigneurialism in 1790 turns up on later lists of Chouans. (I thank Sutherland for sharing this important datum with me.)

Table 7.13. Occurrence of One Form of Insurrection Before August 31, 1789, and the Same or Other Forms After that Date in the Same *Bailliage* (Q-coefficients)

Event Occurs Before August 31, 1789	Event Occurs After August 31, 1789							
	Antiseigneurial	Religious	Anti-tax	Subsistence	Land	Wage	Panic	Counterrevolution
Antiseigneurial	.54****	.42***	.42*	.29*	.56****	.27	.19	.26
Religious	.42**	.40**	.48**	.20	.53***	.40	.22	−.25
Anti-tax	.42**	.42**	.58	.36*	.50**	.03	.27	.20
Subsistence	.45****	.53****	.57****	.51****	.55****	.08	.30	.48***
Land	.49**	.43*	.35	.34	.76****	.29	.52	−.10
Panic	.64****	.63****	.32	.66****	.60****	1.00****	−.40*	.38*

*$p < .05$
**$p < .01$
***$p < .001$
****$p < .0001$

Table 7.14. Occurrence of Antiseigneurial and Counterrevolutionary Events in Western *Bailliages*

		Number of *Bailliages* with Antiseigneurial Events	
		No Events	At Least One Event
Number of *Bailliages* with counterrevolutionary events	No Events	14	1
	At Least One Event	15	13

$N = 43$.
$Q = .85$.
$p < .01$ (Fisher's Exact Test).

accumulated experience in creating organizations and choosing targets, by virtue of demonstrating the weakness of authority that inspires others or by virtue of frightening others into mobilizing themselves, one event may be a spark. Rather than an emulatory process, however, the geographical propinquity of events could also be produced by the far-reaching effects of powerful stresses. The urban presence, for example, may generate several events, or even several sorts of events, in close proximity, especially at propitious moments. We can pose the question of emulation versus powerful contexts as causal forces, but we cannot resolve it with the methods employed here.

Center, Periphery, Peripheries

No image of a unified or homogeneous peasantry can survive this chapter's look at the rural revolution(s)' regionalization. France's regions have distinctive patterns of revolutionary action, both in the mix of event-types and in their timing. The early responses of the new revolutionary leadership to the rural crisis, had as a backdrop the revolts of the summer of 1789, in which we have seen the major role played by peasants of the North. The dramatic moment in the latter part of June when the National Assembly took the plunge of declaring its own existence against the king was almost immediately followed by the great rising of Parisian militants and a number of incidents of plebeian violence in Paris that their memoirs and correspondence show to have been deeply upsetting to the legislators.[150] Immediately

150. The impact on the legislators of the violence around them is taken up in Timothy Tackett's *Becoming a Revolutionary: The Deputies of the French National Assembly and the Emergence of a Revolutionary Culture (1789–1790)* (Princeton: Princeton University Press, 1996), 165–69.

on the heels of these Parisian events, the deputies were hearing a rising crescendo of reports of rural turbulence from around the country; but we have seen how concentrated in the nearby North the events of that particular moment were. The Assembly in early August came up with a package that appeared to meet the needs of that moment; how frustrating and puzzling that, a few months later, the very different peasantries of the Southwest and South-Center rose and were not to be placated by explanations of the benefits brought by the new laws.[151]

Not only did a good deal of the Revolution's dynamism derive from below and beyond the horizons of the urban elites but each region of France played its special part. The French-speakers of the relatively prosperous plain around and north of Paris who had formed the human resources on which Capetian kings enlarged their realm down through the great seventeenth-century expansion in the Northeast, North, and Southeast—the *Staatsvolk,* if one may employ so un-French a term—had their moments, but the leading edge of peasant pressure on the revolutionary state more often came from farther off: antiseigneurial actions in Quercy, Rouergue, Périgord, and Provence; land seizures in Alsace; counterrevolution in Maine and Brittany (and in the Southeast as well). These were not just rural events, but took place far from Paris and even French speech, took place not so much in central villages as those with more scattered livings (but also in and near the large semi-urban Mediterranean villages), took place not so much in the more literate as in the less literate places of the kingdom.

Consider one specific element of the peasant revolts that has sparked some good research: It was in Périgord, Rouergue, and Quercy that the maypole first emerged as a sign of insurrection. The use of maypoles in antiseigneurial actions diffused gradually through the countryside in the West and South. The government eventually appropriated and tamed it as the "tree of liberty." The anxious fascination with these genuinely plebeian actions on the part of educated revolutionary legislators shows up in Bishop Henri Grégoire's extended essay on the meaning and origins of these trees.[152] Grégoire reaches back in time to connect maypoles to sacred trees of antiquity as well as to interpret them as multifaceted symbols of nurturance: the tree shades and shelters, is long-lived and bears fruit. As to its insertion into the history of the Revolution, that was, in Grégoire's account, the work of a local priest, in whom, we may infer, resided a memory of the gods' oaks and groves of antiquity and an appreciation of God's bounty today. This (false) history manages to say everything about these trees except their plebeian origins within the revolutionary context,

151. We shall address the legislature in Chapter 8.

152. Henri Grégoire, "Essai historique et patriotique sur les arbres de la liberté," in *L'Abbé Grégoire, Evêque des Lumières* (Paris: Editions France-Empire, 1988), 192–212.

which has been effaced by a gift of a paternal priest. Grégoire, a clerical legislator, explains to the people a priestly gift and one might almost forget that the actual audience for Grégoire's long essay was a puzzled and anxious urban elite, including his fellow legislators, who were trying to make out what semiliterate southwestern sharecroppers were getting at when they planted these poles on seigneurial lawns. Once the central authorities took up these poles, associated them with liberty, and produced a historical interpretation altogether deplebeianizing them, central standardizing pressures rapidly led to their diffusion throughout the country. Now, finally, the trees took root in the northern countryside.[153]

The national history of the Federation movement of the village National Guards is less well worked out,[154] but resembles that of the tree of liberty in some ways, although the earliest spark is not from the rural periphery. A number of towns began to authorize (in some cases one might speak of "revitalize") armed militias as the sense of disorder mounted. Troyes was an important initiator, as early as April 1788, and several towns followed suit in the winter and spring of 1789,[155] perhaps especially commonly in Provence where the rural mobilization was so intense and threatening.[156] By May and June, fear of attacks on grain harvests led several *intendants* to permit or even promote peasant militias.[157] The attempted formation of a Parisian militia in July helped bring on the attack on the Bastille; the king's subsequent recognition of the Paris National Guard by appointing Lafayette its commander[158] no doubt spread a general legitimation over such bodies. During the urban and rural upheavals of July and August, not only larger towns but many villages formed National Guard units of their own,[159] often spurred, locally, by the Great Fear. The degree to which the Parisian Guard was an inspiring model that diffused into remote villages as opposed to the degree to which the Parisian organization provided a legitimating cover for what some villagers wanted to do anyway is hard to assess. The National Assembly's recognition of militias on August 10, 1789, granted a further legitimation (*AP* 8:378). The election of new local authorities early in 1790 generated a new wave of rural Guards units as these new authorities sought to organize armed force.[160] The National Assembly's recognition that these

153. Vovelle, *La découverte de la politique,* 44–55.

154. Ibid., 38–44.

155. Jacques Godechot, *The Taking of the Bastille, July 14, 1789* (New York: Scribner, 1970), 129, 132, 174.

156. On the formation of town militias in Provence in the spring see Cubells, *Horizons de la liberté,* 111–12.

157. On these early rural militias in Soissonnais, see Ramsay, *Ideology of the Great Fear,* 221–25.

158. Godechot, *Bastille,* 196, 260.

159. The most thorough regional study so far is Dupuy, *La Garde Nationale en Ille-et-Vilaine.*

160. Paul d'Hollander, "Les Gardes Nationales en Limousin (juillet 1789–juillet 1790)," in *Annales Historiques de la Révolution Française* 58 (1992): 471.

new municipal authorities would have paramilitary units under their command provided an opening (and, perhaps, also publicized an organizational possibility).[161] But the National Guards probably had another source as well: the detested militia of the Old Regime.[162] Although, as the *cahiers* make clear (see Chapter 2, p. 39), militia service was loathed, the experience of service in locally recruited, organized, and officered military units—as the militias sometimes were—was very likely an important model for many a villager and many a village to draw on in 1789, and beyond, but now with a far larger voluntary component. Significant numbers of villages might form such bodies. In Limousin, for example, some 10% of communities formed Guards units.[163] In our data set on events, these National Guard units were sometimes an important strike force in antiseigneurial campaigns or other insurrectionary actions. Nancy Fitch's research has unearthed a striking instance near Autun in our North-Central region. In the fall of 1789, the village of Issy-l'Evêque placed its priest in command of its newly formed Guards, who directed them in seizing grain from large producers. The priest's election as mayor by appreciative villagers did not prevent his arrest. (A local petition for his release praised him for putting the National Guards behind ordinary people.)[164] Initiative in antiseigneurial action on the part of Guards units was not always the result of a radical commander. In January 1790, for example, the head of the nearby National Guards unit at Guichen in Brittany twice failed to bring back a satisfactory renunciation of his seigneurial rights from a local lord; that unfortunate commander was pushed aside by his guardsmen, who accused him of selling them out for a

161. The interplay of efforts at central control and grassroots initiative is striking. In the brief parliamentary debate on the proposal for new structures of local government on February 2, 1790, Viscount de Noailles proposed an amendment, immediately adopted, barring "national militias" from meddling in local government and enjoining their obedience to proper officials. Thus the legislation, presumably aimed at controlling local armed groups that were already formed, implicitly accepted the existence of "armed companies under the title of bourgeous militia, national guards, volunteers or under any other denomination" (*AP* 11:417–19). Eleven months later Robespierre waxed enthusiastic over the possibility of a nationwide ensemble of local Guards units, in which membership is open to all regardless of wealth, as "the spectacle of a vast hidden empire of free and armed citizens." But he was quick to stress that local units were to be under judicial or legislative control. The importance he attached to the National Guards may be judged from the length of his discussion and the thoroughness with which he has thought through issues of purpose, relation to the army, membership, control, and even the design of uniforms. Another measure of the significance of the Guards is the debate occasioned by Robespierre's speech to the Jacobins. See Maximilien Robespierre, *Oeuvres,* vol. 6, *Discours 1789–1790* (Paris: Presses Universitaires de France, 1950), 610–55; the quote is from 632.

162. Dupuy makes this argument for Brittany in *La Garde Nationale en Ille-et-Vilaine,* 23–40.

163. Compiled from figures in Paul d'Hollander, "Les Gardes Nationales en Limousin," 469.

164. Nancy Fitch, "Whose Violence? Insurrection and the Negotiation of Democratic Politics in Central France, 1789–1851," presented to the conference on Violence and the Democratic Tradition in France, University of California at Irvine, February 1994, 13–14.

bribe, and who then went on to rip the lord's benches from the nearby church, set fire to the lord's papers, do a good deal of general damage to his *château,* and drink his cider.[165]

Perhaps combating a sense of isolation, such local National Guards sometimes affiliated with one another.[166] The first-known such act of federation seems to have been in the Alps in the fall of 1789.[167] The prospect of an intervillage network of such Guards units, armed and disciplined, must have been very disturbing to some. Dealing with village action that was generally uncoordinated among separate villages was proving hard enough. Towns attempted to seize control of the movement by organizing their own urban-centered federations of the armed citizenry. The urban Guards federation could become a powerful vehicle for, say, a radical city like Marseille to enforce its vision of the Revolution throughout Provence in combat with a precocious southeastern counterrevolutionary mobilization. Ultimately Parisians sought national control of these networks; the Festival of Federation of July 14, 1790, was as much an effort at channeling popular revolution (by organizing it) as it was of celebrating it.

The political clubs of all persuasions that blossomed throughout the French countryside were yet another organizational indicator of the rural periphery's initiative.[168] These signs and seedbeds of rural political activism were often joined by a group of villagers collectively,[169] and in the overall judgment of their historians, were made up of perhaps one-half "cultivators," one-third artisans and shopkeepers, and a sprinkling of local notables, perhaps a lawyer or two. They were far more densely implanted at an early stage in the southern countryside than in the North. The northern clubs did well, to be sure, in district and departmental centers; but in your ordinary northern village this vehicle of a political action was scarce. Not so in the South; in the Department of Vaucluse, a stunning 91% of communities had clubs.[170] In parts of the South, even places with fewer than five hundred persons might well have a club, which meant that these organizations were reaching even more deeply into the depths of the countryside than the religious confraternities of the Old Regime for which the South was famous, which hardly existed in such small places.[171] (A population of two hundred

165. Henri Seé, "Troubles agraires en Haute Bretagne," 319–22.

166. Yoichi Uriu, "Espace et Révolution."

167. Michel Vovelle, ed., "Les fédérations" in Vovelle, ed., *L'état de la France pendant la Révolution* (Paris: Editions de la Découverte, 1988), 216–17.

168. Jean Boutier and Philippe Boutry, *Atlas de la Révolution française,* vol. 6, *Les sociétés politiques* (Paris: Editions de l'Ecole des Hautes Etudes en Sciences Sociales, 1992).

169. Ibid., 59.

170. Ibid., 103.

171. On the role of political clubs and National Guards in rural Auvergne, see Jonathan R. Dalby, *Les paysans cantaliens et la Révolution française (1789–1794)* (Clermont Ferrand: Université de Clermont-Ferrand III, 1989), 258–62.

seems to be the threshold below which villages did not develop clubs either.) Once again, the new state took over the club movement and only then did the northern villagers, taking their cue from the center, form such groupings themselves.

The role of France's peripheries is vital generally. Timothy Tackett has shown the Western urban elite to be unusually prone at the onset of revolution to force a showdown with the church;[172] Lynn Hunt finds the Left more implanted in the periphery;[173] a flurry of recent research on electoral participation, particularly Malcolm Crook's and Melvin Edelstein's, shows not only that early in the Revolution rural participation was generally higher than urban, but that some locations in the rural South and Center compared favorably with the North in voting rates;[174] and I have found that Third Estate and nobility in economically poor and politically peripheral areas were more polarized in their views in the *cahiers* than they were in the economic and political centers of the kingdom.[175]

Tracking the Rural Revolution through Time and Space

Great social movements sometimes seem to follow a regular rhythm. An initial opportunity seized by the hardy opens a breach in the established order that others follow. Those engaged seek new forms of action and eventually find forms that yield some measure of success yet do not bring down too much counteraction from elites or governing authorities. Meanwhile new groups form, taking advantage of the opening; still other

172. Tackett, *Religion, Revolution and Religious Culture*.

173. Lynn Hunt, *Politics, Culture and Class in the French Revolution* (Berkeley and Los Angeles: University of California Press, 1984). Timothy Tackett's work on the National Assembly shows the legislature's emerging Jacobins of 1790 to be disproportionately of rural, southern, and less wealthy backgrounds than their fellow legislators. See Tackett, *Becoming a Revolutionary*, 286.

174. In reviewing a great variety of electoral research by himself and others, Edelstein finds, for example, that in some dozen departments studied, the country people always outvoted the city-dwellers in the elections of May 1790. The urban-rural difference was less sharp one year later. In impoverished Limousin, communities with under five hundred inhabitants had a spectacular turnout of 78% in February 1790 (as compared to the city of Limoges with 47%); by December 1792, Limousin's small villages had fallen to the initial level of Limoges. See Melvin Edelstein, "La place de la Révolution française dans la politisation des paysans," *Annales Historiques de la Révolution Française*, no. 280 (1990): 135–49; Edelstein, "Electoral Behavior During the Constitutional Monarchy"; and Olivier Audevart, "Les élections en Haute-Vienne pendant la Révolution," in Jean Boutier, Michel Cassan, Paul d'Hollander, and Bernard Pommaret, eds., *Limoges en Révolution* (Treignac: Editions "Les Monédières," 1989), 129–38.

175. Shapiro and Markoff, *Revolutionary Demands*, chap. 16.

forces, who initially held back, may eventually enter the fray. Sidney Tarrow's work on social movements has probably given the most cogent such account and his study of Italy in the 1960s and 1970s is probably the most detailed single such treatment along these lines.[176]

Since the location of various configurations of interest and resources is often geographically structured the likelihood that large-scale movements may exhibit spatiotemporal patternings is high and Tarrow's Italian data constitutes a case in point as protest moves from students to workers to clergy and from one town to another. Revolutionary mobilizations may also exhibit such patterns. Marc Ferro observes of the 1917 Russian Revolution that it began in the cities, moved into the forests and their clearings, and then arrived at steppe and mountain.[177]

Our French data suggest some elements of this picture, but deviate from it in the direction of greater complexity. Rather than a movement from center to periphery, we have seen a more intricate interplay of regional initiatives. Much of the more prosperous and literate countryside of northern and eastern France has its great moment only after preliminary skirmishing in the West and a considerable battle in the Southeast (with the Paris region the only northern zone to rival early Provence). In the summer of 1789, however, the rural component of the popular upheaval that was such an important spur to the National Assembly, was concentrated in the North and East. With the Old Regime broken, the main action is elsewhere (and for years) but not in a single place, nor in a single form of conflict, as South-Center, Southwest, Southeast, and West all play various roles. Various locations in the North and East continue to be the centers of battles around subsistence, land, taxation, and wages, but not usually around the numerically most impressive antifeudal actions. But these antifeudal actions only became predominant after that summer.

The temporal pattern of insurrection, both the microrhythms of the weekly cycle and the ebb and flow over the months, gave us some sense of the interplay of traditional and tradition-breaking patterns in the revolutionary countryside (see Chapter 6, pp. 332 et seq.). Spatially, a northern and eastern location for the drama of the summer of 1789 was almost as much an innovation as was the rapidly rising antiseigneurial focus, the move away from Sunday as the favored day for mayhem and the weakening of the codes that limited mutual ruin at harvest-time. The great historical works on the rural revolts of the seventeenth century have made western, southwestern, and southeastern place-names stand for resistance to conscription, resis-

176. Sidney Tarrow, *Democracy and Disorder: Protest and Politics in Italy, 1965–1975* (Oxford: Clarendon Press, 1989).

177. Marc Ferro, *The Russian Revolution of February 1917* (Englewood Cliffs, N.J.: Prentice-Hall, 1967), xi.

tance to taxes; in a word, resistance to the growing state apparatus of extraction. Roland Mousnier's classic *Fureurs Paysannes,* for example, has vivid chapters on the *Croquants* of Saintonge, Angoumois, and Poitou of 1636, the *Croquants* of Périgord of 1637, and the *Nu-Pieds* of Normandy of 1639. (The *Torrébens* of lower Brittany of 1675, exceptionally in Mousnier's account, are even more strongly mobilized around seigneurial questions than taxation).[178] Yves-Marie Bercé goes back a bit further to the *Tard-Avisés* of Limousin and Périgord (1593–95).[179] He identifies the places whose people were known by contemporaries for their hot-blooded ferocity in resisting seventeenth-century taxation: the marshes around Les Sables d'Olonne in Poitou; the woods and wasteland along the Paris-Bordeaux road in Saintonge and Angoumois; a forest south of Périgueux; the plains where Quercy and Limousin meet and where Quercy meets Rouergue; the valleys of the Pyrenees.

After the summer breakthrough in 1789, it is precisely these places (except for Normandy) that appear again and again in our accounts, as Albert Soboul pointed out. The classical heartlands of the seventeenth-century rural tax revolt—Brittany, Périgord, Limousin, Rouergue, Quercy, as well as Provence[180]—are where the peasants came to refuse the abolition of feudalism as the National Assembly defined it in August 1789. For the most part these areas came late to antiseigneurial action (apart from a precocious Provence, already the setting of violent struggle in the spring). Sidney Tarrow has suggested that we see great social movements as initially generating opportunities for innovators in tactics and organization; these movements are later joined by more traditional actors, who see their own opportunities in the initial successes of the pioneers. Our geography of revolt fits, if imperfectly. The traditional heartland of revolt rises, beginning in late fall 1789, not against its traditional target, but the newer one, and after others had pioneered. The deviation from the Tarrowian model here is the early mobilization in Provence, not only early to mobilize at all (the same could be said even more strongly of Brittany) but early to begin the shift toward seigneurial targets. Not all of France's villagers in regions of past strong anti-state militance needed the example of northern innovators to decide to move against the lords. The spatiotemporal rhythms were complex, and were certainly not just themes stated in the center and then responded to with so many variations in the periphery. There were distinct

178. Roland Mousnier, *Fureurs paysannes: Les paysans dans les révoltes du XVIIe siècle (France, Russie, Chine)* (Paris: Calmann-Lévy, 1967).

179. Yves-Marie Bercé, *Histoire des croquants: Étude des soulèvements populaires au XVIIe siècle dans le sud-ouest de la France* (Geneva: Droz, 1974).

180. Provence was a center of seventeenth-century revolts, but René Pillorget's work suggests that these were largely urban affairs. See René Pillorget, *Les mouvements insurrectionels de Provence entre 1596 et 1715* (Paris: A. Pedone, 1975).

peripheries and the social movement was more a polyphonic structure than a sonata.

We have seen many regional differences—Alsatians rising against the lords in the summer of 1789 and remaining calm, mostly, thereafter and peasants of the South-Center and Southwest who do not rise until the end of that year, but prove almost impossible to pacify from then on—but what all these rebellious country people had in common was that they were not just talking to one another, but were in a dialogue with those who administered and those who made the laws. Far from the villages, France's enlightened, revolutionary legislators were an essential part of the polyphonic structure.

We have seen how active was the Breton countryside even before the spring of 1789 and how active was the Provençal countryside that spring—not only active, in fact, but a leader in the shift to antiseigneurial actions. One might point to structural factors: the Provençal heritage of communal solidarities, for example, yet the specifics of time and target seemed elusive. Once we introduced the immediate political context into the discussion, however, we advanced our grasp on what was happening. The intensive campaign for the hearts and minds of Brittany's rural people in the bitter debates that preceded the final decisions on the structures of the Estates-General may help us, as Roger Dupuy suggests,[181] to understand the early mobilization of the Breton countryside; the similarly bitter, complex, elite struggles in Provence, which cast the fief-holding nobility as an intransigent and avowedly reactionary force may help explain not only the early engagement of that province's popular classes, but the early antiseigneurial turn.

If distinctive regional political contexts and regional elite-plebeian dialogues help us grasp popular engagement prior to the summer of 1789, after that summer peasant communities throughout France all had the same powerful interlocutor as each other: the revolutionary legislature. The whole drama from the June declaration that there was a National Assembly through the proclamation of the abolition of the feudal regime in early August, made a national dialogue of village and legislature, of peasants and legislators, at the center of the subsequent revolutionary dynamic. Before the summer of 1789, the varying elite dramas in France's different regions shaped peasant insurrectionary politics differently; after that summer there was a national legislature whose members ached to reconstruct France but found that they had to deal with forty thousand villages.

And innovation came from everywhere. One important village organizational innovation not present in the Old Regime was the National Guards, perhaps appropriated from the Parisian model that lent it legitimacy. It was hard to ban National Guards in the village after accepting them in Paris. Yet

181. Dupuy, *De la Révolution à la Chouannerie*, 24–32.

the village guard probably was taking on a life of its own, threatening to become a grassroots armed force. The cities, appreciative of the threat, moved to repossess the Federation movement, as Paris moved to incorporate the tree of liberty into the revolutionary cult, but on its own terms, under its control. Villagers innovated, emulated, and were emulated.

The Revolution was not the work of Paris, imposing itself on its provinces. It was not the work of an elite promoting modernity. It was not the work of a homogeneous peasantry, nor of a single region. The Revolution was the interplay of peripheral elites and central administrators, of elites and plebeians, of the differently timed pressures from northern villagers and from those far from Paris. The initial breakthrough in antiseigneurial legislation took the nationwide explosion of the summer of 1789 with its strong Paris-area and generally northern participation. Creativity in new organizational vehicles, in actions, and in rejecting the legislators' compromise of August 4, 1789 (see Chapters 8 and 9) were to be found elsewhere. But as peasant rebellions were an essential context for antifeudal legislation, antifeudal legislation was an essential context for peasant action. France's regionally diverse peasantries did not rise in a political vacuum. They were not merely propelled to fight by their varying interests as given by the local conditions of work and the local structures of social relations; they were not merely enabled to fight to different degrees by resources that varied among different kinds of communities. They were not just discovering the possibility of fighting in local opportunities, and they surely were not just expressing their anger, born of local structures and relations in locally varying favorable circumstances. There were forty thousand peasant communities, and in each, people were deciding to act or to stay on the sidelines. The Revolution was engaged in differently in obscure places that few had even heard of fifty kilometers away: Rexpoëde, Saint-Jean-des-Choux, Taradeau, Quézac, Cabris, Jazeneuil, Puyvaladour, Méximieux, Dieu-le-Fit, Saint-Jean-de-Gardonnenque, Saint-Bonnet-Troncet, Chénérailles, and Couëron. Those who lived there were making their own decisions and made them differently but they were not making forty thousand disconnected revolutions. There was a French Revolution. Trying to define, direct, control, and even embody this national revolution was its central legislature. France's villagers were in a dialogue with the lawmakers of France, a dialogue I shall attempt to follow in the chapters to come.

CHAPTER

8

REVOLUTIONARY PEASANTS AND REVOLUTIONARY LEGISLATORS

The "Eternally Celebrated" Night of August 4

Close to two in the morning of August 5, 1789, the National Assembly's cheers for "Louis XVI, restorer of French liberty" were cut off by the session's presiding officer in order to enact a formal decree that briefly summarized the many proposals that had emerged during the long hours of discussion. An exchange of congratulations among legislators and onlookers brought the session to a close. Following some further debate over the next several days, the Assembly adopted on August 11 a more elaborate statement that began with the dramatic words: "The National Assembly destroys the feudal regime in its entirety" (*AP* 8:350, 397–98).

The National Assembly had just been the scene of a sequence of events as unexpected, dramatic, and mysterious as the Great Fear in the countryside. The agenda for early August had called for progress on a Declaration of Rights by way of preface to the Constitution (*AP* 8:339-41). This task was to be interrupted on August 3 by another of the anxious reports on the situation in the countryside that were becoming regular occurrences. There was some talk of defending property rights, of repressive measures and of poor relief (*AP* 8:336–37). On the evening of August 4, Target introduced a measure that addressed "the sacred rights of property and the safety of persons" by reaffirming existing law. Before this rather routine proposal could be debated the floor was seized by viscount de Noailles, who made the first of many radical proposals on rural exactions (*AP* 8:343). Suddenly, one deputy after another began to call for an end to the feudal regime, with some proposing rather drastic measures. What might have seemed a usual round of speeches, if on an unusually central and contentious issue,[1] suddenly altered character as the deputies began to make personal renunciations of their own privileges. A large number of nobles rose to speak—and renounce. The clergy joined in, abandoning some of their own rights. Not to be outdone, members of the Third Estate announced that they were prepared to give up town privileges. Entire regional blocs of delegates declared an end to their own region's special status. Others raised a range of other issues, not all of which were taken up: tax privileges, government stipends, the guilds, slavery. This went on late into the night, wholly defying any attempt to keep track, and before it was over, all manner of other elements of the Old Regime had been offered by someone to the dustbin of history. We know from their letters, journals, and memoirs that many deputies gave themselves over to the exaltation of casting off the past and fusing with others in a primordial experience of fraternization.[2] Others were stunned by the nuttiness about them;[3] still others kept their head but judged it prudent to join in;[4] and others yet again managed to try to steer things one way or another for idiosyncratic motives.[5]

1. Little in the *cahiers* had so set nobility and Third Estate apart. See Chapter 3 as well as John Markoff and Gilbert Shapiro, "Consensus and Conflict at the Onset of Revolution: A Quantitative Study of France in 1789," *American Journal of Sociology* 91 (1985): 44–47.

2. Looking back after a longer experience of revolution, Bailly recalled: "After the troubles that had just excited us, it rested one's soul to see this agreement among the representatives of the nation, this imposing union of the wills of all and this competition in sacrifice for the public good. Beautiful moments, where have you gone?" See Jean-Sylvain Bailly, *Mémoires de Bailly* (Paris: Baudoin, 1821), 2:217.

3. The journalist Charles Lacretelle described the morning after: "The next day most noble and clerical deputies appeared astonished, anxious, almost confused"; *Histoire de la France pendant le dix-huitième siècle* (Paris: Treuttel et Würtz, 1821), 7:142. Many observers, including some deputies, felt that too much dinner wine made a major contribution to the event, a thesis to which Kessel gives some credence; see Patrick Kessel, *La nuit du 4 août 1789* (Paris: Arthaud, 1969), 192–96.

4. On August 7, the marquis de Ferrières, summarizing the tumultuous evening's events in a letter to a good friend, sketched some of the elevated reasons for approving those events and then offers this explanation of his own adherence: "It would have been useless, even dangerous for you,

The rich complexity of events is reflected in the memoirs of A. C. Thibaudeau, a young lawyer who accompanied his father, a Third Estate deputy from Poitou. He describes an "exaltation" that extended to "delirium" in which "I was caught up, like everyone." But it was hard to feel sure one fully understood the course of events. "Was it real? Was it a dream?" Waking the next day, "one thought over the evening's work. Then came the calculation of losses, of vanities, of regret and repentance. How could one have abandoned oneself to this dizzy excess? It was beyond imagination and one felt shame." A bit further on he offers a very different story of noble sacrifice. "The feudal regime did not fall for ignoble reasons: it was worn out, it was violently attacked and it was unsupportable. The nobles felt this. A few generous souls sought the glory of giving it the final blow; most offered their rights to the holocaust in order to save their lands and their persons." And, now, utterly denying any irrationality in the central drama, he adds: "If there was any unreason or madness it was not in abolishing a rotten and odious institution . . . but in giving Louis XVI, for an initiative he had nothing to do with and which must have disgusted him, the title of 'restorer of French Liberty'."[6]

The momentary solidarity found by the legislators (for some more than momentary) and the sense of rising to meet the fearsome challenges around them made the night of August 4 a sort of elite counterpart to the Great Fear, complete with rumors of a plot.[7] In this case the notion of a plot was

had I opposed the general wish of the nation. It would have been to designate you, you and your possessions, as victims of the rage of the multitude; it would have been to expose you to seeing your homes set on fire. The nobles who went along with these sacrifices are losing as much and more than you. . . . Be assured that our little bailliage, until now, is the one that has suffered the least troubles and misfortunes. I dare say that I have tried, through accommodation and prudence, to avoid compromising you. I, therefore, pray that the nobility does not show any regret at the giveaway that has just taken place, that they find no fault publicly with the decree of the National Assembly, and that they show in their speech a prudence, a circumspection on which their own peace depends (and perhaps also the general well-being of the Kingdom)." See Charles-Elie de Ferrières, *Correspondence inédite (1789, 1790, 1791)* (Paris: Armand Colin, 1932), 116–17.

5. Like the duke du Châtelet, who, noticing the bishop of Chartres calling for an abandonment of hunting rights, formed and acted on the wish to go after ecclesiastical payments. ("So, he takes away our hunting; I'm going to take away his tithes," the duke is said to have commented to his neighbors; a bit later he took the floor and made good on his threat.) See Kessel, *La nuit du 4 août,* 154–56; and Jean-Baptiste Grellet de Beauregard, "Lettres de M. Grellet de Beauregard," *Société des sciences naturelles et archéologiques de la Creuse* (1899): 78.

6. Antoine-Claire Thibaudeau, *Mémoires, 1765–1792* (Paris: Champion, 1875), 94–96.

7. At least one deputy speculated that rural insurrection and legislative breakthrough might have been engineered by the same cabal. Recalling August 4, Bertrand Barère observed: "The burning of the châteaux had preceded that day, in the same way that the fear of brigands that was widespread in Paris and the provinces since July 12 caused the organization of the National Guard. . . . I'll never forget the general commotion at Versailles caused by the news of the châteaux in flames. . . . Was this movement caused by the same hand . . . ? Wasn't it a swiftly diffused plan for the formation of the National Guards, conceived by the same mind or by the same party that needed

quite accurate. The Breton Club—the organization forming around the hotheads of the Third Estate of Brittany—had planned a great drama in which the duke d'Aiguillon, one of the wealthiest of lords, would declare for an indemnified phasing-out of seigneurial dues. In the heightened climate of tension and hope in and around the National Assembly, the script was rewritten on the spot as viscount de Noailles, not assigned a part, so it appears, but knowing what was up, jumped the gun on Aiguillon with the far more open-ended and subversive proposal that some seigneurial rights be abolished without compensation, while others be subject to indemnification.[8] For the next week the deputies debated a decree to summarize the tumultuous evening, a week during which it was clear that some, especially among the clergy, had already backed off. The final document adopted on August 11 retained the critical distinction of outright abolition versus compensation, a distinction that structured all subsequent debate and action over the next four years of struggle.

While the journals and letters of the deputies testify to various mixes of impulsive generosity and careful calculation, of exaltation, fear, and cynicism among the full group of participants, the precise mix of motives among the insiders in the Breton Club's catalytic initiative remains a matter of conjecture. The most plausible guess stresses an attempt to save as much as one could through a dramatic gesture of renunciation of what couldn't be saved; the pain of that renunciation, moreover, was to be generously compensated. In the event, the scenario planned at the Breton Club was buried under the response it triggered.

A great deal has been written on the ways in which the revolutionary regime attempted to default on the promise those words seemed to embody: on how peasants were to be permitted to emancipate themselves from some of their major burdens only upon the payment of an indemnity few could afford, on how the revolutionary government itself attempted to collect seigneurial dues attached to the former lands of church or king (which were now administered by the new regime), on how slow was the Paris government to come to terms with the sheer massive refusal of the countryside to continue to pay.[9]

---

the events to justify extraordinary legislative measures?" See Bertrand Barère, *Mémoires* (Paris: Labitte, 1842), 1:269.

8. It is possible that Noailles was part of a second group collectively pushing an agenda different from that proposed by those around Aiguillon—different and far less conservative. See Kessel, *La nuit du 4 août,* 127–32.

9. Henri Doniol, *La Révolution française et la féodalité* (Paris: Guillaumin, 1876); Emile Chénon, *Les démembrements de la propriété foncière en France avant et après la Révolution* (Paris: Recueil Sirey, 1923); Philippe Sagnac, *La législation civile de la Révolution française* (Paris: Hachette, 1898); Alphonse Aulard, *La Révolution française et le régime féodal* (Paris: Alcan, 1919); Marcel Garaud, *Histoire générale du droit privé français,* vol. 2, *La Révolution et la propriété foncière* (Paris: Recueil

It might be convenient to take what was decided on August 4 and in the course of the next week as a baseline to assess the degree to which subsequent actions defaulted on a promise or fulfilled it. To do so, however, may already be attributing a hardness and solidity to what was promised in early August when this itself was subject to negotiation. Kessel has amply documented the degree to which even the participants differed about just what had been decided. Some, in good conscience, informed their constituents that feudal dues needed no longer be paid.[10] Others, in equally good conscience, held the decree to have sharply restricted the rights that no longer had to be honored and thereby to have invited good citizens to cease their riotous behavior; while still others held that the enumeration of rights to be abolished thereby sanctioned the use of force to enforce those rights not so enumerated.[11] The brief summary of the discussion taken down in the early hours of August 5 was a no doubt inevitably selective and sometimes distorted rendering of the general tenor of the discussion;[12] the final decree six days later was not simply an elaboration, formalization, or clarification of the August 4 decision but in some ways broke new ground and in others embodied significant omissions.[13] Some of the deputies

Sirey, 1958); Peter M. Jones, *The Peasantry in the French Revolution* (Cambridge: Cambridge University Press, 1988).

10. On August 8, one clerical deputy wrote home that "we have suppressed the entire feudal regime and the claims derived from it with a solemn decree"; see Kessel, *La nuit du 4 août,* 179.

11. Three deputies from Auvergne wrote home on August 5 that "one must hope that the people will be moved by so much generosity and return to order." Less inclined to hope the people would be moved, the count d'Agoult wrote back to his base in Dauphiné urging the creation of a force to "charge the brigands with bayonets and without mercy." See Kessel, *La nuit de 4 août,* 178; Jean Egret, *La Révolution des notables: Mounier et les Monarchiens* (Paris: Armand Colin, 1950), 105.

12. The summary speaks vaguely of "reforming" the guilds, for example, whereas the only clear statements on the subject uttered in the course of the evening were probably proposals for clear-cut abolition. Proposals voiced in the evening for freedom of worship for non-Catholics, for abolishing the *parlements,* and for extending the emancipation of serfs to include colonial slaves seem to have similarly gotten lost in the shuffle. (This last item was one of the few that aroused notable disapproval. It would take a slave revolt to match the peasant insurrection before the legislature really moved on slavery.) See Jean-Pierre Hirsch, *La nuit du 4 août* (Paris: Gallimard/Julliard), 180–81; Kessel, *La nuit du 4 août,* 157, 169.

13. By the afternoon of August 5 a draft decree was drawn up; it was the basis for the final decree enacted, after an article-by-article debate, on August 11. The August 5 draft has totally dropped all reference to the guilds. On the other hand, it rounds out the previous evening's condemnation of rights over hunting pigeons and rabbits by adding fishing; it declares that clerical stipends *(portions congrues)* are to be raised—an issue omitted in the previous evening's summary—and declares that the National Assembly be given an account of the current state of government stipends to individuals. Kessel provides a convenient comparison of the summary adopted at the end of the session of the fourth, the draft decree of the fifth, and the final text adopted by the eleventh (Kessel, *La nuit du 4 août,* 320–26). The confusion over the guilds led Mathiez to devote an article to whether or not they were slated for abolition on August 4: Albert Mathiez, "Les corporations ont-elles été supprimées en principe dans la nuit du 4 août 1789?" *Annales Historiques de la Révolution Française* 8 (1931): 252–57.

themselves seemed simply baffled like the duke who Condorcet recalled having asked while laughing, "But what have we done? Is there anyone who knows?"[14] Still others, less amused, felt that the confusion of the debate itself permitted cabals to deliberately falsify the intentions of the deputies.[15] The conservative count de Lally-Tolendal thought that many were confusing the night of August 4 itself with later decrees.[16]

It is, then, a bit misleading to speak of the statements of August 4–11 as a promise later evaded. It seems more fruitful to speak of an angry struggle in the months ahead over seigneurial rights in which one of many battlefields was the meaning to be assigned to the August decrees. The claim of an evaded promise was an important weapon for some participants in this struggle; other participants saw a promise being filled.

By virtue of their own sense of the portentiousness of the event, by almost instantly framing the event with the stock phrase "eternally celebrated" (or something very similar),[17] by moving to distribute their views of the event and have their own participation, real, revised, or fictitious, published and disseminated, by terminating the event with the pledge of a memorial to a king who had nothing to do with it, the deputies themselves turned the event into a myth whose interpretation could be contested even before the final decree of August 11 was accomplished. Something that is already born "eternally celebrated" need not wait for the work of deliberate distortion, unconscious selection, misunderstanding, oblivion, and tendentious reinterpretation of the ages.[18]

14. Jean-Antoine-Nicolas de Caritat, marquis de Condorcet, *Mémoires de Condorcet sur la Révolution française* (Paris: Ponthieu, 1924), 2:60.

15. Baron de Gauville had a mixed reaction to the night of the fourth. While it was "more drunkenness than discussion," the drunkenness derived from "patriotism alone." But the next day, he notes bitterly, "everyone was quite astounded at the [summary]. I myself was first among them upon hearing what had taken place last night—rather what they want to have taken place. Several facts were obviously altered. They had extended the abandonment of rights and men of good faith could not recognize their actions in this account"; see Louis-Henri-Charles de Gauville, *Journal du baron de Gauville* (Paris: Gay, 1864), 17–18.

16. "I have heard many complaints about these decrees. But it is not the night of August 4 which must be the object of complaint, it is the extension given those decrees when they were formally drawn up. I restricted myself to listening when it was a matter of subjects foreign to me, but I saw clearly that there was a great difference between . . . the specific abolition of such-and-such a right and the general abolition of the entire feudal regime, within which one might include everything"; Trophime-Gérard, comte de Lally-Tolendal, *Mémoire de M. le comte de Lally-Tolendal ou seconde lettre à ses commettans* (Paris: Desenne, 1790), 113–14.

17. Jean-Pierre Boullé of the Third Estate of Ploërmel, for example, uses the phrase "eternally memorable" in a letter he claims to be writing immediately after the meeting ends early on the 5th; see "Ouverture des états généraux de 1789," *Revue de la Révolution* 15 (1889): 23.

18. Alexandre Lameth remembered "the most laconic decree, yet at the same time the vastest in its consequences that has ever been enacted on human affairs: *The feudal régime is abolished.*" See his *Histoire de l'Assemblée Constituante* (Paris: Moutardier, 1828), 100.

What led the National Assembly not merely to issue a statement on the feudal regime but to issue an eternally celebrated statement whose precise import was to be debated, not merely for months to come, but even before it had been issued? Marquis de Ferrières, noble deputy from Saumur, wrote his wife toward the end of July to describe the considerations that weighed upon him as a legislator. On July 18 he wrote that "the news from the provinces is even more alarming" than what is happening in Paris. He reassured his wife that their own province remained peaceful, a state he has endeavored to maintain by having Saumur's mayor to dinner. Nonetheless, he goes on, "There is a universal insurrection against the Nobility"; it turns out that by "insurrection" here he refers, not to peasant revolt, but to the climate in the National Assembly where short-sighted deputies "don't imagine that they themselves shall be the victims of the uprisings they incite." From here his train of thought strays easily to several nearby sites of popular disturbance; this in turn leads him to remind his wife of how to repair their own moats. As for the actual work of the Assembly, the main task mentioned is the Constitution, viewed with considerable skepticism ("I'm afraid that we are making it so beautiful, so sublime, that it will only look good in books, while in reality it will apply to nothing"). And, explaining his low profile in drafting that document, he defines a noble stance in terms that unself-consciously inverts that proposed by Sieyès for the Third Estate: "I'm nothing and don't want to be anything: that's the only prudent course under the circumstances."[19]

The next day he writes again, even more impressed by the "universal madness, the frantic delirium." He praises his wife's better judgment in not refilling the moats, an act that might arouse too much attention: "They would imagine that I want to defend myself." ("They" have a powerful hold on the marquis' thoughts.)[20] He adds the advice to hire as few hands for the harvest as possible, and preferably domestic servants or known men from nearby. In the next few days, advising his wife on how to protect some money, furnishings, and essential legal documents, he expresses a sense of the discriminating nature of the current violence: "if they come to Marsay, I don't think it will be to burn the *château*—we're too well liked—but to burn the documents which deal with rents and dues." And he again counsels prudent behavior; it is hard to say here if he is advising his wife how to act in the countryside or explaining his own conduct in the National Assembly:

19. Ferrières, *Correspondance,* 99–103. Few deputies would have been unaware of the dramatic opening of the most famous of all the many pamphlets of the convocation period: "1. What is the Third Estate—EVERYTHING. 2. What has it been in the political order until now? NOTHING. 3. What does it ask? TO BE SOMETHING." See Emmanuel Sieyès, *Qu'est-ce que le Tiers état?* (Geneva: Droz, 1970), 119.

20. "They" are major players for many of the other deputies as well. See the passage from baron de Gauville quoted above in note 15.

"The conduct one must adhere to is to say that everything is fine, that the Nobility and Commons are in perfect agreement" (and he adds that one must now avoid the expression, "Third Estate").[21]

Other deputies report their own distinct experiences. Sylvain Bailly's *Memoirs,* probably written down in 1792, suggest a particular sensitivity during July to subsistence disturbances. When he recalls the rumors of the Great Fear, for example, this Third Estate deputy from Paris recalls the tales of bandits cutting unripe grain[22] (perhaps filtered through his own period of responsibility for subsistence as first mayor of revolutionary Paris). Baron de Gauville, stopping on July 27 at his property near Dourdan, whose nobles had chosen him deputy, recalls that peasants "even from my own village" were only restrained by a rumor that the baron was accompanied by a company of dragoons. Fortified, so the baron recalls, by his belief that "the grumbling of the people usually amounts to nothing when an innocent man appears" he passed unarmed and unharmed through the crowd. Adding to the romantic self-portrait the baron recalls riding off in "an awful rainstorm." Fresh from his encounter with the threatening country people at home, the baron informs us that the very first thing he voted for on his return to the National Assembly was a reorganization of the Assembly's guard.[23] (One wonders at how to take a narrative sequence in which the demonstration that innocence is an adequate shield from plebeian violence is followed by strengthening the Assembly's defenses.) For Emmanuel Barbotin, a country priest sent to Versailles by his colleagues from Hainaut, the rural upheaval increased the pains of public service. He writes at the end of August that with taxes uncollectible, the government was not paying the deputies their expected allowance.[24]

For the marquis de Lézay-Marnésia, election as deputy of Aval in Franche-Comté may have seemed an opportunity to participate in realizing the idyllic reforms he had envisioned in his poetry and other writing on rural themes. Recalling his happy country childhood spent with a friend ("a little peasant of the same age as myself") he dreamed, after a military career of twenty-two years, "of exchanging my sword for a spade." In the 1780s, he published *Happiness in the Countryside,* extolling the potential of rustic life but denouncing the injustice of the tax system and the irresponsibility of the nobility, both, in his view, sources of rural poverty. The marquis seems to have given up his own claim to peasant labor on his land and he wrote of his responsibility to his peasant neighbors. Although, like most of his noble neighbors who held serfs, he did not rise to the king's invitation to voluntary

21. Ferrières, *Correspondance,* 103–7; 109–13.

22. Bailly, *Mémoires,* 2:160.

23. Gauville, *Journal,* 13–15.

24. Emmanuel Barbotin, *Lettres de l'abbé Barbotin, député à l'Assemblée constituante* (Paris: Edouard Cornély, 1910), 58.

emancipation in 1779 (see Chapter 9, pp. 549), he was quick to do so when a small group, composed of serfs and lawyers, presented a document to the three estates assembled for the elections of 1789.[25] A month after the August decrees, Lézay-Marnésia saw a France "absolutely disorganized, given over to the most horrible anarchy." And defending the plan to emigrate that he says he shares with eleven other deputies, he asks, "How can one remain in the midst of a people who, out of their lack of understanding, their frivolity . . . have become the cruelest people, the most coldly terrible."[26] And so the marquis emigrates, still traveling toward a land of peace governed by an enlightened elite, which, now, he realizes, lies across the Atlantic.

The common element in these tales in letters, journals, and memoirs of those who sat in the National Assembly is the sense of menace that hung over them in personal ways—as property holders, as residents of particular locales, as holders of particular positions on public issues. The great work of the Constituent Assembly and their personal fortune, their political future, and their physical security were, for the moment, inseparable and what made them inseparable was the mobilization of ordinary people. What happened in the legislature and what happened in the village were now manifestly intertwined. Thus the marquis de Ferrières oscillates between considering his family in the dangerous countryside and thinking about the Assembly, uses "insurrection" to describe the anti-noble animus of the deputies of the Third Estate as well as popular mobilization, and praises prudence equally when advising his wife on talking politics back in Saumur or explaining how he copes with the radical element in the assembly. Thus the baron de Gauville goes from his experience of peasant militance at home ("even in my own village") to concern about guarding Assembly and king. Or consider the abbé Barbotin, whose early letters show him to be sympathetic to reform and animated by considerable distrust of the clerical hierarchy and nobility. For him, the Assembly's assault on the tithe marks a turning point—he is a tithe-holder himself—beyond which his views shift markedly to the right. Both insurrectionary peasants and the Assembly's left are joined together in a common "idiocy."[27]

Now consider the effect on the deputies as a collectivity of this sudden

25. Charles-Louis Chassin, *L'église et les derniers serfs* (Paris: Dentu, 1880), 151–53. During the pamphlet wars of the late 1780s local Third Estate activists included the marquis among the noble defenders of "the people" and called on their less enlightened fellow nobles to emulate them; see Jean Egret, "La Révolution aristocratique en Franche-Comté et son échec (1788–1789)," *Revue d'Histoire Moderne et Contemporaine* 1 (1954): 252.

26. Elisabeth Bourget-Besnier, *Une famille française sous la Révolution et l'Empire: La famille de Lézay-Marnésia* (Paris: Bourget-Besnier, 1985), 15, 16, 18, 19, 25.

27. "Our peasant idiots think they will gain greatly in no longer paying the tithes" and "most members of the Assembly begin to regret the idiocies of the night of the fourth" (Barbotin, *Lettres,* 52, 59.)

accumulation of experience. Figure 8.1 shows the day-by-day detail of how many *bailliages* experienced insurrection during that first dramatic summer of revolution.[28] On July 27, the electoral circumscriptions that sent some sixty-six delegations to the Estates-General were experiencing incidents of panic, or assaults on seigneurial rights, or seizures of transported grain, and so on. The arrival of news at Versailles, however, was not instantaneous. In the normal course of events, mail would take about two days to arrive from Rouen, three from Tours, four from Strasbourg or Lyon, six from Bordeaux, eight from Marseille, eleven from Mauléon.[29] From village France, one would have to add the travel time to the nearest town on a good road. On the other hand, news of the greatest significance might circulate rather more rapidly—it might be worth it to wear out the horses. (We know something, for example, of the rapidity with which the news spread of the king's flight to Varennes[30] or of the rapid spread of the Great Fear.)[31]

Were the deputies in touch with their regions? The answer is not quite obvious since there are many elements of the revolutionary situation that might plausibly have made such contact pointless. The constituent-delegate relationship was far from institutionalized in a country with no tradition of regular elections. Many French theorists of representation, moreover, denied that a deputy represented a constituency, promoting an ideological climate that might have discouraged some from assuming such a role.[32] (A widespread view was that a deputy represented the entire nation.) There was, moreover, no reason to expect a second run for office, which would generate a need for feedback from those one hoped to please (and, in the event, the Constituent Assembly ultimately decreed its own members ineligible to stand for election to the Legislative Assembly). Finally, for the noble deputies specifically, some 40% were not even normally resident in the district they represented, having managed to get elected where their families held property, although living in Paris.[33] Nonetheless, the solidari-

28. This figure has roughly the same shape, but differs conceptually from Figure 6.5, which presented the rise and fall in the number of insurrectionary events.

29. Guy Arbellot and Bernard Lepetit, *Atlas de la Révolution française,* vol. 1, *Routes et communications* (Paris: Editions de l'Ecole des Hautes Etudes en Sciences Sociales, 1987), 41.

30. Ibid., 71.

31. Georges Lefebvre, *La Grande Peur de 1789* (Paris: Armand Colin, 1970).

32. In a valuable overview of current conceptions of representation, Patrice Gueniffey points out that Condorcet was even offended at the notion that deputies "ought to vote not according to reason and justice, but following the interests of their constituents." See Patrice Gueniffey, "Les assemblées et la représentation," in Colin Lucas, ed., *The French Revolution and the Creation of Modern Political Culture,* vol. 2, *The Political Culture of the French Revolution* (Oxford: Pergamon Press, 1988), 233–57.

33. See Timothy Tackett, "Nobles and Third Estate in the Revolutionary Dynamic of the National Assembly, 1789–1790," *American Historical Review* 94 (1989): 276.

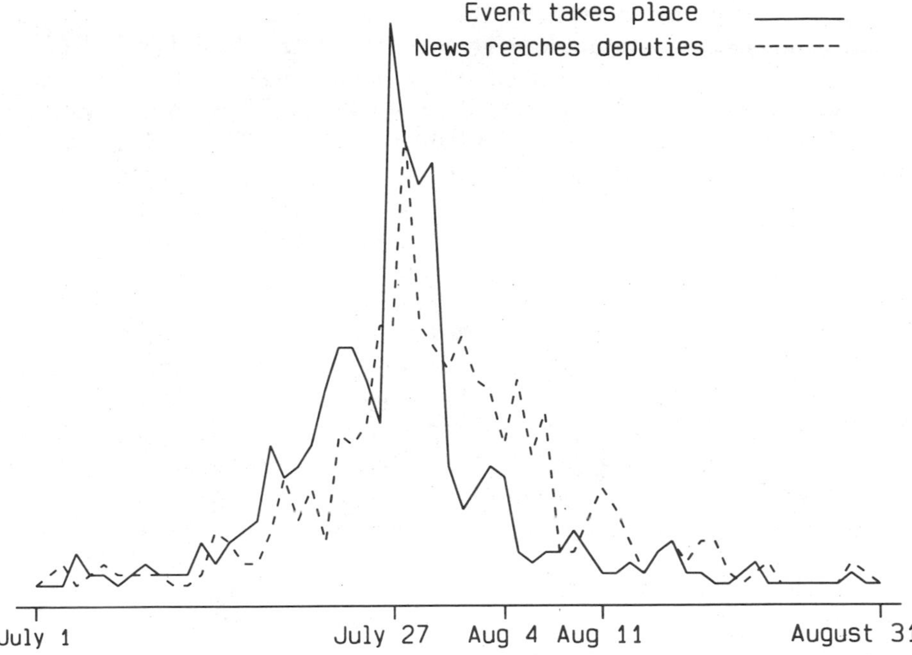

Fig. 8.1 *Bailliages* with Insurrections, July–August 1789

ties forged in the course of the convening of the Estates-General appear to have themselves created a sufficient sense of interdependence and responsibility that even prior to the clear expectation of a regularized politics, many deputies plainly made a practice of regular reports to those who elected them and, in turn, received reports from home.[34]

When did such reports arrive? The broken line in Figure 8.1 is an estimate of the number of *bailliages* whose deputies received, each day in July and August, news that a new insurrection had erupted.[35] Our best guess, then, is that the rising wave of rural insurrection meant that by the earlier part of

34. Timothy Tackett, "Les constituants et leurs commettants," paper presented to the Congrès Mondial pour le Bicentenaire de la Révolution Française, Paris, 1989. The letters to family or constituants of deputies frequently showed a special concern for local issues, although hardly to the exclusion of a national focus. These letters make obvious that many deputies were both oriented to broad, abstract principles, and sensitive to local interests.

35. The time it normally took for news to get from various towns to Paris was taken from the detailed maps of Arbellot and Lepetit, *Routes et Communications*. On the assumption that it might take an extra day, more or less, for events in villages to get to towns on the major roads, I added one to the length of time for news to travel from the major city of a *bailliage* to Paris with the exception of *bailliages* whose major town was itself within a day's travel from Paris. In these latter instances, I assumed that news could travel about as easily from the village to Paris directly as it could via an intermediary town.

July, every day, the delegations of one or two *bailliages* were hearing about deep and disturbing troubles at home. These delegations were generally some variable number of "deputations" (each deputation consisting of one cleric, one noble, and two representatives of the Third) plus a variable number of alternates.[36] Not only was there no letup, but from mid-July on the tempo of such news began to mount rapidly, peaking around July 28 (this is only an estimate, after all), but remaining at quite a high level for the next week or so.[37] At eight in the morning of August 4, for example, most of the deputies from Dauphiné were gathered for a reading of letters from home urging swift action since "the disorders already committed are less frightening than those that some are trying to commit."[38] These deputies had already been through quite a lot; through utterly unique experiences, in fact. They had experienced an election unique in their lifetime. They had seen their excitement at participating in the renewal of France give way as May and June dragged on to the tense tedium of paralysis as the Third could not agree with the others on whether to do business as one body or three. The Third Estate in late June, along with the like-minded among the clergy and a smaller number of nobles, had managed to defy the king and, in their own minds, overturn all of French history by declaring themselves the representatives of the French nation; they had faced down the refusal of the king and the privileged orders to go along and far from being arrested had been saved by the miraculous intervention of the Parisians on July 14. Those who had not gone along with the National Assembly faced the equally unprecedented experience of being ordered to do so by Louis on June 27. (That's what sent nobles like the baron de Gauville back to their constituencies in late July to ask for an extension of their powers so as to honorably comply with the king's new order.)

This, then, was the body that from mid-July on was experiencing, with every day's news, mounting evidence of a country in chaos.[39] Pious hortatory calls to order resounded, rather feebly, to be sure;[40] so did calls for discipline, stern measures, and the like.[41] On the hypothesis of a united elite

36. Of course there were exceptions of which the most important were the Breton delegations that were boycotted by the nobles.

37. Why is the delay between event and news so slight? Recall how many events in the summer of 1789 took place in northern France (see Tables 7.5 and 7.6); and note that the electoral procedures produced disproportionate numbers of northern deputies.

38. Jean Egret, *La Révolution des notables,* 105.

39. "Anarchy" is the usual word used in the letters, diaries, and memoirs of the deputies.

40. See, for example, the declaration that Target, opening the evening session on August 4, proposed to distribute to every parish priest (*AP* 8:343).

41. For example, the deputy who on August 3, fearing a "war of the poor against the rich" while the shortfall in tax revenues mounted, proposed a tough crackdown on those who did not pay taxes, apparently attempting to be sure the poor paid up. The transcript adds that this project went nowhere (*AP* 8:336).

in command of a loyal army one might well imagine the possibility of a consistent strategy of repression. But the elite was far from united, as the marquis de Ferrières noted; and the army's behavior was not simple either.[42] An important group within the National Assembly wished to avoid any concentrated deployment of military force on the likelihood that the first target of any revived capacity for centrally coordinated coercion would be themselves.[43] We have seen that the *cahiers* show the Third Estate—a word out of fashion by late July according to the marquis, always concerned with keeping a low profile[44]—to have been tending by March toward embracing the indemnification option, although with a significant abolitionist component (see Chapter 3). The nobility, on the other hand, tended to keep its own counsel by avoiding much comment; but the more vocal portion of the nobility included a significant component opting for integral maintenance of these seigneurial rights on which they chose to take a stand; while still other nobles proposed a variety of reforms (which, however, differed from those reforms proposed by an equally weighty group within the Third Estate; see Chapter 2, p. 56 and Chapter 3, pp. 67, 126). Let us not underplay the importance of the king himself having abolished serfdom on royal lands in 1779.[45] The significance of this is not so much that the king was much of an ally to antiseigneurial forces, but that prior to his response to the night of August 4, those who wished to think of the king as an ally had a past action on which to pin their present hopes.

It would not be quite apt to say that the peasants, as the French put it, were kicking in an open door. But it certainly was not a securely closed and zealously defended one. It was already partly open, with a variety of guardians pulling and tugging in various directions and in the process, shoving each other a good deal. A very significant number of those guardians, indeed, were proposing to open the door further, if vastly more slowly and cautiously than the besiegers wished. It was hardly a group prepared, as

42. Samuel Scott shows the division within the army and its consequent inconsistent behavior faced with politicized urban crowds. See Samuel F. Scott, *The Response of the Royal Army to the French Revolution: The Role and Development of the Line Army, 1787–1793* (Oxford: Clarendon Press, 1978).

43. One can trace many of the themes mentioned here in the debates around the proposals of Lally-Tolendal, noble deputy of Paris, on July 20 and July 23, to recall France to order and reinvigorate repressive mechanisms; see *AP* 8:252–55, 263–66; Jean-Joseph Mounier, "Exposé de ma conduite dans l'Assemblée Nationale," in François Furet and Ran Halévi, eds., *Orateurs de la Révolution française,* vol. 1, *Les constituants* (Paris: Gallimard, 1989), 922–23.

44. Ferrières, *Correspondance,* 104. Word fashions changed fast. Adrien Duquesnoy, Third Estate deputy from Bar-le-Duc, complained in his journal for May 22 about hideous neologisms borrowed from English like "motion," "amendment," "commons"—as in "House of"—that everybody suddenly seemed to be using. A couple of weeks later his own writing is full of these terms, used quite unself-consciously. See *Journal d'Adrien Duquesnoy* (Paris: Picard, 1894), 1:35.

45. Alphonse Aulard, *La Révolution française et le régime féodal* (Paris: Alcan, 1919), 13–36.

the marquis de Ferrières thought the only reasonable course, to cooperate in shutting the door against a common enemy.[46] The divisions within the legislature provided one significant element of opportunity for peasant action against seigneurial rights to succeed, particularly once a part of the legislature found in the rural threat a useful opportunity to push its own program. But other elements of the Assembly's situation helped enlarge the likelihood of peasant success: the evident need to reestablish taxation on a sound footing opened the possibility of a tacit deal in which the ending of one exaction would be traded for a renewed compliance with the other; the urban upheaval of mid-July added mightily to the pressures on the government for change; and the central experiences of the deputies from mid-June on filled them with exaltation or despair as they thought they discovered that they were at the center of a momentous time when French history could be overturned.

Yet the resistances were real, too. A portion of the National Assembly, after all, was made up of recalcitrant nobles whose constituents were dead set against change in the seigneurial system.[47] While the noble *cahiers,* we saw, are at least as noteworthy for their silence as their intransigeance when it came to seigneurial rights, one could hardly expect that silence, when it had to speak in the National Assembly, to be transmuted into a radical abolitionism.[48] While many Third Estate assemblies, to recall Chapter 3, had an antiseigneurial program, they differed notably from the countryside in their lesser advocacy for uncompensated abolition (see p. 88). There was a considerable group in the Assembly who did not want to go an inch beyond indemnification.[49]

Still others thought the claims of order were more important than any

46. "Among the deputies of the Commons, there are those who hate us without knowing why . . . [T]he people, who they arouse against us, shall fall with even more force against themselves" (Ferrières, *Correspondance,* 100).

47. Rivarol called August 4 "the Saint-Bartholomew's Massacre of property" (Lacretelle, *Histoire de la France,* 7:147).

48. If, with Tocqueville, one sees nobles as harboring conservative tendencies on their own little spot of concerns, and presumes that those in the process of ennoblement (generally by virtue of their occupancy of offices that grant nobility after a given time) eagerly anticipate having access to that spot, it is worth noting that of the 1,315 men who ever sat in the National Assembly 429 were either nobles or on the path of ennoblement. (This number includes nobles chosen by Third Estate assemblies.) See Edna Hindie Lemay, "Les révélations d'un dictionnaire: du nouveau sur la composition de l'Assemblée Nationale Constituante (1789–1791)," *Annales Historiques de la Révolution Française,* no. 284 (1991): 162.

49. Not only did Aiguillon's would-be opening statement only propose indemnification—making no mention whatsoever of the outright abolition of any rights—but the legislation eventually drafted by the Committee on Feudal Rights, the speeches of Merlin and, generally, the central trend in the legislative rhetoric until winter 1792 insisted that rights be honored until indemnification. For example, on June 15, 1791, Merlin insisted that "the most imperious justice forced [the Assembly] to maintain [seigneurial rights] until indemnification" (*AP* 27:242).

decision on the seigneurial regime and the claims of order, at the moment, called for standing firm on substance and using force. Repressive measures were rarely far from the thoughts of some legislators whenever they turned to the peasant question. On August 3, 1789, the Assembly discussed a hortatory proposal for enforcement of laws that carried an implicit threat of force. In the ensuing debate one deputy wanted the more explicit language of "under penalty of extraordinary prosecution and punishment according to the rigor of the ordinances," a euphemism for execution. A week later, the assembly took a break from working on the abolition of feudalism to discuss and pass a very detailed proposal of Target giving local government the authority to call in the new National Guards, the old rural police, and even the army. (There was also to be a list prepared of unemployed and vagabonds in case, one presumes, someone in authority wished to round up the usual suspects.) Soldiers were to be required to swear an oath "between the hands of their commander"—remarkably feudal language for an assembly abolishing feudalism[50]—to keep peace and oppose troublemakers. (Noailles objected to this provision, which he held premature.) This stiffening of the coercive apparatus was to be sent out together with the final form of the reform decree, enacted the next day (*AP* 8:336–37, 378–79). (Others, of course, similarly placing claims of order over the fate of seigneurial rights, opted for a conciliatory strategy.)[51]

Local officials and local holders of seigneurial rights, moreover, in the climate of breakdown of authority, might well attempt to pursue their own policies, either more conciliatory or more repressive than the centrally dictated decision of the moment (a considerable complication throughout the entire history of revolutionary legislation on these rights). The report on conditions in the *département* of Lot, prepared by two commissioners sent

50. On vassal homage, see Marc Bloch, *Feudal Society* (Chicago: University of Chicago Press, 1961), 1:145–46.

51. Bailly, for example, explaining the rationale behind actions taken to appease a crowd of Parisians anxious about a shipment of gunpowder on August 8, seems to sum up his resigned view of how all policy had to be made: "one had to go along; at that time general principles and standard procedures were nothing and tranquility was everything" (*Mémoires,* 1:224). Summing up the actions of the "eternally celebrated" night he writes: "All the propositions were piled up precipitously; not all were decreed and several were decreed too soon. The result was a weakening of all bonds and a crumbling of all lines of authority; our minds didn't grasp the limits of the good we were attempting, these limits were extended by our imaginations and our self-interest and we destroyed everything at once, even what we wished to preserve. During my own administration [as mayor of Paris] that night cost me many problems and many embarrassments. Nonetheless, all those decisions were useful and even necessary. It was the moment for relieving the people of the countryside, almost always or at least for a very long time forgotten. It probably would have been prudent to proceed more slowly and precisely; prudence would have waited until we knew the state of the finances, the extent of the debt and of our resources. But it was necessary to assure the survival of the revolution and to establish the new order of things, and for that, there was only one sure means—winning the support of the people" (2:217–18).

out by the National Assembly to investigate the sources of insurrection there, is a goldmine of information on the significance of such local initiatives. In November 1790, according to their report, the district officials of Gourdon, unimpressed "with the gentle path" decided to call out the troops to tear down the maypoles that had sprouted everywhere in frightening numbers. The commissioners sifted several rival explanations for peasant rebellion; they concluded that it was the battle of the maypoles that was the immediate source of the insurrection (*AP* 25:291, 297–301). The panicky overreaction of district officials that aimed at suppressing outward signs of defiance went well beyond a more cautious approach endorsed by the National Assembly and followed at the *département* level. This local over-zealousness to suppress insurrection, in the commissioners' view, was actually insurrection's major cause. Nearby, around Cahors and Lauzerte, an even more violent and tenacious insurrectionary wave was also, the report contends, fundamentally reactive: this time it was not soldiers under the orders of local officials but armed bands of "gentlemen" who were the provocation. These ex-lords, to be sure, claimed to have only engaged in defensive action in the face of *châteaux* burnings, but the report, sifting the evidence, finds a pattern of antipeasant terrorism, which the peasants were more than able to repay in kind (*AP* 25:301–5).

The upshot was that for all the opportunity the Revolution now presented to rural militance, that opportunity was still fraught with considerable risks. Local military authorities, local police authorities, local judicial authorities, supported by a fluctuating group of legislators and officials at the center, and sometimes even working in parallel with self-defense forces of local ex-lords, continued, intermittently, to attack, arrest, prosecute, and execute peasant insurrectionaries. Other local officials, taking quite the opposite tack, subverted central policies by arriving at their own accommodations with the peasants (who were much closer to them than to the legislators in Paris).[52] The revolutionary climate was more favorable to rural action than ever before: the door was partly open and there were insiders who wanted it opened further. But peasants who took action still ran serious risks; some died.[53]

Arthur Young had just crossed the Alps into France and wrote on December 25, 1789:

52. See Merlin's complaints during the insurrectionary minispurt of June 1791 about "certain administrative bodies" that display "carelessness and weakness that multiply refusals to pay" (*AP* 27:239).

53. While the Revolution's bicentennial was marked by a renewed focus on the violence of the Revolution, this seems rather generally to have meant a focus on the victims of crowd violence or victims of the Terror. Peasants shot, hung, and broken on the wheel—in that first summer Guillotin's machine had not yet been adopted—for hunting, invading fields, and taking food from the lord's stocks seem, as ever, so many incidental details.

> This is the most advantageous entrance into France in respect of beauty of country. From Spain, England, Flanders, Germany or Italy by way of Antibes, all are inferior to this. It is really beautiful and well planted, has many enclosures and mulberries, with some vines. There is hardly a bad feature except the houses . . . [which have] an air of poverty and misery about them. . . . For ten or twelve days past they have had, on this side of the Alps, fine open warm weather with sunshine. . . . Not far from Verpiliere pass the burnt *château* of M. de Veau, in a fine situation, with a noble wood behind it. Mr. Grundy was here in August, and it had then but lately been laid in ashes; and a peasant was hanging on one of the trees of the avenue by the road, one among many who were seized by the *milice bourgeoise* for this atrocious act.[54]

By August 4, 1789, our data suggest, the rural upheaval had settled down considerably in comparison to the previous week, although the level of turbulence remained for a long, long time markedly above prerevolutionary levels. If one gives any credence at all to the estimated delay in the news arriving at the National Assembly, however, Figure 8.1 shows that things probably still appeared quite critical to the deputies on August 4 and for a number of days thereafter. While the actual occurrence of incidents peaked sharply at some 66 insurrectionary *bailliages* on July 27, it is not until August 8 that the number of delegations that might well have been hearing of new troubles each day fell below 20; and not until August 13 did they fall below 10 (for the first time in more than three weeks).

There is much to ponder here. Consider, for one, the effect on the legislators. No sooner did they complete their legislative work on the eleventh than the countryside, almost instantly, subsided into something which if not quite peace was at least far less dramatically threatening than for a long several weeks. Their own words must have seemed to possess magical powers. The sense of bafflement and betrayal with which some deputies (like Merlin de Douai in his speech of June 15, 1791)[55] reacted to renewed waves of rural revolt becomes more understandable—and seems more from the heart, less cynically calculated then if we miss this sensation of having really achieved something on the magical fourth of August, with

54. Arthur Young, *Travels in France and Italy During the Years 1787, 1788 and 1789* (London: J. M. Dent, 1915), 303–4.

55. Merlin speaks of the session of August 4 as having fulfilled "one of the most important missions" ever assigned by "the sovereign will of the French nation." The elaborations of the initial enactment "by the decree of March 15, 1790 seemed to compell a reestablishment of tranquility in the countryside." He then goes on in considerable detail to express his dismay at peasant misunderstanding, in which they are assisted by counterrevolutionaries as well as weak and careless local administrators (*AP* 27:238–42).

only the details to be filled in. Part of the dynamic of the unraveling of this confidence was that the rural rejection of the self-proclaimed total abolition of feudalism was faced by legislators who were by no means united on the meaning of the grand decree of August 4–11 and who differed, moreover, on how they reacted to what they thought it meant.

It is striking that it is in the remaining weeks of August that the sense of polarization in the Assembly grew apace.[56] Timothy Tackett has recently shown that the Assembly's right, largely composed of nobility and clergy, regrouped and recovered considerable ground, as shown by the suddenly conservative nature of the presiding officers, chosen by election at fortnightly intervals.[57] Those lords who had merely gone along with the events of August 4, feeling it unsafe to fight the legislative tide particularly when joined to a mobilized peasantry (like the marquis de Ferrières)[58] or who had felt that under the insurrectionary circumstances in the countryside one might as well concede what could not be defended (like the count de Virieu)[59] had plenty of opportunity to support a detailed interpretation of the abolition of feudalism that would abolish as little as possible.[60] A substantial number of clerical deputies, moreover, had already refused to just go along quietly (let alone with the feigned enthusiasm recommended to holders of losing positions by the marquis de Ferrières) as the notion of an indemnified

56. A sense of a bipolar division among the deputies began to emerge both within the Assembly itself and among journalistic observers during the debates in the days following August 4 and grew sharper as that month went by. By the month's end, the sense of a well-defined right had clearly crystallized (although the press did not use the terms "left" and "right" widely before the end of the year). See Tackett, "Nobles and Third Estate," 285–89; Pierre Rétat, "Partis et factions en 1789: émergence des désignants politiques," *Mots* 16 (1988): 69–89.

57. Tackett, "Nobles and Third Estate," 286.

58. In a letter to a fellow noble on August 7, the marquis goes through a variety of reasons for supporting the "most memorable session in the history of any nation": the new law will show the universe the generosity of the French; it will deal with rural chaos; it creates national unity; it is less injurious to the lords than it at first looks. Then he gets to the bottom line: open opposition by noble deputies would be dangerous, not merely for those deputies, but for the nobility in France as a whole. Ferrières, *Correspondance*, 116–17.

59. Count de Virieu, not yet a noted reactionary, cheerfully joined in the renunciatory drama. Asked to explain his behavior by count de Montlosier, surprised at the right's participation in the "frenzy," he responded that "when the people are delirious, there are only two ways of calming them: generosity and force. We had no force." See François-Dominique de Reynaud de Montlosier, *Mémoires de M. le comte de Montlosier sur la Révolution française, le Consulat, l'Empire, la Restauration et les principaux événemens qui l'ont suivie, 1755–1830* (Paris: Dufey, 1830), 1:239–40.

60. Conservatives were far more prone to put a conservative spin on August 4 than to overtly challenge it. Few of the conservatives openly proposed, as did Duval d'Eprémesnil a year after the event, the explicit abandonment of the principles of August 4–11 ("with the exception of personal servitude, citizens shall have their property restored"). This proposal, coupled with a number of others equally contrary to the spirit of the moment, led Charles de Lameth to immediately propose sending him for a fortnight to the madhouse (*AP* 19:311–12).

end of the tithe (the official summary on August 4) shifted during the next week to an uncompensated abolition.[61] The clerics who now balked included erstwhile allies of the Third Estate, including the abbé Sieyès, the guiding spirit of the very idea of a National Assembly. The lead-off speaker in the clerical attempt on August 6 to alter the article on the tithe before the final decree was Lefrançois, representing the clergy of Caen, who had been an early adherent to the Third Estate's initiative in redefining itself as a National Assembly.[62] Even a cleric as radical as Grégoire was unhappy about the way the tithe legislation was going.[63] There were others who held that initially tentative proposals and individual renunciations advanced in the enthusiasm of August 4 had been frozen into a very radical system over the next week. "There is," observed Lally-Tolendal, "a great difference between indemnifying tithes and their suppression; between the specific abolition of such-and-such a right and the generalized abolition of the entire feudal regime."[64] In the wake of "the abolition of feudalism" and the Declaration of Rights of Man and Citizen (August 26) various elements on the right increasingly found one another. For some, joining the renunciatory throng may have even seemed a form of purging themselves of the taint of earlier acts, now, suddenly, widely defined as crimes.[65] Perhaps there were even

61. Kessel, *La nuit du 4 août,* 211–21; *AP* 8:353–54. The plan to drop indemnification from the tithe legislation mobilized so fierce an opposition that participants were uncertain who would prevail in a vote, the only point at which opinion was so evenly divided in that week of debate. See Jean-François Gaultier de Biauzat, *Gaultier de Biauzat, député du tiers-état aux états-généraux de 1789: Sa vie et correspondance* (Paris: Libraire Historique des Provinces, 1890), 245; Gauville, *Journal,* 19.

62. Kessel, *La nuit du 4 août,* 198.

63. Henri Grégoire, *Mémoires* (Paris: A. Dupont, 1837), 1:78.

64. Lally-Tolendal, *Mémoire,* 113–14. On August 5, Malouet and other deputies from Auvergne wrote a glowing sketch of the previous evening ("Never has a more beautiful night brought to an end so many days of affliction"). They were hopeful of civil peace: "We must hope that the people shall be moved by so much generosity and return to order." Two days later, realizing that some rights were to be abolished without indemnity (they claimed that, in the general excitement, they misheard some of the discussion), they now had misgivings and were a good deal less optimistic about a restoration of rural tranquillity. See Pierre-Victor Malouet, *Correspondance de Malouet avec les officers municipaux de la ville de Riom, 1788–1789* (Riom: Jouvet, n.d.), 110–11.

65. Such at any rate, is the explanation given by the marquis de Ferrières for the improbable participation of the duke du Châtelet on the night of August 4, when he was the third noble to speak. Unlike Noailles and Aiguillon, Châtelet had never been known as a liberal. As a colonel in the French Guards, what he was currently known for, in fact, was having ordered his troops into action in April in the famous disturbance at the Réveillon Factory in Paris's working-class neighborhood of Saint-Antoine. His role in the renunciatory evening was to deliver a particularly "violent" diatribe against the seigneurial regime (or so it was characterized by Duquesnoy), on which Ferrières observes: "Duke du Châtelet, tormented by anxieties and insane terrors, seized an extremely favorable occasion to show himself attached to the interests of the people." Charles-Elie de Ferrières, *Mémoires du Marquis de Ferrières* (Paris: Baudoin, 1821), 1:187; Duquesnoy, *Journal,* 1:266; Kessel, *La nuit du 4 août,* 146–47.

some on the right who eagerly clamored for radical measures in the conviction that anything so bizarre would have to fail.[66]

Was there also a left that was as unhappy about the August events as was the right? If there were any who regarded the decrees as wholly inadequate from the outset, they were quiet.[67] Indeed, there were many deputies who

66. One would not expect any, nor do I know of any, participant who actually claimed to be following what the French call the *politique du pire,* the tactic of supporting what one opposes so that an unviable situation will result. But at least one keen observer of the extreme right deputies that were gathering at her mother's salon in the fall months saw them acting thus: "The rest of the aristocrats only had insults for the popular party and, not dealing with realities, believed themselves doing good through making things worse. Completely wrapped up in justifying their reputations as prophets, they wished their own misfortune in order to enjoy the satisfaction of accurate prediction" (Anne-Louise-Germaine de Staël, *Considérations sur les principaux événements de la Révolution française* [London: Baldwin, Craddock and Joy, 1818], 1:299). Apart from it being generally plausible that some, especially at moments of burning resentment, might vote in order to make a mess of things, at least one important model for some nobles surely embodied such tactics. Louis XVI seems to have explained to one of his ministers that he accepted the Constitution of 1791, thus: "My opinion is that the literal execution of the Constitution is the best way of making the Nation see the alterations to which it is susceptible" (cited in John Hardman, *Louis XVI* [New Haven: Yale University Press, 1993], 208).

67. Immediately after the promulgation of the decrees, the Assembly and its Committee on Feudal Rights received some letters complaining that anything short of total abolition would fail to stem the rural revolt, for the country people would see the right of indemnification as valueless (Kessel, *La nuit du 4 août,* 240–43). The radical journalist Marat held the decrees of August 4–11 a transparent sham: "Let's not be anyone's dupe. If benevolence dictated these sacrifices, one must observe that it waited a bit late to raise its voice. It is only by the light of their burning châteaux that they had the greatness of soul to renounce their privilege of holding in chains those who have recovered their liberty with arms. . . . But we can't deny ourselves some observations that help measure the extent of the sacrifices. Does one have to prove that they are for the most part illusory? And, first of all, the abolition of all the privileges . . . is it real, when it includes as it does, the indemnification of the seigneurial rights, the monopolies, the feudal rights on land?" (*L'Ami du Peaple* [September 21, 1789], 98–100). One might wonder whether there were deputies who shared Marat's view that any abolition was a fake if it included the indemnification option, or deputies who saw August 4–11 as merely the first step. There are occasional hints of more radical views in the Assembly. In the course of debating an exhortation to restore rural peace on August 3 one unnamed deputy insisted that "we mustn't call unjust rights legitimate; they are for the most part founded on violence." This would seem to look ahead to the principles of the legislation of August 1792, not the next day's proceedings (*AP* 8:337). But dissent from the right was far more vocal than from the left, in the press as in the Assembly, in the immediate aftermath of August 4; see Fabio Freddi, "La presse parisienne et la nuit du 4 août," *Annales Historiques de la Révolution Française* 57 (1985): 46–58. If we add to this picture the strength of the indemnification option in the *cahiers* of the Third Estate and the stand-pat option in the *cahiers* of the nobility, it seems a plausible conclusion that the action of August 4–11 was already far more radical than the Assembly would have done without rural violence. The Assembly's attempts in the months ahead to advance a very conservative interpretation of their own action, seems a working-out of the sentiments of the deputies. If I might offer a mechanical analogy: the positions taken during August 4–11 are not the unconstrained equilibrium point of a pendulum that swings under the impulse of the forces internal to the Assembly, but a point rather to the left where that pendulum has been pushed by the

may have had no particular antiseigneurial animus as such but who could embrace such actions as expedients to pacify the peasants—and who might easily shift to a more conservative position later on when the countryside showed itself unwilling to calm down. When such benefits as they were prepared to give, augmented by moral exhortation, failed to pacify the countryside, even deputies with considerable concern about the issue of seigneurialism could counsel force. In his speech of June 15, 1791, Merlin, clearly frustrated by continuing rural turbulence, explained the law on the burden of proof when lord and peasants differ over the validity of a particular seigneurial claim. He had the weary air of one who could not imagine how it could be put more clearly. He presumed that, this time, properly instructed peasants would willingly pay. In the rare cases in which a peasant would not comply, however, he should be held to be "rebel against the law, usurper of another's property, bad citizen, the enemy of all." Military force may be utilized; the Assembly therefore "has reason to expect that the citizens of the countryside, able to appreciate all the good done for them by the Assembly, shall everywhere speedily acquit the obligations from which they are unable to free themselves" (*AP* 27:242).

One concern raised by a turn toward coercive measures was expressed by Adrien Duquesnoy. He feared that proposals for force might be deceptive pretexts to strengthen royal authority and could be used ultimately to reestablish royal tyranny over the Assembly. On the other hand, he conceded, the troubles were quite real: "But, in the end they exist and they must be repressed."[68] Duquesnoy, therefore, wants to be careful that armed force used against urban plebeians be under the control of civil authority to avoid a military-sponsored dictatorship. In the countryside, however, he would give the army a free hand.[69]

Even a single deputy might have several distinct reactions to August 4, as shown in the correspondence of Pinteville de Cernon, noble deputy of Châlons. A week earlier Pinteville had expressed pleased satisfaction at the thought of "sacrifice by those who by their birth are devoted" to protect the nation.[70] This is the image of a warrior nobility now sacrificing itself on the field of fiscal combat. If one were seeking an appropriate occasion for delight in the moral worth of the nobility defined in such terms, August 4 would seem made to order. Pinteville wrote on the fifth that "last evening and night, the French showed great patriotic character whose energy and

disruptive mobilization of the country people; the "natural" equilibrium, without that collective action, is a rightward shift.

68. Duquesnoy, *Journal,* 2:417, 425.

69. Ibid., 2:418.

70. R. Popelin, "Extrait de la correspondance de Pinteville, baron de Cernon," *Mémoires de la Société d'Agriculture, Commerce, Sciences et Arts de la Marne,* ser. 1, 26 (1880–81): 13.

heroism shall astonish Europe—or rather the universe; it is not a matter of sieges nor of battles but of the most complete victory over prejudices and personal interests" (16). But ten days later he reflects on indemnification: "The country people haven't enough money to pay off the principal of the *champart* and the other rights. Take back from them a part of their land: they will gladly sacrifice it to free the rest. . . . [The lord] will acquire in this way some magnificent possessions and a domain whose ownership will be more advantageous to him than [various rights]" (18). In a nine-day span, Pinteville goes from an exalted sense of noble sacrifice to a cool evaluation of seigneurial gain (and peasant sacrifice).

Legislators Talk About Rural Revolt

Late July 1789 may have been the greatest wave of rural revolt in the entire revolutionary period, but it was far from the only one, as we have seen in Chapter 6. If the great July peak produced the great drama of the beleaguered legislature going faster and further than they were at first prepared to go (although going in a direction many wanted to go more slowly or less far), the lesser peaks pushed them further still if in a less frenzied fashion that never repeated the drama of the night of the fourth. Initial responses to subsequent waves of disturbance recalled many of the legislative reactions to the insurrections of the Revolution's first summer: the vain proposals for repression, the pragmatic claims for a conciliatory policy aimed at securing rural assent, the attempts to use the rural disturbances to press particular aims against political opponents.[71] Count d'Agoult thought that the left wanted to prevent any effective pacification "because if the troubles cease, they will lose their influence."[72]

Consider the intertwining of these themes in Alexandre Lameth's reflection on the legislative repercussions of rural turbulence. He was addressing a report to the National Assembly on February 18, 1790, in which the Committee on the Constitution proposed mechanisms for invoking martial law. France was in the peak month of the second great wave of rural insurrection (see Table 6.3). Lameth was skeptical about the effectiveness of martial law in the countryside. It might well work in the towns where there is "a solidarity that derives from the fact that all individuals have

71. The invocation of rural turbulence to cover particular agendas seems to have begun rather earlier than August 4. On July 25, 1789, a deputy from Franche-Comté urged the Assembly to see its disorders as stemming from popular desire to abolish that province's *parlement.* See Jacques Antoine Creuzé-Latouche, *Journal des états-généraux et du début de l'Assemblée Nationale, 18 mai–29 juillet 1789* (Paris: Henri Didier, 1946), 278.

72. Egret, *La Révolution des notables,* 106.

greater or lesser interests in protecting their property and the fruits of their industry; but the countryside is inhabited almost exclusively by proletarians who are naturally led to abuse laws against property held for the most part by nobles or by those who aspire [to become noble]."[73]

Lameth considers at some length various proposals to combine support for protecting property and tax collection on the one hand with avoiding concentrations of force in the hands of potential foes of the Revolution; this leads into a discussion of the legislative fine-tuning of the decrees of August 4 (346–68). Toward the end of that same wave of uprisings of winter 1790, Adrien Duquesnoy points out that "It seems obvious to many that the feudal rights are the great occasion for these movements; it is therefore high time that we worked on this matter and very soon sort these into indemnifiable and non-indemnifiable rights." He points with envy to a peaceful England's capacity to double the rate of taxation that is feasible in France.[74] Two years later as war approached and another great insurrectionary wave was building, Couthon urged the Legislative Assembly to see that the French army would never be effective unless the villagers receive more than fine words from the Revolution. "Do you wish, Messieurs, to assure the prompt recovery of taxes?" his peroration begins, as he admonishes his fellow legislators to ease the terms of indemnification or else see the future of the Revolution threatened by "the mortal indifference of opinion" in the countryside."[75]

The rural disturbances were also rhetorically available to those who sought to generate support for other, often radical, measures. Lameth's account of legislative discussions provoked by the rising of early February 1790, for example, shows Pétion using the occasion to attack primogeniture. Primogeniture is brought into the discussion as a rebellion-triggering facet of the feudal regime "established to give the eldest son the means to meet his responsibility to lead men of arms to war." Lameth plainly sees anti-primogeniture as a vehicle to radically and simultaneously reorganize family relations, social conflict, the French economy, and even state finances. By ending the "shocking differences" in property division, "hatreds among the children" will be avoided, which will lead to a reforging of family ties; by equalizing properties, the number of both "proletarians and colossal properties" will diminish, reducing rural conflict. The disrespect of the laws, characteristic of the ultrarich and ultrapoor, will diminish; and the increased progress of agriculture and industry should permit an increase in state revenues.[76] In the course of another discussion of the same wave of

73. Lameth, *Histoire,* 346.

74. Duquesnoy, *Journal,* 2:417–18. See also his comments on March 6 (2:441).

75. Georges Couthon, *Discours sur le rachat des droits seigneuriaux, prononcé à la séance du mercredi 29 février 1792* (Paris: Imprimerie Nationale, 1792). The quoted passage is on 8.

76. Lameth, *Histoire,* 366.

disturbances, one deputy pointed to the insurrections as the reason for completing the new constitution (*AP* 11:49).

The troubles of November 1792 provided another occasion that could be pointed to on behalf of a radical vision. Although our data show the disturbances that month to be overwhelmingly over subsistence (see Table 6.3), when Robespierre rises to speak on November 30 they become an argument for accelerating the lagging trial of the king (in order to reestablish respect for the Convention's authority).[77] Conservatives, like radicals, could point to rural troubles in making a case for their own concerns. In the course of the insurrectionary wave of the winter of 1789–90, Adrien Duquesnoy noted with amusement and irritation those who exaggerated the threat of peasant movements to try to scare deputies into placing more military force under the king's command.[78]

As a final instance of putting peasant insurrection into the rhetorical service of a political agenda, consider Bertrand Barère's magnificent performance in the Convention on March 18, 1793. Counterrevolution was at its height (see Figs. 6.3 [a]–[d]). Barère paints a tableau in which "passions, intrigues and divisions" among the revolutionary leadership, foreign enemies, émigré nobles, priests, and peasant "fanatics" in the West reinforce one another and encourage poorer peasants to attempt to seize the properties of the wealthy. The rural slide into "anarchy" can only be halted by stern, repressive measures to reassure the rich and generous measures (access to émigré land, division of the commons, poor relief, progressive taxation) to earn the support of the poor; to coordinate all this, while dealing simultaneously with divisiveness at the top, Barère urges, as if it were an afterthought, the creation of "a committee of public safety" (*AP* 60:290–94). Thus rural insurrection becomes the justification for beginning to set up the central institution of the Terror.

What Do You Do After You Have Totally Abolished Feudalism?

Even without continuing rural disturbances, the decrees of August 4–11 would have compelled subsequent legislative action, in order to specify the fate of the myriad of particular rights. But rural disturbances did continue

77. Maximilien Robespierre, *Oeuvres* (Paris: Presses Universitaires de France, 1950), 9:106–9.

78. Duquesnoy, *Journal*, 2:413–14, 418–19, 422–23. The lodging of such force in royal hands was a major goal of conservatives (for example, Maury, Cazalès, Duval d'Eprémesnil) in the debates of February 1790 and a major fear of the developing Jacobin grouping (for example, Robespierre, Pétion).

and legislators repeatedly had to choose a repertoire of actions: repressive actions to halt disruption and avoid concessions; conciliatory actions to satisfy peasants and halt disruption while avoiding repression; and what I suggest we call instructive actions: attempts to convince the peasantry that their interests were already met. In early February, for example, considering reports of violence in the southwestern countryside, one legislator from rebellious Périgord urged firmness ("I surely must be made to pay before I'll pay") while deputies from more peaceful Champagne and Alsace insisted on drawing clear legal distinctions between the abolished and the indemnified so as to "enlighten the people" (*AP* 11:418–19). Debate raged throughout February on two issues: (1) the mix of pedagogic and repressive approaches to the insurrectionary countryside in Brittany and the Southwest; and (2) the division of control over the armed forces between the new local governments and the king. It was a debate that allowed many participants to claim to believe that the people were good but ignorant and led astray; for Jacobins to express fears of royal "dictatorship"; for a part of the right to express admiration for the toughness with which English governments could deal with popular disturbances; and for many to debate the complicity of local officials and rural rioters.[79]

I shall trace the history of the legislation here with an eye on how the legislators coped with rebelling peasants.[80] We shall look again at the August 4–11 decrees seen now as the first in a series of responses to an insurrectionary countryside. In order to gain some perspective on the course of the legislative history of the dismantling of the seigneurial regime, later in this chapter I shall also briefly sketch some of the similar or contrasting features of legislation on two other prime peasant concerns: the tithe and access to land. This set of comparisons will help bring out some of the distinctive elements of the role of seigneurial rights in the Revolution. The major moments of legislative action on these issues are summarized in Table 8.1. It indicates the dates of adoption of the more important pieces of legislation on seigneurial rights, the tithe, and rights over land as well as some of the major statements of position on these matters.[81] (When the seigneurial rights and tithes were covered in the same speech or enactment I joined them under the heading "Feudalism.")

In brief summary, the major turning points in the seigneurial rights

79. *AP* 11:222–24, 365–73, 418–19, 456, 536–38, 613–15, 641, 652–58, 665–85.

80. In Chapter 9 I shall examine the legislation as a conceptual structure.

81. I omitted legislation affecting wage issues as being too small a component of rural actions; I also omitted legislation as well as anxious speeches and reports on subsistence issues since these were complex compounds of urban and rural mobilizations and generally more urban than rural. (Nevertheless the urban popular upheavals had a significant interaction with the largely rural ones in part because rural people took part in urban market events and, in part, because efforts to supply population concentrations caused subsistence problems in smaller places.)

Table 8.1. Principal Legislative Actions on Rural Issues, Summer 1789–Summer 1793

Date	Subject	Brief Summary
August 4–11, 1789	Feudalism	1. Seigneurial rights are divided into two classes: those to be abolished outright and those to be indemnified. The detailed legislation is to follow. 2. Pending indemnification, dues are to be paid. 3. Tithes are to be abolished, detailed legislation to follow.
(September 4, 1789)	Seigneurial rights	Merlin de Douai reports on difficulty of task facing Committee on Feudal Rights
(September 12, 1789)	Seigneurial rights	Preliminary report by Tronchet on rate of indemnification.
November 2, 1789	Sale of national property	Property of secular clergy is to be nationalized.
December 11, 1789	Land ownership	Measures against peasant seizures of forest.
December 19, 1789	Sale of national property	Royal domain (other than forests, *châteaux* and parks) to be sold
(February 8, 1790)	Seigneurial rights	Preliminary report of Committee of Feudal Rights.
March 15–28, 1790	Seigneurial rights	Right are classified as either presumptively illegitimate and therefore to be abolished outright or presumptively legitimate and therefore to be indemnified. In the grey area, burden of proof is on those who pay.
March 15–28, 1790	Tithes	Infeudated tithes are to be assimilated to seigneurial rights, to be indemnified by peasants.
April 14–22, 1790	Tithes	1. Ecclesiastical tithes are to be paid to the state this year, abolished thereafter. 2. Infeudated tithes are to be indemnified by the state.
(April 23–27, 1790)	Seigneurial rights	Discussion of indemnification.

May 3–9, 1790	Seigneurial rights	Setting rates of indemnification.
May 14–17, 1790	Sale of national property	Lands of church and king are to be sold at auction in large blocks.
June 19, 1790	Feudalism	Abolition of hereditary distinctions including coats-of-arms.
(August 1790)	Land ownership	Report on proposal for dividing the commons.
October 23, 1790	Tithes	Infeudated tithes are classified into two categories: Those involving a grant of land are to be assimilated into laws on seigneurial rights; those not involving a land grant are to be indemnified by the state.
November 14–16, 1790	Seigneurial rights	Payers of dues on National Land are allowed to indemnify annual and occasional dues separately
December 1–12, 1790	Tithes	Tenants and sharecroppers are to pay proprietors the value of tithe.
December 10, 1790	Tithes	Various Lutheran tithes are assimilated to basic model.
April 13, 1791	Land ownership	Disputed land is awarded to communities.
April 13–20, 1791	Seigneurial rights	Forty rights are added to the "abolished" category (including weathervanes, church benches, and gallows).
June 1791	Tithes	Clarification of legislation on Lutherans.
September 28–October 6, 1791	Land ownership	Communal grazing rights and individual enclosure rights are both upheld.
(February 19, 1792)	Seigneurial rights	Couthon calls for radical measures.
(March 12, 1792)	Seigneurial rights	Golzart calls for extending law of November 14–19, 1790.
(April 1792)	Seigneurial rights	Discussions of abolition.
(April 11, 1792)	Seigneurial rights	Committee on Feudal Rights proposes new project.

Table 8.1. *(Continued)*

June 18–July 6, 1792	Seigneurial rights	All irregular dues are abolished. Burden of proof in contested cases is placed on lord.
August 14, 1792	Land ownership	Wooded land is to be divided into individual freehold plots.
August 20, 1792	Seigneurial rights	Extension of provisions of law of June 18–July 6, 1792.
August 25, 1792	Seigneurial rights and tithes	1. All seigneurial dues are abolished unless lord can show their consensual character. 2. Infeudated tithes are classified as resembling either "feudal" or "rent-like" payments, and abolished or maintained accordingly.
September 2, 1792	Sale of national property	Emigré land is to be sold.
August 28–September 14, 1792	Land ownership	Common land taken by lord since 1669—legally or not—is awarded to community.
October 11, 1792	Land ownership	August 14, 1792, law is repealed.
March 18, 1793	Land ownership	Death penalty decreed for advocacy of land redistribution
April 24, 1793	Sale of national property	Municipalities are barred from purchasing parcels for resale.
June 3, 1793	Sale of national property	1. Land of émigrés is added to National Lands. 2. Land is to be sold at auction in small blocks.
June 10, 1793	Land ownership	Community is authorized to divide common land among all members of community if one-third so wish.
July 17, 1793	Seingeurial rights and tithes	Abolished.

Note: Major turning points in legislation on seigneurial rights are italicized; debates without immediate legislative actions are in parentheses.

legislation beyond the initial August decree were three: the enactment a half-year later in March 1790 of the proposal of a subcommittee of the Committee on Feudal Rights; the decree of late August 1792, which was profoundly more favorable to those who owed payments; and the decree of July 1793, which constituted the definitive end of the system, at least insofar as anything was definitive.[82] I shall briefly outline here the content of these three acts.

The initial project announced on August 11, 1789, simultaneously proclaimed the complete abolition of the feudal regime as well as a series of sketchy but important promises that were not consistent with such a sweeping claim. Not consistent by any commonsense standards, that is: as we shall see, by some very special definitions of what one might mean by "feudal regime" and "abolish" one could manage to be roughly consistent. Broadly speaking, seigneurial rights were to be divided into two classes: (1) those based on personal servitude or that in some way symbolized that abject status, which were to be simply eliminated; and (2) those rights that were to be regarded as burdens but that were not to be simply removed from their owners until some means of indemnifying those owners was to be worked out. The task confronting Merlin's subcommittee was to distinguish which rights were in which group. A second subcommittee, under Tronchet, was then to report on the modalities of indemnification for those rights to be provisionally maintained.

This outcome of early August 1789 already conceded more to the countryside than all were comfortable with. Quite apart from lords with substantial seigneurial revenues who wanted to hold to an intransigent and integralist position (a viewpoint that informed a significant minority of noble *cahiers*), it is a highly plausible speculation that some of those involved in the eternally celebrated night were quite deliberately attempting to put the best face on things and save what could be saved under the combined

82. The claim to have abolished the feudal regime in its entirety provided peasants with a justification for further insurrection and officials with a justification for holding fast in the years that followed the decrees of August 4–11, 1789. The boundary between legitimate property and illegitimate usurpation was continually shifted in response to political struggle. The line as drawn in July 1793 was definitive, not because of its superior jurisprudential logic, but because subsequent peasant action was containable. One of the fears invoked by the right about August 4–11, 1789, was that once the notion of illegitimate usurpation was raised, who could control how far it would carry? The law of July 17, 1793, attempted to distinguish feudal payments from nonfeudal rent. In providing for the destruction of the legal documents embodying what all now agreed were payments of the first kind, they also were ordering destruction of titles to what most held to be of the second. Some regions then witnessed sporadic peasant attempts to avoid rents. If the lords had once attempted to see seigneurial rights as property and therefore legitimate, some peasants had now learned to see property as itself usurped and as no different than seigneurial claims. As the right had held, to invoke the notion of usurpation to distinguish between legitimate and illegitimate, was to raise the specter of claims that all property was theft.

threats of peasant insurrection, the more radical faction in the National Assembly that wanted to junk the rights anyway, and a pragmatic group of deputies concerned about state finances who accepted the abolition of seigneurial rights as the price to be paid for peasant loyalty, rural tranquility, and a return to tax collection. We see all these concerns surfacing in and around the events of August 4–11: Salomon's alarming report on rural violence on August 3 that introduced a proposed hortatory decree insistent on tax payments;[83] the attempt on the morning of August 4 to continue the Assembly's internally divisive project of preparing a Declaration of Rights (*AP* 8:339–41); Controller-General Necker's elaborate presentation on August 7, right in the middle of the discussions of the feudal regime, reminding everyone of the centrality of the financial situation (*AP* 8:361). And we see division among the movers and the followers of the great drama of August 4, over just how far to go and over what to concede. The triggering mechanism was a plan, elaborated in some detail by the Breton Club—the caucus of the more intransigently radical deputies—for a dramatic call for change in which prestigious figures would lend their names to a major statement on seigneurial rights that would, with luck, secure peasant compliance, undercut the potential for more radical measures, and yet would preserve significant aspects of the seigneurial regime by insisting on continuing payments pending indemnification. Recall, as Alfred Cobban did, that many deputies were themselves holders of seigneurial rights and would have been injured by simple, outright, immediate, and total abolition.[84] Recall as well, as Cobban did not, that the only solution to the financial crisis that anyone was advocating was some form of land sale, with royal and ecclesiastical properties the only ones anyone had the stomach to go after:[85]

83. In the subsequent debate, other deputies variously proposed that any legislative action be postponed pending an investigation of the facts; that "feudal matters" were so difficult and so important that nothing be decreed until a constitution was written; that seigneurial rights be abolished at once, without which such a hortatory declaration would further anger the countryside; that stern punishment be ordered for tax refusal. It was decided to send the matter back to committee (*AP* 8:336–37).

84. Alfred Cobban, *The Social Interpretation of the French Revolution* (Cambridge: Cambridge University Press, 1965), 44–48.

85. The claim that royal lands could be thought of as the property of the nation rather than of Louis was fairly easy although not altogether beyond debate (see *AP* 15:451). Rather more difficult was taking the church's own defense of tax exemption literally; the church did not own the land it used but merely held usufruct rights. The nation, in this reasoning, owned the land, but permitted the church to use its revenues to support its vital work. Thus the revolutionary state's apologists could claim to be within the parameters of tradition in regarding the church as under state supervision and in finding a different use for the land. Indeed, there was some precedent for this very step. Reacting to financial crises and pushed by the Third Estate at the Estates-General of 1560, the government sold off a part of church landholdings between 1563 and 1591. See Emmanuel Le Roy Ladurie, *Les paysans de Languedoc* (Paris: Service d'Edition et de Vente des Publications de l'Education Nationale, 1966), 359–71.

yet the lands of church and king owed a significant part of their value to their associated seigneurial rights. An immediate, total, and uncompensated abolition would seriously compromise the only plan in town for dealing with the state finances. Recall, in the third place, that the relatively "impersonal" ("patriotic," if you will) issue of state finances was indirectly very personal to many deputies who, like many of the well-off of the Old Regime, held significant investments in government annuities of one sort or another and for whom state bankruptcy might be a short step from destruction of the family fortune. The duke d'Aiguillon was a natural as the lead-off speaker: he was a man of almost unimaginable wealth, a good deal of it in the form of seigneurial rights. A plan he endorsed might carry great weight with other rights-holders.[86] On the assumption that the duke's actual performance followed the plan, it is striking to note that he only spoke of indemnification of some rights. Many rights were unmentioned even by implication and the notion of uncompensated abolition for any rights was not mentioned at all.

Indeed, if one were to read Aiguillon's speech out of context it would be a defense of property rights.[87] Popular ferment, the duke began, supported liberty against royal ministers but now "is an obstacle to that same liberty." But one must recognize, he went on, that it isn't just criminals but "the whole people" who have formed "a sort of league to destroy the *châteaux*" and who wildly exaggerate the culpability of the lords. (It is the seigneurial agents who are genuinely blameworthy.) To show the country people one means well, the duke proposed ending tax privileges (including local and regional privileges) and permitting indemnification. Out of context, this would have been seen as a speech offering the countryside tax equality in return for a willingness to settle for the right to buy out the seigneurial obligations (*AP* 8:344). (I stress the right to buy, since the proposed rate was plainly out of the reach of many.)[88]

The event got off to quite a different start, however, when viscount de

86. Barère claimed that he was rebuffed when he approached the group around Aiguillon and Lameth on August 3 and 4 to ask for a part in the action being planned: "They told me that it must be nobles who propose the destruction of feudal rights and judges in *parlement* who propose abolishing venality of office" (Barère, *Mémoires,* 269–70).

87. If one assumes that Aiguillon was unaffected by Noailles's intervention and delivered his original speech as planned, it follows that the lead-off address hatched the night before in the Breton Club was far more of a defense of property rights than it was an attack on anything whatsoever.

88. One might argue that under the conditions that prevailed between May 1790 (when these rates were adopted) and the spring of 1792 (when the laws began to be radically altered) the claim that peasants couldn't pay was not so much an objective reality as a successful social construction by the peasants themselves. Aiguillon proposed reimbursing seigneurial rights at thirty times their annual value (*AP* 8:344). The rates actually adopted were lower—twenty or twenty-five times the annual value depending on the right, for fixed and periodic payouts, and more complex quantities for occasional payments (*AP* 15:365–68). But peasants claimed they couldn't pay and generally speaking did not pay; see Chapter 3, note 73.

Noailles violated the script by taking the floor and introducing the critical distinction between illegitimate rights to be ended outright and those to be subject to indemnification. Nothing could get this distinction off the agenda, once on; nor could the later vast outpouring of personal proposals to renounce various claims be put back in the bottle; nor could the condemnations of seigneurialism that followed be blotted over by Aiguillon's portrait of innocent lords unfairly blamed for the misdeeds of their agents. As if responding to Aiguillon, Le Guen de Kérangal of Brittany pointed out that it was by virtue of the high charges paid to the lord by his agents that those agents were in turn forced to charge the peasants ruinous rates. By contrast to Aiguillon's anodine portrait of lord-peasant relations, Le Guen de Kérangal stressed the humiliating character of some of the rights known in his province, in particular the obligation "to spend nights beating the ponds to prevent the frogs from troubling the sleep of voluptuous lords."[89] We have seen that one of the most important ways of attempting to defend seigneurial rights was to invoke honor: the nobility professed its attachments to its honorific rights, not its lucrative ones, although it might stretch its sense of honor to embrace the profitable (see Chapter 2, p. 47, and Chapter 4, p. 190 et seq.) The counterpart of noble honor, peasant humiliation, was, to be sure, studiously avoided in noble *cahiers* (see Chapter 2, p. 49). Le Guen de Kérangal's evocation of the ritualized humiliations of the Breton countryside was a preemptive rhetorical strike that flavored the evening with feudal barbarism rather than honorable service.[90]

The evening's result: a distinction between two kinds of rights (but which were which?), many to be indemnified (by whom? at what rates?); a claim to abolish feudalism entirely (but what was "feudalism" and what was "abolish"?); and a variety of other claims to be given up, ranging from regional privileges to periodic payments to the papacy. While unquestionably going further than the more intransigent defenders of seigneurial rights wanted, then, and probably going further than the planners of the night of August 4 had aimed at, the results were still very unclear. How the interests of payers and holders of rights were effected would not be clarified until the definitive division of rights between the two categories and the setting of rates of indemnification. These decisions, however, would await the detailed legislation to be prepared by the Committee on Feudal Rights—which would

89. *AP* 8:344. On such humiliations, see Chapter 2, p. 49.

90. Le Guen de Kérangal was followed by a lawyer from Besançon who went beyond the real serfdom of Franche-Comté to depict a world of horrific fantasy in which lords could warm their feet on wintertime hunts in the entrails of their peasants. This speech as well as Le Guen de Kérangal's provided the few points at which the nobles present seemed to feel free to express their indignation at being slandered. See Ferrières, *Mémoires,* 1:187.

then be debated. Conceivably the peasants had won a great victory—and just as conceivably, holders of rights had lost little.[91]

Kessel has shown very clearly that deputies were giving their constituents quite different advice as to what had been voted.[92] Indeed, this very unclarity may have been one of the attractions of the package. The very notion of indemnification had to raise so many questions as to guarantee delay in deciding on any course of action and to ensure confusion in whatever scheme was adopted. Which rights were to be indemnified? How was their value to be reckoned, at what rate were they to be paid off, who was to carry out property assessments, and who was to pay for the assessments? Who, for that matter, was to pay for the indemnification—the state or those subject to the seigneurial rights? If several peasants owed a lord collectively, could they pay separately; or if one peasant owed several lords could they be paid separately; or if one peasant owed one lord multiple dues were the dues to be separable? Was indemnification merely to be permitted or was it to be mandated, conceivably against the wishes of a particular peasant? And what of a peasant and lord who might come to a free agreement on a different rate of payment than the Assembly might propose? Small wonder that the Committee on Feudal Rights, in the middle of the Revolution, took seven months to actually issue a report.[93] By raising a host of tough issues, the central question of who won and who lost what was left hanging. Some conservatives could vote for such a plan with the rationale that it could be rendered meaningless once rural insurrection died down. Some radicals could vote for such a plan as the opening wedge of a real abolition. For some deputies the temporary sense of unity may have afforded an achievement not to be thrown away by speedily clarifying precisely who would benefit and who would lose. For some, the very special climate of noble–Third Estate amity that prevailed at the end of July—when the king asked the nobles to join the National Assembly—already yielded a pleasureable sense

91. One of the arguments the marquis de Ferrières used to try to sell his noble constituents back home on the idea of grinning and bearing it was to contend that carefully read, the legislation was going to cost the nobles a lot less than they might at first think. See Ferrières, *Correspondance,* 116.

92. Kessel, *La nuit du 4 août,* 175–79; 229–43. It would be a miracle if the deputies did have a clear consensus. They had discussed a vast number of issues over a week's time in a huge uncomfortable hall with poor acoustics in the August heat. Their normal working day, as Edna Hindie Lemay has discovered, was very long and an abnormal day like August 4 was even longer. The sketchy summary voted at the end of the evening of August 4 doesn't capture all that was said. The draft under debate from August 5 on was different; and journalistic accounts the delegates might use to prod their no doubt fatigued memories disagreed with each other. See Edna Hindie Lemay, *La vie quotidienne des députés aux états généraux de 1789* (Paris: Hachette, 1987), 204–6.

93. Most of these problems are addressed in a cranky presentation by a committee member, Tronchet, to the Assembly, delivered in a tone of resentment at having been saddled with such an array of impossible questions. See *AP* 12:387–401.

of *fraternité* and one well worth keeping. Timothy Tackett persuasively points out that the immediate result of noble participation for many deputies was an exciting sense of overcoming differences.[94]

In March 1790 the practical meaning, for the National Assembly, of the "abolition" of "feudalism" was much clarified: it was clearly a compromise—and one with an extremely conservative slant. At issue was how Merlin's plan would distinguish those rights to be abolished outright from those to be collected until an indemnity (on terms to be decided later) was paid.[95] On the other hand, many other rights were clearly abolished outright. The justification worked out by Merlin for distinguishing the two classes of rights turned out to be not merely incidental, but integrally woven into the fabric of this complex law. Rights seized by force were regarded as illegitimate and hence abolished outright; rights that derived from a freely consented contract were regarded as legitimate property and therefore as nuisances that could be abolished by a forward-looking state, but only upon payment of adequate compensation. A significant group of rights was abolished outright including those that carried the deepest taint of personal humiliation. The very notion of honorific rights was now anathema. The others, most important, the various payments in cash and kind, were still in force. Merlin's mapping of empirically existing rights into these broad categories rested on the contention that rights of particular kinds could be presumptively assumed to be based on coercion or consent; but the law recognized in practice a third category as well. For rights in this very substantial grey area, there would be a tentative presumption of legitimacy, but peasant communities could mount a court challenge were they able to develop evidence to the effect that the supposedly consensual arrangement was in fact a violent usurpation. Since few peasant communities could in practice demonstrate that any specific monopoly on milling, say, derived from coercion rather than contract, this was hardly an appealing prospect in village France. Let us recall the propensity toward fostering lawsuits that so appealed to the reform-minded in the Third Estate assemblies of the previous March and the indifference to judicial recourse among reform-minded peasant communities (see Chapter 3, pp. 123–24, 129). This issue of the burden of proof in disputed instances was a matter of considerable

94. Tackett, "Nobles and Third Estate," 282, points to the significance of this newfound fraternity in preparing the ground for August 4.

95. The seigneurial courts were slated for an unindemnified suppression by the law of August 11, 1789, but were maintained provisionally pending judicial reorganization. They therefore became assimilated into the National Assembly's work on the French judiciary in general and the timetable for the important subsequent legislative enactments was distinct from the rest of the seigneurial rights: October 8–9, 1789; November 3, 1789; and August 16–24, 1790, are the major dates. I shall not pursue this important institution further here.

importance in the unfolding dialogue of country people and legislators, as we shall see below.

It is probably fair to see Merlin's report as about as conservative as possible without altogether violating the parameters of the August 4–11 decree. In some ways, indeed, it did violate them. The plain language of the August enactment called for the abolition of serfdom and anything with a taint of servile status. Merlin's report invented a new distinction, not introduced at any point in the debates from August 4 to August 11. There were first, Merlin urged, seigneurial obligations that only fell on serfs; second, there were claims that fell on serfs as a matter of empirical fact but that were not inherently servile, and that could be paid by free people (*AP* 11:501–5). These latter, Merlin proposed, were not abolished along with serfdom. In short, serfdom was abolished but with the former serfs now paying as much as possible of what they had always paid.

Given the geographic narrowness of serfdom, far more important to most country people than the maintenance of many burdens of former serfs now defined as free, was the assignment of the burden of proof in contested cases to the peasants. Consider the legislation as of March 1790, in light of the noble *cahiers*. Those noble *cahiers* that defended the rights of the lords had used the language of "honor," stressed their honorific rights, and stretched the boundaries of this category; or, more commonly, they used the language of "property," almost equally elastic (see Chapter 2, pp. 34, 47 and Chapter 3, p. 85). In August and the following March claims of distinctions of honor were now utterly repudiated; the claim of property, however, had a good deal of life left in it. If many noble lords were likely to be unhappy, was peasant satisfaction a reasonable expectation?

If legislators who had hoped that the magic of August 4 would keep the countryside tranquil forever—and certainly (see Fig. 8.1) it did appear to have had an immediate effect—December–February must have been a great disappointment and a great puzzle as well, since these were areas (Brittany, Quercy, Rouergue, Limousin) that hadn't been in the forefront in the spring and summer of 1789.[96] Merlin's draft law was announced in the wake of that new, major rising. Why might the legislators now hope for any better results? Merlin de Douai's carefully crafted report urged the tripartite division into contractual, usurped, and presumptively usurped but subject to (improbable) challenge, described above. I shall comment on the intellectual

96. The extreme uncertainty as to what these new insurrections were all about and what to do about them permeates the extensive legislative discussion of February 9, 1790. The deputies were ultimately puzzled enough about the intractibility of southwestern violence, in fact, to send out an investigative team who produced one of the most interesting documents of the era. See Jacques Godard et Léonard Robin, *Rapport de Messieurs J. Godard et L. Robin, commissaires civils, envoyés par le roi, dans le département du Lot, en exécution du décret de l'Assemblée Nationale, du 13 décembre, 1790* (Paris: Imprimerie Nationale, 1791), 24.

rationale by which he justified these distinctions in Chapter 9; at this point I stress the political convenience. If one goes back to the *cahiers* of the previous March, only one year ago (but what a year!), one finds that the peasants themselves, although with very different rationales than those deployed in the National Assembly, had roughly the same distinctions (see Chapter 3, p. 91; *AP* 11:536–38). In short, I suggest that what made this project viable was less the intellectual persuasion of Merlin's classification, than it was the hope that it would give the peasants enough of what they wanted that they wouldn't fight for more. But the peasants of March 1790 were not the peasants of March 1789 and there was more (and more severe) antiseigneurial contestation ahead.

In any event, the full meaning of Merlin's report might appear very differently in light of the rates of indemnification and the modalities of payment that remained to be set. Could an individual peasant who owed many rights to a lord indemnify them one at a time or did it have to be done as a bloc? Could a group of peasants who collectively owned rights to a lord buy back their rights individually? What would unpaid arrears—quite common in the confusion of 1789—do to all these arrangements? It is symptomatic of the drive to find compromise, already a vital element of August 4, that the National Assembly actually passed this decree without first dealing with the report of Tronchet's subcommittee on indemnification rates; this latter law was not debated and enacted until May. As in August, the National Assembly managed a dramatic action on a central issue of the Revolution while postponing an absolutely essential decision without which it was impossible to say just what that action would mean to anyone. When finally delivered in May, the proposed indemnification option could hardly be called pro-peasant. In brief summary, the May law set terms impossibly difficult in a variety of ways for many peasant communities. Apart from high rates, peasants owing a bundle of obligations could not indemnify them separately nor could a group of peasants collectively responsible to a lord be assigned individual allotments. If one wanted to read "the" meaning of August 4 through the detailed legislation of the following March and May, it would certainly seem to be a plan to give away as little as possible beyond grand statements. (To anticipate the discussion below, the second wave of rural risings from December 1789 through February 1790 had not been accompanied by a great Parisian upheaval that altered the political complexion of the Assembly).

A variety of other measures followed. In mid-June 1790, following closely upon the antiseigneurial, religious, and subsistence disturbances of that month that peaked June 1 and June 9 (refer to Table 6.3), the National Assembly rather dramatically declared an end to all hereditary distinctions (*AP* 16:378). This was a follow-up, rather than a reversal, of the positions of August and March, which declared illegitimate rights based on differential honor, while maintaining those based on some claim of property. The marquis de Ferrières wavered in his reactions. On June 20, he wrote to an alternate deputy from Saumur that the termination of the various privileges of the nobility in tax exemptions and in access to posts, the new inheritance laws, the abolition of seigneurial courts, and the like had already effectively destroyed the nobility in any material sense; the new law aimed at destroying nobility as an idea "that results from a long habit of respect." But this goal will fail "because it is impossible that each man is not the son of his father; because nobility shall be transmitted, as before, by tradition and the link of identity shall always exist between today's noble and his most remote posterity."[97] On the other hand, he writes dejectedly to his wife a few days later, "the last peasant shall hold himself at least as much as a noble and shall believe that he is owed no special regard nor any deference."[98] The marquis's counsel of nonresistance to this odious decree draws on an assessment of the relative strength of the rural movement and of potential forces of order: resistance, he fears, "may become the signal for a general massacre of provincial nobles and for the burning of their *châteaux*. There is no public force able to protect them."[99] Still later, when he set down his memoirs, the marquis identified this abolition of hereditary distinctions, including, specifically, embellishing one's family name with the name of a property, distinctive liveries and coats-of-arms—in a word, the signs "that most recalled the feudal system and the spirit of chivalry"[100] as the particular bitter pill that was beyond the capacity of the nobility to swallow. It was the point at which a nobility, patiently suffering under the damage to their incomes and in the majority accepting the new constitution without regrets, not only turned on the Revolution but came to support a "league unifying the nobility, the clergy and the *parlements,* these three bodies that had detested each other before the revolution."[101] But while those who, like the marquis, thought the June 1790 law a response to the insurrectionary flare-up of that month, it was not a concession that decreased by one sou what any peasant owed any lord. To the extent that it was experienced as, in part, a gift to antiseigneurial peasants, it was a cheap gift. It was also not a gift that the peasants had been pressing for in the spring of 1789, at least

97. Ferrières, *Correspondance,* 206.

98. Ibid., 221.

99. Ibid., 208.

100. Ferrières, *Mémoires,* 2:73.

101. Ibid., 76. Alexandre Lameth, who is among those wealthy nobles singled out by the marquis for blindly betraying the nobility by championing the abolition of the symbols of status distinction, presents an account of the enactment of the law that is remarkably similar, including his judgment of the consequences. The nobility, hitherto divided, now joined together since many were "more sensitive to the loss of their titles than their privileges." Lameth's account only differs from that of Ferrières's in attributing the driving force "not to the people, but to the elite of the Third Estate"; see Lameth, *Histoire,* 1:445–47; Ferrières, *Mémoires,* 2:70, 76.

on the evidence of the *cahiers*. In the early months of 1790, however, the symbolic trappings of lordship were a more prominent target in antiseigneurial actions than they had been the previous year (see Table 8.3). So perhaps this gesture was not wholly out of step with developing rural rebellion.

If the abolition of coats-of-arms and seigneurial titles had hardly been at the center of the peasant grievances of the previous spring, we have seen in Chapters 2–4 how preoccupied the nobility had been with their honor. The general pandemonium of the debate of June 19—complete with cheering spectators, exalted champions of change, and furious nobles (AP 16:374–79)—shows that for many nobles such claims were heartfelt. Noble anger and disgust filled the written complaints they submitted.[102] June 1790, in Timothy Tackett's account, is the point at which significant numbers of the more conservative deputies began to drop out of attempting to moderate the Revolution from within: over the next fifteen months, one noble deputy in five emigrated, many offering their military experience to one or another counterrevolutionary legion forming in exile.[103] One Third Estate deputy saw June 19 as the moment when "most nobles of the kingdom showed themselves irreconcilable enemies of the Constitution."[104]

November 1790 and April 1791 produced some further movement in favor of the peasants: an easing of the indemnification modalities (payers of dues on National Land could now separately indemnify annual and occasional dues) and an addition of specific rights to the class of those to be abolished outright. Such piecemeal improvements, however, began to be called into question by the great wave of antiseigneurial revolt that raged from February into April of 1792. As early as February 29, Couthon called for a far more radical approach than currently in progress and as insurrection mounted into April, others began to speak along the same general lines. The central issue for Couthon was that the current law, far from living up to what he contended was the true spirit of August 4, 1789, actually accepted the legitimacy of important elements of the seigneurial regime. Couthon proposed instead, not merely easing repayment terms, but shifting many more rights out of the presumptively legitimate group of the reimbursable and into the presumptively illegitimate, to be abolished without compensation. This

102. *AP* 16:379–89, 393, 402. Many of the protests use the language of property in expressing their outrage as the nobility had tended to do in defending their rights in the *cahiers;* others cite the limited mandates of their electoral constituencies. It is noteworthy, however, that at this moment, confronting an end to all public emblems of distinction, some refer to descent through blood, others to claims held from God, and one, in the vocabulary of the age, refers to "nature." See the statements of the count de Landenberg-Wagenbourg, count d'Escars, duke d'Havré et de Croÿ, count de Mazancour, and marquis de Laqueuille; *AP* 16:377, 380, 381, 385, 386.

103. Timothy Tackett, *Becoming a Revolutionary: The Deputies of the National Assembly and the Emergence of a Revolutionary Culture* (Princeton: Princeton University Press, 1996), 294–96.

104. Jean-Paul Rabaut-Saint-Etienne, *Précis historique de la Révolution française* (Paris: Treuttel et Würtz, 1807), 265–67.

shift in legitimacy could be institutionalized by a corresponding shift in the burden of proof from peasants to lords. (Couthon's important statement is examined more closely later in this chapter).

According to our data, the high point of this second greatest wave of peasant insurrection peaked on April 5; as in July 1789 this meant that the peak of reports reaching the Legislative Assembly was a few days later; and again a wholly new projected law was proposed in preliminary form almost at once, on April 11. Unlike the plan, carefully constructed out of view in the Breton Club, that failed to control the situation on the floor of the National Assembly on August 4, 1789, the April 11, 1792, project was put forward by an official body, the Committee on Feudal Rights. The peasant movement eased off and it was now a good several months before the law of June 18–July 6 (*AP* 45:336–37) attempted to put out the last word by now presuming all irregular payments to be illegitimate unless the lord had proof to the contrary. Annual payments were still to be reimbursed; but with regard to the very significant and sometimes very heavy group of dues paid upon land transfer due to death or sale, the entire presumption of legitimacy/illegitimacy (or contractual/coercive) had been turned around; the legal burden would now be on the lord.

The overthrow of the monarchy on August 10, 1792, was the death warrant for the Legislative Assembly, which operated by virtue of the monarchical constitution of 1791; that expiring body, however, in its last weeks, now operated under new political circumstances. In the face of yet another wave of rural unrest (this time a combination of antiseigneurial and counterrevolutionary risings; see again Table 6.3), the assembly hastily passed a decree on August 20 further easing the conditions of indemnification.[105] A mere five days later, that decree was entirely superseded by a truly radical extension of the principles that had been pioneered in the law of June 18–July 6. On August 25, 1792,[106] all seigneurial dues were now declared presumptively illegitimate; that is, they were understood to be the result of coercive acts in the barbarous past and were therefore to be abolished outright. Should any lord have evidence to the contrary, he could petition but the burden of proof was his. This law was profoundly different than the initial detailed legislation of March 1790. Not only were fewer rights now subject to indemnification under any circumstances, but the presumption for all seigneurial dues was that they were to be abolished. Moreover, the bitter polarization of French society had advanced so far by the late summer of 1792 that it would seem safe to assume that even those few lords who might actually have some documented case for a contractual

105. Philippe Sagnac and Pierre Caron, *Les comités des droits féodaux et de législation et l'abolition du régime seigneurial* (Paris: Imprimerie Nationale, 1907), 768–72.

106. Ibid., 773–75.

basis for their rights (which means not only that there were some such documents but that these documents had not already gone up in flames in one of the several waves of insurrection) might well fear for their safety should they actually attempt a court case. And what sort of court hearing would they hope for by the fall of 1792?[107]

The great insurrections of the summer of 1789 had pushed the National Assembly to act and assured that the existence of a class of rights to be abolished without compensation could not be sidestepped by a proposal like the duke d'Aiguillon's. The peasant revolts, one might say, got the legislated details to conform a bit more closely to the commonsense meaning of the abolition of feudalism. Something similar seems to have happened in 1792, but with a more radical starting and termination point. The Couthon proposal acknowledged a fundamental illegitimacy to seigneurial rights, yet his specific proposals, and the eventual legislation adopted in June and July and again on August 20 that expanded the number of rights held illegitimate, still left others as "property." What happened between August 20 and August 25 that produced the more drastic shift to an utter reversal of the earlier burden of proof? Unlike the correspondence and memoirs of members of the National Assembly, those who served in the Legislative Assembly have not been very forthcoming on that body's major piece of antiseigneurial legislation. One may presume that the impact of the new political situation together with the rising rural insurrectionary wave that did not peak until September led the expiring Legislative Assembly to go beyond the sort of concrete measures proposed by Couthon and others and to follow his stated principles more completely.

Nonetheless, even this law, while hardly reassuring to holders of seigneurial rights, still deferred to the possibility that, in principle, there might be such an entity as a legitimate seigneurial claim. A lord still had the right to attempt to make a case. It seems improbable that many thought seigneurial rights at all viable in practice at this point. The quantity of antiseigneurial

107. I pose this as a rhetorical question. There is little research on the degree to which ex-lords attempted to use this legal machinery; nor has much been done on peasant lawsuits against lords under the March 1790 law. The earlier law made virtually impossible demands on peasants for documentation (reversed in the later law) so that one presumes that suits must have been scarce. But peasants may have been able to raise questions about documents in the lord's possession and stall. (The scattered and limited research is reviewed by Jones, *Peasantry,* 106–10). If one is willing to assume that petitions to the legislators tap into the same propensity to seek legal redress as petitions to a court (and if one is willing to assume that the selection of such petitions published by Sagnac and Caron is reasonably representative), then it is worth noting that noble petitions seem far down in 1792 from what they were in 1789 and 1790, as if nobles had simply given up on utilizing legal channels to influence policy. For the counts of noble petitions, interesting in spite of the minuscule sample, see Philippe Goujard, "Les pétitions au comité féodal: Loi contre loi," in *La Révolution française et le monde rural* (Editions du Comité des Travaux Historiques et Scientifiques, 1989), 69.

risings fell off after a final—and quite violent—spurt in September (see Chapter 6, pp. 281, 505). Why bother to risk one's neck when one could now almost certainly just stop paying, since no lord could, in practice, get the support of a court? But if antiseigneurial insurrection was dying, peasant activism was hardly at an end. Significant waves of conflict over land were still to come. Wage conflicts, although relatively uncommon were about to rise. And counterrevolution exploded in March. When the next great Parisian intervention hit—the invasion of the Convention on May 31 and June 2, 1793—the subsequent expulsion and arrest of the Girondins once again opened the way to a yet more radical approach to rural issues. The Convention, moreover, organized its work on seigneurial issues quite differently than its predecessors. Following the night of August 4, the National Assembly assigned the drafting of legislation to a specialized committee dominated by highly specialized lawyers, a precedent followed by the Legislative Assembly. The Convention, however, did without such a body, entrusting the work to the more generalist Committee on Legislation.[108] The Convention, then, was organizationally prepared to deal with this area openly as a political problem, rather than shroud it in the mystique of feudal law, the province of specialized professionals. If one sees the work of Merlin and his associates as one of consummate obfuscation—starting with the central distinction of "real" and "personal" rights[109]—one will be inclined to see this organizational shift as favoring a salutary realism. Merlin, on the other hand, regarded the Convention's legislation as unsound, as the mere law of the jungle, not properly done legislation at all.[110] As radical as it was, the law of August 25, 1792, had still maintained the initial distinction of two classes of rights, one of which, legitimate, was to be indemnified, even though the law also ensured that there would be none presumptively in the legitimate group. The law of July 1793, however, found only one class and that one illegitimate.

The history of this new legislation is, in its details, effectively unknown. On June 3—the day after the exclusion of the Girondins—an unnamed deputy proposed burning all documents justifying feudal rights (*AP* 66:4) as part of the next month's celebration of July 14. He was followed by Méaulle who proposed "a general law that completes the destruction of feudalism" (*AP* 66:4). There was no debate (if we credit the written record) and both proposals were referred to the Committee on Legislation.

Six weeks later, the subject came up again, by way of a metaphor that had become a cliché. The seigneurial regime had sometimes been compared

108. Peter Jones points up the significance of the Convention's breaking with a specialized committee (*Peasantry*, 87).

109. The legislation is considered as an intellectual construction in chapter 9.

110. Garaud, *Révolution et propriété foncière*, 227.

to a tree with its slowly growing but impressive trunk, its complexly branching offshoots, its roots sunk deep in French history and culture. Several deputies had discussed the night of August 4 in these terms. On August 5, 1789, describing the elation he, like so many others, felt the night before, the deputy Michel-René Maupetit waxed arboreal: "The famous tree of feudalism was knocked down yesterday and that night all its roots were cut."[111] Nearly four years later, however, Isoré told the Convention that "the tree of feudalism has only been pruned; we must knock it down roots and all, burn it and throw its cinders to the wind" (*AP* 69:19). There seems to have been some debate about a draft law consisting of several articles; the accounts of the debate and the draft differ considerably. Two days later, on July 17, the seigneurial rights were simply declared abolished (*AP* 69:98). The crucial documentation of seigneurial claims was to be destroyed by fire. There appears to have been no debate at all and the law enacted was considerably more elaborate than the draft that some accounts ascribe to Isoré two days earlier. Was there another behind-the-scenes maneuver as before August 4, 1789, only now more successful in controlling discussion? If the path is unknown, however, the outcome is clear: nearly four years after the ever memorable night of August 4, it no longer took a special state of mind or a particular lawyerly logic to find that the law really meant the destruction of the feudal regime in its entirety.

Merlin de Douai, the architect of the intellectual rationale for the indemnification project now in ruins, commented that this was "a law of anger, that, through the breach made in the right of property, exposed those imprudent men who by their clamor had provoked it, to be themselves one day despoiled by a new law made in the same spirit and to lose the properties that they had acquired by extinguishing rights and dues."[112] Merlin saw the danger of sliding further down the slippery slope in which property-owning elites would encourage further radicalism rather than contain it, in terms very similar to those uttered at a much earlier phase by the marquis de Ferrières (see note 19). Yet this time, many legislators were prepared to take steps not to fall further down that slope. The second article of the July 17, 1793, decree made an exception of "nonfeudal" rent (*AP* 69:98). The difficulty of unambiguously distinguishing the one from the other remained. But now there was no geographically widespread grouping of fairly unified peasant communities prepared to disrupt indefinitely. Peasant proprietors had been freed of seigneurial (and ecclesiastical) obligations and stood only to benefit from a renewed capacity to enforce rent-collection.

The sharecroppers of the Southwest, in rebellion since the late fall of 1789, however, had been saddled with the neo-tithe, payable to the same

111. Michel-René Maupetit, "Lettres de Michel-René Maupetit," *Bulletin de la Commission Historique et Archéologique de la Mayenne* 19 (1903): 217.

112. Quoted in Garaud, *Révolution et propriété foncière*, 227.

proprietors who could make claims for "nonfeudal" rents. Their fight went on, but they were not, alone, enough to persuade legislators to go through with the legally mandated auto-da-fé of seigneurial documents that contained rental claims as well. The legislature's concern was not only the abstract claims to property rights of landholders (these had been continually redefined since 1789) but also protecting claims on state-held property. By October 2, 1793, the Convention suspended the burning of these documents. Nonetheless, the will to legislate a narrowed interpretation of the law was gone, in part, perhaps, because of the experience of years of peasant resistance, in part, perhaps because of the aura of sacrality that now hung over the legal document claiming, finally, to have abolished what was left of feudalism. The absence of clear legislative guidance[113] meant that policy was now made by litigation before judges with different views. One court might very strictly rule that any payment "stained in its origins by the lightest mark of feudalism is abolished without indemnity"[114] while another might interpret the law to protect rents.[115]

Southwestern sharecroppers, with several years of tenacious campaigning behind them, continued to resist. In this region all sorts of payments were intertwined, as perhaps is suggested by use of the word "rents" as the "usual term in the area to refer to feudal rights," as Godard and Robin discovered when they toured the Southwest in the winter of 1790–91.[116] The legislature responded with a masterpiece of ambiguity. Landowners could rent land in any mutually agreed upon fashion provided that rental agreements didn't look like seigneurial ones—leaving the varying views of the courts a free hand.[117] From 1789 Merlin had been arguing that much of what the peasants held to be feudal was actually legitimate property; now southwestern peasants argued that some of what elites held to be legitimate property was actually feudal.

How the War Revolutionized the Revolution: Seigneurial Rights Abroad and At Home

Peasant insurrection and war had combined to ruin Merlin's edifice. The war made new demands on the countryside: demands for taxation, for food, for

113. A local official in Moulins wrote to the Legislative Committee for guidance as to whether the law required him to deposit the titles to National Property, presumably prior to burning (Sagnac and Caron, "Les comités des droits féodaux," 789).

114. Garaud, *Révolution et propriété foncière,* 232.

115. Millot, *Le régime féodale en Franche-Comté au XVIIIe siècle* (Besançon: Millot Frères, 1937), 268.

116. Godard and Robin, *Rapport,* 24.

117. Jones, *Peasantry,* 103.

draft animals, and for sons. These alone lent weight to the new approach to seigneurial rights that Couthon had begun to propose as war approached and peasant insurrection broke out again. Couthon's rhetoric was openly political. Rather than a theoretical rationale, Couthon proposed to think about what peasants would not only tolerate but actively support. Rather than complex reasonings the new approach just made a simple and sharp equation of seigneurial rights with violent usurpation, qualified slightly by a few relatively recent contractual arrangements.[118]

But it was not only the material burdens imposed on the peasantry that propelled the change in the structure of the laws but the moral burden the legislators imposed on themselves. In identifying the Revolution with an international crusade against *la féodalité* the legislature made of the abolition of feudal regimes, generally, a national mission. It was part strategic calculation to challenge loyalties of peasant conscripts elsewhere; part self-deception to conceal the aggressive nature of the French side of the war, now renounced in the new Constitution; part genuine identification with "liberty"; and part identification of the French state with a particular set of social institutions whose superiority over the backward institutions of the antagonists was assured by their modernity. By the time of the August 1792 legislation, the antifeudal discourse had emerged from its French cocoon to become a part of the war aims of the revolutionary armies, with the not-so-incidental benefit, so it was hoped (but rarely realized), that rebellious peasants would play havoc with the war-fighting capacities of the Coalition's forces.

In trying to uncover the process of conflating the dismantling of feudalism within France with the confrontation of the new France and the old Europe, we may turn to the language of the legislators in dealing with two early international problems: in considering complaints from across the Rhine, the legislators began to connect their policies at home with troubles abroad; in grappling with a potential war between Spain and Britain a half-year later, the legislators began to cast their country, now rejuvenated, as uniquely moral and principled in world affairs. The complaints of a few German aristocrats hardly threatened war; the threat of Spanish-English war embroiling France was not triggered by anything to do with feudalism; but blend together elements of the two debates and one has the germ of a national mission to end feudalism in the world.

Seigneurial rights became a central element of interstate conflict with the night of August 4. German princes, whose seigneurial claims in Alsace were guaranteed in the treaty of Münster of 1648 hoped to find a powerful backer in the Holy Roman Empire. The landgrave of Hesse-Darmstadt, the bishop of Spire, and the duke of Württemberg had already been at odds with the

118. Couthon, *Discours sur le rachat,* 4–5.

French government over the flurry of institutional innovation of the pre-revolutionary period. The new local and regional assemblies, set up in 1787 with sharply limited representation, already raised the specter of popular sovereignty to these princes. The tax-reform proposals of 1787 and 1788, the judicial reorganization of 1788 that threatened seigneurial courts, and the antifeudal discourse in which public affairs were already being discussed were issues in Alsace even before the Estates-General met.[119] What August 4 did was to raise these tensions, on the French side, from a problem to a national commitment. From a problem that pitted local privileges against monarchical reform and state centralization, this conflict was now transmuted in its more public version into a struggle of the new epoch being born against the lay and clerical lords who fought to keep humanity in chains.

What may have appeared at first as simply the conflicting claims of French and imperial sovereignty, appeared instead to some in the Assembly as a question of whether the sovereignty of the French people (which the legislators took themselves to embody) could be assigned limits under the treaties of past monarchs. When the Committee on Feudal Rights looked into the complaints of German princes that French peasants were failing to honor seigneurial obligations protected by the Treaty of Münster, Merlin, as usual, found a legal principle to sustain the jurisdiction of the National Assembly: the social contract took precedence over all. Since the people of Alsace had never consented to the Treaty of Münster, but had participated in the election of the deputies that enacted the August 4–11 decree, the "treaties of princes" were illegal (*AP* 20:81). The plain implication was that all interstate treaties to date were illegitimate and no European structure of authority, except France's, had the basis in popular consent that made it worthy of respect.[120] Here, as in other pronouncements on seigneurial rights, Merlin's sharp and absolute statement of principle was as radical as the totality of concrete measures was moderate. The Diplomatic Committee, appropriate to its mission, took a more diplomatic view and proposed compensating the princes[121] but the princes refused. As it happened the empire was unwilling to back the princes so that there was no immediate military action (or even an immediate threat),[122] but the linkage of uncompro-

119. Pierre Muret, "L'affaire des princes possessionés d'Alsace et les origines du conflit entre la Révolution et l'Empire," *Revue d'histoire moderne et contemporaine* 1 (1899–1900): 433–56; 566–92.

120. T. C. W. Blanning, *The Origins of The French Revolutionary Wars* (London: Longman, 1986), 74–75.

121. *AP* 20:84. The head of the Diplomatic Committee was Mirabeau who had never liked the developments of the night of August 4 and who had, indeed, been conspicuously absent that evening.

122. Sydney Seymour Biro, *The German Policy of Revolutionary France* (Cambridge: Harvard University Press, 1957), 1:39–42. See also T. C. W. Blanning, *The French Revolution in Germany: Occupation and Resistance in the Rhineland, 1792–1802* (Oxford: Clarendon Press, 1983), 59–69; Muret, "L'affaire des princes possessionés."

mising rhetorical antagonism to seigneurial rights and overturning authority outside of France had been forged.

The next intensive discussion of France as a state among states took place in May 1790.[123] A year earlier, the general harassment of British vessels by Spanish warships off the Pacific coasts of the Americas escalated into a major confrontation at Nootka Sound. When news from this remote edge of European imperial power finally arrived in London and Madrid, the British issued threatening statements, the Spanish sought the backing of France under the Bourbon Family Compact, and the National Assembly found itself asked to support Louis XVI should he follow his sense of French treaty obligations and take his kingdom into war. In a week of highly charged debate, the Assembly argued about the proper locus of the power to engage in war, the proper respect for treaty commitments, the possible consequences for the Revolution of expanding the military or concentrating its command, the proper purposes of warfare, and the triviality or grandeur that underlay the bellicosity of past kings. Unlike the grievances of Rhenish princes, the nature of the Revolution was not directly in question, since the central issue was a quarrel between other states. Nonetheless, many contributors to the discussion managed to connect revolution at home and the European state system: whether France as a "nation" characterized by "freedom"—words much invoked in the arguments—could or should behave like other states was a major axis of debate. Several speakers introduced the notion that a war for some higher purpose would be a different matter entirely than a war over mere "interest" (another frequently invoked concept) let alone a war initiated by the whims of kings. (When one speaker suggested that Henri IV had been prepared to take France into war out of his "insane passion" for Princess de Condé, he triggered an esoteric debate-within-the debate over the minutiae of French history.) (*AP* 15:529–30, 546, 573–74). Pétion spoke of the recent American war as "unjust" because it was not undertaken "to break the shackles of an enslaved people in order to free it." Those who took France into war only "wished to obtain revenge from a rival nation, to humiliate it, to weaken it. Happily, in desiring nothing beyond this goal, they have attained something more noble and more desirable, the only goal that may console the friends of humanity and the public good for the blood and treasure that they expended in this war. They placed the light of liberty in the New World, and this light, although hardly noticed, shall enlighten all the peoples of the earth" (*AP* 15:538).

Many speakers developed the distinction drawn by Merlin a few months before, between the treaties of kings and the treaties of peoples. Fusing this theme with the notion of war in support of moral principle, baron de

123. The debate is found in *AP* 15:510–663. On the background of the Nootka Sound incident, see Blanning, *Origins of the French Revolutionary Wars,* 61–62, 79–80.

Menou's brief contribution pointed to a future profoundly different from the past. He implicitly dismissed the treaty with Spain. The issue for him was the "justice and morality" of the two disputants: "we shall examine which of the two nations is in the wrong. If it is Spain, we must employ our mediation to encourage it to be flexible; if it is England, and if England refuses to do justice, we must arm not fourteen vessels, but all our land and sea forces. And then we shall show Europe what a war is, a war not of ministers but of a nation [applause interrupts the speaker]" (*AP* 15:518).

And, finally, many deputies held that the representatives of a free people had to control the main elements of interstate policy as well as domestic affairs. By the time the discussion had concluded, many deputies had embraced a public rhetoric in which domestic policy, relations with other states, constitutional arrangements at home and position in the European state system were all connected; in which warfare could be justified as support of freedom as well as self-defense, and in which the ways of war-making of a free people were seen as distinguishing that people from its neighbors. The specific crisis passed, but the rhetorical habit of stressing the uniqueness of French institutions and the uniquely moral character of French bellicosity were to infuse all future discussion. And unlike the Nootka Sound incident and the Family Compact, the very sources of tension were largely seen to be France's new institutions and its overthrow of feudalism in particular.

As interstate tensions increased, those in France who favored war convinced themselves that not only would the conscript armies of their enemies crumble when confronting a free people but that the subject peoples of Europe would rise in emulation of the liberated French. Isnard's inflammatory speech of late November 1791 linked French émigrés and German princes in a common concern with lost rights and warned that "if foreign courts try to raise a war of kings against France, we shall raise a war of peoples against kings" (*AP* 35:441–43). When a Prussian radical told the Legislative Assembly in December 1791 that interstate conflict would prompt peasants of Germany and Bohemia to rise against their lords,[124] he was only reaffirming what many were already well prepared to hear. Brissot and his political associates persistently defined the war they advocated as a war against feudalism.[125] There were, to be sure, some who proposed cooling the rhetorical temperature. As war neared in February 1792 the

124. *AP* 36:79. The speaker, Anacharsis Cloots, might have been buoyed by thoughts of the recent peasant rising, in August 1790, in Saxony. See Jerome Blum, *The End of the Old Order in Rural Europe* (Princeton: Princeton University Press, 1978), 337–38.

125. For example, Louvet in December 1791: "swift as lightning let thousands of our citizen-soldiers hurl themselves upon the many domains of feudalism. . . . Let them stop only where servitude ends; let the palaces be surrounded by bayonets; let the Declaration of Rights be deposited in the cottages" (*AP* 36:381).

Diplomatic Committee of the Legislative Assembly reiterated the conciliatory proposal of indemnifying the German princes (*AP* 39:89–90), a proposal dismissed by Mailhe for its weakness (*AP* 39:97). (If it was wrong to indemnify lords across the Rhine, did some of Mailhe's listeners wonder why it was proper to do so on this side?) And Robespierre's attempted deflation of the yoking of liberation and European war is well known.[126] Nonetheless the sense of national mission prevailed. It was to be no more than a playing-out of these notions that saw French armies a few years later support "sister republics" among whose defining attributes were proclaiming the abolition of whatever were the local analogues of seigneurial rights. By late 1792, French forces dominated Belgium and provided a foretaste of what was to come elsewhere: the first article of a proclamation of the founding principles of the new order declared an end to feudal dues, serfdom, and hunting rights.[127]

Until the approach of actual war, most of the legislation on the seigneurial regime still amounted to tinkering with the basic structure embodied in the law of August 4–11, 1789, as elaborated in the enactments of March and May 1790. With the interstate tensions appearing increasingly ominous, peasant insurrection now began to suggest the failure of the existing scheme and the need to strike out in a wholly new direction. As a new wave of rural incidents began to mount in February 1792, ultimately reaching the second largest peak of the revolution in April, Couthon urged a new course in the Legislative Assembly. He reminded his fellow deputies of the great size of the French army. But he urged them to recall that sheer size is far less significant than the moral unity of army and nation. The benefits of the Revolution unfortunately, had not yet been fully received in the French countryside; village France had largely received fine words.

> Each of us has seen that ever memorable night of August 4, 1789, when the Constituent Assembly . . . pronounced in a holy enthusiasm the abolition of the feudal regime. . . . But these striking decisions were soon to present nothing more to the people than the idea of a beautiful dream, whose deceitful illusion left nothing but regrets. It was . . . on August 4, 1789 that a decree was joyously received in all parts of the empire that abolished . . . the feudal regime. Eight months later, a second decree preserved everything of value of this regime, so that far from having served the people, the Constituent Assembly could not even retain the consoling hope of being able to

126. "No one loves armed missionaries"; see Maximilien Robespierre, *Oeuvres* (Paris: Presses Universitaires de France, 1950), 8:81.

127. Robert R. Palmer, *The Age of the Democratic Revolution: A Political History of Europe and America, 1760–1800* (Princeton: Princeton University Press, 1959–64), 2:78.

> one day free themselves from the despotism of the former lords and the exaction of their agents.[128]

Couthon alludes to the earlier work of abolishing the honorific aspects of the regime while insisting on indemnities for lucrative rights: "It is not exactly the honorific aspects of the feudal regime that weigh on the people." These signs of esteem may have outraged, demeaned, and degraded them but it is, Couthon goes on, the dues that are behind the peasant insurrections.[129] If, as now seemed inevitable, war came, it would be only sensible to alleviate sources of peasant discontent—to forestall further episodes of insurrection like those that raged in southeastern France in that winter of 1792.[130] "Do you wish," Couthon goes on, "to assure the prompt return of taxes as well as calm disturbances?"[131] And if one hoped to have villagers submit to the draft and to fight in defense of the Revolution, it would be only prudent to ensure that the Revolution actually met some of their deep aspirations. "We wish," he insists, that the people "believe in the reign of liberty while they remain chained in the dependency on their former lords" (7).

Couthon's speech did not merely call for a new direction in policy, but for a newly pragmatic appreciation of the demands of the countryside. He has no interest whatsoever in any legal theory from which decisions among particular seigneurial rights might appear to derive. One wonders if the "discourse" he refers to as the unappreciated gift of the Revolution to the peasants is intended to refer specifically to the theoretical rationale elaborated by Merlin de Douai (to be discussed in Chapter 9). Against a background of insurrection at home and approaching war abroad, the spirit of Couthon's remarks found support.[132] On March 12 Golzart argued that the Assembly "must finally convince the people of the countryside that the abolition of the feudal regime is not an almost worthless benefit" (*AP* 39:595). He took up Couthon's notion of easing payment terms, but went beyond Couthon in considering having the government reimburse owners of *champart* ("the most revolting" of rights) in order to undercut the appeal of counterrevolutionaries. The Feudal Committee was at once invited "to review all the decrees on indemnification" and to recommend a new course. On April 11, near the great peak of the spring uprisings of that year and virtually on the brink of war, the Committee's report conceded the bankruptcy of the Constituent Assembly's policies. The solicitude shown the lords by the National Assembly made a mockery of claims to abolish the

128. Couthon, *Discours sur le rachat,* 2–3.
129. Ibid., 3.
130. See Table 7.5 on the regional aspects of this wave of insurrection.
131. Couthon, *Discours sur le rachat,* 8.
132. For a general treatment of the political context for the debates of spring 1792, see C. J. Mitchell, *The French Legislative Assembly of 1791* (Leiden: E. J. Brill, 1988), 61–69.

feudal regime: "It is in vain that the Constituent Assembly announced that it was abolishing the feudal regime if, in actual practice, it let the most odious burden continue [the speaker refers here specifically to mutation fees]" (*AP* 41:470–74).

The Committee proposed abolishing mutation fees unless the lord had a title demonstrating the contractual nature of his particular claim. While the Committee's proposal was limited to the specific, but quite onerous, area of mutation fees,[133] let us note the radical shift in where the burden of proof lies. The mutation fees were now presumed illegitimate, a deep reversal that would pervade more sweeping legislation a few months hence. The debate that swirled around this proposal was profoundly symptomatic of a deeply changed climate. If much of the debate around the decrees of August 4–11 had been based on the complaint that they went too far, presaging the contraction embodied in Merlin's law of March 1790, the debate that erupted over the new proposal in the spring of 1792 was around the counterproposal that it didn't go nearly far enough. Taking the legislative history of two years ago as a warning of what was to be avoided at the present moment, one deputy contended that the detailed legislation of March and May 1790 that translated the abolition of the feudal regime into practice actually "validated usurpations rather than suppress them." A new approach to pacifying peasants was needed. Another deputy warned against going too far: only mutation rights were to be covered by new rules (*AP* 41:474, 484–85, 487–88). In the course of that debate, it was clear that defense of "property" still carried very strong claims. The problem, as Couthon stated it, lay in what legitimate property was. The National Assembly, he argued, failed to draw a "sufficiently sharp distinction" between the usurped and the contractual and therefore "produced a decree that the former lords themselves might have dictated."[134]

Such rhetorical minimization of the work of the National Assembly infused many of the contributions to the debates of spring 1792. Describing the *champart* as the seigneurial right most revolting to the inhabitants of the countryside (*AP* 39:595), and speaking of mutation fees as "the most odious burden" (*AP* 41:470–74) (as we have just seen the legislators do) were not very accurate as statements about the place of such rights on the parishes' agenda or the firmness of calls for abolition in the *cahiers* of three years earlier (see Tables 2.5 and 3.4). Yet if one were to eliminate from consideration those rights which had already been effectively abolished by spring

133. In singling out mutation fees from other payments, the Feudal Committee selected precisely the payment most loathed by the peasants and urban elites alike in March 1789 and which had the least support for indemnification (see Tables 3.4 and 3.6.) If there was to be a search for a revision of the laws along the lines Couthon suggested that would do as little as possible and yet that might be enough to satisfy the country people, the *cahiers* data suggest that one couldn't have done better.

134. Couthon, *Discours sur le rachat,* 4–5.

1792 from the tabulations we examined in Chapters 2 and 3, both *champart* and mutation fees would stand near the top of remaining rural concerns. By refusing to credit earlier legislation with meeting any desires of the village, the more radical legislators of 1792 could claim for themselves the achievement of breaking new ground in support of the country people rather than the more modest claim of following through on an earlier breakthrough.

A new draft law was proposed on the brink of the war formally declared by France on April 20. The linkage of the war and the struggle against feudalism continued as a rhetorical commonplace. Condorcet attacked the diplomatic proposals of the Austrian foe for demanding the restoration of "feudal servitude" as part of the price of peace (*AP* 42:21). The rural revolt died down after April, easing the need for immediate action, but when the topic was taken up again in June, Mailhe, a lawyer from Haute-Garonne, who had picked up important career experience as a seigneurial judge,[135] urged his colleagues to see that "the destruction without indemnity of all the rights is the stone that is missing from the foundation of the Constitution" (*AP* 45:18). With the war under way no one could miss the political significance of Mailhe's argument: "When the nation shall have done for its members all that justice commands, then they shall make every effort to do all that the national interest commands." For those who needed a theoretical rationale to counter Merlin's, Mailhe proposed regarding every right as based on an original act of violence. The operational mechanism Mailhe proposed was placing the burden of proof on the lords, should they claim the contrary. As for the criticism that this was a preposterous demand since the lords couldn't prove any such thing, Mailhe countered by pointing out that the identical impossible burden had been put on the peasants in the current law (*AP* 45:17–18).

In mid-June the Girondin leader Louvet joined the position taken by the Montagnard Couthon three months earlier: "We shall never obtain the complete consolidation of our Revolution until the day when the last vestiges of serfdom . . . have forever disappeared." And Louvet went on to denounce the way in which conceptions of property had been used to protect the feudal regime and thereby prevent peasants from fully supporting the revolutionary order: "None of you, Sirs, is ignorant of the fact that it is with this word property that one wished to block our predecessors. . . . Let us see that we don't abuse this word here" (*AP* 45:119–23).

In fact, both sides in these debates of June were vigorously claiming to be

135. Geneviève Thoumas, "La jeunesse de Mailhe," *Annales Historiques de la Révolution Française* 43 (1971): 221–47, and Lenard R. Berlanstein, *The Barristers of Toulouse in the Eighteenth Century (1740–1793)* (Baltimore: Johns Hopkins University Press, 1975), 24. Seigneurial judgeship was often an important part of a legal career. See Maurice Gresset, *Gens de justice à Besançon: De la conquête par Louis XIV à la Révolution française, 1674–1789* (Paris: Bibliothèque Nationale, 1978), 1:100.

the defenders of "property." Prouveur, of the currently peaceful *département* of Nord (see Table 7.5), may have been trying to appeal to ambivalent deputies on the left in quoting Rousseau to the effect that the man who had first said of a plot of land, "This is mine," was the real founder of society; he went on to prophesy social collapse if the legislature did not accept a very broad meaning of property in order to cover feudal rights (*AP* 44:200). But Gohier saw "feudalism" as a disease from which the moral core of property rights had to be rescued, for feudalism meant appropriation by violence, and the passage of the centuries could not retroactively turn that violent act into the freely consented contract that must be honored (*AP* 44:202, 205).

The early months of war saw the overturning of the assumptions of the initial legislation, a process culminating in the August decrees of the Legislative Assembly. The new Convention continued to expound the fusion of struggle against foreign kings and antifeudalism. In November 1792, the Convention discussed "the principles," as Brissot put it, "under which France must protect all the peoples who demand it." Mailhe interjected that whatever else these principles might be, they must include instructing other people "about the natural rights on which the destruction of feudal rights in France was based." And he went on to speak of a national mission: "Citizens, it is in France that feudal rights and their consequences unhappily were born; it is from France that enlightenment must come; it is the French who must raise the thick veil which, among all our neighbors, still conceals the fundamental rights of nature" (*AP* 53:473).

Cambon put it more tersely, "What is the purpose of the war you have undertaken? It is surely the abolition of all privileges. War against the *châteaux,* peace to the cottages" (*AP* 55:70). Even after the new thrust embodied in the antiseigneurial legislation of August 1792, then, the antifeudal language surrounding the war outran the law in France. On December 15, 1792, the Convention decreed the abolition of seigneurial rights with no mention of any provision for lords to appeal in French-controlled areas of Belgium and Germany.[136] A proclamation adopted by the Convention announced French support for peasant insurrection outside of France. "Show yourselves to be free men and we shall protect you against their vengeance."[137]

The new discussions of seigneurial rights were rooted in the war-promoting rhetoric of the Girondins, in statements of war aims, in policy

136. *AP* 55:75. As early as October, General Custine, operating in the Rhineland, had anticipated the legislature in announcing his sympathy to German serfs and his antipathy to "the loathsome feudal rights"; see Sagnac, *Le Rhin français pendant la Révolution et l'Empire* (Paris: Félix Alcan, 1917), 72.

137. *AP* 55:101. See also Suzanne Tessier, *Histoire de la Belgique sous l'occupation française en 1792 et 1793* (Brussels: Librairie Falk fils, 1934).

declarations by generals in Belgium or the Rhineland, in inspirational pep talks to the troops. The rhetorical climate was changing. If the sons of French villagers were to die to free German or Piedmontese villagers from feudal oppression, could the legislators stick to a definition of feudal rights so narrow as to appear an utter fraud in rural France?[138] If the Convention encouraged antifeudal insurrection in France's neighbors, could it manage to prosecute antifeudal peasants at home? If Mailhe not only supported the wartime proclamation of liberation of occupied territories from feudal rights that included protecting peasants from their lords' vengeance but sponsored amending it to include abolishing nobility itself on December 15, it seems but a matter of consistency for him to have advocated, ten days later, that legal proceedings against French peasants rebelling against seigneurialism be dropped (*AP* 55:72–73, 56:65, 74).

The war made it impossible to maintain the disjunction between the sense of a radical rupture in history with a detailed specification that altered little of what peasants owed lords. In presenting the French armies as the agent of liberty in battle against the slave armies of the crowned tyrants,[139] the legislators had to accept the victory of defiant French villagers who doggedly refused the coexistence of the narrow and the broad senses of the abolition of the feudal regime.

Parallels and Contrasts

Legislators Deal with the Tithe

The tithe legislation[140] was in large part an appendage of the seigneurial rights story. The initial legislation recognized that in addition to ecclesiastical tithes in the hands of the church there were the infeudated tithes. These

138. In the fall of 1790, the National Assembly heard of the countryside around Gourdon, where claims were circulating to the effect that the rural National Guards wouldn't enforce decrees held to be fraudulent, that the new laws weren't believed to be the work of the Assembly at all, but of the former lords (*AP* 21:457). Couthon's important speech of February 1792 is a legislator's assertion of a claim made earlier by southwestern sharecroppers, when he dramatically asserts that the former lords could have written the existing legislation.

139. A little past the time-frame considered here, with French armies well beyond the old borders, very traditional sorts of power-enhancing arguments for national expansion were invoked. The same Merlin de Douai who had so dramatically rejected the treaties of princes in 1789 in favor of the will of the people of Alsace, now, on September 22, 1795, championed the annexation of Belgium in order to move the frontier far north of Paris and with no consideration of consulting the Belgians; see Sagnac, *Le Rhin français,* 123.

140. Henri Marion, *La dîme ecclésiastique en France au XVIIIe siècle et sa suppression* (Bordeaux: Imprimerie de l'Université et des Facultés, 1912).

latter were largely assimilated to the antiseigneurial legislation and thereby underwent similar mutations in the rules of indemnification as opposed to outright abolition until finally abolished unconditionally along with the seigneurial rights in July 1793. The ecclesiastical tithes, on the other hand, following some bitter debate, were slated for unconditional abolition by the law of August 4–11, 1789. This outright abolition meant an immediate windfall for somebody and whether that somebody was to be a landowner or that landowner's tenant was a matter of great consequence.[141] The windfall would begin at the date at which the tithe was no longer to be paid, set for 1791 by the law of April 14–20, 1790 (*AP* 12:745). The law (purposely?) did not specify how the windfall was to be distributed, which is reminiscent of the vagueness in the law on seigneurial rights the previous month that had specified the rights to be indemnified but not the rates. Rather than permit a renegotiation of contracts, leaving the distribution of the windfall to the market, the National Assembly awarded the entire windfall to the proprietors (law of December 1–12, 1790).[142] The mechanism for enriching the proprietors was to require that sharecroppers and cash tenants who had previously paid the tithe now were to add its value to their rents. While proprietors might have been quite content with this "neo-tithe," their tenants were unlikely to be so enthusiastic. Thus the revolutionary legislatures helped prepare the way for a shift in the locus of rural conflict away from peasant communities against lords and toward class struggles within those communities.[143]

141. Unlike the case of the infeudated tithe, indemnification was not to be required of peasants, since the state would now take charge of ecclesiastical affairs and finance them out of tax revenues. Note that this is in the general spirit of the parish *cahiers* that grant the tithe to have at least the virtue of supporting a communally valued function (see Chapter 3, p. 109). As with the seigneurial rights, the question of how to actually get peasants to continue to pay any sort of interim tithe pending the definitive abolition was not resolved by all the hortatory injunctions to patriotism, all the reasoned attempts to convince peasants the Revolution was on their behalf, etc.

142. *AP* 21:170. To avoid seeing the legislature as self-consciously stacking the decks in favor of a rural elite even more than they in fact did, we need to recall that the December rule only applied to the allocation of the benefits of the abolition among the parties to current leases. Future terms of tenancy were wide open to the fortunes of lease negotiation. On the other hand, most leases were fairly long-term. While it would be difficult to imagine a group for whom "property" was "sacred" voiding existing contracts, it is possible to imagine a different split of the tithe than 0–100%. (The best account of the "neo-tithe" is Jones, *Peasantry,* 94–103.) As a Third Estate instance of property as "sacred," see the *cahier* of the Third Estate of Cahors, *AP* 3:491; on the sacrality of property for the nobility, see Chapter 2.

143. Complaints received by the Committee on Feudal Rights show a clear expectation that the tithe legislation was planting the seeds of open class conflict in the countryside. According to one analysis "all the proprietors think that the lot of the sharecropper ought in no way be changed for the better;" another contends that "the small farmers . . . say openly that, far from establishing liberty, this measure revives servitude and tyranny" (Sagnac and Caron, *Les comités des droits féodaux,* 347, 353).

The Battle for Land: Landsales and Legislative Initiatives

The trajectory of legislation on ownership of and access to land is considerably more complex than that of the tithe. There is an extensive scholarly literature and one full of disagreement on the nature of conflicts over land policy at both the level of the village and the level of the legislatures. I shall only touch on some of these issues here. Roughly speaking, we may divide the broad question of access to land into four areas of legislative action. There were first of all a host of questions about National Property, the lands of church and king (and later of émigrés) to be sold, simultaneously providing resources to the depleted treasury and creating a class of purchasers committed to the Revolution. Were the terms of sale to be set to favor the state finances or the purchaser's desire for a bargain? Were they to be set to favor larger or smaller acquirers? Second, there were a large number of communities at odds with their lords, especially over the use of pasture and forest; their combat had been taking place in the courts as well as in land invasions. No legislative program on the seigneurial regime could be complete without tackling these associated issues of rights over land. Third, there were issues around the continuation of communal constraints on enclosures, technology, planting dates, and the like; the advanced economic theorists had wanted to eliminate these constraints but had largely been stymied by multiple forms of resistance before the Revolution. Finally, there was the question of the communal land: was it to be preserved as collective property or divided, and if divided, how?

The multiplicity and complexity of these issues assured a vast stream of legislation, which I shall not attempt to trace in any detail[144] but I do want to suggest the major parallel and major contrast with the legislative response to insurrectionary antiseigneurialism. The parallel, first: the legislative actions tended to follow the rhythms of peasant insurrection generally so that major turning points often moved in tandem with legislation on seigneurial rights. The initial law on sale of National Property, for example, provided for the seized lands of church and king to be sold at auction in large plots (*AP* 15:506–8). This major act, plainly favoring the well-to-do, followed almost immediately upon the very conservative legislation setting the terms of seigneurial indemnification (May 3–9). In the wake of August 1792's upheaval, the Convention suddenly made common land other than woods divisible by unspecified mechanisms to be set up at once, still another instance of a dramatic law that deferred central issues to the future. Not having set up any mechanisms, however, the law was revoked in October. On the other hand, the law of August 28–September 14 was more decisive about whose was the contested land in disputes of lords and peasants. Any

144. For excellent surveys, see Jones, *Peasantry,* and Garaud, *Révolution et propriété foncière.*

common land taken by the lord since 1669 with or without a claim legally valid at the time, was awarded to the peasant community.[145] This followed hard upon the reversal of the balance of proof in contested antiseigneurial cases that effectively ended the capacity of most lords to collect most of their rights. By the fall of 1792, then, the antiseigneurial aspect of land law was well developed but the balance of individual and communal claims was oscillating unstably. Following the great political change that left a more radicalized Convention after the Paris militants opened the way by their insurrection of May 31, 1793, for the removal of the Girondins, came the two decrees of June: on June 3, émigré land was now nationalized and added to royal and ecclesiastical property; and National Property was to be sold at auction in small plots, thereby permitting poorer peasant strata than before to compete for land.[146] This was just one month before the definitive antiseigneurial decree. Thus the timing—and the radicalism—of land law roughly paralleled the timing and radicalism of law on seigneurial rights.

The second major point, and the great contrast with the dialogue of peasants and legislators over the seigneurial rights, is the degree to which issues of land access tended to be divisive inside the peasant communities, a divisiveness that grew with the very success of antiseigneurialism. Land conflicts (see Chapter 5) initially in fact were hard to distinguish from communal battles with lay and ecclesiastical lords: peasants would drive their animals over the lord's fields or would cut down trees in a monastery's forests. If one may speak of land conflicts with an antifeudal element, one

145. Georges Bourgin, *Le partage des biens communaux* (Paris: Imprimerie Nationale, 1908), 397, 398–99, 404–5.

146. The laws of June 3, 1793, and September 13, 1793, included two measures that appeared aimed at the poorest rural stratum: first, the right for villagers with no common land to rent émigré land at low rates and, second, the provision of a voucher for 500 livres for the poor to bid for land. But these laws seem to have been sometimes ignored by the peasants and were generally inadequate. Few plots sold for under 500 livres, for example. (See *AP* 66:10, arts. 2 and 3; and Jones, *Peasantry,* 154–61, on these provisions as well as a general assessment of the land sales.) There is a certain parallel here to the gap between word and deed that also permeates the legislation on seigneurial rights. Providing the landless with 500 livre vouchers that couldn't actually purchase anything has some resemblance to a total abolition of feudalism that changed peasant obligation very little. If the poorest benefited little, however, there were many regions where less poor peasants got significant amounts of land (although there were others where they were outbid by urban bourgeois and even ex-lords). Philip Dawson has recently shown that in the region around Paris, not only were the major purchasers prosperous urbanites, even after the law of July 17, 1793, but among peasant purchasers, the lion's share went to the upper stratum of independent proprietors and large renters, the *fermocratie* that Jessenne has shown triumphed in village politics in the 1790s; see "La vente des biens nationaux dans la région parisienne," in *La Révolution française et le monde rural* (Paris: Comité des Travaux Historiques et Scientifiques, 1989), 235–51. On the other hand, Peter Jones has found some important local instances of genuine efforts at putting land in the hands of the landless; see "The 'Agrarian Law': Schemes for Land Redistribution During the French Revolution," *Past and Present,* no. 133 (1991): 96–133.

may observe the rise and fall of such incidents in Figure 8.2 which shows that they follow in very stark form the general antiseigneurial pattern with sharp peaks in July 1789 and April 1792. As communities threw off the hand of the lord the rewards for unity declined. At the same time the differences among villagers became increasingly salient as legislatures made land available to larger, but not smaller, landholders; as the tithe, abolished, turned out, from the point of view of tenants and sharecroppers to continue to exist under the name of rent; and as free-market food policies favored those with a marketable surplus. On land-access questions, then, the legislators were—and increasingly so—dealing with a divided peasant world, by contrast with seigneurial rights.

Figure 8.3 shows an irregularly but clearly rising development of battles over land within the rural community itself. The common interests that had united the villages against the lords were weakening, partly because that battle was being won; it was also, perhaps, because revolutionary legislation favored the endowed of village France. These intracommunal land conflicts by no means ever achieved the numbers of the earlier land struggles against lords and monasteries, but they marked a shift in the nature of rural politics. The intracommunal conflict made it quite difficult for a single measure to satisfy the broad range of peasant interests on land issues once the common

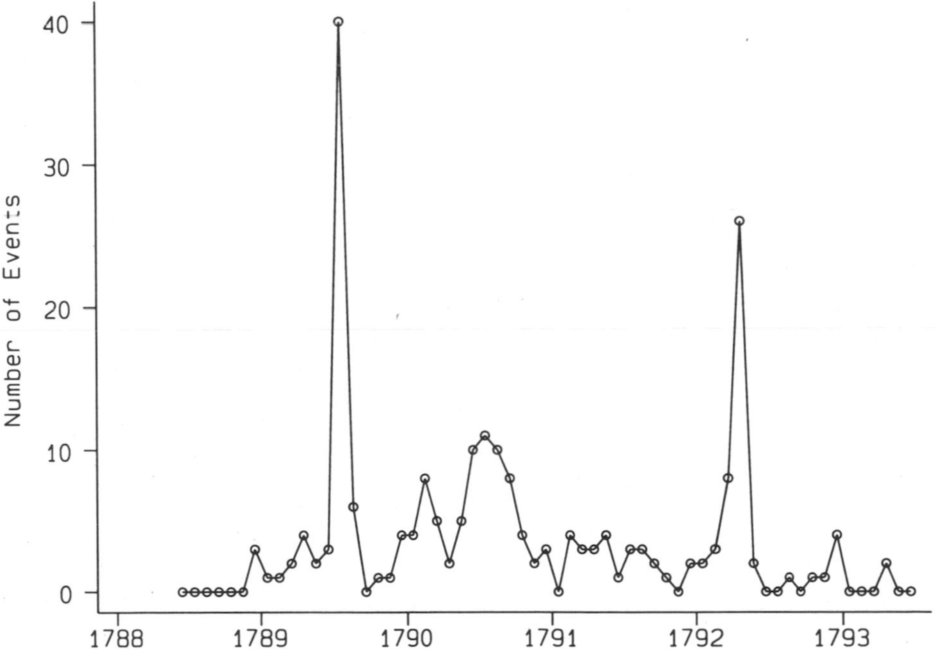

Fig. 8.2 Land Conflict with Feudal Aspect

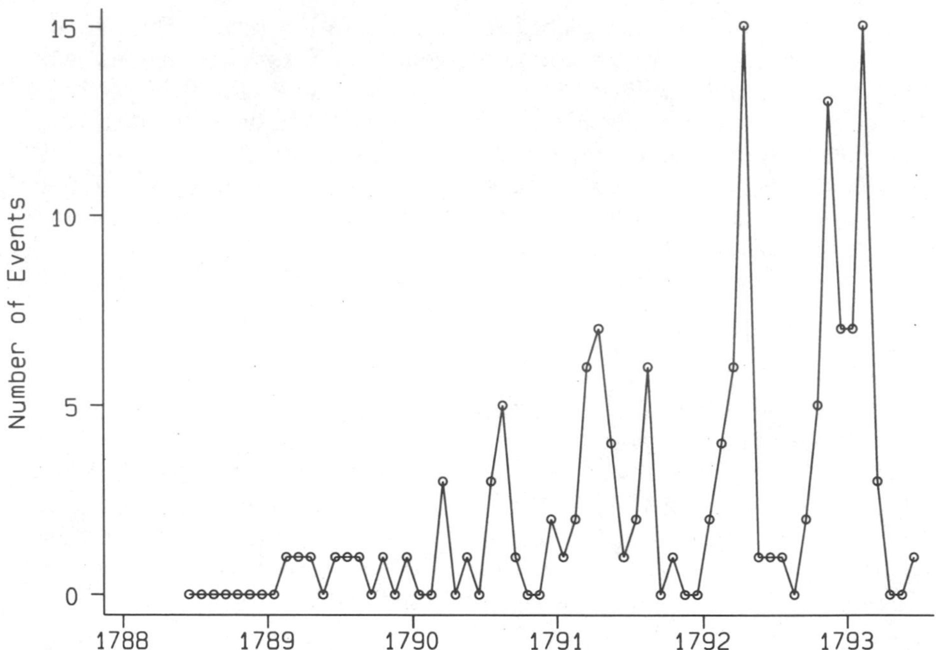

Fig. 8.3 Intracommunal Land Conflict

interest in opposing the lords was exhausted. Legislative action would, therefore, tend to alienate elements of rural France. The political discomfort of the legislators showed up in both delay and contradictory legislation. Although a legislative committee was set up early to draft a comprehensive land law it moved at a pace even slower than the dilatory Committee on Feudal Rights that had taken half a year between August 1789 and March 1790. Only by August 1790 did the committee have a draft land proposal;[147] debate only began eleven months later and not until three more months had elapsed was something actually enacted: the law of September 28–October 6, 1791, which managed to be even more ambiguous than the seigneurial legislation (*AP* 31:431–38). It simultaneously upheld the right of grazing the common herd and the right of enclosure. The more extreme versions of grazing rights—intercommunal grazing—were upheld "provisionally," but, quite unlike the tithe, with no termination date specified.[148]

147. Jones, *Peasantry,* 131.

148. Enclosing takes priority over grazing since it "derives essentially from [the right] of property and may not be challenged" (sect. 4, art. 4). This appears to mean that those with well-founded rights to pasture their animals can continue to do so "provisionally" (sect. 4, art. 2) unless someone doesn't want them to; see *AP* 31:432.

The Battle for Land: Divided Communities and Division of the Commons

The issue of the common lands was a particularly knotty problem. For all the uncompromising agrarian individualism of the *cahiers,* the assemblies found legislation a difficult matter indeed. The Agriculture Committees of all three revolutionary legislatures were, consistently, forums for radically physiocratic views favoring freedoms from communal and governmental constraints for rural property owners (conceived as individual persons rather than collectivities) and, just as consistently, hesitant in the extreme in initiating and promoting legislation.[149] Uncertain as to peasant views, in October 1790 and again in November 1791, the government asked communities for their opinions. They turned out to have many (a circumstance that seems to have further inhibited legislation).[150] But by 1792, intracommunal clashes had risen anyway, despite the legislative efforts to stay out of the way (see Fig. 8.3).

With rising rural disturbances in 1793 again leading to new attention to peasant conflicts, the March peak of counterrevolution was accompanied by the death decree for advocates of redistribution.[151] The notion of an "Agrarian Law," an expression suddenly current that evoked the redistributive policies of the Gracchi two thousand years earlier, was taken as sedition in the extreme, and never more so than under the combination of wartime pressures and counterrevolution.[152] But the Convention also renewed its attention to its own, controlled redistribution in the area of common lands as well as the sales of National Property.[153] Indeed, on March 18 Barère

149. Vida Azimi, "Un instrument de politique agricole: Les comités d'agriculture des assemblées révolutionnaires," in *La Révolution française et le monde rural* (Paris: Comité des Travaux Historiques et Scientifiques, 1989), 483–91.

150. Jones, *Peasantry,* 138–41.

151. "The National Convention decrees the death penalty against whoever proposes an agrarian law or any other law that subverts property, whether territorial, commercial or industrial" (*AP* 60:292).

152. Thomas Lindet, for example, wrote to his brother, currently in the Legislative Assembly (and later member of the Committee of Public Safety), in the wake of the August 1792 overthrow of the monarchy: "The Revolution leads us far: so let's watch out for agrarian law"; Robert-Thomas Lindet, *Correspondance de Thomas Lindet pendant la Constituante et la Législative (1789–1792)* (Paris: Armand Montier, 1899), 370. The connotations of the phrase "agrarian law" are explored in R. B. Rose, "The 'Red Scare' of the 1790s: The French Revolution and the 'Agrarian Law,'" *Past and Present,* no. 103 (1984): 113–30. Fear of redistributionist ideas was central to the Directorial campaign to suppress Babeuf; see R. B. Rose, *Gracchus Babeuf: The First Revolutionary Communist* (Stanford: Stanford University Press, 1978), 221, and Florence Gauthier, "Loi Agraire" in *Dictionnaire des usages socio-politiques (1770–1815)* (Paris: Société Française d'Etude du 18ème Siècle, 1987), 2:65–98.

153. Peter M. Jones, "The 'Agrarian Law': Schemes for Land Redistribution During the French Revolution," *Past and Present,* no. 133 (1991): 96–133.

proposed, along with the death decree, a series of measures that, in conjunction, were explicitly designed to secure the allegiance of both the rich and the poor in the countryside. Arguing that priests and émigrés were encouraging the have-nots to rise against the haves, he not only urged the Convention to protect the well-off by silencing those who might be after their wealth. For the land-poor he urged redistribution of common land with each receiving an equal share regardless of age or sex; dividing National Property into small plots for resale;[154] a progressive income tax; and poor-relief measures. Only the death decree in defense of the rural rich was adopted on the spot (over Marat's objection); the other parts of the package, those that favored the poor, were referred to various committees.[155]

A more comprehensive approach, the termination of this long series of hesitations and false starts, however, followed in the wake of the Girondin expulsion along with the other strong rural measures of June and July 1793. By the law of June 10, 1793 (AP 66:225–30) (one week after the easing of the terms of purchase of National Property), the peasant community was given the right to decide for itself on partition of the commons, thereby avoiding having the government overtly take sides in increasingly active intracommunal conflicts. The long-dormant, but very real, individualistic propensities of the various assemblies, however, were expressed in three ways. In the first place, the decision rule favored division: only one-third had to vote for partition. Second, a decision for partition was irrevocable.[156] Third, in the climate of the summer of 1793 and beyond, fear of the state, whose preferences for "liberty" and against "feudalism" were well known, would seem to have been a strong inducement to vote the politically correct line.

Legislative Silence: Agricultural Labor

In response to the quasi-unity within rural communities and the persistent and numerous mobilizations on seigneurial rights, the legislature drafted many decrees, ultimately acceding to the movement for abolition. In dealing with strife within the village community, the legislators confronted a more divided rural world, one that mounted less persistent and less numerous challenges. Some results are vacillation, contradiction, and delay as we have seen on land issues. Another possible option is silence: a legislative practice by default. The civil code that stabilized under Napoleon, as Serge Aberdam

154. A large proprietor, Barère contended, would not fight counterrevolutionaries to the death to hold onto an addition to his lands but a poor person who acquires a small plot could be counted on.

155. *AP* 60:290–93. It is at the tail end of his series of proposals to secure the support of conflicting rural groups in the face of counterrevolution that Barère broaches the possibility of a new coordinating body, "a committee of public safety."

156. See art. 10, *AP* 66:227.

points out,[157] simply says nothing about rural wage labor or sharecropping arrangements while it does regulate cash tenancy. Both categories of socioeconomic relations, Aberdam suggests, were only implicitly rather than explicitly ordered. Rural wage labor was implicitly taken as a commodity and therefore regulated by portions of the civil code that structured the marketplace for other commodities. In particular, rural laborers were barred from joining forces into defensive or proactive collectivities by the Le Chapelier Law of March 1791. The same Le Chapelier whose improbable election to its presidency on August 3, 1789, gave the National Assembly's left some control over the agenda on the eternally celebrated August 4, lent his name to the law that for a century barred legal recognition of worker associations. The profound element of consistency is the individualistic and anticorporate thrust.

Legislators Respond to Peasants

Let us now survey the overall pattern of agrarian legislation in relation to rural insurrection. In Figure 8.4, I display the timing of major pieces of legislation on the seigneurial regime, the tithe and access to land in the form of short vertical lines at the dates at which the legislature initiated action on the texts we have mentioned. I do not differentiate one enactment from another here, either by subject or importance, other than to make clear the temporal location of the four most significant antiseigneurial moments in the various assemblies. I also display simultaneously some important elements of the insurrectionary context, namely the rise and fall of antiseigneurial events, anti-tithe events, and land conflicts. All three are drawn on scales such that each has an identically tall peak because the relative significance of the three sorts of events is not to the point here. Major clusters of legislation, as we suggested above, follow, with some variation in lag, major bouts of rural activism. The eternally celebrated night of August 4 follows almost immediately upon the great July peak in all three sorts of events; the January 1790 spike of antiseigneurial events is followed a bit later by a rash of decrees of various sorts; so is the June peak in anti-tithe and land conflicts. The April 1792 spike in antiseigneurial events and land conflicts and the anti-tithe rising of the previous month are followed several months later by a variety of major changes. After a little spurt in September 1792, antiseigneurial events fall off for good; and anti-tithe events never rise after

157. Serge Aberdam, *Aux origines du code rural, 1789–1900: Un siècle de débat* (Paris: Institut National de la Recherche Agronomique, 1981–82), 2–4. This paragraph is very indebted to that essay.

March 1792, leaving the field to the moderate peaks in land conflict of late 1792 and early 1793. If some form of rural event is actually impelling the major legislation of June and July 1793, it is surely not any of the events depicted here; presumably it is the great counterrevolutionary wave of March.

It is well worth reflecting on this last point, at once curious and instructive. The August 1792 legislation is followed by an antiseigneurial spurt in September after which antiseigneurialism all but disappears from collective peasant action. The August legislation had effectively ended the seigneurial system in practice, since few lords could produce the evidence now required to even lay claim to indemnification. Even with little peasant pressure now exerted for further legislative change in seigneurial rights, the Convention, finally, declared the total abolition of the feudal regime in July 1793. In fighting counterrevolution and the First Coalition simultaneously, what was left of seigneurialism was to be given up; but generalized land redistribution was not in the cards. In short, the 1793 developments point up one of the features of the dialogue of insurrectionary countryside and revolutionary

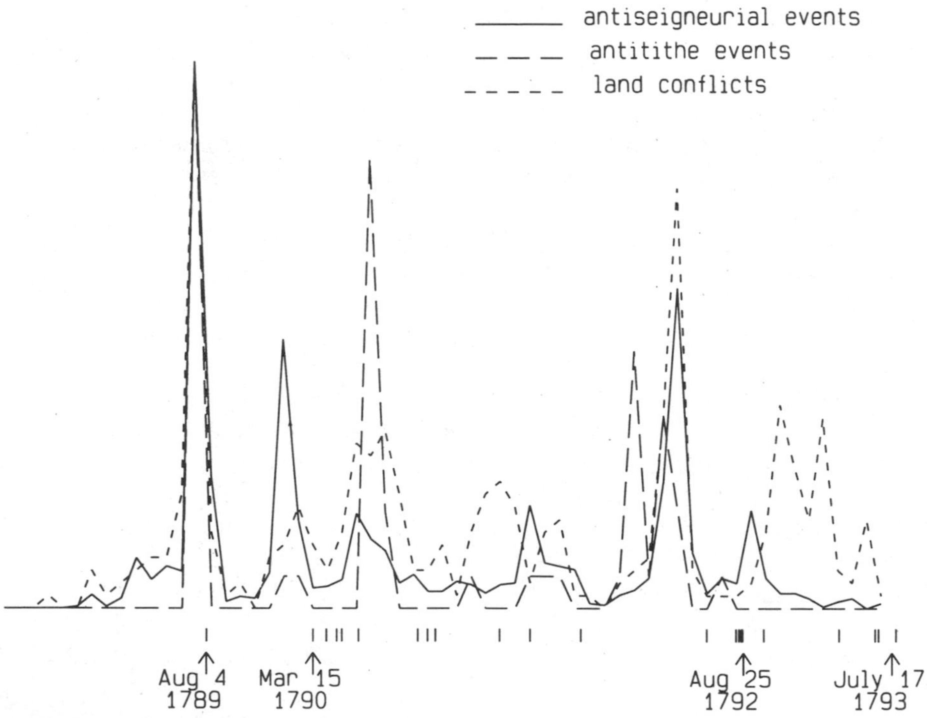

Fig. 8.4 Timing of Major Legislative Initiatives on Seigneurial Regime, Tithe and Access to Land, and of Insurrections over Those Issues

legislature: if the peasants pushed hard, what they got was the abandonment of seigneurial rights even if they pushed in other directions.

Peasants Respond to Legislators

We have focused, so far, in this chapter on the legislative side of the dialogue but there was a peasant side as well. The people of the French countryside altered their actions in light of their assessments of the risks of action and the likelihood of success. To grasp their patterns of mobilization we need, just as we did for the legislators, a sense of their grievances at the onset of the revolutionary process (furnished by the *cahiers*); we need a sense of the variety of targets and forms of action that the varied nature of France's rural worlds fostered; we need to see the ways in which the actions of one rural group altered the world of the others so that through emulation, fear, or rivalry, incidents had a ripple effect. But no account of the contexts of peasant action could begin to be complete if it ignored the ways in which legislative programs altered the forms and targets of France's mobilized countryside. The lesson that, if they dared to fight, it would be on the seigneurial rights that they could well win, was, I suggest, a message that active peasant communities learned.

Such an approach forces us to see the people of the villages as engaged in reasoned action, which by no means implies an absence of emotion or the eschewing of violence. This would not be worth pointing out were it not for the persistent thread in the literature that attributes an unthinking character to them. This attribution was already far advanced in the Revolution itself,[158] as one or another deputy described the frightening rural scene as "anarchy" and its militants as "brigands" whose motives needed only to be deplored

158. On the persistent attribution, by the educated, of disruptive rural politics to peasant lack of "enlightenment" and the consequent proposal to reduce conflict through educational campaigns, see Jean Bart, "Bourgeois et paysans: La crainte et le mépris," in *La Révolution française et le monde rural* (Paris: Comité des Travaux Historiques et Scientifiques, 1989), 459–75. In a study of revolutionary cartoons, Antoine de Baecque suggests that after the first summer of Revolution, in which peasant figures represented either satisfied concord or the revolt of the oppressed, the Revolution was only rarely personified as a peasant. It was a citizen-deputy or an urban *sans-culotte* who was made to stand for the achieved Revolution. The early peasant figure was either a beneficent receiver of revolutionary achievements or a mindless destroyer driven by misery: controlled change was the work of others. See Baecque, "La figure du paysan dans l'imagerie révolutionnaire," in *La Révolution française et le monde rural* (Paris: Comité des Travaux Historiques et Scientifiques, 1989), 477–81. For a similar view see Michel Vovelle, "The Countryside and the Peasantry in Revolutionary Iconography," in Alan Forrest and Peter M. Jones, *Reshaping France: Town, Country and Region During the French Revolution* (Manchester: Manchester University Press, 1991), 26–36.

rather than explored and understood.[159] Such images could even be used metaphorically as in the count de Montlosier's characterization of the night of August 4: "The work of brigands was thus sanctioned by a different brigandage."[160] From the abbé Barbotins's disgust with "peasant idiots"[161] to Merlin's condescension toward understandably resentful cultivators gone astray (*AP* 11:498–99), the revolutionary legislators themselves, when frustrated by rural persistence in undesired actions, found something lacking in the peasants' understanding (rather than in their own). Thus Merlin's contention from 1789 on that most seigneurial dues were property was another confirmation of his brilliant legal mind[162] while sharecroppers' contention after July 1793 that some rents were feudal was another confirmation of their ignorance (see above, p. 469).

Or consider the concerns expressed at the beginning of April 1791 by the lawyer L.-F. Legendre, sent to the Estates-General by the Third Estate of Brest, as he considered the dangers posed by the "fanaticism" of the refractory clergy: "The towns will easily reject the efforts of this intrigue. . . . But how much must we fear the dangerous effects in the countryside where weak intellects may be attracted as Easter nears."[163] The future Montagnard, Thomas Lindet, could write to his brother, the future member of the Committee of Public Safety, of the stupidity of the people of Alsace on which the counterrevolutionaries count.[164] On the brink of the great counterrevolutionary explosion a deputy distinguishes among the rebels in the Sarthe: on the one hand, "the ignorant and credulous majority," on the other, the "disorganizers" and "genuine mischief-makers" (*AP* 58:149). And occasionally the peasants are simple but innately moral: noble savages.[165]

159. Consider this exchange in the National Assembly, engaged in discussing a report on the insurrectionary wave of early 1790 (Maximilien Robespierre, *Oeuvres* [ed. Marc Bouloiseau, Georges Lefebvre and Albert Soboul], vol. 6, *Discours* [Paris: Presses Universitaires de France, 1950], 228):

> ROBESPIERRE: M. Lanjuinais has proposed that we exhaust all possible routes to conciliation before employing military force against the people who burned the châteaux.
> D'EPRESMENIL: They are not the People [one can almost hear the capital *P*]; they are brigands.
> ROBESPIERRE: If you wish I shall speak of citizens accused of having burned the châteaux.
> DE FOUCAULT and D'EPRESMENIL: Say brigands.
> ROBESPIERRE: I shall only use the word "men" and I shall adequately characterize these men when I speak of the crime of which they are accused.

160. Montlosier, *Mémoires,* 1:235.

161. Barbotin, *Lettres,* 52.

162. See, for example, Duquesnoy, *Journal,* 2:426.

163. L.-F. Legendre, "Correspondance de Legendre," *La Révolution Française* 40 (1901): 62.

164. Lindet, *Correspondance,* 252.

165. "The peasant of Brittany, very wild in general, very little civilized, is nevertheless human, good and just" (Duquesnoy, *Journal,* 2:346). Even deputies sympathetic to peasant demands reveal none of the capacity for reflection on their own sense of distance that characterized the famous observation of La Bruyère one century earlier: "One sees certain wild animals, males and females

Alexandre Lameth thought continuing rural unrest due to a combination of rural ignorance and absence of effective force: "The National Assembly has, therefore, resolved to explain the meaning [of its decrees] so that they shall be accessible to all intellects." Martial law was insufficient because the countryside had "a total lack of means of repression"; peasants therefore had to be persuaded.[166]

Finally consider the report of Godard and Robin,[167] dispatched to the Southwest by the National Assembly to investigate the continuing insurrection. They bring back a detailed report urging that the small number of "instigators" be dealt with by force, but that the great majority of peasants, who have been led astray through their misunderstanding of the law, be properly instructed so that they appreciate that under the law of indemnification, their ex-lords have property rights worthy of respect. Thorough investigators as they are, Godard and Robin consider a rival hypothesis offered by local officials. Those officials, the investigators dutifully report, are of the view "that the principal cause of the insurrection, perhaps, is found in the country people's surrender to the desire and the hope to be freed forever of the seigneurial dues" (136). After considering the evidence, gathered in the course of several weeks of speaking with peasants, they still adhere to their own view of a countryside fundamentally docile but misled. But they are not without doubts.

The Revolution itself, then, fostered a view of insurrectionary peasants intellectually incapable of grasping the significance of the wise acts of the lawgivers, particularly when overwhelmed by emotion through the nefarious influence of malicious conspirators. In fact, peasant action was as responsive to developments in the legislatures as legislative action was to news from the countryside. Discussion of legislative politics traveled far and wide. The openness of the sessions themselves, with spectators mingling with legislators in ways that shocked advocates of British parliamentarism;[168] the sudden proliferation of a new journalism whose rapid and public accounts of the high and mighty were sanctioned by the very claims of the revolutionaries to be submitting themselves to the stern scrutiny of the public;[169]

---

alike, scattered through the countryside, foul, discolored like a bruise and thoroughly sunburned, attached to the land that they dig up and stir with an unconquerable stubbornness; they have something almost resembling an articulate voice and when they stand upright they show a human face; and in fact they are human; they withdraw at night into their holes where they live on black bread, water and roots; they spare other men the pains of sowing, laboring and gathering in order to live and they therefore deserve not to lack some of this bread that they have sown"; see Jean de la Bruyère, *Les caractères ou les moeurs de ce siècle* (Paris: Lefèvre, 1843), 333–34.

166. Lameth, *Histoire,* 1:346.

167. Godard and Robin, *Rapport.*

168. Young, *Travels in France,* 315.

169. Jeremy D. Popkin, *Revolutionary News: The Press in France, 1789–1799* (Durham: Duke University Press, 1990); Hugh Gough, *The Newspaper Press in the French Revolution* (London:

the competition among many journalists in claiming accurate reporting of legislative debate;[170] the loosely linked network of thousands of political clubs; the correspondence of deputies and their constituents; and the proliferation of elections for local, departmental, and national positions guaranteed a considerable circulation of news of the center into the periphery. The hunger of local groups for news could lead them to badger weary legislators for more details.[171] To what extent did all this news penetrate the village? If we accept Eugen Weber's vivid image of rural France a century later,[172] with its self-immersed village, isolated in a culture drawing more on folklore than current events, and a politics more local than national, one might wonder whether all this revolutionary news just passed over village France from one urban pocket to another. This is conceivable, and no doubt approximates the reality in some places, but it is extremely doubtful as a generalization. Even modest electoral participation rates show some awareness of national events in the countryside and early in the Revolution those rates were on a par with urban ones—or even surpassed them.[173] The network of political action groups tied to one another in large regional networks extended into some five thousand rural communities.[174] The parish *cahiers* show considerable rural focus on national issues already in place at the onset of the revolutionary process (see Chapter 3, pp. 136 et seq.). Throughout the eighteenth century, indeed, rural communities showed a considerable capacity to identify powerful institutions that fostered or damaged their interests.[175] Even taking into account barriers of language,

---

Routledge, 1988); Claude Labrosse and Pierre Rétat, *Naissance du journal révolutionnaire* (Lyon: Presses Universitaires de Lyon, 1989).

170. Lehodey's technically inventive *Journal Logographique* used a team of observers to try collectively to catch each word of the debates in its bid for an edge over many other periodicals that stressed interpretation. See Popkin, *Revolutionary News,* 106–23; Gough, *Newspaper Press,* 182–83.

171. Legendre, "Correspondance," *La Révolution française* 39 (1900): 528–29.

172. Eugen Weber, *Peasants into Frenchmen: The Modernization of Rural France, 1870–1914* (Stanford: Stanford University Press, 1976).

173. See Malcolm Crook, "'Aux urnes, citoyens!' Urban and rural electoral behavior during the French Revolution," in Alan Forrest and Peter Jones, *Reshaping France: Town, Country and Region during the French Revolution* (Manchester: Manchester University Press, 1991), 152–67; Melvin Edelstein, "La place de la Révolution française dans la politisation des paysans," *Annales Historiques de la Révolution Française,* no. 280 (1990): 113–49, and "Electoral Behavior During the Constitutional Monarchy (1790–1791): A Community Interpretation," in Renée Waldinger, Philip Dawson, and Isser Woloch, eds., *The French Revolution and the Meaning of Citizenship* (Westport, Conn.: Greenwood, 1994), 105–22; Olivier Audevart, "Les élections en Haute-Vienne pendant la Révolution," in Jean Boutier, Michel Cassan, Paul D. Hollander, and Bernard Pommaret, eds., *Limousin en Révolution* (Treignac: Editions "Les Monédières," 1989), 129–38.

174. Jean Boutier and Philippe Boutry, "La diffusion des sociétés politiques en France (1789-an III). Une enquête nationale," *Annales Historiques de la Révolution Française,* no. 266 (1986): 392.

175. Consider, for example, Lianna Vardy's account of the legal strategies pursued by villagers who very accurately discerned effective ways to bring petitions against their lords to the Royal

illiteracy, and remoteness,[176] the likelihood that many villagers were unacquainted with the main lines of legislative action on matters of vital concern to them seems remote. This is not to say that it might not suit country people arrested for sedition to profess ignorance of the law to officials inclined to believe them.

In Table 8.2, I show the changing nature of antiseigneurial actions over time. The dates are chosen to point up the moments of communication of new elite positions on the seigneurial regime. Although the communication of the views of elites was a virtually continuous process, particularly with the great augmentation in the flow of news during the revolutionary period, there are a number of particular moments we may seize as particularly intense. The convocation of the Estates-General was one such moment: not only did French villagers come together and discover their own and each other's views, but they had reason to think deeply about the views of outsiders with whom they would have to deal; these outsiders, moreover, made many efforts to impress those views on the countryside, not merely in the general form of pamphlets of one sort or another circulated widely in the pre-revolutionary crisis,[177] but in the specific form of model *cahiers* which various groups and individuals circulated in the struggle for the hearts and minds of the country people as the elections and *cahiers*-drafting approached. The delegates elected by village communities, then, took their own documents to the main town of their *bailliage* and there actively engaged in (or perhaps shyly hung back from) discussions with town representatives, leading to the election of *bailliage* delegates and the adoption of a *bailliage cahier*. It is hard to see how this process could have failed to acquaint people in the countryside, and particularly those most given to activism, with the views of the urban upper strata that dominated the *bailliage* assemblies.

Beyond this particular moment, we may signal the major turning points in the legislative history: the initial declaration of the abolition of the feudal regime in early August of 1789; the subsequent detailed elaboration in March 1790; the drastic revision of the law that abolished outright many more rights and shifted the burden of proof definitively from peasants to

Council. "Peasants and the Law: A Village Appeals to the French Royal Council, 1768–1791," *Social History* 13 (1988): 295–313.

176. Jeremy Popkin's observations on limits to the diffusion of journalistic accounts are very pertinent (*Revolutionary News,* 78–96).

177. It would be hard to be more direct than Volney's "Letter from the bourgeoisie to the country people, renters, sharecroppers and vassals of certain lords who cheat the people," circulating around Angers in March 1789: "Listen we are good brothers, don't protest so much, we shall share, don't we have the same interests? Don't you have properties like us? Very well, we shall free them, just like ours" (cited in André Bendjebbar, "Propriété et contre-révolution dans l'ouest," in *La Révolution française et le monde rural* [Paris: Comité des Travaux Historiques et Scientifiques, 1989], 287).

Table 8.2. Events with Antiseigneurial Aspects over Time (%)

Time Period	Antiseigneurial Events	Total Events
June 1788–February 28, 1789	12%	(132)
March 1–June 30, 1789[a]	25	(370)
July 1–August 11, 1789[a]	31	(1235)
August 12–December 31, 1789	37	(158)
January 1–March 28, 1790[a]	78	(285)
March 29–May 31, 1790	32	(95)
June 1–June 30, 1790[a]	62	(90)
July 1, 1790–May 31, 1791	49	(403)
June 1–June 30, 1791[a]	69	(89)
July 1, 1791–January 31, 1792	34	(321)
February 1–April 30, 1792[a]	47	(605)
May 1–August 25, 1792	31	(202)
August 26–October 31, 1792[a]	36	(248)
November 1–31, 1792[a]	9	(104)
December 1, 1792–February 28, 1793	14	(118)
March 1–March 31, 1793[a]	3	(158)
April 1–June 30, 1793	12	(77)

[a]Insurrectionary peaks (from Table 6.3).

lords for the remaining indemnifiable rights in August 1792; and finally the ultimate, final abolition of July 1793. Table 8.2 uses these dates as markers. In addition, I distinguish peak insurrectionary times from more quiet times. The ebb and flow of antiseigneurial events, reported in Chapter 6, is considerably clarified by this table. We see that during the initial period of mounting insurrectionary intensity—from June 1788 until the convocation—the percentage of those insurrections that are directed against the seigneurial regime remained relatively small. France's country people were discovering that the costs of insurrection were declining sharply and the potential rewards were rising, but only a little more than one rebellious act in eight had anything to do with the seigneurial regime until the electoral period with its tremendous intensification of contact with the well-to-do. As pamphleteers floated model *cahiers,* as village activists sought out information on what was happening in the towns, as urban and semi-urban advice-givers sometimes helped out in the crafting of the parish documents, the French countryside became more aware and more accurately aware of the extent of antiseigneurial sentiment within the elites. Rural delegates by the hundreds at one *bailliage* meeting after another could not have helped discovering the elaborate antiseigneurial programs of the dominant urban strata of the Third Estate, which, while perhaps disappointing in their emphasis on indemnification, were surely very promising in the degree to which the subject was not only broached, but broached in detail—often in much greater detail, indeed, than in the country documents themselves. Furthermore, the rhetorical temperature of these urban texts was often very elevated, in their depiction of the barbarous past and the generally abusive nature of the system. The country delegates were not only certain to discover all this as they sat at these meetings. They were also fairly likely to discover as well a good deal about the position of the local nobility; there was often much contact between the two orders and occasional (and sometimes successful) attempts to adopt a joint document. And in the weeks before the *balliage* meetings noble propagandists, like those of the Third Estate, had had pamphlets and model *cahiers* distributed. Peasant delegates to the town might well have noted that for all the conservative thrust of the noble *cahiers* the nobility were not prepared to mount a full-blown defense of seigneurial rights in many, many *bailliages* but were choosing silence as the course of prudence. And the villagers were no doubt discovering as well in many *bailliages* that sympathetic parish priests were triumphing over the bishops and canons of the big towns in the clerical elections and were triumphing also over the delegates of the monasteries that often were the most important ecclesiastical lords.[178]

It hardly seems surprising, then, that the proportion of insurrections targeting the seigneurial regime now doubled in the spring. The country people were discovering that if they pushed hard there would be at least some support from significant portions of the Third Estate and an important portion of the clergy and they were probably aware of the divided and ineffective capacity of the nobility to defend themselves. As spring gave way to summer, the first and greatest peak of peasant actions exploded. In spite of how many different sorts of targets were attacked and in spite of the fierce concentration of peasant energies in panics during the peak of July–early August, the antiseigneurial character of the peasant movements rose further still. The percentage of antiseigneurial actions in the summer of 1789 was two and one-half times what it was before the elections.

As the news of the National Assembly's dramatic actions of early August spread, many rural communities gained still further evidence that revolutionary legislators were willing to move on seigneurial rights. To the extent that accurate information on the actions of the nobility and upper clergy diffused in France, the sense that the more conservative forces were hardly prepared for a life-and-death struggle to maintain themselves could only be buttressed. The observation that Condorcet is said to have made of August 4 to the effect that the nobility of France was committing suicide[179] must have

178. Two-thirds of clerical deputies were parish priests (Lemay, "Les révélations d'un dictionnaire," 171).

179. Condorcet, *Mémoires,* 2:60.

occurred to some peasants. Certainly a good deal of information about the August 4–11 actions was sent out very quickly.[180] But, more broadly, the countryside was learning where and how it could expend its energies and which risks were worth running. Deputies whose image of themselves as commanding instant obedience to their laws must have been disappointed, but the laws displayed points of vulnerability. Revolutionary legislation revealed, suggested, and created opportunities for action not necessarily in accord with the legislators' wishes. Here is Bailly: "The National Assembly's decree removing the right to a monopoly in hunting was poorly understood by the multitude who, perhaps, did not want to understand it."[181] He pictures the rural population as going far beyond the Assembly's intentions like a temporary flood at "the opening of a dike holding back the waters." But if the people of the countryside are no longer held in by the old constraints imposed from above and (temporarily) have refused to accept the new ones of the Assembly, they clearly have their own self-imposed discipline; Bailly notes that the great wave of peasant hunting is staying clear of the lands of the "patriot princes" like the duke of Orléans (2:244).

Unlike the liberal Bailly who saw the country people as actively reading the Assembly's acts for their own purposes, the reactionary count de Montlosier saw them almost as unthinking automata that react to the stupidities of the elite. Elite action for the conservation of "this collection of ancient debris"—such is his characterization of the Old Regime—had to be done quietly, if it were to be done at all: "When you are in Alpine passes subject to avalanches, it's good advice to avoid any noise."[182] He goes on to characterize the work of the National Assembly in August 1789 as first encouraging crimes, then "hurrying to regularize these crimes by registering them as laws" (1:235). In their differing ways, then, some of the legislators saw that they themselves had an impact on the countryside. If the new Assembly raised the rewards for insurrection, however, we need to consider other peasant options that also opened up. Against the risks of collective action one must consider the option of unannounced nonpayment. Particularly for those who stressed the famous phrase about the complete destruction of the feudal regime, nonpayment may have already seemed to have acquired the color of law. And claiming that the National Assembly could be taken at its word—or rather, at what villagers would like the complete destruction of feudalism to mean, quite a different matter than what Merlin de Douai wanted it to mean—was a good way to begin to make the reality one wanted. Claiming to believe that the National Assembly had abolished feudalism was a way of making the National Assembly mean what the

180. Kessel, *La nuit du 4 août,* 175–79, 229–36.
181. Bailly, *Mémoires,* 2:244.
182. Montlosier, *Mémoires,* 1:160.

peasants would have liked their words to mean. And for many others in the countryside, determining whether it was indeed the reality, would have been well worth testing—and a lot less likely to get yourself hanged than storming the local *château*. Certainly this is more than just peasant ignorance of legal niceties: some of the legislators themselves, in fact, had immediately communicated such an interpretation of events to their constituents.[183] Other country people, however, may well have judged that circumstances were such that undemonstrative nonpayment was a much-preferred alternative under the current weaknesses of repressive forces, the administrative confusions, and the capacity to claim to have believed that the legislation had abolished feudalism. (Playing the simple-minded peasant, as often, offered its rewards.)[184]

For the next three years, we have an alternation among three different patterns. There were periods of several months of relative peace—relative to the peaks, that is, but surely much more contentious than before 1789—during which between one-third and one-half of insurrections had an antiseigneurial element. There were also stretches of one or several months during which rural conflict rose steeply (see Chapter 6); during these peak episodes the antiseigneurial element was sharply emphasized. In early 1790, some 78% of insurrections were antiseigneurial (and if we restrict the field to the peak month of January, 87%); in the lesser peaks of June 1790 and June 1791, antiseigneurial events still made up an impressive two-thirds. The lowest antiseigneurial propensity in any of the peak times during the three years following the legislative breakthrough of August 1789 is the "mere" half of all events during the great wave of February–April 1792. Even in this wave, on the peak day of February 5, we see that 91% of events were antiseigneurial. Finally we have the insurrectionary peaks that follow the subsidence of antiseigneurial action after the summer of 1792. Since the eruptions of November 1792 and March 1793 were focused on quite different targets (subsistence and counterrevolution), in these two waves antiseigneurial events made the least contribution to peasant rebellion since the autumn of 1788.

The dramatic falloff in antiseigneurial action from the fall of 1792 on, I

183. On August 8 one deputy wrote home to Alsace that "with a solemn decree, we have suppressed the whole feudal regime and all the resulting obligations" (Kessel, *La nuit du 4 août,* 179); on August 12, Arthur Young heard people in Clermont joyously discussing "the great news just arrived from Paris, of the utter abolition of tithes, feudal rights, game, warrens, pigeons, etc." (*Travels in France,* 190).

184. Kessel quotes a mayor in the *département* of Oise on public readings—in church after mass—of the laws: "in general they understand nothing and when the law fit their interests, their imagination went well beyond the law, because they did not understand it" Kessel, *La nuit du 4 août,* 232). But is this the failure of the peasants to understand . . . or their success in putting one over on the mayor?

suggest, was the simple result of the outright abolition of many rights and the near impossibility, after the legislation of late August, of a lord's collecting what, in principle, remained. It is probable that few lords could have actually produced the documentation now required of them to defend many of their rights, all of which were presumed illegitimate. But even if they had such papers, one would hardly need the level of caution of the marquis de Ferrières to realize the risks one ran in attempting to use the Revolution's courts to obtain from French peasants the sorts of claims from which French armies were now liberating France's neighbors. In the wake of the August 1792 legislation, then, the temptation of simply not paying would seem to have been very great indeed. Perhaps this is why even the September 1792 peak, atypically, is no more than 36% antiseigneurial (see Table 6.3). And surely it is the reason why beyond this spurt, certainly from November on, antiseigneurial actions have fallen way back, down as low as they were before the spring of 1789. The law of July 1793, finally declaring that nothing need be paid, appears as something of an anticlimax.

But France's rural citizens had a wider repertoire of responses to the legislative climate than simply the decision on whether or not to challenge the lords openly: how those lords were to be challenged also underwent mutations and these mutations, in part, also seem responses to the terms set by revolutionary legislatures. In the summer and fall of 1788 and into the winter of 1789 (see column 1 of Table 8.3) antiseigneurial actions were largely focused on a few very specific elements of the seigneurial regime: they concerned rights in land (and in wooded land in particular) and the lord's "recreational" privileges: the rights to raise potentially destructive creatures and the monopoly on hunting. Such actions may well have improved the living conditions, at least for the moment, of those who risked the severe consequences of getting caught, but they hardly challenged the claims of the lords in any central way. Resistance to these claims of the lord, indeed, had long coexisted with the seigneurial regime and may be spoken of as highly institutionalized. Poaching had an extensive history, but, while altering a bit the imbalance in nutrients available to lords and peasants, it was more an adaptation than a challenge: poaching depends on someone else's stocking game preserves. By the eighteenth century conflicts over land use, and over forests in particular, were now often pursued in the legal arena as lords and peasant communities sued one another. The seigneurial system, in effect, had absorbed the notion that specific allocations of land rights might be contested; after all, lords eager to take advantage of skyrocketing wood prices were no more eager than peasant communities to accept the claims of immemorial tradition. In the eighteenth century, then, some peasants poached and some lords usurped; and both peasants and lords sued each other. The boundary between the rights of peasant communities and lords was not fixed. It is striking that the first forms of contestation in the revolutionary crisis were not head-on challenges to the seigneurial regime but rather an intensification of forms of conflict that had become part and parcel of it. Of course, even a peripheral attack might be pursued with great intensity or bitterly resisted. That even this early we find some violence against persons should remind us that even such limited actions involved risks. (The relevant seigneurial employee who tended to be attacked at this stage seems to have been a guard of some sort—very likely a game warden.)

As the great electoral process unfolded in March and beyond, the antiseigneurial movement not only grew in size but began an evolution. The conflicts over recreational privileges continued, but now a significant number of grain seizures and other subsistence-oriented actions occurred. Lay and ecclesiastical lords were being "visited" by country people seeking food. As we come to understand better the history of French food riots, it is becoming clear that the coupling of a seigneurial target and an action aimed at food resources was a relatively late development. Cynthia Bouton's research (see Chapter 5, p. 246) indicates that such actions were pioneered in the course of the Flour War of 1775. If one might see the Flour War as a harbinger of the rural struggles of the Revolution in the sense that out of the major form of illegal, oppositional, mobilizational collective action—the struggle over subsistence—a new form of antiseigneurial action was nurtured; if subsistence struggles in their traditional, "classic" forms of market invasion and transport blockage were the dominant mode of action in the opening wedge of rural mobilization from the summer of 1788 into the winter of 1789 (see Fig. 6.3), then perhaps we may see in these events of the spring the bridge between the relatively familiar world of popular mobilization and the new, revolutionary antiseigneurialism that came to the fore in the Revolution. Subsistence events themselves were falling off by spring, but they had opened the way.

In the spring we also see the very beginnings of a more generalized attack: on the lord's legal titles, on the symbols of seigneurialism, on the religious link of lord and God; and, as part and parcel of the beginnings of a head-on assault, the very place in which the lord dwells was now subject to the power of the rural community. All of these forms of contestation, tried out, as it were, in the spring, would grow in the months to come. Now legal documents began to be at issue: sometimes it was the lord's own documents that were demanded and often destroyed; in other instances the lord was forced to publicly renounce his claims, a renunciation generally taken down on paper. Such actions mounted a fundamental challenge to the lord's capacity to collect any of his rights. They did so indirectly: they altered the relative capacities of lord and community to induce state action on their behalf by removing from the lord (or giving to the community) the sorts of documents required by the courts. Let us note that the power of these

Table 8.3. Antiseigneurial Events with Selected Characteristics over Time (%)

Characteristics of Antiseigneurial Events	June 1788– February 28, 1789	March–June 1789	July 1– August 11, 1789	August 12– December 31, 1789	January 1– March 28, 1790	March 29– May 31, 1790	June 1– June 30, 1790
Land invasions	31%	10%	9%	7%	6%	23%	16%
Rights in woods challenged	25	2	4	2	3	13	2
Recreational privileges challenged	44	48	5	10	4	7	0
Subsistence issues	0	21	5	5	11	13	2
Renunciation of rights	0	9	8	10	10	30	50
Titles seized or destroyed	0	6	29	9	12	7	31
Symbolic aspects of regime attacked	0	2	4	10	27	3	0
Religious aspects to event	0	14	5	9	24	20	48
Seious damage to *château*	0	4	32	10	11	13	4
Any attack on or penetration of *château*	0	20	67	28	48	40	55
Violence against persons	6	14	7	10	8	7	5
Dues at issue	19	21	9	33	12	20	68
(*N*)	(16)	(94)	(382)	(58)	(223)	(30)	(56)

Characteristics of Antiseigneurial Events	July 1, 1790– May 31, 1791	June 1–June 30 1791	July 1, 1791– January 31, 1792	February 1– April 30, 1792	May 1– August 25, 1792	August 26– October 31, 1792	November 1, 1792–June 30, 1793
Land invasions	11%	2%	12%	11%	3%	2%	18%
Rights in woods challenged	14	0	5	3	0	1	18
Recreational privileges challenged	11	5	26	4	0	2	5
Subsistence issues	7	2	0	7	0	11	11
Renunciation of rights	5	7	6	1	0	15	0
Titles seized or destroyed	3	10	3	19	0	0	5
Symbolic aspects of regime attacked	13	31	9	13	23	8	5
Religious aspects to event	15	7	26	18	18	0	0
Serious damage to *château*	9	21	12	43	34	46	37
Any attack on or penetration of *château*	24	56	20	77	50	81	53
Violence against persons	6	3	5	3	0	1	3
Dues at issue	24	43	30	10	31	6	13
(*N*)	(198)	(61)	(110)	(282)	(62)	(89)	(38)

actions derived from their recognition of a state that had achieved the capacity to act as arbiter. We may recall from Chapter 3 (pp. 100 et seq., p. 141) that the *cahiers* of the rural parishes treated taxation as if the state's existence was an accepted fact, and therefore, what was at issue was the reform of that state.

Attempting to seize the lord's papers or scaring a renunciation out of him were considerably more invasive of the lord's dwelling and person than looting his rabbit-warren or dovecote, driving one's animals onto his fields, or cutting down his trees. No doubt the lord or his family or his servants were more likely to resist; no doubt, too, a peasant gathering prepared to drag the lord out onto the lawn for a public renunciation was also more prepared, itself, for violence than a group seizing wood in the forests. It is worthwhile noting, then, that the increase in violence against persons is not up far more than it is in the spring; indeed, looking across the table, one can see no point at which violence against persons occurs in more than a fairly small proportion of such events. (This is by no means to deny the terrifying impact on victims and those who feared to be victims, the utter disgust of the right with the failure of the government to effectively prevent such horrors[185] and the general silence of the left.)[186]

As observed in Chapter 5 (see p. 228), the mobilized peasant group seemed to be aiming at eliminating a social role far more than a person. Of course there was more serious damage to the *châteaux* now that the group was penetrating it, rather than confining its assault to the woods and fields. In itself, this does not make invading crowds murderous. Why bother to kill the lord if what makes him a lord is the pieces of paper with the legal formulas—which can be burned? The marquis de Ferrières, for one, had an answer: durable patterns of deference, anchored, not in particular claims or pieces of paper, but in "opinion."[187] If seigneurial domination was not a mere

185. See, for example, Montlosier, *Mémoires,* 1:222–39.

186. Even on the left, it is hard to find expressions of empathy when rural violence was concerned, in stark contrast to such supporting statements as Barnave's famous mocking response to those who had expressed horror at an urban lynching: "Was this blood, then, so pure?" Perhaps rural popular violence was profoundly frightening to all who were well off in a property-dominated society (an observation of Colin Lucas).

187. See Ferrières, *Correspondance,* 207. The lawyer Grellet de Beauregard, Third Estate deputy of Guéret, consoled a noble friend by letter on July 20, 1790: "just as among those with no privilege, people distinguish the man of good family background from one without this advantage, opinion will return to the Nobility a part of the prerogatives that have been taken from it. When the circumstances that have led to the suppression of the orders no longer obtain, we shall be less pained to see distinctions that appeared odious. . . . Some great lords, instead of rubbing out their coats-of-arms, have covered them with plaster, convinced themselves that we shall see them without animosity when the plaster, fallen in decay, lets them reappear. But someone (whose name I've forgotten) replaced the coat-of-arms with a hot air balloon . . . from which ballast is being thrown and on which one reads this device: 'The more they take from me, the higher I rise' " (Grellet de Beauregard, "Lettres," 90).

emanation of words on paper, but inhered in the lord's person, one might expect either the prediction of the optimistic marquis, to the effect that deference would outlast upheaval, or, alternately, a more exterminatory approach on the part of communities seeking their emancipation. But well before the marquis was trying to cheer his wife with the thought that a mere legislature could not reshape "opinion," rural communities were developing other ways of challenging the structures of deference that were built into the system. The most striking is the very penetration of the *château* itself, taking place in about one event in five in the spring of 1789, but already on its way to becoming the central act of defiance. Once inside one could demand not only food but to be fed, then and there. Just as the derelict state might be held to its responsibilities to its people in many of the state-oriented subsistence events, so might the lord be held to a vision of the patrimonial provider and host. In mocking the symbolic pretension of lordship, however, the existence of lordship was still acknowledged, whereas an as yet small number of challenges went further and began to attack the symbolizations of the very idea of lordship: the coats-of-arms, the weathervanes, the (often merely decorative) turrets, the weapons, the church benches—all the material objects that represented what distinguished a lord from his neighbors.

The precise mix of these targets shifted over time. At those moments when attacks on seigneurial institutions increased radically in numbers, larger proportions of those larger numbers saw the *châteaux* entered: in 67% of all antiseigneurial incidents in July–early August 1789; 45% in January 1790; 55% in June 1790; 56% in June 1791; 77% in February–April 1791; a remarkable 81% in August–September 1792; and 56% in November 1792%. These may be compared with an overall rate of 27% for our entire data series. With increasing propensities to enter the lord's dwelling also came, unsurprisingly, increasing reports of serious damage: the insurrectionary waves of 1792, both February–April and August–September were especially prone to generate such reports.

For all their energy and violence, however, the peasant mobilizations were by no means unreflective actions driven by vengeful passion: they responded to the ways in which the revolutionary legislatures continued to redefine the fate of the seigneurial regime. The issue of burden of proof in disputed cases was first raised by the National Assembly in its law of March 1790 that placed that burden on peasant communities. It therefore became far more important for peasant communities to have some documentary basis on which to bring cases before a court. Frightening a lord into dictating such a document was an instant reaction: the spring of 1790 saw nearly one-third of all events involve a coerced renunciation; in the spurt of antiseigneurial events in June of that year, that proportion rose to as many as half of all events. The National Assembly's action increased the incentive for peasants, not only to attack the seigneurial regime, but to intimidate the lord into producing a statement. By setting the rates for indemnification as high as they were set in May 1790, the National Assembly probably increased the incentives for many communities to run the risks of violence in obtaining the needed documents. Hence the law of May was followed by the particular form of lawlessness of June. The lawless countryside was by now highly motivated to seek by violent means the documents required by the law.

Coerced renunciations fell off sharply in the summer of 1790 and stayed low, apart from a flare-up in the fall of 1792; perhaps those to whom such a document would appear useful had already obtained it by the summer of 1790. The corresponding exploration of seizure and destruction of seigneurial archives is more difficult to assess because some of the archive destruction is plainly subsumed under destruction of the *châteaux* as a whole. If a fire in the lord's archives led to the whole building being destroyed, it could easily be the case that the only known fact about that particular incident would be its overall destructiveness. The blurring of detail in our sources is, in this matter, compounded by the likelihood that some peasant gatherings opted to destroy the records flamboyantly by torching the whole building. While all our subcategories of antiseigneurial action are undoubtedly underreported, archive destruction, then, has the added element of being sometimes concealed under a different label.

But the lord's documents might be a target of peasant action for two quite different reasons. The community may wish to destroy the lord's capacity to mount a legal case; alternatively, the community may hope to find evidence useful for its own case.[188] The first is more likely by far, I would suggest, to eventuate in a burning *château,* while the second is rather similar to coerced renunciation. Now my contention here is that the March 1790 laws raised the value to the community of obtaining documents, but did nothing in particular to encourage destroying the lords'. Thus not only were coerced renunciations running high in the June outburst but so were title seizures—without any increase in serious *château* damage. Let us now jump ahead to the opportune winter of 1792, as members of the French legislature were beginning to connect their own talk about France's mission to liberate Europe from feudalism with the villages of their own country, as the probability of an unprecedented military mobilization grew day by day. The most striking feature that Table 8.3 shows us is the focus on the *château* itself: more than three-fourths of peasant events make the *château* a target;

188. This is a point overlooked in Philippe-Jean Hesse's path-breaking article on the modalities of antiseigneurial revolts. See "Géographie coutumière et révoltes paysannes en 1789: Une hypothèse de travail," *Annales Historiques de la Révolution Française* 51 (1979): 280–306. See also Albert Soboul, "Le brûlement des titres féodaux (1789–1793)," in his *Problèmes paysans de la Révolution, 1789–1848* (Paris: Maspero, 1983), 135–46.

more than two-fifths, by my crude reckoning, do serious damage there. These figures exceed those for any previous point, including the previous high in these particulars, the summer of 1789. While a substantial proportion of these incidents involve land or titles, the symbolic aspects of seigneurialism or its religious connection, the movement of winter 1792 is not unique for any of these, but for its focus on the spatial center of the seigneurial regime, the lord's headquarters and home. From this point on, indeed, the antiseigneurial movement maintains these traits: the seriously damaging attack on the *château* remains its most distinctive feature. We are far from the focus on the peripheral outposts of seigneurialism of but a short time before.

Consider now the tail end of the antiseigneurial movement: events taking place after the legislation of August 1792 had shifted the burden of proof onto the lords. We find that renunciations were on a downward trajectory, vanishing by the end of November. By way of contrast, incidents described as including serious destruction were quite high, only exceeded during the insurrectionary peaks earlier in 1792. Indeed, it was the highest rate of serious damage to *châteaux* other than during major peaks of antiseigneurial activity. What is so striking about this stretch of time from December 1792 into June 1793 is that even without any strikingly high points of attacks on the lords (no doubt, many peasant communities were just avoiding complying) when there were such attacks they tended to be quite destructive of property. There were two distinctive elements that characterize the antiseigneurial events that follow the legislation of August: first, the pattern of continued intensive activity into September and then a radical falloff in the numbers of incidents; and second, the continuation of the high proportion of attacks on the *château* among the few remaining antiseigneurial events. Two rather different ways of explaining this configuration suggest themselves. In the first of these, we might conjecture that those still fighting seigneurial rights in 1792 were the most bitterly opposed in the country. Thus, as other villagers who accepted the earlier legislation fell away from risky mobilization, those left were angrier and were unwilling to give up opportunities to burn the *château,* even beyond August, when the regime was essentially dismantled. A second hypothesis, however, would downplay burning anger and look to the changing configuration of interest and opportunity. The law of August 25 set up a structure in which the only reason to take collective action, now, would be to deny the lords the use of relevant documents should they choose a court contest. Let me note that the Convention itself seemed to acknowledge a wave of attacks on archives at this point by ordering public officials to take this task out of the hands of the people and organize, instead, public burnings.[189]

189. Article 6 of the Law of July 17, 1793: "Former lords . . . and other holders of titles that

Perhaps both processes were at work. The legislation of August 1792 encouraged destruction of the lord's archives within the very tense climate of war and mounting counterrevolutionary activity.[190] Amid a general rise in the level of violence, a point to which I shall return in a moment, those who now went after the lord's archives did not bother to limit the property damage. In the spring of 1790, the laws had encouraged seizure as well as destruction of seigneurial documents: some peasant communities might well have wished to use the lord's documents to make their case in court. But with the burden of proof now shifted to the lords by the new law of 1792, there was no reason to seize archives and much reason to demolish them.

If this is correct, it is remarkable how low the rate of violence against persons remained. By way of contrast, consider the course of religiously oriented incidents, which we already know from Chapter 5 to have more than their share of personal assault (see p. 232). Now look at Figure 8.5. As anti-tithe action declined with victory and as the Civil Constitution of the Clergy generated a frequent mismatch of clerical and communal political leanings, violence against clerics rose sharply. By late 1790 the likelihood of personal injury in clashes over religious issues was far above what typified clashes over seigneurial rights. This was so even after the violence of antiseigneurial actions rose in 1792. To reiterate the point made in Chapter 5: the people of the countryside do not personalize the seigneurial regime. Lords may be hurt, but generally in order to force a written document from them. In spite of a climate of mounting tension, war, and rhetorical demonization by revolutionary elites, the personal attacks stay low. Another striking sign: there is no point at which the agents of the lord, often held to be lightning rods for popular anger, are very frequent targets. The largest such percentage, 10% in the March 29–May 31, 1790, stretch, seems to involve assaults on notaries in attempts to get them to write down a lord's renunciation or to seize the lord's papers stored in his office.

Peasants, Legislators, and the Boundary of State Action

Peasant actions often seemed to flow into the space vacated by the state. The government's failure to assure food within proper prices, to constrain

create or recognize rights suppressed by the present decree . . . shall be obliged to deposit them within three months of the publication of the present decree, at the municipal registers. Those deposited before August 10 shall be burned on that day in the presence of the communal council and the citizens; the remainder will be burned at the end of three months" (*AP* 69:98–99).

190. August–September 1792 had many such counterrevolutionary events, alongside the antiseigneurial ones; see Figure 6.4.

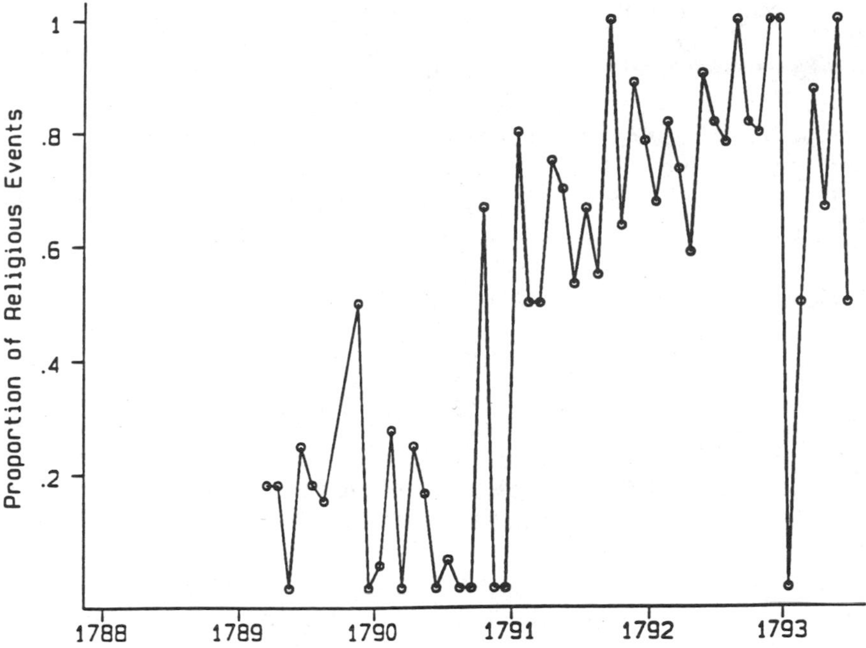

Fig. 8.5 Religious Events: Violence Against Persons

lords to honor communal claims to gather what they could on the forest floor, or to compel those with the right to hunt to abide by the customary restrictions provoked an array of actions readily seen when the state's coercive forces faltered (see Chapter 5, p. 263). Peasants set prices, reoccupied the forests, and cleared their surroundings of predators. But they also overflowed the traditional channels. Lords were not merely compelled to honor traditions (perhaps mockingly as in the coerced meal). The very centers of seigneurialism were challenged: the community announced itself as the source of justice in its erection or removal of gallows; it seized the words on which the lord's claim rested; it destroyed the benches that made the lord more than just a fellow parishioner and tore down the weathervane, turrets, and coats-of-arms that made the *château* something more than a large house. All these actions were eventually reappropriated by the state: the state declared the end of coats-of-arms and weathervanes; it permitted hunting; it authorized nonpayment; and it ordered the burning of seigneurial titles. In the timing of its own actions, the state followed the waves of peasant mobilization. And whatever the rationale the lawyers claimed to underlie the distinctions among rights—those to be abolished outright and those to be indemnified—the particular rights in those categories in March 1790 corresponded, at least roughly, to distinctions found in the parish *cahiers*. The people of the countryside did a great deal more than move into a space left empty by state collapse. They also carved into that space the channels that structured the ways in which the state, in its turn, would move back in. And state reappropriation, in its turn, was not mere restoration. In reversing their free-market propensities, the revolutionary elites did not restore the Old Regime economic controls, but instituted the most thoroughgoing regulation of prices in French history. And in exemplary violence against persons, the new state, with its tens of thousands of headless corpses and hundreds of thousands incarcerated, was multiplying a hundredfold the plebeian violence being displaced.

A Peasant-Bourgeois Alliance

By the spring of 1789, a program of liberal reform had emerged. The *cahiers* show how deeply this program had penetrated the French elites, although there were important differences, on the whole, between Third Estate and nobility, as well as important variation within each estate from one *cahier* to the next. The great crisis of the late 1780s was seen by some as more than a problem, but also as an opportunity for the enactment of the program(s). The misfortunes that broke the habits of obedience, destroyed the sense that tomorrow would be very much like today, provided, at the same time, an opportunity, an opening. The financial crisis was a cause for both despair and hope. As the Third Estate of Draguignan put it in their *cahier:* "The most disastrous period of the monarchy is becoming the most memorable and days of peace and happiness are going to follow this time of disorder" (*AP* 3:254).

Within the various legislatures, however, there was a range of views from opponents of reform to proponents of very radical measures indeed. The rural turbulence provided an opportunity for the enactment of measures more radical than might otherwise have seen the light of day. Peasant uprisings kept rural France on the legislative agenda and drowned out the tendencies to silence on seigneurial rights that characterized much of the nobility. The evident needs of the state for resources and of individual legislators for personal security for country property and family safety might, in some circumstances, have suggested a repressive option. But the strength of one or another reform program adhered to by many in the legislatures made this a losing proposition as far as seigneurial rights were concerned. Peasants running the risks of insurrection could keep bringing seigneurial rights to the fore in spring and summer 1789, winter 1789–90, spring and again summer of 1792 (and less sharply in June 1790 and June

1791). This peasant pressure, however, considered out of the context of the multiple forces at work, did not guarantee a legislative movement along favorable lines. But when rural upheaval was seconded by Parisian insurrection, the forces in the legislature counseling concessions to the peasantry carried the day over the advocates of holding the line.

Perhaps the composition of the National Assembly, which governed until the fall of 1791, enacted the initial decrees and, generally, set the tone for the legislature-countryside dialogue, contributed significantly both to mutual misunderstanding and the potential of an alliance of urban legislative radicals and northern villagers. Timothy Tackett's research shows the Third Estate deputies to be overwhelmingly well-off, from large cities and northerners (this last a quirk of the creation of numerous electoral divisions in northeastern France). One would be hard-put to create a greater social distance from the poorer country people who made war on the lords, largely southerners after the crisis of the summer of 1789 (see Tables 7.5 and 7.6). And Tackett shows as well that those deputies with agricultural backgrounds, as well as the rural clerical deputies, spoke up very little after that summer, perhaps showing a sense of being out of place. (In the early internal debates among the clerical deputies, in Tackett's account, bishops insulted priests by calling them "sons of peasants.") Quite tellingly, the Jacobin grouping, whose coalescence in 1790 Tackett traces, deviates from the general picture profoundly. It not only included the Assembly's few semiplebeians,[191] but had its center of gravity in small towns and rural areas. Almost two-fifths of the Jacobins came from places with fewer than two thousand persons and a majority were from the South. Such delegates, one may conjecture, would be far more likely to have some understanding of the rural resistance, perhaps had some sympathy, and probably had the local personal and political connections to advise them on the sorts of legislation that peasants in Provence or Limousin might settle for.[192]

The legislators were loath to bid for support in the countryside at the cost of alienating others in that same countryside. Initially they sought compromise between peasants and holders of seigneurial rights; but after they began to travel down the road of committing themselves to those who paid, they were reluctant to favor one portion of the peasantry over another (although when they took sides it would be in a direction consistent with their own leanings to agrarian individualism). Since seigneurial rights constituted one area where something could be given to peasants without

191. The deputy whose world was closest to the peasants was probably Pierre-François Lepoutre of Flanders, whose sons worked in the fields and whose daughters labored as servants. He, like the sprinkling of propertyless lawyers, sat with the left.

192. See Timothy Tackett, *Becoming a Revolutionary*, 42, 46, 130, 231, 286.

embroiling legislators in intracommunal struggles, this became a very attractive option indeed[193]—and ultimately an option chosen in the face of insurrection even when the object of insurrection was not seigneurial rights. When counterrevolution exacerbated the strains of wartime mobilization, the Convention responded to counterrevolutionary peasants with force—with force of such an extent, ultimately, that some today have taken up the language of genocide.[194] But not with force alone. We have already looked at Barère's opening a discussion of a broad range of benefits to richer and poorer peasants as well as force in mid-March (see p. 450). But even the absence of a significant antiseigneurial movement did not prevent the newly radicalized Convention (after the Parisian rising of late May and early June 1793) from advancing well beyond the legislation of the previous August, securing, as it were, the tolerance of those many country people who would never seek a return to the domination of the lords—and, with luck, achieving an easier time getting their sons to fight their fellow country people in the West as well as the sons of other country people from Germany and Austria and Spain.

Table 8.4, perhaps in an overschematic fashion, summarizes some of

Table 8.4. Major Legislative Turning Points, Major Peasant and Parisian Insurrections

Date of Major Legislation on Seigneurial Regime	Character of Legislation in Relation to Existing Law: Concessions or Firmness	Date of Major Wave of Rural Insurrection	Is Antiseigneurialism a Major Component in Insurrectionary Wave?	Date of Major Parisian Insurrection
August 4–11, 1789	Concessions to countryside	Summer 1789	Yes	July 1789
No new legislation	No new legislation	No wave of rural insurrection	No wave of rural insurrection	October 1789
March 15–28, 1790	Firmness toward countryside	Winter 1789–90	Yes	No Parisian insurrection
August 25, 1792	Concessions to countryside	Spring 1792 and Summer 1792	Yes	August 1792
July 17, 1793	Concessions to countryside	Spring 1793	No	May 31–June 2, 1793

193. Moving more radically against seigneurial rights was made more attractive by meshing with the Revolution's steadily deepening antinoble thrust; see Patrice L.-R. Higonnet, *Class, Ideology and the Rights of Nobles During the French Revolution* (Oxford: Clarendon Press, 1981).

194. Reynald Secher, *La génocide franco-français: Vendée-Vengé* (Paris: Presses Universitaires de France, 1986). For a telling critique, see Charles Tilly, "State and Counter-revolution in France," in Ferenc Fehér, *The French Revolution and the Birth of Modernity* (Berkeley and Los Angeles: University of California Press, 1990), 49–68.

these relationships for the major legislative turning points. The table emphasizes the following points:

- The greatest waves of rural insurrection were all followed by major legislative acts. Seigneurial rights were placed on the agenda by insurrection.
- In the absence of Parisian insurrection, the direction of legislation did not make concessions to peasants. The act of March 15–28, 1790 (and the associated decisions on the modalities and rates of indemnification of early May) gave a markedly conservative spin to the stirring but ambiguous pronouncements of the previous August. One might take the contrasting roles of one deputy in the enactments of summer 1789 and spring 1790 as emblematic. Le Chapelier presided over the sessions of August 4 and the subsequent days during which concerns over property were integrated into the language of emancipation, renunciation, and regeneration. In the debates occasioned by the risings in the Southeast and Brittany of February 1790, leading up to the March legislation, Le Chapelier reported for the Committee on the Constitution on a proposal concerning the proper quantity and modalities of pacificatory force for protecting rural property (*AP* 11:653).
- Parisian insurrection without peasant insurrection did relatively little insofar as legislation on rural issues is concerned. We recall the march to Versailles on the famous October days; October 5–6, 1789, was as dramatic as any urban upheaval in the entire Revolution. Angry Parisians—women on breadlines, militant artisans, and shopkeepers—marched out to Versailles and not only menaced the royal family, but terrified many legislators as well. The National Guard under Lafayette stepped in, assuming an ambiguous mediating role, and escorted the king to Paris. (Did the Guard save the king from the people or did it seize the king on behalf of the people?) The legislature now moved itself to Paris and both legislature and king were much more dangerously close to volatile Parisian politics. These vivid events may have broken the impasse over the king's stalling on the promulgation of the decrees of August 4–11, but they broke no new legislative ground.
- For peasant insurrection to lead to concessions to the countryside on seigneurial rights, it was not necessary for the insurrection to have antiseigneurial themes, only that it be large and widespread. In 1793 there were very few antiseigneurial actions, and the risings of the spring were dominated by counterrevolution, yet the new law of July 1793 was as definitive an abolition of the feudal regime as the Revolution was to achieve.

The risings in the countryside, then, constituted opportunities for liberals in power to move against the lords; and for those who were even more liberal than most to move much faster than most originally intended. The urban notables' program of freeing up the marketplace was realizable, thanks to the great opportunity presented by the deficit from 1787 on; and then, from the summer of 1789 on, by the deficit combined with peasant insurrection; and still later, by the deficit, peasant insurrection, and interstate warfare. Yet the notables' vision of the sovereign market was not equally easy to bring about in the countryside in all of its aspects. It was most quickly launched on the antiseigneurial front. Cohesive peasant communities rose against their lords. Peasants armed themselves and quickly remembered or rediscovered the arts of planning, surveillance, intimidating, and destroying the capacities of the lords to continue. This was not a propitious moment for legislative attack on those communities as such. The notables' project of freeing property from communal as well as seigneurial restrictions, therefore, was initially shelved. As the battle against the lords began to be won; as contending political forces offered their services to particular segments of rural France in their own search for allies, divisions began to appear within those very communities, and these divisions, now, began to provide an opening for enactment of anticommunal measures as well. If the peasant movement at first seemed to make antiseigneurialism salient, appeared to put it on the agenda, the same could be said, more weakly, for the relationship of intracommunal conflicts and questions revolving around the support for individualistic or communalistic conceptions of rural social relations on the part of French elites. Thus, the peasant movement, by its united thrust in one arena and by its division in a second, constituted opportunities for determined groups among the power-holders to act.[195]

I write "*seemed* to make antiseigneurialism salient"; the salience of antiseigneurialism involved a double process. First of all, the legislature was oriented to seeing things in an antiseigneurial light, so its interpretation of rural events tapped into a particular reading of French social relations. One reason Barnave so early sketched the main lines of what came to be known as the "Marxist" thesis is that a great deal of the upper Third Estate had already assigned seigneurial rights a central role in their interpretation of French society (see Chapters 4 and 9).

But antiseigneurialism became salient in a second way. Just as the legislators reacted to peasant action, so, too, did peasants respond to the power-holders. We have seen that early in the Revolution the antiseigneurial

195. And, let it be noted, that this chapter, including our analysis of Table 8.4 in particular, has shown that the peasant-legislature dialogue was at moments critically affected by circumstances external to that dialogue: the outbreak of warfare, the rhythms of Parisian insurrection. The consequences of rural conflict, then, were linked to urban struggles; and since those urban struggles are not treated here, it is as if an offstage presence suddenly enters center stage. The intertwining of urban and rural conflict is a theme that would fill another book.

element within the broad insurrectionary current was a growing one. It grew because it seemed a fruitful direction in which to push. The general thrust and the divisions among the power-holders provided opportunities for rural militants. The division, most obviously, created the rapid undermining of coercive capacities, totally reorienting the possibilities of bargaining. What was usually off the agenda could now be placed upon it and everything from surreptitious evasion to collective, overt, and vocal battle was undertaken. But undertaken on behalf of what? Country people differed from one another in their aims (as the *cahiers* show) and a single community might have many aims. And the variety of potential rural targets was great (see Chapters 5–7). Given the willingness of the legislatures to give ground on seigneurial rights, however, this quickly came to be a particularly fruitful area in which to push.

Consider rural communities in time of revolution debating the prudent course, perhaps early Sunday afternoon, after Mass. If rural actions early in the spring of 1789 involving invasion of the lord's fields seemed to pay off, should the next step be to push land issues more broadly, or antiseigneurial ones? If the spring of 1789 showed the potential of raids on the lord's foodstocks, was this to be developed along its subsistence dimension or its antiseigneurial one? What lessons were peasant communities learning from their own insurrectionary struggles? The elections for the Estates-General, first of all, and then the enactments of the various legislatures were teaching them that the seigneurial regime was the opportune target. By interpreting peasant action as antiseigneurial, the lawgivers taught peasants to fit their future actions to this mold. Invading the lord's fields and compelling the lord to feed them, paid off for angry peasants on the eternally celebrated night of August 4 in the total abolition of the feudal regime; it did not pay off in promises of land for the land-short or food for the hungry. On the contrary, the legislatures initially sought to protect property rights and free up the grain market.

Marxists for a long time have spoken of an alliance of country people and bourgeoisie against feudalism, although all elements of this formulation have been subject to challenge.[196] I believe the present evidence supports these challenges insofar as it shows that, for all the antiseigneurial elements in the *cahiers* of both groups, no Third Estate–peasant convergence was yet very far advanced in March 1789. During that March only 28% of insurrections had antiseigneurial elements (already significantly up from prior months).

196. Alfred Cobban doubted the antifeudalism of the Third Estate deputies but accepted that of the peasants. George Taylor doubted the initial significance of peasant antifeudalism but accepted that of the Third Estate. In Chapters 2 and 3 I have debated both of these positions. The core element of both positions (with which I am in agreement) is that the countryside and the urban notables *differ* in their evaluations of the seigneurial regime and in their proposals for change. But I read the *cahiers* as identifying two different antiseigneurialisms.

But peasants and legislators found each other. Peasant militants, seeking to exploit the opportunities of the collapse of the old order learned to move against the lords more broadly and single-mindedly until the battle was won; and legislative factions learned to find in the peasant movements a potent resource for pushing an antiseigneurial program that increasingly went beyond what the Third Estate had put in its *cahiers*.[197]

The antiseigneurial alliance was not simply just there, a by-product of structural change impelling an urban notability and a peasantry on convergent courses. There were such structural changes, to be sure. The urban elite had forged a program to free up the market and curtail privileges. The countryside proposed reforming state taxation in the interests of utility and fairness while consigning the hopelessly useless or unfair taxes to the trashcan. While much of the seigneurial regime was to be abolished as utterly worthless, a significant rural minority held that those seigneurial rights capable of reform were to be reformed. Thus the bourgeoisie and the peasants in March 1789. The antiseigneurial alliance rested, then, on positions held on both sides, but those positions (on both sides) changed. The insurrectionary peasants of March 1790 did not accept the relatively conservative legislated compromise that, in many ways, fit their program of the year before; the peasants of March 1790 were not the peasants of March 1789. And the legislators changed as well as they dealt with one another, with Parisian militance, and with royal immobilism. The antiseigneurial alliance, then, was not simply there, not simply a given, not simply the by-product of culture or ideology, and rooted in structural conditions and conjunctural circumstance. The alliance was made. It was made as rural communities and legislative factions each learned how to use the other. What unfolded, then, was a process of bargaining in which the energies expended and risks taken in pursuit of objectives were calibrated to shifting expectations of the likely chances of success and the costs of failure as legislators divided in some ways (on seigneurial rights) and united on others (on the defense of wealth) confronted a subject rural population itself with its own points of unity (on seigneurial rights, for example) and of division (on property claims).

197. We would not expect to find cautious peasants openly defining themselves as following a strategy of violating the law in order to reform it. A petition to the National Assembly from a village in the Somme Valley comes about as close as one could imagine in a document permeated by respect for such catchwords as "property" and "equality" when they point out that if they have to continue to meet their obligations to the local duke they will not have the funds to pay their taxes. In its preference for taxes over seigneurial dues this village of some three hundred souls is like any other village; in its almost open attempt to get the legislators to accept a trade, it is unusual. See Bryant T. Ragan Jr., "Rural Political Activism and Fiscal Equality in the Revolutionary Somme," in Bryant T. Ragan Jr. and Elizabeth Williams, eds., *Recreating Authority in Revolutionary France* (New Brunswick, N.J.: Rutgers University Press, 1992), 44.

The alliance came to exist as radical legislators and militant peasants both seized the moment. The Revolution was not, however, a single moment, but a prolonged series of moments when the actions of a subject population and a group of power-holders created new opportunities for each other.

CHAPTER

9

WORDS AND THINGS: THE FRENCH REVOLUTIONARY BOURGEOISIE DEFINES THE FEUDAL REGIME

As it carried on its dialogue with the countryside, the legislature continually reconstructed a rationale for what it was doing. The conceptual center of these discussions was the term "feudal," used quite commonly at the onset of the Revolution to indicate a presumably delimited collection of claims of one party upon another (feudal rights), rather less commonly to indicate, holistically, a particular form of social order that was historically specific ("*the* feudal regime" but never "*a* feudal regime") and, increasingly commonly, and, even more abstractly, an organizing principle of social relations, with no very exact English equivalent (*féodalité*).

The seigneurial rights could hardly be discussed in the three legislatures that wrote and rewrote the laws without referring to conceptions of the feudal. In this chapter we sketch the evolution of these conceptions. In the last chapter we saw how legislators undertook actions under pressure from the countryside and from the militants of Paris. Legislators sought rationales for these actions. Such rationales were not to be constructed out of whole cloth, for the deputies did more than simply react to pressures: they had their own agenda and program and a set of justifications for that agenda and program. These justifications rested on a number of conceptions: conceptions of the sanctity of property and ideas about the meaning of the term "property"; ideas of French retardation, barriers to progress and the role of seigneurial rights among those barriers; and a sense of the present as a potential turning point in which properly calibrated legislation could shift the future of France onto a different track. The ways in which seigneurial rights were conceived at the onset of revolution by the urban notable strata as well as the nobility were examined in some detail in Chapter 4. We are concerned in the present chapter with how these conceptualizations of seigneurial rights—and particularly their relation to the "feudal"—evolved as the deputies coped with the rural insurrection.[1]

We have stressed above, in our examination of the *cahiers* in Chapters 2 and 3, how peasants, nobles, and urban notables conceived of the seigneurial rights as a bundle of distinguishable claims to be differentially evaluated. We saw, indeed, that one of the hallmarks of the staking-out of positions in the French countryside was precisely the careful delineation of such distinctions. By contrast with a peasantry exquisitely sensitive to the realities of each and every claim as it empirically existed in their own immediate experience, the various revolutionary legislatures were necessarily concerned with the elaboration of principles that could guide administrative action in a wide diversity of individualized locales. The categories employed by these bodies in drafting and debating legislation for the country as a whole were likely, then, to employ a simpler set of distinctions, although conceivably more mysterious ones. The tendency to abstract categorization that was part and process of the professional socialization of the numerous body of lawyers among the legislators made them eminently suited to the task of developing the categories needed to deal with this variegated body of rights on a national basis.

In examining the dilatory character of the legislation on the seigneurial rights in Chapter 8 we considered the economic and political interests at play. In this chapter I consider the legislation as an intellectual construction. One element in the endless legislative delay (it was, for example, seven months after the August 4–11 decrees established the distinction between simple abolition and indemnification that the legislature clarified which rights were in which category and yet another two months before the indemnification rates were set) may well have been the sheer intransigeance of the intellectual tasks.

1. The following discussion draws on John Markoff, "Słowa i rzeczy: burżuazja rewolucyjna definiuje system feudalny," in Andrzej Zybertowicz and Adam Czarnota, eds., *Interpretacje Wielkiej Transformacji. Geneza kapitalizmu jako geneza współczesności* (Warsaw: Kollegium Otryckie, 1989), 357–82.

From the beginning, the seigneurial rights were regarded as interpretable through the prism of "feudal" rights and the working out of the relationship of the one to the other category became one of the central conceptual matters to be worked through in the search for legislative coherence. The seigneurial rights, assimilated to the category of the feudal, then, were legislated about in accord with the elaboration of a discourse about "feudalism." Now the question perplexing those members of the assembly charged with drawing up the detailed legislation following the night of August 4 was discovering, deducing, or inventing the meaning of the feudal.

The general *cahiers* of the Third Estate already showed some elements of a global conception of the "feudal" elements in France. As we saw in Chapter 4, the seigneurial rights were implicitly seen as a totality in that *cahiers* discussing any seigneurial right were prone to discuss the others (and this may be contrasted with the nobility who experienced two distinct groups of seigneurial rights). The Third Estate, moreover, often explicitly addressed "seigneurial rights" as a whole, that term being used more-or-less synonymously with "feudal rights." Finally, this whole was seen as related to other institutions to be altered. While Third Estate assemblies, then, like the parishes or nobles, carefully distinguished one right from others, they also showed evidence of a global conception that was distinctly theirs.

My intention here is to underline a paradox. The revolutionary leadership in Paris tirelessly announced to themselves and to others the existence of a clear rupture with the past, a past that was frequently associated with the term feudal; that, moreover, insofar as this system burdened the country people, they, the lawgivers of the new France, were the rational and conscious agents of a transformation in which the country people, in their blind, violent, and destructive way were also participating; and finally, that, the new world in the making, while not as yet clearly defined, could be seen as the antithesis of the darkness of the past. On the level of the most general statements then we find a contrast of past darkness and future light, not a world of shadows.

The paradox: when we look beyond these more abstract and emotion-laden formulations, everywhere we find nothing but shades of gray, which I will indicate under three broad headings. First, in the period preceding the Revolution, one finds the use of "feudal" instruments of domination for purposes that are not archaic in the least. The actions of France's rural lords, as the Revolution approached, in many ways demonstrate a participation in quite a modern set of economic relationships, even though the legal language through which their actions were enforced used the jargon of the Middle Ages.

Second, when we turn our attention to the mental universe of those who upheld the claims of the rural lords prior to the Revolution, we discover that the justification of those rights, by the late eighteenth century, was often expressed in terms already as thoroughly bourgeois as one could imagine. If one were to conceive of the Revolution as in part the replacement of an archaic aristocratic culture by a modern bourgeois one, in which new sets of justifications for new forms of economic activity laid the ideological groundwork upon which a modern capitalist order would be constructed, one would be disappointed: whatever there was that might reasonably be dubbed "feudal" in the late eighteenth century was already justified on bourgeois grounds, well before the angry people of the countryside set fire to the *châteaux*.

Third, when we examine the details, rather than the broad claims of those who saw themselves as modern Solons giving the Law to the new society, we discover the extent to which change was to consist in renaming things, and how little in altering the material content of the obligations of the rural population to those with claims upon them (at least in the short run.) I shall return to each of these points below.

Let us pretend for a moment that the powerful pressures on the legislature that loomed so large in Chapter 8's account of the legislative history did not exist. We thereby, again for the moment, ignore the rural insurrections that they had to deal with, the Parisian pressures that altered the political configuration of the assemblies, the financial disaster, and the rising tensions that ultimately became large-scale warfare. If one were to limit one's scrutiny to the various revolutionary legislatures in this way, one might well describe the assemblies as groping for a definition of feudal rights and then trying to apply that definition to the specific claims of French lords in order to distinguish those to be abolished from those to be treated otherwise. This would be to present the legislative history as though it derived from a conception of what was and what was not feudal. The *cahiers* make quite clear that in the bright new modern world, what was feudal had no place. The "feudal" evoked a world of fragmented sovereignty, civil violence, and economic retardation as well as local, corporate, and personal privilege. These were to be done away with in the name of national unity, humanity, economic advance, and juridical equality of citizens. In this very general sense, abolishing feudal rights undoubtedly fit the general conceptions of many deputies about what was desirable in the new world in the making. If, however, we look more closely at how "abolish" and "feudal" were defined in actual legislative practice after the ringing declarations of August 1789, one finds quite a different process. Instead of actions being driven by ideas, the ways in which the detailed legislation defined "feudal" were quite plainly attempts at constructing a rationale from which actions to be taken could appear to be derived. And those definitions-in-practice were exceedingly narrow ones.

If it pleased the deputies to sweep away "the sad remnants of the feudal regime" and experience themselves, sometimes exhilaratingly, as moving France from darkness to light, it was also pleasing to define the feudal regime so that it fit what was being swept away (and did not fit what the deputies hoped to preserve). The clarity with which the deputies hoped to define the feudal, so that the light could appear in the greatest contrast to the dark, was difficult to reconcile with the concrete complexity of institutions.

It is the coexistence of a broad (and ever broader) notion of a feudal past whose total abolition is a moment of world transformation with a narrow definition that left many peasant obligations substantially unaltered (but that was subject to change under pressure) that gives the intellectual history of the concept of the feudal its own special dynamic. The legislators could proclaim to themselves and their enthusiastic supporters how radically they had changed the world and could also sternly tell the peasants how much they still owed the same people as before. The people of the countryside, however, could use the broader conception to try to resist the narrower one—and thereby, after bitter battle, make the broader one more real. This conjunction bequeathed to the future in which we live a rich and powerful conceptual heritage: the present was born in a sharp break with the past; the contribution of educated elites to the Revolution was in the realm of ideas and that of plebeians was violence; the fusion of those ideas and that violence effected the transformation of the old into the new.

From Fiefs to Epochs: A Word Expands

In the spring of 1789 a good number of assemblies were already using the term "feudal" (not, let me stress, "seigneurial") as a generic term for a kind of society, and a particularly repugnant kind indeed. "Feudal" and "seigneurial" were often used as interchangeable variants, but the former was sometimes used to indicate some sort of social totality (as in "feudal regime") whereas the latter generally had the more concrete reference of an aggregate of specific rights.[2] One frequently finds the word feudal forming

2. The following draws on Régine Robin, "Fief et seigneurie dans le droit et l'idéologie juridique à la fin du XVIIIe siècle," *Annales historiques de la Révolution française* 43 (1971): 554–602; Claude Mazauric, "Note sur l'emploi du 'régime féodal' et de 'féodalité' pendant la Révolution Française," in *Sur la Révolution Française: Contributions à l'histoire de la Révolution bourgeoise* (Paris: Editions Sociales, 1970), 119–34; Alain Guerreau, "Fief, féodalité, féodalisme. Enjeux sociaux et réflexion historienne," *Annales: Economies, Sociétés, Civilisations* 45 (1990): 134–66; Rolf Reichardt and Eberhard Schmitt, "La Révolution Française—rupture ou continuité? Pour une conceptualisation plus nuancée," in Rolf Reichardt and Eberhard Schmitt, eds., *Ancien Regime: Aufklärung und Revolution* (Munich: Oldenbourg, 1983), 4–71; Diego Venturino, "La naissance de l'Ancien Régime," in Colin Lucas, *The French Revolution and the Creation of a Modern Political Culture,* 2:11–40; Ernst Hinrichs, " 'Feudalität' und Ablösung. Bemerkungen zur Vorgeschichte des 4. August 1789,"

part of a picture of an odious past that unfortunately is not altogether dead, and that therefore needs to be given the final blow. The Third Estate of Poitou for example: "If, for many centuries, France languished in ignorance, anarchy and confusion, those were the centuries of the feudal regime, when the *seigneurs,* enjoying their usurped authority, crushed possessions and persons alike under an equal servitude. The odious time of personal servitude has at last disappeared; or, if in some parts of the realm, the right of *mainmorte* still exercises its empire, this right . . . cannot fail to disappear soon in its turn" (*AP* 5:412).

"Feudal regime" as used here identifies a historical epoch with a set of social institutions, rather than a phase in an unfolding history of the relationship of God and humanity.[3] Sacred history has become transmuted into social history. Instead of time divided into an old order and a Christian era by the appearance of God, the will of the French people was dividing time into a barbarous past and a future (present?) of liberty. The existing seigneurial institutions embodied for many the vestiges of barbarism in their reminiscences of ancient degradation. The honor of humanity, the Third Estate of Avesnes declares, "requires that even the memory of such barbarian practices be lost" (*AP* 2:153).

But of course the memory was not to be lost at all: for the revolutionaries, the vision of feudal barbarism became precisely the standard against which the achievements of the present age and the perfection of those achievements in the near future were to be measured. Consider the *cahier* of the Third Estate of Draguignan. It is against the background of the "still existing vestiges of the servitude of our fathers" that this present "moment of the rebirth of the rights of man" is set in relief. A reference to "the usurpation carried out under the weak successors of Charlemagne" serves to quickly sketch a set of social practices that, we are told, it would be outrageous to describe by the term "legitimate." It is by contrast that one can glimpse the vision of a world of voluntary agreements that might, in the contemporary France of 1789, deserve such a characterization. We get some idea of what liberty, property, and progress in the useful arts might be by contrasting these principles with the barriers to "natural liberty." "The dignity of man" is portrayed by contrast to various claims of the lords; and the concept of "the interest of the state" is seen as requiring a remedy for the "mortal wound" worked by the seigneurial rights (*AP* 3:260–61).

This single document just cited managed to combine many of the current major critiques of "the sad remnants of the feudal regime" into a single

in Eberhard Schmitt, ed., *Die Französische Revolution* (Cologne: Kiepenheuer und Witsch, 1976), 124–57; Gerd van den Heuvel, "Féodalité, Féodal," in Rolf Reichardt and Eberhard Schmitt, eds., *Handbuch politisch-sozialer Grundbegriffe in Frankreich 1680–1820* (Munich: Oldenbourg, 1988), 10:7–54.

3. Guerreau, "Fief, féodalité, féodalisme."

series of paragraphs: that it constituted an affront to individual liberty and to human dignity; that it hindered commerce and devastated agriculture; that it fragmented state authority; that it was incompatible with the rights of property. All that is missing for the particular text to constitute a complete litany of the complaints laid at the door of the feudal regime (as of 1789) would be to couple it with ecclesiastical abuses.[4]

For what we find in the *cahiers* of the Third Estate considered together is a very strong tendency to link the existing seigneurial rights (sometimes described as the remnants of the feudal past, sometimes not) with a wide variety of other criticisms of the social order. To again recall Chapter 4: the many proposals for economic liberalism, largely directed against state hindrances to the market are similarly, if perhaps secondarily, directed against seigneurial claims of various sorts, notably monopolies, tolls, and *corvées*. The champions of a unitary state, on the other hand, are particularly hostile to manifestations of a fragmented sovereignty and wish the dismemberment of the seigneurs' claims to administer justice in their own courts. The proponents of agricultural growth are hostile to the irrationality of the lords' claims on the harvest, which destroy any incentive to innovate. What there is in the way of antagonism to aspects of the activities of the Church is linked to a critique of the lords as well. All this can be seen in the *cahiers* of the spring.

In their explicit usage, terms such as *droits féodaux* or *droits seigneuriaux* refer, of course, to various obligations owed a lord, but it is striking that implicitly these terms had acquired already by the spring of 1789 a very much broader if inexplicit significance. Those documents that speak with particular bitterness or at particular length about these rights also tend to devote themselves to discussions of other institutional arenas and issues, specifically those we have just mentioned: issues of economic blockage, of ecclesiastical abuse, of a wide-ranging structure of privilege in all arenas of French society. Although any number of medievalists have attempted to assure us that the term "feudal" has little meaning when applied to the late eighteenth century,[5] Chapter 4 has shown that the *droits féodaux* were experienced as an absolutely central institution, profoundly linked to many other concerns for social change. The intense and nationwide discussion of French institutions seems to have tightened these linkages. The sense that

4. For a survey of eighteenth-century antifeudal literature, see John Q. C. Mackrell, *The Attack on "Feudalism" in Eighteenth-Century France* (London: Routledge and Kegan Paul, 1973). This eighteenth-century literature itself had a long ancestry as the champions of royalism from at least the sixteenth century excoriated the benighted past. On pre-eighteenth-century antifeudal history-writing, see Harold A. Ellis, *Boulainvilliers and the French Monarchy. Aristocratic Politics in Early Eighteenth-Century France* (Ithaca: Cornell University Press, 1988), 31–51.

5. See, for example, Robert Boutruche, *Seigneurie et féodalité, le premier âge des liens d'homme à homme* (Paris: Aubier, 1968).

this was a moment of transition, a moment when France seemed poised between disintegration and rebirth, was expressed by (and also fueled by) the widespread deployment of neologisms, whose jarring newness reflected (but also stimulated) the sense of institutional flux.[6] And old words could be dusted off for use and in use be themselves transformed: "democracy,"[7] "revolution,"[8]—and "feudal rights."

By August 4, the incorporation of a range of institutions under the "feudal" had broadened. First of all certain specific institutions were associated with the seigneurial rights under the feudal rubric in ways that were not yet in place the previous March. Thus the discussion on August 4 touched on many matters and the summary statement includes tax privileges, venal officeholding, the expenses of obtaining justice, the privileges of provinces and towns, improperly obtained government pensions, various payments to the Vatican, and the guilds. The draft legislation presented on the following day as a basis for discussion adds the *casuels* of the clergy, the increase of the *portion congrue,* and the practice of holding multiple benefices. The ringing opening sentence of the final decree voted on August 11 gives what is being destroyed a broader name than "feudal," let alone "seigneurial," rights. It is now some more generic entity of which these rights are a component, it is a feudal "regime" that is entirely destroyed.[9] It is to a lexically appropriate Committee on Feudal (not Seigneurial) Rights that the task of spelling out the details was confided.

In the sense of a generic term denoting not a particular structure of economic ties, political authority, or military obligation but an entire state of civilization, embracing, to be sure, economic ties, political authority, and military obligation, the precedent was set a half-century earlier by the writings of Boulainvilliers,[10] who was attempting to defend the position of

6. Philippe Roger, "Le dictionnaire contre la Révolution," *Stanford French Review* 14 (1990): 72.

7. "Democrat" seems to have emerged from the theoretical treatises of classically educated intellectuals into the discourse about contemporaneous events in the low countries in the 1780s. See Robert R. Palmer, *The Age of the Democratic Revolution* (Princeton: Princeton University Press, 1959), 1:15.

8. Keith Michael Baker, "Inventing the French Revolution," in his *Inventing the French Revolution: Essays on French Political Culture in the Eighteenth Century* (New York: Cambridge University Press, 1990), 203–23; Roger Barny, "La formation du concept de 'révolution' dans la Révolution," in Michel Vovelle, ed., *L'image de la Révolution française: Communications presentées lors du Congrès Mondial pour le Bicentenaire de la Révolution,* 1:433–39; Alain Roy, *"Révolution": Histoire d'un mot* (Paris: Gallimard, 1989); Rolf Reichardt and Hans-Jürgen Lüsebrink, "Révolution à la fin du 18e siècle. Pour une relecture d'un concept-clé du siècle des Lumières," *Mots* 16 (1988): 35–68.

9. A convenient comparative summary of the three texts is in Patrick Kessel, *La nuit du 4 août 1789* (Paris: Arthaud, 1969), 320–26.

10. François Furet and Mona Ozouf, "Deux légitimations historiques de la société française au XVIIIe siècle: Mably et Boulainvilliers," *Annales: Economies, Sociétés, Civilisations* 34 (1979): 438–50.

the nobility against the various forms of royal usurpation carried out over the centuries, indeed, in his view, from the very beginnings of the Capetian monarchy. While no one had yet explicitly spelled out the conception of an entire feudal society (to appropriate the title of Marc Bloch's great book), the grievance lists of the spring of 1789 embody such a notion implicitly.

The term "feudal," like all reference to the Middle Ages, took on a denunciatory quality. "Gothic," like "feudal," came to stand for the rejected past. In condemning those engaged in destroying the artworks of France's cultural heritage, one revolutionary legislator probably invented the modern use of "vandalism."[11] And most strikingly we see the degree to which in their public pageantry, their invocations of heroic names, their literary metaphors, the revolutionary bourgeoisie leaped back over the Middle Ages to embrace Greek and Latin antiquity. In short, "the feudal regime" was already by the summer of 1789 becoming a summary term that evoked almost the entire social order being destroyed. This was a considerable broadening of the term in only a few months. "The feudal regime" in that first summer of Revolution did not yet embrace the monarchy, the king being celebrated as "the restorer of French liberty" in the final article of the decree of August 11—but 1789 was not yet 1793.[12]

As the principles developed in the legislation of March 1790, however, gave way to the radical shift anticipated in the spring of 1792 and more fully embodied in the laws of the following August—the shifting of the burden of proof in contested cases to the lords as well as making more rights subject to uncompensated abolition (see Chapter 8, p. 465)—the lexical climate shifted again. By August 1792, as Claude Mazauric has pointed out, "feudal regime" gave way to the even more abstract "féodalité," which had come to be freely employed as a rather generalized pejorative for all that was absurd, illegitimate, or backward in the Old Regime.[13] When Grégoire came to issue his important report on the French language, he spoke of the future as "the epoch when these feudal idioms shall have disappeared."[14]

11. Catherine Volpillac, Dany Hadjadj, and Jean-Louis Jam, "Des vandales au vandalisme," in Simone Bernard-Griffiths, Marie-Claude Chemin, and Jean Ehrard, *Révolution française et "vandalisme révolutionnaire"* (Paris: Universitas, 1992), 15–27.

12. Rethinking the image of collective madness evoked by the night of August 4 from a vantage point a few years down the road past the king's trial, the lawyer A.-C. Thibaudeau considered that, in retrospect, the most genuinely deranged element of that night's many unusual acts was honoring Louis XVI (Antoine-Claire Thibaudeau, *Mémoires, 1765–1792* [Paris: Champion, 1875], 96). We shall consider below how monarchy came, for the revolutionaries, to join the feudal regime.

13. *L'abolition de la féodalité dans le monde occidental* (Paris: Editions du Centre National de la Recherche Scientifique, 1971), 2:502–3.

14. Henri Grégoire, "Rapport sur la nécessité et les moyens d'anéantir les patois et d'universaliser l'usage de la langue française," in Michel de Certeau, Dominique Julia, and Jacques Revel, eds., *Une politique de la langue. La Révolution française et les patois: L'enquête de Grégoire* (Paris: Gallimard, 1975), 302.

We have then the image of a radical break with the past, energized by the wisdom of the lawgivers in conjunction with the anger of the country people. There is an illustration in the Cabinet des Estampes of the Bibliothèque Nationale that magnificently represents this image of the alliance against a broad concept of feudalism.[15] Labeled "the night of August 4–5 or patriotic exaltation," it depicts the muscular arms of the country people wielding agricultural implements to strike at a pile of noble and clerical objects. Perhaps a grouping of three men in breeches pounding away is to remind us of the patriotic representatives of the three orders who, as the National Assembly, passed the historic decree. (Other engravings of the day show a very similar threesome in dress that clearly identifies them with the three orders; here the trio has a distinctly rustic and popular cast.) Already broken by the blows are several swords; a coat-of-arms is being trampled, bishops' staffs and clerical garb are on the ground, too, but not yet damaged as far as I can see (and an unmolested village church stands serenely in the background). We have here the violence of the people represented as fused with the actions of the National Assembly. That violence is directed against the symbols of noble and clerical privilege (but not the church as such) rather than against anything specifically restricted to seigneurial payments.

Now that the lawgivers had risen to their historic mission, to be sure, further popular violence would be harder to regard as having a place in the necessary destruction of the old order.

Lawyers Make Distinctions: A Word Contracts

But while the National Assembly in the summer of 1789 was elaborating an image of a total break with a past for which "feudal regime" was a convenient summary label, the Committee on Feudal Rights of that very same assembly, in the course of preparing the detailed legislation on *precisely* what was abolished, was pursuing a very different tack.

By September 1789, when the term feudal had already taken on for many the broadest of associations, the chair of the Committee on Feudal Rights, Merlin de Douai, reported on the necessity for some definitional precision. While such terms as *droits féodaux,* he pointed out, "in their most rigorous sense only designate those rights that derive from a fief contract" (*AP* 8:524), plainly something broader was intended, something he designates, apparently lacking an appropriate French phrase, by following the sixteenth-

15. A reproduction appears on the cover of Jean Nicolas, ed., *Mouvements populaires et conscience sociale, XVIe–XIXe siècles* (Paris: Maloine, 1985).

century jurist Dumoulin's expression *complexum feudale.* In the invocation of Dumoulin's two-centuries-old Latin, moreover, there is a significant intimation that Dumoulin himself was describing something already quite old, but that continued to be barely alive in a later century. If the dead skin of social relations that constituted the *complexum* could be stripped off, some fully up-to-date institutions could emerge, for which meaningful French names could be noted; unlike the struggle to find a name for these dessicated institutional ruins, the new names would be obvious. Yet the difficulty of naming what it was that shall be the object of legislation did not suggest to Merlin any potential for ambiguity or arbitrariness: "The object of our work is unequivocal" (*AP* 8:524).

Just as the broadening of "feudal" into a generalized condemnation of the old order was prefigured in the *cahiers* of the spring, so was Merlin's approach to a more restricted meaning, which would not, however, be the antiquarian restriction of regarding "féodal" as the adjectival form of "fief." The *cahiers* of the spring, in fact, bear eloquent testimony to the lack of interest in "droits féodaux" in Merlin's most rigorous sense: as we saw in Chapter 2 there were few discussions of the various institutions that to the legal-minded signified a vassal's acknowledgment of his lord and even less interest in the lord's occasional attempted exercise of his alleged prerogative to temporarily seize the land of those who withheld such acknowledgment. Nor were discussions involving the distinctions between fiefs and other forms of tenure *(censives, alleux, emphytéoses)* much of a subject for lively discussion (see Chapter 2, pp. 52, 60).

To the extent that the urban notables in their *cahiers* meant something specific by *droits féodaux,* then, it was hardly limited to fiefs and indeed had little to do with fiefs at all. As the term "feudal" was taking on ever broader implications in political discourse, the lawyers found no sense whatever in a narrower usage derived from the archaic bonds among the members of a dominant warrior class. If they shared with some twentieth-century medievalists the view that such a usage had little bearing on the modern eighteenth century, they were also participating in a historical moment in which the term was a fixture of ordinary speech, perhaps more so than ever before—or since. In the course of his work with the Committee on Feudal Rights following the August 4–11 decrees, Merlin therefore takes it to be his conceptual task to distinguish those rights that are fully part of the *complexum feudale* and therefore are to simply disappear, from those that partake of the saving grace of legitimate private property and are therefore to be eliminated only upon payment of an indemnity. This was a daunting task indeed: in spite of Merlin's confident announcement in September that the identity of the *complexum feudale* was unequivocal, it surely was equivocal in the extreme.

Both in daily practice and in ideological justification, "feudal" and modern practices and conceptions were so completely intertwined that the attempt to abolish the former in order to emancipate the latter was, on the level of detail, a hopeless project. The only realization of this project was on the level of an abstract conception of a total break between two clearly distinguishable social orders. Rather than a sharp distinction of bourgeois and feudal forms and practices, what we find on the level of detailed reality as well as detailed discussion is an intertwining of the two: not so much the clear opposition suggested by the abstract condemnations of pre-revolutionary publicists or the revolutionary decrees but an everyday blend verging on syncretism.

A Feudal-Modern Mélange

I shall enlarge upon the foregoing observations under two broad headings that together provide a context for appreciating Merlin's intellectual construction.

- The specific claims that were made on peasant resources cannot be divided into those that were part of an archaic economy and those that were part of a modern economy.
- The language of disputes about particular claims did not appear as a conflict between archaic principles and modern ones; rather, all specific disputes tended to be debated in modern terms.

The result of these two propositions was that one could "abolish" the "feudal" by relabeling it as "property." The changes in certain peasant obligations that were held to follow from the abolition of feudalism were therefore quite modest.

Traditional Claims and Modern Purposes (or Using the Old to Obtain the New)

The machinery to enforce traditional claims was being used for quite modern purposes. A generation of historians devoted much energy and ingenuity to debating the thesis of a feudal reaction according to which the weight of feudal or seigneurial burdens was actually stepped up in the immediately pre-revolutionary period.[16] A great deal of the debate concerns not the

16. The alleged seigneurial reaction has sometimes been seen as part of a broader and even more debatable "aristocratic reaction" in which the old orders struggled increasingly for control of the state, for restrictions on the advancement of commoners as well as a reinforced structure of

reality, but the novelty, of the augmentation of seigneurial claims, with some historians seeing a cyclical pattern rather than a distinctively pre-revolutionary one and others seeing a long-term and quasi-permanent process. What is of interest here is the diversity of mechanisms employed by the lords of the late eighteenth century: the remaking of land surveys itemizing their proper claims; the employment of legal specialists to discover every last sou that could be squeezed out of the peasantry; the employment of the right of option by virtue of which a lord could purchase any land a peasant dependent attempted to sell; the enforcement (or even the invention) of claims on pastures and forests that crippled the access of peasants to formerly available collective resources of the rural community; the deliberate failure to enforce dues over a number of years, followed by a legally enforceable demand that the arrears be paid at once; the attempt to enclose the lord's own fields and thereby remove this land from the collective access of the rural community (and if some peasants were thereby thrown from poverty into desperation, their land might be purchased by the lord).

It is far from clear, however, that this is very meaningfully characterized as a "feudal" reaction in any of the senses in which that term is likely to be used by today's historians. For all the medieval terminology employed by the lawyers who served the lords as defenders of such actions, it is at least as reasonable to see these activities as the attempt of a landowning class to increase its capacity to produce for a growing national market. As cities flourished; as road networks grew; as the standing army consumed more horses, food, textiles; as the state bureaucrats continued their elaborate shipbuilding program in the vain hope of rivaling England on the seas—the demands for grain, meat, leather, hemp, and wood rose dramatically. We are not dealing here so much with lords trying to revive an aging medieval economy but with landholders trying to position themselves to take advantage of expanding market opportunities. By dispossessing their peasant dependents, gaining increasing and undivided control of land, and making peasant smallholding as precarious as possible (thereby forcing peasants to sell out), the substantial landholders not only expanded and consolidated their own holdings but also expanded the landless rural proletariat who were needed as agricultural laborers on those expanded holdings (or who worked for urban merchants in the expanding rural cottage-based textile industries).[17]

---

the collection of seigneurial dues. For various positions, see William Doyle, "Was There an Aristocratic Reaction in Pre-Revolutionary France?" in Douglas Johnson, ed., *French Society and the Revolution* (Cambridge: Cambridge University Press, 1976), 3–28; Reichardt and Schmitt, "Rupture ou continuité?"; Albert Soboul, "Sur le prélèvement féodal," in his *Problèmes paysans de la Révolution, 1789–1848* (Paris: Maspero, 1983), 89–115; and D. M. G. Sutherland, *France, 1789–1815: Revolution and Counterrevolution* (New York: Oxford University Press, 1986), 70–72.

17. Rural industry was probably expanding as merchant-employers reduced labor costs by

The forms and language surrounding an expansion of the lord's activities may have been "feudal," but what of the content? If the dominant rural strata were able to use the customary claims embodied in the terminology of the medieval past to increase their capacity to rationalize production on their own estates for the market, if they could employ the language of the Middle Ages while abandoning whatever there might once have been by way of patrimonial responsibilities to the underclass, ought we to speak of "feudalism" at all? The answer is yes if we want to employ the vocabulary of the Old Regime, but is very likely no if we are trying to identify a social order sharply differentiated from the capitalist era.

When the French peasantry rose against the so-called feudal and seigneurial rights in 1789, therefore, we might well wonder whether this was not so much as part of a triumphant vanguard action in alliance with the revolutionary bourgeoisie against a dying feudalism, as it was a rearguard struggle against a developing rural capitalism.[18] Indeed there is a considerable recent polemical literature on this question.[19] The debate could go on a long time, since the intertwining of "feudal" and "capitalist" actions was so profound that contemporary historians have no greater success in achieving any consensus on the assignment of French institutions to one or another

avoiding the urban guilds as well as hiring workers embedded in rural families with some revenue from agricultural labor.

18. Georges Lefebvre has some particularly pointed remarks on the anticapitalist aspect of peasant action in 1789 and beyond. See Georges Lefebvre, "La Révolution française et les paysans," in *Etudes sur la Révolution Française* (Paris: Presses Universitaires de France, 1963), 343. That the actual exploitation of noble holdings was carried out in as bourgeois a spirit as can be imagined is shown in several works of Robert Forster: *The Nobility of Toulouse in the Eighteenth Century* (Baltimore: Johns Hopkins University Press, 1960); "The Noble Wine Producers of the Bordelais in the Eighteenth Century," *Economic History Review* 14 (1961): 18–33; "The Provincial Noble: A Reappraisal," *American Historical Review* 68 (1963): 681–91. For appraisals of the debate around Lefebvre's viewpoint, see Peter M. Jones, "Georges Lefebvre and the French Revolution: Fifty Years On," *French Historical Studies* 16 (1990): 645–63; Peter McPhee, "The French Revolution, Peasants and Capitalism," *American Historical Review* 5 (1989): 1265–80. Barrington Moore, reviewing his own comparative examination of revolution and rural class relations from seventeenth-century England to twentieth-century Asia, has formulated a mournful generalization: "The chief social basis of radicalism has been the peasants and the smaller artisans in the towns. From these facts one may conclude that the wellsprings of human freedom lie not only where Marx saw them, in the aspirations of classes about to take power but perhaps even more in the dying wail of a class over whom the wave of progress is about to roll"; see his *Social Origins of Dictatorship and Democracy: Lord and Peasant in the Making of the Modern World* (Boston: Beacon, 1966), 505.

19. In addition to the works cited in the previous note, see Florence Gauthier, *La voie paysanne dans la Révolution française: L'exemple de la Picardie* (Paris: Maspero, 1977); Ado, *Krest'ianskoe dvizhenie;* Albert Soboul, ed., *Contributions à l'histoire paysanne de la Révolution française* (Paris: Editions Sociales, 1977); Guy-Robert Ikni, "Le mouvement paysan en Picardie: Meneurs, pratiques, maturation et signification historique," in Florence Gauthier and Guy-Robert Ikni, eds., *La Guerre du Blé au XVIIIe siècle: La critique populaire contre le libéralisme économique au XVIIIe siècle* (Montreuil: Editions de la Passion, 1988), 187–203.

category than did Merlin in finding a classification of seigneurial rights into "feudal" versus "legitimate property" that could retain widespread assent when challenged.

Defending Old Rights with New Ideas (or Using the New to Maintain the Old)

If the actual enforcement of the *droits féodaux* seems to fit a capitalist model of social relationships about as well as it does a feudal one, the same may be said for the justificatory legitimations invoked by defenders of the seigneurial system. One certainly does find what we may call the aristocratic defense of the structures of rural domination: namely the claim that the seigneurial rights are a constituent part of a structure of hierarchical domination on which a proper social order depends, in which each has his proper place but in which there are many different places (see Chapter 3, p. 86). Consider the language used in a lawsuit brought by the marquis of Castelmoron in 1776 against peasant violators of his exclusive rights to bear arms and hunt: "the natural liberty to hunt having been limited and restrained by the mores of peoples and the laws of sovereigns and a few other persons, he nevertheless observes with pain that there are vile and mechanical persons who undertake hunting, with firearms and otherwise, on the land and *seigneurie* of the said Castelmoron where the *seigneur* has the right of high, middle and low justice and consequently the capacity to forbid hunting and to hunt himself."[20]

Assertions of the essential character of status distinction do sometimes make their appearance in the noble *cahiers,* quite literally in the case of the nobility of Bazas, which, in its discussion of seigneurial rights, contends "that it is of the essence of monarchical government that there be distinctions of status, so that moderation in ideas may be maintained and subordination in the behavior and conduct of all men may be preserved" (*AP* 2:268). (This is the line of argument that Montesquieu had pursued with a special vigor.)[21]

The nobles of Nivernais et Donzois add that being publicly singled out by virtue of clear and visible status distinctions makes nobles feel they must live up to the qualities of their ancestors (*AP* 4:253). Here we find something close to the argument that the recognition of privilege need not merely be seen as a reward for responsibility, but that it is also a spur to, a source of

20. Cited in Anne-Marie Cocula-Vaillières, "La contestation des privilèges seigneuriaux dans le fonds des Eaux et Forêts. L'exemple acquitain dans la seconde moitié du XVIIIe siècle," in Jean Nicolas, ed., *Mouvements populaires et conscience sociale, XVIe–XIXe siècles* (Paris: Maloine, 1985), 211.

21. *De l'esprit des lois* (Paris: Société Les Belles Lettres, 1950), book 5, chap. 9.

responsibility. Help us put on the mask of authority, the Nivernais nobles urge, and our faces will grow to fit that mask.[22]

In one of the most careful efforts of Louis XVI to align himself with the new order of things, the king embraced the abandonment of the three estates yet maintained that a valuable and hereditary distinction adhered to the nobility: "everything that reminds a nation of the antiquity and continuity of the services of an honored race constitutes a distinction that nothing can destroy." He concluded that "those who, in all classes of society, aspire to serve their country effectively, and those who have already had the happiness of serving it, have an interest in respecting this transmission of titles or of memories, the most beautiful of all the legacies one can pass on to one's children" (*AP* 11:430).

Such an aristocrat's defense of the rural social order is unsurprising, to be sure; far more interesting is the degree to which the defenders of seigneurial claims had, by the spring of 1789, thoroughly assimilated the notion of private property as a sacred area beyond the legitimate reach of marauders (agents of the state most pointedly included) and worthy of defense by any properly constituted governing authority (see pp. 34, 86, 188). We are likely to associate the modern idea of property, when we consider the fragmented nature of rights over land embodied in the "sad remnants of the feudal regime" of the eighteenth century, with the physiocrats' advocacy of an absolute property, all rights over which are the owner's.[23]

From this point of view, what is striking about many of the *cahiers* in which the nobility defend their claims on peasant revenues and deference, is that the claim rests precisely on assimilating the feudal or seigneurial rights to private property, thereby conceiving of them as inviolable. Even the nobles of Bazas, cited above for their defense of a hierarchical social order, also speak of their "distinctions and prerogatives" as "property which no power on earth may infringe" (*AP* 2:267–68). Or consider the nobles of Saintonge, so insistent that their property rights (conflated with their "liberty") be defended by their deputies and for whom property includes a long list of seigneurial claims including fiefs (*AP* 5:665).

One of the few noble *cahiers* actually to defend the continued existence of fiefs, then, mounts its defense in the language of property rights. Are they defending "feudalism"? Embracing "capitalism"? The nobles of this district, like many of their fellows, have mounted a defense of feudal claims (even in

22. The arresting image of a face conforming to a mask is used to good effect in James Scott's magnificent essay *Domination and the Arts of Resistance: Hidden Transcripts* (New Haven: Yale University Press, 1990), 10–11. Scott got it from George Orwell's "Shooting an Elephant," in *Inside the Whale and Other Essays* (Harmondsworth: Penguin, 1962), 95–96.

23. For an interesting recent exposition, see Elizabeth Fox-Genovese, *Origins of Physiocracy,* 200–201, 228.

the most rigorous sense of rights associated with fiefs) in terms that are quite "bourgeois." This characteristic of their *cahiers* is not merely a desperate last-ditch attempt by the nobility on the eve of the Revolution to adopt the terms of their enemies. Regine Robin[24] has shown that eighteenth-century manuals and treatises on feudal and seigneurial rights had already adopted such bourgeois terms of discourse by deriving obligations from contracts freely entered into by two parties. The defenders of the "feudal" were already close to speaking of a world of creditors and debtors engaged in legitimate interchanges between freely consenting equals, structured by property relations. Neither the manuals studied by Robin nor most of the noble *cahiers* I have explored defend a social order in which landholding was part of a hierarchical system of political domination bound together by obligations of mutual support among unequals in which the superior party provided protection, the inferior aid.

The *cahiers* of the Third Estate are close in spirit. Consider the *cahier* adopted by the Third Estate of Nemours, largely written by a liberal noble whose official duties placed him among those in high office in charge of economic development. We read in this document of the powerful advantages of strengthening property rights: the more fully one is a proprietor, the more one is motivated to invest, thereby increasing yields. It is in the public interest that landowners not be burdened with seigneurial payments. On the other hand, seigneurial rights are themselves property. However, no one's property claims extend beyond the grave. A father, this *cahier* goes on, lacks the right "to commit his children to a semi-servitude." To contract an agreement that one's heirs will pay a seigneurial right forever with no possibility of redemption is to agree to give away what belongs to another and is therefore invalid. A full understanding of property rights must include others' rights and therefore a full respect for property requires an indemnification option (*AP* 4:197). The claim that seigneurial rights are property, then, while not fully acceptable without certain qualifications, has enough force that the compromise formula of indemnification, rather than outright abolition, is in order.

Notions of property were serviceable to defend the old order as well as attack it;[25] by giving due weight to the property rights of both those who paid and those who were paid seigneurial rights, moreover, one appeared to be led in the direction of indemnification. All positions, then, could be—and

24. Robin, "Fief et seigneurie." James Whitman has called attention to a significant current among Old Regime legal theorists that resisted treating the seigneurial regime as a body of debts among equals. See James Q. Whitman, " 'Les seigneurs descendent au rang de simples créanciers': Droit romain, droit féodal et Révolution," *Droits: Revue Française de Théorie Juridique* 17 (1993): 19–32.

25. To recall Chapter 2, the *cahiers* of the nobility are actually rather more likely to mount a defense of property rights than the *cahiers* of the Third Estate (66% vs. 50%).

were—justified in terms of property rights. Not only were rationalized forms of agricultural practice being developed in part through the use of medieval legal terminology to pressure recalcitrant peasant communities, but the jurists of the late eighteenth century were prone to see in seigneurial rights a form of private property rather than a mere obstacle to the full development of what many might hold to be the quintessentially capitalist institution. If the Revolution's champions were fond of the claim that the revolutionary order meant the entire destruction of the feudal regime, the detailed intertwining of the damned "feudal" and the sacralized "property" was very tight. The development of a rationale for detailed legislation in the countryside would be a very delicate problem.

Merlin Defines the Feudal Regime

The selection of Merlin de Douai as head of the National Assembly's committee charged with drawing up such legislation was symptomatic; Merlin had made his reputation before the Revolution through his ingenuity in the defense of lords' claims against their peasants. Merlin, for example, gained legal recognition for one lord's right to enlarge the roads through the local communal lands and to compel nearby peasant communities to pay the wages of the road crews.[26] His contributions to a major manual on seigneurial rights were, in the estimate of Georges Lefebvre,[27] very rigorous in their support of seigneurial domination. His legal rigor notwithstanding, Merlin saw the task confided him by the Assembly as fundamentally a political one: avoiding the hopeless alienation of the lords on the one hand and of the peasants on the other: "It is necessary to give the people a law whose justice will force into silence the egotistical feudatory who, for the last six months, has been screaming so indecently about spoliation, and a law whose wisdom may return to the course of duty the cultivator who has, for the moment, strayed out of resentment of long oppression" (*AP* 11:498–99). The very choice of Merlin for such a role may have been intended to reassure lords who worried about the meaning of August 4: Merlin's rigorous mind would be applied to finding a set of principles under which August 4 would turn out not to have expropriated the lords. Those principles would have to be found, for the claim that the "feudal regime" had been abolished could not very well be retracted—not if the National Assembly were to hope for a pacified countryside and not if the National Assembly were to continue to fulfill its own hopes of breaking with a past for which "feudal" was becoming a global summary.

Now the intellectual task facing Merlin and his committee was how to

26. Georges Lefebvre, *Les paysans du Nord,* 155, 158.
27. Ibid., 158.

keep the peasants paying the legitmate claims of property owners (good) and yet maintain the vision of a decisive break with a feudal past (bad) when the two were in practice and in eighteenth-century legal thought so closely bound together. Merlin developed the distinction between those claims of the lords that were founded on a violent usurpation and those deriving from a freely consented contract. The former, the operational specification of "feudal" for Merlin, were of course to be abolished (since the "entire feudal regime" was abolished, after all). The latter, however, were property, and not to be touched without proper compensation.

The possibility of adjusting the terms of indemnification to meet the political needs of the moment made this an especially tempting option indeed. If the rate were set sufficiently high so that no one could conceivably pay, the National Assembly could adhere to its claim to have made peasant emancipation possible without actually altering peasant burdens in the slightest; if the rate were set just low enough so that payment was conceivable, then those who genuinely wished the long-term elimination of the *droits féodaux* could see that goal realized with minimal embitterment of the holders of those rights (not to mention the lucrative rewards for themselves to the extent that these very legislators were seigneurs); and, should peasant resistance be greater than anticipated, the indemnification rate could be set lower still.[28] The very complexity of the indemnification issue guaranteed considerable delay in implementation,[29] which by itself might have recommended it to many deputies who were uncertain as to how to deal with rural France.

The contractual versus the usurped: this remarkable formulation of the committee on Feudal Rights had a double beauty. In the first place, since no one could establish the consensual or coerced nature of any particular claim, the lords' rights could be assigned to one or the other category as seemed expedient at the moment. On one level, this may be seen as an attempt to recover what seems to have been the initial goal of the plan hatched in the Breton Club on August 3: the promise of abolition and the reality of indemnification at rates yet to be decided, but under appropriate political conditions fixable at a rate unpayable by the peasantry. Once viscount de

28. The history of the most striking precedent, if reflected upon by the deputies, would surely have suggested the possibilities of fine-tuning within an indemnification framework. In 1762, the duke of independent Savoy freed peasants to indemnify their lords for certain rights. After a period of what was judged inadequate peasant response, the terms were reset in the peasants' favor in 1771. Noble and clerical protest led to further modification in 1778. (In 1790, the peasants of Savoy, like their French neighbors, rebelled against the inadequate reforms.) See Max Bruchet, *L'abolition des droits seigneuriaux en Savoie (1761–1793)* (Annecy: Hérisson, 1908); Jean Nicolas, *La Révolution française dans les Alpes: Dauphiné et Savoie, 1789–1799* (Toulouse: Privat, 1989), 103–10.

29. See the complaints of a spokesman for the Committee on Feudal Rights on the difficulties of fixing the rates of indemnification: *AP* 12:387.

Noailles broke into the script and introduced the distinction between abolition with and without compensation it was no longer possible to abolish nothing whatsoever; once the flood of emotion, resignation, and calculation introduced the discussion of all sorts of other claims, more genuine change in who paid what to whom was unavoidable. Merlin's committee's work, then, may be read as a remarkable attempt to put most of a cat back into a bag. If the feudal regime is limited, verbally, to what is already "completely abolished" then it follows, does it not, that whatever claims on peasants remain are not part of the feudal regime?

Almost from the beginning of his assignment, then, Merlin placed the total destruction of the feudal regime in the recent past rather than the indefinite future. In a statement defining the task of the Committee on Feudal Rights on September 4, 1789, Merlin pondered the immediate consequences of terminating the feudal regime. (For example, "As soon as the feudal regime is destroyed, does it follow that one ought no longer to render *foi et hommage* [etc.]?" *AP* 8:575). The destruction was still located in an indefinite future. But by February 8, Merlin placed it in the past[30] and therefore—and from then on—his speeches would focus on the rationale for indemnification and strategies to assure payment until that indemnification is effected. If it isn't feudal it must be "property," to be respected and collected. Thus, the Merlin project, by insisting upon the entire abolition of the feudal regime as already accomplished, amounted to a legitimation of all other payments.

Merlin's committee recommended wiping out the surface rust of feudalism to reveal the shiny property not far beneath. Merlin repeated the hypnotic refrain "there are no more fiefs, therefore . . ." many times—and the conclusion that followed from the abolition of fiefs, was that payments due lords were no longer feudal (the feudal regime being entirely destroyed) and therefore must be paid (*AP* 11:500). Invoking the awesome overturning of the "antique oak" of the feudal regime that had grown over the kingdom, Merlin went on to describe "the conceptual center" of the legislation: "The feudal rights, by virtue of the destruction of the feudal regime, have been converted into simple ground rents" (*AP* 11:498, 500). In Merlin's reasoning, therefore, the very image of a decisive rupture became transformed into the justification for collecting the same sums from the same burdened country people. As his countrymen still say, "Plus ça change, plus c'est la même chose."

It is possible, then, to read Merlin's project of March 1790 (and perhaps the original intent of the duke d'Aiguillon and his fellows on August 4, 1789) as effecting the transformation of "lords" into "proprietors" by shifting the

30. Note that this coincides with the insurrectionary wave of December 1789–February 1790. See *AP* 11:498–518.

juridical rationale for their claims without in any substantial way diminishing those claims themselves. This verbal sleight-of-hand was not simply the clever innovation of Merlin, but was rooted in important ways in the intellectual habits of the jurists of the late eighteenth century. Such, in any event, is the interpretation of these intellectual acts given by Régine Robin.[31] Studying some of the more significant prerevolutionary manuals of seigneurial rights (including one of which Merlin was co-author), Robin notes the degree to which such manuals were already permeated with "bourgeois" concepts. The seigneurial rights were conceived as property; their acquisition was seen as "contractual." Rather than evoke, as a legitimating context, an image of a properly hierarchical world in which men and their lords entered into relationships in which each filled appropriate obligations to the other, with the nature of those obligations depending on one's role within the superior-subordinate pair, the eighteenth-century jurists had already slipped into the language of property legitimately exchanged by freely contracting juridical equals.

Merlin merely makes this reasoning explicit by superimposing upon the distinction between the violently coerced (= "usurped") and the contractual (= "payment for a concession of land") a second distinction made in the terminology of Roman law. Merlin distinguishes between "personal rights" and "real rights." Personal rights derive from a hierarchical relationship among unequals; since they are rooted in the greater power of the one over the other, they are explicitly or implicitly coercive. They have their origins in an era when sovereignty was parceled out into feudal anarchy and are, in the enlightened eighteenth century, wholly illegitimate. On the other hand, there are the "real rights," which do not derive from the superior status of one man over another, but are, in their origins, freely consented contractual arrangements among juridical equals. A balance of public purpose and private property was achieved by recognizing state appropriation of property in return for adequate compensation, tacked on at the last minute as the final article of the Declaration of the Rights of Man and Citizen,[32] adopted two weeks after the declarations on seigneurial rights. By declaring the greater part of the seigneurial rights to be presumptively within the "contractual" category, Merlin, in effect, imagines the social relations at the time the rights originated to have permitted a freely consented contract.[33] A class of lords, who once might have proudly proclaimed their personal superiority

31. Robin, "Fief et seigneurie." See also Régine Robin, *Histoire et linguistique* (Paris: Armand Colin, 1973), 181–83.

32. Georges Lefebvre, *The Coming of the French Revolution,* 147.

33. If the feudal past carried a burden of anarchic violence for Merlin and many of his contemporaries, one might well wonder why so many of the seigneurial rights are presumptively contractual. But no one demanded that Merlin produce a coherent picture of the political economy of medieval landholding.

and on the basis of that superior status defended their prerogatives, were now redefined as merely the juridical equals of their peasants, who, having freely consented in the past, must now be held to continue to pay in the present, unless, of course, they paid adequate compensation.

This line of defense of seigneurial rights was widely taken up. A creative effort to establish a contractual aspect to a claim on publicly displayed deference, for example, is found in a letter to a noble friend written by Grellet, deputy of Haute-Marche, on June 2, 1790. (He has just stopped signing himself Grellet de Beauregard). He comments that the seigneurial claim to a family bench in church "cannot be preserved" if it is held to derive from being a seigneur; if, however, it can be made out that one is a "patron," "it seems to me that [the benches] are presumed to have been granted as the price of a concession and benefit." The church bench would be redefined from a sign of the superiority of one man over others, now illegal, to an object acquired by contract. ("This motive is to my eyes infinitely more respectable.") But Grellet adds that he doesn't know if this reasoning will work.[34]

This example suggests the historically arbitrary character of the assignment of specific rights to one or the other category.[35] "Historically" arbitrary in that one presumes that rights are coerced or contractual when no proof one way or the other was possible in most cases. The law recognized such a gray area in principle: the presumptive categorization of some rights could be challenged in court by allowing one party to have the right to produce documents that in practice could only rarely be produced. What was historically arbitrary could be categorized in accord with political judgment. We saw in Chapter 3 that the countryside showed some support for indemnification of periodic rentlike dues, and relatively little or even no support for indemnifying other rights. The law of March 15–28, 1790, roughly parallels this pattern, suggesting that when Merlin proposed indemnification for *champart*, say, there was some sense of at least the possibility of peasant acquiescence.

The arbitrary character also permitted the moving of rights from one

34. Jean-Baptiste Grellet de Beauregard, "Lettres de Grellet de Beauregard," *Société des sciences naturelles et archéologiques de la Creuse* (1899): 84.

35. The decisions being taken by legislators on a national scale concerning broad classes of rights were being replicated in miniature around the country as thousands of lords made political decisions and intellectual distinctions in deciding precisely what to attempt to collect and what to abandon. In the summer of 1790, the council that administered the vast holdings of the duke de Penthièvre, for example, pondered an annual obligation of the village of Essay near Châteauvillain to make an annual payment, a sum of twenty-three livres and one chicken. Out of some combination of legal scholarship and political judgment, they decided that the chicken was "personal" and thereby abolished while the "real" claim of cash was to be paid, pending indemnification; see Jean Duma, "Le Conseil du duc de Penthièvre et le mouvement populaire (1789–1792)," in Jean Nicolas, ed., *Mouvements populaires et conscience sociale, XVIe–XIXe siècles* (Paris: Maloine, 1985), 665.

category to the next. Thus successive moments of insurrection between March 1790 and the spring of 1792 led the assembly to shift categories by way of accommodation. The law of April 13–20, 1791, enumerated some forty rights to be abolished that were not specifically indicated in the original classification (*AP* 25:4–7). Finally, intellectual inconsistencies in even the initial laws seem calibrated to meet some sense of what the countryside might tolerate. Thus, improbably, *mainmorte réele* ("real" mainmorte) is lumped with the "personal" rights and therefore abolished without indemnification (as the peasants demand) (*AP* 12:173). Perhaps, but doubtfully, the Committee just tripped on the intellectual complexity of the task. But we may have even less doubt when we consider the Committee's actions on seigneurial usurpations of common lands. The Committee initially urged—and the Assembly adopted—a moratorium of thirty years. Usurpations that took place further back were not annulled even though the central explicit statement of principles required the law to claim that other usurpations back into the Middle Ages were now to be undone. Of course, as we saw in the previous chapter, all the revolutionary legislatures were politically skittish about land ownership issues and tended to hunt for compromises (especially if compromises could be slanted toward larger owners). Thus all "usurped" rights were to be abolished even if usurped a thousand years before—unless it was the hot topic of the commons that was at issue.[36] The abstract rationale of dividing rights into the violently usurped and the contractual was not, then, consistently practiced even on the conceptual level, quite apart from its empirically preposterous character.

The dramatic alterations in the laws brought on by the wartime mobilization in conjunction with continuing peasant disturbances (see Chapter 8) radically altered the options facing peasant and lord. The series of laws enacted by the Legislative Assembly in spring and summer (especially June 18, August 20, and August 25 of 1792), reversed the burden of proof. Now the lords were in the situation of having to prove the contractual nature of their claims. (The very few lords who might actually have an original contract—the "primordial title"—would have to consider the probably foolhardy act of trying to sue a peasant community before a revolutionary judge in order to claim the same sorts of rights his neighbor's sons were fighting to overturn in Belgium, Germany, and Italy.) But the overarching legal theory was still maintained: that there were contractual and there were coerced seigneurial claims.

Not until the law of July 17, 1793, did an even more radicalized Convention grant the abolition of the entire structure when confronted with counterrevo-

36. These inconsistencies in legal reasoning are pointed to by Philippe Sagnac and Pierre Caron, *Les comités des droits féodaux et de législation et l'abolition du régime seigneurial (1789–1793)* (Paris: Imprimerie Nationale, 1907), xii–xiii.

lution, although no longer facing down significant antiseigneurial actions. And what of the rationale for the law of July 1793? The existing written record indicates no debate, nothing but a brief preliminary mention of a law in preparation on June 3 and again on July 15. Was there another behind-the-scenes preparation as on August 3, 1789? We know nothing but that after several years of public rhetoric saturated with Merlin's distinctions, the seigneurial rights were now to be thrown away; one cannot say "unceremoniously thrown away," for the titles, when they existed, were to be very ceremoniously burned. All seigneurial rights were now regarded as violently obtained (and any purported evidence to the contrary was to be eliminated by fire.) We have some hints that the lexical practices of the deputies, even when focused on seigneurial rights rather than the broad meaning of the Revolution, were overflowing their own effort at a narrow definition of the feudal. The preface to the law of August 20, 1792, spoke of the need to emancipate property to assure "the absolute independence of citizens."[37] It went on to urge a speeding-up of this emancipation by easing "the indemnification of formerly feudal rights." By implication, at least some of these rights that were not initially abolished outright were "feudal" (until they became "formerly"). And on June 3, 1793, a deputy called for completing "the destruction of *la féodalité*" (*AP* 66:4), indicating, again, that not all encompassed within the feudal had actually been destroyed by the acts of August 4–11, 1789. The narrow definition, though promoted with great energy, was failing even in the legislature, let alone the village.

And even after July 17, 1793, attempts to control words failed to control events. One telling symptom of the impossible intellectual task, if undertaken seriously, of the initial plan to separate with clarity "property" from "feudal rights" was the storm of protest against the legislated burning of the seigneurial records from holders of what almost no one (except some southwestern sharecroppers?) denied were property claims. These very same documents sometimes also contained the only valid records of the ex-lords' claims to rent.

Merlin's Reasoning and Noble Ideology

Merlin's reasoning may have appealed precisely because it systematized the way the nobility were already inclined to defend the seigneurial rights. Let us consider what the nobility did not do. Régine Robin's research on seigneurial manuals depicts an aristocracy that has largely abandoned the claims of God's immutable hierarchy as the basis for justification of its

37. Sagnac and Caron, *Les comités des droits féodaux*, 768.

holdings, as revealed in the language of practitioners of feudal law in the eighteenth century. We may review some further evidence on this point largely drawn from the *cahiers* of the nobility. There are at least three significant elements that the *cahiers* reveal to us. The nobility did not express a vision of a profoundly hierarchical social totality, they did not ground their social vision in divine sanction, and they did not maintain a structure of mutual support with the human bearers of God's word.

To elaborate each point in turn: first, we find only the most minimal interest in retaining any of the hierarchical structure of "feudalism." When Merlin contended that something besides fiefs was the object, at that moment, of discussions of "the feudal regime," the *complexum feudale* that he borrowed from Dumoulin is not something broader than the structure of fiefs and the relations of lord and vassal (in the original sense of that term) but which includes those fiefs and those social relationships. Merlin's *complexum feudale* turns out to be not so much an expansion of a concept to cover more than the fiefs, but something quite different than the world of the fiefs altogether.

The fiefs themselves, in fact, can easily be abolished because no one, including the nobility, cares any more. More generally, the *cahiers* display very little concern over those rights that involve formal recognition of one's location within a network conceived of as linking men unequal in status. The nobility that thus presents itself in the *cahiers* has a sense of the nobility-commoner divide as a significant marker to be retained; but internally the nobility is unstructured. Not many noble *cahiers* make this claim explicitly, but their almost total failure to mention the minutiae of status gradations show the degree to which the nobility of present and future are conceived as equal among themselves, if perhaps superior collectively to the Third Estate (see Chapter 3, p. 61).

Although noble *cahiers* retain the language of devotion to the king, it is striking how little this language has to do with a feudal hierarchy. They still speak of their respect, gratitude, love, fidelity, devotion, attachment, and obedience to their king and the king to some extent still preserves the medieval attributes of "goodness" and, to a lesser extent, "prudence." Nonetheless, the king is practically never located at the apex of a feudal hierarchy.[38] The nobility of St. Mihiel are unusual in recognizing Louis "in his quality as suzerain" but hardly honor him for it because he is thereby implicated in the extortion to which all local possessors of fiefs are subject

38. Medieval French kings were conventionally ascribed "three qualities which were those of God himself: *bonitas, sapientia,* and *potentia.*" Note that the third member of this particular trinity—power—is almost wholly missing in the *cahiers'* invocation of Louis XVI. See Bernard Guénée, *States and Rulers in Later Medieval Europe* (Oxford: Basil Blackwell, 1988), 71; Shapiro and Markoff, *Revolutionary Demands: A Content Analysis of the Cahiers de Doléances of 1789* (Stanford: Stanford University Press, 1997), chap. 19.

(*AP* 2:236). If a minuscule number of *cahiers* address him as *seigneur,* an equal number use a much newer model of authority, the citizen-king.[39] And perhaps the marquis de Ferrières expressed what others felt when he found, as compensation for social democratization, that at least others would no longer so easily be able to look down on him.[40]

Second, the claim that social order rested on divine warrant, had been supplanted to a large extent in the *cahiers* of Third Estate and nobility alike by arguments from history or functional utility.[41] The Third Estate of Nemours, for example, championed indemnification by invoking "natural law," that ambiguous way-station between God and a desanctified world: natural law, the text suggests, requires that debtors be able to pay off their debts (and therefore perpetual payments are improper). But this natural-law argument is almost submerged by utilitarian appeals to the increase in agricultural yields sure to follow on termination of seigneurial payments (*AP* 4:197). The particular dangers of arguments from history and utility were, to be sure, that others might have their own interpretations of that history and their own evaluations of that utility.

Third and finally, there was a weakening, if not a breakdown, in the lord-church nexus. The symbolization of the interpenetration of the religious realm with immutable social hierarchy manifest in such practices as the lord's church-bench and the monasteries' claim to seigneurial rights had long helped weave the sense of divine warrant into the seigneurial fabric. But the first two orders were far from standing shoulder to shoulder in their *cahiers* and beyond on defense of each others' rights. The *cahiers* reveal a certain lack of mutual support between the first two orders. The noble *cahiers* do not defend peasant payments to clerics, for example (see Table 3.1). And church prelates on the night of August 4 were more than willing to sacrifice the pleasures of lay seigneurs. The marquis de Ferrières well expressed

39. Nobility of Clermont-Ferrand: "A citizen King invites us to come . . . and work to reform the abuses" (*AP* 2:766).

40. Ferrières, reflecting wistfully to his sister on August 10, 1789, on the losses of the nobility, finds some consolation in a more democratic climate: "all in all, I prefer that the man in the street think he's my equal than to see a Great Lord think me his inferior and treat me like those he pays and feeds"; see Charles-Elie de Ferrières, *Correspondance inédite (1789, 1790, 1791)* (Paris: Armand Colin, 1932), 120.

41. I will not comment here on the *cahiers* of the clergy, which, unfortunately for the discussion at hand, were not included in the Shapiro-Markoff *cahiers* data archive. Those who controlled the periodic assemblies of the clergy of France appear to have maintained a consistent image of a linkage of throne and altar throughout the century; it is worth asking whether the clergy's assemblies in 1789, when the hierarchy was so profoundly challenged, maintained the sacred connection beyond the weakened forms it retains in the noble and Third Estate texts. See Michel Péronnet, "La théorie de l'ordre public exposée par les assemblées du clergé: Le trône et l'autel (seconde moitié du XVIIIe siècle)," in Jean Nicolas, ed., *Mouvements populaires et conscience sociale, XVIe–XIXe siècles* (Paris: Maloine, 1985), 625–34.

the indifference with which a portion of the nobility regarded the problems of church in revolution. He supported the nationalization of church land of November 2, 1789; castigated as intolerant and fanatic those priests who treated the juring clergy with disdain; and found the clergy to be responsible for much of the conflict of the Revolution.[42] (To be sure, the staunch Catholicism of other nobles and the noble origins of the clerical hierarchy provided an important nucleus of persons and an ideological coloration to the counterrevolution.)[43]

Legislators Maintain a Broad Definition and a Narrow One; Peasants Misunderstand

The developing tendency of the defenders of seigneurial rights to eschew religious linkages, disdain a feudal hierarchy, and adopt a contractual view of legitimation provided only the weakest of buttresses against the onslaught of those determined on removing impediments to progress in the name of precisely the same principles of unencumbered property rights. It did, however, also furnish the possibility of the particular illusionary legislative strategy of Merlin: to denounce rights grounded in the hierarchical principles now sloughed off and *therefore* to regard what was left—namely, most of what peasants directly paid lords—as unassailable.

In a remarkable statement to the National Assembly on June 15, 1791—(does the timing respond to the spurt of unrest in that month? see Table 6.3), Merlin insisted on the moral basis for enforcing seigneurial payments. He began by celebrating the abolition of the feudal regime, understood as rights of one person over another. But rights arising from concessions of land that are subsumed under "the sacred and inviolable rights of property" are a different matter entirely. The legislators quite naturally expected that rural peace would have been restored. But peasant disturbances have continued, Merlin acknowledged, and for two reasons. The first is that "enemies of the Revolution" have misled the country people into disorder. And second, some local administrators responsible for National Property have lacked the courage to go on collecting seigneurial rights and thereby have spread a spirit of insubordination. Merlin went on to describe the proper procedure for contesting a seigneurial claim that had not, perhaps,

42. See Aulard's introduction to Ferrières, *Correspondance*.

43. See Timothy Tackett, *Becoming a Revolutionary: The Deputies of the French National Assembly and the Emergence of a Revolutionary Culture (1789–1790)* (Princeton: Princeton University Press, 1996), on the religious aspect of the National Assembly's right.

been properly understood "although very clear." (This was followed by a score of very dense paragraphs that it is difficult to believe could have been grasped by a listener, particularly on a warm June day in a stuffy hall with poor acoustics.) He expressed the belief that the proper understanding of the law "will bring all difficulty to an end." If that fails, however, one must look to the judiciary, the local administrations, the National Guard, and the army. But force "shall surely be rarely necessary" for the citizens of the countryside shall appreciate the benefits of the Revolution "and they shall all feel since they have become the equals of their former lords in rights, that these former lords, by that fact alone, must peacefully enjoy their properties, just like themselves" (*AP* 27:238–42).

Merlin is a schoolmaster here: he hopes and expects that the peasants can be taught to see their errors. They have misunderstood the law, not having grasped the distinction between personal and real rights. They have not seen the benefits the Revolution has given them. They have not seen the justice in the property rights of former lords. But the schoolmaster can be stern. Pointing out the coercive capacities that can be marshaled, he expects that the people of the countryside "will not cause the National Assembly to regret the benefits" it has accorded them; even those who do not appreciate the justice of the new law or who simply misunderstand it, can understand the pointlessness of resistance and "will hurry" to pay "what they cannot escape." Merlin thus grants the villagers the capacity to understand force (*AP* 27:242).

In the legislative rhetoric the radical break in history effected by the rapid and total destruction of an institution so central that it penetrated all the nooks and crannies of the national existence coexisted with the unending efforts at restricting change and limiting the threat from below. The emotional exaltation of overthrowing history coexisted with carefully thought-out measures of damage control.

What coexisted for legislators could be experienced as contradictory for peasants. If continuing peasant insurrection seemed, to puzzled legislators, a sign of incomprehension, ingratitude, or "sedition," peasants could find the legislation equally baffling and equally in need of explanation. On December 7, 1790, anxious officials in Cahors wrote to the Assembly that extensive peasant turbulence has been in considerable measure provoked by the claim that the decrees on seigneurial rights were fake: they were not, so it was rumored locally, the real acts of the National Assembly, but fraudulent versions put out by the former lords (*AP* 21:457). A very thorough report on that situation put out by two investigators sent by the Assembly to explain the local disturbances never directly asked why such a claim might seem plausible in the countryside.[44]

44. Jacques Godard and Léonard Robin, *Rapport de Messieurs J. Godard et L. Robin, commissaires*

In February 1790 Merlin had explained how total was the break with the past: "Messieurs, in destroying the feudal regime; in overturning, to use a well-known expression of Montesquieu, this antique oak whose branches covered the entire surface of the French empire while its unknown roots reach back into the customs and government of the barbarians who expelled the Romans from Gaul. . . . You have taken on a great task" (*AP* 11:498). But three insurrection-filled years later Isoré commented on the floor of the Convention that the Revolution had not destroyed the tree of feudalism, but only pruned it (*AP* 68:19).

One way of describing the compromise of March 1790, then, was as an arrangement in which the lords would either keep most of their claims on direct payments (because the peasants couldn't pay back at the high rates and stringent modalities), now justified in terms of the new ideals of property, or, sometimes, receive generous financial returns for their abolition. The peasants were to get the generous knowledge that what they were paying was now consented by them rather than coerced from them: now they were to pay and like it. And how disappointing that they didn't seem to like it!

The tone of some of the subsequent angry, hurt, frustrated, and surprised legislators discovering that country people were not more prone to pay legitimate property claims than they had been to make the same payments when they were illegitimate and feudal was surely sometimes put on, but sometimes it appears to be genuine puzzlement. At least some legislators seemed to really think this plan would work. It is as if the delegates felt that renaming things truly constituted a change in their essences, as if words had magical properties.[45] At least one deputy saw it that way from the start. In describing, two days later, the plan worked out on August 3, Parisot tells us that rather than take the fruitless route of introducing just another motion, a group of about one hundred decided "to use a kind of magic."[46] Let us recall how rapidly the insurrections were dropping off, just as soon as the declaration was issued (see Fig. 8.1). Would not such an apparent reward for their efforts be experienced by some legislators as a validation of the efficacy of their words?

civils, envoyés par le roi, dans le département de Lot, en exécution du décret de l'Assemblée Nationale, du 13 décembre, 1790 (Paris: Imprimerie Nationale, 1791).

45. Consider, for example, Grégoire's comment on his own coining of "vandalism" ("I created the word to kill the thing") or the proposal of a deputy in the Thermidorean Convention "to exclude the word 'revolutionary' from the language," killing the thing, one might say, by uncreating the word. And sometimes the thing might cause the word. Stanislas de Clermont-Tonnerre told the National Assembly: "Everything is new for us. We are heading towards regeneration and have created words to express new ideas." See Henri Grégoire, *Mémoires* (Paris: A. Dupont, 1837), 1:346; Ferdinand Brunot, *Histoire de la langue française de ses origines à nos jours,* vol. 9, *La Révolution et l'Empire* (Paris: Armand Colin, 1967), part 2, 656; *AP* 9:603.

46. Quoted in Lefebvre, *The Coming of the French Revolution,* 136.

We need also to see the degree to which, in the heightened atmosphere of 1789, intellectuals in public life in France found power in words; indeed, were drunk on words.[47] There are all the neologisms of the revolutionary era: the imports, generally from England (like "commons"), the retrieving of words from classical educations and, dusting them off for application to the struggles of the hour (like "democrat" or "agrarian law"), the infusion of richer meanings into initially limited terms (like "revolution"), the metaphors used for the unprecedented (like "left" and "right"). Philippe Roger has shown how word-obsessed both revolutionaries and counterrevolutionaries were. As revolutionaries coined new terms, counterrevolutionaries, pioneering deconstructionists, issued debunking dictionaries.[48] Eventually the terms for space and time were changed (the metric system, the revolutionary toponomy, the new calendar). And if altering the language of the French was difficult enough, other languages were to be seen as beyond reform; as Barère was to put it in a much-cited speech: "federalism and superstition speak Breton; emigration and hatred for the Republic speak German; counterrevolution speaks Italian and fanaticism speaks Basque" (*AP* 83:715).

The Revolution was many things and one of them was, as Philippe Roger observes, a logomachy, a war about words. Talleyrand spoke for many when he characterized the National Assembly "that surely knows . . . the power of the word and that knows the extent to which words are the stuff of empire or rather how much effect they have upon ideas and through ideas upon habits."[49] In such a logogenetic view of social transformation, to define feudalism is to control human action.[50] And, therefore, peasants who rebel are mostly diagnosed as not understanding. As chair of the Committee on Reports, charged with keeping track of sedition, Grégoire reported some five causes of the peasant risings of winter 1789–90 in Brittany and the Southwest, first and foremost of which was "ignorance of the language" (*AP* 11:536). He proposed mobilizing the parish priesthood in an instructional campaign. Investigators Godard and Robin, sent to the Southwest, were prepared from the beginning to see rural resistance as composed of a small number of "instigators" to be dealt with by force and a much larger number

47. The starting point for study of revolutionary language is still Brunot, *Histoire de la langue française*.

48. Philippe Roger, "Dictionnaire contre Révolution"; "La langue révolutionnaire au tribunal des écrivains," in R. Campagnoli, ed., *Robespierre & Co.* (Bologna: CLUEB, 1988), 1:175–93; "Le débat sur la 'langue révolutionnaire,' " in Jean-Claude Bonnet, *La Carmagnole des muses: L'homme de lettres et l'artiste dans la Révolution* (Paris: Armand Colin, 1988), 157–84; Roger Barny, "Les mots et les choses chez les hommes de la Révolution française," *La Pensée,* no. 202 (1978): 96–115.

49. Quoted in Roger, "La langue révolutionnaire," 160–61.

50. A novelist would be reproached for straining credibility if he invented a revolutionary elite, ready to see words controlling things, who, searching for a chief architect of "a kind of magic," came up with someone named Merlin as its master magician.

of the "misled" who need only proper instruction.[51] True to their views of peasants errant by ignorance, Godard and Robin reported any number of incidents where they instructed peasants on their responsibilities, on the meaning of the law, on the benefits of the Revolution. The peasants, in their report, invariably were grateful for the civics lessons thus offered them. Like many other teachers, Godard and Robin don't inquire whether their pupils might be buttering them up by helping them see themselves as successful instructors. Rabusson-Lamothe, a deputy to the Legislative Assembly from Puy-de-Dôme, commented on subsistence disturbances during the insurrectionary wave of winter 1792 that the only solution to popular disturbance was patient education "that may in time show the misled their true interests."[52] For his part, Merlin generally sees the failure to comply with his carefully crafted edicts as misunderstandings. Control over words is central to the legislators' conception of control over deeds.[53] So Merlin is puzzled as to why the peasants' deeds don't accord with the legislators' words. A fundamentally pedagogic stance was also embodied in *La Feuille Villageoise,* the Revolution's Parisian-authored newspaper that aimed, highly unusually, at a peasant audience, and whose editorial committee included a deputy to the National Assembly from Nîmes, Rabaut Saint-Etienne. In 1791, a "Notice to all subscribers" offered the observation that "village disorders have hardly any origin other than ignorance."[54] Even the king could attribute rural disturbances to the misled (*AP* 11:430–31).

The legislators on August 4 and on any number of other occasions felt they were making history at the moment they acted. We have here some sense of the power of words to be more than words. Consider the contention of Boissy d'Anglas in the Convention: "To dictate the destiny of the world, you need only will. You are the creators of a new world: say that there shall

51. Godard and Robin, *Rapport,* for example, 13 (and passim).

52. Antoine Rabusson-Lamothe, *Lettres sur l'Assemblée Législative (1791–1792)* (Paris: Aubry, 1870), 115.

53. One wonders to what degree this attribution of power to language is rooted in the intellectual culture of the eighteenth century and to what degree in the specific context of the revolutionary legislatures where a large number of people met in a vast chamber, with poor acoustics, for long hours. Only a master of words could get any attention at all and in the unsettled turmoil of 1789 and beyond, among the revolutionary elites, words were power. Memoirs of prominent revolutionaries are full of self-presentations (and of remembrances of others) in which verbal brilliance plays a great role. "When so-and-so said this, how rich, witty, pointed was my reply" is a prominent theme in these texts.

54. Béatrice Didier "La Feuille Villageoise: Un dialogue Paris-Province pendant la Révolution," in Robert Chagny, ed., *Aux origines provinciales de la Révolution* (Grenoble: Presses Universitaires de Grenoble, 1990), 267–78. For more on this newspaper, see Melvin Edelstein, *La Feuille Villageoise. Communication et information dans les régions rurales pendant la Révolution* (Paris: Commission d'Histoire Economique et Sociale de la Révolution, 1977).

be light and there shall be light."[55] The deputies could create "the feudal regime": it was in their power to conceive of a set of institutions they believed they had destroyed and to thereby experience the Revolution as creating the wholly new. They could not, however, so easily create the experience of the people of the French countryside. The feudal regime of the peasants was not "the feudal regime" that was "abolished in its entirety" between August 4 and August 11. The deputies could invent words but they couldn't invent the country people (although they could invent "the people" as well as "the brigands," "the peasant idiots," "the fanatics"). Insurrectionary peasants who refused to be invented and insurrectionary Parisians who kept shaking up the legislatures were recalcitrant realities to which the legislature ultimately adapted by going much farther than it initially planned.

Monarchy

One of the central dramas of the Revolution's early years was the unraveling of the arrangement that institutionally placed an elected legislature side by side with a hereditary monarch. Ideologically there was a tension between finding the fount of legitimate authority in popular sovereignty and nonetheless retaining a place in public life for a man whose own claims to authority had heretofore rested on divine sanction. Historians have tended, recently, to emphasize the elements in the revolutionaries' outlook that made stable compromise unlikely: in the transference of a sense of sovereignty from king to assembly, the new political order was from the beginning latently republican, particularly as monarchical political culture had accustomed participants to speak of sovereignty as unshared:[56] from a monarch who fully embodies sovereignty to an assembly that does so was a less radical transition than any notion of institutional compromise and negotiation. The hope of balancing the power of the king and the rights of the nation "by a just equilibrium"[57] would have required enormous care and forebearance on both sides. Within such a structure, Louis refused to dutifully play his part and ultimately provoked his removal and death. When we look a bit more closely at the actions of the king that intensified legislative ill-will, we find that one of the initial difficulties was over the fate of seigneurial rights. Just

55. Quoted in Mona Ozouf, "La Révolution française et l'idée de l'homme nouveau," in Colin Lucas, ed., *The French Revolution and the Creation of Modern Political Culture,* vol. 2, *The Political Culture of the French Revolution* (New York: Pergamon Press, 1988), 220.

56. This is a common enough phrase in the *cahiers*. See, for example, the nobles of Etain, *AP* 2:214.

57. Third Estate of Cahors, *AP* 5:409.

as the night of August 4 led to tensions with Rhenish princes, which in turn became an opportunity for interstate tension to be couched in terms of the opposition of the Revolution to feudalism, the falling-out of king and legislature also came to align Louis with the defenders of the feudal regime.

There is little that was overtly antimonarchical at the onset of revolution. The assemblies in large numbers spoke of their respect, gratitude, and love for their paternal king and in somewhat smaller numbers of their fidelity, devotion, attachment, and obedience to their just and benevolent monarch.[58] A substantial number of noble and Third Estate *cahiers* still described the king as "sacred" (although one may well wonder what they meant by this). Desired change was presented as happening together with the king, under his auspices or through his agency. For some assemblies, indeed, the Estates-General was described as a vehicle for bringing the French, through representatives, into contact with the sovereign whose personal healing touch was now to "remedy the ills of the kingdom and soothe the oppressed class."[59] Well into the fall, the lively press was associating a beneficent and paternal king with the renewal of France, although after the October days, a few journalists, especially on the right, began to see king and Revolution as opposed.[60]

Those who hoped to bring about change together with the king could draw upon current understandings of the trajectory of French history as well as recent events in bolstering an image of a monarchy in tandem with a reformed seigneurialism. To begin with, many writers on the history of the monarchy for the past half-century had counterposed that monarchy to an earlier epoch of savage feudalism that had been brought under control by the imposition of state discipline.[61] Louis XVI, in particular, was associated

58. The noble deputy count Beugnot, whose memoirs have a number of interesting observations on the drafting of the *cahiers* of his *bailliage,* quotes a very exceptional parish *cahier* that he turned over to the relevant authorities for criminal prosecution: "We give our deputies power to ask the lord-king's consent to the preceding demands; and should he grant it, to thank him, but should he refuse, to unking him." See Jean-Claude de Beugnot, *Mémoires du Comte Beugnot, 1779–1815* (Paris: Hachette, 1959), 94.

59. Third Estate, Charolles, *AP* 2:618. On the king in the *cahiers* see Shapiro and Markoff, *Revolutionary Demands,* chap. 19.

60. Labrosse and Rétat, *Naissance du journal révolutionnaire,* 253–56. The history of the vitriolic antiroyalist campaign that developed in part of the popular press is imperfectly known, but does not seem noticeable earlier than the winter of 1791. See Ouzi Elyada, "La représentation populaire de l'image royale avant Varennes," *Annales Historiques de la Révolution Française,* no. 297 (1994): 527–46.

61. See, for example, the jurist Henrion de Pansey's portrayal of past violence and usurpation later tamed by the monarchy; "Eloge du Dumoulin" in Pierre-Paul-Nicolas Henrion de Pansey, ed., *Traité des fiefs de Dumoulin analysé et conféré avec les autres feudistes* (Paris: Valade, 1773), esp. 7–8. Indeed, one may see much history-writing from as far back as the sixteenth century as imbued with a monarchical triumphalism that condemned the anarchic, feudal past. We saw in Chapter 4 that the king was not associated with seigneurialism for the authors of the *cahiers.*

with two significant reform efforts. In 1779, apparently responding to a vigorous campaign against serfdom, the king abolished *mainmorte* on his own domains.[62] The preamble of the royal decree appealed to a common humanity: "we have not been able to see without pain the remaining elements of servitude that continue in several of our provinces; we have been affected by considering that a great number of our subjects, servilely attached to the land, are regarded as constituting a part of the land and, so to speak, as confounded with it." Moving from the language of sentiment to the language of proper procedure: the royal decree proclaimed a respect for property that forbade a national abolition without compensation while asserting an absence of funds for such compensation. The king, therefore, expressed the hope that other lords would voluntarily follow his example.[63] Not much resulted from the initiative.[64] The second area of royal antiseigneurial action was in the judicial realm as part of the two great antiparlementary reform packages of the late Old Regime. The Maupeou program of 1771 was in part directed at increasing the efficacy with which the courts pursued criminal matters by removing those matters from seigneurial to royal courts, if necessary, more expeditiously than in the past.[65] The Lamoignon measures of 1788 went further still in permitting either party to civil litigation to insist on a hearing before a royal court.[66] Small wonder, then, that discussions of the king are not associated in the *cahiers* with the seigneurial regime (see Chapter 4, p. 162).

Antiseigneurial forces might optimistically read such actions as indicating the possibility of royal support for more wide-ranging measures, particularly if indemnification was at the center of any plan. Those moved by the preamble to the limited emancipation edict of 1779[67] might hope for what the beneficent king could do now that revolutionary forces had unfettered him from the hold of a retrograde aristocracy. And committed royalists,

62. Alphonse Aulard, *La Révolution française et le régime féodal* (Paris: Alcan, 1919), 5–36; F.-A. Isambert, *Recueil général des anciennes lois françaises depuis l'an 420 jusqu'à la Révolution de 1789* (Paris: Gregg Press, 1966), 26:139–42 (August 1779). At virtually the onset of revolution, Henrion de Pansey had nothing but enthusiasm for the king's emancipatory actions; see *Dissertations féodales: Traité du pouvoir municipal et des biens communaux* (Barrois, 1789), 2:185.

63. The king would not "buy back this right from the lords" because of "the regard we have always had for the laws of property that we consider the most secure foundation for order and justice"; see Jacques Necker, *Oeuvres complètes* (Paris: Treuttel and Würtz, 1820), 3:492.

64. Millot, *Le régime féodal en Franche-Comté au XVIIIe siècle* (Besançon: Millot Frères, 1937).

65. Jules Flammermont, *Le Chancelier Maupeou et les parlements* (Paris: Picard, 1883), 279, 281.

66. Jacques-Henri Bataillon, *Les justices seigneuriales du bailliage de Pontoise à la fin de l'Ancien Régime* (Paris: Sirey, 1942), 161–65; Isambert, *Recueil des anciennes lois,* 29:541–42 (May 8, 1788). The relevant edict insisted that the lord's courts were property and therefore not to be abolished.

67. At least one diarist was so moved. The abbé de Véri thought the preamble "more touching" than poetry. But Véri also noted how few were the royal serfs who would actually be helped. See Joseph Alphonse de Véri, *Journal de l'abbé de Véri* (Paris: Tallandier, 1928–30), 2:238.

regardless of their specific positions on the seigneurial regime, might hope to enlist the king on the side of—and at least nominally at the head of—the Revolution. The notion of an antifeudal king could draw sustenance, moreover, from the intransigent resistance to royal policy of the Besançon Parlement, which protected serfdom in Franche-Comté to the extent of withholding registration of the royal reforms—and thereby opposing emancipation even on royal estates—until forced to do so in the crisis of 1788.[68] In this confrontation, the target of the defenders of feudalism was royal policy. A more pessimistic reading of the monarch's behavior might note that on the most detested aspect of seigneurialism, serfdom, the king was not prepared to force anybody to emancipate anyone from virtually anything[69] and that property rights, which in the king's view covered the seigneurial regime, were the highest priority. This latter element was clearly reiterated by the king on June 23, 1789.[70]

It was by no means strange, then, that a noble of the *monarchien* group, the count de Lally-Tolendal, succeeded, toward the end of the night of August 4, in securing the king's association with the evening's drama in the form of a commemorative medal and a Te Deum honoring Louis "the Restorer of Liberty."[71] Both proponents and opponents of the events of August 4 could lay claim to one or another dubious statement of Louis's actual reaction. In one rather unlikely account, the duke de Liancourt left the session to inform his king and received a supportive statement from him;[72] but there is also a letter of uncertain authenticity, that Louis may have sent on August 5, in which he adamantly refuses to consent to the spoliation of "my clergy, my nobility."[73]

68. Millot, *Le régime féodal en Franche-Comté,* 138 et seq.

69. In the antiserfdom decree, the right of "pursuit," under which the possessions of a serf who had left could be seized by the lord, was, exceptionally, abolished throughout the kingdom for all serfs who had established a domicile. In Necker's recommendation to the king, he advised Louis not to worry about property issues in this case because the right of pursuit was "truly revolting." Louis's decree did manage to invoke property, nonetheless, by stressing the defense of the goods of serfs (Necker, *Oeuvres,* 3:490, 494, 496).

70. "All properties are to be continually respected and his Majesty understands expressly under the name of property the tithes, *cens, rentes,* seigneurial rights and duties and, generally, all the rights and prerogatives, whether income-producing or honorific, that are attached to fiefs and lands." See Philippe-Joseph-Benjamin Buchez and P.-C. Roux, *Histoire parlementaire de la Révolution francaise* (Paris: Paulin, 1834), 2:17.

71. Trophime-Gérard Lally-Tolendal, *Mémoire de M. le comte de Lally-Tolendal, ou seconde lettre à ses commetans* (Paris: n.p., 1790), 1:112–13. Many deputies were quite pleased at associating the king with these measures as shown by cries of "vive le roi" or expressions of satisfaction in their correspondance; see Ferrières, *Correspondance,* 115; François-Joseph Bouchette, *Lettres de François-Joseph Bouchette (1735–1810): Avocat à Bergues. Membre de l'Assemblée Constituante* (Paris: Champion, 1909), 241–42.

72. Kessel, *La nuit du 4 août,* 173–74.

73. Buchez and Roux, *Histoire parlementaire,* 2:248.

By early August, however, many had already discovered that their Revolution was being made against the king, not with him. The formation of the National Assembly defied the king as well as the aristocracy; the problem about suppressing peasant insurrection with force, for some on the left, was not so much that it would fail but that organizing such force might lead the king to move against themselves. The months ahead were to make clear that Louis would do what he could to oppose the resolutions of August 4–11; he opposed them in such a way that a contentious procedural issue over the powers of the king in the new Constitution being written and the antifeudal package became yoked together. The bitterly debated constitutional question was whether the king was to be invested with an absolute veto over legislative enactments, a suspensive veto that could delay legislation but could, in turn, be overridden or no veto.[74] At stake were varying theories of where sovereignty was lodged. Giving this question added urgency was the immediate problem of what veto, if any, the king was to have over the Constitution itself and over quasi-constitutional legislation such as the enactments of August 4–11 appeared to be. The way in which the issue of the role of the king in the new order and the specific issues surrounding the abolition of feudalism became conflated was around the question of what role, if any, was Louis to play in the enactments of early August. Was his approval needed for these measures to become law? These questions were posed as early as the debates on August 6, when a clerical deputy insisted that abolishing the tithe would be illegitimate without royal concurrence (*AP* 8:353). Had Louis actually supported the measures, no doubt some painless subterfuge could have been found under which those who held his approval necessary could feel he had given it and those who held his approval unnecessary could ignore it. But Louis's tactic was to give whatever minimal assent could be gotten away with: to offer comments on the legislation when asked for approval, to offer to publish the decree without authorizing its execution, to have it printed but not disseminated, etc.[75] Rather than go along with the enthusiasm with which, on August 4, the National Assembly associated his name with a measure he had no part in, Louis had managed simultaneously to show himself willing to obstruct the abolition of feudalism and to demonstrate the nefarious aspect of any royal veto. The October rising, which saw the king ushered back to Paris by the distrustful crowd, resolved this particular impasse.

The count de Montlosier testifies to the hostile response triggered by Louis's tepid and qualified initial reaction to the decrees: "This response—so

74. Ran Halévi, "Monarchiens," in François Furet and Mona Ozouf, *A Critical Dictionary of the French Revolution* (Cambridge: Harvard University Press, 1989), 376–78.

75. On the struggle over "promulgation," see Philippe-Antoine Merlin, *Recueil alphabétique des questions de droit* (Brussels: Tarlier, 1829), 4:238–40; Kessel, *La nuit du 4 août,* 253–64; Egret, *Necker,* 358–64.

prudent, so generous, so reasonable, but offering an uncertain consent, strongly affected the Assembly. For a moment it remained silent. Then: 'What an insidious and perfidious reply,' said Muguet de Nantou. For his part, Duport characterized it as dangerous. Goupil de Préfelne called it alarming. Robespierre declared that it was destructive."[76] By mid-September, some in the Assembly saw the king as in league with the recalcitrant nobility and clergy who aimed to undo the events of August 4 and were only deterred by fear of further risings.[77] This confrontation had a while to run yet, but by the time the king accepted that he had no choice but to go along with the August decrees, he had gone far down the road to associating the monarchy with the feudal regime. And he had gone down the road as well to demonstrating to some that negotiations about royal authority, like negotiations about the feudal regime, only progressed under the threat of insurrection.[78]

Tocqueville made much of the degree to which the Revolution, in sweeping away the remnants of the feudal order, actually completed the historic task of Louis's forebears. Mirabeau's frustrated efforts to persuade the king that the Revolution was in the interests of the monarchical state were shrewdly seized on by Tocqueville for their ironic insight.[79] Yet we see that at least as early as June 1789 Louis was committing himself to the "feudal" world about to be swept away; in so doing, he rendered the political alignment dear to revolutionary royalists like Mirabeau unworkable, while easing the task of constructing a more radical vision of a thoroughgoing rupture in which the royal and feudal, in their mutual embrace, would be seen as indistinguishable aspects of a single, worn-out, and unenlightened past. But even as late as the beginning of 1790, a reservoir of goodwill was there for royal tapping. Duquesnoy, who often described his legislative colleagues with a certain sarcasm, renders their views shortly before a royal appearance: "although the king doesn't have extensive learning nor a profound intellect and although he expresses himself with some difficulty, he has a sense of fairness, some clear ideas, but above all, an infinitely honest soul, a good and sensitive heart and a burning desire for the good."[80]

76. François-Dominique de Reynaud de Montlosier, *Mémoires de M. de Comte de Montlosier sur la Révolution française, le Consulat, l'Empire, la Restauration et les principaux événements qui l'ont suivie, 1775–1830* (Paris: Dufey, 1830), 1:244–45; see also Alexandre Lameth, *Histoire de l'Assemblée Constituante* (Paris: Moutardier, 1828), 1:142.

77. Adrien Duquesnoy, *Journal d'Adrien Duquesnoy,* 1:349; Lameth, *Histoire,* 1:140.

78. "The king, ceding to the wishes of the representatives of the people and perhaps also to the force of circumstances, gave them his pure and simple approval [to the August decrees] that they had asked for" (Lameth, *Histoire,* 1:143).

79. Alexis de Tocqueville, *The Old Régime and the French Revolution* (Garden City, N.Y.: Doubleday, 1955), 8. Mirabeau had even contended that "monarchy only begins with the revolutionary epoch." See Honoré-Gabriel de Riquetti, comte de Mirabeau, *Lettres du comte de Mirabeau à ses commettants* (Paris: Imprimerie du Patriote François, 1789–1791).

80. Duquesnoy, *Journal,* 2:254.

For quite some time, any gestures that Louis made toward embracing the Revolution and toward honoring the National Assembly were not only greeted with relieved acceptance, but were experienced by the legislators, even by much of the left, as moving. In the midst of the winter 1790 wave of rural disturbances, Louis appeared at the National Assembly, eschewed elaborate ceremonial deference, spoke with warmth of the Assembly's work and with sympathy of the frustrations stemming from renewed insurrectionary action when one had expected peace. Capturing the Assembly's passion for education as the path to the new world, Louis announced "in concert with the Queen, who shares all my sentiments, I shall, at an early moment, prepare the mind and heart of my son for the new order of things that circumstances have brought. I shall give him the habit, from his early years, of being made happy by the happiness of the French, and of recognizing always . . . that a wise constitution shall protect him from the dangers of inexperience." Their public debate and personal letters show the Assembly deeply moved.[81] A half-year later, when Louis publicly appeared to embrace the role of the constitutional, revolutionary "king of the French"[82] on the first anniversary of the attack on the Bastille, many in the National Assembly were delighted to have him on board.[83]

The event-filled years that followed 1789 were to show how persistently some hoped to make the Revolution with Louis rather than against him and how persistently he had to opt for the most conservative forces to wreck these hopes beyond repair. Far down the road, a significant group still backed a constitutional monarchy in the Legislative Assembly even with the monarch brought back from failed flight into captivity. Even the monarch's plain disavowal of the Revolution was not enough to end notions of a monarchical Revolution.[84] Many of those who from the first opposed the feudal only very gradually found that they opposed the monarchical as well.

Just as the international scene came to be understood as a conflict over feudalism versus liberty, the conflict of king and assembly was in part a conflict over feudalism. Small wonder that, ultimately, royalism and feudalism seemed to go hand in hand and could enter jointly into a global concept of the "Old Regime."[85] The law of July 17, 1793, reappropriated from

81. *AP* 11:429–32; Duquesnoy, *Journal,* 2:347–52; 354–57. For more details on this revealing event, see Tackett, *Becoming a Revolutionary,* 275–77.

82. Peter R. Campbell, "Louis XVI, King of the French," in Colin Lucas, ed., *The French Revolution and the Creation of Modern Political Culture,* vol. 2, *The Political Culture of the French Revolution* (Oxford: Pergamon Press, 1988), 161–82.

83. Tackett, *Becoming a Revolutionary.*

84. C. J. Mitchell, *The French Legislative Assembly of 1791* (Leiden: E. J. Brill, 1988), 208–20.

85. François Furet, "Ancien Régime," in François Furet and Mona Ozouf, *A Critical Dictionary of the French Revolution* (Cambridge: Harvard University Press, 1989), 604–15; Diego Venturino, "La naissance de l'Ancien Régime."

popular rage the seigneurial documents, now to be ceremonially burned. Burned when? On August 10, the first anniversary of the attack on the king's palace by radical Parisians and provincial National Guards that pulled the now captive king from his throne (*AP* 69:98). So completely had the royal and feudal become fused in their joint death that one could celebrate the first anniversary of the overthrow of the one by completing the destruction of the other.

The Rupture

If one only focuses on the fate of the seigneurial dues, "the complete destruction of the feudal regime" looks like nothing else but a pathetic fraud,[86] the work of the relevant committees of the various legislatures appears so much hypocritical casuistry, and any enduring benefits to the peasantry appear as seized from an unwilling new elite.[87] If we note the genuineness of the exaltation, alongside the undeniable hypocrisy, in the legislatures, we might add some notion of self-delusion. If we note the immediate and genuine suppression of the purely honorific rights, of such import to elite commoners and of such little importance to the peasantry (see Chapter 2, p. 47), we might be led to comment as well on elite misperceptions of the countryside; we also would see that the legislators had effected a break in what counted for them (especially if we recall the undercurrent of attention to humiliation on the night of August 4) (see Chapter 8, p. 458). If, however, we see the seigneurial rights as a part of the "feudal regime" and consider the enactments of August 4–11, 1789, and the subsequent work of the legislators across the full range of what was held to be "feudal," matters appear quite otherwise. I believe there are two essential points to note here: first, the seigneurial dues were only a part of the multiform complex of seigneurial rights; and second, the seigneurial rights were but a part of the broad sense of the feudal. I shall elaborate a bit on each of these points.

Although the decrees of August 4–11 (as elaborated in March and May 1790) prompted an indemnificatory scheme for dues that country people resisted for years, much of the seigneurial regime was actually abolished outright, at least in principle. Perhaps, as Couthon noted in his speech of February 29, 1792, the pure claims to honor, the most decisively suppressed, were of relatively little interest in the countryside. But the same

86. See the evidence marshaled by Reichardt and Schmitt, "Rupture on continuité?"

87. But let us recall that rural opinion, expressed in the spring of 1789, did actually show less pressure for outright abolition of payments to the lord than for almost any other aspect of the seigneurial regime; see Chapter 3, p. 73.

cannot be said for those honors that entailed material harm to the peasants (the right to compulsory labor, to hunt and to raise pigeons, rabbits, fish), which, on the evidence of the parish *cahiers,* were plainly detested. The seigneurial courts, also abolished outright, had weighed heavily on France's rural communities in some regions (although not others) (see Chapter 3, p. 114). Removing seigneurial tolls and controls over markets may have been appreciated by the more commercial peasant strata; and ending monopolistic control of milling and baking and grape-pressing (unless the lord could demonstrate a consensual origin) was also of some significance.

The seigneurial regime, moreover, hardly exhausted the scope of those August measures. In attacking the bases of financing the church and of staffing government posts by sale of office, in moving against guilds as well as the privileges of order and province, the entire structure of privilege and the corporate conception of society were attacked.[88] In declaring an end to tax privilege and privileged access to posts and careers, the fundamental equality of the new citizens was being established, and some of the most important implications of that equality spelled out. In subjecting government pensions and subsidies to scrutiny, the removal of ultimate authority from the person of the king was affirmed. One might protest that the subsequent indemnification of venal officeholders (in parallel to the plan to indemnify the lords) was a good deal for the Old Regime's officialdom. True enough, but what was created, at one stroke, was a society of juridical equals whose relations were not governed by claims of tradition or immutable hierarchy but by their autonomous wills entering into voluntary contracts. And as individuals, all were to be equal: universal rather than particular law (= "privilege") would follow. To whatever extent this immediately altered anyone's material circumstances, it was a conceptual break with the past.

On the one hand there was the sovereign individual, secure in his absolute property, absolute in the sense of rights unconstrained by traditional, communal, or corporate organization; on the other hand, there was the new revolutionary state, also unconstrained by such intermediary structures. The ambiguity of the dual sovereignty of individual and state was to be encapsulated in a definition in Napoleon's Civil Code: "Property is the right to enjoy and dispose of goods in the most absolute manner, provided that one does not make any use of these goods that are prohibited by the laws and regulations."[89] In this light, as François Furet and Ran Halévi urge,[90] the sense of bringing an epoch to an end and of creating the social world

88. This point is stressed by Michael P. Fitzsimmons, "Privilege and the Polity in France, 1786–1789," *American Historical Review* 92 (1987): 269–95.

89. André-Jean Arnaud, *Les origines doctrinales du code civil français* (Paris: Librairie Générale de Droit et de Jurisprudence, 1969), 179.

90. François Furet and Ran Halévi, *Orateurs de la Révolution française,* vol. 1, *Les constituants* (Paris: Gallimard, 1989), lxvii–lxxii.

anew is readily graspable. Personal obligations are now held to derive from voluntary contracts among equals and seen as exchanges of property of one sort or another rather than the inherent deference of inferiors to their masters. For the legislators, it was epochal. It is in this light that we need to see Merlin's puzzlement that the country people do not acknowledge the great change of redefining the same payments as consequences of property rights rather than feudal violence.

A Cultural Legacy

If it has seemed to many, in the bourgeois world that coalesced after the Revolution, that an abstract notion of a modern economy was necessarily locked in battle with feudal anachronisms, enterprising lords in the eighteenth century often, in practice, utilized the seigneurial apparatus in their seizure of market opportunities. And conversely even the very concept of private property, we have observed, served the rearguard as well as the vanguard. The work of Georges Lefebvre posed the question of the extent to which the peasant risings were directed against something that might be called a consolidating, modern, capitalist order as opposed to a dying, traditional, feudal one. This modern order, however, utilized the existing seigneurial rights and armed itself with feudal lawyers. And when the nobles spoke, they not only looked to the responsibilities of their public service as the feudal warrior class as justification for their rights but to the *ultima ratio* of the bourgeois order.

If seigneurial dues were no longer paid from 1789 on it was not because the National Assembly, as the self-conscious leaders of the violent masses seized their historic mission of effecting the famous transition from feudalism to an as yet unnamed social form, but because in the disintegration of the coercive apparatus of the state, the country people burnt the *châteaux,* terrorized the lords, pillaged the legal documents, utterly refused to participate in the indemnification scheme and, probably as significantly if less dramatically, simply stopped paying when they discovered no one could compel them to do so.[91]

But it is hard to see the seigneurial machinery of the late eighteenth century as unambiguously *pre*capitalist; it is impossible to see the National Assembly as creating a bourgeois rural order when that had already largely been in place; it is hard to see them as overthrowing one economic system

91. At least one legislator was less full of the usual self-congratulation than many of his fellows: "we would never have gotten to the point of applying and carrying out our principles except after long and lively discussions, which would have been interminable, if the people hadn't cut them short and completed for itself its own emancipation" (Thibaudeau, *Mémoires,* 96).

and replacing it with another when they struggled so hard to change as little of the peasants' obligations to the dominant strata as possible—at least in the short run in which human beings actually live. Only gradually did the revolutionary legislatures face up to the reality that no one could govern France without accepting that the peasants weren't paying any more. And as we saw in Chapter 8, it was the war that compelled the Legislative Assembly and then, more profoundly, the Convention to abandon the policy of ecstatic words of self-praise for having abolished history combined with exhortation—backed by (inadequate) coercion—to keep on meeting the traditional obligations. To the extent that peasants were freed of traditional burdens, it was in large part because they freed themselves. And even then, large proprietors sometimes managed to subsume old payments under the newer and thoroughly legitimated rental contracts, thereby achieving precisely the vision of Merlin and the Committee on Feudal Rights. Even quite archaic forms of seigneurial obligation were occasionally enforced well into the new era.[92]

The Revolution's legislators did have their own antiseigneurial agenda: freeing market forces from the shackles of the past; strengthening the authority of the state over a more uniform institutional structure; advancing the movement toward a vision of juridically equal individuals freely entering contracts and policed by a state itself grounded in a primal contract, the written Constitution. This latter achievement of necessity entailed the repudiation of a vision of collectivities with corporate rights (such as the village community), of essential inequalities of status recognized in law, of parcelized sovereignty and of personal rulership ultimately supported by divine sanction. Claims of custom were seen as masks for initial acts of coercion and were no longer to be admissible in a future society whose people, seen as individuals, were held to be bound together only by virtue of their uncoerced consent. The Third Estate *cahiers* show a modal tendency for a generally indemnified phasing-out of seigneurial rights that would simultaneously bring about the desired social transformation, would respect those aspects of seigneurialism that were assimilable to notions of property, would strike a balanced compromise, would put money in the pockets of some legislators themselves, and would protect the plan of selling National Property (with seigneurial rights attached) from ruin. When this program was dramatically announced on August 4, 1789, and then developed in detail in March 1790, there were those who rejected the consensus. Initially dissenting on one side were those legislators, largely noble, who refused

92. Pierre Massé, "Survivances des droits féodaux dans l'Ouest (1793–1902)," *Annales Historiques de la Révolution Française* 37 (1965): 270–98; Albert Soboul, "Survivances 'féodales' dans la société rurale française au XIXe siècle," *Annales: Economies, Sociétés, Civilisations* 23 (1968): 965–86.

even a slow and indemnified phase-out, taking their stand on property rights. And, less vocal at first but ultimately dissenting on the other side, were those who found all aspects of seigneurialism illegitimate, also taking their stand on claims of property rights. The original plan foundered in part because no path to a new role for the king could be found; in part because the reorganization of the place of the church could not be peacefully accomplished; in part because the pressures from Parisian popular forces continued to remake the political balance of the legislatures; and, in very large part, because some of the people of the countryside, seizing the opportunities opened by the weakening of the coercive apparatus, the search for a new institutional order among the new revolutionary elites, and the openness to change of some sort on the part of the preponderance of the new claimants to authority, refused to demobilize without obtaining a much more extensive and rapid dismantlement of the seigneurial regime.

But in their early insistence that they had made a decisive break the revolutionaries in Paris helped define the Revolution as a rupture; in their sense of the feudal regime as not merely the seigneurial rights, but as an institutional complex reaching into every corner of social life, they convinced themselves and future generations of intellectuals that the present was born in a radical break with the past. In evoking the broad connotations that permitted an undefined "feudal" to come to characterize a social totality (even as their lawyers were groping for a restricted definition in the unsuccessful attempt to achieve the assent of the rural population), those who spoke for the Revolution told themselves that the world they were making was in every way a new creation, a creation born from the marriage of violence and reason. The great medievalist Marc Bloch observed that whenever we think about "feudalism" today, "[i]n the background there is always a reflection of the firing of châteaux during the burning summer of '89."[93] For future revolutionaries, in the nineteenth century and beyond, the Revolution suggested the possibility of new such ruptures. And there was a legacy for the human sciences as well. A sense of a disjunction between past and present preceded the Revolution, as seen in the eighteenth-century development of economics and history. But the dramatic intensity of the revolutionary experience served to concentrate the thoughts of European observers on the meaning of the Revolution and amplified a thousandfold the sensation of that upheaval. From the 1790s on, a European could hardly think about social issues without thinking about the French Revolution.[94] The vision of the revolutionaries thus made a powerful contribution to

93. Marc Bloch, *The Historian's Craft* (New York: Vintage Books: 1953), 172.

94. Ronald Paulson brilliantly shows how images drawn from the revolutionary experience permeated nineteenth-century art and literature. See Paulson, *Representations of Revolution, 1789–1820* (New Haven: Yale University Press, 1983).

the conception of a traditional/modern dichotomy that became the central problematic for the nineteenth-century founders of sociology.

The development of the contemporary social sciences was powerfully shaped by the sense, already widespread in Western Europe in the eighteenth century and experienced much more intensely in the era that followed, that the world of contemporary experience differed strikingly from the world of the past; that change in social relationships, institutions, and patterns of thought was an ongoing process; and that to some extent the direction of change was subject to human will. Intellectuals differed greatly in their evaluation of this state of affairs; but whether one regarded the passing of the old with dismay or looked to the future with hope, the passionate and concerned sense of the present social order as radically distinct energized the variety of reflections on our collective life that became the social sciences. Thus we may roughly date modern economics from Adam Smith's sense of the advanced commercial society of England as one that both drew upon and liberated the natural human tendency "to truck, barter and exchange." The emergence of the modern discipline of history surely owes much, as Krzysztof Pomian has contended, to a sense of the past as genuinely past and gone, and thereby able to yield up its documents to the scrutiny of scholars who claim to be motivated by a disinterested desire to understand.[95] And sociology was powerfully shaped by a sense of an institutional and cultural divide that separated status from contract, *Gemeinschaft* from *Gesellschaft* and so on through a large number of such paired conceptions, including the terms that have shaped and misshaped the outlook of generations of American sociologists, the gap between the traditional and the modern. Perhaps no set of paired images has been more widely influential than feudalism/capitalism and no problem more vexing than the transition that led from the one to the other.

The image of a temporal rupture that separated two forms of social life was a legacy that guided, inspired, and blinded more than the scholar. It galvanized a way of acting in the world by providing a secularized transformation of a Christian universe in which a worldly city was opposed to a City of God, in which the flow of time underwent breaks between the Old and the New, in which history advanced toward godliness in jumps as revealed in the transition from one such epoch to the next. By retaining the emotive power of such imagery, but substituting national history for sacred history; by tracing the defining characteristics of an age to the transformation of institutions rather than the workings of the Holy Spirit; by imagining change as the working-out of human rather than divine will; by locating sacrality in rights that could be legislated rather than in royal persons divinely conse-

95. Krzysztof Pomian, "Les historiens et les archives dans la France du XVIIe siècle," *Acta Poloniae Historica* 26 (1972): 109–25.

crated, the way was open for new generations in distant lands to create local versions of this no longer specifically Christian vision. Much of the thinking behind this was taking place in Western Europe and its colonial offshoots between the very religious (and therefore culturally specific) English Revolution of the 1640s and the French Revolution of 1789. But the passionate conviction that here and now we have actually carried out the total destruction of the feudal regime and with that destruction an entire state of civilization was transformed almost at once into something new has remained a powerful model of what was possible.

CHAPTER

10

CONCLUSION: FROM GRIEVANCES TO REVOLUTION

A Serf Meets Legislators

October 23, 1789. In the weeks that followed the impassioned discussions touched off on the night of August 4, the National Assembly was absorbed in its very full agenda. Many sessions began with a reading of letters from various communities announcing their adhesion to the work of national regeneration. On this particular morning, the Assembly welcomed a live guest from serf country: an "old man of one hundred twenty years, born at Mont-Jura: he wishes to see the Assembly that has freed his country from the bonds of servitude." The legislators had developed the keenest sensitivities as to who might sit before whom, whose hats were to be doffed and whose not, and the like, as the representatives of a free people continuously renegotiated such ceremonial issues with the representative of the king. For the nobles among them, having been—or not been—presented to the king would at one point have been the weightiest of matters. Now the old serf, on crutches, and, according to the biography that instantly appeared,[1] blind and hard of hearing, helped by his family, was introduced and the legislators, at Grégoire's suggestion, stood. When the old man took his seat and put on his hat "[t]he hall rang with applause" (AP 9:484). The honored guest displayed his baptismal record, which, indeed, read 1669.

One deputy called for a modest sum to be raised (the count de Praslin soon presented 8,377 livres on behalf of an infantry regiment); another announced a plan for an exemplary model of the respect youth owed age in the form of having young children assist the former serf (especially those "whose fathers were killed in the attack on Bastille"). Mirabeau interjected, "Do what you want for this old man, but leave him alone." Perhaps cutting off further comments, the chair expressed his concern about exhausting the distinguished visitor and added that the Assembly "desires that you enjoy for a long time the sight of your country completely freed" (*AP* 9:484). One contemporary was so moved that he went on to write a biography of this man, an honor, like the ceremonial deference shown by legislators, that used to be for the kings of this world.[2] His biographer sees him as eminently worthy of emulation, attributing his long life to piety, hard work, clean living, and the avoidance, until recently, of the medical profession.

Although the legislators were moved by their guest and by their own participation in completely freeing their country, one may well wonder at how thankful other villagers in Franche-Comté were when the legislation of March and May 1790 fixed just how much they still owed their former lords. Did they take the same satisfaction in paying rents rather than servile obligations as the deputies did in thus redefining their status? Perhaps,[3] but other peasants, as we have repeatedly seen, were not at all satisfied. When the old man died two months after his visit to the Assembly, a new wave of peasant insurrection was building up steam in Brittany and the Southwest.

A grateful serf honored by legislators proud of their legislative achievements; peasants in one province accepting the new laws, while peasants elsewhere were renewing their fight—elements of the dynamic, evolving relationships of those at the centers of visible authority who wrote the laws and those in near and distant villages who were pleased, who acquiesced or who complained, deceived and openly challenged. If the dialogue of peasants

1. Jean Joseph Pithou, *Vie de Jean Jacob, vieillard de Mont-Jura, âgé de 120 ans, pensioné de Sa Majesté à laquelle il a été présenté depuis peu ainsi qu'à l'Assemblée Nationale* (Paris: Valleyre, 1789).

2. Apart from police reports on the mutinous, biographies of prerevolutionary French plebeians can be counted on the fingers of one hand.

3. The lawyer Christin, deputy from Aval and former partner of Voltaire in the struggle for freeing the serfs, thought that former serfs from his province were not only grateful, but deserving of praise for "their submission to the laws, and their most profound respect for properties, even for those of the canons of Saint-Claude, who had for so long unjustly oppressed them"; quoted in Alphonse Aulard, *La Révolution française et le régime féodal* (Paris: Alcan, 1919), 116–17. Grateful serfs of Saint-Claude did thank the king; see Kessel, *La nuit du 4 août 1789* (Paris: Arthaud, 1969), 242–43.

and legislators was complex, "peasants" and "legislators" were themselves complex entities. Country people variously lived in regions that grew wheat, supported domestic textile production, raised animals; carried out production through the labor of smallholders, sharecroppers, and wage laborers; were more or less densely endowed with roads, royal officials, literacy, communal and provincial self-government; and had different local traditions of resistance.

A peasant community might be more highly stratified or more egalitarian and have more or less serious divisions among landowners, renters, and the landless, producers for the market and consumers, those rooted in the community and seasonal workers, older peasants with legal title to land and younger ones dependent on fathers and bosses. In one village, a past triumph over a tax collector might be a proud memory; in another, the pain of judicial punishment following a challenge to grain prices might be on people's minds. Peasants in different regions and in different locations in the village world sometimes had common interests and sometimes divergent ones; on some issues and at some times they acted, without explicit coordination, in mutual support; at other times they pulled in different directions.

The legislators, too, differed among themselves in their visions of a future France, the place of the countryside in that future and the tactics to achieve that end. And from one moment to the next, the ensemble of issues the legislators confronted was altering, and altering with it their sense of how to handle the rural rebels. To understand legislature and countryside, both, we need a sense of their points of division: at one moment some provinces, but not others, nurtured movements with some targets but not with others and challenged a legislature confronting particular constellations of other challenges with particular internal divisions. We have tried to see this multiplex dialogue by tracking the intertwined trajectories of peasant insurrection and revolutionary legislation.

A Peasant-Bourgeois Alliance

Revolutionary peasants and revolutionary legislators together ended the seigneurial regime. How was this antiseigneurial convergence achieved? In the historical literature, there are two principal grand narratives of the Revolution within which this joining of forces has an important place, a Marxian story and a Tocquevillean one. In what is generally characterized as a Marxist account,[4] transformations in the material conditions of existence

4. The identification of this particular narrative as *the* Marxist account is subject to challenge in

are held to bring about new structures of interest. These structures align people in new patterns of conflict as they come to have a sense of their commonalities of interest with some and their antagonistic interest in relation to others. The sense of identity that thereby develops is deepened to the extent that people organize themselves for the purposes of advancing the interests of their group against others.

The advance of the marketplace as an organizing principle for social relations provided one of the most important institutional frameworks around which group interests, group allegiances, and group antagonisms formed in early modern Europe; within this matrix an antifeudal alliance of a cramped bourgeoisie and a threatened peasantry was forged. In Albert Soboul's version, a wealthy and cultivated urban bourgeoisie came to occupy "the leading position in society, a position which was at variance with the official existence of privileged orders."[5] An enormously active and prosperous class of financiers, merchants, and manufacturers were poised to take advantage of economic change, Soboul continues. Material transformation had a cultural counterpart: "[t]he economic base of society was changing, and with it ideologies were being modified" (66). A critique of the existing order was elaborated on behalf of individual rights, property, equality before the law, rationality, progress, and freedom. A developing body of professionals—legal professionals in particular—proved increasingly capable of representing these new interests and new ideas (45–46). The whole movement came to resent the multiple injuries of what was left of feudalism: its limitations on property rights and individual initiative, its deleterious effect on agricultural progress, its identification with the irrational past rather than the rationality of the future.

The peasantry were equally if differently hostile to seigneurialism. Although there were important differences of interest within individual peasant communities and important regional differences in the social structures that developed in the rural world, there was a broad unity in distress at the high levels of burden imposed by state, church, and lord, among which the claims of the lord were the most resented. In the eighteenth century the lords, moreover, utilized the structures of seigneurialism to enhance their capacity

---

several ways: one might debate whether it is distinctively Marxist rather than shared with a broad school of nineteenth-century French liberal historiography; one might debate whether it captures what is most interesting in how Marx understood the Revolution or is even accurate as a statement of his views; and one might point to the great diversity of thinking among those who locate themselves as Marxists. See François Furet, *Marx and the French Revolution* (Chicago: University of Chicago Press, 1988); Eric Hobsbawm, "The Making of a Bourgeois Revolution," in Ferenc Fehér, *The French Revolution and the Birth of Modernity* (Berkeley and Los Angeles: University of California Press, 1990), 30–48; George C. Comninel, *Rethinking the French Revolution: Marxism and the Revisionist Challenge* (London: Verso, 1987).

5. Albert Soboul, *The French Revolution, 1789–1799: From the Storming of the Bastille* (New York: Vintage Books, 1975), 44.

to take advantage of the development of the market. Exactions, Soboul goes on, were tightened to force peasants to sell out so that the lord's holdings could be rationalized and enlarged; communal rights of various sorts came under attack as lords, encouraged by the new doctrines of the physiocrats, aimed at increasing their incomes still further (58–67). As for the chief beneficiaries of the old order, the nobility were in the deepest disarray. Some embraced the forms of economic activity being opened up and others championed liberal reform; still others, however, reacted to threat by more scrupulously collecting their traditional sources of income at peasant expense and by reasserting their traditional claims against growing state rationalization (34–38).

Tocqueville, too, saw a coincidence of peasant and bourgeois interests against seigneurial rights, but he located the matrix of this tacit alliance in a cultural shift that was in turn rooted in the enlargement of state power and authority.[6] The long process of central state development, Tocqueville argued, eroded the basis on which others would accept the positions of nobles and lords in French society. State development also entailed a cultural transformation of the nobility itself which came rather close to preparing them for their own elimination as a social force. With regard to the first point, Tocqueville presented a detailed analysis of the legitimacy of the social order as a question of services. One's sense of justice is not violated, in this view, to the extent that greater rewards accrue to those who perform greater services. To the extent that the nobility were central in the provision of services through their responsible domination of public affairs, to the extent that noble lords furnished protection from violence, maintained the roads, policed economic transactions, succored the poor, supported the true Church and dispensed justice among the contentious, the privileges of the nobility and of the lords could be seen as so many deserved benefits. The lords' social role was substantial, they bore the costs of performing that role and they were, perhaps, seen as indispensable. But as these functions passed into the hands of the central state, the entire justification for noble and seigneurial privilege evaporated. As, for example, the legitimate exercise of violence became the task of the royal army or as the policing of the economic life of the kingdom passed into the hands of government inspectors and planners, the moral acceptability of a special noble or seigneurial status was eroded, even though the king's generals and the king's economic managers were themselves recruited from the nobility.[7]

6. For a discussion of Tocqueville's *Old Regime* as an account of cultural transformation see Sasha R. Weitman, "Regime Practice and Mass-Political Dispositions: Reflections on the Old Regime and the Revolution," paper presented to the Bicentennial Conference on the French Revolution, George Washington University, May 1989. See also the same author's "The Sociological Thesis of Tocqueville's *The Old Regime and the Revolution*," *Social Research* 33 (1966): 389–406.

7. Alexis de Tocqueville, *The Old Regime and the French Revolution* (Garden City, N.Y.: Doubleday, 1955), 32–41.

As the nobles' public responsibilities were being whittled away, royal policy tended to leave their privileges intact in the hope of obtaining their assent to the changing institutions of France. Indeed, one may speak of the growth of new areas of privilege, for the nobility often succeeded in assuring itself privileged consideration for the positions opened up by the expanding central government. (The more powerful and potentially dangerous nobles were often granted government subsidies.)

In its own adjustment to the new social context in which royal bureaucrats were beginning to impose something of a universalistic and antitraditionalist approach to public life, the nobility itself underwent a profound moral change. The actions and thoughts whose center was the Paris-based bureaucracy increasingly refused to recognize the sanctity of local and regional distinctions, or birth-based differences among the king's subjects, or of anything but impersonal and technical criteria for the making of decisions. The emerging state was beginning to recognize isolated individuals rather than long-standing, hierarchical, and corporate bodies as the true components of the social order. Even the nobility participated as highly placed agents of the bureaucratizing government. The many nobles who were negotiating with the state and trying to adjust to it, were, in Tocqueville's view, largely won over to its values. Their own worldview was increasingly indistinguishable from that of other well-to-do persons. The centralized character of France "had cast the minds of all in the same mold and given them the same equipment." They did not differ in values from the bourgeoisie but only in privilege (*Old Regime,* 81). While elite commoners resented noble distinctions, the nobility enjoyed participating in an intellectual culture fundamentally antithetical to their own prerogatives (142). In the Middle Ages, "the nobles enjoyed invidious privileges and rights that weighted heavily on the commoner, but in return for this they kept order, administered justice, saw to the execution of the laws, came to the rescue of the oppressed, and watched over the interests of all. The more these functions passed out of the hands of the nobility, the more uncalled for did their privileges appear—until at last their mere existence seemed a meaningless anachronism" (30).

As for the peasantry, the military and political erosion of the lord's role had turned a once-genuine protector into an exploiter. Tocqueville here is elaborating a particular French instance of a process commonly discussed in much of the recent comparative literature on peasant revolt. Do local landholders have responsibilities toward their dependents? Subjection to increasingly effective bureaucratic states or, for that matter, to the market, is held to erode traditional clientelistic rural relationships. The position of the local elites shifts radically as their communal responsibilities becomes a memory, as opportunities for them to profit by greater exactions combines with greater pressures on them to do so, and as their capacity to call on the coercive apparatus of effective central authorities decreases their need to live up to traditional legitimating images of the good lord. The work of James Scott in particular touched off quite a lively debate. Scott depicted a "moral economy" that had once protected the claims to subsistence of the peasant community. Landowning elites, bound by that moral economy, performed a vital role, but one that ultimately succumbed to the forces of change.[8]

Both interpretive frameworks make sense of a peasant-bourgeois alliance against the lords.[9] But, as Lynn Hunt tellingly points out, neither grapples with the Revolution itself as a political process.[10] The peasant-bourgeois alliance is seen as a rather straightforward by-product of the common interest of peasants and bourgeois in dismantling the seigneurial regime. Long-term structural change reoriented group interests in turning an envious commoner elite and a subordinate peasantry against the lords of France: revolutionary antiseigneurialism, given this context, was a foregone conclusion[11] and one can only debate the relative contribution of peasants and legislators to that end. Thus critics of one or another of these structuralist accounts deny the antiseigneurialism of the countryside (Taylor) or of the bourgeoisie (Cobban) or deny the impact of antiseigneurial insurrection (Root). As we shall soon see, while some populist accounts make peasant

8. James Scott, *The Moral Economy of the Peasant: Rebellion and Subsistence in Southeast Asia* (New Haven: Yale University Press, 1976); Samuel Popkin, *The Rational Peasant: The Political Economy of Rural Society in Vietnam* (Berkeley and Los Angeles: University of California Press, 1979); Charles F. Keyes, ed., "Symposium: Peasant Strategies in Asian Societies," *Journal of Asian Studies* 42 (1983): 753–868; Theda Skocpol, "What Makes Peasants Revolutionary?" *Comparative Politics* 14 (1982): 351–75; Hy Van Luong, "Agrarian Unrest from an Anthropological Perspective: The Case of Vietnam," *Comparative Politics* 17 (1985): 153–74.

9. There are other broad interpretative frameworks, most notably the claim that the motor of revolution was a demographic increase in collision with institutional inertia: rapid population growth generated intractable problems for state revenues that were difficult to increase given the rigidities of the tax system; the children of the elites were threatened with blocked career opportunities since appropriate elite positions were expanding more slowly than the numbers of young elite members seeking their fortunes; and the standard of living of rural populations was threatened, a process that showed up in deteriorating lease terms, declines in real wages, and land scarcities. These three processes exacerbated each other. This thesis has the virtue of integrating state fiscal crisis, elite division, and popular mobilization into a single process. (The skeptical might see this as a vice.) While rather effective in explaining the timing of the Revolution, this demographic-structural approach sheds no light on the specific issues around which conflict arose. For the most impressive analysis of the Revolution along these lines, see Jack A. Goldstone, *Revolution and Rebellion in the Early Modern World* (Berkeley and Los Angeles: University of California Press, 1991), 170–348.

10. Lynn Hunt, *Politics, Culture and Class in the French Revolution* (Berkeley and Los Angeles: University of California Press, 1984), 1–16.

11. The phrase is used in the title of Tocqueville's final chapter: "How, given the facts set forth in the preceding chapters, the Revolution was a foregone conclusion" (*Old Regime and Revolution,* 203); a Marxian equivalent is the evocation of the chains which, having to be broken, were broken; see Karl Marx and Frederick Engels, "Manifesto of the Communist Party," in Marx and Engels, *Selected Works* (Moscow: Foreign Languages Publishing House, 1955), 1:39.

insurrection everything, carrying a hypocritical elite of footdraggers before it, other scholars, stressing elite political discourse, deny that rural insurrection added very much to an essentially legislative breakthrough.

The evidence that we have examined, however, suggests a rather different way of thinking about the dismantling of the seigneurial rights. Certainly there were long-term changes of the sorts dear to both Marxists and Tocquevilleans: the market and the state both expanded in significance and became increasingly weighty in village lives. Important elements of both accounts were also part of the self-understandings of some revolutionary participants. The Third Estate of Arbois adds a supplement to the *cahier* of Aval that embodies a Tocquevillean outlook when they write: "All dues and all rights that are part of the old feudalism that communities pay to their lords by reason of services no longer owed by the lords shall be suppressed."[12] So do their fellows of Annonay in calling for the indemnification of some rights while reserving abolition without compensation for "those for which the reason no longer exists" (*AP* 3:52). As for the Marxian thesis, we have noted its Barnavian preincarnation, which stressed the power of commerce to transform social institutions (see Chapter 4, p. 180). We also see in the *cahiers* a pattern of opinion that at points seems what one would expect in the Marxist account and at other points fits the Tocquevillean model. Marxists, for example, would find it easy to understand the combination of a focus on market restrictions and a focus on privilege that characterizes the *cahiers* of the Third Estate; Tocquevilleans would find similarly clear the nobles combining a concern with civil liberties with a concern for state finances (see Chapter 2, pp. 29, 35). The geography of insurrection also suggests that some weight be given to market forces and some to statemaking. Marxists, for example, would feel on familiar ground observing how regions of market activity sparked a wide range of peasant insurrections, as would Tocquevilleans observing the insurrection-generating qualities of areas where the central administration's control was unimpeded by a politically weighty aristocratic corps (see Chapter 7, pp. 375, 377, 396, 407). And the available evidence on long-term change over time in patterns of stating grievances and staging rebellions since the seventeenth century points to the shift toward attacking the seigneurial regime that both the Marxian and Tocquevillean frameworks insist upon. The comparison of the *cahiers* of 1789 to the *cahiers* of 1614 brings out clearly that a focus on the exactions of the state was down while a focus on the lords was up (see Chapter 3, p. 134). As for insurrections, their frequency was not only rising toward the end of the Old Regime but their targets were increasingly seigneurial (see Chapter 5, p. 265).

12. Beatrice Fry Hyslop, *A Guide to the General Cahiers of 1789, with the Texts of Unedited Cahiers* (New York: Octagon Books, 1968), 217.

Nonetheless, there are limitations to the explanatory power of an exclusive focus on long-term structures.[13] Although the development of the state and the market may have decreased the tolerance of many for the lord's prerogatives, we have reviewed ample evidence that, in themselves, these structural changes did not bring either urban notables or peasants to the point of totally overthrowing the seigneurial regime. In the first place the *cahiers* show that even if seigneurial rights were a weightier agenda item than they had been in 1614, they were, still, a lesser concern than taxation at the outset of revolution (see Chapter 5, p. 265). There were also many demands for reform or indemnification as well as abolition in all three groups of documents (see Chapter 3). The study of the early insurrections, moreover, shows how insignificant, at first, were actions against the lords, particularly when these are seen in comparison to subsistence events (see Figs. 6.3 [a]–[d]). And if we turn to the legislative arena early in the Revolution, we note that the general tone of radical break that hovered over the night of August 4, 1789, was consistent with a very conservative stance on many of the seigneurial rights (see Chapters 8 and 9). The intricate dance by which peasants came to make their chief target the seigneurial rights while legislators revamped their enactments had to be invented. It was in no way given at the outset.

Recapitulation

Let us review the steps in the argument. Chapter 2 examined the *cahiers de doléances* in order to identify the place of the seigneurial rights on the agendas of the country people, the urban notables, and the nobility. The three faced the Revolution differently. While all had in common considerable attention to the broad questions of taxation, the nobility were quite distinctive for their attention to the constitutional issues posed by the advance of the central state. They were sensitive to issues of civil liberties, of the authority of the Estates-General, of the rule of law (see p. 29). A Tocquevillean would surmise that their sense of identification with an imagined past autonomy was the glue that held together these notions of rights threatened by arbitrary state authority. Developing the sense that controls of various sorts needed to be put on the swelling state—a constitution, a legal code, stable judicial procedures, a representative legislative body, regional

13. I believe this to be the core point in the critiques by George Taylor and William Doyle of previous writing on the overall course of the Revolution. When Taylor suggests that what began as a "political" process turned into a "social" one, he is urging us to look for a revolutionary dynamic; similarly for Doyle when he urges us to see revolutionaries "created by the Revolution," rather than the reverse; Taylor, "Revolutionary and Nonrevolutionary Content"; Doyle, *Origins,* 213.

authorities with defined powers, supervision over finances, ministerial responsibility—the nobles also put forth the concept of a personal sphere on which the state is not to intrude: property (see p. 34). On the seigneurial rights, many noble *cahiers* maintained a discreet silence (see p. 56). (Were they uncertain, divided, prudent—or embarrassed?) When they did speak of these rights, however, they tended to stress their honorific rather than their lucrative aspects (see pp. 47–50). Or at least they tended to claim they did so: when, to glance at Chapter 3, one looks rather closely at what some of the noble *cahiers* purport to be issues of honor one can see that significant material claims are sometimes involved (see p. 80 et seq). The nobility seem quite unconcerned with aspects of seigneurialism that suggest a finely graded status hierarchy among the lords themselves. They defended their rights, then, as "property" (when they didn't invoke their "honor") (see pp. 79–85). A Marxist might see in this noble rhetoric the prerevolutionary triumph of the worldview of the bourgeois order; a Tocquevillean might think of a cultural adaptation to the antihierarchical leveling of the modernizing state bureaucracy.

One might situate this issue more broadly within the debate on the social bases of the Enlightenment: where a Marxist view sees the language of individuality and liberty as an intellectually coherent moral rationale for the profit-making, antitraditional, and rationalizing thrust of a developing capitalism chafing under legal structures and social practices that inhibit the full flowering of the marketplace,[14] a more Tocquevillean view might suggest that we see, as Denis Richet does,[15] the Enlightenment program as an aristocrat's reaction to the threat of autonomy posed by the growing state, a reaction later joined by (rather than initiated by) flourishing commercial interests. In any event, when it is not downright silent on seigneurial rights, the noble defense had already accepted the central terms of the discourse of property and individual liberty with which those rights were attacked.

The most distinctive aspects of the Third Estate's agenda were its concerns with privilege and with market hindrances (see pp. 35, 50–52, 62). Where the nobility tended to focus on issues of liberty in the sense of freedom from an arbitrary state the Third tended to focus on freedom to

14. Albert Soboul entitles a chapter on the Enlightenment "The Philosophy of the Bourgeoisie." He tells us that "the intellectual origins of the Revolution are to be sought in the philosophy that the bourgeoisie elaborated since the 17th century." We learn in the next few pages that Voltaire's aim was "to give the government over to bourgeois proprietors" while Rousseau may be seen as expressing "the political and social ideal of the petite bourgeoisie." Soboul goes on to find the unity of French Enlightenment thought in its "opposition to aristocracy." As for their constitutional views we are told that "the upper bourgeoisie was aware that the development of capitalism required a transformation of the State"; Soboul, *La Révolution française* (Paris: Editions Sociales, 1962), 1:69–79.

15. Denis Richet, *La France moderne: L'esprit des institutions* (Paris: Flammarion, 1973).

participate in the market, unconstrained by state, communal, or seigneurial barriers. The juridical equality of all within the national community, their other major distinctive focus, intersected this first concern in numerous ways (see p. 35). To eliminate fiscal privilege meant that special taxes on noble land that distorted land transactions would have to go; to eliminate privileged, even monopolistic, access to high-level careers would mean that those with skills could trade those skills for income and responsibility in a sort of job market ("the career open to talent"); to abandon regional privilege would advance the task of integrating the national market. With regard to the seigneurial rights, consistently enough, it was seigneurial claims to limit the market via monopolies, to have private claims on tolls and to command peasant labor that aroused the urban notables' greatest concern (see pp. 50–52). The attack on privilege ("private law" in its root meaning) necessarily entailed attacking many elements of the seigneurial regime, often seen, in the historical accounts of the day, as the legacy of a violent era of privately appropriated sovereignty.[16] Rather than an image of a society composed of hierarchically related corporate groups with distinct rights and obligations, whose structure was given by God and tradition, and which was supervised by the state, the new society would be seen as composed of formally equal individuals who could invent and reinvent their relationships through freely consented contracts and to whom the state was responsible. Marxist historians would readily recognize the growing market opportunities as the likely root of many of these Third Estate concerns. The antiprivilege aspect of the distinctive Third Estate agenda, however, is even more readily assimilable into the Tocquevillean argument about the leveling effect of a growing state that wipes out the meaningfully everyday character of local difference and personal privilege.

The peasants' agenda is far simpler to characterize. As shown in the parish *cahiers,* they were not particularly concerned with constitutional arrangements; they were focused on the details of the claims upon them by state, church, and lord. Nearly half of their grievances involve one or another burden, a strikingly larger figure than for the nobility or Third Estate (see Table 2.2). The peasants show relatively little concern for the symbolizations of status, far less than the Third does, which, to look ahead, may help to explain why many peasant communities seemed so indifferent to an abolition of just those rights that was so proudly proclaimed by the revolutionary legislature in August 1789 (see p. 48, Table 2.4, and p. 475). The peasants also seemed little interested in the lord's agents, surprising in

16. The Third Estate of Poitiers speaks of the authority that the lords usurped during the centuries of "ignorance, anarchy and confusion." For the Third of Auray, the rights "recall for us the centuries of rage and blindness." The Third of Toul sees many rights as "extorted before joining in the union with the crown." For the Third of Vitry-le-françois, monopolies and *corvées* "have no other principle than as the old vestiges of barbarism and slavery" (*AP* 5:412; *AP* 6:13, 115, 219).

light of a literature that has often argued that by giving the seigneurial regime a human face, these agents deflected attention from the lords (see p. 53). But we saw little personalization at all, as if the peasants clearly grasped the systemic character of seigneurialism, rather than focusing on individual wrongdoers.

The antiseigneurial element in the *cahiers* of the Third Estate, coupled with a nobility a significant portion of whose assemblies offered no public defense at all while others put forward a defense mounted in terms of the property rights so dear to the Third Estate, jointly constituted an important opening for peasant action. And peasant antiseigneurialism, in its turn, constituted an important opening for action on the part of the antiseigneurial elements of the urban notability. The potential for an antiseigneurial alliance of peasants and legislators was there in the *cahiers*. But only the potential: far more peasant attention in the spring of 1789 was given to taxation, the antiseigneurialism of the urban notables was far from identical to that of the peasantry and aspects of the Third Estate's position were antithetical to the interests of significant rural segments.

Chapter 3 took up the programs of the three groups. We saw considerable openness to change among all three groups and little support for the unreformed preservation of most institutions (see, e.g., Table 3.3). While the nobility were appreciably more conservative than the Third Estate, their embrace of change is striking and not readily compatible with those many versions of the basic Marxian model, which would have the nobility attached to a way of life under attack;[17] the pervasive embrace of change seems more easily consistent with Tocqueville's notion of a general cultural transformation. On the seigneurial rights, however, a significant portion of the nobility (and only the nobility) did indeed dig in its heels.

We saw that the seigneurial regime was less likely than most areas of French life to have attracted proposals for reform (see Tables 3.1 and 3.2). In this regard it differed profoundly from taxation, which, although the subject of many more grievances, also attracted many reform proposals. The peasants seem to have considered, not merely the weight of particular burdens, but the value of associated services and, sometimes, the fairness of the distribution of those burdens. The state, by the eve of the Revolution, was seen as a provider (or at least a potential provider) of vital services; the lord, his genuine public role eroded as the state advanced, had seen his claims upon the peasants redefined from the costs of appreciated services

17. Noble embrace of change is, however, quite compatible with a view of the nobility as itself in large part assimilated to the bourgeoisie. If the theoretical opposition between "bourgeois" and "aristocrats" is not empirically exemplified by "Third Estate" and "nobility" because the French nobility had become bourgeois, the theoretical problem posed by noble liberalism collapses. Noble conservatism (for example, the intransigeance of a minority on seigneurial rights) can be dealt with by speaking of an incomplete *embourgeoisement*.

to parasitism. This pattern explains why individual taxes, ecclesiastical exactions, and seigneurial rights differ from one another in the degree to which the peasants would consider some sort of reform. Among taxes, generally speaking, the indirect taxes, seen as lining the pockets of the rich rather than meeting the needs of state actions, are about as hopelessly illegitimate as the seigneurial rights (see p. 102). And among seigneurial rights, those tied to a communally valued service tend to attract significant, if minority, support for some sort of reform measures (see p. 110). Seigneurial courts, for example, are relatively reformable because some sort of judicial function was a recognized necessity of village life; after all, peasants disputed land use with one another as well as with lord and state (see p. 111). And why should the peasants prefer the king's distant and none-too-reliable justice over the nearer, cheaper and (if suitably reformed) competent judgment of one who knew well the particular community? The character of peasants' reform proposals depends a good deal on the particular exaction in question. Those many demands to reform taxation, especially direct taxation, assume the existence of a service and concentrate on the attainment of equity. Those few demands for reforming seigneurial rights rarely concern such equity issues; it is a matter of assuring the services (and avoiding the associated disservices).[18]

When we compare the reform strategies of our different groups, we are also struck by how frequently the Third Estate endorsed some sort of legal procedure, as in their proposals to support peasant communities in lawsuits as a mechanism to enforce desired change (see p. 129). We may see here a harbinger of years of conflict to come, conflicts in which puzzled or angry legislators managed to convince themselves that the peasants were failing to recognize the generous benefits that they had received, while the peasantry, often rejecting being swallowed up along the legal route, mounted thousands of insurrections (see Chapter 9, pp. 542–47). And until well into 1792, one of the principal ways in which revolutionary legislators tried to cope with rural turbulence was by altering the terms under which peasant communities or lords could sue each other (see Chapter 8).

There are other significant ways in which the peasant demands of the spring of 1789 are echoed in the legislation of the following August and March. The seigneurial rights for which the peasants were most likely to propose measures other than simple abolition included many of the payments to the lord (see Tables 3.4, 3.6, and 3.11); perhaps this explains in part the confidence (or at least the hope) of many legislators that a program conceived along the lines of August 1789 and March 1790 might actually achieve sufficient peasant support to be viable. Some rights were slated for

18. A community might, for example, accept the hunting rights but only if it is possible to protect fields from destruction. See Chapter 3, p. 118.

indemnification, others for outright abolition—and the distinctions adopted in March 1790 were rather close to the expressed peasant wishes of March 1789. We can now recognize, however, that the peasantry, by March 1790, were not as they had been one year previously and were prepared, in many parts of France (see Chapter 7), to go on fighting. Certainly, some sense of the possibility of a moderate compromise would seem consistent with the views expressed in the parish *cahiers* in which significant rural factions opted for reform, others for indemnification, and still others contented themselves with expressions of hostility without any specific proposal at all (let alone a radical one) (see p. 136).

This pattern of peasant grievances is utterly inconsistent with any notion of a mindless countryside, in thrall to either an unthinking tradition or an unreflective radicalism. Peasant communities seem to have distinguished carefully among rights according to their possible value to the community (see p. 132) as well as the feasibility of the compromise indemnification project (see pp. 90–94). Restating some important results from Chapter 2, we see that the peasants showed little interest in the strictly honorific aspects of seigneurialism and surprisingly little in the agents of the lord. Many grievances, moreover, appear to have been national in scope, or, in any event, did not specify any region or locality (see p. 136). It seems likely that peasants engaged in careful and rational calculations of costs and rewards, right by right; that they had a sense of fairness as well as burden; that they had an abstract conception of a seigneurial system rather than limiting their thinking to their own, known, particular lord; that they had a certain acceptance—however resignedly that might have been—of state authority (as indicated by how rare demands to abolish the tax system were compared to demands for reform) (see Table 3.1); that, in short, they had some sense of public service, of equity, and of citizenship. It is, however, also the case that peasant communities were more likely than the elites to have locally oriented demands as well as to have nonspecific sources of resentment (see Table 3.1). Plainly, the battles for the hearts and minds of the country people was still up for grabs at the onset of the Revolution.

If we may glance ahead for a moment at Chapters 5 and 6, we get powerful supporting evidence from Roger Chartier's comparison of the rural *cahiers* of one *bailliage* in 1789 with their predecessors' complaints in 1614 as well as from the long-term study of rural contestation from 1661 to 1789 carried out by the team working under Jean Nicolas and Guy Lemarchand. We do see a shift in grievances away from the claims of the state and toward the claims of the lords, but the claims of the state are still far more numerous (see p. 266). The Nicolas-Lemarchand data show, similarly, that antiseigneurial events were only a small proportion of all riotous action at their seventeenth-century starting point and that the proportion of antiseigneurial events was rising late in the Old Regime (see p. 264).

Nonetheless, more "traditional" forms of peasant action—the classic anti-tax rebellions and the eighteenth century's up-and-coming subsistence events—still claimed the lion's share. Other, usually more geographically circumscribed, studies confirm the general picture. Among these, Cynthia Bouton's work on the changing nature of subsistence events deserves special notice; she shows that, by the 1770s, subsistence actions were being carried out in a way that went beyond the usual patterns of market invasions and convoy blockages; in addition to these standard forms of action, peasants now also mounted a preeminently rural cluster of attacks on producers, large landholders, prosperous peasants, large-scale tenants and sometimes even lords and monasteries. This is a shift away from seeing the state and its agents as the ultimate culprits and ultimate saviors in scarcities; now the institutions of civil society were accountable and among the new actions in which the community went directly to the problematic points, rather than called for state intervention, there were some seigneurial targets (see p. 247). All this evidence is clear: late in the Old Regime, an antiseigneurial shift in word and deed occurred in the French countryside, strongly enough to suggest that our notion of the "prerevolution" as a largely elite process is in need of some revision (see p. 335). While it is probably fair to say that we do not yet know the full scope of this rural and plebeian prerevolution, it is also clear that it had not gone nearly far enough by the spring of 1789 to account, in itself, for the full range and intensity of the antiseigneurial insurrections.

In Chapter 3 we also explored the *cahiers* of those one might think most likely to defend Old Regime institutions in general and seigneurial rights in particular. When we examined the noble program at the onset of revolution, we were struck not merely by how open to change they were generally, but that even on the seigneurial rights, where a significant minority of assemblies took an unyielding stand and an even larger number avoided discussion altogether, there was still a rather significant body of reform sentiment, not weaker indeed than the reform sentiment among the peasants and urban notables (see Table 3.1) The nobles, then were about as divided as could be; indeed, by one measure, the seigneurial rights were among the subjects that exhibited the greatest noble division.[19] When we shifted from considering the seigneurial regime as a whole to specific seigneurial rights, the study of the actions demanded only reinforced some of the conclusions of Chapter 2. There was simply no interest in defending any elaborate noble hierarchy (see p. 84); defense of the system, while sometimes couched in terms of honor, was often constructed out of notions of property rights (see pp.

19. John Markoff and Gilbert Shapiro, "Consensus and Conflict at the Onset of Revolution: A Quantitative Study of France in 1789," *American Journal of Sociology* 91 (1985): 43.

79–88), the very same notions with which its theoretically minded opponents were combating the seigneurial regime.

A basis for a peasant-bourgeois alliance against "feudalism" existed at the onset of revolution, although the work of forging it was not yet accomplished. Chapter 4 explores the degree to which the revolutionary notion(s) of that feudalism were already present to the assemblies in the spring of 1789. And just as the peasant-bourgeois alliance was not born whole, but was made, we saw that the full web of associations of seigneurialism, as used on August 4, 1789, was only partly woven a half-year earlier (not to speak of what was "feudal" in 1792).

There was, at the time of drafting of the *cahiers,* a sense among the assemblies of the Third Estate that seigneurial rights belonged in the same discussion as each other: in the most literal sense, Third Estate *cahiers* that discussed one right tended to discuss others as well (see p. 148). In this regard the nobility were rather different: they tended to think of two groups of rights, the honorific ones, which they claimed to defend, and what I call here the lucrative ones. Noble discussions of particular honorific rights tended to evoke discussions of other such rights, but did not tend to evoke discussions of lucrative rights, and vice versa (see p. 190).

Returning to the Third Estate documents and searching for which other institutions tend to have been treated along with seigneurial rights, we see that ecclesiastical exactions were associated with seigneurial ones (see p. 154). Indeed, religious issues generally tended to be more discussed in documents in which discussion of the seigneurial regime was more extensive (see Table 4.7). Taxation on the other hand was generally not so associated, although certain specific taxes were (*franc-fief, centième denier,* the royal *corvée,* and the *aides*) (see p. 158). More broadly and in brief summary we find that some of the institutions later brought along with seigneurial rights into the discussion of "feudalism" were, while other were not, so associated at the onset of the Revolution. One very important missing element was any derogatory lumping-together of the royal and the feudal (see p. 162). Not only, then, was the alliance of bourgeois and peasant no more than incipient but anything that could be conceptualized as an antifeudal coalition would be hard to imagine without further elaboration of what was meant by the feudalism such a movement is claimed to have targeted. What the study of the *cahiers* suggests, in other words, is that to the extent that there was some meaningful action participated in significantly by both a peasantry and a revolutionary bourgeoisie, some sort of important negotiations or quasi-negotiations took place after the spring of 1789; and that to the extent that revolutionary discourse conceived of that alliance as directed against "feudalism," some sort of conceptual elaboration of that notion took place after that spring as well.

But such processes hardly started from zero. There was a very significant peasant antiseigneurialism in the *cahiers* and the same could be said of the Third Estate; there also was a considerable sense, in the *cahiers* of the Third Estate, of the centrality of the seigneurial regime. Seigneurial rights were seen, to some extent, to hinder economic growth; to be an important part of a regime of privilege; to be intimately linked to the church. The nobility, on the other hand, did not seem to see the seigneurial regime at all. Not only did many of its *cahiers* say nothing, but those that did speak did not seem to see a whole, but two halves (see p. 190): an honorable part and an income-producing part. (Was it a self-destructive conceptualization to have thus dissociated its own sense of honor from its income?) The income-producing part was often defended by an expansive notion of honor and the honorific part by claims of property. The claims of some immutable hierarchy, or of any finely graded hierarchy immutable or otherwise, were hardly taken up at all.

Having explored the positions taken at the Revolution's onset, we turned to the ensuing dialogue of legislators and peasants. In Chapters 5–7 we examined the peasant half of that dialogue: the propensities to undertake various types of action in Chapter 5, the unfolding rhythms of conflict in Chapter 6 and the regional patterns in Chapter 7. Antiseigneurial events proved to be the most common (more than one-third the total) over the entire time span from summer 1788 to summer 1793. Subsistence events came in second with one-quarter, followed by religious events, then panics, counterrevolution, land conflict; only then do we get to the formerly flourishing anti-tax events. Conflicts over wages proved to be the least numerous category in our sample (see Table 5.1). It was quite consistent with the *cahiers* that there was remarkably little personal violence in the antiseigneurial events,[20] consistent with how little here is by way of personification in those documents: the lord's agents were far more rarely the subject of grievance than one might well have expected on the basis of the historical literature (see Chapter 2, p. 53). In our tabulations of rebellion, we found that the particular lord himself is also seriously injured far less often than one might have expected given the intensity of mobilization for thousands of incidents. Indeed, personification of the targets of peasant anger seems to have been generally rather limited in other sorts of conflict as well. (The great exception was the religious domain, in which a large proportion of all events have an individualized clerical target (see p. 230); might one see here something of the primal, perhaps primitive, character of communal religious identity, to suggest a Durkheimian conjecture?) This low general level of personalization is consistent with an interpretation of

20. See Table 5.2 and 225–26. (Of course, even if severe injuries resulted from only a small proportion of events, if there were thousands of events there could still be a lot of pain—and there was.)

the *cahiers* that sees France's villagers supporting an abstract conceptualization of a social system become unjust rather than an aberrantly malicious evildoer causing ill.

Let me stress how small a portion of revolutionary events were constituted by anti-tax actions (see Table 5.1). With all due reservations about the data, which very likely do understate the extent of such events (see pp. 233–37), it appears that paying taxes was less unpalatable in the revolutionary years than was paying seigneurial dues. Let us recall that in light of the ease of tax evasion, the fact that anyone paid taxes at all was just shy of miraculous. Recall again the *cahiers,* in which taxation, the most widely discussed of French institutions, differed profoundly from the seigneurial rights in that taxation was, on the whole, seen as reformable (see Table 3.1). I contended that the *cahiers* show a certain acceptance of the state in the countryside—and a contrasting intolerance for the further existence of seigneurial rights; the pattern of insurrectionary actions revealed in Chapter 5 is consistent with such a view.

The forms of peasant action were variations within known patterns: the destruction or seizure of power-giving documents; sacking the residence of wrongdoers; the rescue of one's fellow from the clutches of authority; the reappropriation of usurped rights; severing the enemy's sacred ties; redistribution of resources; imposing costs on violators of community solidarity. While there were important innovations, ranging from displays of particular colors (like Bourbon white, for example) to the deployment of unfamiliar symbols (such as the maypole, mysterious and threatening to revolutionary elites), for the most part these were familiar-enough routines. This very familiarity, this very drawing on a culturally present tradition, was no doubt utterly essential to easy comprehension and ultimately rapid diffusion of insurrectionary forms (see pp. 261–64, and Chapter 7). Nonetheless, the deployment of these forms of action against the lords, in anything like the concentration reached during the Revolution, was utterly without precedent. The central thrust of seventeenth-century risings was antitaxation; in the relatively peaceful eighteenth century, subsistence issues were added as central foci of protest. In the last prerevolutionary years, antiseigneurial actions, while rising, still lagged far behind. And this picture is reinforced by the *cahiers.*

How, then, did it come about that so many peasant insurrections were directed, first and foremost, at the lords? Chapter 6, on the rhythms of contention, showed enormous month-to-month variation in the intensity of conflict (see Fig. 6.1). The peak month for the entire half-decade was July 1789 and large numbers of insurrectionary events took place as well in January 1790, April 1792, August 1792, and March 1793, with lesser peaks in June 1790 and June 1791. The rapid and radical oscillation in conflict intensity testifies to the volatile nature of collective action in risky situations.

As potential participants reevaluated the likelihood of success and the likelihood of danger in light of insurrectionary developments elsewhere as well as ever-changing news from the legislative and local governments, people rapidly mobilized and demobilized.

Although the overall intensity of conflict fluctuated wildly, however, one may discern some clear temporal patterns in the concentration of the French countryside upon particular targets. In the summer of 1788 subsistence events were overwhelmingly dominant and antiseigneurial events were nearly nonexistent (see Figs. 6.2 [a]–[d]). Attacks on the rights of the lords began to rise in the late autumn of 1788. The great spike of July 1789 was nearly one-third composed of antiseigneurial events. By the burst of insurrectionary action in the winter of 1789–90, antiseigneurial events had become the dominant component of peak periods of rural mobilization and remained so through the spring of 1792. By the wave of late summer 1792, however, the antiseigneurial focus was beginning to fade: the proportion in September 1792, for example, was a little over one-third. Beyond this point, attacks on the rights of the lords fell off rapidly: the late fall minipeak was dominated, as in the early phases of the Revolution, by subsistence events; the spring 1793 peak was overwhelmingly made up of counterrevolution (see Table 6.3). If any sort of peasant action can be said to have opened the way for later developments, then, it was the subsistence events. But an antiseigneurial movement grew strong and stayed strong until the fall of 1792.

Chapter 7 took up the spatial dimension of the insurrectionary waves. By thinking of the variations in social, political, and economic structures across the map of France, it was possible to assess many of the claims that have been made about the social circumstances nurturing peasant insurrection and, more particularly, peasant antiseigneurialism. Thus, the heaviness of the hand of the Paris-centered royal administration was quite different in the directly administered *pays d'élections* from what it was in the *pays d'états* where some greater measure of autonomy had been preserved in the form of Provincial Estates. The pressures and opportunities of the marketplace can be approximated by the extent of major road and navigable river, the size of towns and the nature of the local crops; the mobilizational impact of immediate economic crisis by variations in the price of grain; and the like. We find, in that first spring and summer of Revolution, that indicators of both market involvement and of state penetration increased the propensity to insurrection. The long-term processes undermining peasant acquiescence dear to both Marxists and Tocquevilleans have some explanatory force and thereby help us understand some of the long-term processes that mobilized peasants to crack the Old Regime in the spring and summer of 1789. Indeed, market opportunities seem to have fostered virtually every sort of insurrectionary event (see Table 7.8). The presence of a specifically antiseigneurial thrust within that movement of the early Revolution, however, is less well explained by such structural conditions. As we move forward in time, moreover, the explanatory power of these particular enduring structures shifts: antiseigneurial actions were no longer primarily rooted in the openfield of the North and East as well as the coastal zones of Provence as they had been in the spring and summer of 1789. Mapping the changing locations of uprising shows such shifts clearly. After that great wave of uprising in the summer of 1789 and the self-consciously epochal decrees of August, areas of France not notably mobilized for antiseigneurial action at first (and sometimes not notably mobilized—at first—for any sort of action at all) entered the fray. At the tail end of 1789 and the beginning of 1790, peasants in "backward" areas like Brittany and the Southwest not only rose but took on the seigneurial regime (see Tables 7.5 and 7.6). One might almost say that the new antiseigneurial zones were quite similar to the classic regions of the anti-tax revolts of the seventeenth century, but they were now rising against a target not generally associated with those regions' more well-known past movements. The spatiotemporal analysis, then, reveals something of the structures that nurtured revolts of various sorts and permits us to sift and evaluate some of the classical theses about what the important structural changes were. But that analysis also suggests some of the limits of a purely structural approach, since the spatial shifts once again demonstrate that there are short-term processes at work as well.

We also see how distinctive is each province's revolution. Provence, for example, is both an early and a late center of antiseigneurialism. And we see as well that there was no single geographic center of insurrectionary innovation. The development of organizational vehicles (National Guards, political clubs), symbolizations (trees of liberty) or targets might remain locally or regionally bound at one point and then be taken up elsewhere. On the other hand, if we consider the entire period our data covers, antiseigneurial events prove to be among the least regionally restricted of the forms of conflict we have tracked. Legislators groping for simple but effective formulas to deal with complex realities might well find in antiseigneurial legislation a key to coping with France's many different peasantries.

Peasants, urban elites, and nobles each with their own distinct sense of the salient aspects of the seigneurial regime and their own programs for change; thousands of acts of rural rebellion directed against many distinct targets—these are the data we have been studying. How did it come about, starting from the various positions set forth in 1789, that the pattern of insurrection was one increasingly focused on the seigneurial regime until deep into 1792 and which the legislators themselves understood as part of the overthrow of something called "feudalism"? Why didn't the French peasants remain focused on taxation and subsistence issues, the central concerns of most rebellious peasants in the seventeenth and eighteenth centuries for a long time now? We have urged that in part (but only in part) the answer lies in structural changes that increased acceptance of the central state and decreased the tolerability of the seigneurial regime. Beyond this important first step, however, this book has argued that the actions of revolutionary peasants and revolutionary legislators opened possibilities for each other. As rural communities discovered the strengths of antiseigneurial sentiment in the upper Third Estate during the electoral campaign and within the National Assembly during the summer of 1789, they discovered the great payoff to insisting on legislative progress; after the decrees of August 4–11 in which many legislators hoped to have found the key to rural pacification, the seigneurial regime stood revealed as even more vulnerable and many peasants continued to ignore the proffered civil peace (see Chapter 8). Ultimately the legislature went along and yielded in practice to much of what the country people were demanding: the legislation of August 1792 yielded in practice to the peasant attacks and the following July the legislature yielded in principle to the commonsense meaning of abolition of feudal rights. For its part the legislators had the most diverse motives in constructing the August 1789 package: the search for a compromise; the genuine belief in turning history around; the attempt to reconcile their own pocketbook interest with removing a hindrance to social and economic progress; the hope of satisfying the country people without undermining the value of the royal and church properties that they hoped to sell; the possibility of delay through redefining the social meaning of August 4 retrospectively by future manipulation of the terms of indemnification. Disappointed, angry, and frustrated that significant peasant mobilization continued to take place, the legislature continued to tinker with the law (see pp. 450–65) while at the same time convincing themselves that feudalism, which they claimed to have abolished, was the central institution of the Old Regime and was central, too, to the increasingly hostile relations with the other European powers. With the commencement of war, the attempt to convince themselves that, pending indemnification, some combination of coercion and persuasion could get French peasants to continue to pay, broke down as the conscription of French villagers to liberate Belgian and German villagers from feudalism seemed an impossible matter without recognizing that for French villagers the liberation of France from feudalism was as yet a promise; try as they might, the legislators had failed to persuade their own villagers that their liberation from feudalism had already been achieved (see pp. 469–79). Revolutionary legislators encouraged revolt and revolutionary peasants forced the legislators to live up to the commonsense meanings of their own rhetoric.

While the legislators let the relatively united peasant communities push them much further than they had originally intended on seigneurial rights, on issues much more divisive within those same communities (land conflicts primarily; wage conflicts were relatively scarce), the legislature never acted with the clarity that obtained—ultimately—in the seigneurial arena. (Perhaps the failure of the sharecroppers' movement in the Southwest that clearly emerged after the battle over seigneurial rights was generally won, is another good example. Joined with other peasants elsewhere, the southwestern sharecroppers' tenacious refusal of the initial revolutionary legislation made a significant contribution to the antiseigneurial movement's success. Isolated, later, they obtained much less.)[21]

In the course of their dialogue with the peasantry the legislators attempted a narrow definition of feudalism, initially exempting many payments from immediate and uncompensated abolition on the grounds that such payments were inherently based on proper contracts (see Chapter 9). At the same time, the affective power of the claim to have abolished feudalism came not from the joys of such a delimited abolition, but from an increasingly broad and vague notion of feudalism, virtually coextensive with the entire Old Regime and thereby part of the claim to have overturned French history (and to be fundamentally at odds with the European powers where feudalism still held the day). It was the simultaneous development of the narrow and the broad senses of "the abolition of feudalism" that gives the legislators' talk about feudalism its special quality: its evidently frequent (though not always) and deeply felt sense of having, godlike, brought light where there had been darkness through the power of words coexisting with a condescension, nervousness, and hostility toward the country people who wanted changes that were meaningful in their own lives. The intertwining of creating a new world and quibbling about indemnification modalities, of the generously grand and the stingily petty gave these revolutionary debates their special character. In the course of ultimately yielding to the countryside, the revolutionaries disseminated one of their most profound conceptual constructions: the sense of "revolution" as a willed rupture of the fabric of history, of a total repudiation of a past on behalf of a better future, an image of the time of the lords as a social order totally overthrown that has continued to permeate the polarities of the past and the present in the social sciences.

Elites and Plebeians

As in many other historical episodes of conflict and change, the Revolution's chroniclers have long wrestled with the social location of the impetus for recreating institutions. Does the energy for destruction and reconstruction, perhaps along with the vision to imagine the new, well up out of the popular

21. See Peter M. Jones, *The Peasantry in the French Revolution* (Cambridge: Cambridge University Press, 1988), 99–103.

classes? Or do those accustomed to the uses of power seize some epochal opportunity to impose their own vision of social reformation? The relative weights of the actions and projects of revolutionary elites and French villagers in dismantling the seigneurial regime have been variously characterized. For Alfred Cobban (see p. 594), a Marxist notion of a bourgeois-peasant antifeudal alliance was doubly nonsensical: first, because the leadership of the Third Estate were in fact quite conservative on seigneurial rights. Their only distinction from the intransigent portion of the nobility, in Cobban's view, was their clever ploy of indemnification, a protective smokescreen behind which seigneurial rights were to continue. In the second place, the notion of an antifeudal Revolution was nonsensical because there was no very meaningful feudalism to destroy to begin with. For George Taylor, on the contrary, there was not very much radicalism anywhere initially, but to the extent that there was, it was lodged in the world of the urban elites and made up no part at all of rural attitudes.[22] Albert Soboul saw the driving force of the rural aspect of the Revolution in the actions of peasants themselves,[23] particularly insofar as they, along with the urban popular classes, were able to obtain an adequately responsive government in 1793: "The peasant and popular revolution was at the very heart of the bourgeois revolution and carried it steadily forward."[24] François Furet and Ran Halévi, on the contrary, are impressed by the initial radicalism of 1789, seen in large part as a conceptual break with the past (including the very conception of a conceptual break), and carried by a bourgeoisie energized by their vision of overturning French history.[25] While the radicalism that interests Soboul is most closely realized in 1793, making the interplay of Jacobin dictatorship and popular movements the central thing to be explained, Furet and Halévi want us to appreciate, again, that initial break, and to see the radicalism of 1789 as deeper (and as a deeper mystery) than that of 1793 (xcv); that initial radicalism is exhibited centrally in the language of legislators, and popular movements play only an auxiliary role.[26]

It is probable, indeed, that similar debates go on about most other historical moments that combine a great sense of conflict with a great sense of transformation. If we move away from the discipline of history to

22. Taylor speaks of the "docility shown by the peasants towards the seigneurial system" in their *cahiers;* see his "Revolutionary and Nonrevolutionary Content in the *Cahiers* of 1789: An Interim Report," *French Historical Studies* 7 (1972): 495.

23. "The most active wing of this revolution was not so much the commercial bourgeoisie . . . , but the mass of small direct producers whose surplus was seized by the feudal aristocracy with the full support of the judiciary and the means of constraint available to the state under the Ancien Régime" (Soboul, *The French Revolution,* 8).

24. "The political instrument of change was the Jacobin dictatorship of the lower and middle section of the bourgeoisie, supported by the popular classes" (ibid).

25. François Furet and Ran Halévi, *Orateurs de la Révolution française,* vol. 1, *Les constituants* (Paris: Gallimard, 1989), lxvii–lxxvi.

26. Soboul's masterpiece is, appropriately, *The Parisian Sans-Culottes in the Year Two.* Nowhere

the social sciences more likely to be self-consciously concerned with the formulation of generalizations, we can see, in North America at any rate, a curious disciplinary division in emphasis. Until fairly recently, sociology was where social movements were studied: sociologists have devoted great energy to unearthing the sources of recruitment into movements, the variety of ways in which movement organizations are structured, the historical settings within which movements emerge, the ways in which movements organize the lives of their members, and, to a lesser extent, the transformative effect of movement participation on participants. Given notably short shrift, however, until quite recently, was anything resembling comparable attention to the power-holders of whom those movements made demands.[27] Quite the contrary could be said for the field of political science: political scientists, students of every nuance of government, lovingly attentive to governmental organization, the social origins of government personnel, the nature of policymaking and policy implementation, the ideologies of governing elites and the like, have been almost completely neglectful of social movements.[28] This division of intellectual labor means that almost no one was studying the interplay of states and movements.

But what seems to emerge from our examination of peasants, lords, and legislators is precisely that a great deal of what propelled the Revolution in the countryside was the interplay of peasant and legislator, plebeian and elite, periphery and center. Peasants and legislators altered their actions in response to the other. As legislators, for example, attempted to cope with the failure of previous legislation to demobilize rural activism, they altered the terms on which disputed cases would be fought out in the courts in order to increase the frequency of peasant victory in litigation by shifting the burden of proof from peasant to lord (see Chapter 8, p. 465). The peasants, in turn, to pursue this particular matter, reacted to the increased significance of seigneurial documents implied by the shifting burden of proof, not so much by moving into the legal arena, as by becoming increasingly prone to seize or destroy those documents (see Chapter 8, p. 504). This miniprocess, a small piece of a much larger and richer dialogue, could not be adequately captured by summarizing it as "really" a peasant initiative or a legislative one; both parties took their own initiatives with an eye on the other's.

---

has Furet so imaginatively deployed evidence on behalf of his view of the Revolution as in his introduction with Ran Halévi to their collection of revolutionary oratory, just cited. See Albert Soboul, *Les Sans-culottes parisiens en l'an II: Mouvement populaire et gouvernement révolutionnaire, 2 Juin 1793–Thermidor an II* (Paris: Librairie Clavreuil, 1958).

27. To some extent the picture just drawn had been ameliorated by the new focus on "bringing the state back in." See Peter B. Evans, Dietrich Rueschemeyer, and Theda Skocpol, *Bringing the State Back In* (Cambridge: Cambridge University Press, 1985).

28. The great exception is Sidney Tarrow. See, for example, *Democracy and Disorder: Protest and Politics in Italy, 1965–1975* (Oxford: Clarendon Press, 1989).

We see at every turn that the movement in the villages and the politics of the legislatures converged on an increasingly radical antiseigneurialism. Major waves of peasant actions were the occasion for antiseigneurial legislation even when the peasant actions were not overwhelmingly antiseigneurial (as in summer 1789 and spring 1793). Thus the antiseigneurial propensities of the legislators and their ideological construction of feudalism led them to deal with peasant problems by going further in dismantling the seigneurial regime. In March 1790, perhaps with an eye on the peasant demands of one year earlier, they were tougher on some seigneurial rights than others; but the legislative assault on the symbolics of noble honor of June 1790, so horrifying to the nobles and moving to the well-to-do commoners, was far less important to the countryside.[29] Peasant rebellion got seigneurial rights on the legislative agenda, again and again, but whether the legislators followed the peasant program or not varied a good deal from moment to moment. Peasant disruption yielded legislative responses, but not necessarily the responses desired. Ultimately, the legislators, pressed by war, began to take note of the stress of material burdens, not symbolics, in the peasant position.

Students of social movements, one might comment here, have sometimes noted a similar pattern in diverse contexts. Elite actions open the door to social-movement challengers who push the door further open still—and sometimes tear it off its hinges altogether; social movements get issues on elite agendas; elite actions in dealing with those agendas frequently diverge from the intentions of movement participants.[30] We have a dialogue, not two monologues.

If we look to the realm of ideas, we find again an irreducibly interactive component. Public positions staked out in the *cahiers* at the beginning of the Revolution were altered as the opportunities and constraints changed rapidly. The *cahiers* of the Third Estate, even when supplemented by considering the more conservative views of the nobility, are a very imperfect predictor of the legislation actually drafted by the National Assembly (let alone by subsequent legislatures); the positions staked out by France's forty thousand rural communities in the spring of 1789 are an even less perfect predictor of what the country people would or would not settle for as little as one year later. Why not? The *cahiers* are not a magic window opening onto the souls of peasants or urban notables. They are public statements, hammered out with an eye on the possibilities and risks of the moment;[31] some of those possibilities and risks were the same one year later, but

29. See Chapters 2–4 on the honorific rights in the *cahiers*.

30. Sidney Tarrow, *Struggle, Politics and Reform: Collective Action, Social Movements and Cycles of Protest* (Ithaca: Cornell University Center for International Studies, 1989).

31. See Chapter 2, pp. 26–28; Gilbert Shapiro and John Markoff, *Revolutionary Demands: A Content Analysis of the Cahiers de Doléances of 1789* (Stanford: Stanford University Press, 1997).

many had changed. The very concept of "the feudal regime," a major conceptual tool with which the revolutionary elites interpreted the world to themselves and explained their actions to the world, was itself in flux and modified in the course of the interaction of peasants and legislators.

Is such an entity as a purely peasant or legislative discourse ever conceivable? When peasants speak or act it is to make an impact on someone; the same for legislators. Unless we adopt some notion of purely expressive acts, with no element of calculation whatsoever, we must concede that there is always an other to whom one speaks, whether the form of that speech is in grievances, insurrection, legislation. The habits of discourse are themselves, moreover, shaped interactively. We have had many occasions to note the powerful impact of a culture of legal professionalism on both peasants and lords, not to mention the upper reaches of the Third Estate. As compared to the *cahiers* of 1614 the parish documents of 1789 were coherently ordered and employed categories at once understandable by the administrative personnel to whom those late eighteenth-century rural communities had plainly become accustomed.[32] Both peasants at one extreme and nobles (see pp. 34, 84–85) at the other employed rhetoric in which the language of contract, property, voluntary consent, and rational negotiation were central. (We may speculate whether the nobility's position was doomed in advance by its conversion to the terms of discourse of the bourgeois world.)

The village, even in relatively quiet times, was rarely, if ever, a self-contained world. The all too scarce memoirs of those who had known this eighteenth-century rural community from within all offer eloquent testimony to that effect. Pierre Prion, a down-on-his-luck notary's son who took employment with a Languedocian marquis in the earlier part of the century; Monsieur Nicolas, who had left the home of his father, a prosperous peasant risen to seigneurial judge in Burgundy, to become the "Rousseau of the gutter"; the desperately poor boy who escaped the sort of stepmother who provided the model for many a folk-tale, ultimately to become Captain Coignet in Napoleon's army—they show us a world of villagers coming and going, collectively challenging a lord or individually fleeing the recruiting sergeant, divided in its adherence to France's rival religious currents, with an upper stratum importing urban notions and tastes, appreciative of those among them versed in the ways of law and administration.[33]

Even the analysis of the insurrections themselves demands a sense not just of the roots of peasant actions but of interactions. Conflict is not only, as the

32. Roger Chartier, "Cultures, lumières et doléances: Les cahiers de 1789," *Revue d'histoire moderne et contemporaine* 28 (1981): 68–93.

33. Emmanuel Le Roy Ladurie and Orest Ranum, eds., *Pierre Prion, Scribe: Mémoires d'un écrivain de campagne au XVIIIe siècle* (Paris: Gallimard-Julliard, 1985); Nicolas-Edmé Restif de la Bretonne, *My Father's Life* (Gloucester: Sutton, 1986); *Les cahiers du Capitaine Coignet, 1799–1815* (Paris: Hachette, 1968).

phrase goes, as old as history but, like other quintessentially interactive phenomena, is virtually incomprehensible without a historical narrative. Like the tango, conflict is the sort of thing it takes at least two to do: one party attempts to injure another, to seize something from another, to defend itself from another, to demand that another do something (perhaps to or for a third party). As the second party responds (and perhaps third, fourth, and other parties as well), the first responds in turn to those responses. The choice among future actions is made in light of expectations that draw on past experience, on the continual rediscovery of how the other parties react to one's own actions, on the continual reassessment of tactics and goals. Conflict exists in time as parties interact and, in interacting, change. Conflicts, therefore, are processes and as processes have histories. The central evidence on which to develop an understanding of conflict, then must be historical.

When we note that rural communities lived, not in hermetically sealed compartments, but continually interacted with priests, lords, government administrators, and (hardly the least) lawyers, we are very far from embracing any thesis of inherent rural incapacity to formulate their own interests. Just as the evidence of the *cahiers* shows considerable nuance in distinguishing one tax from the rest, one seigneurial right from the rest, so, too does the shifting choice of targets of insurrection display a reasoned and continual reevaluation of their situation.

In action and reaction, in seizing opportunities and in coping with threats posed by the other, legislators and peasants made the Revolution antiseigneurial. Can one say that the plebeian contribution was violence, the legislative conceptual? This has been a common notion, at first the property of the political right as conservative legislators held good country people seduced by a seditious, educated stratum and later, in the nineteenth century, appropriated by a left who saw a vital role for a theory-bearing stratum to speak for the voiceless. Consider the following vivid passage of François Furet. "But the decrees of August 4 to August 11 number among the founding texts of modern France. They destroyed aristocratic society from top to bottom, along with its structure of dependencies and privileges. For this structure they substituted the modern, autonomous individual, free to do whatever was not prohibited by law. August 4 wiped the slate clean by eliminating whatever remained of intrasocial powers between the individual and the social body as a whole."[34] Since structures weren't "destroyed' in a week's time—Furet's own work is testimony to continuity in political struggle over a century[35]—this paragraph is most plausible as a statement on the level of conceptualization. The National Assembly can be

34. François Furet, "Night of August 4," in François Furet and Mona Ozouf, *Critical Dictionary of the French Revolution* (Cambridge: Harvard University Press, 1989), 112.

35. François Furet, *La Révolution de Turgot à Jules Ferry, 1770–1880* (Paris: Hachette, 1988).

credited with a new image of French society. Even so, this seems far too strong: the history of women's rights shows plainly that even conceptually, the National Assembly did not wholly do away with intrasocietal hierarchies; the free, autonomous, individual citizens were a band of brothers whose women were still dependent.[36]

Amending Furet to allow more weight to the plebeian role, we seem to have plebeian violence plus elite conceptualizations as the revolutionary motor. But recall how often we have seen an interplay of peripheral and central, plebeian and elite, initiative: in the National Guards, in the diffusion of Trees of Liberty, in the locus of antiseigneurial violence. Why *assume* that radical lawyers had the ideas, ideas that ultimately impressed themselves on a welcoming or hostile population? If, as Hilton Root has suggested,[37] lawyers representing peasant communities against their lords had forged an antiseigneurial judicial discourse, was the direction of influence only from lawyer to peasant community? This seems a dubious proposition, if perhaps not quite so dubious as a notion of a pristine peasant community, unaffected by legal/administrative contexts. This would be to follow the legislators in seeing the action of intellect in Merlin's distinctions and ignorance in those of southwestern sharecroppers, violence in the actions of the sharecroppers and not in those of Merlin and his fellow legislators. The writing of history tends to quote the words of the legislators more than the words of the sharecroppers, but that tells us nothing about the ultimate sources of ideas and practices. The evidence presented here is that the abolition of seigneurial rights was a complex process, and a collective, but not a consensual, one, that grew from differences between village and legislature (and differences among villages and among legislators) as much as it grew by convergence, commonality, diffusion.

There are two important, opposed challenges to this picture of plebeian/elite dialogue that still need some comment: first, the charge, quite common in the 1990s, that the plebeian violence was but a tragic sideshow in a history primarily driven by elite reform. The second, the view that the elite reform was nothing but a fraud.

Did It Matter?

In the summer of 1989, heads of state gathered in France to participate in the celebration of the Revolution's Bicentennial.[38] Since the revolutionary

36. Carol Pateman, *The Sexual Contract* (Stanford: Stanford University Press, 1988); Lynn A. Hunt, *The Family Romance of the French Revolution* (Berkeley and Los Angeles: University of California Press, 1992).

37. Root, *Peasants and King in Burgundy: Agrarian Foundations of French Absolutism* (Berkeley and Los Angeles: University of California Press, 1987), 183–93.

38. This section draws on John Markoff, "Violence, Emancipation and Democracy: The Countryside in the French Revolution," *American Historical Review* 100 (1995): 360–86.

events were so divisive and still capable of providing touchstones for all that continued to divide France's left, right, and center, the consensus-promoting government of François Mitterrand chose to stress the theme of the Revolution's impact on the world. Britain's Margaret Thatcher, irritated at the torrent of French self-congratulation for having been a wellspring of liberty in the world, remarked that her country played at least as significant a role in liberty's history and without having undergone one of those nasty revolutions.[39] This earned her a public history lesson from Christopher Hill who reminded her of England's own seventeenth-century upheaval.[40]

Two hundred years after the Revolution, it was not only a British prime minister who doubted that plebeian violence had contributed to human advance. Many a historian was wondering the same thing, and in one or another form was elaborating the ironic point of Thatcher that social progress had not only not required revolutionary violence but was retarded by it. The trickle of dissent from what Cobban and Taylor in the 1960s and 1970s had taken as the celebratory orthodoxy of the political left became, by the late 1980s, a flood tide of debunking. The Revolution's effects were now seen as perverse (as in the claim that far from eliminating barriers to French economic advance, the Revolution so damaged the French economy as to augment the already developing British lead and thereby ensure British economic dominance)[41] or nonexistent (as in the claim that the advances often attributed to the Revolution were actually being carried out by the reforming elites of the Old Regime to begin with).[42] And when there were results worthy of respect, these were increasingly held to have been carried primarily by mutations in elite political culture rather than by mass action.[43]

39. *Le Monde* (July 13, 1989): 1.

40. Christopher Hill, "Mrs. Thatcher set to rights," *Guardian* (July 15, 1989).

41. François Crouzet, *De la supériorité de l'Angleterre sur la France: L'économique et l'imaginaire, XVIIe–XX siècles* (Paris: Librairie Académique Perrin, 1985), esp. 248–98; Pierre Chaunu, *Le grand déclassement: A propos d'une commémoration* (Paris: Laffont, 1989), 265–84; René Sédillot, *Le coût de la Révolution* (Paris: Librairie Académique Perrin, 1987).

42. From Simon Schama's preface to *Citizens:* "The drastic social changes imputed to the Revolution seem less clear-cut or actually not apparent at all. The 'bourgeoisie' said in the classic Marxist accounts to have been the authors and beneficiaries of the event have become social zombies, the product of historiographical obsessions rather than historical realities. Other alterations in the modernization of French society and institutions seem to have been anticipated by the reform of the 'old regime.' " See Schama, *Citizens: A Chronicle of the French Revolution* (New York: Vintage Books, 1990), xiv.

43. For surveys of this recent literature, see Sarah Maza, "Politics, Culture and the Origins of the French Revolution," *Journal of Modern History* 61 (1989): 704–23, and Jack Censer, "The Coming of a New Interpretation of the French Revolution," *Journal of Social History* 21 (1987): 295–309. The Bicentennial became an occasion for the expression of these issues, a theme magnificently developed in Steven Laurence Kaplan, *Farewell Revolution, Disputed Legacies: France, 1789/1989* (Ithaca: Cornell University Press, 1995), and *Farewell Revolution, The Historians' Feud: France, 1789/1989* (Ithaca: Cornell University Press, 1995).

Let us look at the questions being raised in the specific instance of the seigneurial rights. Did the Revolution benefit peasants? The Revolution's impact on the people of the countryside is complex, contradictory, and not fully known: important changes occurred in landholding, taxation, local government, market outlets, inheritance law, demography, the role of the church, judicial institutions, and patterns of deference that, even if fully researched, would defy ready summary.[44] For the seigneurial rights considered alone, however, it seems clear that the principal beneficiaries were peasant proprietors who had owed the lord periodic payments and mutation fees; but tenants and laborers would seem to have benefited along with peasant owners from the ending of tolls, compulsory labor, monopolies, pigeon- and rabbit-raising and hunting rights not to mention the innumerable affronts to dignity. We may dismiss the charge that the Revolution's accomplishments, on the whole, were in this area nonexistent or downright perverse;[45] we need, however, to address the question of whether the Revolution, and popular mobilization in particular, was in some sense a necessary part of dismantling the seigneurial regime. Not only might a debunker point to the pre-revolutionary beginning made by the king in abolishing serfdom on royal holdings (see Chapter 9, p. 549), but, far more powerfully, one could point to the very elaborate antiseigneurialism in the *cahiers* of the Third Estate.

Was a more peaceful termination of seigneurial rights, carefully controlled by a forward-looking elite, imaginable? Such a question demands of us that we try to speculate about the consequences of an elite-driven antiseigneurial project pursued without the threat of effective peasant disruption. Such counterfactual speculation is fraught with no end of hazards. In this particular case, however, we have some important parallel experiences to draw on if we look eastward at other European projects for the removal of broadly similar rights. Elite desires to partially or wholly dismantle antiseigneurialism drew on many sources apart from fears of rebellion: the conviction that agricultural productivity could be advanced, that state revenues would increase, that an emancipated peasantry was more reliable in wartime, that

44. For recent statements of the issues, see Jones, *Peasantry,* 248–70; Timothy J. A. LeGoff and Donald M. G. Sutherland, "The Revolution and the Rural Economy," in Alan Forrest and Peter M. Jones, eds., *Reshaping France: Town, Country and Region During the French Revolution* (Manchester: Manchester University Press, 1991), 52–85.

45. But we ought by no means to dismiss the charge that the benefits varied profoundly from region to region and that peasants in some regions may have been more injured by tax equalization than they were helped by ending seigneurial claims. See the case made by Donald Sutherland in *The Chouans: The Social Origins of Popular Counter-Revolution in Upper Brittany, 1770–1796* (Oxford: Clarendon Press, 1982), 8–9, 134–43. This would be particularly true of tenants who benefited far less than proprietors from the ending of seigneurial rights and tithes, particularly since demographic pressures probably permitted landlords to raise rents and thereby gain a good part of whatever extra resources the abolition of seigneurial rights potentially left in the tenants' hands.

a civilized country such as one hoped to feel one belonged to required a juridical commitment to personal freedom and that at least some seigneurial claims cost more to extract than they were worth even to the seigneurs. We have seen that French elites did have an antiseigneurial program at the onset of revolution, although one well short of what many French villagers would accept. It is, then, conceivable that there were rural emancipations elsewhere pushed by elite reformers in which fear of rural plebeians was minimal. Conceivable, but did it happen? Anywhere?

Jerome Blum's comparative survey of the formal emancipations of continental Europe's rural populations shows that almost everywhere it was a protracted process.[46] Three states preceded France.[47] Savoy's duke freed his own serfs in 1762 and went beyond the later similar act of Louis XVI by decreeing an indemnified redemption for other peasants. In 1772 the indemnification terms were altered in favor of the peasants, but the incapacity of the country people to buy their freedom led the process to drag on until the French army entered two decades later and ordered an immediate and unindemnified abolition.[48] Baden's initial proclamation dates from 1783, but seigneurial claims did not definitively end until 1848.[49] After a series of false starts going back as early as 1702, Denmark proclaimed an effective abolition in 1788, but did not complete the process until 1861.[50]

Emancipations hardly proceeded any more rapidly in those many instances in which reform began in the wake of the Revolution. A few princes in western Germany announced preemptive reforms as early as the fall of 1789.[51] Emancipation decrees were issued in Prussia, Württemberg, Mecklenburg, Bavaria, and Hesse between 1807 and 1820 but the processes were not completed until the revolutionary wave of 1848. Still other

46. Given the extreme variety of rights lords held over peasants, there is ambiguity in defining just which measure should be taken as initiating effective emancipation (does one date France's process from the decree of August 4–11, 1789, for example, or from the king's limited abolition of serfdom on his own holdings in 1779?). The ambiguities of dating the end points of emancipation is even more hazardous: many emancipatory processes trailed off with monopoly rights or tolls or sometimes other claims still alive and well, for example. As a guide through these and other difficulties in comparative observation I have largely relied on Blum.

47. One might also wish to include as a fourth instance the Swiss canton of Soluthurn, which freed all serfs without indemnities in 1785, but I have not been able to learn anything of the circumstances in which this enactment took place, nor of its consequences.

48. Max Bruchet, *L'abolition des droits seigneuriaux en Savoie (1761–1793).* (Annecy: Hérisson, 1908).

49. Blum, *The End of the Old Order in Rural Europe* (Princeton: Princeton University Press, 1978), 386.

50. Ibid., 219–20, 385–86. Unmarried male servants could not leave their employer until 1840 and even then only if they were over twenty-eight years old.

51. In Nassau-Saarbrücken and Saarwerden, tithes, *corvées,* and hunting monopolies were abolished. See Eberhard Weis, "Révoltes paysannes et citadines dans les états allemands sur la rive gauche du Rhin, de 1789 à 1792," *Francia* 3 (1975): 354.

emancipatory processes did not even commence until the pressures of the agitated early 1830s as in Hannover or Saxony and others awaited the still more intense pressures of 1848 as in Austria, Saxe-Weimar, and Anhalt-Dessau-Köthen (Austrian officials were keenly affected by a Galician revolt in 1846).[52] All of these emancipations outside France involved indemnifications. Many were limited to some but not other peasants. Denmark's 1788 law, for example, did not free serfs between fourteen and thirty-six years old; its 1791 law denied landless farmworkers the right to seek other employment.[53] Some of these indemnified emancipations required the consent of both lord and peasant, which enabled these lords who wished to retain their rights to do so, at least until, as invariably happened, subsequent legislation removed the voluntary element.[54] The rapidity of the French transition from a process in large part indemnificatory to one that was thoroughgoingly abolitionist stands out as utterly unique among all European cases that commenced prior to 1848.

Apart from Savoy, Baden, and Denmark, moreover, the initial impulse for all the pre-1815 cases was French. French arms sometimes brought varying degrees of rural emancipation as in Belgium at the very start of the long war, the Helvetic Republic, and various western German states in 1798, the Grand Duchy of Warsaw in 1807, and various north German states in 1811; these actions in turn might trigger preemptive emancipation by fearful neighbors as in a number of German instances in 1807. Some of the other pre-1848 cases, moreover, were hardly independent examples, to say the least. The knowledge of the dangers of revolution in which French peasants instructed the world certainly helped spur some of the nineteenth-century cases.[55] And in 1848 itself insurrectionary peasants may have more rapidly won concessions in German-speaking lands because many governments felt that they had learned from 1789 to 1793 the futility of half-measures in the countryside: thus the termination of several decades-long emancipatory processes and the commencement and rapid completion of others in 1848–49. (In Hungary in 1848, the Diet appears to have been panicked into abolishing serfdom by a false report of 40,000 mobilized peasants.)[56] In other words, in central and western Europe through the mid-nineteenth

52. Blum, *End of the Old Order,* 364.

53. Ibid., 384–85.

54. Ibid., 406.

55. This is not to deny that, at points, elites made fearful by the French example may well have delayed or aborted emancipation processes. In Austria, for example, the French Revolution further energized a conservative current that was already successfully combating the reforms of Joseph II. See Ernst Wangermann, *From Joseph II to the Jacobin Trials: Government Policy and Public Opinion in the Habsburg Dominions in the Period of the French Revolution* (Oxford: Oxford University Press, 1969).

56. G. Spira, "La dernière génération des serfs de Hongrie: l'exemple du comitat de Pest," *Annales: Economies, Sociétés, Civilisations* 23 (1968): 353–67.

century there are many instances of elite-driven reforms but not a single one that actually came to completion without the presence of the French army in its revolutionary or Napoleonic forms, the specter of popular insurrection, or both.

I think we are on fairly strong ground in asserting that without the determined, violent, and frightening popular battle, French peasants would still have been responsible for seigneurial obligations at the middle of the nineteenth century—at the very least. If we consider the role of popular uprising in prompting the initial decrees of August 4–11, 1789, in the first place, one might well wonder if one could be sure that any serious emancipation would even have taken place at all. Even the positions taken in the Third Estate *cahiers* of the spring of 1789 were surely taken with an awareness of the riots rising in the French countryside; the assemblies, moreover, although dominated by urban notables, had a significant number of village delegates. The positions taken in the Third Estate *cahiers* already reflect rural pressures.

Looking beyond France in an even more speculative vein, there seems some reason for doubting that many of the emancipations in the 1831–32 and 1848–49 waves would have taken place nearly so rapidly without the prior historical experience of France in the 1790s. These cases only terminated in 1848–49 because of the fear of upheaval—but would that fear have been so great without the experience of France's revolutionary decade and the consequent belief in the power of an alliance of liberal reformers and violent popular forces to tear the fabric of national history? The other European powers, when triumphant over French arms, sometimes showed an acceptance of the French definition of the international struggle as a war over feudalism by attempting to undo the emancipatory reforms, as in Hannover, Hesse-Cassel, or the Napoleonic Kingdom of Westphalia.[57]

Things not only went much faster in France than elsewhere, but the terms ultimately adopted were substantially more favorable to the peasants. The long period in other countries during which indemnification was the rule meant that more peasants actually paid out an indemnity. In some cases peasants did not fully obtain the land they had worked: In Prussia, for example, peasants exchanged part of their land for freedom from seigneurial obligations while in Denmark, "freed" peasants were not turned into proprietors but into renters.[58] Outside of France, particularly in regions beyond the easy reach of French armies, freedom from dues did not necessarily coincide

57. Ibid., 362. The most interesting such restoration attempt was in the Austrian-occupied portion of northern France in 1793–94. Under the merely half-hearted support of the Austrian army, lords and ecclesiastics attempted to collect, but were largely stymied by peasant evasion of payment; see Georges Lefebvre, *Les paysans du Nord pendant la Révolution française* (Paris: Armand Colin, 1972), 551–55.

58. Blum, *End of the Old Order,* 398–99.

with a thoroughgoing assault on all seigneurial rights nor with a generic attack on privilege. Lords often could continue their economic monopolies, retain their judicial and police authority, and enjoy their tax exemptions even after emancipatory decrees.[59]

Is there any plausibility to the notion that rural popular violence accomplished nothing that wasn't coming anyway? To the extent that we can speculate about alternate worlds on the basis of evidence about what happened in our world, it looks as if exactly the opposite was the case: the emancipation of the countryside from the lords in the first half of the nineteenth century—not just the French but the west and central European countryside generally—looks much less likely without the half-decade of uncontrollable rural uprising in France. Indeed, given the extent to which the lords of France were adapting "feudal" claims to the developing marketplace, it is not obvious that without the popular insurrection that joined the forces of its greatest victims to the reforming dreams of the elites, there ever would have been any necessity to totally abolish seigneurial rights. Lords could "modernize" their operations and were doing so. Elite-driven reform efforts, in short, would have been inadequate in France without the fear of popular insurrection and probably in much of western and central Europe as well.[60]

Was There Only a Popular Revolution? A Note on a Thesis of Cobban

François Furet has devoted some energy to making sure that we give proper recognition to the elite component in forging a revolution; that we see, in particular, the genuinely revolutionary character of the decrees of August 4–11, even in their most conservative aspect in which dues are indemnified.[61] He argues that the hold on scholars of the socialist critique of bourgeois individualism is such that "the rupture of the bourgeois revolution

59. Ibid., 406–17. The formal retention of such rights, however, must be contrasted with the capacity of France's rural elites to find ways to continue such practices in effect despite their apparent termination in law. In other words, the comparison of legislation alone may exaggerate the relative advantages gained by French country people over those further east. See Albert Soboul, "Survivances 'féodales' dans la société rurale du XIXe siècle," *Annales: Economies, Sociétés, Civilisations* 23 (1968): 965–86.

60. As late as the 1870s, the seigneurial rights could still be imagined vividly enough that republican politicians courted peasant votes by playing on their fears of a revival. See Sanford Elwitt, *The Making of the Third Republic: Class and Politics in Rural France, 1868–1884* (Baton Rouge: Louisiana State University Press, 1975), 76.

61. Furet, "Night of August 4," 112.

is devalued by comparing it to the rupture that remains to be carried out, that of the truly social revolution."[62] Furet then goes on to make an important case for the significance of August 4, presumably challenging belittling Marxists for whom the liberal revolution is but a step on the way to (and a forerunner of) the real revolution to come. It is not, however, any Marxist who elaborated the most influential critique of the thesis of a significant bourgeois participation in an antifeudal movement, but the very anti-Marxist Alfred Cobban. For Cobban, far more than for the Marxists both he and Furet attack, the rural revolution was overwhelmingly a peasant affair.

Cobban caused a stir two and a half decades ago when he proposed, in the course of a provocative critique of what he took to be the prevailing, Marxist conception of the Revolution, several surprising reinterpretations.[63] In attacking the claim that the French Revolution was a watershed in the triumph of a modern bourgeois order over the feudal past, Cobban asserted: "If 'feudalism' in 1789 did not mean seigniorial rights, it meant nothing."[64] Moreover, he argued, the attack on seigneurial rights was not a bourgeois project at all. "The abolition of seigniorial dues was the work of the peasantry, unwillingly accepted by the men who drew up the town and *bailliage cahiers,* and forced on the National Assembly through the fear of a peasant revolt. It follows that the 'overthrow of feudalism by the bourgeoisie' takes on very much the appearance of the myth I suggested it was in a lecture some eight years ago."[65] The upper reaches of the Third Estate—including members of the National Assembly and, most particularly, the members of the Committee on Feudal Rights—were, he contended, frequently seigneurs themselves, with the most urgent material interests in retaining the system and in only giving in to peasant rebellion as grudgingly as possible. Cobban's thesis is important, for it is a serious challenge to the notion that a revolutionary elite, imbued with antifeudal notions, joined forces with peasant militants in dismantling the seigneurial regime. Cobban denies the Third Estate any antiseigneurial views to speak of and he denies that the legislatures engaged in meaningful antiseigneurial legislation except insofar as they were pushed by rural insurgents.

Although there certainly is a case for dilatory tactics in the National

62. Furet and Halévi, *Orateurs de la Révolution,* lxxxiv.

63. *The Social Interpretation of the French Revolution* (Cambridge: Cambridge University Press, 1965) and several articles collected in *Aspects of the French Revolution* (New York: Norton, 1968): "The Myth of the French Revolution," 90–111; "Political *versus* Social Interpretations of the French Revolution," 264–74; and "The French Revolution: Orthodox and Unorthodox Interpretations," 275–87.

64. Cobban, *Social Interpretation,* 35.

65. Ibid., 53. The lecture Cobban refers to is "The Myth of the French Revolution."

Assembly, for years of obfuscation and foot-dragging,[66] Cobban's portrait, our data show, is oversimple to the point of total distortion. A glance at the tables comparing the actions demanded by the Third Estate and nobility[67] shows beyond question that the urban notables were not by any stretch of the imagination committed to the integral maintenance of the system. Where the nobles were either silent or defensive, the Third Estate was vocal and on the attack. Among Third Estate *cahiers* discussing monopolies on ovens and winepresses, compulsory labor services, the right to raise rabbits, serfdom, seigneurial tolls, and the seigneurial courts a majority called for uncompensated abolition. This is very far from nothing, no matter how one interprets the push for indemnification. And if one looks beyond the *cahiers,* to the foot-dragging of the legislatures, it was not primarily in these areas that the feet dragged, but in the area of payments to the lords. The monopolies, the tolls, the animal-raising, the hunting monopoly, and the courts did in fact go rather fast. If indemnification was a smokescreen for those afraid to call for maintenance, it was a smokescreen that only covered a part of the seigneurial complex. A very important part, to be sure; but it is extremely misleading to identify the indemnification proposals as a spirited, if covert, defense of the whole system. And if the Third Estate's attack was markedly weaker than that of the peasants, they were notably even more vocal: less likely to abolish, but more likely to discuss at all.

Cobban's summary claim with regard to "the men who drew up the *cahiers* in the towns and the members of the *tiers état* in the National Assembly" is that "there can be no doubt of their opposition to the abolition of seigneurial dues and rights."[68] On the contrary, there can be the gravest of doubts. They were, after all, more likely to propose abolition than they were indemnification (see Table 3.1). That a portion, even (perhaps)[69] a large portion, of the urban notables enjoyed seigneurial rights does not mean that they did not have other interests as well, in particular, an ideological commitment to freeing the market in land and labor.[70] Their

66. For partisans of the legislation of March 1790, what to some seems "foot-dragging" was the sacred defense of property and the claim of obfuscation is merely the ignorant failure to understand Merlin's clarifications. See Chapters 8 and 9.

67. See Tables 3.1 and 3.4. For another critique of Cobban's evidence, by Gilbert Shapiro, see Shapiro and Markoff, *Revolutionary Demands,* chap. 14.

68. Cobban, *Social Interpretation,* 43.

69. I am unable to see that Cobban presents any evidence on the frequency with which these urban notables were seigneurs, nor do I know of any that is definitive. This is not even to raise the question of what role seigneurial income played in the total wealth of those deputies of the Third Estate who were lords. Recent prosopographical work by Timothy Tackett (*Becoming a Revolutionary: The Deputies of the National Assembly and the Emergence of a Revolutionary Culture (1789–1790)* [Princeton: Princeton University Press, 1996]) is both suggestive and makes one wary of any claim, like Cobban's, of certain knowledge of this important matter.

70. The bearing of this commitment on proposals about the seigneurial regime was treated in Chapters 2 and 4.

personal stake in the system complicated their position[71] and no doubt was a part of the foot-dragging, but it can hardly explain a full-scale defense of seigneurial rights (which they never mounted). The indemnification project that distinguishes the *cahiers* of the Third Estate from the others was indeed precisely a magnificent vehicle to reap the advantages of abolishing the system at the same time as profiting from one's personal stake in that system. But if the strength of support for indemnification separates the urban notables from the peasants, it hardly identifies them as defenders of the system. As we saw in Chapters 8 and 9, both the indemnification option in particular and the overall structure of the National Assembly's actions in general were as far from the more intransigent positions of some of the noble deputies as they were from the desires of peasant communities that continued in rebellion past the summer of 1789. A study of indemnification in practice in Charente-Inférieure, for example, confirms the lack of noble enthusiasm for indemnification. A clear majority of seigneurs, approached with the legally mandated offer, either refused to accept it or avoided being found and served with legal documents.[72] In other words, faced with the actual legislation, the behavior of the seigneurs shows clearly that indemnification was not their position.

Opposition to indemnification is also demonstrated in the reaction to Pierre-François Boncerf's attack on the seigneurial regime. Boncerf had

71. There were more impersonal stakes as well that Cobban ignores: the desire for order in the countryside held by some to be best served by an inflexible attitude on peasant demands; the financial state of the government. With regard to the latter, a report to the National Assembly on March 28, 1790, from the Committee on Feudal Rights shows a concern for the sale of royal and church property—a central element in the struggle to solve the financial crisis that precipitated the Revolution—whose value was clearly affected by the terms on which attached seigneurial rights could be indemnified (*AP* 12:39). In the discussions of the negative consequences of the law of July 17, 1793, one important issue was the reduction of the value of National Property; see Philippe Sagnac and Pierre Caron, *Les comités des droits féodaux et de législation et l'abolition du régime seigneurial (1789–1793)* (Paris: Imprimerie Nationale, 1907), 787–88, 789–90. While an interest in public revenues may help explain the lack of enthusiasm of revolutionary legislators for uncompensated abolition, this is rather remote from the private financial concerns that Cobban sees as their central motivation.

72. Jean-Noël Luc, "Le rachat des droits féodaux dans le département de la Charente-Inférieure (1789–1793)," in Albert Soboul, *Contributions à l'histoire paysanne de la Révolution française* (Paris: Editions Sociales, 1977), 318. The seigneur's "absence" half the time strikes one as a continuation into the revolutionary era of the noble abstention so striking in the *cahiers* (see Chapter 2). Those seigneurs who actually went on record, moreover, as refusing to accept the terms offered were far more numerous than those who agreed not to contest the idemnity offer. This is also consistent with the *cahiers*. The seigneurs also mounted an effective passive resistance against attempts to indemnify them in Franche-Comté; see Jean Millot, *L'abolition des droits seigneuriaux dans le département du Doubs et la région comtoise* (Besançon: Imprimerie Millot Frères, 1941), 174–76. It was not only peasants, but lords as well who waged an effective campaign to undermine the revolutionary laws. Peasants resisted by not paying as well as by attacking the *châteaux;* lords resisted by avoiding being served legal documents, as well as organizing counterrevolution.

urged indemnification at a rate far more generous than provided in the later revolutionary legislation.[73] He devoted much effort to persuading the lords that his scheme was in their interest: not only would they be generously compensated, but the endless financial drain of supervision, records, surveys, and the unending litigation would be wiped out.[74] In spite of the reasoned argument and the generous terms, neither the hostility of the *parlement* of Paris to this work nor the failure of the noble *cahiers* to espouse its arguments suggests that the seigneurs were at all persuaded. Yet Cobban would have us identify the indemnification policy of the National Assembly (far less generous than what Boncerf's sketchy proposal had offered) as a camouflage for seigneurial interest. Certainly the nobles of Quesnoy did not see this option as a veiled defense of seigneurial interests when they observed: "Involuntary indemnification, that is to say, what is not done by the free choice of the possessor of any rights whatsoever, is every bit as much an encroachment on property" (*AP* 5:504).

Nor did the assembly of the Third Estate of Poitou seem aware that they were supporting the seigneurial regime when they proposed, with the most obvious reluctance, to indemnify the current possessors of rights they plainly held loathsome. This indemnification project was too much for the thirty-two delegates who appended their denunciation of the majority to the *cahier:* "to reverse the social order instead of establishing it, to attack property instead of defending it, to seek in appearance the peace that is so desired while fanning the flames of discord, would be to substitute license for liberty and agitation for patriotism" (*AP* 5:415).

Since Cobban's would-be demolition of the Marxist interpretation of the bourgeois-peasant alliance against feudalism (identified by Cobban with Soboul's version) was so influential and became one of the inspirations for a large number of scholars who feel confident that an old saw has now been overthrown, it is worth pausing over some of the fundamental flaws in Cobban's argument. Cobban could equate indemnification with maintenance only because he never compared the noble *cahiers* with the Third Estate *cahiers;* only because, within the Third Estate *cahiers,* he failed to distinguish one right from another; and, only because, underlying these two weaknesses, he had a habit of making quasi-quantitative statements without actually counting anything.

In arguing that the Third Estate notables were not pushing for the dismantling of the system, Cobban argues that "a further indication of the attitude of the towns is to be found in the fact that there was one seigneurial

73. The rates of indemnification under discussion kept getting more favorable to the peasants. Boncerf's pamphlet of 1776 proposed 50 or 60 times their annual value, the duke d'Aiguillon suggested 30 times on August 4, 1789, and the rate established in May 1790 was 20 to 25, depending on the particular right; see Pierre-François Boncerf, *Les inconvéniens des droits féodaux* (London: Valade, 1776), 11: *AP* 8:344; *AP* 15:365–66).

74. Boncerf, *Inconvéniens des droits féodaux,* 11, 12, 26, 52.

right, if it can be called such, which they commonly opposed. But this was franc-fief, and it was a payment not to the *seigneur* but to the crown, due after land that was part of a fief passed from noble into non-noble possession."[75] Now it is perfectly correct that the *droit de franc-fief,* a royal tax, is discussed by more *cahiers* of the Third Estate (72%), than any of the seigneurial rights we have been examining. We would suggest that to insist that an institution be taken up by almost three-quarters of the *cahiers* before we speak of it as "commonly opposed" is to set a very stringent standard indeed, but not necessarily an indefensible one. But when we read a few pages later that the *feudistes,* who advised the lords on their valid claims, were "bitterly attacked in the *cahiers*"[76] we are astonished. Table 2.4 showed that discussion of all seigneurial agents, including the *feudistes,* is not even among the dozen most frequently discussed aspects of the seigneurial regime. We are not so much protesting that Cobban has exaggerated the degree to which the seigneurial agents were a focus of attack, but that, in the absence of the discipline imposed by a quantitative methodology, the polemical needs of the moment can dictate his standard of what it means to say something is vigorously attacked in the *cahiers.* To argue that the system was hardly attacked at all, he invokes the *franc-fief* as a standard of comparison. To show that it was in its increasingly bourgeois characteristics rather than in its feudal residue that the system was condemned, he invokes the *feudistes,* far less widely discussed, in fact, than many seigneurial rights.[77]

Cobban's evidence is elusive even when he is not deploying quasi-quantitative claims. In discussing the *bailliage* of Mirecourt, he tells us that the town *cahier* fails to mention seigneurial rights, by contrast to the rural documents. This clearly supports his thesis that the attack on the seigneurial regime is the work of the countryside, and not of the urban notables at all. But a few sentences earlier he supported his claim by telling us that "the

75. Cobban, *Social Interpretation,* 38.

76. Ibid., 49.

77. There are a number of other misleading claims by Cobban. He asserts that "the best preserved, and most universally hated, of the seigneurial rights, were the *banalités* of mill, wine or olive press, and oven" and that "the right of the banal mill" was "the most widely denounced abuse in the *cahiers*" (ibid., 50). Table 2.5 shows that for the Third Estate, even the monopoly on milling is less widely discussed than the exclusive right to hunt, the right to raise pigeons, seigneurial tolls, compulsory labor services. The other monopolies are even less discussed. Nor is the monopoly on milling the most frequent target of parish grievances (although those who discussed it did loathe it). Nor is Table 3.4 consistent with the claim of Third Estate reluctance to abolish these monopolies (ibid., 51). Nor for that matter, can the *banalité du four* be grouped among the "best preserved" of rights. It was often in grave difficulty; see Jean Bastier, *La féodalité au siècle des lumières dans la région de Toulouse (1730–1790)* (Paris: Bibliothèque Nationale, 1975), 169–71, for evidence. The point here is not to enumerate Cobban's lesser errors as an issue in itself but to show how unreliable his sort of impressionistic quasi-quantitative argument can be.

peasants of Neuborg in Normandy complain of the *taille* but not of the seigneurial regime."[78] It is as if he feels his thesis is supported when peasants oppose seigneurial rights and when they don't. To say the least, it is not obvious what is the relevance of the views of Neuborg's inhabitants.

Even harder to grasp, and far more fundamental to his argument, is the evidence for his contention that well-to-do commoners, having so frequently acquired seigneuries, are indistinguishable from noble seigneurs in regard to their interests in seigneurial rights.[79] But, as mentioned above, he totally fails to complement his reading of Third Estate *cahiers* with a study of the nobles' documents. (Our own study shows quite dramatic differences.) Methodologically, Cobban failed to establish any benchmarks from which to gauge Third Estate opinion. On these grounds alone his case would be suspect.

One final point: Cobban is certainly correct when he points to the existence of non-noble lords. But he misses the point of view of the actors for whom "nobles" and "lords" were closely related social categories. The sense of the seigneurial rights as a sort of abstract collective possession of the nobility is quite clear in many *cahiers*. The nobles of Limoges, for example, discuss "seigneurial courts and other honorific rights" under the heading: "Of Noble Privileges"; the nobles of Berry under a similar heading go even farther and take up all seigneurial rights. The parish of Domjulien in Mirecourt, under the heading of "seigneurial rights," begins to discuss the "domination of the seigneurs" but shifts to the "domination of the Nobility." The nobles of Soule go so far as to characterize the seigneurial rights as "essentially noble," and to speak of "tithes" as "the oldest and most precious possession" of the local nobility; they even refer to seigneurial monopolies as "our rights." The parish of Bucey-en-Othe in Troyes conflates the two terms in discussing seigneurial rights under the heading "concerning the Nobility and the *seigneurs*."[80] In such an ideational matrix, it is not obvious that Third Estate texts that urge compensation are invariably motivated by the protection of what they see as their own private interests, rather than by a more abstract respect for property (which of course protects *other* interests of theirs).

Speaking

If we are to see the joint action against the lords as the product of an interaction of peasants and legislators, we need a somewhat different

78. Cobban, *Social Interpretation*, 37.

79. Ibid., 44–48.

80. *AP* 3:569–70; 2:322; 5:779; E. Martin, *Cahiers de doléances du bailliage de Mirecourt* (Epinal: Imprimerie Lorraine, 1928), 61–62; Jules-Joseph Vernier, *Cahiers de doléances de bailliage de Troyes (principal et secondaires) et du bailliage de Bar-sur-Seine pour les états généraux de 1789* (Troyes: P. Nouel, 1909), 1:466–67.

methodological toolkit than we would if we could confidently root peasant actions in a pristine peasant opinion alone, legislative action in the pristine views of legislators, solely modified, at most, to conform to the interests of their more influential constituents. We need to see the speech of both sides as in significant degree strategic; that is, as calculated to produce certain effects and avoid others. We cannot see the *cahiers* as simply the outcome of interests that are fixed by social structures nor can we see insurrection as the outcome of certain external structures alone. The making of grievances involves some sense of the likely consequences of placing certain statements in a *cahier;* the making of collective actions involves some sense of the consequences of attacking a socially defined target in a particular way. Political speech is to be seen as instrumental as much as it is expressive.

When the two parties differ as much in resources as did France's peasants and officials (the king's and the revolutionary legislatures'), there are some specific features of their exchanges that James Scott's work helps us grasp. On the peasant side, we should expect a great deal of caution that might show up in many ways: the avoidance of open challenges to the norms and values publicly advocated by the dominant strata, the attempt to define situations of challenge as involving mitigating circumstances that lessen risk when failure occurs, and an acute sensitivity to even slight modulations of the tone of elite discourse. The last thing we should expect from rational peasants is a coherent, integrated, and explicit ideological challenge to the premises of the social order. When we fail to find it, we ought not to be overquick to assume that they are intellectually incapable of grasping their interests. I submit that the ways in which the country people distinguished among their various burdens (see Chapters 2 and 3) is not only, in itself, a sign of reflection upon their situation but is also an appropriately cautious way of making claims. Even so, it was an act of some courage in the spring of 1789 to defy the seigneurial judges who presided over so many of the assemblies in practice[81] (although not nearly so universally as one might expect from the letter of the law)[82] and in many communities those judges appear to have been defied.[83] Calling for a mix of abolition, indemnification,

81. The inhabitants of Vellaux, in the *bailliage* of Aix, for example, plainly and bitterly expressed fears of retaliation by the seigneur in response to the condemnation of seigneurial institutions in their outspoken *cahier* (*AP* 6:438).

82. See Shapiro and Markoff, *Revolutionary Demands*, chap. 9.

83. In one parish in Quimper, the *procureur fiscal* of the local seigneurial court took pains to indicate that his signature merely verified his legally required presence, and in no way indicated his approval of the document over whose adoption he presided, but some of whose articles he abhorred—especially those dealing with "property." The *bailliage* of Rennes seems to have seen many such incidents, perhaps because it combined an active seigneurial judiciary with great peasant hostility to the seigneurial regime. In one parish, the *procureur fiscal* tried to hold an assembly at the lord's *château,* where he intended to promote a very pro-noble text. The peasants refused to attend, and held their own assembly—which he refused to chair—elsewhere. Also in Rennes we find places where the peasants stuck to their guns even though the chairman refused to sign the

and reform in the spring was much safer than calling for the abolition of everything and surely far less likely to panic the state into repressive measures, yet it was risky enough to annoy many a presiding judge. A year later, when the National Assembly had abolished much of seigneurialism, while still keeping many kinds of dues pending an (improbable) indemnity payment, the climate of elite acceptance, the absence of any significant seigneurial counterthrust, and the deterioration of state repressive capacity, suggested to many peasant communities that they not accept the legislative package, however much it resembled a distillation of what they and 40,000 other village communities had asked for.

Defiance often took the form of surreptitious evasion of payment. When a more visible challenge was mounted, however (and, no doubt, our own sample of 1,687 antiseigneurial incidents was but a fraction of those that occurred) a variety of time-tested routines for the avoidance of full responsibility in the event of failure was incorporated into peasant actions and in the talk surrounding those actions. There were the misunderstandings of the laws; there were the claims that the king had authorized some action (or, in the newer version of political correctness, there were the claims that the revolutionary legislature had done the authorizing). There was the claim that the villagers believed that the legislature's laws were false, as in the Southwest where villagers said that the basic law earmarking many rights for indemnification was actually written by the lords (see *AP* 21:457). Whatever the power of such a claim to enroll peasants for open mobilization, its flamboyantly preposterous character made it all the more compelling as an emblem of peasants being led astray. Quite widespread throughout the whole period of antiseigneurial struggles was the claim to only wish to see the lord's titles. This not only appeared far more moderate than a demand for immediate root-and-branch abolition, but it simultaneously appeared to identify peasants with the cause of legality in the abstract (probably a good tack to take with revolutionary lawyer-legislators) as well as with support for the specific legal framework erected by those legislators in which titles assumed so much importance. That most lords couldn't produce the papers demanded, that seigneurial resistance could easily lead to great property destruction, that once produced the document itself could be destroyed meant in practice that the seigneurial regime would disintegrate if actually forced to try to cough up this piece of paper. This last point can be seen when we note that once the state reappropriated the peasant complaint and demanded, in effect, that the lords come up with the documents—by shifting

document. See Jean Savina and Daniel Bernard, eds., *Cahiers de doléances des sénéchaussées de Quimper et de Concarneau pour les états généraux de 1789* (Rennes Imprimerie Oberthur: 1927), lviii; Henri Sée and André Lesort, eds., *Cahiers de doléances de la sénéchaussée de Rennes pour les états généraux de 1789* (Rennes: Imprimerie Oberthur, 1909–12), 1:lxi–lxiv.

the burden of proof to the lords in the legislation of August 1792—the seigneurial regime was at once near death (see Chapter 8, p. 465) and, after a final spurt, peasant communities for the most part halted antiseigneurial mobilization (see p. 497). By such devices, the French peasants who pushed the Convention to abolish seigneurialism in principle without indemnities, could, when arrested, be treated as merely ignorant and misled.

And in a turbulent climate where the powerful saw conspiracies everywhere, peasants could portray themselves as simple people misled by a sinister, educated leadership. Viscount de Mirabeau passed on to the National Assembly an "eyewitness" account of antiseigneurial violence. A Breton gentleman informed the legislators that local peasants not only denied having anything to do with the violence, but that the initial small nucleus of the pillaging band was "led by intelligent men, whose faces were not worn down by rural labor." And he goes on, "there were some among them speaking Latin."[84]

The methodological point is to be neither too quick to see in any set of documents the authentic voice of these peasants nor too simple-minded in judging their wishes. All we ever actually see is the expression of wishes under particular circumstances. Wishes evolve over time in a dialogic process as changing circumstances, which may have altered in part as a result of a prior expression of wishes, encourage reformulations of those wishes. Claims of motivation are often post hoc reconstructions designed to give a certain plausible narrative coherence to a stream of events by placing them all in relation to some presumed goal.

From the point of view of how peasants and legislators took each other in, the report of two agents sent out to the *département* of Lot is a gold mine.[85] Assigned the task of getting to the roots of the puzzling violence that had resisted the best efforts of local administrators (*AP* 21:456–58), the earnest investigators arrive in Cahors at the very end of 1790 and immediately discover that far from having exaggerated the local difficulties, the tale told by departmental officials considerably understates the difficult reality (*Rapport,* 10–12). Around Gourdon the peasant forces have defeated the line army and district officials have fled in terror; around Lauzerte ex-nobles have formed an armed body to which peasants respond by incinerating several *châteaux* every day; the garrison in Cahors sees itself "in

84. *AP* 11:368. The plausibility of this tale to the legislators may be indicated by the response of Grégoire, a radical cleric perhaps sensitive to the implication that the nucleus of insurrection was supplied by radical clerics—who else would be speaking Latin? He does not dismiss the anonymous eyewitness out of hand but observes that the Committee on Reports has seen no supporting evidence (*AP* 11:536).

85. Jacques Godard and Léonard Robin, *Rapport de Messieurs J. Godard et L. Robin, commissaires civils, envoyés par le roi, dans le département de Lot, en execution du décret de l'Assemblée Nationale, du 13 décembre 1790* (Paris: Imprimerie Royale, 1791). Subsequently cited as *Rapport.*

open war against the inhabitants" and considerable fear is experienced in Montauban and Figeac. Matters are grave enough to demand considerable thought: "Before acting, it was necessary to study the events, the character of the inhabitants and the principles that must govern a newly freed people in order to find the proper means to put down excess and restore order" (*Rapport,* 12). Nothing daunted, the two legislators prepare their advice for the departmental officials—and we are astonished to note that it is only January 1, 1791, exactly one day after they have presented their credentials to local officials. How quick were agents of "enlightened" legislators, to use a favorite term of self-praise, to feel their conceptual frame gave them a handle on particular events! At that point, however, news of a series of pillages makes them decide to delay their recommendations until they've actually talked to some peasants. And so the two travel, unarmed and unescorted (they wouldn't have it any other way), through a devastated countryside, bringing the true word to the country people who have lost their way.[86] They learn of peasants who claim that the laws requiring payment pending indemnities are fabrications (*Rapport,* 19); they find that everywhere peasants employ at least some of the proper lawyers' language ("These words—'primordial title'—came at the same time out of every mouth when we spoke of seigneurial dues");[87] they hear peasants justify not paying current dues on grounds that the lords owe them vast restitutions for improperly collected dues in the past and that, therefore, even implicitly accepting the legality of the lords' claims, the lords owe them more than they owe the lords (*Rapport,* 25). As for whether or not maypoles are a sign of sedition—a matter of some debate among the legislature's would-be peasantologists (*AP* 21:457–58)—peasants questioned on the meaning of the maypole reliably give the politically correct response that it's a "sign of rejoicing for liberty" (*Rapport,* 30). When asked whether they held to the fantastic idea "as several people told us, that when a maypole was planted for a year and a day, you were, at the end of this time, freed from payment of seigneurial rights," the villagers smile at such a silly idea (*Rapport,* 30–31). While some maypoles are decorated with seditious emblems (a

86. Just as peasants may have adjusted their speech to the expectations of the two investigators, the duo may have similarly sought the right language for their own audience. In a letter explaining their task to the local priests, they speak of "the ministry of peace" with which they have been entrusted; "such a doctrine is that of the Evangelist whom you preach and our present mission resembles yours in some ways"; they "pray" that the priests will explain the important "mission" to their parishioners (*Rapport,* 15–16).

87. *Rapport,* 24. Far to the north, peasant petitioners also knew how to use the proper legal language about seigneurial rights when they addressed the National Assembly; see Bryant T. Ragan Jr., "Rural Political Activism and Fiscal Equality in the Revolutionary Somme," in Bryant T. Ragan Jr. and Elizabeth A. Williams, eds., *Recreating Authority in Revolutionary France* (New Brunswick: Rutgers University Press, 1992), 44.

weathervane yanked from a *château*'s roof, for example), most are respectably adorned, if adorned at all: "maypoles are not in themselves signs of sedition." Yet Godard and Robin note, in one of their many moments of recognizing that empirical realities are violating their expectations, that the number of maypoles multiplied rapidly "after the triumph that the peasants obtained over the troops of the line."[88] Other peasants professed themselves unwilling participants in events: if they planted maypoles it was because they were afraid of insurrectionary neighbors; if they failed to pay dues or joined in the attack on Gourdon, it was for the same reason (*Rapport,* 34). While disorder rages on all sides, and even re-emerges in locales they have lately quitted, the two legislators are delighted that their personal appearance recalls the peasants to reason: "When we've spoken to the people about their excesses, they have acknowledged their wrongdoing and have shown the most sincere contrition" (*Rapport,* 49).

Through all of this, the two commissioners maintain their belief that a small number of "instigators" have misled the great majority of peasant activists. An effective pacificatory policy, then, must contain a pedagogic dimension: "We thought, in a word, that if, in the cities, generally speaking, people understand the laws more easily than in the countryside, and if they are observed there with more exactitude (unless some party spirit misleads the citizens), it is because education is more widespread there. It is necessary therefore to diffuse it equally in the countryside" (*Rapport,* 57).

The view of the country people as simple but fundamentally respectful of the revolutionary institutions that permeates this report and permits its authors to take their peasant interviewees at face value much of the time was in no way shared by the anxious and frightened local officials who maintained consistently that "the principal cause of the insurrection, perhaps the only one, is found in the desire and the hope to which the country people have imprudently given themselves up, the desire to be freed forever from the seigneurial dues" (*Rapport,* 136). While acknowledging the case for such an alternative explanation of the pervasive insurrectionary climate, the investigators stick to their own view, a view that favors a patient attitude by the authorities more than it does a punitive one, in order to allow time for a proper civic education to make the use of force against the rural communities superfluous. In a tone of pride, they recount some of their lessons to those of good heart but uninstructed. They tell the country

88. *Rapport,* 32. When questioned about a maypole condemning a particular seigneurial obligation, the members of the nearby village profess astonishment: "They have never heard this inscription mentioned. They responded that they did not know it existed and that they could not even imagine that it even could exist since most of them had already paid the dues and the others were ready to pay" (ibid., 56). For their part, the two commissioners are surprised that the municipal government of Cahors "whose zeal and whose activity nothing escapes, was unaware of such a deed" (ibid).

people, so they tell us, that now that all are free and equal, the rights of ex-lords need be respected (*Rapport,* 31–33); they even praise peasant suspicion of legislative intent, since the new revolutionary openness means that "everything must be scrutinized by all" (*Rapport,* 21); they promise that those genuinely devoted to overturning the Revolution will be dealt with severely but that the great majority need little more than better information. The language of liberty and equality is used to extract rural assent to a program that had left intact important peasant obligations, but that is experienced as epochal by the investigative duo. At no point in their journey in the insurrectionary zone do they encounter peasants who announce their defiance of the National Assembly and precious few who, openly, go an inch beyond announcing their credentials as partisans of the new order. Everywhere, they report, the peaceful peasants, sometimes full of remorse, show their desire to obey the law. Yet as they move on to new villages, those behind them sometimes explode once again. And as they prepare their report, back in Paris, the local authorities write that the region is not at all pacified (*Rapport,* 136–38).

What permits such a dialogue is a common framework, differently interpreted. The law, the National Assembly, liberty and equality are significant touchstones, but all intersect the notion of property. That one's property—including one's property in oneself—is beyond arbitrary government action is an essential element of the sense of a rule of law as it appears in the *cahiers;* liberty is the capacity to freely dispose of property (always including one's own energies and capacities); and equality can be the claim of equal rights in law, the very counterclaim to "privilege." We have seen repeatedly how deeply an image of a society of individuals, equal in rights, none of whom possess coercive resources of their own and all of whom count on the state to enforce the rights of all permeates the *cahiers*—including the nobles' texts which make very little attempt at any defense of a corporate, hierarchical, and immutable order. The language of rights and the language of property are nearly fused in the *cahiers* of the elites. A fundamentally contractual view of social relations is everywhere: the elites see property as exchangeable in freely consented contracts and hence can imagine legitimizing many seigneurial rights in the spring of 1790 by claiming a voluntary and contractual aspect to lord-peasant relations. The villagers, too, in their own documents, evaluate taxation, church exactions, and seigneurial rights in terms of services rendered in return for compensation. While far less prone than the elites to discuss the abstract principles of rights and how those rights might best be embodied in a new constitution in the making, they nonetheless express a quasi-contractual view of their relations with those who extract resources from them, and quasi-contracts should be abrogated when the service goes unfilled (unless, in the view of some, it seems feasible to compel the lords to fill the service).

An Emerging Political Profession

Alongside contractual images, the hand of the legal professions seems everywhere: in the orderly character of peasant *cahiers,* a dramatic contrast with 1614; in the arrangement of articles in noble *cahiers,* a notable, if perhaps lesser, contrast (see Chapter 2, p. 84); in the stress on crafting the constitution to be written rather than rediscovering the constitution that has always been. Innumerable parish *cahiers* show long familiarity with rule-bound royal bureaucracies and noble *cahiers* justify seigneurial rights with notions of contractual legality rather than divine will. One of the most widely discussed topics in the *cahiers* was the tax on legal documents—the *droit de contrôle* (see Table 2.1)—which, unlike most indirect taxes, was widely held worthy of reform (see Table 3.7). The people of the countryside recognize some value to a bureaucratized registry of transactions, displaying simultaneously their acceptance of a rationalized state[89] and a society of individuals entering into freely consented contracts. We know that law schools were producing far more graduates[90] than could be readily assimilated into traditional legal roles; perhaps this is where some of those lawyers came from who took on the cases of peasant communities in what appear to be rising numbers of lawsuits[91] against the lords in the course of which, to follow Hilton Root's suggestion, villagers and lawyers together forged the language of the antiseigneurial discussions of 1789.[92] Even the Revolution's insurrections carried a legalistic strain in appropriating elements of the state's administrative and judicial practice as well as in subsiding when the state in its turn appropriated the insurrectionary practice. We've noted Godard and Robin marveling at how the villagers of the rebellious Southwest spoke the legalese of "primordial titles" and we have noted Merlin's disparagement (see Chapter 8, p. 468) of the Convention's taking the burning of such titles back from the people (see also Chapter 5, p. 263). Legal professionals are everywhere in the late Old Regime: most dramatically, they are center stage in promoting a notion of a public as a sort of tribunal before which the

89. John Markoff, "Governmental Bureaucratization: General Processes and an Anomolous Case," *Comparative Studies in Society and History* 17 (1975): 479–503.

90. Richard Kagan, "Law Students and Careers in Eighteenth-Century France," *Past and Present* 68 (1975): 38–72.

91. Colin Jones speaks of "a Golden Age of Peasant Litigiousness"; see his "Bourgeois Revolution Revivified: 1789 and Social Change," in Colin Lucas, ed., *Rewriting the French Revolution* (Oxford: Clarendon Press, 1991), 87. For a regional instance see Maurice Gresset, *Gens de justice à Besançon de la conquête par Louis XIV à la Révolution française, 1674–1789* (Paris: Bibliothèque Nationale, 1978), 2:731–34.

92. Hilton Root, *Peasants and King in Burgundy: Agrarian Foundations of French Absolutism* (Berkeley and Los Angeles: University of California Press, 1987), 183–93.

misdeeds of the high and mighty are to be judged.[93] In the course of inventing such a public opinion, the legal professionals are also inventing the notion of a dispassionate commitment to public service; that is, what their own activism is held to be.[94] And under a vision of a society of individuals, whose arrangements are freely negotiated contracts, enforced in impartial courts where rights are equal, legal professionals, the experts in the crafting and interpretation of valid contracts, constitute a sort of social lubricant that makes society run. In such a view, the crafting of a constitution (in which, of course, lawyers can play a major role) becomes the primal political act. In our own time the notion of a society as a body of individuals whose different claims were to be harmonized by a properly crafted constitution has been giving way to a more managerial vision of a collectivity needing to be properly directed: constitution-writing is far less spoken of today as essential to democratic consolidation, having been largely supplanted by the crafting of economic policy as the foundation of political life.[95] But in France two centuries ago, the radical break was experienced as tied to the notions of liberty, property, and law.

The complex electoral process of 1789 dramatically thrust lawyers to the fore. Merchants, government officers, medical men and, most dramatically, members of the legal professions, were to be found in the *bailliage* assemblies much more often than in either the primary assemblies or the general population. Indeed, virtually every opportunity to select deputies in the multiple phases of the electoral process for the Third Estate augmented the proportion of lawyers and legally trained officials. Peasants chose a significant

93. Keith Michael Baker, "Politics and Public Opinion under the Old Regime: Some Reflections," in Jack R. Censer and Jeremy D. Popkin, eds., *Press and Politics in Pre-Revolution France* (Berkeley and Los Angeles: University of California Press, 1987), 204–46; Sara Maza, "Le tribunal de la nation: Les mémoires judiciaires et l'opinion publique à la fin de l'Ancien Régime," *Annales: Economies, Sociétés, Civilisations* 42 (1987): 73–90. For more on lawyers as vanguard social critics see Sarah Maza, "Domestic Melodrama as Political Ideology: The Case of the Comte de Sanois," *American Historical Review* 94 (1989): 1249–64, and "The Rose-Girl of Salency: Representations of Virtue in Prerevolutionary France," *Eighteenth Century Studies* 22 (1989): 395–412; Hans-Jürgen Lüsebrink, "L'affaire Cléreaux (Rouen, 1786–90): Affrontements idéologiques et tensions institutionelles autour de la scène judiciaire au XVIIIe siècle," *Studies on Voltaire and the Eighteenth Century* 191 (1980): 892–900; David A. Bell, "Lawyers into Demogogues: Chancellor Maupeou and the Transformation of Legal Practice in France, 1771–1789," *Past and Present,* no. 130 (1991): 107–41, and *Lawyers and Citizens: The Making of a Political Elite in Old Regime France* (New York: Oxford University Press, 1994); Lenard R. Berlanstein, "Lawyers in Pre-Revolutionary France," in Wilfred Prest, ed., *Lawyers in Early Modern Europe and America* (London: Croom Helm, 1981), 164–80.

94. Lucien Karpik, "Lawyers and Politics in France: 1814–1950: The State, the Market and the Public," *Law and Social Inquiry* 13 (1988): 707–36; "Le désintéressément," *Annales: Economies, Sociétés, Civilisations* 44 (1989): 733–51. See also Maurice Gresset, *Gens de justice à Besançon,* 2:626–33.

95. See John Markoff and Verónica Montecinos, "The Ubiquitous Rise of Economists," *Journal of Public Policy* 13 (1993): 37–68.

number of men of law, such as notaries, lawyers, even seigneurial judges, as well as peasant notables to send to *bailliage* assemblies. When representatives of the various guilds met to draft a town *cahier,* the drafting committee had proportionally more lawyers than the town assembly as a whole, and this is true also of the town's delegation to the *bailliage* assembly. The commissioners drafting *bailliage cahiers* favored lawyers and royal officers; if, in accordance with the convocation regulations, a reduction in the number of deputies from lower assemblies was carried out, the proportion of lawyers rose still further. And, finally, three-fifths of Third Estate delegates at Versailles were legal professionals.[96] Legal professionals continued to be weighty in the Legislative Assembly[97] and Convention[98] as well.

As peasant revolt and legislative action challenged and then overwhelmed the world that had grown up around the lords, legal professionals and their professional close kin were both cast loose from their familiar routines and seized opportunities to create new ones. Some remade themselves and others found themselves close to insurrectionary collective action. One reads, for example, of the meeting of the municipal council of Dôle in March 1789, interrupted by "several hundred scoundrels, twenty with hatchets and one or two with pistols" and led by "attorneys."[99] Many found themselves entering (and inventing) modern political roles. François-Noël Babeuf had pursued a career as a local *feudiste,* successfully advising local lords despite his own plebeian origins. The Revolution opened many things but shut down

96. François Furet, "Les états généraux de 1789: Deux bailliages élisent leurs députés," in Fernand Braudel, ed., *Conjoncture économique, structures sociales: Hommage à Ernest Labrousse* (Paris: Mouton, 1974), 433–48; Ran Halévi, "La monarchie et les élections: Position des problémes," in Keith Michael Baker, ed., *The French Revolution and the Creation of Modern Political Culture,* vol. 1, *The Political Culture of the Old Regime,* 387–402; Abel Poitrineau, "Les assemblées primaires du bailliage de Salers en 1789," *Revue d'Histoire Moderne et Contemporaine* 25 (1978): 419–41; Roger Chartier, "Cultures, lumières, doléances"; Michel Naudin, "Les élections aux états-généraux pour la ville de Nîmes," *Annales Historiques de la Révolution Française* 56 (1984): 495–513; Edna Hindie Lemay, "Les révélations d'un dictionnaire: du nouveau sur la composition de l'Assemblée Nationale Constituante (1789–1791)" *Annales Historiques de la Révolution Française,* no. 384 (1991): 159–89; Gresset, *Gens de justice à Besançon,* 2:759–63.

97. From Kuscinski's sketchy indications of their backgrounds, I calculated that a minimum of 39% of the members of the Legislative Assembly were lawyers of some sort. Since Kuscinski often indicates only the current public office (for example, "administrator of the district directory") rather than all positions held, past and present, and does not identify those with legal backgrounds who never practiced, one may be certain that the number is larger. See August Kuscinski, *Les députés à l'Assemblée Législative de 1791* (Paris: Société de l'Histoire de la Révolution Française, 1900).

98. Alison Patrick, *The Men of the First French Republic* (Baltimore: Johns Hopkins University Press, 1972), 263–65. From Patrick's figures (259), I calculated that at least 48% of the numbers of the Convention were lawyers. Since she relied on Kuscinski for data on professions, this must be regarded as a minimum figure for the reason stated in the previous footnote. See August Kuscinski, *Dictionnaire des Conventionnels* (Brueil-en-Vexin: Editions du Vexin Français, 1973).

99. Jean Egret, "La Révolution aristocratique en Franche-Comté et son échec," *Revue d'Histoire Moderne et Contemporaine* 1 (1954): 266.

that career; in a transformation that has defied the explanatory powers of his biographers,[100] Babeuf became a champion of peasant causes, first achieving considerable prominence in anti-tax movements but ultimately becoming identified with the idea of a radical redistribution of land, the "agrarian law" for which Barère had successfully asked the Convention to vote the death decree (see Chapter 8, p. 485). Babeuf claimed to speak for those who repudiated the limits of revolutionary legislation on peasant affairs and on their behalf joined in organizing a clandestine movement for "another, far greater, far more solemn revolution, which will be the last."[101] Philippe-Antoine Merlin,[102] on the contrary, stood, if any single person did, precisely for the wisdom of that very legislation, as the major architect and chief defender of the detailed decrees by which the National Assembly implemented the breakthrough of August 4–11. For a Babeuf, even the complete abolition of seigneurialism was woefully inadequate to the assurance of a just society; for a Merlin, it was way too much, since a proper respect for legitimate property demanded that a significant element of indemnification be part of any antiseigneurial program. Merlin's repute as a legal thinker was great before the Revolution (as a collaborator on a major treatise whose second edition of 1784 made it one of the very late pre-revolutionary works on feudal law to appear), considerable during the upheaval, and extended way beyond (when he drafted yet another vast treatise, *Questions of Law,* whose first edition appeared under the Consulate).

In the months after the fall of Robespierre in Thermidor, Babeuf, like much of the left, was very much a marginal figure;[103] renewed publication of his radical journal, *The People's Tribune,* led to an arrest order from the minister of justice—none other than Merlin, whose own political star was rising.[104] Babeuf went to his death and Merlin capped his political career as a director. Returning to his love of multivolume legal reference works, he brought out his second such manual, organized around likely questions posed by the practicing attorney.[105] In spite of a seventeen-year exile as a

100. R. B. Rose, *Gracchus Babeuf: The First Revolutionary Communist* (Stanford: Stanford University Press, 1978); Victor M. Daline, *Gracchus Babeuf à la veille et pendant la grande Révolution française) (1785–1794)* (Moscow: Editions du Progrès, 1976).

101. The words are Sylvain Maréchal's. See François Furet, "Babeuf" in François Furet and Mona Ozouf, eds., *A Critical Dictionary of the French Revolution* (Cambridge: Harvard University Press, 1989), 184.

102. See Louis Gruffy, *La vie et l'oeuvre juridique de Merlin de Douai* (Paris: Librairie de Jurisprudence Ancienne et Moderne, 1934).

103. Isser Woloch, *Jacobin Legacy: The Democratic Movement Under the Directory* (Princeton: Princeton University Press, 1970), 11–79.

104. Rose, *Gracchus Babeuf,* 220–21.

105. The very first question of feudalism Merlin proposes to answer for the curious postrevolutionary lawyer who, seeking his advice, consults the fourth edition of *Questions of Law,* is whether a feudal contract entered into after August 11, 1789, but prior to the November promulgation of

regicide in the wake of Napoleon's defeat,[106] he kept up his scholarly pursuits, and continued to put out revised versions of his major manuals, reminding the nineteenth century what the feudal regime once had been.[107]

that edict by the king, was a valid contract. Merlin, consistent with his position in the fall of 1789, replies with a strong negative, for the king had no power to approve or disapprove this act of the National Assembly. If the juxtaposition with Babeuf leads to simply seeing the extremely conservative side of Merlin, it is worth remembering that the logic of his own unyielding position on "feudalism" was radical enough for him to have very early embraced the legal theory of royal disempowerment and ultimately to have consistently cast his votes on several questions that decided the fate of Louis XVI with the regicides. See Philippe-Antoine Merlin, *Recueil alphabétique de questions de droit* (Brussels: Tarlier, 1829), art. "féodalité."

106. See Edna Hindie Lemay, *Dictionnaire des constituants, 1789–1791* (Paris: Universitas, 1991), 659–62.

107. The prerevolutionary *Répertoire de jurisprudence* had a third edition that began to appear in 1807, a fourth in 1812, a fifth, prepared in Belgian exile, in 1827. The second edition of *Questions de Droit* appeared in 1810, a third in 1819, a fourth began to appear in 1827. On the publishing history see Gruffy, *Merlin,* 249–77.

Appendix: Sources for Peasant Insurrection Data

Ado, Anatoly V. "Munitsipal'nye vybory pervichnye sobranaya i sotsial'naya bor'ba vo frantsuzskoi derevnye (1790)." *Frantsuzskii Ezhegodnik* 7 (1964): 57–95.

———. *Krest'ianskoe dvizhenie vo Frantsii vo vremia velikoi burzhaznoi revoliutsii kontsa XVIII veka.* Moscow: Izdatel'stvo Universiteta Moskovskovo, 1971.

Archelet, Jehan d'. "Les émeutes d'Issoudun contre les aides et octrois." *Revue de Berry et du Centre* 20 (1916): 250–83.

Arches, Paul. "La Grande Peur à Dieppe." *Annales Historiques de la Révolution Française* 30 (1958): 72–73.

———. "La Garde Nationale de St-Antonin et les fédérations de Rouergue et du Bas-Quercy (juillet 1789–juillet 1790)." *Annales du Midi* 77 (1965): 375–90.

Aulard, Alphonse. *La Révolution française et le régime féodal.* Paris: Alcan, 1919.

Baudens, G. *Une petite ville pendant la Révolution.* Toulouse: n.p., 1891.

Bercé, Yves-Marie. *Croquants et Nu-Pieds: Les soulèvements paysans en France du XVIe au XIXe siècle.* Paris: Gallimard/Julliard, 1974.

Bois, Paul. *Les paysans de l'Ouest: Des structures économiques et sociales aux options politiques depuis l'époque révolutionnaire dans le département de la Sarthe.* Le Mans: Imprimerie M. Vilaire, 1960.

Bouis, R. "La Grande Peur à Vendôme." *Annales Historiques de la Révolution Française* 44 (1972): 121–23.

Bouloiseau, Marc. "La Grande Peur dans le Haut-Maine." *Annales Historiques de la Révolution Française* 32 (1960): 199–207.

Bourgin, Georges. *Le partage des biens communaux: Documents sur la préparation de la loi de 10 juin 1793.* Paris: Imprimerie Nationale, 1908.

Boutier, Jean. "Jacqueries en pays croquant. Les révoltes paysannes en Acquitaine (décembre 1789–mars 1790)." *Annales: Economies, Sociétés, Civilisations* 34 (1979): 760–86.

———. *Campagnes en émoi: Révoltes et Révolution en bas-Limousin, 1789–1800.* Treignac: Editions "Les Monédières," 1987.

Brugal, Simon. "La Jacquerie dans le Vivarais de 1789 à 1793." *Revue de la Révolution* 3 (1883): 338–48, 361–76.

Bruneau, Marcel. *Les débuts de la Révolution dans les départements du Cher et de l'Indre.* Paris: Hachette, 1902.

Bussière, Georges. *Etudes Historiques sur la Révolution en Périgord.* Vol. 3, *Révolution bourgeoise: l'organisation spontanée. La Révolution rurale: la fin de la féodalité.* Bordeaux: Librairie Historique des Provinces, 1877–1903.

———. "La Révolution en Périgord. L'organisation spontanée (mai à octobre 1789)." *La Révolution Française* 11 (1891): 385–423.

Cardenal, L. de. "La liquidation des impôts directs de l'Ancien Régime. (Exercises 1788 et 1789)." *Révolution Française* (1934): 292–324.

Caron, Pierre. "Le mouvement antiseigneuriale de 1790 dans le Sarladais et le Quercy." *Bulletin d'Histoire Economique de la Révolution* (1912): 353–86.

———. *Les massacres de septembre.* Paris: La Maison du Livre Français, 1935.

Chassin, Charles-Louis. *Les élections et les cahiers de Paris en 1789: Documents recueillis, mis en ordre et annotés.* Vol. 4, *Paris hors les murs.* Paris: D. Jouast, 1889.

———. *La préparation de la guerre de Vendée, 1789–1793.* Paris: Imprimerie Paul Dupont, 1892.

Chomel, Vital, ed. *Les débuts de la Révolution française en Dauphiné, 1788–89.* Grenoble: Presses Universitaires de Grenoble, 1988.

Clère, Jean-Jacques. *Les paysans de la Haute-Marne et la Révolution française: Recherches sur les structures foncières de la communauté villageoise (1780–1815).* Paris: Editions du Comité des Travaux Historiques et Scientifiques, 1988.

Conard, Pierre. *La Grande Peur en Dauphiné (juillet–août, 1789).* Paris: Société Nouvelle de Librairie et de l'Edition, 1904.

Dalin, Victor M. *Grakkh Babef: Nakanune i vo vremia velikoi frantsuzskoi revoliutsii, 1785–1794.* Moscow: Izdatel'stvo Akademii SSSR, 1963.

Darsy, François-Irénée. *Amiens et le département de la Somme pendant la Révolution: Episodes historiques tirés des documents administratifs.* Amiens: Douillet, 1878–83.

Defresne, Arsène, and Fernand Evrard. *Les subsistances dans le district de Versailles de 1788 à l'an V.* Rennes: Imprimerie Oberthur, 1921–22.

Delon, Pierre J.-B. *La Révolution en Lozère.* Mende: Imprimerie Lozérienne, 1922.

Descadeillas, René. *Le fédéralisme méridionale pendant la Révolution: Le comité civil et militaire de Narbonne (24 avril 1793–9 nivôse an II).* Carcassonne: Imprimerie et Lithographie E. Roudière, 1939.

Diné, Henri. *La Grande Peur dans la généralité de Poitiers, juillet–aôut, 1789.* Paris: Chez l'auteur, 1951.

Dinet, Henri. "La Grande Peur en Hurepoix, juillet 1789." *Paris et Ile-de-France: Mémoires* 18–19 (1970): 152–202.

———. "Les peurs du Beauvaisis et du Valois, juillet 1789." *Paris et Ile-de-France: Mémoires* 23–24 (1975): 199–302.

———. "Quelques paniques postérieures à la Grande Peur de 1789." *Annales de Bourgogne* 48 (1976): 44–51.

———. "Les peurs de 1789 dans la région parisienne." *Annales Historiques de la Révolution Française* 50 (1978): 34–44.

———. "Recherches sur la Grande Peur dans la Bourgogne septentrionale: La peur de Bernon." *Annales de Bourgogne* 50 (1978): 129–73.

———. "Craintes, brigandages et paniques inédites des années 1789–1791." *Annales Historiques de la Révolution Française* 53 (1981): 304–16.

———. "L'année 1789 en Champagne," *Annales Historiques de la Révolution Française* 55 (1983): 570–95.

Directoire du Département de la Charente-Inférieure. Various documents. *Archives Historiques de la Saintonge et de l'Aunis* 36 (1906): 61–89.

Dommanget, Maurice. "Les grèves de moissoneurs du Valois sous la Révolution Française." *Annales Historiques de la Révolution Française* 1 (1924): 519–44.

Dorigny, Marcel. "Crise des institutions municipales et émergence d'un 'parti patriote': L'exemple de la ville d'Autun (1787–1790)." In *Aux origines provinciales de la Révolution,* edited by Robert Chagny, 111–22. Grenoble: Presses Universitaires de Grenoble, 1990.

Duchemin, Victor, and Robert Triger. *Les premiers troubles de la Révolution dans la Mayenne.* Mamers: Fleury et Dargin, 1888.

Dupuy, Roger. *La Garde Nationale et les débuts de la Révolution en Ille-et-Vilaine (1789–Mars 1793).* Rennes: Université de Haute-Bretagne, 1972.

———. *De la Révolution à la Chouannerie: Paysans en Bretagne, 1788–1794.* Paris: Flammarion, 1988.

Duval, Louis. *Archives révolutionnaires du département de la Creuse, 1789–1794.* Guéret: Chez l'auteur, 1875.

Evrard, Fernand. "Les paysans du Maconnais et les brigandages de juillet, 1789." *Annales de Bourgogne* 19 (1947): 7–121.

Faye, Henry. "L'anarchie spontanée en Touraine." *Revue de la Révolution* 5 (1885): 447–60; 6 (1885): 23–32.

———. *La Révolution au jour le jour en Touraine (1789–1800).* Angers: Germain et Grassin, 1903.

Fleury, Gabriel. *La ville et le district de Mamers durant la Révolution (1789–1804).* Vol. 1. Mamers: Fleury, 1909.

Forot, Victor. *Episodes révolutionnaires: L'année de la peur à Tulle.* Paris: Librairie Paul Cheronnet, 1906.

Forrest, Alan. *Conscripts and Deserters: The Army and French Society During the Revolution and Empire.* New York: Oxford University Press, 1989.

———. *The Soldiers of the French Revolution.* Durham: Duke University Press, 1990.

Gavignaud, Geneviève. "La propriété privée des terres en Roussillon: Respect et contestations de 1789 à 1849." In *Mouvements populaires et conscience sociale, XVIe–XIXe siècles,* edited by Jean Nicolas, 253–59. Paris: Maloine, 1985.

Gerbaux, Fernand, and Charles Schmidt. *Procès-verbaux des comités d'agriculture et de commerce de la Constituante, de la Législative et de la Convention.* Vol. 1, *Assemblée Constituante.* Paris: Imprimerie Nationale, 1906–10.

Girardot, Jean. "L'insurrection populaire de juillet 1789 dans le bailliage d'Amont." *Société d'Agriculture, Lettres, Sciences et Arts du Départément de la Haute-Saône* (1932): 18–57.

Goujard, Philippe. *L'abolition de la "féodalité" dans le Pays de Bray (1789–1793).* Paris: Bibliothèque Nationale, 1979.

Hesse, Philippe-Jean. "Géographie coutumière et révoltes paysannes en 1789: Une hypothèse de travail." *Annales Historiques de la Révolution Française* 51 (1979): 280–306.

Hollander, Paul d'. "La levée des trois cent mille hommes en Haute-Vienne (mars 1973)." *Annales du Midi* 101 (1989): 73–89.

Huot-Marchand, Ch. "Le mouvement populaire contre les châteaux en Franche-Comté (juillet 1789)." *Annales Franc-Comtoises* 16 (1904): 193–204.

Ikni, Guy-Robert. "Documents: Sur la loi agraire dans l'Oise pendant la Révolution française." *Annales Historiques Compiègnoises* 19 (1982): 19–26.

———. "Sur les biens communaux pendant la Révolution française." *Annales Historiques de la Révolution Française* 54 (1982): 71–94.

———. "La crise agraire dans le Valois de la fin de l'Ancien Régime à la Révolution." *Annales Historiques Compiègnoises* 31 (1985): 21–32.

Jacob, Louis. "La Grande Peur en Artois." *Annales Historiques de la Révolution Française* 10 (1936): 123–48.

Johnson, Hubert C. *The Midi in Revolution: A Study of Regional Political Diversity, 1789–93*. Princeton: Princeton University Press, 1986.

Jolivet, Charles. *La Révolution dans l'Ardèche (1788–1795)*. Marseille: Lafitte Reprints, 1980.

Jones, Peter M. *Politics and Rural Society: The Southern Massif Central c. 1750–1880*. Cambridge: Cambridge University Press, 1985.

Jouanne, R. "Les émeutes paysannes en Pays Bas-Normand." *Les Pays Bas Normands* 1 (1957): 2–85.

Karéiew, N. I. *Les paysans et la question paysanne en France dans le dernier quart du XVIIIe siècle*. Geneva: Slatkine-Megariotis Reprints, 1974.

Lacoste, M. "Le partage des communaux sur le territoire du département de la Meurthe avant la loi de 10 juin 1793." *Annales de l'Est* 1 (1953): 51–78, 155–75, 283–314, 321–49.

Lauvergne, Hubert. *Histoire de la Révolution française dans le département du Var depuis 1789 jusqu'à 1798*. Marseille: Lafitte Reprints, 1974.

Lefebvre, Georges. "Documents sur la Grande Peur: Clermontois, Valois et Soissonais." *Annales Historiques de la Révolution Française* 10 (1933): 167–75.

———. "Documents sur la Grande Peur de 1789 dans la région parisienne." *Annales Historiques de la Révolution Française* 11 (1934): 152–67.

———. *Etudes orléanaises*. Vol. 2. Paris: Commission d'Histoire Economique et Sociale de la Révolution Française, 1962.

———. "Le meurtre du comte de Dampierre (22 juin 1791)." In *Etudes sur la Révolution française*, 393–405. Paris: Presses Universitaires de France, 1963.

———. *La Grande Peur de 1789*. Paris: Armand Colin, 1970.

———. *Les paysans du Nord pendant la Révolution française*. Paris: Armand Colin, 1972.

LeGoff, Timothy J. A. *Vannes and its Region: A Study of Town and Country in Eighteenth-Century France*. Oxford: Clarendon Press, 1981.

Legrand, Robert. *Grèves et incidents dans la Santerre*. Abbeville: Imprimerie Lafosse, 1960.

———. "Babeuf en Picardie (1790–1792)." *Annales Historiques de la Révolution Française* 32 (1968): 458–70.

Lemarchand, Guy. "Les troubles de subsistances dans la généralité de Rouen (seconde moitié du XVIIIe siècle)." *Annales Historiques de la Révolution Française* 35 (1963): 401–27.

———. *La fin du féodalisme dans le pays de Caux: Conjoncture économique et démographique et structure sociale dans une région de grande culture de la crise du XVIIe siècle à la stabilisation de la Révolution (1640–1795)*. Paris: Editions du Comité des Travaux Historiques et Scientifiques, 1989.

Lerch, Ch.-H. "Un document inédit sur la Grande Peur dans la région de Vesoul." *Annales Historiques de la Révolution Française* 42 (1970): 667–70.

Leymarie, M. "Les redevances seigneuriales en haute Auvergne." *Annales Historiques de la Révolution Française* 40 (1968): 298–380.

———. "Féodalité et mouvement populaire à Maurs (Cantal) et aux environs en 1789 et 1790." *Annales Historiques de la Révolution Française* 44 (1972): 92–97.

Lorain, Ch., ed. *Les subsistances en céréales dans le district de Chaumont de 1788 à l'an V.* Vol. 1. Chaumont: R. Cavanol, 1911.

Luc, Jean-Noël. *Paysans et droits féodaux en Charente-Inférieure pendant la Révolution française.* Paris: Comité des Travaux Historiques et Scientifiques, 1984.

Marion, Marcel. *Histoire financière de la France depuis 1715.* Vol. 2, *1789–1792.* Paris: Librairie Rousseau, 1914.

———. "Le recouvrement des impôts en 1790." *Revue Historique* 121 (1916): 1–47.

Massiou, D. *Histoire politique, civile et religieuse de la Saintonge et de l'Aunis.* Vol. 6. Saintes: A. Charrier, 1846.

Mathiez, Albert. *La vie chère et le mouvement social sous la Terreur.* Paris: Payot, 1927.

Mavidal, Jérôme, and E. Laurent. *Archives parlementaires de 1787 à 1860.* Ser. 1. Paris: Librairie Administrative de Paul Dupont, 1862.

Mazel, Henri. "La Révolution dans le Midi: L'incendie des châteaux du bas Languedoc." *Revue de la Révolution* 8–9 (1886–87): 142–57, 307–19, 380–91, 456–69.

Michaud, Alain. *Histoire de Saintes.* Toulouse: Privat, 1989.

Mège, Francisque. *La dernière année de la province de l'Auvergne: La Grande Peur en Auvergne.* Clermont-Ferrand: Albert Bouy, 1901.

Millot, Jean. *L'abolition des droits seigneuriaux dans le département du Doubs et la région comtoise.* Besançon: Imprimerie Millot Frères, 1941.

Moriceau, Jean-Marc. "Les 'Baccanals' ou grèves de moissoneurs en pays de France (seconde moitié du XVIII siècle)." In *Mouvements populaires et conscience sociale, XVIe–XIXe siècles,* edited by Jean Nicolas, 421–34. Paris: Maloine, 1985.

Mourlot, Félix. *La fin de l'Ancien Régime et les débuts de la Révolution dans la généralité de Caen.* Paris: Société de l'Histoire de la Révolution Française, 1913.

Nicolas, Jean. *La Révolution française dans les Alpes: Dauphiné et Savoie, 1789–1799.* Toulouse: Privat, 1989.

———. "Une jeunesse montée sur le plus grand ton d'insolence. Les tumultes juvéniles en France au XVIIIe siècle." In *Aux origines provinciales de la Révolution,* edited by Robert Chagny, 137–56. Grenoble: Presses Universitaires de Grenoble, 1990.

Perrier, Antoine. "Les troubles à Nexon en Mars 1792." *Bulletin de la Société Archéologique et Historique du Limousin* 91 (1965): 193–98.

———. "La Grande Peur à Brive." *Annales Historiques de la Révolution Française* 49 (1973): 138–39.

Porée, Charles. *Sources manuscrites de l'histoire de la Révolution dans l'Yonne.* Vol. 1. Auxerre: Imprimerie Coopérative Ouvrière "L'Universelle," 1918.

Port, Célestin. *La Vendée angevine: Les origines—L'insurrection (janvier 1789–31 mars 1793).* Paris: Hachette, 1888.

Richard, Antoine. "Les troubles agraires des Landes en 1791 et 1792." *Annales Historiques de la Révolution Française* 4 (1927): 564–77.

Richard, Jean. "La levée des 300,000 hommes et les troubles de mars 1793 en Bourgogne." *Annales de Bourgogne* 33 (1961): 213–51.

Rocher, G. *Le district de Saint-Germain-en-Laye pendant la Révolution*. Paris: F. Rieder, 1914.

Rose, R. B. "Tax Revolt and Popular Organization in Picardy, 1789–1791." *Past and Present* 43 (1969): 92–108.

———. "Jacquerie at Davenescourt in 1791: A Peasant Riot in the French Revolution." In *History from Below: Studies in Popular Protest and Popular Ideology in Honor of George Rudé,* edited by Frederick Krantz, 163–76. Montreal: Concordia University, 1985.

Rouault de la Vigne, René. "Les débuts des troubles de Vernon en 1789 d'après une lettre inédite." In *Actes du 81 Congrès Nationale des Sociétés Savantes: Section d'Histoire Moderne et Contemporaine,* 437–42. Paris: Presses Universitaires de France, 1956.

Rouvière, François. *Histoire de la Révolution française dans le département du Gard.* Marseille: Lafitte Reprints, 1974.

Roux, Marie, marquis de. *La Révolution à Poitiers et dans la Vienne*. Paris: Nouvelle Librairie Nationale, 1911.

Sagnac, Philippe, and Pierre Caron, eds. *Les comités des droits féodaux et de législation et l'abolition du régime seigneurial (1789–1793)*. Paris: Imprimerie Nationale, 1907.

Sée, Henri. "Les troubles agraires en Haute-Bretagne, 1790–91." *Bulletin d'Histoire Economique et Sociale de la Révolution Française* (1920–21): 231–373.

———. "Les troubles agraires dans le bas-Maine en juillet, 1789." *Annales Historiques de la Révolution Française* 2 (1925): 528–37.

Seyve, Michel. "Mutation des structures municipales à la ville et à la campagne en Dauphiné drômois." In *Aux origines provinciales de la Révolution,* edited by Robert Chagny, 83–93. Grenoble: Presses Universitaires de Grenoble, 1990.

Soboul, Albert. "La Peur en bas-Languedoc." *Annales Historiques de la Révolution Française* 31 (1959): 162–63.

Sol, Eugène. *La Révolution en Quercy*. Paris: Picard, 1926 and 1930.

Solakian, Daniel. "Mouvements contestataires de communautés agro-pastorales de Haute Provence au XVIIIe siècle dans le témoignage écrit et le mémoire collective." In *Mouvements populaires et conscience sociale, XVIe–XIXe siècles,* edited by Jean Nicolas, 241–52. Paris: Maloine, 1985.

Soreau, Edmond. *Ouvriers et paysans de 1789 à 1792*. Paris: Société d'Edition "Les Belles Lettres," 1936.

Tanné, Claude. "Sur la Grande Peur en Champagne méridionale." *Annales Historiques de la Révolution Française* 32 (1960): 208–10.

Thuillier, André. *Economie et société nivernaises au début du XIXe siècle*. Paris: Mouton, 1974.

Veron-Réveille, Antoine Armand. *Histoire de la Révolution française dans le département du Haut-Rhin 1789–1795*. Paris: Durand, 1865.

Viguier, Jules. *Les débuts de la Révolution en Provence (24 janvier 1789–30 septembre 1791)*. Paris: Lenoir, 1895.

———. *La convocation des états généraux en Provence*. Paris: Lenoir, 1896.

Vitalis, J. "Une émeute des journaliers agricoles de Saint-Nicolas-de-la-Grave, en mars 1793." *Annales Historiques de la Révolution Française* 28 (1956): 295–98.

Vovelle, Michel. "Les campagnes à l'assaut des villes sous la Révolution." In *Ville et campagne au 18e siècle: Chartres et la Beauce,* edited by Michel Vovelle, 227–76. Paris: Editions Sociales, 1980.

———. "Les troubles sociaux en Provence de 1750 à 1792." In *De la cave au grenier: Un itinéraire en Provence au XVIIIe siècle. De l'histoire sociale à l'histoire des mentalités,* edited by Michel Vovelle, 221–62. Quebec: Serge Fleury, 1980.

Wahl, Maurice. *Les premières années de la Révolution à Lyon: 1788–1792.* Paris: Armand Colin, 1894.

Walter, Gérard. *Histoire des paysans en France.* Paris: Flammarion, 1963.

REFERENCES

Aberdam, Serge. *Aux origines du code rural, 1789–1900: Un siècle de débat.* Paris: Institut National de la Recherche Agronomique, 1981–82.

Aberdam, Serge, and Marie-Claude al Hamchari. "Revendications métayères: du droit à l'égalité au droit du bénéfice." In *La Révolution française et le monde rural,* 137–52. Paris: Editions du Comité des Travaux Historiques et Scientifiques, 1989.

L'abolition de la féodalité dans le monde occidental. Paris: Editions du Centre National de la Recherche Scientifique, 1971.

Ado, Anatoly V. *Krest'ianskoe dvizhenie vo Frantsii vo vremiia velikoi burzhuaznoi revoliutsii kontsa XVIII veka.* Moscow: Izdatel'stvo Moskovskovo Universiteta, 1971.

———. "Le mouvement paysan et le problème de l'égalité, 1789–1794." In *Contributions à l'histoire paysanne de la Révolution française,* edited by Albert Soboul, 119–38. Paris: Editions Sociales, 1977.

———. *Krest'iane i velikaia frantsuzskaia revoliutsiia. Krest'ianskoe dvizhenie v 1789–1794 godu.* Moscow: Izdatel'stvo Moskovskovo Universiteta, 1987.

Agulhon, Maurice. *Pénitents et francs-maçons de l'ancienne Provence.* Paris: Fayard, 1968.

———. *La vie sociale en Provence intérieure au lendemain de la Révolution.* Paris: Société des Etudes Robespierristes, 1970.

———. *La République au village: Les populations du Var de la Révolution à la Deuxième République.* Paris: Seuil, 1979.

Almanach Royal, Année Commune MDCCLXXXIX. Paris: Debure, 1789.

L'Ami du Peuple. 21 September 1789.

Appolis, Emile. *Le diocèse civil de Lodève: Etude administrative et économique.* Albi: Imprimerie Coopérative du Sud-Ouest, 1951.

Arbellot, Guy, and Bernard Lepetit. *Atlas de la Révolution française.* Vol. 1, *Routes et communications.* Paris: Editions de l'Ecole des Hautes Etudes en Sciences Sociales, 1987.

Arbois de Jubainville, P. d', ed. *Cahiers de doléances des bailliages de Longuyon, de Longwy, et de Villers-la-Montagne pour les états généraux de 1789.* Nancy: Société d'Impressions Typographiques, 1952.

Ardant, Gabriel. *Théorie sociologique de l'impôt.* Paris: Service d'Edition et de Vente des Publications de l'Education Nationale, 1965.

Arnaud, André-Jean. *Les origines doctrinales du code civil français.* Paris: Librairie Générale de Droit et de Jurisprudence, 1969.

Arrêt de la cour de parlement, qui condamne une brochure intituleé: Les inconvéniens des droits féodaux. London: Valade, 1776.

Aubin, Gérard. "La crise du prélèvement seigneurial à la fin de l'Ancien Régime." In *Aux origines provinciales de la Révolution,* edited by Robert Chagny, 23–33. Grenoble: Presses Universitaires de Grenoble, 1990.

Audevart, Olivier. "Les élections en Haute-Vienne pendant la Révolution." In *Limousin en Révolution,* edited by Jean Boutier, Michel Cassan, Paul d'Hollander, and Bernard Pommaret, 129–38. Treignac: Editions "Les Monédières," 1989.

Aulard, Alphonse. *La Révolution française et le régime féodal.* Paris: Alcan, 1919.

Azimi, Vida. "Un instrument de politique agricole: Les comités d'agriculture des assemblées révolutionnaires." In *La Révolution française et le monde rural,* 483–91. Paris: Editions du Comité des Travaux Historiques et Scientifiques, 1989.

Babeau, Henry. *Les assemblées générales des communautés d'habitants en France du XIIIe siècle à la Révolution.* Paris: Rousseau, 1893.

Baecque, Antoine de. "La figure du paysan dans l'imagerie révolutionnaire." In *La Révolution française et le monde rural,* 477–81. Paris: Editions du Comité des Travaux Historiques et Scientifiques, 1989.

Bailly, Jean-Sylvain. *Mémoires de Bailly.* Paris: Baudoin, 1821.

Baker, Keith Michael. "Politics and Public Opinion under the Old Regime: Some Reflections." In *Press and Politics in Pre-Revolutionary France,* edited by Jack R. Censer and Jeremy D. Popkin, 204–46. Berkeley and Los Angeles: University of California Press, 1987.

———. "Inventing the French Revolution." In *Inventing the French Revolution: Essays on French Political Culture in the Eighteenth Century,* edited by Keith Michael Baker, 202–23. New York: Cambridge University Press, 1990.

Balencie, Gaston, ed. *Cahiers de doléances de la sénéchaussée de Bigorre pour les états généraux de 1789.* Tarbes: Imprimerie Lesbordes, 1925.

Barber, Elinore G. *The Bourgeoisie in 18th-Century France.* Princeton: Princeton University Press, 1955.

Barbotin, Emmanuel. *Lettres de l'abbé Barbotin, député à l'Assemblée Constituante.* Paris: Edouard Cornély, 1910.

Barère, Bertrand. *Mémoires.* Paris: Labitte, 1842.

Barnave, Antoine-Pierre-Joseph-Marie. *Power, Property and History: Barnave's Introduction to the French Revolution and Other Writings.* New York: Harper and Row, 1971.

Barny, Roger. "Les mots et les choses chez les hommes de la Révolution française." *La Pensée,* no. 202 (1978): 96–115.

———. "La formation du concept de 'Revolution' dans la Révolution." In *L'image de la Révolution française. Communications présentées lors du Congrès Mondial pour le Bicentenaire de la Révolution,* edited by Michel Vovelle, 2:433–39. Paris: Pergamon, 1989.

Bart, Jean. "Bourgeois et paysans: la crainte et le mépris." In *La Révolution française et le monde rural,* 459–75. Paris: Editions du Comité des Travaux Historiques et Scientifiques, 1989.

———. "Encore un mot sur les curés de campagne . . ." In *Aux origines provinciales de la Révolution,* edited by Robert Chagny, 157–68. Grenoble: Presses Universitaires de Grenoble, 1990.

Bastier, Jean. *La féodalité au siècle des lumières dans la région de Toulouse (1730–1790).* Paris: Bibliothèque Nationale, 1975.

Bataillon, Jacques-Henri. *Les justices seigneuriales du bailliage de Pontoise à la fin de l'Ancien Régime.* Paris: Sirey, 1942.

Bates, Robert H., and Da-Hsiang Donald Lien. "A note on taxation, development and representative government." *Politics and Society* 14 (1985): 53–70.

Beck, Thomas D. *French Legislators, 1800–1834: A Study in Quantitative History.* Berkeley and Los Angeles: University of California Press, 1974.

Behrens, C. B. A. "Nobles, Privileges and Taxes in France at the End of the Ancien Régime." *Economic History Review,* 2d ser., 15 (1963): 451–75.

Bell, David A. "Lawyers into Demogogues: Chancellor Maupeou and the Transformation of Legal Practice in France, 1771–1789." *Past and Present,* no. 130 (1991): 107–41.

———. *Lawyers and Citizens: The Making of a Political Elite in Old Regime France.* New York: Oxford University Press, 1994.

Bendjebbar, André. "Propriété et contre-révolution dans l'ouest." In *La Révolution française et le monde rural,* 287–300. Paris: Editions du Comité des Travaux Historiques et Scientifiques, 1989.

Bercé, Yves-Marie. *Histoire des croquants: Étude des soulèvements populaires au XVIIIe siècle dans le sud-ouest de la France.* Geneva: Droz, 1974.

———. *Fête et révolte: Des mentalités populaires du XVIe au XVIIIe siècle.* Paris: Hachette, 1976.

Berlanstein, Lenard R. *The Barristers of Toulouse in the Eighteenth Century (1740–1793).* Baltimore: Johns Hopkins University Press, 1975.

———. "Lawyers in Pre-Revolutionary France." In *Lawyers in Early Modern Europe and America,* edited by Wilfred Prest, 164–80. London: Croom Helm, 1981.

Bernard-Griffiths, Simone, Marie-Claude Chemin, and Jean Ehrard. *Révolution française et vandalisme révolutionnaire.* Paris: Universitas, 1992.

Bertaud, Jean-Paul. *The Army of the French Revolution: From Citizen-Soldiers to Instrument of Power.* Princeton: Princeton University Press, 1988.

Béteille, Roger. "Les migrations saisonnières sous le Premier Empire: Essai de synthèse." *Revue d'Histoire Moderne et Contemporaine* 17 (1970): 424–41.

Beugnot, Jean-Claude de. *Mémoires du comte Beugnot, 1779–1815.* Paris: Hachette, 1959.

Bien, David D. "La réaction aristocratique avant 1789: L'exemple de l'armée." *Annales: Economies, Sociétés, Civilisations* 29 (1974): 23–48, 505–34.

Biro, Sidney Seymour. *The German Policy of Revolutionary France.* Cambridge: Harvard University Press, 1957.

Blanning, T. C. W. *The French Revolution in Germany: Occupation and Resistance in the Rhineland, 1792–1802.* Oxford: Clarendon Press, 1983.

———. *The Origins of the French Revolutionary Wars.* London: Longman, 1986.

Bloch, Camille, ed. *Cahiers de doléances du bailliage d'Orléans pour les états généraux de 1789.* Orléans: Imprimerie Orléannaise, 1906.

Bloch, Marc. "La lutte pour l'individualisme agraire dans la France du XVIIIe siècle." *Annales d'Histoire Economique et Sociale* 2 (1930): 329–81, 511–56.

———. *The Historian's Craft.* New York: Vintage Books, 1953.

———. *Feudal Society*. Chicago: University of Chicago Press, 1964.

———. *French Rural History. An Essay on Its Basic Characteristics*. Berkeley and Los Angeles: University of California Press, 1966.

———. *Les caractères originaux de l'histoire rurale française*. Paris: Armand Colin, 1968.

Blum, Jerome. *The End of the Old Order in Rural Europe*. Princeton: Princeton University Press, 1978.

Bohstedt, John. "The Moral Economy and the Discipline of Historical Context." *Journal of Social History* 26 (1992): 265–84.

Bois, Paul, ed. *Cahiers de doléances du tiers état de la sénéchaussée de Château-du-Loir pour les états généraux de 1789*. Gap: Imprimerie Louis-Jean, 1960.

———. *Les paysans de l'Ouest: des structures économiques et sociales aux options politiques depuis l'époque révolutionnaire dans la Sarthe*. Le Mans: Imprimerie M. Vilaire, 1960.

Boncerf, Pierre-François. *Les inconvéniens des droits féodaux*. London: Valade, 1776.

Bordes, Maurice. *L'administration provinciale et municipale en France au XVIIIe siècle*. Paris: Société d'Edition d'Enseignement Supérieur, 1972.

Bosher, J. F. *The Single Duty Project: A Study of the Movement for a French Customs Union in the Eighteenth Century*. London: Athlone Press, 1964.

———. *French Finances, 1770–1775: From Business to Bureaucracy*. Cambridge: Cambridge University Press, 1970.

Bouchette, François-Joseph. *Lettres de François-Joseph Bouchette (1735–1810): Avocat à Bergues. Membre de l'Assemblée Constituante*. Paris: Champion, 1909.

Boullé, Jean-Pierre. "Ouverture des états généraux de 1789." *Revue de la Révolution* 15 (1889): 13–28, 99–104.

Bouloiseau, Marc. "Elections de 1789 et communautés rurales en Haute-Normandie." *Annales Historiques de la Révolution Française* 28 (1956): 29–47.

———, ed. *Cahiers de doléances du tiers état du bailliage de Rouen pour les états généraux de 1789*. Rouen: Imprimerie Administrative de la Seine-Maritime, 1960.

Bourget-Besnier, Elisabeth. *Une famille française sous la Révolution et l'Empire: La famille de Lézay-Marnésia*. Paris: Bourget-Besnier, 1985.

Bourgin, Georges. *Le partage des biens communaux: documents sur la préparation de la loi du 10 juin 1793*. Paris: Imprimerie Nationale, 1908.

Boutier, Jean. *Campagnes en émoi: Révoltes et Révolution en bas-Limousin, 1789–1800*. Treignac: Editions "Les Monédières," 1987.

———. "Un autre midi. Note sur les sociétés populaires en Corse (1790–1794)." *Annales Historiques de la Révolution Française*, no. 268 (1987): 158–75.

Boutier, Jean, and Philippe Boutry. "La diffusion des sociétés politiques en France (1789–an III). Une enquête nationale." *Annales Historiques de la Révolution Française*, no. 266 (1986): 365–98.

———. *Atlas de la Révolution française*. Vol. 6, *Les sociétés populaires*. Paris: Editions de l'Ecole des Hautes Etudes en Sciences Sociales, 1992.

Bouton, Cynthia A. "Les victimes de la violence populaire pendant la guerre des farines (1775)." In *Mouvements populaires et conscience sociale, XVIe–XIXe siècles*, edited by Jean Nicolas, 391–99. Paris: Maloine, 1985.

———. "L'économie morale et la guerre des farines de 1775." In *La Guerre du Blé au XVIIIe siècle: La critique populaire contre le libéralisme économique au XVIIIe siècle,* edited by Florence Gauthier and Guy-Robert Ikni, 93–110. Paris: Editions de la Passion, 1988.

———. "Gendered Behavior in Subsistence Riots: The Flour War of 1775." *Journal of Social History* 23 (1990): 735–54.

———. *The Flour War: Gender, Class and Community in Late Ancien Régime Society.* University Park: Pennsylvania State University Press, 1993.

———. "Regions and Regionalism: The Case of France." Paper presented to the meetings of the American Historical Association, San Francisco, 1994.

Boutruche, Robert. *Seigneurie et féodalité: Le premier âge des liens d'homme à homme.* Paris: Aubier, 1968.

Braudel, Fernand. *L'identité de la France.* Paris: Flammarion, 1986.

Brette, Armand. *Receuil de documents relatifs à la convocation des états généraux de 1789.* Paris: Imprimerie Nationale, 1894–1915.

Bruchet, Max. *L'abolition des droits seigneuriaux en Savoie (1761–1793).* Annecy: Hérisson Frères, 1908.

Brunet, Michel. *Le Roussillon face à la Révolution française.* Perpignan: Trabucaire, 1989.

Brunot, Ferdinand. *Histoire de la langue française de ses origines à nos jours.* Vol. 9, *La Révolution et l'Empire.* Paris: Armand Colin, 1967.

Brustein, William. "Regional Social Orders in France and the French Revolution." *Comparative Social Research* 9 (1986): 145–61.

Buchez, Philippe-Joseph-Benjamin, and P.-C. Roux. *Histoire parlementaire de la Révolution française.* Paris: Paulin, 1834.

Bussière, Georges. *Etudes historiques sur la Révolution en Périgord.* Paris: Librairie Historique des Provinces, 1877–1903.

Cameron, Iain A. *Crime and Repression in the Auvergne and the Guyenne, 1720–1790.* Cambridge: Cambridge University Press, 1981.

Campbell, Peter R. "Louis XVI, King of the French." In *The French Revolution and the Creation of Modern Political Culture.* Vol. 2, *The Political Culture of the French Revolution,* edited by Colin Lucas, 161–82. Oxford: Pergamon, 1988.

Caron, Pierre. "Le mouvement antiseigneurial de 1790 dans le Sarladais et le Quercy." *Bulletin d'Histoire Economique de la Révolution* (1912): 352–86.

Castan, Nicole. *Les criminels de Languedoc: Les exigences d'ordre et les voies du ressentiment dans une société prérévolutionnaire (1750–1790).* Toulouse: Association des Publications de l'Université de Toulouse-Mirail, 1980.

———. *Justice et répression en Languedoc à l'époque des lumières.* Paris: Flammarion, 1980.

———. "Contentieux sociale et utilisation variable du charivari à la fin de l'Ancien Régime en Languedoc." In *Le Charivari,* edited by Jacques Le Goff and Jean-Claude Schmitt, 197–205. Paris: Ecole des Hautes Etudes en Sciences Sociales, 1981.

Castan, Yves. "Attitudes et motivations dans les conflits entre seigneurs et communautés devant le Parlement de Toulouse au XVIIIe siècle." In *Villes de l'Europe Méditerranéenne et de l'Europe Occidentale du Moyen Age au XIXe siècle,* 223–39. Nice: Centre de la Mediterranée Moderne et Contemporaraine, 1969.

Caussy, Fernand. *Voltaire, seigneur de village.* Paris: Hachette, 1912.

Censer, Jack. "The Coming of a New Interpretation of the French Revolution." *Journal of Social History* 21 (1987): 295–309.

———. "The French Revolution After Two Hundred Years." In *The Global Ramifications of the French Revolution,* edited by Joseph Klaits and Michael Haltzel, 7–25. Washington, D.C.: Woodrow Wilson Center Press, 1994.

Champion, Edmé. *La France d'après les cahiers de 1789*. Paris: Armand Colin, 1897.

Charmasse, Anatole de, ed. *Cahiers des paroisses et communautés du bailliage d'Autun pour les états généraux de 1789*. Autun: Imprimerie Dujussieu, 1895.

Chartier, Roger. "Culture, lumières et doléances: Les cahiers de 1789." *Revue d'Histoire Moderne et Contemporaine* 28 (1981): 68–93.

———. "De 1614 à 1789: Le déplacement des attentes." In *Représentation et vouloir politiques: Autour des états généraux de 1614,* edited by Roger Chartier and Denis Richet, 101–11. Paris: Editions de l'Ecole des Hautes Etudes en Sciences Sociales, 1982.

———. *The Cultural Origins of the French Revolution*. Durham: Duke University Press, 1991.

Chartier, Roger, and Jean Nagle. "Paroisses et châtellenies en 1614." In *Représentation et vouloir politiques: Autour des états-généraux de 1614,* edited by Roger Chartier and Denis Richet, 89–100. Paris: Ecole des Hautes Etudes en Sciences Sociales, 1982.

Chassin, Charles-Louis. *L'église et les derniers serfs*. Paris: Dentu, 1880.

———. *La préparation de la guerre de Vendée, 1789–1793*. Paris: Imprimerie Paul Dupont, 1892.

Chastel, André. *Le château, la chasse et la forêt*. Bordeaux: Editions Sud-Ouest, 1990.

Chaunu, Pierre. *Le grand déclassement: A propos d'une commémoration*. Paris: Laffont, 1989.

Chaussinand-Nogaret, Guy. *La noblesse au XVIIIe siècle: De la féodalité aux lumières*. Paris: Hachette, 1976.

Chénon, Emile. *Les démembrements de la propriété foncière en France avant et après la Révolution*. Paris: Recueil Sirey, 1923.

Clère, Jean-Jacques. *Les paysans de la Haute-Marne et la Révolution française: Recherches sur les structures foncières de la communauté villageoise (1780–1815)*. Paris: Editions du Comité des Travaux Historiques et Scientifiques, 1988.

Clout, Hugh D. "Agricultural Change in the Eighteenth and Nineteenth Centuries." In *Themes in the Historical Geography of France,* edited by Hugh D. Clout, 407–46. New York: Academic Press, 1977.

———. *Agriculture in France on the Eve of the Railway Age*. London: Croom Helm, 1980.

Cobban, Alfred. *The Social Interpretation of the French Revolution*. Cambridge: Cambridge University Press, 1965.

———. *Aspects of the French Revolution*. New York: Norton, 1968.

———. "The French Revolution: Orthodox and Unorthodox Interpretations." In his *Aspects of the French Revolution,* 275–87. New York: Norton, 1968.

———. "The Myth of the French Revolution." In his *Aspects of the French Revolution,* 90–111. New York: Norton, 1968.

———. "Political *versus* Social Interpretations of the French Revolution." In his *Aspects of the French Revolution,* 264–74. New York: Norton, 1968.

Cocula-Vaillières, Anne-Marie. "La contestation des privilèges seigneuriaux dans le fonds des Eaux et Forêts. L'exemple acquitain dans la seconde moitié du XVIIIe siècle."

In *Mouvements populaires et conscience sociale, XVIe–XIXe siècles,* edited by Jean Nicolas, 209–16. Paris: Maloine, 1985.

———. "Les seigneurs et la forêt en Périgord aux temps modernes." In *Le château, la chasse et la forêt,* edited by André Chastel, 101–4. Bordeaux: Editions du Sud-Ouest, 1990.

Coignet, Capitaine [Jean Roch]. *Les cahiers du capitaine Coignet 1799–1815.* Paris: Hachette, 1968.

Comninel, George C. *Rethinking the French Revolution: Marxism and the Revisionist Challenge.* London: Verso, 1987.

Condorcet, Jean-Antoine-Nicolas de Caritat, marquis de. *Mémoires de Condorcet sur la Révolution française.* Paris: Ponthieu, 1824.

Corvisier, André. *L'armée française de la fin du XVIIe siècle au ministère de Choiseul: Le soldat.* Paris: Presses Universitaires de France, 1964.

Corvol, Andrée. "Forêt et communautés en basse Bourgogne au dix-huitième siècle." *Revue Historique* 256 (1976): 15–36.

———. "Les délinquances forestières en basse-Bourgogne depuis la réformation de 1711–1718." *Revue Historique* 259 (1978): 345–88.

———. *L'homme et l'arbre sous l'Ancien Régime.* Paris: Economica, 1984.

———. "La coercition en milieu forestier." In *Mouvements populaires et conscience sociale, XVIe–XIXe siècles,* edited by Jean Nicolas, 199–207. Paris: Maloine, 1985.

———. *L'homme au bois: Histoire des relations de l'homme et de la forêt (XVIIe–XXe siècles).* Paris: Fayard, 1987.

Couthon, Georges. *Discours sur le rachat des droits seigneuriaux, prononcé à la séance du mercredi 29 février 1792.* Paris: Imprimerie Nationale, 1792.

Crebouw, Yvonne. "Les salariés agricoles face au maximum des salaires." In *La Révolution française et le monde rural,* 113–22. Paris: Editions du Comité des Travaux Historiques et Scientifiques, 1989.

Creuzé-Latouche, Jacques-Antoine. *Journal des états-généraux et du début de l'Assemblée Nationale, 18 mai–29 juillet 1789.* Paris: Henri Didier, 1946.

Crook, Malcolm. " 'Aux urnes, citoyens!' Urban and Rural Electoral Behavior during the French Revolution." In *Reshaping France: Town, Country and Region during the French Revolution,* edited by Alan Forrest and Peter M. Jones, 152–67. Manchester: Manchester University Press, 1991.

Crouzet, François. *De la supériorité de l'Angleterre sur la France: L'économique et l'imaginaire, XVIIe–XXe siècles.* Paris: Librairie Académique Perrin, 1985.

Cubells, Monique. "L'émeute du 25 mars 1789 à Aix-en-Provence." In *Mouvements populaires et conscience sociale, XVIe–XIXe siècles,* edited by Jean Nicolas, 401–8. Paris: Maloine, 1985.

———. *Les horizons de la liberté: La naissance de la Révolution en Provence, 1787–1789.* Aix: Edisud, 1987.

Dakin, Douglas. *Turgot and the Ancien Regime in France.* New York: Octagon Books, 1965.

Dalby, Jonathan R. *Les paysans cantaliens et la Révolution française (1789–1794).* Clermont-Ferrand: Université de Clermont-Ferrand III, 1989.

Daline, Victor M. *Gracchus Babeuf à la veille et pendant la grande Révolution française, 1785–1794.* Moscow: Editions du Progrès, 1976.

Darnton, Robert. *The Kiss of Lamourette.* New York: Norton, 1990.

Davies, James Chowning. "The J-Curve of Rising and Declining Satisfactions as a Cause of Revolution and Rebellion." In *Violence in America: Historical and Comparative Perspectives,* edited by Hugh Davis Graham and Ted Robert Gurr, 415–36. Beverly Hills, Calif.: Sage Publications, 1979.

Davis, Natalie Zemon. "The Reasons of Misrule." In her *Society and Culture in Early Modern France,* 97–123. Stanford: Stanford University Press, 1975.

———. "The Rites of Violence." In her *Society and Culture in Early Modern France,* 152–87. Stanford: Stanford University Press, 1975.

Dawson, Phillip. *Provincial Magistrates and Revolutionary Politics in France, 1789–1795.* Cambridge: Harvard University Press, 1972.

———. "La vente des biens nationaux dans la région parisienne." In *La Révolution française et le monde rural,* 235–51. Paris: Editions du Comité des Travaux Historiques et Scientifiques, 1989.

Delumeau, Jean. *Catholicism between Luther and Voltaire: A New View of the Counter-Reformation.* Philadelphia: Westminster Press, 1977.

Desplat, Christian. "La forêt béarnaise au XVIIIe siècle." *Annales du Midi* 85 (1973): 147–71.

———. "Le peuple en armes dans les Pyrénées occidentales françaises à l'époque moderne." In *Mouvements populaires et conscience social, XVIe–XIXe siècles,* edited by Jean Nicolas, 217–27. Paris: Maloine, 1985.

Dewald, Jonathan. *Pont-St.-Pierre, 1398–1789: Lordship, Community and Capitalism in Early Modern France.* Berkeley and Los Angeles: University of California Press, 1987.

Didier, Béatrice. "La Feuille Villageoise: un dialogue Paris-province pendant la Révolution." In *Aux origines provinciales de la Révolution,* edited by Robert Chagny, 267–78. Grenoble: Presses Universitaires de Grenoble, 1990.

Dion, Roger. *Essai sur la formation du paysage rural français.* Neuilly-sur-Seine: Guy Durier, 1981.

"Doléances, plaintes et remontrances du tiers état du bailliage royale de Château-Salins en Lorraine." *Annuaire de la Société Historique et Archéologique Lorraine* 16 (1904): 220–27.

Doniol, Henri. *La Révolution française et la féodalité.* Paris: Guillaumin, 1876.

Dontenwill, Serge. *Une seigneurie sous l'Ancien Régime: L' "Etoile" en Brionnais du XVIe au XVIIIe siècle.* Roanne: Editions Horvath, 1973.

Dorvaux, N., and P. Lesprand, eds. *Cahiers de doléances des bailliages des généralités de Metz et de Nancy pour les états-généraux de 1789.* 2d ser., vol. 7, *Cahiers du bailliage de Thionville.* Bar-le-Duc: Société d'Histoire et d'Archéologie Lorraine, 1922.

Doyle, William. "Was There an Aristocratic Reaction in Pre-Revolutionary France?" In *French Society and the Revolution,* edited by Douglas Johnson, 3–28. Cambridge: Cambridge University Press, 1976.

———. *Origins of the French Revolution.* Oxford: Oxford University Press, 1980.

Duby, Georges. *The Three Orders: Feudal Society Imagined.* Chicago: University of Chicago Press, 1980.

Duchemin, Victor, and Rober Triger. *Les premières troubles de la Révolution dans la*

Mayenne: Etudes sur l'état des esprits dans les différentes régions de ce département. Mamers: Fleury et Dangin, 1888.

Duma, Jean. "Le conseil du duc de Penthièvre et le mouvement populaire (1789–1792)." In *Mouvements populaires et conscience sociale, XVIe–XIXe,* edited by Jean Nicolas, 659–70. Paris: Maloine, 1985.

———. "Place de l'élément féodal et seigneurial dans la fortune d'un 'grand': L'exemple des Bourbon-Penthièvre." In *La Révolution française et le monde rural,* 55–66. Paris: Comité des Travaux Historiques et Scientifiques, 1989.

Dupâquier, Jacques. "Structures sociales et cahiers de doléances. L'exemple du Vexin français." *Annales Historiques de la Révolution Française* 40 (1968): 433–54.

Dupuy, Roger. *La Garde Nationale et les débuts de la Révolution en Ille-et-Vilaine (1789–mars 1793).* Rennes: Université de Haute-Bretagne, 1972.

———. "Les émeutes anti-féodales de Haute-Bretagne (janvier 1790 et janvier 1791): Meneurs improvisés ou agitateurs politisés." In *Mouvements populaires et conscience sociale, XVIe–XIXe siècles,* edited by Jean Nicolas, 449–56. Paris: Maloine, 1985.

———. *De la Révolution à la Chouannerie: Paysans en Bretagne, 1788–1794.* Paris: Flammarion, 1988.

Duquesnoy, Adrien. *Journal d'Adrien Duquesnoy.* Paris: Picard, 1894.

Durand, Yves. *Les fermiers généraux au XVIII siècle.* Paris: Presses Universitaires de France, 1971.

Edeine, Bernard, ed. *Les assemblées préliminaires et la rédaction des cahiers de doléances dans le bailliage secondaire de Romorantin.* Blois: Imprimerie Raymond Sille, 1949.

Edelstein, Melvin. "Vers une 'sociologie électorale' de la Révolution française: La participation des citadins et campagnards (1789–1793)." *Revue d'Histoire Moderne et Contemporaine* 22 (1975): 508–29.

———. *La Feuille Villageoise: Communication et modernisation dans les régions rurales pendant la Révolution.* Paris: Commission d'Histoire Economique et Sociale de la Révolution Française, 1977.

———. "L'apprentissage de la citoyenneté: participation électorale des campagnards et citadins (1789–1793)." In *L'image de la Révolution française: Communications lors du Congrès Mondial pour le Bicentenaire de la Révolution,* edited by Michel Vovelle, 1:15–25. Paris: Pergamon, 1989.

———. "La place de la Révolution française dans la politisation des paysans." *Annales Historiques de la Révolution Française,* no. 280 (1990): 135–49.

———. "La reception de la Révolution en Bretagne: Etude électorale." Paper presented at conference on Pouvoir Local et Révolution. Rennes, 1993.

———. "Electoral Behavior during the Constitutional Monarchy (1790–1791): A 'Community' Interpretation." In *The French Revolution and the Meaning of Citizenship,* edited by Renée Waldinger, Philip Dawson, and Isser Woloch, 105–22. Westport, Conn.: Greenwood, 1994.

Egret, Jean. *La Révolution des notables: Mounier et les monarchiens.* Paris: Armand Colin, 1950.

———. "La Révolution aristocratique en Franche-Comté et son échec." *Revue d'Histoire Moderne et Contemporaine* 1 (1954): 245–71.

———. "La prérévolution en Provence, 1787–1789." *Annales Historiques de la Révolution Française* 26 (1954): 97–126.

———. "Les origines de la Révolution en Bretagne (1788–1789)." *Revue Historique* 213 (1955): 189–215.

———. *La pre-révolution française, 1787–1788*. Paris: Presses Universitaires de France, 1962.

———. *Necker, ministère de Louis XVI*. Paris: Champion, 1975.

Ellis, Harold A. *Boulainvilliers and the French Monarchy: Aristocratic Politics in Early Eighteenth-Century France*. Ithaca: Cornell University Press, 1988.

Elwitt, Sanford. *The Making of the Third Republic: Class and Politics in Rural France, 1868–1884*. Baton Rouge: Louisiana State University Press, 1975.

Elyada, Ouzi. "La représentation populaire de l'image royale avant Varennes." *Annales Historiques de la Révolution Française,* no. 297 (1994): 527–46.

Etienne, Charles, ed. *Cahiers de doléances des bailliages des généralités de Metz et de Nancy pour les états généraux de 1789*. 1st ser., vol. 1, *Cahiers du bailliage de Vic*. Nancy: Imprimerie Berger-Levrault, 1907.

———, ed. *Cahiers de doléances des bailliages des généralités de Metz et de Nancy pour les états généraux de 1789*. 1st ser., vol. 2, *Cahiers du bailliage de Dieuze*. Nancy: Imprimerie Berger-Levrault, 1912.

———, ed. *Cahiers de doléances des bailliages de Metz et de Nancy pour les états généraux de 1789*. 1st ser., vol. 3, *Cahiers du bailliage de Vézelise*. Nancy: Imprimerie Berger-Levrault, 1930.

Evans, Peter B., Dietrich Rueschemeyer, and Theda Skocpol. *Bringing the State Back In*. Cambridge: Cambridge University Press, 1985.

Facó, Rui. *Cangaceiros e fanáticos: Gênese e lutas*. Rio de Janeiro: Editora Civilização Brasileira, 1972.

Farge, Arlette, and Jacques Revel. *Logiques de la foule*. Paris: Hachette, 1988.

Feierabend, Ivo K., and Rosalind L. Feierabend. "Aggressive Behavior Within Polities, 1948–1962: A Cross-National Study." *Journal of Conflict Resolution* 10 (1966): 249–71.

Fel, André. "Petite Culture, 1750–1850." In *Themes in the Historical Geography of France,* edited by Hugh D. Clout, 215–45. New York: Academic Press, 1977.

Ferradou, André. *Le rachat des droits féodaux dans la Gironde, 1790–1793*. Paris: Sirey, 1928.

Ferrières, Charles-Elie de. *Mémoires du marquis de Ferrières*. Paris: Baudoin, 1821.

———. *Correspondance inédite (1789, 1790, 1791)*. Paris: Armand Colin, 1932.

Ferro, Marc. *The Russian Revolution of 1917*. Englewood Cliffs, N.J.: Prentice-Hall, 1967.

———. "The Aspirations of Russian Society." In *Revolutionary Russia,* edited by Richard Pipes, 143–57. Cambridge: Harvard University Press, 1968.

———. "The Russian Soldier in 1917: Undisciplined, Patriotic and Revolutionary." *Slavic Review* 30 (1971): 483–512.

Festy, Octave. *L'agriculture pendant la Révolution française: Les conditions de production et de récolte des céréales; Etude d'histoire économique*. Paris: Gallimard, 1947.

Fitch, Nancy. "Whose Violence? Insurrection and the Negotiation of Democratic Politics in Central France, 1789–1851." Paper presented at conference on Violence and the Democratic Tradition in France. University of California, Irvine, 1994.

Fitzsimmons, Michael P. "Privilege and the Polity in France, 1786–1789." *American Historical Review* 92 (1987): 269–95.

Flammermont, Jules. *Le Chancelier Maupeou et les parlements.* Paris: Picard, 1883.

Fleury, Michel, and Pierre Valmary. "Les progrès de l'instruction élémentaire de Louis XIV à Napoléon III d'après l'enquête de Louis Maggiolo (1877–1879)." *Population* 12 (1957): 71–92.

Ford, Franklin L. *Robe and Sword: The Regrouping of the French Aristocracy after Louis XIV.* New York: Harper and Row, 1965.

Forrest, Alan. *Conscripts and Deserters: The Army and French Society During the Revolution and Empire.* New York: Oxford University Press, 1989.

———. "Regionalism and Counter-Revolution in France." In *Rewriting the French Revolution,* edited by Colin Lucas, 151–82. Oxford: Clarendon Press, 1991.

Forster, Robert. *The Nobility of Toulouse in the Eighteenth Century: A Social and Economic Study.* Baltimore: Johns Hopkins University Press, 1960.

———. "The Noble Wine Producers of the Bordelais in the Eighteenth Century." *Economic History Review* 14 (1961): 18–33.

———. "The Provincial Noble: A Reappraisal." *American Historical Review* 68 (1963): 681–91.

———. *The House of Saulx-Tavanes: Versailles and Burgundy, 1700–1830.* Baltimore: Johns Hopkins University Press, 1971.

———. "The 'World' Between Seigneur and Peasant." In *Studies in Eighteenth-Century Culture,* edited by Ronald C. Rosbottom, 5:401–21. Madison: University of Wisconsin Press, 1976.

———. "Seigneurs and their Agents." In *Vom Ancien Régime Zur Französischen Revolution: Forschungen und Perspektiven,* edited by Ernst Hinrichs, Eberhard Schmitt, and Rudolf F. Vierhaus, 169–87. Göttingen: Vandenhoeck und Ruprecht, 1978.

———. *Merchants, Landlords, Magistrates: The Depont Family in Eighteenth-Century France.* Baltimore: Johns Hopkins University Press, 1980.

Fournier, Georges. "Société paysanne et pouvoir local en Languedoc pendant la Révolution." In *La Révolution française et le monde rural,* 381–96. Paris: Editions du Comité des Travaux Historiques et Scientifiques, 1989.

Fox-Genovese, Elizabeth. *The Origins of Physiocracy: Economic Revolution and Social Order in Eighteenth-Century France.* Ithaca: Cornell University Press, 1976.

Franzosi, Roberto. "The Press as a Source of Sociohistorical Data: Issues in the Methodology of Data Collection from Newspapers." *Historical Methods* 20 (1987): 5–16.

Frayssenge, Jacques, and Nicole Lemaître. "Les émotions populaires en Rouergue au XVIIIe siècle." In *Mouvements populaires et conscience sociale, XVIe–XIXe siècles,* edited by Jean Nicolas, 371–81. Paris: Maloine, 1985.

Frêche, Georges. *Toulouse et la région Midi-Pyrénées au siècle des lumières (vers 1670–1789).* Paris: Cujas, 1976.

Freddi, Fabio. "La presse parisienne et la nuit du 4 août." *Annales Historiques de la Révolution Française* 57 (1985): 46–58.

Furet, François. "Les états généraux de 1789: Deux bailliages élisent leurs députés." In *Conjoncture économique, structures sociales: Hommage à Ernest Labrousse,* edited by Fernand Braudel, 433–48. Paris: Mouton, 1974.

———. *Marx and the French Revolution*. Chicago: University of Chicago Press, 1988.

———. *La Révolution de Turgot à Jules Ferry, 1770–1880*. Paris: Hachette, 1988.

———. "Night of August 4." In *A Critical Dictionary of the French Revolution,* edited by François Furet and Mona Ozouf, 107–14. Cambridge: Belknap Press of Harvard University Press, 1989.

———. "Babeuf." In *A Critical Dictionary of the French Revolution,* edited by François Furet and Mona Ozouf, 179–85. Cambridge: Belknap Press of Harvard University Press, 1989.

———. "Ancien Régime." In *A Critical Dictionary of the French Revolution,* edited by François Furet and Mona Ozouf, 604–15. Cambridge: Belknap Press of Harvard University Press, 1989.

Furet, François, and Ran Halévi. *Orateurs de la Révolution française*. Vol. 1, *Les constituants*. Paris: Gallimard, 1989.

Furet, François, and Jacques Ozouf. *Lire et écrire: L'alphabétisation des français de Calvin à Jules Ferry*. Paris: Les Editions de Minuit, 1977.

Furet, François, and Mona Ozouf. "Deux légitimations historiques de la société française au XVIIIe siècle: Mably et Boulainvilliers." *Annales: Economies, Sociétés, Civilisations* 34 (1979): 438–50.

Furet, François, and Denis Richet. *La Révolution française*. Paris: Fayard, 1973.

Garaud, Marcel. *Histoire générale du droit privé français*. Vol. 1, *La Révolution et l'égalité civile*. Paris: Recueil Sirey, 1953.

———. *Histoire générale du droit privé français*. Vol. 2, *La Révolution et la propriété foncière*. Paris: Receuil Sirey, 1958.

Garraud, Robert. *Le rachat des droits féodaux et des dîmes inféodées en Haute-Vienne*. Limoges: Imprimerie Dupuy-Moulinier, 1939.

Gaultier de Biauzat, Jean-François. *Gaultier de Biauzat, député du tiers-état aux états généraux de 1789: Sa vie et correspondence*. Paris: Librairie Historique des Provinces, 1890.

Gauthier, Florence. *La voie paysanne dans la Révolution française: L'exemple de la Picardie*. Paris: F. Maspero, 1977.

———. "Loi agraire." In *Dictionnaire des usages sociopolitiques (1770–1775),* 2:65–98. Paris: Société Française d'Etude du 18ème Siècle, 1987.

Gauville, Louis-Henri-Charles de. *Journal du baron de Gauville*. Paris: Gay, 1864.

Gérard, Alain. *Pourquoi la Vendée?* Paris: Armand Colin, 1990.

Gerbaux, Fernand, and Charles Schmidt. *Procès verbaux des comités d'agriculture et de commerce de la Constituante, de la Législative et de la Convention*. Paris: Imprimerie Nationale, 1906–10.

Giesey, Ralph. "State-Building in Early Modern France: The Role of Royal Officialdom." *Journal of Modern History* 55 (1983): 191–207.

Giffard, André. *Les justices seigneuriales en Bretagne au XVIIe et XVIIIe siècles (1661–1791)*. Brionne: Montfort, 1903.

Gindin, Cl. "Aperçu sur les conditions de la mouture des grains en France, fin du XVIIIe siècle." In *Contributions à l'histoire paysanne de la Révolution française,* edited by Albert Soboul, 159–88. Paris: Editions Sociales, 1977.

Godard, Jacques, and Léonard Robin. *Rapport de Messieurs J. Godard et L. Robin, commissaires civils, envoyés par le roi, dans le département du Lot, en exécution du décret de l'Assemblée Nationale, du 13 décembre, 1790*. Paris: Imprimerie Nationale, 1791.

Godechot, Jacques. *The Taking of the Bastille, July 14, 1789*. New York: Scribner, 1970.

———. "Les municipalités du Midi avant et après la Révolution." *Annales du Midi* 84 (1972): 363–67.

Godfrin, Jean, ed. *Cahiers de doléances des bailliages des généralités de Metz et de Nancy pour les états généraux de 1789*. 1st ser., vol. 4, *Cahiers du bailliage de Nancy*. Paris: Librairie Ernest Leroux, 1934.

Goldstone, Jack A. *Revolution and Rebellion in the Early Modern World*. Berkeley and Los Angeles: University of California Press, 1991.

Goubert, Pierre. *L'Ancien Régime*. Vol. 1, *La société*. Paris: Armand Colin, 1969.

———. *The Ancien Régime: French Society, 1600–1750*. New York: Harper, 1973.

———. "Sociétés rurales françaises du 18e siècle: Vingt paysanneries contrastées. Quelques problèmes." In *Clio parmi les hommes: Recueil d'articles*, edited by Pierre Goubert, 63–74. Paris: Mouton, 1976.

Gough, Hugh. *The Newspaper Press in the French Revolution*. London: Routledge, 1988.

Goujard, Philippe. "L'abolition de la féodalité dans le district de Neuchâtel (Seine-Inférieure)." In *Contributions à l'histoire paysanne de la Révolution française*, edited by Albert Soboul, 363–73. Paris: Editions Sociales, 1977.

———. *L'abolition de la "féodalité" dans le pays de Bray, 1789–1793*. Paris: Bibliothèque Nationale, 1979.

———. "Les pétitions au comité féodal: Loi contre loi." In *La Révolution française et le monde rural*, 67–81. Paris: Edition du Comité des Travaux Historiques et Scientifiques, 1989.

Grégoire, Henri. *Mémoires*. Paris: A. Dupont, 1837.

———. "Rapport sur la nécessité et les moyens d'anéantir les patois et universaliser l'usage de la langue française." In *Une politique de la langue: La Révolution française et les patois: L'enquête de Grégoire*, edited by Michel de Certeau, Dominique Julia, and Jacques Revel, 300–317. Paris: Gallimard, 1975.

———. *L'abbé Grégoire, Evêque des Lumières*. Paris: Editions France-Empire, 1988.

Grellet de Beauregard, Jean-Baptiste. "Lettres de M. Grellet de Beauregard." *Société des Sciences Naturelles et Archéologiques de la Creuse* (1899): 53–117.

Gresset, Maurice. *Gens de justice à Besançon: De la conquête par Louis XIV à la Révolution française, 1674–1789*. Paris: Bibliothèque Nationale, 1978.

Gross, Jean-Pierre. "Progressive Taxation and Social Justice in Eighteenth Century France." *Past and Present*, no. 140 (1993): 79–126.

Gruffy, Louis. *La vie et l'oeuvre juridique de Merlin de Douai*. Paris: Librairie de Jurisprudence Ancienne et Moderne, 1934.

Guénée, Bernard. *States and Rulers in Later Medieval Europe*. Oxford: Basil Blackwell, 1988.

Gueniffey, Patrice. "Les assemblées et la représentation." In *The French Revolution and the Creation of Modern Political Culture*, vol. 2, *The Political Culture of the French Revolution*, edited by Colin Lucas, 233–57. Oxford: Pergamon, 1988.

Guerreau, Alain. "Fief, féodalité, féodalisme. Enjeux sociaux et réflexion historienne." *Annales: Economies, Sociétés, Civilisations* 45 (1990): 134–66.

Gullickson, Gay. *The Spinners and Weavers of Auffay: Rural Industry and the Sexual*

Division of Labor in a French Village, 1750–1850. Cambridge: Cambridge University Press, 1986.

Gurr, Ted Robert. *Why Men Rebel*. Princeton: Princeton University Press, 1970.

Gutton, Jean-Pierre. *Villages du Lyonnais sous la monarchie (XVIe–XVIIIe siècles)*. Lyon: Presses Universitaires du Lyon, 1978.

———. *La sociabilité villageoise dans l'Ancienne France: Solidarités et voisinages du XVIe au XVIIIe siècle*. Paris: Hachette, 1979.

Halévi, Ran. "La monarchie et les élections: position des problèmes." In *The French Revolution and the Creation of Modern Political Culture,* vol. 1, *The Political Culture of the Old Regime,* edited by Keith Michael Baker, 387–402. Oxford: Pergamon, 1987.

———. "Monarchiens." In *A Critical Dictionary of the French Revolution,* edited by François Furet and Mona Ozouf, 376–78. Cambridge: Belknap Press of Harvard University Press, 1989.

Hampson, Norman. "The Idea of the Nation in Revolutionary France." In *Reshaping France: Town, Country, and Region During the French Revolution,* edited by Alan Forrest and Peter M. Jones, 13–25. Manchester: Manchester University Press, 1991.

Hardman, John. *Louis XVI*. New Haven: Yale University Press, 1993.

Harsany, Zoltan-Etienne, ed. *Cahiers de doléances des bailliages des généralités de Metz et de Nancy pour les états généraux de 1789*. 1st ser., vol. 5, *Cahiers du bailliage de Pont-à-Mousson*. Paris: Librairie Paul Hartmann, 1946.

Heckscher, Eli F. *Mercantilism*. New York: Macmillan, 1955.

Henrion de Pansey, Pierre-Paul-Nicolas. *Traité des fiefs de Dumoulin analysé et conféré avec les autres feudistes*. Paris: Valade, 1773.

———. *Traité du pouvoir municipal et des biens communaux: Dissertations féodales*. Barrois: 1789.

Herbert, Sydney. *The Fall of Feudalism in France*. New York: Barnes and Noble, 1921.

Herlihy, P. "L'abolition de la dîme inféodée (1789–1793)." In *Contributions à l'histoire paysanne de la Révolution française,* edited by Albert Soboul, 377–99. Paris: Editions Sociales, 1977.

Hervé, François. *Theorie des matières féodales et censuelles*. Paris: Knapen, 1785–88.

Hesse, Philippe-Jean. "Géographie coutumière et révoltes paysannes en 1789: Une hypothèse de travail." *Annales Historiques de la Révolution Française* 51 (1979): 280–306.

Heuvel, Gerd van den. "Féodalité, Féodal." In *Handbuch politisch-sozialer Grundbegriffe in Frankreich 1680–1820,* edited by Rolf Reichardt and Eberhard Schmitt, vol. 1: 7–54. Munich: Oldenbourg, 1988.

Higonnet, Patrice L.-R. *Class, Ideology and the Rights of Nobles during the French Revolution*. Oxford: Clarendon Press, 1981.

Hill, Christopher. "Mrs. Thatcher Set to Rights." *Guardian*. 15 July 1989.

Hincker, François. *Les français devant l'impôt sous l'Ancien Régime*. Paris: Flammarion, 1971.

Hinrichs, Ernst. " 'Feudalität' und Ablösung. Bemerkungen zur Vorgeschichte des 4. August 1789." In *Die Französische Revolution,* edited by Eberhard Schmitt, 124–57. Cologne: Kiepenheuer und Witsch, 1976.

Hirsch, Jean-Pierre. *La nuit du 4 août.* Paris: Gallimard/Julliard, 1978.

Hobsbawm, Eric. "The Making of a Bourgeois Revolution." In *The French Revolution and the Birth of Modernity,* edited by Ferenc Fehér, 30–48. Berkeley and Los Angeles: University of California Press, 1990.

Hollander, Paul d'. "La levée des trois cent mille hommes en Haute-Vienne (mars 1793)." *Annales du Midi* 101 (1989): 73–90.

———. "Les Gardes Nationales en Limousin (juillet 1789–juillet 1790)." *Annales Historiques de la Révolution Française,* no. 290 (1992): 465–89.

Hood, J. N. "Revival and Mutation of Old Rivalries in Revolutionary France." *Past and Present* 82 (1979): 82–115.

Houdaille, J. "Les signatures au marriage de 1740 à 1829." *Population* 32 (1977): 65–90.

Hufton, Olwen H. *The Poor of Eighteenth-Century France: 1750–1789.* Oxford: Clarendon Press, 1974.

———. "Le paysan et la loi en France au XVIIIe siècle." *Annales: Economies, Sociétés, Civilisations* 38 (1983): 679–700.

Hunt, Lynn A. "Committees and Communes: Local Politics and National Revolution in 1789." *Comparative Studies in Society and History* 18 (1976): 321–46.

———. *Politics, Culture and Class in the French Revolution.* Berkeley and Los Angeles: University of California Press, 1984.

———. *The Family Romance of the French Revolution.* Berkeley and Los Angeles: University of California Press, 1992.

Hutt, Maurice. *Chouannerie and Counter-Revolution: Puisaye, the Princes and the British Government in the 1790s.* Cambridge: Cambridge University Press, 1983.

Hyslop, Beatrice Fry. *Répertoire critique des cahiers de doléances pour les états généraux de 1789.* Paris: Ministère de l'Education Nationale, 1933.

———. *Supplément au répertoire critique des cahiers de doléances pour les états généraux de 1789.* Paris: Ministère de l'Education Nationale, 1952.

———. *L'apanage de Philippe Egalité, Duc d'Orléans (1785–1791).* Paris: Société des Etudes Robespierristes, 1965.

———. *A Guide to the General Cahiers of 1789, with the Texts of Unedited Cahiers.* New York: Octagon Books, 1968.

Ikni, Guy-Robert. "Le mouvement paysan en Picardie: meneurs, pratiques, maturation et signification historique." In *La guerre du blé au XVIIIe siècle: La critique populaire contre le libéralisme économique au XVIIIe siècle,* edited by Florence Gauthier and Guy-Robert Ikni, 187–203. Montreuil: Editions de la Passion, 1988.

Isambert, F.-A. *Recueil général des anciennes lois françaises depuis l'an 420 jusqu'à la Révolution de 1789.* Ridgewood, N.J.: Gregg, 1964.

Jessenne, Jean-Pierre. *Pouvoir au village et Révolution: Artois, 1760–1848.* Lille: Presses Universitaires de Lille, 1987.

Joanne, Paul. *Dictionnaire géographique et administrative de la France et de ses colonies.* Paris: Hachette, 1890.

Johnson, Hubert C. *The Midi in Revolution. A Study of Regional Political Diversity, 1789–1793.* Princeton: Princeton University Press, 1986.

Jones, Colin. "Bourgeois Revolution Revivified: 1789 and Social Change." In *Rewriting the French Revolution,* edited by Colin Lucas, 69–118. Oxford: Clarendon Press, 1991.

Jones, Peter M. "Parish, Seigneurie and the Community of Inhabitants in Southern Central France During the Eighteenth and Early Nineteenth Centuries." *Past and Present* 91 (1981): 74–108.

———. *Politics and Rural Society: The Southern Massif Central, c. 1750–1880*. Cambridge: Cambridge University Press, 1985.

———. *The Peasantry in the French Revolution*. Cambridge: Cambridge University Press, 1988.

———. "A Response to Hilton Root, 'The Case Against Georges Lefebvre's Peasant Revolution.' " *History Workshop* 28 (1989): 103–6.

———. "Georges Lefebvre and the French Revolution: Fifty Years On." *French Historical Studies* 16 (1990): 645–63.

———. "The 'Agrarian Law': Schemes for Land Redistribution During the French Revolution." *Past and Present*, no. 133 (1991): 96–133.

Juillard, Etienne. *La vie rurale dans la plaine de Basse-Alsace*. Strasbourg: Le Roux, 1953.

Julia, Dominique. "La réforme post-tridentine en France d'après les procès verbaux des visites pastorales: Ordre et résistances." In *La società religiosa nell'età moderna*, 311–415. Naples: Guido Editori, 1973.

Kagan, Richard. "Law Students and Careers in Eighteenth-Century France." *Past and Present* 68 (1975): 38–72.

Kaplan, Steven L. *Bread, Politics and Political Economy in the Reign of Louis XV*. The Hague: Martinus Nijhoff, 1976.

———. *La Bagarre. Galiani's "Lost" Parody*. The Hague: Martinus Nijhoff, 1979.

———. *The Famine Plot Persuasion in Eighteenth-Century France*. Philadelphia: American Philosophical Society, 1982.

———. *Provisioning Paris*. Ithaca: Cornell University Press, 1984.

———. *Farewell Revolution. Disputed Legacies: France, 1789/1989*. Ithaca, N.Y.: Cornell University Press, 1995.

———. *Farewell Revolution. The Historians' Feud: France, 1789/1989*. Ithaca, N.Y.: Cornell University Press, 1995.

Karéiew, Nikolai Ivanovich. *Les paysans et la question paysanne en France dans le dernier quart du XVIIIe siècle*. Paris: V. Giard and E. Brière, 1899.

Karpik, Lucien. "Lawyers and Politics in France: 1814–1950: The State, the Market and the Public." *Law and Social Inquiry* 13 (1988): 707–36.

———. "Le désintéressément." *Annales: Economies, Sociétés, Civilisations* 44 (1989): 733–51.

Kennedy, Michael L. *The Jacobin Clubs in the French Revolution: The First Years*. Princeton: Princeton University Press, 1982.

Kessel, Patrick. *La nuit du 4 août 1789*. Paris: Arthaud, 1969.

Keyes, Charles F., ed. "Symposium: Peasant Strategies in Asian Societies." *Journal of Asian Studies* 42 (1983): 753–868.

Knight, Alan. *The Mexican Revolution*. New York: Cambridge University Press, 1986.

Kriedte, Peter, Hans Medick, and Jürgen Schlumbohm. *Industrialization Before Industrialization: Rural Industry in the Genesis of Capitalism*. Cambridge: Cambridge University Press, 1981.

Kuscinski, August. *Les députés à l'Assemblée Législative de 1791*. Paris: Société de l'Histoire de la Révolution Française, 1900.

———. *Dictionnaire des conventionnels.* Brueil-en-Vexin: Editions du Vexin Français, 1973.

La Bruyère, Jean de. *Les caractères ou les moeurs de ce siècle.* Paris: Lefèvre, 1843.

Labrosse, Claude, and Pierre Rétat. *Naissance du journal révolutionnaire, 1789.* Lyon: Presses Universitaires de Lyon, 1989.

Labrousse, Camille-Ernest. *Esquisse du mouvement des prix et des revenus en France au XVIIIe siècle.* Paris: Librairie Dalloz, 1933.

———. *La crise de l'économie française à la fin de l'Ancien Régime et au début de la Révolution.* Paris: Presses Universitaires de France, 1944.

Lachiver, Marcel. *Vin, vigne et vignerons en région parisienne du XVIIe au XIXe siècle.* Pontoise: Société Historique et Archéologique de Pontoise, du Val d'Oise et du Vexin, 1982.

Lacretelle, Charles. *Histoire de la France pendant le dix-huitième siècle.* Paris: Treuttel et Würtz, 1821.

Lalanne, Ludovic. *Dictionnaire historique de la France.* Geneva: Slatkine-Megariotis Reprints, 1977.

Lally-Tolendal, Trophime-Gérard, comte de. *Mémoire de M. le comte de Lally-Tolendal; ou, Seconde lettre à ses commetants.* Paris: Desenne, 1790.

Lameth, Alexandre. *Histoire de l'Assemblée Constituante.* Paris: Moutardier, 1828.

Lane, Frederic C. "Economic Consequences of Organized Violence." In *Venice and History: The Collected Papers of Frederic C. Lane,* 412–428. Baltimore: Johns Hopkins University Press, 1966.

Langlois, Claude. "La fin des guerres de religion: La disparition de la violence religieuse en France au 19e siècle." Paper presented at conference on Violence and the Democratic Tradition in France, University of California, Irvine, 1994.

Lassaigne, Jean-Dominique. *Les assemblées de la noblesse de France aux dix-septième et dix-huitième siècles.* Paris: Cujas, 1965.

Laurent, Gustave, ed. *Cahiers de doléances pour les états généraux de 1789.* Vol. 1, *Bailliage de Châlons-sur-Marne.* Epernay: Imprimerie Henri Villers, 1906.

Lebigre, Arlette. *Les Grands Jours d'Auvergne: Désordres et répression au XVIIe siècle.* Paris: Hachette, 1976.

LeBras, Hervé, and Emmanuel Todd. *L'invention de la France: Atlas anthropologique et politique.* Paris: Livre de Poche, 1981.

Lefebvre, Georges. *The Coming of the French Revolution.* Princeton: Princeton University Press, 1947.

———. "La Révolution française et les paysans." In his *Etudes sur la Révolution française,* 338–67. Paris: Presses Universitaires de France, 1963.

———. "Le meurtre du comte de Dampierre (22 juin 1791)." In his *Etudes sur la Révolution française,* 393–405. Paris: Presses Universitaires de France, 1963.

———. "La Révolution française dans l'histoire du monde." In his *Etudes sur la Révolution française,* 431–43. Paris: Presses Universitaires de France, 1963.

———. *La Grande Peur de 1789.* Paris: Armand Colin, 1970.

———. *Les paysans du Nord pendant la Révolution française.* Paris: Armand Colin, 1972.

———. *The Great Fear of 1789: Rural Panic in Revolutionary France.* New York: Vintage Books, 1973.

Legendre, L.-F. "Correspondance de Legendre." *La Révolution Française* 39 (1900): 515–58; 40 (1901): 46–78.

LeGoff, Timothy J. A. *Vannes and Its Region: A Study of Town and Country in Eighteenth-Century France*. Oxford: Clarendon Press, 1981.

LeGoff, Timothy J. A., and Donald M. G. Sutherland. "The Revolution and the Rural Economy." In *Reshaping France: Town, Country and Region During the French Revolution*, edited by Alan Forrest and Peter M. Jones, 52–85. Manchester: University of Manchester Press, 1991.

Lemaître, Nicole. *Un horizon bloqué: Ussel et la montagne limousine au XVIIe et XVIIIe siècles*. Ussel: Musée du Pays d'Ussel, 1978.

Lemarchand, Guy. "Les troubles de subsistances dans la généralité de Rouen (seconde moitié du XVIIIe siècle). *Annales Historiques de la Révolution Française* 35 (1963): 401–27.

———. "Le féodalisme dans la France rurale des temps modernes: Essai de caractérisation." *Annales Historiques de la Révolution Française* 41 (1969): 77–108.

———. "La féodalité et la révolution française: Seigneurie et communauté paysanne (1780–1799)." *Annales Historiques de la Révolution Française* 242 (1980): 536–58.

———. "Vols de bois et braconnage dans la généralité de Rouen au XVIIIe siècle." In *Mouvements populaires et conscience sociale, XVIe–XIXe siècles*, edited by Jean Nicolas, 229–39. Paris: Maloine, 1985.

———. *La fin de féodalisme dans le pays de Caux*. Paris: Editions du Comité des Travaux Historiques et Scientifiques, 1989.

———. "Troubles populaires au XVIIIe siècle et conscience de classe. Une préface à la Révolution française." *Annales Historiques de la Révolution Française*, no. 279 (1990): 32–48.

Lemay, Edna Hindie. *La vie quotidienne des députés aux états généraux de 1789*. Paris: Hachette, 1987.

———. "Les révélations d'un dictionnaire: du nouveau sur la composition de l'Assemblée Nationale Constituante (1789–1791)." *Annales Historiques de la Révolution Française*, no. 384 (1991): 159–89.

———. *Dictionnaire des constituants, 1789–1791*. Paris: Universitas, 1991.

Le Monde. 13 July 1989.

Le Roy Ladurie, Emmanuel. *Les paysans de Languedoc*. Paris: Service d'Edition et de Vente des Publications de l'Education Nationale, 1966.

———. "Révoltes et contestations rurales en France de 1675 à 1788." *Annales: Economies, Sociétés, Civilisations* 29 (1974): 6–22.

Le Roy Ladurie, Emmanuel, and Orest Ranum, eds. *Pierre Prion, Scribe: Mémoires d'un écrivain de campagne au XVIIIe siècle*. Paris: Gallimard/Julliard, 1985.

Lesprand, P., and L. Bour, eds. *Cahiers de doléances des prévôtés bailliagères de Sarrebourg et Phalsbourg et du bailliage de Lixheim pour les états généraux de 1789*. Metz: Imprimerie P. Even, 1938.

Lesueur, Frédéric, and Alfred Cauchie, eds. *Cahiers de doléances du bailliage de Blois et du bailliage secondaire de Romorantin pour les états généraux de 1789*. Blois: Imprimerie Emmanuel Rivière, 1907.

Letaconneux, Joseph. *Le régime de la corvée en Bretagne au XVIIIe siècle*. Rennes: Plihon et Hommay, 1905.

Levi, Margaret. *Of Rule and Revenue*. Berkeley and Los Angeles: University of California Press, 1988.

Levine, Robert M. *Vale of Tears: Revisiting the Canudos Massacre in Northeastern Brazil, 1893–1897.* Berkeley and Los Angeles: University of California Press, 1992.

Lewis, Gwynne. *The Second Vendée: The Continuity of Counterrevolution in the Department of the Gard, 1789–1815.* Oxford: Clarendon Press, 1978.

Ligou, Daniel, ed. *Cahiers de doléances du tiers état du pays et jugerie de Rivière-Verdun pour les états-généraux de 1789.* Gap: Imprimerie Louis-Jean, 1961.

Lindet, Robert-Thomas. *Correspondance de Thomas Lindet pendant la Constituante et la Législative (1789–1792).* Paris: Amand Montier, 1899.

Locke, John. *Of Civil Government, Two Treatises.* London: J. M. Dent, 1924.

Lorcin, Marie-Thérèse. "Un musée imaginaire de la ruse paysanne: La fraude des décimables du XIVe au XVIIIe siècles dans la région lyonnaise." *Etudes Rurales,* no. 51 (1973): 112–24.

Luc, Jean-Noël. "Le rachat des droits féodaux dans le département de la Charente-Inférieure (1789–1793)." In *Contributions à l'histoire paysanne de la Révolution française,* edited by Albert Soboul, 309–52. Paris: Editions Sociales, 1977.

———. *Paysans et droits féodaux en Charente-Inférieure pendant la Révolution française.* Paris: Commission d'Histoire de la Révolution Française, 1984.

Lucas, Colin. "The Problem of the Midi in the French Revolution." *Transactions of the Royal Historical Society* 28 (1978): 1–25.

———. "Résistances populaires à la Révolution dans le sud-est." In *Mouvements populaires et conscience sociale, XVIe–XIXe siècles,* edited by Jean Nicolas, 473–85. Paris: Maloine, 1985.

———. "The Crowd and Politics." In *The French Revolution and the Creation of Modern Political Culture,* vol. 2, *The Political Culture of the French Revolution,* edited by Colin Lucas, 259–85. Oxford: Pergamon, 1988.

———. "Aux sources du comportement politique de la paysannerie beaujolaise." In *La Révolution française et le monde rural,* 345–65. Paris: Editions du Comité des Travaux Historiques et Scientifiques, 1989.

Luong, Hy Van. "Agrarian Unrest from an Anthropological Perspective." *Comparative Politics* 17 (1985): 153–74.

Lüsebrink, Hans-Jürgen. "L'affaire Cléreaux (Rouen, 1786–1790): Affrontements idéologiques et tensions institutionelles autour de la scène judiciaire au XVIIIe siècle." *Studies on Voltaire and the Eighteenth Century* 191 (1980): 892–900.

Mackrell, John Q. C. "Criticism of Seigneurial Justice in Eighteenth-Century France." In *French Government and Society, 1500–1850,* edited by J. F. Bosher, 123–44. London: Athlone, 1973.

———. *The Attack on "Feudalism" in Eighteenth-Century France.* London: Routledge and Kegan Paul, 1973.

Malouet, Pierre-Victor. *Correspondance de Malouet avec les officiers municipaux de la ville de Riom, 1788–1789.* Riom: Jouvet, n.d.

Marion, Henri. *La dîme ecclésiastique en France au XVIIIe siècle et sa suppression.* Bordeaux: Imprimerie de l'Université et des Facultés, 1912.

Marion, Marcel. *La Garde des Sceaux Lamoignon et la réforme judiciaire de 1788.* Paris: Hachette, 1905.

———. *Histoire financière de la France depuis 1715.* Paris: Rousseau, 1914.

———. "Le recouvrement des impôts en 1790." *Revue Historique* 121 (1916): 1–47.

———. *Dictionnaire des institutions de la France depuis 1715*. Paris: Picard, 1969.

———. *Les impôts directs sous l'Ancien Régime, principalement au XVIIIe siècle*. Geneva: Slatkine-Megariotis Reprints, 1974.

Markoff, John. "Governmental Bureaucratization: General Processes and an Anomalous Case." *Comparative Studies in Society and History* 17 (1975): 479–503.

———. "Suggestions for the Measurement of Consensus." *American Sociological Review* 47 (1982): 290–98.

———. "The Social Geography of Rural Revolt at the Beginning of the French Revolution." *American Sociological Review* 50 (1985): 761–81.

———. "Contexts and Forms of Rural Revolt: France in 1789." *Journal of Conflict Resolution* 30 (1986): 253–89.

———. "Literacy and Revolt: Some Empirical Notes on 1789 in France." *American Journal of Sociology* 92 (1986): 323–49.

———. "Some Effects of Literacy in Eighteenth-Century France." *Journal of Interdisciplinary History* 17 (1986): 311–33.

———. "Allies and Opponents: Nobility and Third Estate in the Spring of 1789." *American Sociological Review* 53 (1988): 477–96.

———. "Images du roi au début de la Révolution." In *L'image de la Révolution française: Communications présenteés lors du Congrès Mondial pour le Bicentenaire de la Révolution,* edited by Michel Vovelle, 1:237–45. Paris: Pergamon, 1989.

———. "Słowa i rzeczy: rewolucyjna burżuazja francuska definiuje system feudalny." In *Interpretacje wielkiej transformacji: Geneza kapitalizmu jako geneza współczesności,* edited by Adam Czarnota and Andrzej Zybertowicz, 357–82. Warsaw: Kolegium Otryckie, 1989.

———. "¿Cuál es la cuestión? Algunos comentarios sobre la transición hacia el capitalismo." *AREAS* 11 (1989): 37–46.

———. "Peasant Grievances and Peasant Insurrection: France in 1789." *Journal of Modern History* 62 (1990): 445–76.

———. "Peasants Protest: The Claims of Lord, Church and State in the *Cahiers de Doléances* of 1789." *Comparative Studies in Society and History* 32 (1990): 413–54.

———. "Prélèvements seigneuriaux et prélèvements fiscaux: sur l'utilisation des cahiers de doléances." In *Mélanges de l'Ecole Française de Rome* 103 (1991): 47–68.

———. "Violence, Emancipation and Democracy: The Countryside and the French Revolution." *American Historical Review* 100 (1995): 360–86.

Markoff, John, and Verónica Montecinos. "The Ubiquitous Rise of Economists." *Journal of Public Policy* 13 (1993): 37–68.

Markoff, John, and Gilbert Shapiro. "The Linkage of Data Describing Overlapping Geographical Units." *Historical Methods Newsletter* 7 (1973): 34–46.

———. "Consensus and Conflict at the Onset of Revolution: A Quantitative Study of France in 1789." *American Journal of Sociology* 91 (1985): 28–53.

Markoff, John, Gilbert Shapiro, and Sasha R. Weitman. "Towards the Integration of Content Analysis and General Methodology." In *Sociological Methodology 1975,* edited by David Heise, 1–58. San Francisco: Jossey-Bass, 1974.

Martin, E., ed. *Cahiers de doléances du bailliage de Mirecourt.* Epinal: Imprimerie Lorraine, 1928.

Martin, Jean-Clément. *La Vendée et la France.* Paris: Editions du Seuil, 1987.

Marx, Karl. "The Eighteenth Brumaire of Louis Bonaparte." In *Selected Works,* by Karl Marx and Frederick Engels, 1:247–344. Moscow: Foreign Languages Publishing House, 1955.

Marx, Karl, and Frederick Engels. "Manifesto of the Communist Party." In *Selected Works,* by Karl Marx and Frederick Engels, 1:21–65. Moscow: Foreign Languages Publishing House, 1955.

Massé, Pierre. "Survivances des droits féodaux dans l'Ouest (1793–1902)." *Annales Historiques de la Révolution Française* 37 (1965): 270–98.

Massereau, T., ed. *Recueil des cahiers de doléances des bailliages de Tours et de Loches et cahier général du bailliage de Chinon aux états généraux de 1789.* Orléans: Imprimerie Moderne, 1918.

Mathiez, Albert. *La vie chère et le mouvement social sous la Terreur.* Paris: Payot, 1927.

———. "Les corporations françaises ont-elles été supprimées en principe dans la nuit du 4 août 1789?" *Annales Historiques de la Révolution Française* 8 (1931): 252–57.

———. *The French Revolution.* New York: Grosset and Dunlap, 1964.

Matthews, George T. *The Royal General Farms in Eighteenth-Century France.* New York: Columbia University Press, 1958.

Maupetit, Michel-René. "Lettres de Michel-René Maupetit." *Bulletin de la Commission Historique et Archéologique de la Mayenne,* 2d ser., 17 (1901): 302–27; 18 (1902): 133–63, 321–33, 447–75; 19 (1903): 205–50; 20 (1904): 88–125, 358–77; 21 (1905): 446–51; 22 (1906): 67–95, 213–39, 349–84, 454–93; 23 (1907): 87–115.

Mavidal, Jérôme, and E. Laurent. *Archives parlementaires de 1787 à 1860.* 1st ser. Paris: Libraire Administrative de Paul Dupont, 1862–.

Maza, Sarah. "Le tribunal de la nation: Les mémoires judiciaires et l'opinion publique à la fin de l'Ancien Régime." *Annales: Economies, Sociétés, Civilisations* 42 (1987): 73–90.

———. "The Rose-Girl of Salency: Representations of Virtue in Prerevolutionary France." *Eighteenth Century Studies* 22 (1989): 395–412.

———. "Domestic Melodrama as Political Ideology: The Case of the Comte de Sanois." *American Historical Review* 94 (1989): 1249–64.

———. "Politics, Culture and the Origins of the French Revolution." *Journal of Modern History* 61 (1989): 704–23.

Mazauric, Claude. "Note sur l'emploi du 'régime féodal' et de 'féodalité' pendant la Révolution française." In *Sur la Révolution française: Contributions à l'histoire de la Révolution bourgeoise,* edited by Claude Mazauric, 119–34. Paris: Editions Sociales, 1970.

Mazel, Henri. "La Révolution dans le Midi: L'incendie des châteaux du bas Languedoc." *Revue de la Révolution* 8 (1886): 142–57, 307–19, 380–91, 456–69.

McManners, John. *French Ecclesiastical Society under the Ancien Régime: A Study of Angers in the Eighteenth Century.* Manchester: Manchester University Press, 1960.

———. *The French Revolution and the Church.* New York: Harper and Row, 1969.

McPhee, Peter. "Electoral Democracy and Direct Democracy in France, 1789–1851." *European History Quarterly* 16 (1986): 77–96.

———. "The French Revolution, Peasants and Capitalism." *American Historical Review* 5 (1989): 1265–80.

———. "Peasant Revolution, Winegrowing and the Environment: The Corbières Region of Languedoc, 1780–1830." *Australian Journal of French Studies* 29 (1992): 153–69.

Meadwell, Hudson. "Exchange Relations Between Lords and Peasants." *Archives Européenes de Sociologie* 28 (1987): 3–49.

Merlin, Philippe-Antoine. *Recueil alphabétique des questions de droit.* Brussels: Tarlier, 1829.

———. *Répertoire universel et raisonné de jurisprudence.* Paris: Garnery, 1827–1828.

Merritt, Richard L. *Symbols of American Community, 1735–1775.* New Haven: Yale University Press, 1966.

Millot, Jean. *Le régime féodal en Franche-Comté au XVIIIe siècle.* Besançon: Imprimerie Millot Frères, 1937.

———. *L'abolition des droits seigneuriaux dans le département du Doubs et la région comtoise.* Besançon: Imprimerie Millot Frères, 1941.

Ministère de l'Instruction Publique. *Statistique de l'instruction primaire.* Paris: Imprimerie Nationale, 1880.

Ministère des Travaux Publics, de l'Agriculture et du Commerce. *Statistique de la France.* Paris: Imprimerie Royale, 1837.

Mirabeau, Honoré-Gabriel de Riquetti, comte de. *Lettres du comte de Mirabeau à ses commettans.* Paris: Imprimerie du Patriote François, 1789–1791.

Mitchell, C. J. *The French Legislative Assembly of 1791.* Leiden: E. J. Brill, 1988.

Molinier, Alain. *Une paroisse du bas Languedoc: Sérignan, 1650–1792.* Montpellier: Imprimerie Dehan, 1968.

Montesquieu, Charles de Secondat, baron de la Brède et de. *De l'esprit des lois.* Paris: Société Les Belles Lettres, 1950.

Montlosier, François-Dominique de Reynaud de. *Mémoires de M. le Comte de Montlosier sur la Révolution française, le Consulat, l'Empire, la Restauration et les principaux événemens qui l'ont suivie, 1755–1830.* Paris: Dufey, 1830.

Moore, Barrington. *Social Origins of Dictatorship and Democracy: Lord and Peasant in the Making of the Modern World.* Boston: Beacon, 1966.

Moriceau, Jean-Marc. "Les 'Baccanals' ou grèves de moissoneurs en pays de France (seconde moitié du XVIIIe siècle)." In *Mouvements populaires et conscience sociale, XVIe–XIXe siècles,* edited by Jean Nicolas, 421–34. Paris: Maloine, 1985.

Morel, O. "Les Assises ou Grands Jours dans le justice seigneuriales de Bresse à la fin de l'Ancien Régime (1768–1789)." *Annales de la Société d'Emulation et de l'Agriculture de l'Ain* (1934): 311–44.

Mounier, Jean-Joseph. "Exposé de ma conduite dans l'Assemblée Nationale." In *Orateurs de la Révolution française,* vol. 1, *Les constituants,* edited by François Furet and Ran Halévi, 908–97. Paris: Gallimard, 1989.

Mousnier, Roland. *Fureurs paysannes: Les paysans dans les révoltes du XVIIe siècle (France, Russie, Chine).* Paris: Calmann-Lévy, 1967.

Muret, Pierre. "L'affaire des princes possessionés d'Alsace et les origines du conflit entre la Révolution et l'Empire." *Revue d'histoire moderne et contemporaine* 1 (1899–1900): 433–56, 566–92.

Naudin, Michel. "Les élections aux états-généraux pour la ville de Nîmes." *Annales Historiques de la Révolution Française* 56 (1984): 495–513.

Necker, Jacques. *Compte rendu au roi.* Paris: Imprimerie Royale, 1781.
———. *De l'administration des finances.* Paris: n.p., 1784.
———. *Oeuvres complètes.* Paris: Treuttel and Würtz, 1820.
Nicolas, Jean. "La dîme: Contrats d'affermage et autres documents décimaux." In *La pratique des documents anciens: Actes publics et notariés, documents administratifs et comptables,* edited by Roger Devos, Robert Grabion, Jean-Yves Mariotte, Jean Nicolas, and Christian Abry, 173–94. Annecy: Archives Départementales de la Haute-Savoie, 1978.
———. "Le paysan et son seigneur en Dauphiné à la veille de la Révolution." In *La France d'Ancien Régime: Etudes réunies en l'honneur de Pierre Goubert,* 2: 497–507. Toulouse: Privat, 1984.
———. "Un chantier toujours neuf." In *Mouvements populaires et conscience sociale, XVIe–XIXe siècles,* edited by Jean Nicolas, 13–20. Paris: Maloine, 1985.
———, ed. *Mouvements populaires et conscience sociale, XVIe–XIXe siècles.* Paris: Maloine, 1985.
———. "Les émotions dans l'ordinateur: Premiers résultats d'une enquête collective." Paper presented at University of Paris VII, October 1986.
———. *La Révolution française dans les alpes: Dauphiné et Savoie, 1789–1799.* Toulouse: Privat, 1989.
———. "Une jeunesse montée sur le plus grand ton d'insolence. Les tumultes juvéniles en France au XVIIIe siècle." In *Aux origines provinciales de la Révolution,* edited by Robert Chagny, 137–56. Grenoble: Presses Universitaires de Grenoble, 1990.
Noël, Jean-François. "Une justice seigneuriale de Haute Bretagne à la fin de l'Ancien Régime: La châtellenie de la Motte-de-Gennes." *Annales de Bretagne* 83 (1976): 127–67.
Oberschall, Anthony. *Social Conflict and Social Movements.* Englewood Cliffs, N.J.: Prentice-Hall, 1973.
Orwell, George. *Inside the Whale and Other Essays.* Harmondsworth: Penguin, 1962.
Ozouf, Mona. *La fête révolutionnaire, 1789–1799.* Paris: Gallimard, 1976.
———. "La Révolution française et l'idée de l'homme nouveau." In *The French Revolution and the Creation of Modern Political Culture,* vol. 2, *The Political Culture of the French Revolution,* edited by Colin Lucas, 213–32. Oxford: Pergamon, 1988.
Page, Joseph A. *The Revolution that Never Was: The Brazilian Northeast, 1955–1964.* New York: Grossman, 1972.
Paige, Jeffery M. *Agrarian Revolution: Social Movements and Export Agriculture in the Underdeveloped World.* New York: Free Press, 1975.
Paiva, Vanilda. *Igreja e questão agrária.* São Paulo: Edicões Loyola, 1985.
Palmer, Robert R. *The Age of the Democratic Revolution: A Political History of Europe and America, 1760–1800.* Princeton: Princeton University Press, 1959–64.
Pasquier, Félix, and François Galabert, eds. *Cahiers paroissiaux des sénéchausées de Toulouse et de Comminges en 1789.* Toulouse: Privat, 1925–28.
Pateman, Carol. *The Sexual Contract.* Stanford: Stanford University Press, 1988.
Patrick, Alison. *The Men of the First Republic.* Baltimore: Johns Hopkins University Press, 1972.
———. "French Revolutionary Local Government, 1789–1792." In *The French Revolution and the Creation of Modern Political Culture,* vol. 2, *The Political Culture of the French Revolution,* edited by Colin Lucas, 399–420. Oxford: Pergamon, 1988.

Paulson, Ronald. *Representations of Revolution, 1789–1820*. New Haven: Yale University Press, 1983.

Pelzer, Eric. "Nobles, paysans et la fin de la féodalité en Alsace." *La Révolution française et le monde rural,* 41–54. Paris: Editions du Comité des Travaux Historiques et Scientifiques, 1989.

Peret, Jacques. *Seigneurs et seigneurie en Gâtine poitevine: Le Duché de la Meilleraye, XVIIe–XVIIIe siècles*. Poitiers: Société des Antiquaires de l'Ouest, 1976.

Péronnet, Michel. "La théorie de l'ordre public exposée par les assemblées du clergé: Le trône et l'autel (seconde moitié du XVIIIe siècle)." In *Mouvements populaires et conscience sociale, XVIe–XIXe siècles,* edited by Jean Nicolas, 625–34. Paris: Maloine, 1985.

Petitfrère, Claude. *Blancs et bleues d'Anjou (1789–1793)*. Lille: Atelier Reproduction des Thèses, 1979.

———. *La Vendée et les vendéens*. Paris: Gallimard, 1981.

Peyrard, Christine. "Peut-on parler du jacobinisme dans l'Ouest? (Maine, bas Normandie)." In *La Révolution française et le monde rural,* 367–80. Paris: Editions du Comité des Travaux Historiques et Scientifiques, 1989.

Pigeonneau, Henri, and Alfred de Foville. *L'administration de l'agriculture au contrôle des finances (1785–1787). Procès-verbaux et rapports*. Paris: Guillaumin, 1882.

Pillorget, René. *Les mouvements insurrectionels de Provence entre 1596 et 1715*. Paris: A. Pedone, 1975.

———. "Les mouvements insurrectionels de Provence (1715–1789)." In *Mouvements populaires et conscience sociale, XVIe–XIXe siècles,* edited by Jean Nicolas, 351–60. Paris: Maloine, 1985.

Pimenova, Ludmila. *Dvorianstvo nakanune velikoi frantsuzskoi revoliutsii*. Moscow: Izdatel'stvo Universiteta, 1986.

———. "Das sozialpolitische Programm des Adels am Vorabend der französischen Revolution." *Jahrbuch für Geschichte* 39 (1989): 179–201.

———. "La noblesse à la veille de la Révolution." In *La grande Révolution française,* 37–63. Moscow: Editions Naouka, 1989.

Pipes, Richard. *Russia Under the Old Regime*. New York: Scribner, 1974.

Pithou, Jean Joseph. *Vie de Jean Jacob, vieillard de Mont-Jura, âgé de 120 ans, pensioné de sa Majesté à laquelle il a été présenté depuis peu ainsi qu'à l'Assemblée Nationale*. Paris: Valleyre, 1789.

Plongeron, Bernard. *Conscience religieuse en Révolution: Regards sur l'historiographie religieuse de la Révolution française*. Paris: Picard, 1969.

Poitrineau, Abel. "Aspects de la crise des justices seigneuriales dans l'Auvergne." *Revue Historique de Droit Français et Etranger* (1961): 552–70.

———. *La vie rurale en Basse-Auvergne au XVIIIe siècle, 1726–1789*. Paris: Presses Universitaires de France, 1965.

———. "Les assemblées primaires du bailliage de Salers en 1789." *Revue d'Histoire Moderne et Contemporaine* 25 (1978): 419–41.

———. "Le détonateur économico-fiscal et la charge des rancoeurs catégorielles profondes, lors des explosions de la colère populaire en Auvergne, au XVIIIe siècle." In *Mouvements populaires et conscience sociale, XVIe–XIXe siècles,* edited by Jean Nicolas, 361–70. Paris: Maloine, 1985.

Pomian, Krzysztof. "Les historiens et les archives dans la France du XVIIe siècle." *Acta Poloniae Historica* 26 (1972): 109–25.

Popelin, R. "Extrait de la correspondance de Pinteville, baron de Cernon." *Mémoires de la Société d'Agriculture, Commerce, Sciences et Arts de la Marne,* 1st ser., 26 (1880–81): 7–25.

Popkin, Jeremy D. *Revolutionary News: The Press in France, 1789–1799.* Durham: Duke University Press, 1990.

Popkin, Samuel. *The Rational Peasant: The Political Economy of Rural Society in Vietnam.* Berkeley and Los Angeles: University of California Press, 1979.

"Populations des villes suivant les états envoyés par Messieurs les intendants de Province, années 1787–1789. Eléments ayant servi à la formation des Etats de Population du Royaume de France." Archives Nationales, Série Div bis, Dossier 47.

Porée, Charles, ed. *Cahiers de doléances du bailliage de Sens pour les états généraux de 1789.* Auxerre: Imprimerie Coopérative Ouvrière l'Universelle, 1906.

Port, Célestin. *La Vendée angevine: Les origines—l'insurrection (janvier 1789–mars 1793).* Paris: Hachette, 1888.

Pothier, Robert J. *Traité des fiefs, avec un titre sur le cens.* Orléans: Chez la veuve Rouzeau Montaut, 1776.

Prince, Hugh. "Regional Contrasts in Agrarian Structures." In *Themes in the Historical Geography of France,* edited by Hugh D. Clout, 129–84. New York: Academic Press, 1977.

Quéniart, Jean. *Les hommes, l'église et Dieu dans la France du XVIIIe siècle.* Paris: Hachette, 1978.

Rabaut-Saint-Etienne, Jean-Paul. *Précis historique de la Révolution française.* Paris: Treuttel et Würtz, 1807.

Rabusson-Lamothe, Antoine. *Lettres sur l'Assemblée Législative (1791–1792).* Paris: Aubry, 1870.

Radkey, Oliver. *The Agrarian Foes of Bolshevism: Promise and Defeat of the Russian Socialist Revolutionaries, February to October, 1917.* New York: Columbia University Press, 1958.

Ragan, Bryant T., Jr. "Rural Political Activism and Fiscal Equality in the Revolutionary Somme." In *Recreating Authority in Revolutionary France,* edited by Bryant T. Ragan Jr., and Elizabeth A. Williams, 36–56. New Brunswick, N.J.: Rutgers University Press, 1992.

Ramon, G. *La Révolution à Péronne: Troisième série (1789–1791).* Péronne: J. Quentin, n.d.

Ramsay, Clay. *The Ideology of the Great Fear: The Soissonnais in 1789.* Baltimore: Johns Hopkins University Press, 1992.

Reddy, William M. "The Textile Trade and the Language of the Crowd at Rouen, 1752–1871." *Past and Present* 74 (1977): 62–89.

———. *The Rise of Market Culture: The Textile Trade and French Society, 1750–1900.* Cambridge: Cambridge University Press, 1984.

Reichardt, Rolf, and Hans-Jürgen Lüsebrink. "Révolution à la fin du 18e siècle. Pour une relecture d'un concept–clé du siècle des Lumières." *Mots* 16 (1988): 35–68.

Reichardt, Rolf, and Eberhard Schmitt. "La Révolution française—rupture ou continuité?

Pour une conceptualisation plus nuancée." In *Ancien Regime: Aufklärung und Revolution,* edited by Rolf Reichardt and Eberhard Schmitt, 4–71. Munich: Oldenbourg, 1979.

Reinhard, Marcel. "Sur l'histoire de la Révolution française." *Annales: Economies, Sociétés, Civilisations* 14 (1959): 555–58.

Reinhardt, Steven G. *Justice in the Sarladais, 1770–1790.* Baton Rouge: Louisiana State University Press, 1991.

Renauldon, Joseph. *Traité historique et pratique des droits seigneuriaux.* Paris: Despilly, 1765.

———. *Dictionnaire des fiefs et droits seigneuriaux utiles et honorifiques.* Paris: Delalain, 1788.

Restif de la Bretonne, Nicholas-Edmé. *My Father's Life.* Gloucester: Sutton, 1986.

Rétat, Pierre. "Partis et factions en 1789: Emergence des désignants politiques." *Mots* 16 (1988): 69–89.

Reuss, Rodolphe. "L'antisémitisme dans le Bas-Rhin pendant la Révolution (1790–1793)." *Revue des Etudes Juives* 68 (1914): 246–63.

Richet, Denis. "Autour des origines idéologiques lointaines de la Révolution française: élites et despotisme." *Annales: Economies, Sociétés, Civilisations* 9 (1969): 1–23.

———. *La France moderne: L'esprit des institutions.* Paris: Flammarion, 1973.

Richez, Jean-Claude. "Emeutes antisémites et Révolution en Alsace." In *Révolte et Société,* edited by Fabienne Gambrelle and Michel Tribitsch, 1:114–21. Paris: Histoire au Présent, 1988.

Riley, James C. *The Seven Years War and the Old Regime in France: The Economic and Financial Toll.* Princeton: Princeton University Press, 1986.

Rives, Jean. *Dîme et société dans l'archevêché d'Auch au XVIIIe siècle.* Paris: Bibliothèque Nationale, 1976.

Robespierre, Maximilien. *Oeuvres,* vol. 6, *Discours, 1789–1790;* vol. 7, *Discours, janvier-septembre 1791;* vol. 8, *Discours, octobre 1791–septembre 1792;* vol. 9, *Discours, septembre 1792–27 juillet 1793.* Paris: Presses Universitaires de France, 1950.

Robin, Régine. *La société française en 1789: Semur-en-Auxois.* Paris: Plon, 1970.

———. "Fief et seigneurie dans le droit et l'idéologie juridique à la fin du XVIIIe siècle." *Annales Historiques de la Révolution française* 43 (1971): 554–602.

———. *Histoire et linguistique.* Paris: Armand Colin, 1973.

Roger, Philippe. "Le débat sur la 'langue révolutionnaire.' " In *La Carmagnole des muses: L'homme de lettres et l'artiste dans la Révolution,* edited by Jean-Claude Bonnet, 157–84. Paris: Armand Colin, 1988.

———. "La langue révolutionnaire au tribunal des écrivains." In *Robespierre & Co.,* edited by R. Campagnoli, 1:175–93. Bologna: CLUEB, 1988.

———. "The French Revolution as 'Logomachy.' " In *Language and Rhetoric of the Revolution,* edited by John Renwick, 4–24. Edinburgh: Edinburgh University Press, 1990.

———. "Le dictionnaire contre la Révolution." *Stanford French Review* 14 (1990): 65–83.

Root, Hilton. *Peasants and King in Burgundy. Agrarian Foundations of French Absolutism.* Berkeley and Los Angeles: University of California Press, 1987.

———. "The Case Against George Lefebvre's Peasant Revolution." *History Workshop* 28 (1989): 88–102.

———. "Root's Response to Jones." *History Workshop* 28 (1989): 106–10.

———. "Politiques frumentaires et violence collective en Europe au XVIIIe siècle." *Annales: Economies, Sociétés, Civilisations* 45 (1990): 167–89.

Rose, R. B. "Eighteenth Century Price Riots, the French Revolution and the Jacobin Maximum." *International Review of Social History* 4 (1959): 432–41.

———. "Tax Revolt and Popular Organization in Picardy, 1789–1791." *Past and Present* 43 (1969): 92–108.

———. *Gracchus Babeuf: The First Revolutionary Communist.* Stanford: Stanford University Press, 1978.

———. "The 'Red Scare' of the 1790s: the French Revolution and the 'Agrarian Law.' " *Past and Present,* no. 103 (1984): 113–30.

Rosenthal, Jean-Laurent. *The Fruits of Revolution: Property Rights, Litigation and French Agriculture, 1700–1860.* Cambridge: Cambridge University Press, 1992.

Rouvière, François. *Histoire de la Révolution française dans le département du Gard.* Marseille: Lafitte Reprints, 1974.

Roy, Alain. *"Révolution": Histoire d'un mot.* Paris: Gallimard, 1989.

Rudé, George. "La taxation populaire de mai 1775 à Paris et dans la région parisienne." *Annales Historiques de la Révolution Française* 28 (1956): 139–79.

Sabatier, Gérard. "De la révolte de Roure (1679) aux Masques Armés (1783): La mutation du phénomène contestataire en Vivarais." In *Mouvements populaires et conscience sociale, XVIe–XIXe siècles,* edited by Jean Nicolas, 121–47. Paris: Maloine, 1985.

Sagnac, Philippe. *La législation civile de la Révolution française.* Paris: Hachette, 1898.

———. *Le Rhin français pendant la Révolution et l'Empire.* Paris: Félix Alcan, 1917.

Sagnac, Philippe, and Pierre Caron. *Les comités des droits féodaux et de législation et l'abolition du régime seigneurial (1789–1793).* Paris: Imprimerie Nationale, 1907.

Saint Jacob, Pierre de. *Les paysans de la Bourgogne du Nord au dernier siècle de l'Ancien Régime.* Paris: Société Les Belles Lettres, 1960.

Sauvageon, Jean. "Les cadres de la société rurale dans la Drôme à la fin de l'Ancien Régime: Survivances communautaires, survivances féodales et régime seigneurial." In *Aux origines provinciales de la Révolution,* edited by Robert Chagny, 35–44. Grenoble: Presses Universitaires de Grenoble, 1990.

Savina, Jean, and Daniel Bernard, eds. *Cahiers de doléances des sénéchaussées de Quimper et de Concarneau pour les états généraux de 1789.* Rennes: Imprimerie Oberthur, 1927.

Schama, Simon. *Citizens: A Chronicle of the French Revolution.* New York: Vintage Books, 1990.

Schmale, Wolfgang. *Bäuerlicher Widerstand, Gerichte und Rechtsentwicklung in Frankreich: Untersuchungen zu Prozessen zwischen Bauern und Seigneurs vor dem Parlament von Paris (16.–18. Jahrhundert).* Frankfurt am Main: Klostermann, 1986.

Scott, James C. *The Moral Economy of the Peasant: Rebellion and Subsistence in Southeast Asia.* New Haven: Yale University Press, 1976.

———. *Weapons of the Weak: Everyday Forms of Peasant Resistance.* New York: Vintage Books, 1985.

———. "Resistance without Protest and without Organization: Peasant Opposition to the Islamic Zakat and the Christian Tithe." *Comparative Studies in Society and History* 29 (1987): 417–52.

———. *Domination and the Arts of Resistance: Hidden Transcripts.* New Haven: Yale University Press, 1990.

Scott, Samuel F. *The Response of the Royal Army to the French Revolution: The Role and Development of the Line Army, 1787–1793.* Oxford: Clarendon Press, 1978.

Secher, Reynald. *Le génocide franco-français: Vendée-Vengé.* Paris: Presses Universitaires de France, 1986.

Sédillot, René. *Le coût de la Révolution française.* Paris: Perrin, 1987.

Sée, Henri. "La rédaction et la valeur historique des cahiers de paroisses pour les états-généraux de 1789." *Revue Historique* 103 (1910): 292–309.

———. "Les troubles agraires en Haute-Bretagne, 1790–1791." *Bulletin d'Histoire Economique de la Révolution Française* (1920–21): 231–373.

Sée, Henri, and André Lesort, eds. *Cahiers de doléances de la sénéchaussée de Rennes pour les états généraux de 1789.* Rennes: Imprimerie Oberthur, 1909–12.

Sewell, William H., Jr. *Work and Revolution in France: The Language of Labor from the Old Regime to 1848.* Cambridge: Cambridge University Press, 1980.

———. "Collective Violence and Collective Loyalties in France: Why the French Revolution Made a Difference." *Politics and Society* 18 (1990): 527–52.

———. *A Rhetoric of Bourgeois Revolution: The Abbé Sieyes and What Is the Third Estate?* Durham, N.C.: Duke University Press, 1994.

Shapiro, Gilbert. "Les demandes les plus répandues dans les cahiers de doléances." In *L'image de la Révolution française: Communications présentées lors du Congrès Mondial pour le Bicentenaire de la Révolution,* edited by Michel Vovelle, 1:7–14. Paris: Pergamon, 1989.

Shapiro, Gilbert, and Philip Dawson. "Social Mobility and Political Radicalism: The Case of the French Revolution of 1789." In *The Dimensions of Quantitative Research in History,* edited by William O. Aydelotte, Alan G. Bogue, and Robert W. Fogel, 159–92. Princeton: Princeton University Press, 1972.

Shapiro, Gilbert, and John Markoff. "L'authenticité des cahiers." *Bulletin d'Histoire de la Révolution Française* (1990/91): 17–70.

———. *Revolutionary Demands: A Content Analysis of the Cahiers de Doléances of 1789.* Stanford: Stanford University Press, 1997.

Shapiro, Gilbert, John Markoff, and Silvio Duncan Baretta. "The Selective Transmission of Historical Documents: The Case of the Parish *Cahiers* of 1789." *Histoire et Measure* 2 (1987): 115–72.

Shapiro, Gilbert, John Markoff, and Sasha R. Weitman. "Quantitative Studies of the French Revolution." *History and Theory: Studies in the Philosophy of History* 12 (1973): 163–91.

Shorter, Edward. *The Making of the Modern Family.* New York: Basic Books, 1975.

Siegfried, André. *Tableau politique de la France de l'Ouest sous la Troisième République.* Paris: Armand Colin, 1964.

Sieyès, Emmanuel. *Qu'est-ce que le tiers état?* Geneva: Droz, 1970.

Singer, Brian. "Violence in the French Revolution. Forms of Ingestion/Forms of Exclusion." In *The French Revolution and the Birth of Modernity,* edited by Ferenc Fehér, 201–18. Berkeley and Los Angeles: University of California Press, 1990.

Skidmore, Thomas E. *The Politics of Military Rule in Brazil, 1964–1985.* New York: Oxford University Press, 1988.

Skocpol, Theda. *States and Social Revolutions: A Comparative Analysis of France, Russia and China.* Cambridge: Cambridge University Press, 1979.

———. "What Makes Peasants Revolutionary?" *Comparative Politics* 14 (1982): 351–75.

Smith, Adam. *An Inquiry into the Nature and Causes of the Wealth of Nations.* London: Everyman's Library, 1910.

Snyder, David, and William R. Kelly. "Conflict Intensity, Media Sensitivity and the Validity of Newspaper Data." *American Sociological Review* 42 (1977): 105–23.

Snyder, David, and Charles Tilly. "Hardship and Collective Violence in France, 1830–1960." *American Sociological Review* 37 (1972): 520–32.

Soboul, Albert. *Les sans-culottes parisiens en l'an II: Mouvement populaire et gouvernement révolutionnaire, 2 Juin 1793–Thermidor an II.* Paris: Librairie Clavreuil, 1958.

———. *La Révolution française.* Paris: Gallimard, 1962.

———. *Précis d'histoire de la Révolution française.* Paris: Editions Sociales, 1962.

———. "Survivances 'féodales' dans la société rurale française au XIXe siècle." *Annales: Economies, Sociétés, Civilisations* 23 (1968): 965–86.

———. "Sur le mouvement paysan dans la Révolution française." *Annales Historiques de la Révolution Française* 45 (1973): 85–101.

———. *The French Revolution, 1787–1799. From the Storming of the Bastille To Napoleon.* New York: Vintage Books, 1975.

———. "De l'Ancien Régime à la Révolution: Problème régional et réalités sociales." In *Régions et régionalisme en France du dix-huitième siècle à nos jours,* edited by Christian Gras and Georges Livet, 25–54. Paris: Presses Universitaires de France, 1977.

———, ed. *Contributions à l'histoire paysanne de la Révolution française.* Paris: Editions Sociales, 1977.

———. "Sur le prélèvement féodal." In *Problèmes paysans de la Révolution, 1789–1848,* edited by Albert Soboul, 89–115. Paris: Maspero, 1983.

———. "Le brûlement des titres féodaux (1789–1793)." In *Problèmes paysans de la Révolution, 1789–1848,* edited by Albert Soboul, 135–46. Paris: Maspero, 1983.

Solakian, Daniel. "Mouvements contestataires de communautés agro-pastorales de Haute-Provence au XVIIIe siècle dans le témoignage écrit et la mémoire collective." In *Mouvements populaires et conscience sociale, XVIIe–XIXe siècles,* edited by Jean Nicolas, 241–52. Paris: Maloine, 1985.

Spira, György. "La dernière génération des serfs de Hongrie: l'exemple du comitat de Pest." *Annales: Economies, Sociétés, Civilisations* 23 (1968): 353–67.

Staël, Anne-Louise-Germaine de. *Considérations sur les principaux événements de la Révolution française.* London: Baldwin, Craddock and Joy, 1818.

Stinchcombe, Arthur L. *Creating Efficient Industrial Organizations.* New York: Academic Press, 1974.

———. *Economic Sociology.* New York: Academic Press, 1983.

Stone, Lawrence. "Literacy and Education in England, 1640–1900." *Past and Present,* no. 42 (1969): 69–139.

Sutherland, Donald M. G. *The Chouans: The Social Origins of Popular Counter-Revolution in Upper Brittany, 1770–1796.* Oxford: Clarendon Press, 1982.

———. *France, 1789–1815: Revolution and Counterrevolution.* New York: Oxford University Press, 1986.

———. "Violence and the Revolutionary State." Paper presented at the conference on Violence and the Democratic Tradition in France, University of California, Irvine, 1994.

"Table Ronde: Autour des travaux d'Anatoli Ado sur les soulèvements paysans pendant la Révolution française." In *La Révolution française et le monde rural,* 521–47. Paris: Editions du Comité des Travaux Historiques et Scientifiques, 1989.

Tackett, Timothy. *Priest and Parish in Eighteenth-Century France: A Social and Political Study of the Curés in the Diocese of Dauphiné, 1750–1791.* Princeton: Princeton University Press, 1977.

———. "The West in France in 1789: The Religious Factor in the Origins of the Counterrevolution." *Journal of Modern History* 54 (1982): 715–45.

———. *Religion, Revolution, and Regional Culture in France: The Ecclesiastical Oath of 1791.* Princeton: Princeton University Press, 1986.

———. "Les constituants et leurs commetants." Paper presented to the Congrès Mondial pour le Bicentenaire de la Révolution Française, Paris, 1989.

———. "Nobles and Third Estate in the Revolutionary Dynamic of the National Assembly, 1789–1790." *American Historical Review* 94 (1989): 271–301.

———. *Becoming a Revolutionary: The Deputies of the French National Assembly and the Emergence of a Revolutionary Culture (1789–1790).* Princeton: Princeton University Press, 1996.

Tarrow, Sidney. *Struggle, Politics, and Reform: Collective Action, Social Movements and Cycles of Protest.* Ithaca: Cornell University Center for International Studies, 1989.

———. *Democracy and Disorder: Protest and Politics in Italy, 1965–1975.* Oxford: Clarendon Press, 1989.

———. "Political Opportunities, Cycles of Protest and Collective Action: Theoretical Perspectives." Paper presented at Workshop on Collective Action Events and Cycles of Protest, Cornell University, 1990.

Taylor, George V. "Noncapitalist Wealth and the Origins of the French Revolution." *American Historical Review* 72 (1967): 469–96.

———. "Revolutionary and Nonrevolutionary Content in the *Cahiers* of 1789: An Interim Report." *French Historical Studies* 7 (1972): 479–502.

Tessier, Suzanne. *Histoire de la Belgique sous l'occupation française en 1792 et 1793.* Brussels: Librairie Falk fils, 1934.

Thibaudeau, Antoine-Claire. *Mémoires, 1765–1792.* Paris: Champion, 1875.

Thomas-Lacroix, P., ed. *Les cahiers de doléances de la sénéchaussée d'Hennebont. (Extrait de Mémoires de la Société d'Histoire et d'Archéologie de Bretagne,* vol. 25). Rennes: Imprimerie Bretonne, 1955.

Thompson, E. P. "The Moral Economy of the English Crowd in the Eighteenth Century." *Past and Present* 50 (1971): 71–136.

———. " 'Rough Music' and Charivari. Quelques réflexions complémentaires." In *Le Charivari,* edited by Jacques Le Goff and Jean-Claude Schmitt, 273–83. Paris: Ecole des Hautes Etudes en Sciences Sociales, 1981.

Thoumas, Geneviève. "La jeunesse de Mailhe." *Annales Historiques de la Révolution Française* 43 (1971): 221–47.

Tilly, Charles. "Some Problems in the History of the Vendée." *American Historical Review* 67 (1961): 19–33.

———. "Reflections on the Revolutions of Paris: An Essay on Recent Historical Writing." *Social Problems* 12 (1964): 99–121.

———. *The Vendée.* Cambridge: Harvard University Press, 1964.

———. "Collective Violence in European Perspective." In *The History of Violence in America,* edited by Hugh Davis Graham and Ted Robert Gurr, 4–44. New York: Bantam Books, 1969.

———. "How Protest Modernized in France, 1845–1855." In *The Dimensions of Quantitative Research in History,* edited by William O. Aydelotte, Allan G. Bogue, and Robert W. Fogel, 192–255. Princeton: Princeton University Press, 1972.

———. "Food Supply and Public Order in Modern Europe." In *The Formation of National States in Western Europe,* edited by Charles Tilly, 380–455. Princeton: Princeton University Press, 1975.

———. "Speaking Your Mind without Elections, Surveys or Social Movements." *Public Opinion Quarterly* 47 (1983): 461–78.

———. *The Contentious French.* Cambridge: Belknap Press of Harvard University Press, 1986.

———. "State and Counter-revolution in France." In *The French Revolution and the Birth of Modernity,* edited by Ferenc Fehér, 49–68. Berkeley and Los Angeles: University of California Press, 1990.

———. "Contentious Repertoires in Great Britain, 1758–1834." *Social Science History* 17 (1993): 255–80.

———. *Popular Contention in Great Britain, 1758–1834.* Cambridge: Harvard University Press, 1995.

Tilly, Louise. "The Food Riot as a Form of Political Conflict in France." *Journal of Interdisciplinary History* 3 (1971): 23–57.

Tocqueville, Alexis de. *The Old Regime and the French Revolution.* Garden City, N.Y.: Doubleday, 1955.

———. *The European Revolution and Correspondence with Gobineau.* Garden City, N.Y.: Doubleday, 1959.

Trénard, L. "Communication de M. Trénard." In *L'abolition de la féodalité dans le monde occidental,* 2:589–605. Paris: Editions du Centre National de la Recherche Scientifique, 1971.

Uriu, Yoichi. "Espace et Révolution: Enquête, grande peur et fédérations." *Annales Historiques de la Révolution Française,* no. 280 (1990): 150–66.

Vardy, Lianna. "Peasants and the Law: A Village Appeals to the French Royal Council, 1768–1791." *Social History* 13 (1988): 295–313.

Venturino, Diego. "La naissance de l'Ancien Régime." In *The French Revolution and the Creation of Modern Political Culture,* vol. 2, *The Political Culture of the French Revolution,* edited by Colin Lucas, 11–40. Oxford: Pergamon, 1988.

Véri, Joseph Alphonse de. *Journal de l'abbé de Véri.* Paris: Tallandier, 1928–30.

Vernier, Jules-Joseph, ed. *Cahiers de doléances du bailliage de Troyes (principal et secondaires) et du bailliage de Bar-sur-Seine pour les états généraux de 1789.* Troyes: P. Nouel, 1909.

Viallet, Gérard. "La Journée des tuiles: Accident de l'histoire ou première manifestation politique populaire à la veille de 1789?" In *Les débuts de la Révolution française en Dauphiné, 1788–1791,* edited by Vital Chomel, 63–94. Grenoble: Presses Universitaires de Grenoble, 1988.

Vidal de la Blache, Pierre. *Tableau de la géographie de la France.* Paris: Hachette, 1911.

Viguier, Jules. *La convocation des états-généraux en Provence.* Paris: Lenoir, 1896.

Villard, Pierre. *Les justices seigneuriales dans la Marche.* Paris: Librairie Générale de Droit et de Jurisprudence, 1969.

Volpillac, Catherine, Dany Hadjadj, and Jean-Louis Jam. "Des vandales au vandalisme." In *Révolution française et "vandalisme révolutionnaire,"* edited by Simone Bernard-Griffiths, Marie-Claude Chemin, and Jean Ehrard, 15–27. Paris: Universitas, 1992.

Voltaire. *Oeuvres complètes.* Paris: Garnier Frères, 1877–85.

Vovelle, Michel. *Les métamorphoses de la fête en Provence de 1750 à 1820.* Paris: Aubier/Flammarion, 1976.

———. "Les troubles sociaux en Provence de 1750 à 1792." In *De la cave au grenier: Un itinéraire en Provence au XVIIIe siècle. De l'histoire sociale à l'histoire des mentalités,* edited by Michel Vovelle, 221–62. Quebec: Serge Fleury, 1980.

———. "Y a-t-il eu une Révolution culturelle au XVIIIe siècle? A propos de l'éducation populaire en Provence." In *De la cave au grenier: Un itinéraire en Provence au XVIIIe siècle. De l'histoire sociale à l'histoire des mentalités,* edited by Michel Vovelle, 313–67. Quebec: Serge Fleury, 1980.

———. "Les campagnes à l'assaut des villes sous la Révolution." In his *Ville et campagne au XVIIIe siècle: Chartres et la Beauce,* 227–76. Paris: Editions Sociales, 1980.

———. *Ville et campagne au XVIIIe siècle: Chartres et la Beauce.* Paris: Editions Sociales, 1980.

———. "Les fédérations." In *L'état de la France pendant la Révolution (1789–1799),* edited by Michel Vovelle, 216–17. Paris: Editions de la Découverte, 1988.

———. *L'image de la Révolution française: Communications presentées lors du Congrès Mondial pour le Bicentenaire de la Révolution.* Paris: Pergamon, 1989.

———. "The Countryside and the French Peasantry in Revolutionary Iconography." In *Reshaping France: Town, Country and Region during the French Revolution,* edited by Alan Forrest and Peter M. Jones, 26–36. Manchester: Manchester University Press, 1991.

———. *La découverte de la politique: Géopolitique de la Révolution française.* Paris: Editions de la Découverte, 1993.

Walter, Gérard. *Répertoire de l'histoire de la Révolution française (Travaux Publics de 1800 à 1940).* Vol. 2, *Lieux.* Paris: Bibliothèque Nationale, 1951.

Wangermann, Ernst. *From Joseph II to the Jacobin Trials: Government Policy and Public Opinion in the Habsburg Dominions in the Period of the French Revolution.* Oxford: Oxford University Press, 1969.

Webb, Eugene J., Donald T. Campbell, Richard Schwartz, and Lee Sechrest. *Unobtrusive Measures: Nonreactive Research in the Social Sciences.* Chicago: Rand McNally, 1966.

Weber, Eugen. *Peasants into Frenchmen: The Modernization of Rural France, 1870–1914.* Stanford: Stanford University Press, 1976.

Weber, Max. *Economy and Society.* New York: Bedminster, 1968.

Weis, Eberhard. "Révoltes paysannes et citadines dans les états allemands sur la rive gauche du Rhin, de 1789 à 1792." *Francia* 3 (1975): 346–58.

Weitman, Sasha R. "The Sociological Thesis of Tocqueville's *The Old Regime and the Revolution.*" *Social Research* 33 (1966): 389–406.

———. "Bureaucracy, Democracy and the French Revolution." Ph.D. diss., Washington University, 1968.

———. "Regime Practice and Mass-Political Dispositions: Reflections on the Old Regime and the Revolution." Paper presented to the Bicentennial Conference on the French Revolution, George Washington University, May 1989.

Werner, Robert. *Les Ponts et Chaussées d'Alsace au dix-huitième siècle.* Strasbourg: Imprimerie Heitz, 1929.

Weulersse, Georges. *Le mouvement physiocratique en France (de 1756 à 1770).* Paris: Félix Alcan, 1910.

———. *La physiocratie sous les ministères de Turgot et de Necker (1774–1781).* Paris: Presses Universitaires de France, 1950.

———. *La physiocratie à l'aube de la Révolution (1781–1792).* Paris: Editions de l'Ecole des Hautes Etudes en Sciences Sociales, 1985.

Whitman, James Q. " 'Les seigneurs descendent au rang de simples créanciers': droit romain, droit féodal et Révolution." *Droits: Revue Française de Théorie Juridique* 17 (1993): 19–32.

Wolf, Eric. *Peasant Wars of the Twentieth Century.* New York: Harper and Row, 1973.

Wolikow, C. "Communauté et féodalité. Mouvements anti-féodaux dans le vignoble de Bar-sur-Seine, fin de l'Ancien Régime." In *Contributions à l'histoire paysanne de la Révolution française,* edited by Albert Soboul, 283–308. Paris: Edition Sociales, 1977.

Woloch, Isser. *Jacobin Legacy: The Democratic Movement Under the Directory.* Princeton: Princeton University Press, 1970.

———. "Republican Institutions, 1797–1799." In *The French Revolution and the Creation of Modern Political Culture,* vol. 2, *The Political Culture of the French Revolution,* edited by Colin Lucas, 371–87. Oxford: Pergamon, 1988.

———. *The New Regime. Transformations of the French Civic Order, 1789–1820s.* New York: Norton, 1994.

Woronoff, Denis. "Les châteaux, entreprises forestières et industrielles aux XVIIe et XVIIIe siècles." In *Le château, la chasse et la forêt,* edited by André Chastel, 115–26. Bordeaux: Editions Sud-Ouest, 1990.

Young, Arthur. *Travels in France and Italy During the Years 1787, 1788 and 1789.* London: J. M. Dent, 1915.

———. *Voyages en France en 1787, 1788 et 1789.* Paris: Armand Colin, 1976.

Zald, Mayer N., and John D. McCarthy. *The Dynamics of Social Movements: Resource Mobilization, Social Control and Tactics.* Cambridge, Mass.: Winthrop, 1979.

———. *Social Movements in an Organizational Society: Collected Essays.* New Brunswick, N.J.: Transaction Books, 1987.

Zink, Anne. "Parlementaires et entrepreneurs: à propos des événements à Bascoms (1776–1782)." In *La France d'Ancien Régime: Etudes réunies en l'honneur de Pierre Goubert,* 2:715–24. Toulouse: Privat, 1984.

Index